Cradle of Conflict

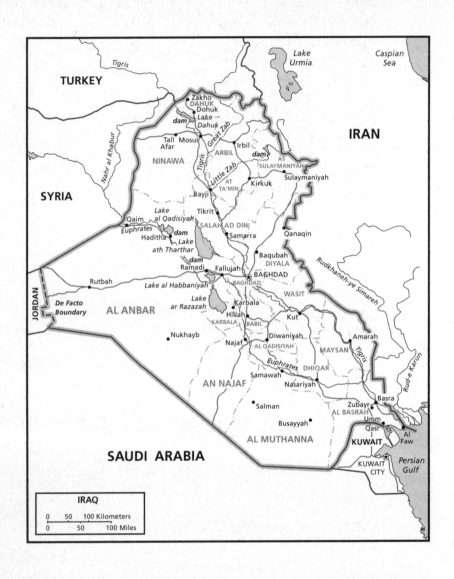

TURKEY

Tigris

Lake Urmia

Caspian Sea

IRAN

Zakho
DAHUK
Dohuk
dam
Lake Dahuk

Great Zab

Tall Mosul
Afar

ARBIL

Irbil

dam

AS SULAYMANIYAH

NINAWA

Tigris

Little Zab

Kirkuk

Sulaymaniyah

AT TA'MIN

SYRIA

Bayji

Nahr al Khabur

Qaim
Lake al Qadisiyah

Tikrit

SALAH AD DIN

Samarra

Qanaqin

Euphrates
Haditha
dam
Lake ath Tharthar

Baqubah
DIYALA

Rudkhaneh-ye Simareh

dam
Ramadi
Fallujah

BAGHDAD
BAGHDAD

Rutbah

Lake al Habbaniyah

WASIT

JORDAN

De Facto Boundary

AL ANBAR

Lake ar Razazah

Karbala

KARBALA

Hillah
BABIL

Kut

Nukhayb

Najaf

Diwaniyah

AL QADISIYAH

Amarah

Tigris

MAYSAN

Rud-e Karun

Euphrates
Samawah

DHIQAR

AN NAJAF

Nasariyah

Salman

Basra

Zubayr
AL BASRAH
Umm
Qasr

Busayyah

AL MUTHANNA

KUWAIT

Al Faw

SAUDI ARABIA

KUWAIT CITY

Persian Gulf

IRAQ

0   50   100 Kilometers
0   50   100 Miles

CRADLE
OF
CONFLICT

IRAQ AND THE BIRTH OF MODERN U.S. MILITARY POWER

MICHAEL ANDREW KNIGHTS

Naval Institute Press
Annapolis, Maryland

Naval Institute Press
291 Wood Road
Annapolis, MD 21402

ISBN 1-59114-444-2

Printed in the United States of America

TO MARIA

Contents

Preface

As Iraq represented the cradle of civilization to the ancient world, it has represented the cradle of conflict in the post-Cold War world. It is a little known fact that the United States and her allies have been involved in combat operations in Iraq every year since 1991, a period of U.S. military engagement that is longer even than America's direct military involvement in the Vietnam War. U.S. bombs and missiles have impacted inside Iraq every year for over a decade. For many people born in peaceful countries of the West or the troubled states of the Near East at the end of the 20th century, Iraq was their formative experience of war in the modern world. No sooner had the Cold War threat posed by the Warsaw Pact expired than a new adversary arose in the shape of Saddam Hussein's Baathist regime in Iraq. Fifteen years after the United Nations Security Council imposed sanctions and militarized containment on Iraq, U.S. forces continue to battle remnants of the former regime and a range of other adversaries inside Iraq. The Baathist regime's decades-spanning campaign to resist U.S. military pressure was the crucible on which the post-Cold War U.S. military was forged and given its keen edge. Careful study of this fifteen-year struggle offers a unique prism through which to study the strengths and limitations of U.S. military power in the post-Cold War era, generating lessons that are useful in guiding the future development and proper use of U.S. military power in the 21st century. Doctrinal and procurement decisions being made now will affect the status of U.S. military power for the next half-century, so it is vital to draw the right lessons from the contemporary history of U.S. military operations in Iraq. Focusing on how the U.S. uses military force in *practice* rather than in *theory*, this book looks at how the combination of new technologies and operational concepts interacted with the real-world threats and real-world political constraints facing the U.S. government.

For most people, the history of U.S. military involvement in Iraq is a tale of two wars. First there was the technological wizardry of the morally clear-cut and apparently bloodless Operation Desert Storm in 1991, which seemed to represent the zenith of military execution. Twelve years later, there followed the controversial and protracted project to invade Iraq and replace the Baathist regime—Operation Iraqi Freedom—eclipsed the earlier operation. In 1991, the set-piece campaign took 43 days to achieve its limited objectives, and devastated Iraq in the process. In 2003, the lightweight and fast-moving Operation Iraqi Freedom took 26 days to remove the regime of Saddam Hussein, overrunning much of Iraq and causing highly selective damage to regime targets. In fact, the twin wars are not so much discrete events as bookends that mark the beginning and end of almost fifteen years of continuous military containment and periodic armed clashes. No analysis of either the 1991 or 2003 wars in Iraq is complete without detailed consideration of the political and military events that separated the two campaigns. It is impossible to judge the political and military effectiveness of Operation Desert Storm in 1991 without examining the post-war survival of the Baathist government and the decade of Iraqi intransigence that followed. Likewise, it is impossible to understand the apparent ease with which the Baathist regime was removed during Operation Iraqi Freedom without understanding the continual military operations being undertaken against Iraq since 1991. The U.S. military confrontation with Iraq should not be viewed as two wars, but rather as one meandering conflict that spanned a fifteen-year timespan. By probing the shrouded history of U.S. military operations in Iraq between the two wars, this book tells the complete story for the first time.

At the political level, the conflict with Saddam Hussein's regime represents a critical and pervasive influence on the broader history of the early post-Cold War era. Between 1991 and 2003, the Baathist regime's resistance to the constraints imposed on it through ceasefire terms and United Nations (UN) resolutions transformed Iraq into an international pariah state, and had far-reaching effects on the development of post-Cold War international relations.

After providing a shining example of UN solidarity in the collective defense of Kuwait's right to self-determination, Iraq's ability to flout UN resolutions spotlighted the limited realization of a rules-based New World Order. Iraqi defiance split the UN Security Council and caused lasting damage to attempts to establish non-proliferation norms concerning weapons of mass destruction in the post-Cold War system. Meanwhile, the humanitarian impact of sanctions on Iraq, the periodic use of force against Iraq, and the maintenance of substantial U.S. forces in the Persian Gulf exacerbated and perhaps accelerated tensions developing between Western and Islamic cultures. Iraq remains a decisive battlefront for both those who support and those who oppose the development of more moderate and globalized Islamic societies. After over a decade of commanding center-stage at the UN, the March 2003 invasion of Iraq also witnessed the first operational application of the post-9/11 U.S. strategy of strategic pre-emption. Although U.S. leaders such as Vice President Richard Cheney and Secretary of Defense Colin Powell previously opposed the toppling of Saddam Hussein's government in 1991 as Secretary of Defense and Chairman of the Joint Chiefs of Staff respectively, they now publicly supported the war. A key question remains: What accounts for this change? Why was regime change considered unnecessary and unwise in 1991, but prudent and achievable in 2003? What happened in the intervening decade to make policy decision-makers argue that the removal of the Baathist regime was such a pressing necessity? What role did the regime's unstinting resistance play in this transformation?

At the military-technical level, fifteen years of military operations focused on Iraq represent a uniquely rich operational environment from which to extract lessons about the strengths and limitations of U.S. military power and its application in complex emergencies. Exclusive focus on the lessons of the 1991 and 2003 wars expose the analyst to charges that the lessons from Iraq may not be transferable in an age when large-scale mechanized warfare, territorial annexation, and regime change are the exception rather than the rule in international conflicts. A broader focus on the continuum of operations against Iraq presents a different picture and a more valid sample of U.S. military responses to post-Cold War challenges. Iraq was the setting for the first post-Cold War humanitarian intervention within the territory of a sovereign state, witnessing the establishment of safe-havens to protect the Kurds in April 1991 and the imposition of two no-fly zones. Throughout the 1990s, the U.S. military undertook repeated coercive air and missile strikes to reduce Iraq's intransigent rejection ceasefire terms and UN resolutions. The United States rolled back Iraq's resilient air defenses and carried out selective strikes on its leadership, weapons of mass destruction facilities, and terrorist havens during a decade of intense military activity sandwiched between the two Gulf wars. Even before the Baathist regime had fallen in April 2003, U.S. forces in some parts of Iraq had transitioned to stabilization and humanitarian support operations, then again transitioned to fight a counterinsurgency campaign. The scope of U.S. military challenges in Iraq runs the gamut of post-Cold War missions when the period is viewed as a continuum of conflict.

The chronological retelling of America's conflict with Iraq is divided into an account of three sections. Part One relates the beginning of the confrontation between the U.S. and Iraq, reflecting on Iraq's metamorphosis from uncomfortable U.S. ally to post-Cold War adversary between 1980 and 1991. It is titled "The Challenge" to reflect two key features of this period. On the one hand, it brings to mind the challenge that Saddam Hussein posed to the United States at the very moment it emerged as the last standing superpower, necessitating a forceful response. On the other hand, this period also saw the U.S. military face the challenge of adapting to the post-Vietnam and post-Cold War eras. Chapter 1 ("Raising the Shield") describes how the U.S. military was forced into a hasty transition from its settled Cold War garrisons to expeditionary warfare in a new and unfamiliar theater of war. Following the frantic deployment to screen Saudi Arabia from a possible Iraqi attack, this portion of the story describes how U.S. commanders assessed the balance of forces required to evict Iraq's army from Kuwait. The U.S. military which faced Saddam's large armed forces awaited its first major test of arms since Vietnam, reliant on untested Cold War training, technologies, and operational concepts. As Chapter 2 ("Forging the Sword") recounts, the mission of these forces in Operation Desert Storm was simple but demanding, involving the neutering of Saddam Hussein's offensive military capabilities. In addition to massing huge U.S. and coalition forces to dislodge the Iraqi occupation, U.S. planners relied on deception, offensive maneuver, and aerial preparation throughout the depth of the battlespace to tip the odds in the coalition's favor. In the event, what emerged from the planning process was not merely a scheme to evict Iraq's army from Kuwait and remove its long-term offensive capabilities, but instead an incredibly detailed and intensive effort to dismember a regime and paralyze an industrialized society.

Chapters 3 ("Strategic Attack") and 4 ("Air-Land Battle") relate the execution of Operation Desert Storm, looking beneath the surface of this tremendous display of military power. This operation provided powerful validation of the U.S. way of warfare that was under development at the close of the Cold War. The opening moments of Operation Desert Storm indelibly inked themselves on the witnessing generation and the short duration and low cost of the subsequent war set the standard for post-Cold War U.S. military operations. The forty-three-day aerial and one-hundred-hour air-land phases were hailed as the leading edge of a more decisive, surgical, and information technology-intensive style of warfare. Yet, the outcomes of Operation Desert Storm were not as one-sided as many analyses suggested. In certain fields of the conflict, Iraq's forces displayed strong abilities to limit U.S. military power, creating air defense sanctuaries, frustrating U.S. intelligence collection, and blunting U.S. air attacks. Although decisively outmatched in land combat, the Iraqi military regularly fought its ground. Most importantly, although Iraq was successfully evicted from Kuwait, it retained vital portions of its offensive capabilities and quickly turned these on internal rebels to assure that the regime survived to resist the United States another day.

Part Two of the book is titled "The War Between the Wars" and deals with the constant military confrontations that took place between the high-profile military campaigns in 1991 and 2003. Each chapter represents the first detailed unclassified examination of this period of U.S. military history. Chapter 5 ("After the Storm") charts the Baathist regime's post-war survival, followed by its immediate resumption of resistance against the obligations placed upon it by ceasefire terms and United Nations resolutions. In just under two years after Operation Desert Storm, Saddam Hussein's regime resisted UN inspections and reignited military clashes with the United States following the imposition of no-fly zones over northern and southern Iraq. The chapter closes by looking at the January 1993 crisis, in which Saddam Hussein sought to strike out at U.S. forces for the first time since Operation Desert Storm. These new modes of resistance were more difficult for the Pentagon to confront decisively, and the fecklessness of the response ordered by outgoing President George Herbert Walker Bush in early 1993 hinted at many of the key limitations on U.S. military power in the post-Cold War era. Chapter 6 ("Tomahawk Diplomacy") provides the first detailed account of the cruise missile-only operations launched under the first administration of President Bill Clinton. The chapter demonstrates that rather than the character of the Clinton administration, the preferences of military decision-makers and the lack of regional host nation support for U.S. operations were the key drivers behind these types of limited response to the limited threat posed by the Baathist regime. The chapter focuses on the difficulties of using limited displays of U.S. military power to deter resistance by determined regional adversaries. Time and again in the 1993–1996 period, Iraq suffered little harm after provoking a U.S. military response. After riding out the June 1993 cruise missile strike of intelligence headquarters, the Baathist regime twice tested U.S. patience by saber-rattling on the Kuwaiti border on October 1994 and successfully overrunning the Kurdish safe haven in northern Iraq in September 1996. These episodes displayed Iraq's ability to generate tactical surprise, move its forces with great rapidity, and display military power at a time when the Baathist regime was beginning to undermine the U.S.-backed policy of containment.

Chapter 7 ("Cheat and Retreat") provides the first authoritative account of U.S. military planning and operations during Iraq's series of obstructions of UN inspections between October 1997 and December 1998. Building on the partial normalization in Iraq's commercial relations with many countries as the UN-administered Oil-for-Food Program began generating funds and contracts, Saddam aimed to wear down international resolve to maintain sanctions by drawing the United States into a series of military standoffs. These "cheat and retreat" tactics were simple but effective: the United States would be drawn into expending political capital at the UN Security Council and carrying out costly military deployments to the Gulf, but each time Saddam would back down shortly before the United States resorted to the use of force. This chapter describes the challenges facing the U.S. military planning community as they were tasked to develop military options in the absence of clear political objectives or targeting intelligence. The result was Operation Desert Fox in December 1998, a four-day series of air-strikes characterized in equal measure by military-technical brilliance and political ineffectiveness. To conclude Part Two, Chapter 8 ("Prelude to War: The No-Fly Zones after Desert Fox") discusses Saddam's use of no-fly zones as a forum for resistance after UN inspection ceased in 1998. A frustrated Clinton administration stepped up to the challenge, triggering an escalating series of military clashes as the Baathist regime traded blows with U.S. aerial patrols over Iraq. When Iraq's air defenses showed signs of dangerous adaptation and Iraq's leadership maintained the challenge, it was the U.S. military that decided to de-escalate but found that Iraqi resistance could not be scaled back. The chapter finishes with the 9/11 attacks on the United States, a development which signaled a temporary cessation of effective policing of the no-fly zones and had a profound effect on the evolution of the U.S. conflict with Iraq.

The third and final part of the story is titled "Ending Resistance," reflecting the effort made during this period to realize the U.S. government's long-standing policy of seeking regime change in Iraq. Chapter 9 ("Transitioning to War") traces the development of the operational scheme used in Operation Iraqi Freedom, including the first detailed insider account of the integration of more aggressive "peacetime" no-fly zone policing into the wartime operational plan, an effort known as Operation Southern Focus. This perspective frames Operation Iraqi Freedom in a different light, representing not the start of a new war, but the beginning of the end of one that had started over a decade before. In reviewing the war, the chapter highlights the way by which fleeting intelligence drew the U.S. military into a running start, dislocating carefully planned air operations in an effort to exploit decapitation opportunities and protect threatened oilfields. Chapter 11 ("The March of Baghdad") picks up the story as U.S. forces speed toward Operation Iraqi Freedom's main objective: the enemy's presumed center of gravity at Baghdad. The chapter delves below the obvious success story of the rapid U.S. penetration of Baathist-controlled territory and the scattering of enemy fielded forces to ask tough questions about the operational effects achieved in the campaign and the ability of the modern U.S. military to fight network-centric warfare or develop real situational awareness with the use of technical intelligence collection assets. Chapter 12 ("Ending Resistance") begins by discussing the Baathist regime's role in continuing resistance during the post-war insurgency in Iraq. The chapter views Operation Iraqi Freedom for what it was—a highly effective "movement to contact" that necessarily placed the U.S. military in close proximity with its adversaries as well as a large number of undecided Iraqi citizens, but nonetheless preceded the decisive defeat of the long-term resistance strategy devised by the Baathist regime. Although the story of the post-war period will receive a far fuller treatment in the years to come, this chapter sheds light on the effects that early errors in the stabilization effort played in fostering resistance. After tracking the U.S. military's struggle with the requirements of counterinsurgency in 2003, the book looks at the lessons learned during the year of battles fought in 2004 and ends with the complex and broadly successful effort to secure elections on 31 January 2005.

Above all, the conflict with Iraq is a tale of the attempts of a regional adversary to resist and frustrate U.S. military power in the post-Cold War era. With anti-hegemonic and anti-Western sentiment rising in every region of the globe, further resistance is bound to occur, and the case if Iraq is rich in surprising insights. In the epilogue that follows, key trends concerning the most pressing military problems facing the 21st Century U.S. military are extracted from the marathon U.S. military engagement with Iraq. Should serious threats to U.S. interests be contained through an admixture of diplomatic, economic, and military means until such adversaries atrophy, or must they be met with pre-emption and regime removal? How do regional adversaries learn to blunt U.S. military power and frustrate U.S. intelligence collection? What social, political, and economic drivers and circumstances mould the asymmetric operational styles of individual regional adversaries?

What emerges from a survey of U.S. military operations in Iraq is a new and constructive critique of U.S. military power in the post-Cold War era. At the military-technical level, the basic formula adopted by the U.S. military—maneuver, deception, and precision strike, enabled by network-centric warfare—is clearly the right way to go. At a political-military level, U.S. military forces excelled at satisfying the demanding but relatively simple political objectives of ejecting Saddam Hussein's forces from Kuwait in 1991 and deposing the Baathist government in 2003. The efficacy of U.S. military activism is less clear in the complex missions undertaken between and since these great campaigns, however, witnessing U.S. strategic and tactical failures on a number of occasions. The plain truth is that Iraq frequently managed to prevent the U.S. military from achieving the political and military objectives that it set between 1991 and 2003. Resistance against UN inspections and U.S. military containment was never suppressed. Why was this? It is both crude and logically unsustainable to suggest that the cause of U.S. military frustrations in this period was due to the character of any single U.S. president or their administration. Limited post-Gulf War air and missile strikes were first ordered by President George Herbert Walker Bush, and continued throughout the administrations of President Bill Clinton and President George Walker Bush with uniformly unimpressive political results.

Instead, the fifteen years of U.S. military operations in Iraq are rich in lessons about the limits on technologically based U.S. military power in limited war scenarios and protracted engagements. Careful analysis of this period unearths important lessons concerning the negative effect that insufficient intelligence, limited host nation support, and unclear political objectives can have on U.S. military power in the 21st Century. Looking at the 1990–2005 period as a continuum of conflict shows that given enough time, developing-world militaries are adept at improvising resistance strategies that make it increasingly hard for U.S. forces to achieve decisive effects in limited military operations. The accepted wisdom to have emerged from post-Cold War military operations is Western forces will become increasingly capable by harnessing information technology and precision strike technologies, while developing world adversaries will migrate to the opposite end of the spectrum, eschewing conventional military hardware to engage in terrorist-type asymmetric warfare. A detailed survey of U.S. military operations in Iraq suggests that there is a middle road that future developing world adversaries are more likely to take, involving ongoing use of their machine-age inventories of conventional military equipment alongside new asymmetric tactics. Similarly, claims that Operation Desert Storm represented a new, cleaner, and more decisive form of warfare need to be critically assessed, as does the emerging claim that the leaner and purportedly smarter forces used in Operation Iraqi Freedom validated the value of technology-enabled network-centric warfare. Although the history of U.S. military operations in Iraq includes the first operational use of almost all the intelligence sensors, advanced information processors, and precision strike technologies to have emerged since the end of the Cold War, the tale is a cautionary one. The United States will require more than advanced technologies to truly transform itself into the dominant military power of the 21st Century. In a troubled age when the United States will be required to engage at all levels of conflict and display global reach, much more must be done to develop intelligence dominance to match the other areas of U.S. military dominance; to garner multilateral support; and to underpin the use of force with clear and attainable military objectives.

Acknowledgments

One of the aims of this book was to allow the U.S. soldiers, sailors, and airmen to tell the story of America's military involvement in Iraq in their own words. Wherever possible, this book has used unclassified interview materials with eye-witness participants to render its account of command decision-making in U.S. military operations in Iraq. Where such accounts did not exist, the author developed them by embarking on a wide-ranging interview program while visiting U.S. military facilities and living in Washington DC from 2002 to 2004. No outsider to the U.S. military community can embark on such a venture without allies on the inside who believe in their work. This study would not have been possible without the intellectual and logistical support of the U.S. military. First, however, I would like to recognize the debt of gratitude I owe to members of British defense academia. Professor Philip Sabin of the Department of War Studies at King's College London and Peter Gray, head of Defence Studies at the Royal Air Force, provided my initial introduction to one of the intellectual brain-trusts of the U.S. military, the U.S. Air Force's Air University at Maxwell Air Force Base, Alabama. At the Air University, I was provided with a seat at the School of Advanced Airpower Studies (SAAS) by Professor Denny Drew, who supported me throughout my months of residence at Maxwell.

While at SAAS I was able to access a vast body of interview material on Operations Desert Shield and Desert Storm, which was unclassified

ACKNOWLEDGMENTS

but accessible at the Air Force Historical Research Agency (AFHRA). In addition to accessing dozens of otherwise inaccessible interview-led theses by U.S. officers, I catalogued and noted over three thousand pages of interview transcripts at Maxwell, making the first use of interview materials generated (but not used) by USAF College for Aerospace Doctrine, Research and Education (CADRE) researchers Richard Reynolds and Edward Mann. These gentlemen introduced me to Major General David Deptula, the central air campaign planner in Operation Desert Storm and then Director of Plans and Programs at Air Combat Command (ACC), who proved instrumental to this study. The Air Force Historian Support Office (AFHSO) ran a parallel research programme to the CADRE effort, focusing instead on mining the written record surrounding Desert Shield and Desert Storm, and Richard Hallion of AFHSO was kind enough to provide me with pre-release transcripts from this research effort. With connections forged at Maxwell, AFHSO, and later during a sponsored stay at ACC, I executed an extensive interview program throughout the community of senior officers with command experience in Iraq. In addition to these serving officers, a range of former military and civilian decision-makers provided key support and deserve individual recognition, including but not limited to Anthony Lake, Kenneth Pollack, Bruce Riedel, Rear Admiral John Sigler, and General Anthony Zinni. I would like to thank my interviewees for setting aside so much valuable time. All in all, I was staggered by the hospitality shown to me by the U.S. Department of Defense and the U.S. Air Force in particular. The individuals I met in these organizations were truly the finest community of Americans I encountered during my twenty-nine months in the States.

I also received generous support from the military fellows at the Washington Institute for Near East Policy. Research director Patrick Clawson and head of military studies Michael Eisenstadt provided moral as well as intellectual leadership throughout the writing process of this book. Retired Defense Intelligence Agency analyst Jeffrey White provided key insights from his own long experience of watching the development of regional militaries and insurgent movements. The Washington Institute's unparalleled background in Near Eastern affairs gave me a platform to meet and exchange ideas with Iraq specialists such as U.S. Central Command's senior analyst Gregory Hooker and the U.S. Army's foremost authority on counterinsurgency, Dr. Steven Metz, as well as meeting a number of U.S. Army divisional commanders and Coalition Provisional Authority officials who had recently returned from command positions in Iraq.

Such a long period of research would not have been possible without the kind assistance of a number of friends who supported me during my initial year of U.S.-based research in 2002. Jonathan and Rachel Micah-Jones allowed me to hit the ground running when I first arrived in Washington D.C., making me a home from home in their Dupont Circle apartment. Thereafter, Royal Air Force Group Captain Bryan Collins and his wife Vita gave me a marvelous family environment in which to soak up the mass of valuable data at Maxwell Air Force Base in Alabama. Jim and Sonya Dorschner gave me a soft landing on my second visit to the States, granting me the space I needed to write up my interview materials by turning over their basement to me for three months. You each deserve my deepest thanks. On the home front, my friends sustained me. In particular, Jamie and Ed; thanks for keeping my chin up. Whilst I may lack taste in many things, I have always had good taste in friends. I would also like to thank my parents, Michael and Marion, and my sister Debbie for giving me the best possible family environment to begin my studies. Even if I never had any degrees or awards, I'd still be the luckiest son and brother in the world.

Finally, I want to thank my wife Maria for supporting me through the darker episodes of the writing process. When the book took all my energy, she gave me her own. No man had a greater partner or co-author.

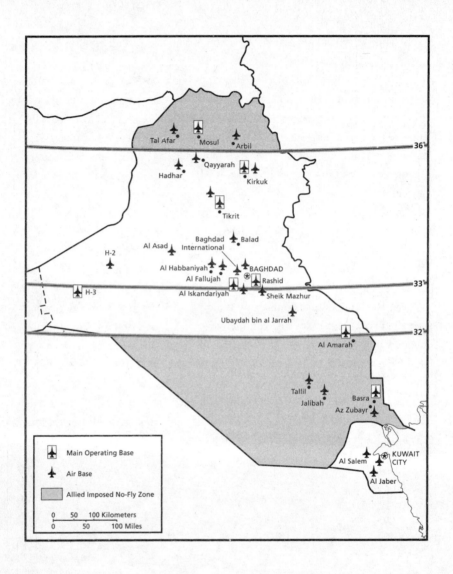

Tal Afar •   Mosul   • Arbil   36

Qayyarah

Hadhar •

Kirkuk

Tikrit •

Baghdad   • Balad
International

Al Asad

H-2

Al Habbaniyah
Al Fallujah   BAGHDAD
Rashid

H-3   33

Al Iskandariyah   Sheik Mazhur

Ubaydah bin al Jarrah

32

Al Amarah •

Tallil
Jalibah   Basra •
Az Zubayr

Al Salem   KUWAIT
CITY

Al Jaber

Main Operating Base

Air Base

Allied Imposed No-Fly Zone

0   50   100 Kilometers
0   50   100 Miles

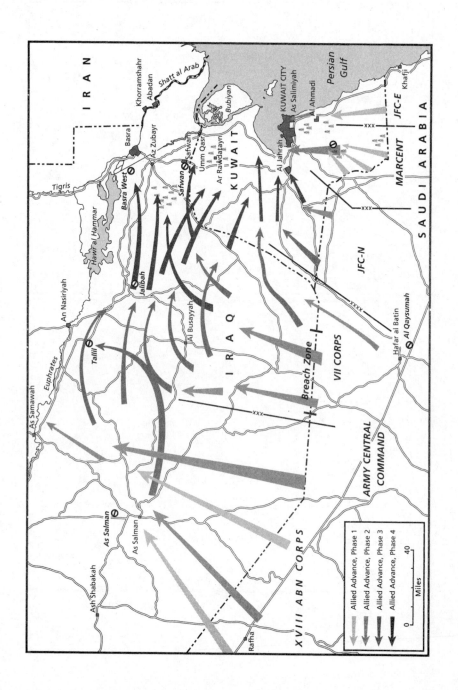

IRAN

Khorramshahr
Abadan
Shatt al Arab

Basra

Az Zubayr

Tigris

Basra West

Hawr al Hammar

Jalibah

An Nasiriyah

Talili

Euphrates

As Samawah

Ash Shabakah

As Salman

Rafha

XVIII ABN CORPS

ARMY CENTRAL COMMAND

Safwan

Umm Qasr

Bubiyan

Ar Rawdatayn

KUWAIT CITY
As Salimiyah

Al Ahmadi

Persian Gulf

Khafji

JFC-E

KUWAIT

Al Jahrah

Al Jaber

MARCENT

SAUDI ARABIA

JFC-N

Breach Zone

VII CORPS

Hafar al Batin

Al Qaysumah

I R A Q

Al Busayyah

Allied Advance, Phase 1
Allied Advance, Phase 2
Allied Advance, Phase 3
Allied Advance, Phase 4

0   40
Miles

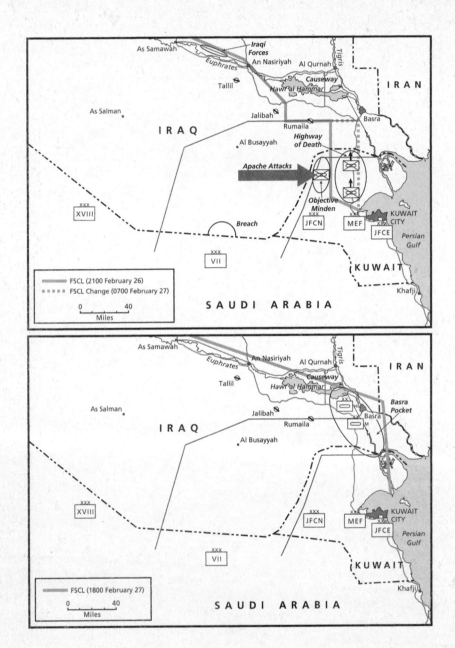

Top map labels:

As Samawah · *Iraqi Forces* · An Nasiriyah · Al Qurnah · *Tigris* · IRAN · *Euphrates* · Tallil · *Causeway* · *Hawr al Hammar* · As Salman · IRAQ · Jalibah · Rumaila · Basra · Al Busayyah · *Highway of Death* · Apache Attacks · *Objective Minden* · KUWAIT CITY · *Breach* · XXX XVIII · XXX JFCN · MEF · JFCE · *Persian Gulf* · XXX VII · KUWAIT · Khafji · SAUDI ARABIA

FSCL (2100 February 26)
FSCL Change (0700 February 27)

0   40
Miles

Bottom map labels:

As Samawah · An Nasiriyah · Al Qurnah · *Tigris* · IRAN · *Euphrates* · Tallil · *Causeway* · *Hawr al Hammar* · As Salman · IRAQ · Jalibah · Rumaila · Basra · *Basra Pocket* · Al Busayyah · XXX XVIII · XXX JFCN · MEF · KUWAIT CITY · JFCE · *Persian Gulf* · XXX VII · KUWAIT · Khafji · SAUDI ARABIA

FSCL (1800 February 27)

0   40
Miles

PART ONE
The Challenge

1

Raising the Shield

I t was a death foretold when Iraqi forces began their lightning assault on the tiny emirate of Kuwait in the first hours of August 2, 1990. For more than a year, U.S. intelligence agencies had closely followed rising tensions among Iraq and the smaller Gulf Cooperation Council (GCC) nations. In 1988, Iraq had emerged victorious from the Iran-Iraq War, a military misadventure that Saddam Hussein conceived of as a short, limited act of aggression when he began the war in September 1980. Instead, the war raged until August 1988, consuming the lives of 375,000 Iraqis and as many as a million Iranians, and the strategic fruits of the war were paltry when compared to the sacrifices made by the Iraqi nation.

Iraq finished the war with the largest and most effective military in the Gulf, but defense spending and infrastructure damage had inflicted grievous damage on Iraq's economy. Saddam considered these near-term costs well worth paying because his own political and physical survival was the ultimate outcome of the war. When Iraq's invasion of southwestern Iran met unexpected levels of resistance from post-revolutionary Iran, Saddam's survival instinct drove him to quickly seek a negotiated peace in return for his withdrawal from Iranian territory. However, the newly installed theocratic government in Tehran refused all entreaties and drove Iraqi forces back into Iraq, thereby threatening the Baathist regime's survival and forcing Saddam to expend liberal quantities of blood and treasure to force the Islamic Republic of Iran to sue for peace.

It was during Iraq's dark years between 1982 and 1984, with Iranian forces pressing into Iraq, that the United States was drawn into a strategic relationship with Saddam Hussein's government. It was never a warm relationship, however, not least because relations between the two countries had been frosty for decades. In 1958, King Faisal, the pro-Western Hashemite monarch of Iraq, had been overthrown, and Iraq joined the growing ranks of Soviet-sponsored Arab republics. During the 1967 Arab-Israeli War, Iraq broke off diplomatic relations with the United States in protest of the growing U.S.–Israeli strategic alliance and pursued a massive rearmament drive in the 1970s, which culminated in the initiation of a nuclear weapons program late in the decade. Relations between Baghdad and Washington were further soured when Israeli strike aircraft bombed the Osiraq nuclear reactor near Baghdad on June 7, 1981, using targeting information surreptitiously gleaned from the United States. Yet, if the United States had enjoyed frosty relations with Iraq, its relations with the Khomeini government were positively glacial in 1980 following the revolution, the seizure of U.S. hostages, and the failed hostage rescue bid in April 1980.

In March 1982, the United States took its first steps toward closer relations with Baghdad by removing Iraq from the U.S. State Department list of state sponsors of terrorism in return for some relatively minor concessions (such as the expulsion of Palestinian terrorist Abu Nidal). On November 26, 1983, President Ronald Reagan signed National Security Decision Directive (NSDD) 114, which expressed concern about Iranian successes in the Iran-Iraq War and opened the path for closer relations with Baghdad. In December 1983 and March 1984, President Reagan sent Donald Rumsfeld, then a private citizen and trusted former government official, with letters to Saddam Hussein. According to declassified reports of their December 1983 meeting, Rumsfeld told the Iraqi president, "It was not in the interest of the region or the West for the conflict to create greater instability, or for the outcome to be one that weakened Iraq's role, or enhanced the interests and ambitions of Iran."[1]

These meetings were followed on April 5, 1984, by NSDD 139, titled "Measures to Improve U.S. Posture and Readiness to Respond to Developments in the Iran-Iraq War," which called for a plan of action to "avert an Iraqi collapse," including alterations to the U.S. "intelligence collection posture."[2]

The latter feature referred to the beginning of the regular provision of U.S. military intelligence to Iraq, including satellite imagery, construction plans of Iranian air bases, and warnings of impending offensives. In November 1984, full diplomatic relations were restored between the United States and Iraq.

As noted, the relationship with Saddam Hussein's regime was never a comfortable experience for the United States. Against a constant background of tension and mutual suspicions, there were periodic spikes in tension, such as the March 17, 1987, missile attack on the USS *Stark*, when the U.S. ship was apparently mistakenly attacked by Iraqi aircraft, causing the deaths of thirty-nine sailors. Although Iraq had been removed from the state sponsors of terrorism list, U.S. officials had little doubt that Baghdad continued to sponsor acts of terror and to shelter international terrorists who presented a threat to American interests and those of its allies. In June 1982, the assassination of Shlomo Argov, Israel's ambassador to the United Kingdom was linked to an Iraqi intelligence officer, and the Iraqi government sent arms and funding to various Palestinian factions throughout the 1980s. In 1985, Iraq gave shelter to terrorists involved in the hijacking of the *Achille Lauro* cruise ship and the murder of the wheelchair-bound U.S. citizen Leon Klinghoffer. In that same year, two Iraq-based terrorist suspects were detained in Rome, en route to U.S. targets in Europe that they were planning to attack.[3]

Saddam's Iraq was also blatantly pursuing the capability to build weapons of mass destruction (WMD), which threatened to decisively alter the regional military balance. The Israeli strike at Osiraq had set back Iraq's pursuit of nuclear materials but had not removed the regime's basic desire to develop a nuclear arsenal. In the meantime, Iraq initiated the first use of chemical weapons in the Iran-Iraq War and employed them from August 1983 onward. Although lethal chemical weapons had been used on other modern battlefields—by Nasserite forces in the Egyptian-Yemeni fighting in the 1960s and by Soviet occupation forces in Afghanistan during the 1980s—they were employed in the Iran-Iraq War on a scale not seen since World War I. In the midst of forging closer covert relations with Iraq, the United States was forced to condemn Iraqi battlefield use of chemical weapons on March 5, 1984. Despite this, Iraq would continue to use a variety of chemical weapons throughout the war.

When a series of devastating offensives by a reformed and professionalized Iraqi military destroyed Iranian military strength in April–July 1988, thereby bringing an end to the war, the United States was quick to disengage from Iraq. In late August 1988, as the fighting between Iran and Iraq trailed off, Saddam moved quickly to evict any Iranian influence on his northern borders with Iran and to punish the Kurdish communities that had sided with Iran during the war. On August 25, 1988, the Iraqi regime launched a massive chemical attack on the town of Halabja, resulting in the death of an estimated five thousand civilians.

Against a backdrop of international protest, U.S. criticism was initially muted but began to grow in early 1989 as the U.S. media exposed details of Iraq's growing chemical and biological weapons programs. In March 1989, with the Soviet threat fading and the offensive capability of the Iranian military effectively destroyed, CENTCOM (U.S. Central Command) identified Iraq as the next major regional threat in its area of responsibility. A strong piece of evidence for this designation was a mammoth arms fair in Baghdad, which gave further indications of Iraq's intent to enlarge its foreign purchases of advanced armaments while simultaneously developing a range of advanced ballistic missile systems for its own use and for export sales.

In August 1989, CENTCOM began the long process of designing contingency plans to confront possible Iraqi actions. Three Defense Intelligence Agency (DIA) analyses were created to kick-start the process. In November 1989, DIA issued an intelligence briefing titled "The Iraqi Threat to the GCC" and an intelligence assessment titled "Iraqi Military Developments through 1992." The latter document downplayed the possibility that Iraq would aggressively expand so soon after the Iran-Iraq War. It stated that "Iraq is unlikely to launch military operations against any of its neighbors over the next three years" and added "to protect its image of moderation, Iraq is unlikely to take military action against Kuwait." Having assessed Iraq's intentions, DIA followed up with an assessment of its capabilities in February 1990 with the DIA intelligence study, "Iraqi Ground and Air Doctrine, Tactics and Operations."[4]

The DIA products indicated that Iraq retained the capability, and the long-term intent, to militarily threaten its smaller neighbors in the Gulf, particularly Kuwait. Since 1961, when Britain ended its protectorate in Kuwait, Iraq's government had claimed suzerainty over the small emirate and claimed it was an "integral part of Iraq" because of its status as part of the Ottoman-era province of Basra. In July 1961, only the timely deployment of British forces to Kuwait prevented an Iraqi attempt at annexation, and since then the Kuwaiti nation had lived under the shadow of its northern neighbor.

During the Iran-Iraq War, Kuwait had informally loaned Iraq at least $17 billion, provided on a grant basis but with the expectation of eventual repayment. Kuwait had also provided wartime berthing for ships bearing Iraqi imports and exports, thereby drawing Iranian missile and air attacks on a number of occasions.[5] After the end of the Iran-Iraq War, Saddam had placed increasing pressure on Kuwait (and to a lesser extent the other GCC nations) to write off Iraqi loans and to reduce their oil-production quotas to raise the price of oil by claiming that Iraq had bankrupted itself fighting the Iran-Iraq War on behalf of all Arabs and that the GCC nations were exacerbating Iraq's bankruptcy.

In comparison with Saddam's largely rhetorical threats to other GCC nations, the danger to Kuwait was clear and present. In an effort to widen the very narrow aperture through which Iraq could access the Persian Gulf, Saddam emphasized Iraq's right to control two Kuwaiti islands—Warbah and Bubiyan—in order to provide an alternative export route to the Shatt al-Arab (SAA) waterway, which was once shared by Iran and Iraq but was clogged by the detritus of war and impassable to commercial traffic in 1989. Iraq also claimed that Kuwait was excessively drawing from shared Iraqi-Kuwaiti oil reservoirs that stretched beneath and astride the border area. In anticipation of some form of confrontation, the U.S. military held a number of war games that dealt with the possibility of an Iraqi invasion of Kuwait. In February 1990, the Naval War College Strategic Studies Group held a war game dealing with an Iraqi invasion of the GCC nations, and at the same time CENTCOM designed a May 1990 war game and its annual command post exercise (CPX) war game around an Iraqi invasion of Kuwait. The CPX, called Internal Look 90, was designed between August 1989 and July 1990 and was intended to sharpen the CENTCOM plan to defend the Arabian Peninsula against an Iraqi attack, an operational plan called OPLAN 1002-90.

IRAQI "SABER-RATTLING"

When Internal Look 90 was played on July 20–28, 1990, at MacDill Air Force Base in Florida, CENTCOM planners noticed disturbing parallels between the scenario unfolding in the war game and real-life events taking place in the Gulf. In the six months prior to Internal Look 90, CENTCOM and DIA had adjusted their program of intelligence collection in the Middle East to closely watch Iraq for signs of military mobilization. Beginning on February 24, 1990,

U.S. satellites imaged Iraqi logistical and military hubs, searching for unusual activity that might betray preparations for offensive operations. Starting in mid-June, a string of indicators pointed to an unusual level of Iraqi military activity, and during July 16–17, these developed into the unmistakable signs of a major military deployment, including the southerly movement of Iraq's most modern battle tanks, Soviet-supplied T-72 models, and the steady development of logistics and communications networks in the Basra area.[6]

On July 17, Saddam issued a scathing critique of Kuwait and the United Arab Emirates (UAE) for bringing the price of oil down through increases in oil production. On this occasion, Iraq looked set to finally back its words by deeds. By July 21, U.S. satellite imagery showed that most of the elements of eight elite Iraqi Republican Guard divisions had deployed by rail and road to the Kuwaiti border in only fourteen days, some moving more than seven hundred kilometers from their depots.[7]

The U.S. intelligence community found it hard to interpret Saddam's motivation and ultimate intent during the July crisis. Was Saddam merely "saber-rattling," did he intend a limited incursion, or would he really carry out the long-threatened annexation of Kuwait? CIA Director Richard Kerr stated, "It would be unprecedented for one Arab state to attack another," and while this was not strictly true (there had been low-key clashes, often involving tribal or rebel proxies, between Egypt and Yemen, Yemen and Saudi Arabia, and Jordan and Syria), an invasion of Kuwait would be a blatant and unparalleled breach of inter-Arab solidarity.[8] Yet, as the military indicators increased in seriousness, DIA assessments began to reflect recognition that military action was a possibility—Saddam's deployment went far beyond what was necessary to either threaten Kuwait or perform deployment exercises.

In a nation where the fear of coup attempts meant that military forces were rarely allowed to deploy from barracks or to receive issues of ammunition, this form of military deployment could only mean that some form of military action was under consideration in Baghdad. But what kind? On July 20, the DIA *Defense Intelligence Digest* stated, "Iraq is unlikely to use significant force against Kuwait, such as occupation of Warbah or Bubiyan Islands. . . . Small-scale incursions are possible." Five days later, with sufficient Iraqi forces in place to overrun Kuwait, the twice-daily DIA defense special assessment stated that Iraq was still "unlikely to use military pressure" but could now "occupy limited objectives" in forty-eight hours or occupy "all of Kuwait in five days."[9]

Even so, it was difficult for the U.S. intelligence community to accept that Saddam planned to annex Kuwait and to take the exceptionally rare step of removing a sovereign country from the roster of nations. According to Bob Woodward, DIA Director General Harry Soyster "just did not find it conceivable that Saddam would do something so anachronistic as an old-fashioned land grab. Countries just didn't go around doing things like that anymore."[10]

As the world should have learned from Iraq's conduct in the 1980s and as it was fated to learn again in August 1990, the Baathist dictatorship in Baghdad paid little heed to international conventions such as the United Nations (UN) charter and even less to the apparent Western attempt to begin forging a post–Cold War modus vivendi—a more peaceful New World Order in which wars of aggression were a thing of the past. Saddam Hussein was unaware of the relief that most of the world felt as the Cold War ended or of the fleeting opportunity to reforge international relations. Instead, he still lived in a Hobbesian "state of nature," where life was "nasty, brutish, and short." For him, nothing had changed, the debts remained, and Iraq needed a new conquest. As Bruce Jentleson wrote, Saddam chose to move "into Kuwait, not into the family of nations."[11]

On August 1, 1990, Iraq's Republican Guard moved into position. According to Pat Lang, the DIA defense intelligence officer for Middle East, South Asia, and Terrorism, "All three Iraqi armored divisions had uncoiled and moved dramatically forward to within three miles of the Kuwaiti border. It was breathtaking, a beautiful military maneuver. . . . Hundreds of tanks were on line—all facing towards Kuwait, spaced some 50–75 yards apart. It was a genuine line of death, miles long. . . . Command tanks had taken the traditional battlefield position in the rear of the line in the center of each division. . . . The Iraqis had moved some eighty helicopters closer to the border in a classic Air-Land assault posture."[12]

At 0100 on August 2, the armored divisions struck out across the border while overhead the Iraqi Air Force (IrAF) launched air strikes on Kuwaiti air bases. At 0130, two brigades of the Republican Guard Special Forces Division made a helicopter assault on Kuwait City while an amphibious force made a seaward assault on palaces where the Kuwaiti royal family was believed to be in residence. The campaign to wipe Kuwait off the map began with a ruthless attempt to kill its royal family. Across Kuwait City, elements of the Emiri Guard launched small counterattacks to reclaim royal palaces, and at the Dasman Palace, one of the emir's brothers, Sheikh Fahd al-Ahmed Al-Sabah, was killed by Iraqi Special Forces. Elsewhere the Emiri Guard fought delaying actions to allow the emir and the rest of the royal family to escape to Saudi Arabia.

The Republican Guard's armored advance was momentarily checked by the Kuwaiti 35th Armored Brigade at the pivotal al-Jahrah crossroads and hindered by Kuwaiti Air Force jets that were able to drop a single set of ordnance each before falling back on Saudi air bases. However, by 0800 the Iraqi armored columns had linked up with their heliborne special forces in Kuwait City, which sealed the country's immediate fate.[13] In this initial lunge, Iraq's armored spearhead traveled eighty kilometers in the first ten hours of the attack and moved an additional seventy-five kilometers to the Saudi-Kuwaiti border in the next twenty-four hours.[14]

By the end of August 2, DIA assessed that Iraq had massed a sufficient number of offensive forces to continue its thrust into Saudi Arabia, whose most important oil fields were arrayed a little more than a hundred kilometers farther down the Kuwait-Saudi coastal road. By August 6, the Iraqi military had deployed eleven divisions to Kuwait; four days later, they had established an integrated air-defense system within the country and based IrAF interceptor, reconnaissance, and strike aircraft at captured Kuwaiti air bases. On August 8, Iraq announced that its forces would stay in Kuwait, which would be annexed and absorbed within Iraq as the country's 19th province.

Iraq's "old-fashioned land grab" in Kuwait immediately captivated world attention and drew strong international criticism. Kuwait's important role in global oil markets undoubtedly played a role in focusing the mind of the international community on the Iraqi invasion. Iraq's own oil production represented 3 percent of world production and almost 10 percent of proven global reserves. With Kuwaiti oil, Saddam would control 5 percent of world production and 19.6 percent of proven global reserves. Were Saddam to continue his advance into the world's largest oil producer, Saudi Arabia, he would eventually have held ransom 15.8 percent of world production and a staggering 43.5 percent of proven global reserves, thereby providing him with turnkey control over the growth of the global economy and sufficient funding to guarantee his emergence as a new regional superpower. As a result, Saddam's invasion of Kuwait represented the most serious challenge to date to the 1980 Carter Doctrine, which states that "any attempt by any outside force to gain control of the Persian Gulf region will be regarded as an assault on the vital interests of the United States of America. And such an assault will be repelled by any means necessary, including military force."[15]

Although the Carter Doctrine, in large part, had been developed to warn off Soviet incursions into the Gulf, Saddam's invasion of Kuwait came in the first blooming of the post–Cold War thaw in U.S.–Soviet relations and was met with a united front that would probably have been impossible to achieve during the Cold War years. No major power was willing to trust Saddam Hussein at the helm of global oil production. During the prior decade, Saddam had shown that neither the United States nor the Soviet Union could control him, and he struck a strongly independent line whenever it suited him. Nor was Saddam a loyal or creditworthy business partner, as France, the Soviet Union, and a host of international-export credit agencies discovered to their cost.

Thanks to Iraq's eight-year war against Iran, Saddam's stewardship of Iraq's massive oil reserves had been an unmitigated disaster, marking Saddam as one of the least predictable people in whom to entrust a controlling share in the most precious material commodity on the planet. Coming at the close of a decade of war, the invasion of Kuwait showed that Saddam was simply not a man with whom one could do business anymore. On August 2, 1990, the UN Security Council (UNSC) passed Resolution 660, which condemned the invasion and called for Iraq to withdraw from Kuwait. Eleven additional UN resolutions were passed in the months between August and November 1990, including the authorization of "all necessary means" to liberate Kuwait, which underlined the unprecedented level of international solidarity evoked by Iraq's invasion.[16]

Saddam's invasion came at what was termed the "unipolar moment" of the United States—the last superpower standing—and it was U.S. leadership that focused international concern and made concerted action possible. The motivations of President George H. W. Bush's administration bear some commentary. With as many as three thousand U.S. citizens held as "guests" in Iraq and Kuwait, the U.S. government faced a delicate situation and might not have been faulted for circumspection in its approach to the Gulf crisis. Yet, as early as August 5, President Bush stated that Iraq's actions constituted "naked aggression" and vowed "this will not stand, this aggression against Kuwait."[17]

In what Bob Woodward called "Act One of the New World Order," the president was attempting to trace the lines of acceptable conduct in the post–Cold War world.[18] A World War II aviator, President Bush reacted to Iraq's act of aggression in a way that reflected his generational perspective on the dangers of appeasing ascendant regional dictators, and Bush's reading material during the crisis—Martin Gilbert's *The Second World War: A Complete History*—appears to have framed his thinking on the crisis.[19] On August 5, Bush phrased U.S. objectives as securing the "immediate, complete, and unconditional withdrawal of all Iraq forces from Kuwait" and the restoration of the Kuwaiti government. Three days later, Bush stated, "If history teaches us anything, it is that we must resist aggression or it will destroy our freedoms."[20] In an interview with David Frost aired just before Operation Desert Storm, the president stated, "We have such a clear moral case. . . . It's that big, it's that important. [There's been] nothing like this since World War Two. Nothing of this moral importance since World War Two."[21]

BUILDING THE FORCES: OPERATION DESERT SHIELD

Thus, from the outset, U.S. military planners could count on strong political support from national-level decision makers and an unprecedented degree of solidarity in the international community. Yet, in early August 1990, what they needed most were forces in place in the Gulf to deter a potential Iraqi move into Saudi Arabia. Although no evidence has since emerged to suggest that Saddam planned to undertake this course of action, at the time it seemed as though little could be done to stop Saddam's military from taking control of the most critical oil fields in the world. For a four-day window after the invasion of Kuwait, the northern Saudi oil fields—a two-day drive from Iraqi frontline forces—were solely defended by a single Saudi Arabian brigade. Although a U.S. aircraft carrier battle group was ordered to the Gulf on August 2, its aircraft were not within effective range of the Saudi-Kuwait border until August 6, at which time a senior Department of Defense (DoD) delegation had arrived in Saudi Arabia to discuss the deployment of U.S. forces within the kingdom.

After fifteen years of U.S. deployments to land bases in the GCC nations, it is easy for the present-day reader to forget that in 1990 the deployment of Western forces was a novel and threatening prospect for the Gulf nations, most of all for Saudi Arabia, whose royal family were the custodians of Islam's holiest shrines, Makkah and Medina. As Bob Woodward noted, "It was unheard of for the Saudis to ask the United States for forces. . . . We would be asking the Saudis to confront a decision that they had spent their lifetimes shying away from. It would be a radical departure to accept a force of any size."[22]

Other Gulf nations expressed similar concerns, notably the United Arab Emirates (UAE). The UAE took great pains to conceal the Operation Ivory Justice deployment of U.S. tanker aircraft to the country in July (by making sure their tall tail fins could not be seen over airfield walls, for example), despite the ostensible purpose of the deployment, which was to provide a visible deterrent against Iraqi threats.[23] Although the UAE leadership wanted to demonstrate its ability to call on U.S. protection, it dared not communicate that same message to its people, whose unease about a U.S. military presence would linger throughout the following decade.

In the aftermath of Iraq's shocking annexation of another GCC nation, however, traditional GCC resistance to a U.S. military presence quickly disappeared, and a steady flow of aircraft began to arrive in each of the Gulf nations from August 7 onward, the date that marked the official beginning of Operation Desert Shield. Within forty-eight hours, one squadron of F-15C/D fighters from the 1st Tactical Fighter Wing at Langley Air Force Base had joined U.S. carrier aviation in establishing combat air patrols over northern Saudi Arabia, while seven B-52 bombers of the 42nd Bombardment Wing provided bomber cover from the Indian Ocean island of Diego Garcia, a British possession leased to the U.S. military. Within five days, five fighter squadrons plus Airborne Warning and Control System (AWACS) aircraft had landed in the Gulf and a brigade combat team of the 82nd Airborne Division was digging in along the Saudi–Kuwaiti border. The opening days of the deployment marked a moment of dramatic vulnerability for U.S. forces. As Brig. Gen. Patrick Caruana of Strategic Air Command observed, the screen might not have held if Iraqi forces had made a determined effort to breach it. He noted, "How effective we would have been with B-52s against an armored column was marginal at best."[24] The troopers of the 82nd Airborne depreciatingly referred to themselves as "Iraqi speed-bumps."[25] Had Iraq been able to lodge itself in Saudi Arabia's oil-rich provinces and denied the Coalition access to key Saudi ports and air bases, it could have seriously derailed the complex Coalition deployment process. This prompted Caruana to note: "If Saddam Hussein had been smart, he would have done that. That would have complicated things tremendously for us."[26]

While the heavy ground forces of the Cold War U.S. military slowly made their way to theater—held up by rail and sealift bottlenecks as they made their way from bases in Europe and the continental United States (CONUS)—an air-heavy deterrent force faced the growing number of Iraqi forces in Kuwait throughout August. CENTCOM Commander-in-Chief (CINC) Gen. Norman Schwarzkopf adapted the flow of forces to theater in the Time-Phased Force Deployment Directive to ensure that high numbers of tank-killing platforms arrived in the Gulf during the weeks following the invasion. These included ten squadrons of A-10 ground-attack aircraft, two squadrons of U.S. Marine Corps AV-8B Harriers, plus four squadrons of Army AH-64 Apache helicopters and two squadrons of Marine AH-1W Cobra attack helicopters. According to Col. Steve Wilson, who was present throughout the early bed-down period of Desert Shield, on August 14 the Joint Force Air Component Commander (JFACC), Lt. Gen. Charles "Chuck" Horner, guided the Central Command Air Forces (CENTAF) staff "to build a campaign plan to attack the Iraqi army guys right along the border" in attacks that would deliberately keep the pressure up all through the night by "stretching out Time-on-Targets [ToTs]."

The so-called D-Day Plan, completed by August 20, included these features, with all available aircraft making a "hard initial thrust" against the Iraqi forces for the first seven hours of an invasion. For Lieutenant General Horner, one of the elements of the D-Day Plan that caused the most concern was the very real possibility that Iraqi forces would overrun Saudi airfields used by the United States. Therefore, once the initial attacks were launched, the plan included provision for land-based aircraft to relocate while the aircraft carriers USS *Eisenhower* and *Independence* would apply "continuous pressure" for an additional thirty-six hours, focusing both on Iraqi armored spearheads and likely choke points in the Iraqi lines of supply. The plan involved few fixed targets—for which targeting materials did not yet exist anyhow—and instead matched the constantly increasing force pool to a set of kill boxes thirty by thirty miles wide that would be mapped over the Kuwait-Saudi border. Only strike packages with electronic support packages would probe deeper and attack key logistical nodes from the slender forty-four-target CENTAF joint target list.[27] The plan was sound, but there was no comfort for U.S. planners, as Horner recalled: "I will never forget those long dark nights in August 1990, when we struggled desperately to build up our forces, knowing that at any time the Iraqi army could easily push across Saudi Arabia's border and capture not only the majority of the world's oil supply, but also the air bases and ports necessary for deploying our forces."[28]

By the time the heavy forces of the 24th Mechanized Infantry Division deployed to Saudi Arabia in September 1990, the imminent risk of Iraqi invasion had passed and the immediate objective of Desert Shield was fulfilled. The U.S. military had passed its first major post—Cold War challenge—a challenge that presented a mixture of the familiar and the novel. The establishment of a defensive system that could repel the lead elements of an armor-heavy attacker, while simultaneously striking deep at advancing follow-on forces, perfectly mirrored the task for which the U.S. military had prepared throughout the previous decade, namely, a follow-on forces attack (FOFA). By creating a miniature Fulda Gap in the Saudi desert, the U.S. military had raised the shield.

The geographical context, on the other hand, was vastly different. As in other contemporaneous U.S. military operations in Grenada (1983), Libya (1986), and Panama (1989), the United States was required to quickly refocus on an area outside its core military theaters in Central Europe and Korea. Unlike in those cases, however, the United States faced a threat that required the deployment of major heavyweight U.S. Army formations. The Saudi desert was, in the words of Lt. Gen. Fred Franks, "a very strange, unfamiliar, and harsh place" for the European and CONUS-based cold warriors who deployed there in the fall of 1990.[29]

INTELLIGENCE PREPARATION OF THE BATTLEFIELD

The U.S. military had been a garrison force for forty-five years, but now a sizable portion of it had to pick up and move. When U.S. forces deployed to Saudi Arabia, the kingdom represented what might be termed an immature theater, because although Saudi air bases provided ample ramp space and hardened aircraft shelters for the burgeoning numbers of arriving U.S. combat and transport aircraft, everything else had to be built from scratch, ranging from personnel shelters and sanitation, to water and food supplies, training ranges, mail deliveries, and rest and relaxation (R&R) opportunities. This was even more true for the development of an intelligence system to support CENTCOM, which received a low priority from the outset of Desert Shield until initial defensive forces were in place by October 1990. For the first sixty days of Operation Desert Shield, the shipment of desperately needed combat forces were prioritized over support elements, which included CENTCOM's intelligence directorate (J-2), plus the intelligence directorates of individual U.S. components (such as the air component, CENTAF).[30] The formal intelligence system took many months to recover from this delay, as illustrated by the late development of the CENTCOM J-2 directorate, which was "a mere shell" up to four months after the invasion of Kuwait.[31] CENTCOM had always been different from other U.S. regional commands in that it did not maintain a permanent forward headquarters, operating instead from MacDill Air Force Base in Florida. As a result, its peacetime headquarters and intelligence elements were lightly manned outfits; by November 1990, CENTCOM J-2 had merely 43 staff members, and it took until January 1991 for that number to reach its wartime manning of 670 personnel.[32] CENTCOM's peacetime "over-the-horizon" posture meant that no U.S. communications network existed in theater in August 1990. Instead, an all-new, theater-wide communications system needed to be improvised and slowly deployed, piece by piece, throughout the fall of 1990.

Although the system gradually increased connectivity among individual components and tactical formations, CENTCOM J-2, and the national intelligence providers, it became hopelessly clogged with routine message traffic as Desert Shield unfolded.[33] As formal channels became swamped, U.S. combat commanders and intelligence officers in the Gulf developed a range of informal and improvised workarounds. This parallel intelligence system operated before and after the formal system—which used CENTCOM J-2 as the clearinghouse for national and theater intelligence products—started to function effectively in January 1991. Months before the establishment of the rapidly overwhelmed Automatic Digital Network (AUTODIN) special-intelligence communications network, key planning and intelligence hubs in Saudi Arabia gained the ability to communicate directly with the national intelligence agencies in Washington, D.C.: the Central Intelligence Agency (CIA), DIA, individual service intelligence agencies, and the National Security Agency (NSA). This connectivity was achieved either through the self-contained satellite communications capability of the DIA National Military Intelligence Support Teams (NMISTs) deployed to major (component and corps) headquarters in Saudi Arabia, or through other less advanced means, including secure telephone, fax, e-mail (to a lesser extent), or courier delivery of information in electronic disk or hard-copy format.[34]

National-level intelligence agencies proved to be the best providers of all-source intelligence products for a host of reasons. In the first case, until CENTCOM J-2 was deployed and adequately manned to assign, collect, and analyze intelligence, there was no alternative. As Gen. Michael Ryan noted in 1991, "when you have a theater that is immature, it is very hard to deal with any other place but in Washington."[35] Just as important, national-level intelligence-collection systems (satellites, high-altitude spy planes, and human agents) were best positioned to collect new intelligence data on Iraq during the preconflict phase because border patrols by tactical collection systems (scouts and airborne surveillance aircraft) were considered to be too provocative in the buildup period. Coalition naval forces were restricted to operations seventy-two miles south of the Kuwaiti-Saudi border, and Coalition air forces were restricted from operating within fifty-five miles of the border. Even when U-2R surveillance missions were launched from farther south, it was like patrolling the East German border or the parallel separating North and South Korea all over again. Coalition aircraft were frequently "painted" by Iraqi radar or shadowed by Iraqi fighters, and Iraq launched a series of shallow incursions by its aircraft into Saudi Arabia.[36] As a result, neither U.S. naval vehicles nor tactical aerial reconnaissance systems (such as the venerable RF-4C) could effectively surveil Iraq or occupied Kuwait. Other tactical intelligence-gathering capabilities (U.S. Army and Marine Corps signals-intelligence [SIGINT] assets) were either not fully deployed or were again limited in their ability to reach into enemy territory or to translate communications intercepts in Arabic.[37] Defections of enemy prisoners of war (EPWs)—a key source of tactical intelligence—were uncommon in the preconflict period. As a result, intelligence during Desert Shield predominantly flowed down from the national level and frequently failed to trickle down as far as the tactical levels.[38]

An early priority for the ad hoc intelligence system was the development of updated maps and other geospatial analyses of the terrain and physical environment in Saudi Arabia, Kuwait, and Iraq. As Desert Storm began, the U.S. Defense Mapping Agency was poorly prepared to provide geographical intelligence on these areas because the DoD and Joint Chiefs of Staff (JCS) continued to prioritize mapping of areas in Europe and the Union of Soviet Socialist Republics (USSR).[39] Existing maps were too few and typically four to ten years old, which led the United States to task multispectral imagery satellites with developing a brand-new range of up-to-date 1:50,000 and 1:100,000 scale maps of the theater. During the course of Desert Shield, the U.S. military would deliver 80 million maps to Coalition forces.[40] Yet, what maps could not always tell tactical commanders was the load-bearing capacity of certain areas, which led U.S. Army intelligence officers to undertake a series of terrain-reconnaissance efforts. Between September and November 1990, U.S. ground forces planners used multispectral imagery to identify areas of Saudi terrain with similar qualities to terrain found in southern Iraq, and then performed a series of trafficability tests on the Saudi terrain, thereby assessing the Iraqi terrain's ability to support tracked and wheeled vehicle movements.[41] U.S. ground forces commanders who had spent the majority of their careers planning or rehearsing the terrain-based defense of Germany or Korea were used to being able to spend days walking the actual terrain on which they planned to fight defensive battles. This practice was fine for the defense of Saudi Arabia, but it would be impossible in the context of offensive operations into Kuwait or Iraq, where very little ground-level terrain analysis could be provided. As Brig. Gen. John Stewart, the senior intelligence officer (G-2) for the U.S. Third Army in 1990–91 noted, "Knowledge of precisely the kind of desert we faced was sketchy. In the years we had official relations with Iraq, not one military attaché had apparently walked the terrain south of the Euphrates to the Saudi Arabian border."[42] To reduce the effects of this shortfall, bedouin in the employ of the CIA carried out nocturnal, long-range patrols to probe the load-bearing capacity of *sabquas*, corridors of soft sandy terrain, and took low-light video footage of boulder fields and other potential obstacles to armored movement.[43]

KNOWING THE ENEMY

The second immediate intelligence requirement that most U.S. commanders faced was a need to get a feel for the capabilities and intentions of the Iraqi military. Unlike other regional commands, CENTCOM did not have military forces permanently allocated to it in 1990, and its units were instead drawn as required from Europe, CONUS, and other theaters from around the world. These men and women had primarily trained to defend against Soviet, Warsaw Pact, or North Korean opponents. Although this meant that most of them could readily characterize the capabilities of Iraq's large arsenal of Eastern Bloc military equipment, only a tiny fraction of them had deployed to the

Middle East before. Still fewer had any impression of the intangible cultural and historical factors that provided added pointers to the type of adversary Iraq threatened to be.

Although CENTCOM's small standing staff had gained some degree of familiarity with the Iraqi order of battle (ORBAT) during the months of alerts and war games that preceded the invasion of Kuwait, the real expertise on the military threat from Iraq resided in DIA, which had published its timely intelligence study "Iraqi Ground and Air Doctrine, Tactics and Operations" in February 1990.[44] This assessment drew on the work of the U.S. Army Intelligence Agency (AIA)'s Intelligence and Threat Analysis Center (ITAC); other assessments of Iraq's air and coastal defense capabilities would be provided by the U.S. Air Force Intelligence Agency and the U.S. Navy Operational Intelligence Center, respectively.[45]

The recent Iran-Iraq War had provided eight years during which U.S. military attachés and observers could observe the Iraqi military at close range, particularly as intelligence-sharing arrangements and military-to-military ties deepened in the mid-1980s. Since the end of that war, the U.S. intelligence community had increasingly focused its technical collection assets on Iraq, although this remained largely limited to tasking satellite surveillance of Iraq's logistical and transportation hubs to glean indicators of military mobilization. The swift and brutal annexation of Kuwait gave the United States a current picture of the offensive capabilities of Iraq's Republican Guard forces. As a result, using both historical data and ongoing intelligence collection, the United States quickly developed an image of Iraq's military potential.

Following the erection of a minimum deterrent force screening Saudi Arabia, Coalition military planners and intelligence analysts began to anticipate the mission of liberating Kuwait. Few U.S. military commanders were willing to bet that offensive airpower would successfully coerce an Iraqi withdrawal from Kuwait, which placed Iraq's land-warfare capability at the front and center of U.S. military capability (MILCAP) analyses. Time after time, Iraqi ground forces had displayed bravery, logistical efficiency, and tactical ineptitude in equal measure during both the 1948 and 1973 Arab-Israeli wars and a running series of battles with Kurdish separatists during 1961–70 and 1974–75. Yet, the U.S. intelligence community was ultimately more interested in the development of Iraq's advanced land-warfare capabilities since the mid-1970s. This period witnessed a doubling of the size of Iraq's military and its increasing dedication to the mission of guaranteeing external security. In 1989, Iraq was assessed to have a million-man standing military plus 850,000 reservists. Its land forces' ORBAT included fifty-three divisions, twenty special-forces brigades, and numerous regional militias. In raw numbers, Iraq was believed to maintain holdings of 5,500 tanks, more than 3,000 artillery pieces, strong air defenses, and approximately 700 combat aircraft and helicopters.[46] By any account it was a monstrous military, the fourth-largest standing army in the world and of comparative size to the U.S. Army. In addition, it was modernizing. Following early battlefield reverses in the first two years of the Iran-Iraq War, the Baathist regime moved slowly but inexorably to reduce the politicization of the Iraqi officer class, improve unit cohesion, and develop better-trained armed forces. During the 1980–88 Iran-Iraq War, Baghdad effectively forged a three-tier military: eleven high-quality Republican Guard or regular-army armored or mechanized divisions, an additional fifty-two regular-army infantry divisions, and a 150,000-strong regional militia called the Popular Army.[47]

DEFENSE-IN-DEPTH: IRAQI LAND-WARFARE CAPABILITIES

The Iran-Iraq War, particularly its last six months, saw the ultimate development of Iraq's military abilities in the fields of defense-in-depth and counteroffensive operations. Both of these areas were supported by the battlefield employment of chemical weapons, and thus were of great significance to U.S. planners. As Iranian offensive operations frequently penetrated Iraqi defenses—bypassing Iraqi strongpoints or infiltrating between them at night—Iraq employed layered defensive networks of ever-increasing sophistication as the war unfolded. By the end of the Iran-Iraq War, the Iraqi armed forces developed a three-stage defensive concept of operations.

The first stage involved the development of parallel defensive lines that continuously covered the breadth of the battlefront and extended to a depth of thirty-five kilometers or more, thereby reducing the risk of flanking or infiltration. Basra, for instance, was covered by six concentric defensive belts. At times, the development of Iraqi defenses involved extensive modification of peacetime geography. In the summer of 1982, Iraqi engineers flooded a set of fisheries east of Basra known as Fish Lake, expanding the body of water, sowing it with mines and barbed wire, and electrifying some sections with coils of exposed power lines.[48] As CENTCOM planners and intelligence analysts perused imagery of the Kuwait theater of operations (KTO) and southern Iraq, it was clear from an early stage that Iraq was building a defensive system of comparable scale. The so-called Saddam Line was more than 240 kilometers long, including 80 kilometers that extended west of the trilateral Kuwaiti-Iraq-Saudi border. To sustain the defensive network, 2,000 kilometers of roads were etched out of the Kuwaiti and Iraqi deserts and hundreds of kilometers of new railway tracks and water pipelines extended southward from Iraq.[49]

Beginning 5–15 kilometers north of the Saudi border, a series of platoon- and company-sized strongpoints, barbed wire, and mixed antitank and antipersonnel mine belts extended throughout this deep security zone, which served as an early-warning and delaying mechanism for Iraq's main defense line. The security zone was typically separated from the main defensive position by a continuous sand berm, nearly 3 meters tall, backed on the enemy side by a deep antitank trench. The double barrier of the berm and ditch sought to ensure that Iraqi gunners would have two opportunities to target the weaker belly armor of Coalition vehicles as they crested the berm and then emerged from the ditch. Where oil pipe lines ran close to the trench, preparations were made for crude oil to be diverted into the ditch and to be ignited if Coalition forces breached the barrier. On the Iraqi side of the berm, a total of twenty-three Iraqi infantry divisions were identified and located by U.S. SIGINT and imagery intelligence (IMINT). Each division was deployed on a 15–20 kilometer frontage to a depth of approximately 10 kilometers. According to the Congressional report *The Conduct of the Persian Gulf War*, the main defense line constituted "an almost unbroken line of mutually supporting brigade-sized defensive positions, composed of company trench lines and strong points."[50]

Extensive supplies of ammunition appeared to have been positioned with these units to enable them to continue fighting even if isolated, and each of their dozen or so battalions was deployed within a triangular fighting position. Roughly 2,500 meters across on each side, the positions included company-sized strongpoints at each corner and a central redoubt in which armored vehicles were sheltered from horizontal ground-level targeting by a tall sand wall and nestled within horseshoe-shaped berms to guard against the effects of near misses by air strikes or artillery.[51] An additional 45 kilometers of Kuwait's coastline was also extensively fortified against amphibious invasion. In addition to offshore minefields and underwater beach obstacles, barbed wire, and belts of antipersonnel mines on the beach and dune areas, three Iraqi infantry divisions had dug themselves into the semiurban sprawl along the Persian Gulf coast. They fortified civilian high-rise buildings and condominium complexes and developing elaborate schemes to simultaneously detonate a series of liquid chlorine, natural gas, and petroleum plants along the seafront in the event of an amphibious assault.[52]

Once attacking forces had become entangled in the defensive system, the second stage of Iraq's defensive doctrine in the Iran-Iraq War called for the use of massed artillery fires and, to a lesser extent, close air support (CAS) to inflict heavy casualties on the enemy. Iraqi defensive systems were designed to channel attacking forces into "kill sacks," predictable areas that had been preregistered by Iraqi artillery and aerial units and which—lacking any reliable form of over-the-horizon targeting[53]—would otherwise have been incapable of bringing fire to bear on a mobile opponent. In addition to conventional munitions—high-explosive shells and rockets, cluster bombs, and fuel-air explosives—Iraq's artillery and CAS helicopters or aircraft were also highly proficient in using chemical weapons against enemy units snagged on Iraqi defensive lines.

During the Iran-Iraq War, the Baathist government demonstrated Iraq's ability to deliver large quantities of blister agents (such as mustard gas) and was the first and only nation to use nerve gasses (such as Sarin and Soman) in battle.[54] In the course of these operations, the Iraqis had learned that the heat of the desert quickly evaporated chemical agents and the unpredictable desert winds often dispersed them or carried them back toward Iraqi lines. By 1988, they had learned to use chemical weapons early in the morning, when the desert was cool and the air still. Lacking the type of human intelligence (HUMINT) sources within the Iraqi leadership that could give a definitive impression of Iraqi intent to use chemical weapons, the Army Intelligence Agency (AIA) issued an estimate in December 1990 that stated Iraq would use chemical weapons against Coalition forces, perhaps as early as initial Coalition breaching attacks on the main defensive belt of the Saddam Line, and certainly if Republican Guard forces came under effective attack.[55] Given Iraq's past form and the lack of hard data on Iraq's operational intentions, it was the only responsible assessment that could be made.

Iraqi artillery units located up to thirty-two kilometers from each kill sack represented the key threat, both in terms of conventional and chemical-munitions delivery, and indeed Iraq's frontline infantry divisions had been bolstered with additional army and Republican Guard artillery battalions during Desert Shield. In addition to these potential sources of Iraqi firepower, the helicopters of the Iraqi Army Aviation Corps (IrAAC) and the tactical aircraft of the IrAF could also launch conventional or chemical attacks on the kill sacks from greater ranges. Although unresponsive by Western standards, massed Iraqi CAS against key enemy concentrations could be requested by Iraqi corps and divisional commanders. When employing conventional munitions, such attacks were unlikely to cause serious losses to Coalition forces and amounted to little more than the massed salvo-firing of unguided rockets and bombs. Iraqi had experimented with air-delivered fuel-air explosives, which theoretically flooded targeted areas with an explosive aerosol that, on ignition, produced extremely destructive overpressures, although the difficult art of achieving the fuel-air mix had apparently never been perfected by the Iraqis.[56] By 1987–88, Iraq's helicopters and aircraft had developed increased proficiency in delivering "annihilation insecticides," as the Iraqi leadership referred to chemical weapons, by utilizing aerial bombs, rockets, and spray tanks.[57] As Desert Shield developed, U.S. intelligence monitoring of Iraqi airfields appeared to show preparation of chemical munitions at a number of air bases that boasted distinctive S-shaped or cruciform chemical-weapons storage bunkers.

The third stage of Iraq's defensive concept of operations was the use of reserves to launch counterattacks against enemy penetrations of the main defense line. During the Iran-Iraq War, an armored "tactical reserve" stood immediately behind the infantry divisions of each Iraqi corps, and during Desert Shield the same principle appeared to be in preparation. Nine Iraqi regular-army divisions were held to reinforce the main defensive line, including three armored divisions (the 10th, 12th, and 52nd), while the 5th Mechanized Division was held to reinforce Iraq's coastal defense line. These formations, the cream of the Iraqi regular army, were thought to be most likely to undertake simple and direct counterattacks against enemy breakthroughs. To counter more serious breakthroughs during the Iran-Iraq War, Saddam had developed a set of "operational reserves" that could be held well back from the main defensive line and switched back and forth along the excellent four- and six-lane highways that paralleled the Iran-Iraq border. By using rail transport in addition to the highways, Iraq could swiftly move its armor on an enormous fleet of three thousand heavy-equipment transporters (HETs), a force six times as large as the U.S. fleet.[58]

The Republican Guard's armored and mechanized divisions were the linchpin of this capability and were inevitably compared to Nazi Germany's *Waffen SS* divisions. Enlarged from just a single brigade of regime security forces in 1981, the Republican Guard was a twenty-eight-brigade miniature army by 1988.[59] Grown from the regime's palace praetorian, the Republican Guard was pampered from the outset with preferential access to Iraq's most modern military equipment and far more attractive pay, billeting, and feeding arrangements. Like the *Waffen SS*, Republican Guard divisions were given symbolic names drawn either from Mesopotamian history (Hammurabi, Nebuchadnezzar) or from significant Iraqi cities or battle honors of the Republican Guard. The Republican Guard's "fire brigade" role honed its offensive military capabilities. Utilizing Iraq's most modern offensive land-warfare platforms—T-72 tanks and self-propelled artillery and air defenses—the Republican Guard developed unparalleled all-arms cooperation (tank, infantry, and artillery) and was undoubtedly "the world's most seasoned [army] in carrying out assaults preceded by chemical attacks."[60] As the lightning invasion of Kuwait had shown, the Republican Guard had maintained its keen edge two years after the last offensive of the Iran-Iraq War.

Iraq's apparent ability to undertake sophisticated offensive operations that penetrated deep into enemy territory concerned U.S. commanders. *The Conduct of the Persian Gulf War* noted: "During the last six months of the Iran-Iraq war, the Iraqi army had demonstrated a capability to conduct multi-axis, multi-corps, combined-arms operations deep into hostile territory. The staff could conduct long-range planning; coordination of air and artillery preparations; timing of movements and operations; coordination of complicated logistics requirements; and movement of supplies, equipment, and troops to the right place at the designated time. They had developed excellent operational security and deception."[61]

Iraq's inclination toward "deep attacks" mirrored key elements of late–Cold War Soviet and U.S. land-warfare doctrine, which sought to attack the enemy throughout his strategic depth. As early as 1984, Iraq's army aviation had launched attack helicopter raids with up to fifty Mi-25 Hind-D gunships to a depth of seventy-five kilometers behind Iranian lines, and the helicopter arm of the IrAAC arguably developed into the most effective component of Iraq's armed forces. By 1988, Iraq was using its Brazilian-supplied Astros-II multiple-launch rocket system to dispense cluster bombs against logistical choke points up to sixty-five kilometers behind enemy lines.[62] In offensives in

1988 and 1990, Iraq had demonstrated its ability to conduct deep helicopter- and amphibious-assault operations to secure operational objectives.

"KARI": IRAQ'S INTEGRATED AIR-DEFENSE SYSTEM

To protect Iraq's ground forces and national infrastructure, by 1990 Iraq had developed one of the most intricate integrated air-defense systems (IADS) in the world. A French-designed automated command-and-control (C2) system called KARI (Iraq spelled backward in French) provided the backbone of an extensive network of 100 radar sites, approximately 210 radar-guided surface-to-air missile (SAM) sites, 500 dedicated IrAF interceptor aircraft protected by a system of 594 hardened aircraft shelters, and a dense low-altitude air-defense system comprising 6,000 antiaircraft artillery (AAA) guns and tens of thousands of shoulder-launched heat-seeking SAMs, known as manportable air defense systems (MANPADSs).[63] Israeli and Iranian air attacks on Iraq during the 1980s had exploited weaknesses in low-altitude Iraqi radar coverage, which led Iraq to employ unguided barrages of low-altitude antiaircraft fire to force attackers up to higher altitudes, where their bombing attacks would be less effective and their aircraft more vulnerable to interception by radar-guided SAMs and aircraft. In the air, as on the ground, Iraq had learned to employ defense-in-depth and channel the enemy into prepared killing grounds.

Integration and electronic data transfer were the key to KARI's sophistication. The national Air Defense Operations Center, housed in an underground bunker in Baghdad, coordinated the system. Five sector operations centers, including a new one in occupied Kuwait, maintained local situational awareness (SA) of the "air picture." Each was capable of tracking up to 120 air contacts simultaneously and of matching weapons to targeting solutions, including automatically targeting SA-2 and SA-3 radar-guided SAM on enemy contacts. Alternately, SAM sites could operate autonomously, tracking incoming attackers using their own tracking and fire-control radars. Fourteen Intercept Operations Centers (IOC) located in bunkers at IrAF air bases provided radio guidance to airborne IrAF interceptor aircraft, a procedure known as ground-controlled intercept (GCI).

Although the Iraqi air force had engaged in intense air-to-air combat during the entire eight years of the Iran-Iraq War, it had emerged with a mixed record. On the one hand, they had taken part in more than a thousand air-to-air engagements, including the first large-scale beyond-visual-range combats using active and semiactive radar-guided missiles. On the flipside, however, Iraqi air-to-air interception skills had not developed beyond the use of ambushes and short, sharp, high-speed slash attacks and were characterized by an overreliance on GCI support. This dependency developed during the Iran-Iraq War, when Iraqi pilots were encouraged to rely entirely on the IOCs for almost every detail of air-to-air warfare, as Farhad Bishop and Tom Cooper graphically described: "The Iraqis in general depended heavily on GCI for the entire duration of an engagement: they were trained to fly an intercept course according to GCI instructions, to maneuver according to GCI instructions, and to finally activate their radars and fire when the GCI would tell them to do so."[64] Furthermore, although the IrAF stepped up its activity levels and defensive patrols between August 1990 and January 1991, it had already lost much of the keen edge that it developed during the Iran-Iraq War as a result of postwar purges, politicization, and the lack of useful training program.

The KARI system had never been required to manage a major massed attack on Iraq since its completion in 1986, nor had it ever been directly subjected to sustained attack itself. As a result, it was unclear to U.S. planners and intelligence analysts how well it would function under these conditions. In the absence of data on the recent performance of Iraqi air defenses, U.S. threat estimates focused on the technical characteristics of the individual components of KARI. Iraq deployed most of the same SAM systems as the Soviet Union, including an estimated 135 of the capable and survivable SA-6 self-propelled systems; it also deployed a range of European medium-altitude point-defense SAMs. The IrAF, meanwhile, boasted up to 820 aircraft delivered by the Soviet Union between 1980 and 1987, including late-export models of the MiG-29 interceptor, which the U.S. intelligence community then classified as a dangerous "fourth-generation" fighter.[65] In addition, France had only recently delivered seventy "3.5-generation" Dassault F-1EQ-5 interceptors, complete with limited quantities of advanced French "Super" R-530F air-to-air missiles (AAMs), and fifty advanced R-550 Magic II AAM had been captured from the Kuwaiti air force in August 1990.[66]

U.S. assessments focused disproportionately on these small numbers of platforms and munitions because of their capability to cause tactical surprise wherever they appeared. Far less attention was focused on the lower profile but arguably more significant features of military power—training and equipment maintenance—that represented areas of Iraqi weakness. The final U.S. assessment of KARI reflected the prevailing belief that the system presented a serious threat to Coaliton freedom of action over Iraqi-held territory, as noted by *The Conduct of the Persian Gulf War*: "The Iraqi air defense system was formidable, combining the best features of several systems. The multi-layered, redundant, computer-controlled air defense network around Baghdad was more dense than that surrounding most Eastern European cities during the Cold War, and several orders of magnitude greater than that which had defended Hanoi during the later stages of the Vietnam War."[67]

IRAQ'S LONG-RANGE STRIKE CAPABILITIES

The final element of Iraq's military forces were its long-range strike assets, which gave Iraq the ability to strike enemy shipping, economic, or military infrastructure, and populations centers at ranges of up to 650 kilometers, with varying degrees of accuracy. Employing land- and air-launched antiship missiles, Iraq had engaged in coercive strikes on oil tankers bound for Iranian waters throughout the Iran-Iraq War. Indeed, the U.S. military had experienced the potential reach of IrAF antiship strikes on May 17, 1987, when the frigate USS *Stark* was mistakenly targeted by an Iraqi Dassault F-1EQ-5. The short-warning strike resulted in two direct Exocet missile hits and the deaths of thirty-nine U.S. sailors.[68] Antiship strikes represented one way that Iraq could try to keep U.S. forces at a safe distance from Iraq and Kuwait, a military mission that would later be termed "antiaccess and area denial," or A2AD.[69]

Strikes on Saudi Arabian air bases or other critical military infrastructure were a second option that Iraq might use to disrupt Coalition military operations. Yet, using conventional munitions, Iraq's capabilities were highly limited in this sphere, as the failure of Iraq's surprise air strikes that were launched at the outset of the Iran-Iraq War had indicated. When Iraq attacked eight Iranian airfields and five airports on September 22, 1980, it had complete surprise. However, it failed to duplicate the devastating Israeli achievements of 1967, when huge numbers of Egyptian, Syrian, Jordanian, and Iraqi aircraft were destroyed on the ground. Lacking the ability to surge sufficient numbers of sorties and operating without suitable munitions to disable Iranian runways or penetrate their hardened aircraft shelters, the preemptive attack was a dismal failure. Even after a decade of experience in airfield attacks, during which time Iraq developed a remarkable level of experience in the employment of laser-guided bombs (LGBs), the Iraqi air force lacked the ability to carry out effective deep strikes against Saudi Arabian airfields and other military infrastructure defended by Coalition air defenses.[70]

U.S. planners considered it more likely that a desperate Iraqi leadership might use chemical or biological weapons (CBWs) to perform A2AD attacks against key Saudi bases. During the final offensives of the Iran-Iraq War, the Iraqi armed forces had systematically targeted Iranian command-and-logistics hubs with chemical weapons. DIA assessments highlighted the possibility that airfields within 300 kilometers of the Iraqi border (Dharan, King Fahd, and King Abdulaziz) could be targeted for chemical attacks by massed IrAF fighter-bombers and that smaller packages of F-1 and MiG-23 strike aircraft could feasibly deliver chemical attacks on Coalition headquarters in Riyadh if Iraq utilized the in-flight refueling capabilities of these types. Although the IrAF would suffer heavy losses piercing the Coalition air-defense screen, the DIA noted that "such an attempt cannot be overlooked, especially if Iraq were on the verge of a defeat," and stated that such attacks held the potential to "inflict extensive casualties in command facilities and degrade Desert Shield command and control, at least temporarily."[71]

As an alternative, DIA noted, Iraq might employ some of its arsenal of short-range ballistic missiles (SRBMs), which had seen extensive use during the latter months of the Iran-Iraq War. Prior to early 1988, Iraq had lacked a means of striking at the distant and well-defended target of Tehran and had conceived of a number of long-range strike projects. Some failed, like the 600-kilometer "supergun,"[72] whereas others succeeded. Iraqi modifications to its arsenal of 300-kilometer SS-1C Scud-B missiles reduced their explosive payload to a mere 396-lb warhead and engineered a faster fuel burn rate.[73] This lighter and longer-ranged variant, the al-Hussein, had a range of 600–650 kilometers, which allowed missiles to be used for the first time against Tehran in February 1988. Although of greatly reduced military utility because of their tiny warheads and reduced accuracy and reliability, the al-Hussein Scuds caused panic in Tehran when the first sixteen missiles unexpectedly fell from the sky on February 29, 1988.

During the so-called War of the Cities between February and April 1988, two hundred al-Hussein missiles were fired at Tehran, which caused an esti-mated quarter of the city's population to evacuate and demonstrated the terror value of Iraq's missile force.[74] Scud attacks were particularly unsettling for residents of Tehran and Isfahan because, unlike air attacks, they could neither be intercepted nor detected in time to alert the public through municipal networks of air-raid sirens and because of the risk that chemical weapons might be employed.

Since the end of the Iran-Iraq War, Iraq's missiles had increasingly been trained on Israel, an implacable foe of Saddam Hussein's regime following Iraq's involvement in two Arab-Israeli wars, Israel's destruction of the Osiraq nuclear reactor in 1980, and a host of Iraqi retaliatory terrorist activities in the decade that followed. With evidence mounting that Iraq was developing rapidly in all fields of WMD research, the chance of an Israeli strike similar to the Osiraq raid seemed to be mounting and prompted Iraq to react aggressively. In the months before the Iraqi invasion of Kuwait, tensions with Israel had worsened after the Baathist regime executed British journalist Farzad Bazoft on March 19, 1990, for allegedly spying for Israel. On April 2, Saddam Hussein made plain Iraq's unwillingness to suffer another Osiraq-style Israeli strike, claiming "we have the binary chemical weapon. . . . We will make a fire to eat up half of Israel."[75]

Israel was convinced in 1990 that al-Hussein and al-Hijarah missiles (the latter meaning "the stones," a reference to the rock-throwing resistance of Palestinian youth in the first intifada during the 1980s) would be launched against Tel Aviv and other Israeli cities if war broke out.[76] To placate Israeli fears, knowing that Israeli military action against Iraq could dissolve Arab involvement in the carefully crafted international coalition facing Iraq, U.S. Secretary of Defense Richard Cheney stressed Iraq's Scud capabilities as an important planning factor as early as August 1990, when he tasked the intelligence community to keep fixed Scud launch sites under continual surveillance and committed valuable intelligence resources to the issue. From September, Cheney drove the generation of Operation Scorpion, a plan to seize the western Scud launch sites using ground forces, formally ordered development of the plan on October 12, and ordered supporting satellite and photoreconnaissance imagery on October 24.[77]

The U.S. military, focusing on the technical features of Iraq's Scud variants, came to a different assessment and downgraded the significance of Iraq's missile fleet. From a military standpoint, the Scud fleet looked likely to be a persistent irritant but not a priority. Iraq's extended-range missiles frequently broke up in midair because of their imperfect modification, and each had a two- to three-thousand-meter circular error of probability (CEP), meaning that only 50 percent of missiles could be expected to arrive within this radius. In Soviet service, Scud missiles were primarily intended as chemical-, biological-, or nuclear-munitions-delivery systems, but Iraq had a range of more effective and better-tested deployment options for CBWs. In addition, Iraq was not assessed to have developed even a single crude (and heavy) nuclear device by 1990, which, in any case, could not have been reduced to the size and weight of the small warheads carried by Iraqi extended-range missiles. An initial survey of Iraq's fixed Scud launch sites and Scud-related industries was completed between August 17 and September 30, but by mid-October the DIA had asked for and received permission from CENTCOM J-2 to reduce its heavy collection effort against the Scud target set.

The issue of Iraq's Scud missiles was perhaps the first indication of the post–Cold War requirement for U.S. military commanders to weigh the strategic as well as the operational and tactical consequences of their actions and those of the enemy. The secretary of defense twice more sought to focus CENTCOM on the Scud threat by reordering surveillance on all Scud launch sites every two days, beginning on October 24. Then, during a December 20 visit to Saudi Arabia that followed three Iraqi Scud test launches earlier in the month, Cheney demanded reassurances that Scud launches would be suppressed. CENTAF Commander Horner candidly told Cheney that he could not give assurances that Iraq's unknown numbers of mobile transporter erector launchers (TELs) would be found and destroyed in time to prevent Scud launches.

To military men, this was an expensive and inefficient diversion of resources and not a military mission they wanted to undertake. Horner admitted after the war, "The point I missed about the whole operation is the terror the Scud induced in the people in Israel, Bahrain and Saudi Arabia, it was almost overwhelming" and conceded, "I'm not as politically sensitive as I should be."[78] Summing up the prewar U.S. military assessment of the Scud, CENTCOM commander (CINCCENT) General Schwarzkopf stated: "Saying that Scuds are a danger to a nation is like saying that lightning is a danger to a nation. I frankly would be more afraid of standing out in a lightning storm in southern Georgia than I would standing out in the streets of Riyadh when the Scuds are coming down."[79]

In the post–Cold War world, however, the U.S. military would increasingly have to get used to fighting the kinds of missions that they were given rather than the military tasks for which they had prepared.

COLD WARRIORS IN THE DESERT

Schwarzkopf's comments reflected the Cold War mind-set that prevailed in the U.S. military as Desert Shield unfolded. For nearly two decades after the end of the Vietnam War, the U.S. military had been focused primarily on the deterrence of Soviet expansionism in Europe and North Korean aggression against South Korea. In the context of these total war scenarios—particularly the former, where limited and even intercontinental nuclear exchanges were a distinct possibility—a militarily ineffective weapon such as Iraq's al-Hussein Scud force was unlikely to impress U.S. combatant commanders such as Schwarzkopf and Horner. Yet, as events would show, war with Iraq would unfold in a post–Cold War, limited-war context, where the public opinions of the United States and regional countries mattered and would continue to matter through the coming decade.

The prospect of war with Iraq presented a strange blend of limited objectives and high stakes. The United States had fought other limited wars in the years between the end of the Vietnam War and the invasion of Kuwait—ground forces deployments to Lebanon, Grenada, and Panama, aerial strikes and air or naval skirmishes against Libya and Iran—but never had the stakes been higher or the threat so advanced. At the political level, Iraq's invasion of Kuwait posed a critical challenge to U.S. national prestige. Throughout the 1980s, the United States experienced a renewed blossoming of national confidence, a national revival that was capped by America's success in outlasting the Communist Bloc and seeing the Berlin Wall and many Eastern Bloc regimes come crashing down at the end of the decade. When Iraq invaded Kuwait, it threatened to besmirch what might be termed America's "unipolar moment" when the United States stood as the sole superpower and the ultimate guarantor of peace and stability in the Gulf. All eyes were on America.

As the executive branch responsible for providing force to back up the resolute words of the president, all eyes were also focused on the performance of the U.S. DoD. The U.S. military now had to simultaneously prepare for action in an immature theater and respond to a regional threat that was unprecedented in scale and seriousness since the Korean War. The U.S. commitment to the liberation of Kuwait initiated the largest U.S. expeditionary deployment for decades and created the credible possibility of U.S. involvement in the first major theater war since the Korean War, which had began forty years prior—well beyond the living memory of most of the U.S. service personnel involved in Desert Shield. Compared to the small but important 1980s operations of the U.S. military, a war to liberate Kuwait represented the first real test of the combined arms capabilities of the revitalized post-Vietnam U.S. military and its focus on superior training, doctrine, and equipment.

Dual impulses wracked U.S. commanders and their advisers when assessing the military balance developing in the Gulf and calculating the forces required to eject Iraq from Kuwait. The U.S. military sought to develop an accurate but confident appraisal of enemy strengths and weaknesses, much as the U.S. military developed vis-à-vis the Soviet threat in the 1970–80s. Unlike the modern Soviet military, which had not been involved in a high-intensity war since the World War II, the Iraqi military had been extensively employed in high-intensity combat operations throughout most of the decade that preceded Operation Desert Shield, which gave the United States some opportunity to gauge the overall effectiveness of Iraqi armed forces.

Even so, the U.S. military faced many of the same uncertainties as it had during the Cold War military standoff with the USSR. How good was the enemy, and how good were we? U.S. military thinking in the late Cold War had trained commanders to seize and exploit the predicted qualitative weaknesses of Soviet armed forces and doctrine, and the same methods of assessment were applied to the Iraqi forces. When CINCCENT Schwarzkopf briefed President Bush and other national-security decision makers as early as the Camp David meeting on August 4, 1990, he started out by reassuring the civilian decision makers that "they're not ten feet tall."[80] According to Schwarzkopf, Iraq's strength lay in its ground forces—in the quantitative advantage that a million-man land force conferred, in their deployment of high-quality, late-model Soviet tanks, artillery, and fighting vehicles, and in their willingness and proven ability to use chemical weapons on the battlefield. In making this assessment, Schwarzkopf could almost have been describing the threat from the group of Soviet forces in Germany. Possessed of more than eight hundred late-model Soviet aircraft plus advanced French aircraft and munitions, Iraq's air and naval forces nevertheless posed a lesser threat to General Schwarzkopf, whose confidence lay in the qualitative and technological edge enjoyed by U.S. forces in the air and naval environments. In the land warfare environment, however, Schwarzkopf was less sure that quality and technological superiority could substitute for raw numbers or fully negate the power of an enemy willing to make battlefield use of WMDs. A conflict with Iraq promised to put the late–Cold War U.S. doctrine of quality over quantity to the ultimate test and to provide Iraq's armed forces with their most sophisticated military challenge to date.

On the positive side, Schwarzkopf told the National Security Council attendees, the United States could count on several key advantages over the Iraqi ground forces. Command and control, intelligence, surveillance, and reconnaissance (C2ISR) was the first key area of Coalition superiority. On the first count, C2, U.S. intelligence analysts predicted that Iraqi commanders would be unable to fight a war of mobility; they would, rather, be tied through ability and habit to "a war of position, tied to fortifications [and] communications nets" and would lack the ability to "think rapidly or improvise in the heat of battle."[81] In December 1990, the AIA predicted the Iraqis would employ a static defense with little operational movement, fixated on the defense of Kuwait City and Basra.[82]

On the ISR side, increasingly intense sharing of intelligence during the Iran-Iraq War had given Iraq and the United States a relatively detailed understanding of each other's intelligence-gathering capabilities—a factor that later bolstered Iraq's ability to deceive the U.S. intelligence community but also gave Schwarzkopf cause for optimism as the Gulf crisis began. Iraq relied almost entirely on the United States for high-quality imagery intelligence (IMINT) during the last five years of the Iran-Iraq War, particularly after DIA established a satellite-imagery dissemination team in Baghdad in 1986.[83] In the last year of the war, Iraq had also purchased commercial satellite imagery from the French *Systeme Pour l'Observation de la Terre* (SPOT) constellation, but this type of imagery was embargoed along with all other military or dual-use imports to Iraq. Although Iraq had developed a small fleet of airborne early-warning aircraft and made limited use of tactical reconnaissance aircraft and domestically produced remote-piloted vehicles, its ability to operate these systems during wartime was thought to be strictly limited. Similarly, although Iraqi SIGINT-collection capabilities were assessed to be good,[84] its ability to gather other forms of electronic intelligence (ELINT) or emissions intelligence (EMINT) were thought to be extremely limited. Put together, Iraqi military intelligence was configured to fight a purely "visual range war," whereas U.S. systems had a critical advantage at looking "over the hill."[85] Intelligence superiority and air superiority went hand in hand, and Schwarzkopf told the Camp David meeting that Iraqi ground forces would be uniquely exposed to air attack if war came. The desert, Schwarzkopf predicted, would provide a "target-rich environment," in which ground targets could be observed from some distance and conditions for air attack would be optimal. Moreover, the CINC noted, Iraq had no experience of operating under massed air attacks of the sort that the United States would launch, and there would be a significant morale effect against Iraqi rear echelons, which had never had to experience systematic aerial interdiction in the past.[86]

Alongside the systematic assessment of Iraqi strengths and weaknesses lay a parallel, more instinctive reaction to the potential challenge posed by Iraq's armed forces—the fear of underestimating the enemy and applying too little force to win decisively and with as few casualties as possible. The United States may have won the Cold War, but the U.S. military still had much to prove and the ghosts of America's military withdrawal from Vietnam loomed large in military deliberations. The U.S. flag officers and colonels commanding operational units in Operation Desert Shield had been the field-grade officers in Vietnam: platoon or company commanders or combat pilots. As Tom Clancy wrote about Lieutenant General Franks, the U.S. VII Corps commander, "Fred Franks' experience of Vietnam had influenced him on this matter. If he erred, he wanted to err on the side of overestimating his enemy. He wanted to be sure that, this time, the results would be different."[87]

2
Forging the Sword

INITIAL PLANNING

As the U.S. military stepped up to the challenge posed by Iraq, one of the first practical steps it took was to calculate what kind of deployment of U.S. forces was required. To do this, it needed to formulate military objectives. As early as August 11, 1990, key U.S. military decision makers were maneuvering to ensure that the long-term threat from Iraq would be neutralized in the event of war. According to Lt. Col. Ron Stanfill, who was present at Chairman of the Joint Chiefs of Staff (CJCS) Gen. Colin Powell's first meeting with offensive planners in mid-August, if war came, the chairman did not want to merely push the Iraqis out and thereby leave them free to threaten the region again as soon as Coalition forces redeployed back to their home bases. Instead, Powell wanted the Iraqi military trapped on the "beaten ground" of Kuwait and destroyed while the opportunity was available. At that time the bare Kuwaiti desert appeared to offer a smorgasbord from which Coalition airpower could feed. Powell knew the United States would never have a better opportunity to curtail Iraq's long-term military potential.[1] Powell's oft-quoted comment from the August 11, 1990, meeting summed up the chairman's view: "If we go this far in the air campaign, I want to finish it. Destroy the Iraqi Army on the ground. . . . I don't want them to go home. I want to leave smoking tanks as kilometer posts all the way to Baghdad."[2]

CINCCENT Schwarzkopf took Powell's directive to heart. He knew that the Republican Guard divisions were the mainstay of Iraq's offensive military capabilities and prioritized an effort to cut them off inside the KTO and kill them. As JFACC Lieutenant General Horner noted, when he and Schwarzkopf talked about isolating the battlefield in the KTO, "we were not talking about isolating the battlefield from supplies coming in; we were talking about the Republican Guard leaving. I think, in retrospect, Powell was very concerned about this. . . . I think that [Schwarzkopf] promised Powell that he was going to annihilate the Republican Guards."[3]

In keeping with Schwarzkopf's initial Camp David assessment of the Iraqi military threat, the second pillar of Iraq's offensive potential—nuclear, biological, and chemical (NBC) weapons programs and munitions—were to be hit as hard as possible during any offensive operation to liberate Kuwait. By the time Operational Order 91-001 was issued on the eve of war—January 17, 1991—a complex and ambitious set of military objectives had been set for CENTCOM to achieve. In addition to the principal tasks of ejecting the Iraqi armed forces from Kuwait and assisting the restoration of the legitimate government of Kuwait, the destruction of the Republican Guard and of all known Scud and NBC targets were central aims. This reflected the United States' desire to set back Iraqi offensive capabilities for the foreseeable future.[4]

BALANCE OF FORCES

As offensive planning for the liberation of Kuwait began in the early fall of 1990, the U.S. military was forced to face the key question it had pondered for more than a decade prior to Iraq's invasion of Kuwait: could a numerically superior Soviet-style opponent be defeated by high-quality and technologically advanced Western forces that utilize surprise and offensive maneuvers to destroy enemy frontline forces while using deep fires to destroy the reinforcing combat and logistical forces of the enemy rear echelon?

This concept, known as air-land battle, was developed at the U.S. Army Training and Doctrine Command (TRADOC), which was established in 1973 and which had spearheaded the post-Vietnam revitalization of the U.S. military. TRADOC focused on increasing the realism and effectiveness of U.S.

military training and leadership development and on developing doctrine that would allow the U.S. military to "fight outnumbered and win." The air-land battle concept was first recognized in the U.S. Army *Field Manual* (*FM*) 100-5 in 1976, and the concept was adopted by the U.S. Army and NATO in the ten years that followed.[5] It rested on a set of principles. Active defense, offensive maneuver, and maintenance of the initiative were required to "set or change the terms of battle." Agility, meaning the ability to think and act faster than the enemy, was a second decisive factor in warfare. U.S. forces would need to "think and fight deep," undertaking a FOFA against enemy reinforcements and logistical support.

The *Conduct of the Persian Gulf War* report summarized:

> The essence of Air-Land Battle is to defeat the enemy by conducting simultaneous offensive operations over the full breadth and depth of the battlefield.... Commanders must fight concurrently what are known as close, deep, and rear operations, all as interrelated parts of one battle. Commanders fight close to destroy enemy forces where the battle is joined. They fight deep to delay or attack enemy reserves. These operations are intended to disrupt the enemy's plan and create opportunities for success in close operations. They fight rear, behind forward units, to protect [support] assets and to retain freedom of action for friendly sustainment and movement of reserve forces.[6]

Finally, the U.S. armed services were expected to fight as closely knit combined arms teams. The Goldwater-Nichols Department of Defense Reorganization Act of 1986 sought to reduce the damaging effects of interservice rivalry on U.S. military operations by enforcing a culture of "jointness." Since Vietnam, congressional impetus had existed for a reduction in the role of the individual armed service chiefs and their staff in combat operations because of indications that interservice rivalries resulted in competition rather than cooperation among the services. Goldwater-Nichols created a clear separation of roles in which the individual armed services were limited to *organizing, training, and equipping* U.S. armed forces. The National Command Authorities (NCA), the CJCS, the regional CINCs, and their air, land, or naval component commanders *employed* armed forces in military operations.[7] The only exception to Goldwater-Nichols was the U.S. Marine Corps, which negotiated an omnibus agreement to the act in 1986. The marines retained operational control over 50 percent of U.S. Marine Corps aircraft sorties scheduled to be placed under the control of the theater JFACC and these aircraft sorties, along with other marine assets, were instead operationally controlled by a Marine Air-Ground Task Force (MAGTF) commander who reports directly to the theater CINC.[8]

The air-land battle concept had developed synergistically alongside a crop of new military platforms, munitions, and sensors that had been developed since the 1970s. In keeping with the air-land battle's focus on offensive maneuvers, a number of highly mobile land-warfare platforms had been developed to provide the United States with increased operational and tactical maneuverability.[9] The M1A1 Abrams main battle tank and the M2A and M3 Bradley fighting vehicles provided fast, well-protected armored capability. Each was mounted with cutting-edge sensors and antiarmor weapons capable of out-ranging and out-shooting their Soviet-built counterparts. Further mobility was provided by the high-mobility multipurpose wheeled vehicle (HMMWV) and the Blackhawk helicopter. CAS to U.S. forces had greatly improved through the development of the advanced AH-64 Apache attack helicopter, the modernization of the AH-1F Cobra attack helicopters, and development of advanced antiarmor munitions (the CBU-87 combined-effects munition, the CBU-89 air-delivered Gator mine, and the AGM-65D Maverick missile) available for carriage on fixed-wing CAS platforms such as the A-10, F-16, AV-8, and F/A-18 aircraft. Alongside U.S. Army systems such as the multiple-launch rocket system (MLRS) and increasingly networked and automated artillery-fire control systems, these deep-strike technologies provided a range of "assault breaker" capabilities to support the FOFA concept of operations.[10]

Just as the Soviet offensive threat was fading, the United States was beginning to deploy a range of new ISR and targeting sensors to facilitate all-weather or nighttime FOFA strikes. Two prototype E-8A joint surface targeting and acquisition radar system (JSTARS) that were rushed into U.S. service for Operation Desert Shield used a ground moving-target indicator (GMTI) to detect large-scale enemy vehicle movements. These and TR-1/U-2 reconnaissance aircraft also carried synthetic aperture radar (SAR) that could develop wide-area coverage or detailed "spot" images of areas of particular interest. Also important, GMTI and SAR could image regardless of light conditions, cloud cover, or other obscuration. In addition to the night-vision equipment mounted on AH-64 helicopters and their supporting OH-58D Kiowa scouts, a range of U.S. tactical aircraft were also developing night-strike capabilities. The F-111F strike aircraft carried the Pave Tack infrared navigation and targeting system, which enabled it to carry out night interdiction missions. Navigation and targeting pods were also being rushed into service for carriage in limited numbers of F-15E and F-16C aircraft.

DESIGNING AN OFFENSIVE PLAN

Despite the technological edge developed by the United States over the Soviet or regional militaries, many doubts plagued the Coalition commanders who were developing offensive plans. First, would high-technology systems take the strain of high-tempo warfare, especially in the austere operating conditions of the desert? Assuming the qualitative edge of U.S. technology and doctrine worked as advertised, to what extent could it offset the presumed advantages of the defending Iraqi force? In the absence of real proof concerning how well air-land battle and its supporting suite of technologies would work, the Coalition instead assumed qualitative parity between U.S. and Iraqi forces and sought to build a man-for-man advantage over the enemy. During the key period when planning for offensive ground operations was undertaken— roughly September 18 until November 14—CENTCOM J-2 and the DIA estimated that 500,000 Iraqi troops were deployed in the KTO, along Iraq's border with Saudi Arabia, or held in operational reserve on the Saudi-Kuwaiti border.[11] Because the Coalition could not remotely sense the actual strength of Iraqi units, the estimate prudently assumed that all identified Iraqi divisions were fully manned.

A time-honored and broadly accepted maxim was that an attacker required a three-to-one numerical advantage over the defender to ensure success.[12] This would mean that a Coalition force of approximately 1.5 million soldiers would need to be fielded, a force that was larger than the entire U.S. Army. Instead, the attacking force would instead be 540,000-strong, even after the VII Corps from Europe was deployed on November 9, 1990. This was little better than a 1:1 ratio. Furthermore, the enemy enjoyed an advantage (called a force multiplier) because "his [Saddam's] combat engineers, rated among the best in the world, had months to construct their defenses."[13]

In addition, the Coalition had to achieve its objectives at minimum cost. Although some prewar predictions provided figures as high as 7,000 dead and 13,000 wounded, the Coalition planning guidance issued in late December 1990 called for total casualties no higher than the equivalent of three companies per Coalition brigade (equating to roughly 15 percent casualties in the forces involved).[14]

Evolving to meet the mission of liberating Kuwait at acceptable cost would set the U.S. military on the path toward a post–Cold War transformation. The Soviet and Korean threats induced the U.S. military to bolster deterrence through the demonstrated capability to defensively fight "outnumbered and win," but if deterrence failed and the fighting came, the struggle on the World War III battlefield would be anything but limited. Tremendous casualties—including friendly and noncombatant casualties—would be inevitable.

As the Iraqi situation came to war, the U.S. military had been put on the offensive and given the tasks to fight a deeply entrenched enemy of equal size and to win with low casualties to friend and noncombatant alike, which were harbingers of the increasingly challenging and complex missions that would characterize the post–Cold War military environment.

To find means of leveraging Coalition capabilities into decisive advantages at critical points on the battlefield, General Schwarzkopf recognized the need to prepare or "shape" the battlefield. This generally consists of a series of actions that "seize the initiative from the enemy, forcing him to fight in accordance with your plan rather than his, thus allowing the attacker to exploit the enemy's weaknesses and to maneuver more freely on the battlefield."[15] Preparation or shaping of the battlefield has two basic components. The first was preparation to deceive and demoralize the enemy through psychological operations. This form of preparation was integral to the offensive ground operations that would liberate Kuwait. To develop the plan for the ground war, Schwarzkopf employed a team of graduates from the U.S. Army School of Advanced Military Studies (SAMS), experts in the operational level of warfare, called the CENTCOM J-5 Special Planning Group (CCJ5-SPG).[16] These planners, known as the "Jedi Knights," designed the preferred concept of a two-corps attack option in which both corps would thrust across the Iraqi border at the extreme western end of the Saddam Line: the U.S. XVIII Airborne Corps would drive north to the Euphrates River while the armor-heavy U.S. VII Corps would thrust northeast to destroy the Republican Guard in the area south of Basra and trap the majority of the Iraqi army in Kuwait.

The plan required a force of two U.S. Marine divisions and four divisions provided by Islamic nations to pin Iraqi frontline forces along the Saudi-Kuwaiti border. The westward relocation of XVIII and VII Corps—390 and 220 kilometers, respectively—would need to be undertaken in conditions of the greatest secrecy, screened from the prying eyes of Iraq's ISR assets. Deception operations were designed to draw Iraqi attention away from the western end of the Saddam Line. Before the war, the 13th Marine Expeditionary Unit (MEU) would undertake well-publicized amphibious rehearsals off the coast of Oman in January 1990. During military operations, the Coalition would launch a series of feints against Iraqi forces in Kuwait, including amphibious raids and apparent preparations for an assault on the Kuwaiti coast, thereby probe Iraqi forces at the triborder area of Wadi al-Batin. Eventually the MEF and the two Islamic Corps would launch a major pinning attack along the Saudi-Kuwaiti border.[17]

The Jedi Knights calculated that pinning Iraqi forces and pitting the Coalition's strength against Iraqi weaknesses would result in attacker–defender ratios of 1.3 to 1 in the attack on the Saudi-Kuwaiti coast and 2.4 to 1 in the VII Corps attack on the Republican Guard.

ROLE OF AIR POWER IN OFFENSIVE PLANNING

A second feature of Schwarzkopf's preparation of the battlefield would be the physical degradation of the defending Iraqi forces—a factor that offered an additional means of improving attacker/defender ratios. A period of preliminary bombardment by Coalition air forces and other deep-strike assets would be the principal means used to physically prepare the battlefield ahead of a ground offensive. In addition to reducing the effectiveness of Iraqi combat forces, a preliminary aerial campaign would seize air superiority. This would prevent Iraqi airborne reconnaissance from identifying the westward shift of U.S. forces and fixing Iraqi frontline forces, plus tactical and operational reserves, in place.

Air forces would build up much faster than Coalition ground forces. Thus, it was also a practical matter that air operations should start first, especially considering that the plan was modified on November 9, 1990, to call for a second U.S. Army corps. This second corps necessitated a 120-day deployment of VII Corps to Saudi Arabia, which set back the ground forces' timetable. For these reasons, the concept of a phased campaign to liberate Iraq, initiated by a preliminary air campaign and followed by an air-land warfare phase, was broadly accepted, although there were attempts by U.S. Air Force and U.S. Army planners to promote air-only offensives or simultaneous air and ground offensives, respectively, during the planning process.

In early August, as CENTAF fought to deploy screening forces to theater and to attend to the logistical details of the bed-down in Saudi Arabia, the XOXW (warfighting concepts) section of the U.S. Air Force Air Staff was handed the task of preparing offensive air-power-led retaliatory options if, in General Schwarzkopf's words, "a heinous act was committed." According to Air Force historian Diane Putney, Schwarzkopf considered attacks on U.S. hostages in Kuwait or Iraq or the use of chemical weapons as "heinous acts" likely to draw a response from the United States.[18]

Led by U.S. Air Force Col. John Warden, XOXW (known informally as "Checkmate") was charged with developing long-term war-fighting concepts, represented a mix of operations personnel and planners, and was known for encouraging independent thinking and analysis on important future U.S. Air Force missions. By August 10, 1990, Checkmate had developed an 84-target air campaign called Instant Thunder, which was more aggressive and better developed than the range of other retaliatory options presented for consideration in early August.[19] These other options consisted of a navy option that relied primarily on the unfamiliar and operationally untried Tomahawk land-attack missile (TLAM);[20] the "demonstration plan," an escalating series of coercive strikes conceived by the U.S. Air Force Tactical Air Command (TAC);[21] and CENTAF's own "punishment Air Tasking Order" (ATO), a small 44-target option that used a motley assortment of targets in Iraq and Kuwait developed for use in the Internal Look war game in July 1990.[22]

Although elements of Instant Thunder would ultimately prove to be highly influential on air-campaign design, when the concept of operations was presented in August 1990, it suffered from the fatal flaw of promising to coerce Iraq into leaving Kuwait within a six-to-nine-day period. It had clearly been conceived as an air-only option to which no land-warfare sequel would theoretically be required. Early iterations of Instant Thunder presented to Schwarzkopf and Powell on August 10–11 focused on eight strategic target sets—the IADS, Scud missiles and other long-range strike assets, WMDs, leadership, communications, electricity, oil, and transport—but did not envisage striking the Iraqi ground forces in Kuwait unless they attacked Saudi Arabia.[23]

Although Powell directed that Instant Thunder be expanded to incorporate a second phase of air attacks within the KTO, including attacks on Iraqi armored forces and WMD-delivery systems, Instant Thunder remained at heart a strategic air campaign that focused almost entirely on targets in Iraq. When Warden and a Checkmate team delivered the plan to theater on August 20, it was roundly condemned by Lieutenant General Horner for three reasons: its inability to merge into a thorough preparation of the battlefield if Iraq did not withdraw after nine days, its minimal focus on the possible need to repel an Iraqi invasion of Saudi Arabia, and, perhaps most important, its failure to meet one of the key unofficial U.S. objectives—the opportunistic destruction of the long-term offensive threat posed by Iraqi ground forces.[24]

THE "AIR-POWER COMPROMISE"

Although an air-only option had few supporters among the senior U.S. military decision makers, neither did a simultaneous commencement of air and ground operations. During the Cold War, the near-simultaneous beginning of air and land operations was an assumed feature of air-land battle, if for no other reason than attacking Warsaw Pact forces would have given U.S. forces little warning and thus little choice in the matter. As Edward Mann noted, Air Force planners at TAC had developed a "wait-and-see" attitude: wait for the U.S. Army to communicate its scheme of maneuver and then develop aerial support to match.[25]

Yet, by the fall of 1990, U.S. Army officers such as Powell and Schwarzkopf saw the necessity of a prolonged period of aerial preparation of the battlefield as ground forces deployed to theater and shifted westward. When Schwarzkopf and Powell conferred at MacDill on August 14, the CINC indicated his commitment to an air-first but not an air-only option. Schwarzkopf noted, "I could see that the plan being briefed could double with the offensive planning we were doing."[26] The air campaign that emerged from the planning effort in the fall of 1990 was neither Colonel Warden's air-only attack on strategic targets nor a narrow attempt to destroy Iraqi ground forces in the KTO, but was instead the unprecedented development of an air campaign that promised to unleash near-simultaneous attacks across the full range of strategic and tactical targets identified by U.S. targeteers—who specialize in selecting and developing air-strike targets—which Mann termed the "airpower compromise."[27]

Although Checkmate's Col. Warden returned to Washington, D.C., three of his Air Staff planners—Lt. Col. David Deptula, Lt. Col. Ben Harvey, and Lt. Col. Ron Stanfill—remained in Saudi Arabia to form the core of the offensive air-campaign planning cell, known as the Special Planning Group (SPG) or, informally, "the Black Hole." Horner appointed U.S. Air Force Brig. Gen. Buster Glosson from outside CENTAF to command the SPG and gave him the title of special assistant to the JFACC. By September 2, the team had developed a new iteration of Instant Thunder, now called "Offensive Campaign—Phase One."[28] One of Warden's key concepts—the maintenance of an exclusive focus on strategic targets in Iraq—was gone, and the plan now sought to prepare the ground for a potential sequel phase that specifically focused on preparation of the battlefield in the KTO.

Horner borrowed from U.S. Army doctrine when he set the objective of this phase to be reducing the strength of targeted Iraqi divisions by 50 percent, the point at which the U.S. Army classified a formation combat ineffective.[29] This level of degradation would theoretically give the pinning assaults along the Saudi-Kuwaiti border an attacker/defender ratio of 2.8 to 1 and VII Corps would smash into the Republican Guard with a 4.8 to 1 advantage. The integration of targets aimed at causing prompt damage to Iraq's fielded armed forces in the earliest sequence of strikes indicated a fundamental shift from the absolutist principle of Instant Thunder—that there should be no diversion of air strikes against fielded armed forces—to a more flexible and responsive planning effort.

At the same time, many elements of Instant Thunder survived and profoundly changed the way that the air war would be executed. Although the preparation of the battlefield was to be the ultimate aim of the air campaign and thereby facilitate the destruction of Iraqi offensive capabilities and the liberation of Kuwait, the SPG designed a campaign that began with a massive series of strikes on strategic targets in both Iraq and Kuwait. This was termed "parallel attack." Using the force multipliers of selective targeting and precision-guided munitions (PGMs) in addition to unmanned cruise missiles and stealth aircraft, the attack would be compressed in time: it would strike all strategic target sets simultaneously and go straight into the air-defense fortress of Baghdad from the first night of air strikes.

So-called "inside-out" attacks on strategic targets were designed to cause cascading effects on Iraq's ability to direct defensive activities in the KTO and southern Iraq. Each of these ideas was controversial in 1990 and had been critiqued by Horner at the August 20 meeting with Warden, yet they became centerpieces of the offensive air campaign. How did this occur?

The simple answer is that air-campaign planners made it easy for Horner to take a chance on "parallel-attack" and "inside-out" warfare by reducing the amount of the JFACC's total aerial resources required to undertake them. Lieutenant Colonel Deptula, one of the three Checkmate officers that formed the core of the SPG, was the primary driver behind the incorporation of these advanced concepts. From the outset, Horner had been impressed by the overwhelming and sustained application of airpower advocated by Instant Thunder, and he would have supported any offensive air option that was to be massive in scale and highly integrated. Deptula's "effects-based targeting" offered a means of multiplying the effects of a relatively small number of U.S. strike sorties through the selection of only the most critical aimpoints. As Deptula noted, effects-based targeting could cause paralysis in an adversary, "temporarily destroying the cohesion of an entire nation, including its fielded forces.... The aim is to suppress function across a system; individual nodes are not the focus, hence less bombs per target but targeting is more widely spread geographically and more concentrated temporally."[30]

Through its focus on temporary effects, the new targeting model also seemed to offer the potential for relatively finessed targeting of national infrastructures, which would allow air-campaign planners to limit long-term damage to Iraq's economic and oil-export infrastructure. This approach required U.S. air-campaign planners to tear up the approach used in the Cold War rule books for targeting, the *Joint Munitions Effectiveness Manuals* (*JMEM*), which stressed the node-by-node destruction of every element of every target set to ensure the permanent loss of functionality to the target system.[31]

Although this type of targeting went against the grain of the training and habits of CENTAF/IN targeteers, Deptula carefully controlled target selection and the numbers of aircraft and munitions assigned to each target. This forced CENTAF/IN targeteers to very carefully select aimpoints, or designed mean points of impact (DMPIs). Deptula recalled: "Here's how I did it.... I'm the one who designated how many airplanes and how many weapons systems were associated with a particular target, that's in the master attack plan.... That was the regulator for [CENTAF/IN], so if I only assigned one F-117 against a particular target, they could only put two bombs on it."[32]

Such guidance to CENTAF/IN targeteers was contained in SPG's daily target-planning worksheets, which were intended to prevent targeteers from turning to the *JMEM*. The *JMEM* laid out suggested numbers of DMPIs based on Cold War requirements for permanent destruction. Deptula hoped DMPI selection would be "asset led" rather than "*JMEM* led."[33] Throughout the fall of 1990, the JFACC came to see the efficiency of an effects-based approach.

Deptula needed to convince Horner and other air planners of another key element of the Instant Thunder approach—the central role of PGMs. On

August 20, Horner had disagreed with one of Checkmate's key assumptions: that parallel attack, simultaneity, and massed effects relied on the extensive use of PGMs. As anachronistic as it may seem in hindsight, Horner believed, along with many other U.S. Air Force generals in 1990, that low-altitude "precision delivery"—dropping unguided bombs from stable, highly accurate platforms such as the F-16—could provide sufficient accuracy for most strike missions, thereby deemphasizing the importance of PGM-capable aircraft.[34] Additionally, the form of precision munitions with which most U.S. Air Force and Army planners of the air-land-battle era were most familiar was the AGM-65 Maverick series, which is useful primarily in the CAS role. The planners thought laser-guided bombs (LGBs) were more esoteric tools used for attacks on point targets such as bridges.

This difference of opinion initially put the SPG at odds with theater and Washington decision makers over which types of aircraft to flow into theater. In the early months of Desert Shield, for example, Checkmate and the SPG had to overcome objections to secure the deployment of a second batch of 24 F-117A stealth fighters and the first 32 F-111F strike aircraft.[35] The SPG eventually saw the deployment of 229 U.S. aircraft capable of either self-designating and delivering PGMs or delivering PGM using a "buddy-lasing" partnership with a laser-designating aircraft.[36] Throughout the air-campaign planning process, effects-based targeting became more and more ambitious as a result of the growth of available PGM-capable assets and a growing confidence in their ability to hit targets more efficiently than other platforms. For instance, in the iteration of Instant Thunder that was current on August 16, 1990, sixteen F-117 were due to be targeted on two complexes (eight aircraft per target), whereas in the final prewar air-campaign plan, thirty F-117 were targeted against forty-nine target complexes, meaning that three aircraft were tasked against every five targets.[37]

In addition to compressing the timescale of air attacks, PGMs promised other advantages over unguided munitions. The first was the limitation of collateral damage, which President Bush had flagged as a guiding feature of air-campaign planning as early as the August 4, 1990, Camp David meeting of the National Security Council. He had stressed that the United States had "no quarrel with the Iraqi people."[38] Although PGM had missed their targets in the past—for instance, during U.S. attacks on Libya in 1986 (when the French embassy was struck) and in Panama in 1989 (when F-117A strikes went astray)—guided weapons still offered a more reliable means to strike critical targets collocated with civilian communities. Furthermore, the incorporation of stealth aircraft and Tomahawk missiles allowed attacks to be planned on Baghdad targets from the first night and for the maintenance of some strikes throughout the day.[39] This overcame reservations about the dangers of operating nonstealthy or manned aircraft over the Iraqi capital that were raised by the U.S. Navy's SPEAR (Strike Projection Evaluation and Anti-Air Warfare Research) think tank and the U.S. Air Force Center for Studies and Analysis.[40] The net effect was that PGMs, plus stealthy or unmanned platforms, gave the United States the ability to reach into sensitive or heavily defended areas and deny sanctuary to the enemy assets within them.

As the following chapter notes, however, U.S. decision makers were never entirely convinced that PGMs could deliver the results promised by the SPG or that they represented a far better option than precision delivery of unguided ordnance until some days into the war itself. Although their views of PGMs would be sharply adjusted during offensive operations against Iraq, the prewar debate over PGMs soon became largely academic: the sheer scale of the Desert Shield deployment—some four thousand Coalition military or leased civilian aircraft and helicopters—reduced the need for air-campaign planners to make difficult choices about targeting and the allocation of assets. As William Arkin noted, "Horner had so many assets, he could accommodate everyone's theory."[41] Brig. Gen. Glosson described the resources at his disposal: "The Gulf coalition forces at my disposal were unrealistically large. I had almost twice as many airplanes as I needed, excluding tankers. But as far as fighters, I certainly had at least 30 or 40 percent more airplanes than I needed . . . [and] realistically, the biggest challenge we were facing was trying to cram so much into every 24 hours."[42]

The wealth of assets caused the planned phases to be telescoped, resulting in an order of parallelism and simultaneity *above and beyond* that laid out in the Instant Thunder plan, which envisaged a small, highly discriminate strike against eighty-four targets. PGM droppers could deal with the deep war against strategic targets, while a mass of CAS and battlefield air-interdiction platforms would roam the KTO and southern Iraq preparing the battlefield. Eventually, all target sets, including Republican Guard and fielded armed forces, would be struck to greater or lesser degrees from the outset of the war and throughout the duration of the conflict.

AN AUDACIOUS PLAN

The air campaign that emerged from the Desert Shield planning effort promised to inflict hitherto unparalleled levels of strategic and operational disruption on the Iraqi war machine. It took the objectives espoused by air-land battle to a new level by striking the enemy throughout the depth and breadth of the entire battlespace, which now included the enemy's home nation.

Phases I to III of the offensive campaign would be fought almost exclusively by the air component, with attacks on each and every target set undertaken from the first night of the operation. For the first week of air attacks, phases I (the strategic air campaign) and II (air superiority in the KTO) would receive the lion's share of sorties. These phases aimed to isolate the Iraqi leadership, gain and maintain air superiority, and destroy as much of Iraq's NBC and offensive military capabilities as possible. Phase III (preparation of the battlefield) would also begin on the first night of the war, initially targeting the command posts and logistical underpinnings (supply dumps, railways, and bridges) of Iraqi ground forces. It would then undertake increasing numbers of direct strikes on Iraqi forces as battlefield preparation became the main effort during the second week of air operations.[43]

According to Checkmate and SPG calculations based on a commitment of six hundred sorties per day, the strength of targeted Republican Guard would be reduced to 50 percent within four days of the main phase III effort and to 10 percent within nine days.[44] After ten to twelve days of phase III preparation, planners anticipated being able to advise CINCCENT Schwarzkopf that the ground was ready for the commencement of phase IV, the air-land operations to liberate Kuwait.

Never before had a nation been so surgically dissected as a target system. To support the air-campaign objective of isolating and incapacitating the Iraqi regime, the U.S. and allied intelligence communities had worked hard to build a more detailed targeting picture of the secretive regime. Diplomats, CIA officers, and former U.S. military attachés who had been stationed in Baghdad joined Iraqi émigrés and defectors in designating the exact buildings and even offices in which key leaders sat.[45] The regime's military-communications architecture and use of the public-telephone network, radio, and television was assessed, mapped, and targeted for systematic destruction. In an attempt to interrupt regime and air-defense communications, the electricity system was carefully targeted so that attacks would cause temporary collapse of the national grid. Using intelligence provided to the CIA by the French engineer who designed the KARI network, the United States planned to disrupt the centralized control and execution afforded by the system, exploit the "creases" in its coverage, blind the radars on which it relied, and overload its ability to transfer data. The Coalition canvassed the French, Japanese, Swedish, Belgian, and Yugoslavian contractors who built the superhardened aircraft shelters used by the enemy, and decided to avoid them. Instead, it would destroy the IOCs, jam the radio communications on which enemy pilots relied, and crater the runways that the Iraqi Air Force used to take off.

Meanwhile, a range of identified chemical-weapon storage and production targets and nuclear installations would be hit alongside a number of suspected biological-weapons facilities. Military production and storage sites, Scud-missile production and storage facilities, oil-refining and distribution facilities, naval ports and facilities, and railroads and bridges would all be struck in an air campaign that promised to leave no stone unturned.[46]

As the countdown to war took place in January 1991, Coalition forces in the Gulf were tense, like a coiled spring ready to lunge forward. Even so, many uncertainties disturbed Coalition commanders and planners alike. The offensive plan relied on a number of new and untried concepts and capabilities to give Coalition forces the decisive superiority that, it was hoped, would allow them to secure victory at an acceptable cost. Would technologies perform under the strain of high-tempo warfare in the harsh desert environment? Would the qualitative edge of the U.S. military survive the shock of combat, the blunting effects of enemy fortifications, numbers, and weight of conventional and chemical bombardments? Would the deception effort and the scheme of maneuver succeed in pitting Coalition strengths against enemy weaknesses? Similar questions had been posed concerning the possible outcome in Cold War scenarios for many years, but this time the U.S. military could count on knowing the answers in short order.

The Cold War military may have trained to fight outnumbered and win, but its key role had been to deter rather than defeat a Soviet or Korean attack. That paradigm changed during Operation Desert Shield, when it became clear that the primary role of the post–Cold War U.S. military would not simply be to deter conflicts but instead to fight them, something U.S. personnel would do on an increasingly regular basis during the coming decade.

3

Desert Storm
Strategic Attack

T he mood of the Coalition forces and the American public was tense as the UN deadline passed on January 15, 1991. On January 14, 1991, U.S. Air Force Chief of Staff Merrill McPeak had lunch with the president and warned him that the keen edge of the fighting forces could be maintained for only so long. The U.S. national command authorities had asked for CINCCENT Schwarzkopf to find the best but also earliest date possible to launch the assault.[1] As JFACC Lieutenant General Horner noted, "The day the air war started was left up to me, and that was a weather and moon decision, but we were also told, if we possibly could, to get on with it."[2] Operation Desert Storm began in the early hours of January 17, 1991, a moonless, clear night chosen because of its ability to hide the F-117A stealth fighters from Iraqi eyes. Although the opening hour of Operation Desert Storm would become emblematic of the beginning of a new era of warfare, Horner's choice of a moonless night and fair flying weather was a reminder that the traditional sources of friction in warfare—the elements, the terrain, and the enemy—still applied as the U.S. military undertook its first major post–Cold War mission.

When President Bush signed the NSDD for Operation Desert Storm on January 15, many hours before the first missiles and bombs would hit, the Coalition moved into action by beginning a meticulously orchestrated opening strike that would stun the watching world as completely as it stunned the enemy. Weeks of feints and training missions had desensitized the Iraqi IADS to Coalition air movements, which allowed the attacking forces to close in on Iraq, prevented the Iraqi leadership from launching last-minute diplomatic gambits, and prevented the Iraqi military from falling into a last-moment defensive crouch. H-Hour was scheduled for 0300 on January 17 in Baghdad, 1900 on January 16 in Eastern Standard Time (EST). The military movement began at 0635 Baghdad time on January 16 as seven B-52G bombers departed from air bases in the United States carrying conventional air-launched cruise missiles (CALCMs). These bombers were beginning a thirty-five hour, twenty-two-thousand-kilometer round trip, which were at the time the longest bomber sorties in history.

On the evening of January 16, Coalition ISR aircraft took up routine orbits over Saudi Arabia and closely monitored the activity and responses of Iraq's IADS and strategic communications. The first strike packages marshaled south of the effective detection range of the Iraqi and Jordanian radar network, working on the premise that King Hussein's pro-Iraqi government might provide Baghdad with early warning. At ninety minutes before H-Hour (H-90), the Aegis air-defense cruiser USS *San Jacinto* (CG56) launched TLAMs from the Red Sea toward Iraq, the first shots of Desert Storm. Moments later a range of U.S. ships in the Persian Gulf began firing the first fifty-two-missile wave of TLAMs toward Baghdad.[3] As cruise missiles skimmed along the Iranian coast and the Turkish mountains, and past recognizable way points programmed into their terrain-comparison guidance systems, F-117A stealth aircraft and the attack helicopters of Task Force Normandy slipped into Iraq unnoticed.

The first indication that Iraqi air-defense operators had of the impending attack came at 0238 (H-22), when U.S. EF-111A jamming aircraft filled the airwaves with intense electronic jamming, making it impossible for Iraqi IADS operators to pick out the minimal but detectable signatures of the inbound F-117s. Although TLAMs were the first weapons to be launched in Desert Storm, the first weapons to impact were Hellfire missiles launched by the nine Apache helicopters of Task Force Normandy against Iraqi early-warning sites. These impacted just as the IADS detected the EF-111A jamming.

The 101st Air Assault Division Apaches had been led scores of kilometers inside Iraq by three U.S. Air Force MH-53J Pave Low special-operations helicopters of the 1st Special Operations Wing, which utilized night-vision goggles and GPS to rendezvous at their desert targets with pinpoint precision and punctuality despite the moonless conditions. Task Force Normandy's attack created a gap in Iraq's surveillance radar along the Saudi border, and twelve minutes later at 0251 (H-9), F-117A struck the Nukayb IOC and suppressed Iraq's ability to provide GCI information to Iraqi fighters operating in the gapped area.[4] The attacks unzipped the KARI network along an axis running perpendicular to the Saudi Arabian border and ending at Baghdad, and exploited and expanded the north–south crease in KARI that had previously been identified.

In less than twenty-four hours' time, the newly established Task Force Proven Force flew from Turkish bases to punch a gap through Iraq's northern early-warning screen by demolishing four key surveillance radars.[5] In the northern Gulf, the USS *Nichols* (FFG-47) executed a sophisticated takedown of Iraqi "spy rigs," oil platforms used as radar outposts.[6]

The first phase of the attack achieved critical mass in the five minutes following H-Hour as dozens of missiles and stealth aircraft simultaneously converged on their targets. The attack unfurled with unprecedented suddenness because of the new efficiencies allowed by PGM-armed stealth aircraft and cruise missiles, which could be surged against targets without overstraining support assets such as jammers and tankers.

At 0300, the AT&T communications tower was destroyed by F-117A precision strikes, thereby crippling the national communications system. In the following five minutes the IrAF headquarters, the national Air-Defense Operations Center, and the Baghdad IOC at Salman Pak were struck.[7] The KARI system reeled and collapsed; from this point until the close of the war, Iraq abandoned the centralized control of air-defense operations; the integrated system had literally been disintegrated.

Twenty-eight electricity targets were hit by electronic-attack TLAMs, which exploded in bursts of electromagnetic energy or dispensed transformer-shorting carbon filaments. This cut off Baghdad's electrical supply by H+10, causing the city to lose all commercial power. Some government and military systems, particularly the integrated air-defense system, reverted to generator backup, but many sustained damage as a result of the massive and repetitive short circuiting of the electrical grid and fell inoperative when the grid failed.[8] All around the world, CNN broadcast the dramatic opening blows of what appeared to be a new way of war, which indelibly changed the expectations and perceptions of those who watched the precision strikes.

A less visible but equally impressive second phase of the attack followed. With the KARI system in disarray and little early warning filtering down from the shattered system, Iraq's SAM operators activated their organic on-site acquisition and tracking radars. They expected the initial blitz to be followed by waves of manned aircraft strikes and were unsurprised to see patterns of radar contacts entering Iraq. In fact, these were unmanned aerial decoys: twenty-five U.S. ADM-141A Navy tactical air-launched decoys (TALDs) in the west and fourteen BQM-74 Scathe Mean drones in southern Iraq.[9]

The Iraqi radar operators needed to crank up the power of their radar systems to drown out the heavy electronic jamming interference. As Williamson Murray and Robert Scales noted, this was "like switching from parking lights to headlights" and clearly identified the position of every major radar system in the western and southern sectors. Behind each set of drones was a trailing group of "Wild Weasel" aircraft, specially equipped with AGM-88 high-speed anti-radiation missiles (HARMs) designed to home in on active radars. The HARMs were drawn to Iraq's cranked-up radars like needles to magnets. The first wave of HARM-firing aircraft launched sixty-seven HARMs and a total of two hundred were fired during the vital first three days of air operations, while the Iraqi leadership and its radar operators were unaware of the scale of destruction and the extent to which the radar network was vulnerable to attack.[10] After these three days, Iraqi radar activity fell off dramatically and registered no more than 20 percent of its daily prewar level of activity in any day during the rest of the conflict.[11]

In a development reminiscent of the Vietnamese reaction to U.S. "Wild Weasel" operations, Iraqi SAM operators began firing precious high-altitude SA-2 and SA-3 missiles ballistically, hoping that their onboard seeker heads would go active at a fortuitous moment. This gave most SAM systems an infinitesimally small chance of a successful interception.[12]

Although the IrAF represented the weaker junior partner in Iraq's strategic IADS, the United States had spared no effort to completely deactivate the airborne-interceptor element of the IADS as a meaningful threat in the opening days of Desert Storm. Gulf War–era CIA military analyst Ken Pollack noted that Iraq's air-force leadership was pragmatic about the IrAF's inability to contest air superiority and instead planned to harass and disrupt Coalition plans.[13] To do this, the IOCs were required to provide GCI to orient silent-running, radar-inactive interceptors to isolated Coalition aircraft. Yet, by H+5 the highly centralized IrAF was decapitated through the physical destruction of its headquarters and two of its key IOCs, as well as by the intense jamming of its air-to-air and air-to-ground communications.

Lacking GCI, the IrAF disintegrated. Pilots became separated from their wingmen without GCI to shepherd them, and the stealthy radar-inactive, GCI-controlled stalk became an impractical tactic. The hunters became the hunted, losing fourteen aircraft in air-to-air engagements in the first week alone and an additional eleven the week after.[14]

Alongside the more visible achievements of the Baghdad strikes, the secret success of the takedown of the strategic IADS was so sudden and so complete that it appeared to constitute a miniature military-technical victory in its own right. As Carlo Kopp noted, the Iraqi IADS was "a good facsimile of the planned-for threat—the Warsaw Pact," and the takedown vindicated late–Cold War U.S. approaches to the suppression and destruction of Soviet IADS. The long-pondered "what ifs" of the Cold War were beginning to find partial answers in the attack on Iraq.[15] The disintegration of KARI and the Iraqi radar network was a particularly significant moment for U.S. aviators, who considered the destruction of the enemy air defenses both a victory over their professional counterparts and an enabler that would make all their other options simpler, safer, and more successful.

The near-extinction of the high-altitude radar-guided SAMs and GCI-controlled fighter threat brought U.S. air campaign planners a sense of relief they had never felt before, a "cognitive freedom of action," to use William Andrews's phrase.[16] In less than a week, high altitude had been transformed from the killing zone of the Cold War to a U.S. sanctuary. It could be used to attack the predominantly large and precisely located phase I strategic targets with near impunity. Coalition aircraft could now enjoy "near-total freedom of action" in most Iraqi areas at altitudes above ten thousand feet, although, as the following chapter discusses, operations at low altitudes were heavily constrained.[17] After the first three nights of preplanned air operations, Saddam's Iraq was at once a house with no roof, and the cost had been mercifully low—three aircraft destroyed, three pilots killed. This was an order of magnitude lower than the thirty losses predicted in Checkmate simulations.

IRAQI WITHHOLDING OF STRATEGIC AIR-DEFENSE EFFORTS

Iraq's response to the disintegration of KARI was to hunker down and wait out the bombardment: an attritional air-defense campaign that would, in its broadest sense, continue throughout the next fifteen years. When Iraq's military leadership recognized the rate at which Iraq's radar systems were being destroyed, it quickly moved to assure the long-term survival of these vital components of the IADS. This was an early indication of the Baathist government's overarching preoccupation with the maintenance of the hard-to-replace elements of its military arsenal. Withholding had been a feature of Iraqi air-defense operations in the Iran-Iraq War—Saddam chose to maintain his air force as a deterrent "force in being"—and now, three days into the war, Iraq voluntarily surrendered its ability to employ many of its radar-guided SAMs in an attempt to protect its future capability.

Giving the first hint of the Iraqi regime's proclivity for dispersal and concealment, Iraq went further than merely turning its radars off; it "dismantle[ed] and camouflage[ed] many [SAMs and radars] to avoid attack."[18] The DIA reported that six days into the war Iraq's use of its remaining active radar-guided SAMs had already become more disciplined.[19] Iraq maintained the threat by sparingly using its radar-guided SAMs to complicate Coalition operations, particularly within the Baghdad Missile Engagement Zone (or "SuperMEZ"). For instance, on the third day of air operations, a large package of seventy F-16s were tasked with destroying a nuclear target within the SuperMEZ, but their HARM shooters had expended all their munitions against enemy radar activity by the time the package reached the target. As a result, the largely unsuppressed strategic SAMs shot down two F-16s during the January 19 daylight raid.[20]

According to Desert Storm planner Maj. David Karns, the losses showed planners that the SuperMEZ remained too hot an environment for nonstealthy aircraft, which led to a number of changes in that night's air-tasking order (ATO).[21] Iraq maintained this capacity until the very end of the war, which forced nonstealthy U.S. aircraft to treat the SuperMEZ with respect. As late as February 25–26, when heavy strategic strikes were renewed on Baghdad, Iraq fired a total of sixty radar-guided SAMs each day, the same daily total that it fired in the first day of the war.[22]

Learning from the early collapse of the GCI system, Iraq also quickly began to withhold its precious air forces: sorties dropped from an average of thirty per day in the first week of the war—an insignificant number for a force of more than two hundred interceptors—to almost complete inactivity by the third week. Although Coalition forces had initiated heavy and ongoing runway-denial attacks on Iraqi air fields, the DIA reported "energetic runway repair," which sometimes resulted in fixes in four to six hours.[23]

The inactivity of the IrAF was instead a deliberate strategy that aimed to preserve Iraq's aircraft as a "force in being." Its most capable types were inactive but protected within more than six hundred Iraqi and Kuwaiti hardened aircraft shelters (HAS), and others were dispersed to highway or desert dispersal fields or even parked singly or doubly alongside mosques, archaeological monuments, schools, and other sensitive targets.[24] This latter form of dispersal was a harbinger of future Iraqi operations; not only did Iraq use noncombatants and off-limit areas to screen its aircraft, but it also moved them frequently, which placed additional strain on U.S. intelligence-collection efforts. But in this game of cat and mouse, would Iraq forever be the mouse?

SHELTER CAMPAIGN

U.S. intelligence community could not assume ongoing IrAF passivity. The United States had identified the possibility of an "Air Tet"—a reference to the 1968 Tet offensive, which was militarily disastrous for the Viet Cong but politically disastrous for the U.S. war effort. "Air Tet" specifically referred to a mass attack by withheld IrAF forces that, although militarily suicidal, could result in either a chemical or biological strike on Coalition bases or a militarily insignificant conventional strike that would nonetheless challenge the U.S. claims to air superiority and damage Coalition morale.[25]

Iraq's combination of energetic runway repair and superhardened aircraft shelters meant that a knockout blow such as the one launched by Israel against its Arab neighbors in 1967 would be impossible against the IrAF. A more attritional effort needed to be launched. As early as January 20, four days into the offensive, Checkmate had identified the slow degradation of IrAF capabilities as a problem and had proposed a bunker-busting campaign to the SPG. Conventional wisdom suggested that such shelters were almost impenetrable, and, upon returning from Iraq, one Soviet flight instructor commented: "I will admit that Iraqi air bases literally overwhelmed me. I had never seen anything like it before, although while serving in the Soviet Union I had been in scores of garrisons. The equipment, shelters, and blast walls—everything was the last word in equipment of outstanding quality. The aerodynamic hardened aircraft bunkers were super-hardened to withstand all conceivable threats. As far as I could see, it would have been virtually impossible to destroy them with tactical weapons, even super-accurate ones, and probably would have required nuclear warheads."[26]

Undeterred, the SPG dug out October 1990 contingency plans for HAS attacks and updated them with Checkmate schematics of Iraqi and Kuwaiti shelters that were gleaned from Belgian and Yugoslavian contractors (approached by CIA operatives at trade shows[27]) and subjected to vulnerability analysis by Defense Nuclear Agency analysts.[28] From January 23–27, 375 of 594 Iraqi HASs and a number of Kuwait shelters were struck and an estimated 117 aircraft were destroyed in the strikes.[29] The physical results were often spectacular:

> Post-strike target photos revealed the progressive destruction of the Iraqi Air Force. Each F-111 carried up to four bombs. In one attack, 20 F-111s made two passes each on an airfield, delivering PGMs directly on command bunkers and aircraft shelters, within seven minutes. This equates to a weapon impact about every five seconds. Most of these case hardened bombs penetrated many feet of reinforced concrete and detonated inside the shelters, causing catastrophic explosions that destroyed the shelters and their contents from the inside out. Concrete and steel blast doors weighing as much as tons were hurled up to 250 feet. In some cases, the bombs penetrated the roof and the floor of the shelter before detonation, crushing aircraft between the floor and ceiling.[30]

The operational results were also impressive. From January 26 to 29, more than one hundred of Iraq's best aircraft relocated to Iran, including its remaining two Adnan airborne-early-warning platforms, Su-24 strike aircraft, and F-1EQ5 and MiG-29 interceptors. Iraq also sought to send its thirteen remaining naval missile combatants to Iran, although only two survived the journey after attacks by Coalition naval aviation.[31] During the Iran-Iraq War, Saddam had flown aircraft to third-country sanctuaries in Jordan and Kuwait, and indeed the United States expected Saddam to relocate some aircraft to Jordan. However, the move to Iran was unprecedented and ultimately disastrous for Iraq because the majority of the aircraft were permanently absorbed into the Islamic Republic of Iran Air Force (IRIAF). Whether lying dead in their shelters, scattered in hiding, or held in Iran, the majority of Iraq's aircraft were functionally ineffective and no sorties were flown in the fourteen days preceding the ground war.

On January 27, CINCCENT Schwarzkopf declared air supremacy. The rapid three-day reassignment of valuable air assets to the bunker campaign, including forty F-111F and sixteen F-15E aircraft,[32] plus PGM-dropping

A-6E U.S. Navy aircraft and Royal Air Force Buccaneers and Tornados,[33] underlined the centrality of the maintenance of air superiority to aviators. As the first week of air operations ended, the Shelter Campaign had second priority only to one other targeting effort—the hunt for Saddam's Scuds.

EMPTY BATTLEFIELD: SCUD-HUNTING IN 1991

Unbeknown to Schwarzkopf and General Horner at the outset of the war, Saddam's Scud missile force was to become the ultimate strategic-target set in Desert Storm because it presented almost no tactical or operational threat yet dominated the strategic outlook of Coalition leaders and the global media. The CIA's assessment of Iraqi intent to launch strikes on Israel was quickly validated when Iraq launched eight al-Hussein Scud variants at Israel on the morning of January 18, less than twenty-four hours into the war.

Saddam had always conceived of the Scud missile as a strategic weapon, using it to coerce the Iranian government and sap the morale of the Iranian people of Tehran and Isfahan. Now he intended to use his al-Hussein fleet to parade his pan-Arab credentials by striking out at Israel, knowing that any Israeli retaliatory strike could shatter the coalition of Western and Arab states facing him. The *Conduct of the Persian Gulf War* noted: "At a minimum, this almost certainly would have led to a war between Israel and Jordan and allowed Saddam Hussein to change the complexion of the war from the liberation of Kuwait to another Arab–Israeli conflict. It might easily have brought down the government of Jordan and replaced it with a radical one. The Coalition's unity would be tested severely, with potentially major repercussions."[34]

After having stressed the importance of the Scud target set for months, Secretary of Defense Cheney was alarmed to find that the counter-Scud effort represented a tiny fraction of the planned air campaign. The SPG had met Cheney's basic requirement: every element of the Scud target set was scheduled to be struck in the first thirty-six hours of Desert Storm, although no TELs had been located with certainty. Twenty-six launch sites, comprising a total of sixty launch pads, were hit by twenty-four F-15E and RAF Tornados within five minutes of H-Hour. They entered Iraq through the gap made by the Task Force Normandy Apache strikes. Poor weather made it impossible to gather bomb-damage assessment (BDA) on these sites. Their ongoing suppression was "a token gesture" of two strike aircraft sorties per night and a B-52 carpet-bombing mission, according to one Desert Storm planner,[35] and after the war,

UN inspectors confirmed that only fourteen of twenty-eight sites had been destroyed.[36] All this was academic, however, because the origins of missile attacks showed that Iraq had already made a decision to rely solely on its mobile launcher fleet.

High-level U.S. representatives such as Deputy Secretary of State Lawrence Eagleburger and Under Secretary of Defense Paul Wolfowitz were flown to Israel to assure Tel Aviv that no effort would be spared to suppress Scud launches.[37] Colonel Trexler, USAF military assistant to Cheney, noted that the secretary of defense demanded more activity: "Cheney effectively told [the military], 'I want to see more airplanes flying against SCUDs. I want to see more activity. I want to be able to tell [Israeli Defense Minister] Arens that we have increased our effort to eliminate the Scuds.'"[38]

From January 20 to 28, the Scud-target set was made the top priority in the air campaign. In addition to receiving intelligence updates from the Tactical Air Command Center (TACC) in Riyadh via a hotline linked to a special Joint Staff planning cell set up at the U.S. embassy in Tel Aviv, Israel, TACC Director Lt. Gen. John Corder, recalled, "I had to give a piece of paper every day to Horner about how we are dealing with the Scuds, how many aircraft we had committed."[39] As Corder noted, the Israelis were quick to spot any reduction in the counter-Scud effort, either through these reports or through their direct monitoring with their own air-defense radars of the number of aircraft flying each night. When Corder pulled a single AC-130 gunship off Scud duty, the action was immediately criticized "right from Powell, because the Israelis were counting every sortie every day."[40]

For the first time during Desert Storm, political decision makers sought to dictate operational detail and passed along Israeli demands for greater and greater effort to suppress the Scuds. During the first week of Desert Storm, Iraq fired thirty-three Scuds at Israel and Saudi Arabia. During this time, CENTAF established twenty-four-hour coverage over both the Western launch "baskets": "Scud Alley," a range of wadis southeast of the Baghdad-Amman highway, and "Scud Boulevard," a network of roads northwest of the highway, near the Syrian border area of al-Qaim.[41] Twelve F-15E aircraft were committed to the baskets at night, each basket was covered by a pair of fighters, and one of each pair carried one of the Coalition's few low-altitude navigation and targeting infrared for night (LANTIRN) targeting pods. The counter-Scud effort was tying up fully half of the twelve prototype laser-designating pods that had been rushed into service for Desert Storm. One squadron of A-10A aircraft were diverted to maintaining the day coverage, and many other high-value PGM- and night-capable aircraft were drawn into the Scud hunt. It consumed 17 percent of Coalition sorties between January 21 and 26: roughly two hundred sorties per day.

SPG planners eventually managed to put a ceiling on the number of aircraft diverted to the Scud campaign by pointing out the uncomfortable truth: no matter how many strike aircraft orbited western Iraq, Scud launches could not even be reduced, let alone stopped, until a means was found to locate Iraq's mobile TELs. Lieutenant Colonel Deptula noted: "We did resist a diversion of resources to an increased effort against Scuds. . . . The presumption of some of the senior U.S. leadership was that we weren't already doing something about the Scuds. What I did was to end up convincing Glosson, . . . Horner, and Schwarzkopf that we were already doing as much as could be done without more intelligence. . . . Part of it was also finally getting hold of the Israeli target list . . . which allowed me to say, 'Look, there's nothing on here we're not already doing.'"[42]

FINDING THE SCUDS

In the lead-up to war, the U.S. intelligence community made sporadic attempts to track the mobile TELs as they shuttled around the western Scud baskets and the two other key Scud baskets near Basra. The TELs took periodic visits to their depot and could not be tracked in any case, because in transit they looked much like any of the thousands of articulated trucks traveling Iraq's busy commercial highways. In 1991, the number of Scud TELs was never known, but probably numbered nine to eleven Soviet-made 9P117 launchers and an additional eight unsatisfactory Iraqi copies.[43]

As the previous chapter noted, it is fair to say that the U.S. military did not believe it could effectively target the mobile TELs, so it presumed that it would not have to do so. Yet, in the post–Cold War military environment, the militarily impossible and the politically imperative would often be one and the same. Centralized tasking of Coalition ISR assets by CENTCOM J-2 facilitated a massive reorientation of ISR platforms that mirrored the shift of combat aircraft to the Scud hunt.[44] Defense Support Program (DSP) early-warning satellites could detect the heat bloom from each mobile Scud launch but provided only a general area to search because of the cloud cover.

U.S. signals-intelligence (SIGINT) satellites, aircraft, and ground stations monitored Iraqi communications but turned up few targeting leads.

On January 21, one of the Coalition's two prototype E-8A JSTARS aircraft was allotted to the Scud hunt in the western desert. Using its wide-area surveillance and moving-target-indicator (MIT) sensors, JSTARS raked back and forth over the western Scud baskets for six days identifying moving vehicles within the area. However, it was an experimental system that was not expected to reach operational units until 1997 and had flown fewer than ten in-theater flights since arriving in Saudi Arabia on January 12. There were problems with the system's ability to manage data flow and automatically filter out types of vehicles that could not be Scud TELs (e.g., vehicles with caterpillar tracks rather than wheels). JSTARS also could not more accurately classify the mobile contacts it monitored using its SAR imager, which could theoretically zoom in to image a four-by-four-kilometer area for target identification: it could not identify a Scud TEL within this scene at this early stage in the system's development.

U-2 and TR-1 reconnaissance aircraft also imaged the Scud baskets using real-time SAR, which was downloaded to a C2 van in the car park of the Coalition headquarters in Riyadh, but the SAR images were not precise enough to differentiate a Scud TEL from the many commercial trucks or other military vehicles using the area.[45]

Because wide-area surveillance systems could not provide sufficient detail, a range of tactical systems and intelligence-gathering capabilities were then cued to image the areas of interest identified by U-2 or satellite intelligence. There was no safe way to do this kind of intelligence gathering. Very-low-altitude road reconnaissance was launched by U.S. Air Force RF-4C and RAF Tornado GR-1A photograph reconnaissance aircraft. During the day, OV-10D and A-10 aircraft loitered over a dangerous missile engagement zone (MEZ) near the H-2 and H-3 airfields, searching with sideways-looking radar and binoculars, respectively, while at night, F-15E and other aircraft used their forward-looking infrared (FLIR) to scan for heat sources. Bad weather complicated the effort by blanketing large areas of the Scud baskets with cloud and fog. Special forces offered one means of getting "under the weather" and close to the Scuds, albeit dangerously close.

On January 20, British Special Air Service (SAS) foot and vehicle patrols were preparing to carry out strategic reconnaissance missions along the Baghdad-Amman highway and other main supply routes when they were given the priority mission of locating mobile TELs operating in the western desert. By February 7, the British special-operation forces (SOFs) were joined by a U.S. Joint Special Operations Task Force (JSOTF) composed of eight hundred troops (two squadrons of U.S. Delta Force operators and a number of U.S. Ranger companies) and the helicopter forces of the 160th U.S. Special Operations Aviation Regiment.

Until February 27, the penultimate day of the war, the SAS combed Scud Alley and the JSOTF operated along Scud Boulevard. Coalition SOF operators could only move at night and were frequently compromised by local civilians and counter-SOF militias. At night SOFs frequently saw Scud launches from a distance of forty kilometers away but had no means of reaching the target quickly or orienting aircraft onto an exact target area.[46] The F-15E loitering overhead, often above the clouds, could also see the Scud launches but were often many minutes of flight time away and also had no way of precisely locating what they had seen. Of forty-two visual acquisitions of Scud launches, only eight could identify a specific area that could be targeted. There is no firm indication that any mobile TELs were destroyed during Desert Storm.[47]

The Coalition's inability to locate and target Iraq's mobile launcher fleet was caused by a combination of highly effective Iraqi tactics and the lack of preparedness of the Coalition intelligence-collection system to find small and relocateable targets or to engage them within a compressed timeframe—what would later be termed time-sensitive targeting (TST). On the first count, Iraq's missile forces ranked as the most professional element of the country's armed forces, as befitted the developing strategic deterrent force of the nation. UN Arms Inspector Scott Ritter recalled that even after the war, the Iraqi Missile Command (Unit 224) displayed all the indicators of high morale, including spit-and-polish presentation and discipline.[48]

A regular recipient of U.S. SIGINT and IMINT throughout the 1986–88 period, Iraq had a clear and relatively current understanding of the strengths and weaknesses of the U.S. intelligence-collection system. As William Studeman, director of the U.S. NSA, noted:

> Having had about four years' or more worth of US delivering intelligence to it with regard to Iran's conduct of the war, Iraq had a substantial knowledge and sensitivity of our capabilities in the area of imaging and other intelligence collection methods such as signals intelligence. If you go back to the first principles of intelligence, we had already failed on the first count. That is, our security had been penetrated because we were

dealing with this target to whom we had spent so many years displaying what our intelligence capabilities were. Add the fact that Iraq is a very secretive country itself, and places a great premium on security, and you then have a target that is probably the most denial-and-deception oriented target that the US has ever faced. It is a country that goes out of its way to create a large number of barriers to allowing any Western penetration of its capabilities and intentions.[49]

Since the end of the Iran-Iraq War, Baghdad had also been intensely concerned about a counterforce strike on its Scud forces by the Israeli military, and indeed Iraq had feared that Israel might try a disarming strike in April 1990. As early as August 10, 1990, the Iraqi leadership issued instructions to its Missile Command that it should focus on "concealment above any other action" and should take immediate steps to "avoid discovery by space photography."[50]

As noted, the Iraqi Missile Command's first decision was to rely fully on mobile launchers because it recognized the vulnerability of fixed sites. General Schwarzkopf noted that it would have been a tall order to find "nine, maybe ten trucks" in an area of twenty-nine thousand square miles under ideal circumstances, and Iraq's countermeasures to Coalition intelligence gathering made the reliable identification of launchers close to impossible.[51] Iraq's missile force moved only at night and rested up during the day in a variety of hides, particularly highway underpasses. Seven launch "baskets" were used, each a large area hundreds of kilometers square with easy access to road systems, where the launchers could merge into the busy Baghdad-Amman traffic. To support this tactic, TELs were camouflaged as commercial trucks, and high-quality East German TEL decoys were deployed to distract loitering Coalition attack aircraft undertaking road reconnaissance missions.[52]

Coalition planers were well aware that sensor acuity was simply not good enough either to differentiate decoys or, indeed, to find camouflaged Scuds; a prewar exercise, Touted Gleam, had shown that even an F-15E had difficulty finding a TEL-sized vehicle in a one-square-mile area, even when the pilot knew exactly where to look.[53] Energetic counter-SOF activities, carried out by both the local Popular Army militias and a specialized Iraqi commando brigade, prevented the SAS or the JSOTF from scouting possible Scud hides during the day.

When the TELs emerged at night, they had at their disposal a large pool of potential launch sites, already surveyed with GPS equipment purchased by

Iraq. Ironically, the U.S. military's reliance on commercial GPS equipment meant that it could not utilize its option of degrading the quality of commercial GPS services, which was unencrypted and thus available for Iraq to use. During Desert Storm, Iraq's al-Hussein and al-Hijarah missile forces shuffled continuously among these many sites, being careful to avoid repetitive reuse of sites and launching attacks at different times each evening.

Missiles were launched at night only, preferably under cloud cover, and numerous steps were taken to reduce the possibility that launch groups would be identified. The number of vehicles in the TEL convoys was kept to an absolute minimum, and communications devices were not allowed to be activated at the same site as the missile launcher. Accuracy was sacrificed to reduce the recognizable signature and timescale of a Scud launch; Iraqi crews dispensed with highly visible weather balloon launches or detectable Flap Board radar emissions. The Gulf War commander of Iraq's missile forces, Lt. Gen. Hazim Abdul-Razzaq Al-Ayubi, stated that Iraqi al-Hussein batteries took thirty-five to forty minutes to set up, fuel a missile, and fire from a surveyed site, which was far shorter than the ninety minutes required for Soviet Scud batteries to halt and carry out a full site survey and telemetry calculations.[54]

TST would become a military buzzword later in the 1990s, when efforts would be made to shorten the sensor-to-shooter "kill chain."[55] Of course, to some branches of the U.S. military, TST was already second nature by 1991. Most often, advanced sensor-to-shooter networks and short kill chains existed in the aerial or naval arenas, which enable missions such as naval antiair warfare (AAW), air-to-air combat, or antisubmarine warfare. During Operation Desert Storm, for example, the U.S. Navy maintained a sophisticated AAW effort in the Persian Gulf. It used a network of ships and aircraft tied together by a theater-wide digital datalink architecture, and monitored more than sixty-five thousand inbound and outbound air sorties and to differentiate inbound Iraqi attackers from Coalition return flights (thereby avoiding fratricide). The system was amazingly successful.[56]

Although TST against ground targets was less common, some kinds of targets were prosecuted by sensor-to-shooter networks with great speed, notably counterbattery fire against enemy artillery systems. On an ad hoc basis, the U.S. military began to experiment with other forms of TST against ground targets during Operation Desert Storm.

In an extension of the highly networked naval AAW system, Coalition naval forces carried out an example of TST against an Iraqi Silkworm antiship-missile site on February 25. The Royal Navy frigate HMS *Gloucester* detected the launch of two Silkworms against Coalition vessels, intercepted one missile, and immediately passed on the rough launch location to a U.S. Navy E-2C aircraft coordinating Coalition air forces on the area. The E-2C tasked an EP-3 surveillance aircraft and other assets to pinpoint the launcher, and then directed an A-6E aircraft to strike the site with twelve Rockeye cluster-bomb munitions.[57] Thanks to the naval requirement for distributed communications and timely air defense, the U.S. Navy was well equipped to complete the complex kill chain in a manageable timeframe.

The U.S. services operating most regularly against ground targets—the Army, Marines, and Air Force—were relative newcomers, however. Early in Desert Storm, one of the two prototype Army tactical missile systems (ATACMS) deployed to theater gave a hint of what would one day be possible when it received an urgent tasking to engage an Iraqi SA-2 emplacement in the KTO. Traveling in convoy, the self-propelled ATACMS launcher slewed out of the column into a hasty firing position, located itself, calculated a firing solution, and fired one of its 165-kilometer munitions at the target.[58]

Although this kind of targeting represented the exception rather than the rule in 1991, twenty years earlier, in a different war, the United States had been rather good at TST against some types of ground targets. Between 1965 and 1971, the United States used a network of special forces and electronic intelligence-gathering systems to detect vehicle and even personnel movement on the Ho Chi Minh trail. The Shining Brass/Prairie Fire system saw SOF operators communicate directly with OH-1 Bird Dog aircraft, which in turn cued airborne strike aircraft onto enemy concentrations within minutes. The fully electronic Igloo White network of seismic, magnetic, noise, and chemical detection sensors, relayed by airborne EC-121R aircraft and QU-22B Pace Eagle unmanned aerial vehicles (UAVs), communicated targeting solutions to aircraft in a mere two to five minutes. The limiting factor was often not targeting intelligence but instead the ability of strike aircraft to reach the target and deliver their munitions in adverse weather conditions. Even so, thirty- to forty-minute kill chains were commonly achieved.[59]

Yet, aside from the aforementioned counterbattery role, highly responsive TST against ground targets had not been a feature of the Cold War mission of the U.S. military. Soviet armored and logistical columns would not be fleeting targets: to the contrary, they would stretch like pulsing veins from the West German border to the Soviet Union. Readjusting to the mobile

Scud target set was thus a major challenge, especially given the lack of prewar focus on the problem.

Lack of "zoomable" wide-area surveillance or high-acuity night sensors meant that the Coalition could not exploit even the thirty-five to forty minutes in which Scud TELs were setting up. Instead, the clock started ticking the moment the Scud engines were ignited and either SOFs or aircraft saw the launch or the DSP satellites registered a "heat event." Although it was able to give some slender early warning to Israeli and Gulf governments, the DSP system took seven to nine minutes to communicate the rough location of the heat bloom to the Coalition TACC, which in turn needed to verbally pass this information on to an AWACS aircraft, which would then verbally task an airborne strike aircraft. Special forces could add little to Coalition SA in this case; even if they took the time to stop and set up their satellite communications or ran the risk of using their detectable high-frequency radios, their report of a Scud launch in the distance would be imprecise and no timelier than the DSP warning.

With a sensor-to-shooter cycle of up to fifty minutes, inbound strike aircraft stood little chance of finding the TELs because of the speed at which Iraqi missile crews could relocate: they could move up to twelve miles within fifteen minutes.[60] One F-15E plot recalled: "AWACS is yelling and hollering for us to get on it and we're heading for the coordinates as fast as we could go. It was about twenty-five miles away from us but when we got there, we went down the road and all I could find in the targeting pod was a hot spot on the ground. It was no longer than five minutes after the launch when we found the hot spot. These guys were fast. They were just like cockroaches that disappear when the kitchen light goes on."[61]

INDIRECT APPROACH TO THE SCUD THREAT

Unable to catch the mobile TELs "red-handed" at their launch sites, the Coalition instead sought to speculatively strike their potential hiding or launching places and to destroy their supporting infrastructure. Eventually, the Coalition spent merely 20 percent of aircraft sorties on TEL hunting and the remaining 80 percent on attacking fixed sites and the supporting infrastructure.[62] Potential Scud hides—particularly highway underpasses and hardened aircraft shelters—were struck with 2,000-pound laser-guided bombs. The two F-15E aircraft on airborne alert flew racetrack patterns over Scud Boulevard at night, dropping 500-pound bombs at random intervals to spook the Scud crews. The SAS in Scud Alley, and later the JSOTF in Scud Boulevard, began direct-action attacks on suspected Scud convoys using their own heavy weapons or cued overhead PGM droppers onto convoys using their laser-designating markers.

Although the DIA claimed that sixty Scuds were destroyed, DIA subsequently claimed that most appeared to be commercial articulated trucks and fuel tankers. On January 30, for instance, a number of Jordanian trucks and petrol tankers were destroyed at a truck stop in the western desert. Although the U.S. government did not admit the collateral damage until 1992, it declared the entire Iraqi stretch of the Baghdad-Amman highway to be a legitimate military target from February 7, 1991 onward.[63]

From February 19 onward, B-52G and F-15E aircraft seeded choke points and suspected launch sites with air-scattered CBU-89 Gator mines. Targeting cues were now originating from unattended seismic, acoustic, and magnetic sensors deployed by SOFs in the launch baskets[64] and from the multispectral-satellite-imagery-fusion cell set up on February 14, which exploited the ability of multispectral imagery to detect repetitive use of ground or the presence of chemical agents and heat signatures.[65]

By this time, Scud launches against Israel and Saudi Arabia had already dropped from their first-week average of 4.7 per day to 1.5 per day. To some extent, the reduced pace appears to have been the result of the general friction of operating at high tempo under wartime conditions—Iraq's missile crews were tired after days of movement and preparation spent in the austere western desert, the threat of SOFs and air attack was growing, and cratered roads and broken communications links made each element of Scud operations a little harder. The memoirs of Iraq's Missile Forces commander, Lieutenant General al-Ayyubi, distinctly give this impression.[66]

Iraq also appears to have deliberately reduced the firing rate, perhaps to withhold its stock of al-Hussein missiles, which was limited because of the effects of Coalition bombing on Scud production facilities. Although strikes were launched on the fixed launch sites and a token number of aircraft were allotted to the search for TELs, Coalition counter-Scud strategy, planned before the war, had focused on destroying Iraq's Scud storage and refueling facilities. Coalition strategists anticipated that missiles could only be kept loaded with their unstable liquid fuel for six weeks before they needed to be emptied and filled with fresh fuel. In the event of a war lasting longer than six weeks, Iraq would find itself effectively disarmed. These planned strikes were carried out against the Latifyah fuel facility and the Shahiyat rocket motor plant at 1300 on January 17 by F-16 aircraft.

In actual fact, Iraq's Missile Command rotated missiles after they had been fueled for just four weeks and new Scud fueling was carried out at a reduced rate throughout the war. Scud firings during the first three weeks of the war were thus carried out using missiles fueled in the weeks preceding the war and then stored all across the country in scores of caches, each of fewer than thirty missiles. A new set of ten missiles were fueled as soon as antiaircraft fire began in Baghdad around 0300 on January 17, providing the stocks that would be fired in the middle of the war.

But what of Iraq's late war firings? Throughout the war the Coalition tasked B-52G and other aircraft against suspected storage facilities, and known Scud-fueling facilities were watched for activity. Hair-trigger rapid-response options were put in place should the Scuds surface. On one occasion, thirteen TLAMs were fired at premensurated targets in response to an intelligence warning that Scud refueling might be underway at a key facility. Yet, fueling of small numbers of Scuds continued during the war using a series of temporary fueling facilities located near Ramadi, which allowed a brief upsurge of launches at the close of the war. Instead of fueling, the key limiting factor for the western-desert Iraqi missile force appeared to be the need to bring the five to seven TELs active at any one time back to loading facilities near Ramadi to take on new Scuds, an operation that continued until January 28–29, when the operation relocated to a new area that was never discovered by Coalition surveillance.[67]

Unaware of this center of gravity for the Scud force, the Coalition instead sought to cut the communications that were presumed to link Scud forces to the political leadership and the military-targeting infrastructure. On the first count, there was little that could be done to interdict the orders to fire. At 1100 on January 17, within thirty minutes of its writing, a letter from the Office of the Presidential Palace (OPP) was hand-delivered to the Iraqi Missile Forces commander that ordered conventional missile strikes against Israel to begin that night and for them to "continue until further notice." Guidance from the Baathist leadership was infrequent; the next letter from OPP on January 29 told Missile Forces to slow down the pace of firing but to continue operations until otherwise instructed.[68] Furthermore, U.S. intelligence analysts made an understandable error in assuming that the Scud force would need to receive telemetry data from Baghdad to maximize the accuracy of each launch. This pattern that would be repeated time and again in the following decade, as Iraq modified standard operational procedures, resulting in improved survivability but reduced or even negated military effectiveness.

Throughout the remainder of the war, the Coalition would hammer away at the communication links between Baghdad and western Iraq—Coalition SOFs would raid desolate communications facilities and the SAS would even dig around with pneumatic drills searching for roadside fiber-optic cables to sever.[69] Meanwhile, the SPG planned in late January to destroy nine Baghdad bridges across the Tigris River, targeting them in large part to sever the fiber-optic cables strung beneath them, all in the name of the Scud campaign.

COSTS AND BENEFITS OF BROADER STRATEGIC TARGETING

The targeting of bridges in Baghdad was emblematic of the costs and benefits that attended strategic targeting in Desert Storm. Like any of the fixed targets that were identified in the six months preceding the war, no Iraq bridge could stand against Coalition precision bombing. If targets could be found, they could be destroyed. Alongside the planned takedown of the Iraqi IADS, and in spite of the diversion of assets to the Scud hunt, strategic bombing of "stable and easily identifiable targets of high value" remained a cornerstone of the prewar plan to impose strategic paralysis on Iraq's military effort.[70]

The DIA reported that by the end of the first week of the war, attacks of the electrical grid had imposed frequent blackouts throughout Iraq. The local grid in Baghdad had shut down after suffering "severe disruption" from the first night of the war. Satellite images and television reports showed a darkened Iraqi capital. Two of Iraq's three largest oil refineries were also "not operable" as a result of Coalition air attacks and the trickle-down effect of electrical failure, which reduced Iraq's ability to refine military and civilian fuels by 50 percent and left the country with an estimated fifty-five days worth of refined oil at prewar consumption rates.[71] Industrial sites had suffered "heavy damage," especially in Iraq's chemicals sector. The DIA assessed that Iraqi ability to manufacture nerve agents and mustard gas had been reduced by 40–50 percent and its chemical-weapons-filling capacity by 70 percent. Suspected biological-weapons research and refrigerated storage sites were struck.[72] A trickle of nuclear targets was engaged throughout the war: first the Isis nuclear reactor, which had been identified before the war, and then nuclear complexes in Mosul and Baghdad as the war continued.

The strategic air campaign ripped through any Iraqi target that could be found, fixed, tracked, and targeted. Reflecting on the ability to destroy these targets and at the same time keep the general fabric of the city and the health of the population intact, Luttwak reflected the tune of many postwar analysts when he exclaimed, "Airpower had finally done it."[73]

In fact, it would take years to untangle what airpower had actually done to Iraq's political and economic infrastructure. PGMs and stealth made attacks on critical infrastructures and military industries remarkably cheap to execute, so they did not represent a major military investment on the part of Coalition commanders. Indeed only 10 percent of Coalition strike sorties were carried out against these targets.[74] As Lieutenant Colonel Deptula noted, by using PGMs, "smaller numbers of aircraft could keep up more focus and pressure on the strategic campaign than is readily apparent from sortie statistics. . . . I capitalised on the general lack of awareness of these facts among the senior commanders to keep pressure on the strategic effort."[75]

However, efficiency does not necessarily equate to effectiveness. Although any disruption of the Iraqi war effort would have some effect on war-fighting capabilities, the near-term benefits from the bombing of core strategic-target sets are difficult to gauge. What would become apparent in Desert Storm was that the cost of strategic attack against economic infrastructures, leadership, and communications would be primarily *political,* not *military*, both in the near and long term.

UNINTENDED LONG-TERM CONSEQUENCES OF STRATEGIC ATTACK

For instance, many of the strategic air campaign's features had been designed to cause long-term damage to specific Iraqi capabilities—NBC and military industries—and would not have a direct influence on the conduct of the war because of its short duration. Others were intended to cause temporary damage to Iraq's ability to function as a state, for instance, the temporary takedown of the electrical grid or the petrol, oil, and lubricants (POL) storage infrastructure.

In the chaos of war, however, it was predictably difficult to maintain such finessed targeting directives. Although the SPG had warned targeteers at wing level to avoid certain types of aimpoints that would cause long-term damage, CENTAF/IN did not pass this DMPI-selection guidance from the SPG to the wings. Lacking guidance and forced to choose only the most lucrative aimpoints because of Deptula's low aircraft-to-target assignment in the daily master attack plan, these targeteers used unit manuals such as the aforementioned *JMEMs* or the *Critical Elements of Selected Generic Installations Handbook*, which focused on permanent damage.

Against the electricity target set, which was attacked from the first to the last day of the war, this resulted in strikes on hard-to-replace generating halls and boilers instead of the SPG's preferred strikes on easy-to-replace transformers and switching yards.[76] Against the POL-target set, the result was that expensive and high-tech distillation or "cracking" towers were attacked instead of stocks of refined oil that had short-term military utility.[77]

In other cases, U.S. Navy aircraft returning to their carriers needed to offload unspent munitions, and, unbeknown to the SPG, critical infrastructure targets including the Basra power station were designated as secondary targets or "bomb dumps."[78] Similarly, the same power-generator sites that had been temporarily knocked out by electronic-attack TLAMs and CALCMs were designated as bomb dumps, nullifying the intended impermanent effect of the attacks.[79] The Bayji thermal-power plant, the largest in Iraq and the key source of Baghdad's power, was critically damaged. The aftereffects of the loss of commercial electricity were devastating. As U.S. Air Force strategic-attack doctrine later commented, "The loss of electricity shut down the capital's water treatment plants and led to a public health crisis from raw sewage dumped in the Tigris River."[80]

No one could have guessed in January 1991 that, restrained by the effects of more than a decade of UN sanctions on Iraq, sewage treatment in Iraq would not return until May 2004 or that it would eventually be restarted by U.S. military engineers. In the interregnum, waterborne diseases caused a decade-long health crisis. Because Iraq is a particularly energy- and technology-dependent developing country, Iraq's civilians suffered gravely from the loss of sewage treatment, running water, refrigeration and air conditioning, and medical services. According to a Harvard University team that visited Iraq months after the war, infant mortality reached 100 percent of premature babies in many hospitals, and tens of thousands of preventable deaths are likely to have occurred in 1991 and subsequent years because of the aftereffects of the war.[81]

Although Instant Thunder's architect, Colonel Warden, noted in 1992 that the strategic air campaign had been "a war waged primarily against things, but one that produced remarkably few casualties," he was right only to a point—Baghdad was no Dresden. Yet, in the years to follow, air-campaign planners would come to learn that collateral damage and civilian deaths come in many different forms, both prompt and long-term.

PROMPT COLLATERAL DAMAGE

In early 1991, however, attention was firmly focused on prompt collateral damage, much of which would be caused by the risky endeavor of seeking to "isolate and incapacitate the Iraqi regime," which meant going after its leadership bunkers and communications. This feature of Instant Thunder had survived as a centerpiece of the Desert Storm air-campaign plan, which drew strong focus on leadership targets, the ultimate "inside-out" target set and the bull's-eye at the center of Colonel Warden's targeting-ring model.

During Desert Storm, this effort would take the form of 260 strikes on the political leadership of Iraq and an additional 1,710 on command, control, communications, and computerization (C4) targets that connected the leadership to the Iraqi military and the people.[82] The effort began in the first five minutes after H-Hour, when Iraq's main presidential palace in Baghdad was destroyed. In the days that followed an additional forty-four fixed leadership targets were attacked in an attempt to deny the regime the use of reliable or high-volume communications networks and the public switching network (PSN).

According to the DIA, one week into the war, the "control function" of the Iraqi government had been disrupted and the leadership "driven underground."[83] It might have been more precise to say that the leadership was on the run, because Coalition bunker busting throughout the duration of the war made Baghdad's underground the last place the Baathist leadership wanted to be. Instead, Saddam used mobility and obscurity. Throughout the war, air-campaign planners kept up an unrelenting hunt for up to twenty-four Wanderlodge conference vehicles, which Saddam was believed to be using as mobile command posts. Mostly, however, Saddam had fallen back on his humble origins and taken to the modest residential districts of Baghdad as protection against air attacks, once again abandoning elaborately and expensively developed military infrastructure to reduce risks. As Bruce Riedel, then the senior CIA analyst on Iraq, recalled, "Since August 1990, we had tried to track this man on a day-to-day basis with little to show. We always search for an enemy's center of gravity, and in a system like Iraq's, this ultimately involves a manhunt."[84]

Saddam and other senior Iraqi leaders were experts at evading such assassination attempts, however, and kept knowledge of their frequent movements within an extremely small circle of trusted loyalists. When Saddam Hussein met with Russian Foreign Minister Yevgeniy Primakov during the war, he did so in a humble residential dwelling. CIA operative Bob Baer recalled an Iraqi defector who described the security measures surrounding Saddam: "You were told to go to a certain street corner in Baghdad and wait, sometimes for up to two or three hours. Eventually a car would stop. You were told to get in the back and lie down on the floor. A blanket would be thrown over your head so that you couldn't see anything. The car would drive around Baghdad for at least an hour. Then the car would stop, and there Saddam would be, waiting for you in front of a very ordinary house, probably commandeered for only that one meeting."[85]

Yet, with residential districts as their only safe refuge, the Coalition felt that it had seriously degraded the Iraqi government's ability to command and control the war. Edward Mann summarized that "it seems implausible to argue that a running, hiding leadership out of normal contact with its citizenry and army could effectively direct a nation-state for long."[86]

As logical as this seems, leadership strikes do not appear to have isolated the leadership to the extent that was hoped. It is true that the loss of real-time, high-volume communications had catastrophic effects on the Iraqi IADS and on Iraq's internal intelligence-collection and regime security capabilities, and the denial of peacetime leadership facilities "greatly disrupted normal government activities," according to the DIA. At the operational level, however, Saddam could still control key elements of Iraq's military, ordering the initiation of Scud strikes and later communicating major decisions such as the order to launch a cross-border incursion into Saudi Arabia as well as a phased retreat from the KTO.

In addition to initiating the aforementioned partially completed series of attacks on all nine of the bridges spanning the Tigris River, air-campaign planners sought permission to carry out a preannounced strike on the Al Rashid and Babylon Hotels—the former of which was occupied by the press corps— to strike a suspected fiber-optic hub in the basement. General Schwarzkopf vetoed the attack, despite the Coalition's intent to warn residents with a preceding leaflet drop.[87]

In fact, the lack of real-time communications arguably forced Saddam to delegate operational decision-making to better-qualified military professionals. The leadership was also not particularly isolated from the broader Arab world or the international community: although the Coalition had destroyed Iraq's ARABSAT terminal early in the war, it used portable satellite transmitters and foreign media to maintain the bearing and appearance of a functioning government.[88]

The Coalition enjoyed the most success in isolating Saddam from the Iraqi people by jamming Iraq's known radio and television facilities until its broadcasts were "weak and sporadic."[89] Although regime security communications could fall back on informal personal communications, much of it depended on telephone communication. There appears to have been a slight loosening of control, evidenced by the ability of many Iraqi frontline deserters to return to their homes and eventually by the major uprisings that flared up in fourteen of Iraq's eighteen provinces after the Gulf War. Some efforts were made to destabilize the Baathist regime as its military defeat became evident to the Iraqi people through a late-war escalation of strikes against the visible symbols of the regime—the Baath Party headquarters, the giant statue of Saddam in Firdos Square, and the Victory monument, four giant, bronze, crossed scimitars held by hands reputedly modeled on Saddam's—although this was not a major focus of Coalition air-campaign planners. It was no longer in use, but the Baath Party building was symbolically struck by twenty-one LGBs on the very last day of the war, three times the number of munitions that had hit it during the entire war up to that point. Permission to destroy the latter two statues was never granted by the White House or CJCS legal counsel.

In an attempt to keep up pressure on the Iraqi leadership, an ongoing series of attacks were mounted against new and identified leadership bunkers, which led to the most-publicized collateral-damage incident of the post–Cold War era—the February 12 destruction of the al-Firdos communications bunker, which killed 350 noncombatants who were sheltering inside.

Desert Storm showed that any attempt to reach into the urban sanctuary of Baghdad was likely to result in a pattern of collateral-damage incidents that reduced the strategic payoff from attacks on leadership or communications targets. Attacks on Baghdad were particularly sensitive because the international media were camped out in the Iraqi capital. Although the February 13 al-Firdos strike was the key event that preempted vetting of Baghdad targets, it must be situated amid a broader sequence of events that caused senior U.S. political and military decision makers discomfort.

On January 30, a failed attack on a Tigris bridge ended in collateral damage to the Iraqi Central Bank. Two days later, a daylight "stream" of TLAMs was filmed by a BBC cameraman passing the Al Rashid Hotel. After that, Iraq claimed that civilians had been killed by a Tomahawk that appears to have crashed after being hit by antiaircraft fire, causing U.S. CJCS Powell to institute a moratorium on Tomahawk shoots into Baghdad. Commenting on this, Brigadier General Glosson stated: "If the Al Rashid had not been used in the Tomahawk flight plan as a turn point, I don't think Tomahawk would ever have been restricted."[90] Although TLAM targeteers continued to nominate targets to Glosson for the duration of the war, the Al Rashid TLAMs were the last to be fired in the war. Casualties quickly mounted. On February 4, a failed Royal Air Force (RAF) attack on a bridge in Nasariyah caused an unspecified number of civilian deaths, and, following the al-Firdos attack on February 13, a failed bridge attack at Fallujiah on February 14 caused approximately 130 civilian deaths.

Iraq was quick not only to exploit accidental civilian deaths but also to fabricate apparent examples of Coalition collateral damage. By February 11, Iraq had feigned the destruction of a mosque in Basra and released pictures of alleged collateral damage that actually showed images of earthquake damage.[91] All strikes on Baghdad were suspended for five days, and thereafter General Schwarzkopf wanted to be notified verbally about all Baghdad targets at the 1900 meeting, including collateral-damage risks and military objectives related to the strike, and later wanted written lists to be submitted, which would then be sent back to Powell.[92] For senior decision makers such as the chairman, the payoff from striking strategic targets had dried up, whereas the liabilities associated with them were increasing. This resulted in tightened criteria for strikes in the Baghdad area.

Although collateral damage came to the forefront of media coverage after the al-Firdos bombing, it had been an issue throughout the war. JFACC Horner is reported to have commented that Desert Storm was "the first war in which every target was reviewed by a military lawyer," and this appears to be the case. Targets were also scrubbed before the war by all the key National Security Council principals, including President Bush, Secretary of Defense Cheney, CJCS Powell, Secretary of State James Baker, National Security Adviser Brent Scowcroft, and State Department adviser Bob Kimmitt.[93]

Rules of engagement (ROEs) for striking ground targets in Desert Storm took strong steps to minimize the risk of collateral damage. As Judge Advocate John Humphries noted: "If a coalition mission's 'fragged' target or an alternative one could not be located, the rules required a pilot to return with their weapons. Similarly, aircrews could attack a target in populated areas only if they were sure of the target's identification and location; otherwise they were not to deliver their ordnance. Consequently, numerous coalition aircraft returned from combat sorties carrying undelivered ordnance. Indeed, approximately 25 percent of all combat missions culminated in undelivered ordnance."[94]

However, it would be a mistake to characterize the ROEs as weak. Mosques, shrines, hospitals, schools, museums, national monuments, and other historical or cultural sites were not to be attacked *except in self-defense*, meaning that an enemy weapon was firing from their vicinity.[95] There would be no sanctuaries for enemy forces demonstrating hostile intent or carrying out hostile acts. All identified Iraqi forces were considered hostile and therefore legitimate targets for engagement, in stark contrast to Vietnam-era ROEs that required hostile intent to be displayed or hostile acts to be committed by some surface targets before engagement.[96]

In line with the military lawyer's principle of proportionality, any potential target in Iraq might be attacked if the strategic payoff were high enough. Judge advocates worked with planners in the SPG to ensure that high-value targets could be included on the JTL regardless of their location. CENTAF Judge Advocate Harry Heintzelmann used the example of the Baghdad nuclear reactor, which had to be destroyed without spreading hazardous materials over the nearby civilian neighborhoods. According to his account, judge advocates encouraged the use of LGBs to destroy the supporting piles of the building so that the reactor core would be buried rather than directly struck. Heintzelmann noted that "in most instances where the proposed target is a military objective, help is needed only in developing a means of attack that meets the criteria of proportionality."

Judge advocates at Heintzelmann's level (the SPG) and below (the tactical wings) provided these means by modifying the axis, timing of attack, the munitions used, or a combination of all three.[97] Such assistance was increasingly vital because Iraq had sought to exploit Coalition ROEs and "no-strike" lists after the Baghdad collateral-damage incidents. Judge Humphries noted, "About 30 days into the air campaign, several events led CENTAF to review the rules of engagement and determine whether certain considerations of the law of armed conflict might require changes in this rules. Iraq began storing military materiel in and near schools, medical facilities, and places of worship. It located command and control centers in schools and public buildings. The Iraqi military scattered antiaircraft weapons throughout residential areas and on rooftops of public buildings. Tanks and artillery pieces were placed near homes in small Iraqi villages. MiG fighters were parked next to the most important archaeological sites within Iraq's borders."[98]

In the coming decade, friendly and inimical manipulations of ROE would become a regular feature of the U.S.–Iraqi military confrontation, and the military lawyers would become an indispensable part of defeating these kinds of asymmetric defensive tactics.

ON BALANCE: THE STRATEGIC AIR CAMPAIGN

The strategic air campaign produced some of Desert Storm's most memorable and visually impressive moments, and it is unlikely that the war would have become such a watershed event without them. The U.S. Air Force was certainly pleased. The civilian secretary of the Air Force, Donald Rice, wrote about the "new era" in which the strategic air campaign had finally come of age, and claimed: "Air power did exactly what the air power visionaries said it could. With roughly one percent of the bombs dropped in eleven years in Vietnam, allied air assets shut down Iraq's gasoline production, electricity, transportation, communications offensive weapons production, and air defenses."[99] Cruise missiles navigated Baghdad's streets and LGBs flew unerringly down ventilation shafts, but what was the real strategic effect of the "inside-out" air campaign?

The strategic air campaign had four main objectives before the war began: gain and maintain air supremacy, isolate and incapacitate the regime, destroy Iraq's NBC capabilities, and eliminate industries underpinning offensive military capabilities. The wartime objective of keeping Israel out of the conflict by suppressing the Scud threat must be added as a fifth objective. The most successful were arguably the first and last. The takedown of Iraq's strategic IADS was a masterstroke, a triumph of crafty planning and synchronized execution. The Scud hunt, although not always effective at a military-technical level, had the desired strategic effect of keeping Israel out of the war.

Success was far less clear in the other three areas, where the resultant wartime and long-term benefits were frequently offset by liability for prompt and long-term collateral damage. Although the Baathist regime required the services of its IADS and Scud forces during the war and thus practiced only partial withholding and dispersal to preserve these assets, the Iraqi government was willing and able to undertake far more extreme defensive measures to protect and preserve its leadership, C2, WMD, and conventional military industries. The UN deadline that triggered Operation Desert Storm gave the Iraqis a window of time in which to prepare to meet the threat, and there are strong indicators that they stripped most government facilities of sensitive and difficult-to-replace equipment and personnel before the first bombs fell. The Iraqis seem to have expected exactly the kind of six- to nine-day blitz proposed in the Instant Thunder plan and were willing to wait out Coalition air attacks before reassembling the critical infrastructures of the Iraqi security state. As Scott Ritter noted, from 1982 to 1985, Iraq's military-intelligence (Istikhabarat) and general-intelligence (Mukhabarat) services had received instruction from the Soviet Union's KGB on the concealment of government facilities from U.S. intelligence-collection methods as well as damage-limitation measures, including wartime relocation of critical components and personnel.[100]

The Coalition's effort to isolate and incapacitate the regime was hampered from the outset not only by the Baathist government's ability to disperse and utilize low-volume means of communication (e.g., personal couriers) but also by the relatively limited understanding that the Coalition managed to develop of the structure and vulnerabilities of Saddam's regime. After the war, JFACC Horner recounted:

I think we learned we need to do a better job of analysis of target systems such as [enemy] "leadership" [sites] in order to have effective attacks, and I do not believe we are strong in the area of understanding other cultures, modes of leadership, and the ways to alter them so as to fit our goals and objectives in a war. We sure didn't succeed in our efforts to disrupt Iraqi leadership, not because we were unable to kill the needed targets, but because we were unaware of what targets we needed to destroy. In terms of bombing the Baath Party headquarters, we looked at Saddam Hussein and the Baath Party as one. We wanted to show weakness in the Baath Party and thus weakness in Saddam Hussein. We wanted to embarrass him in front of his people as well as limit the loss of life. But what we didn't realize was that it doesn't matter what the people think. In the final analysis, we looked at it through American eyes, which was wrong.[101]

Although Coalition attacks undoubtedly inflicted tremendous additional friction on the Iraqi war-fighting effort, they failed to achieve the more ambitious stated aim of "isolating" the regime or the unspoken aim of shaking its foundations and paving the way for a postwar coup. The Iraqi high command maintained strategic direction of the war, successfully initiated Scud attacks, ordered the attack on Khafji, and authorized the withdrawal from Kuwait. Even Colonel Warden admitted that low-technology and low-volume regime-security communications remained "impervious" to Coalition attack.[102]

Iraq's WMD capabilities and military industries also experienced lighter damage than was hoped, which left Iraq with the potential to reconstitute both its nonconventional and conventional arsenals. Successful attacks on Iraq's vulnerable nuclear reactors did greatly reduce Iraq's ability to divert low-enriched uranium into a crash bomb-making program that could have produced a crude nuclear device by summer 1991, and an increasing number of NBC targets were struck throughout the war. Even so, the Coalition failed to find or effectively strike scores of WMD-related sites: merely 30 percent of identified nuclear sites were destroyed or damaged during the war and most nuclear-related headquarters, laboratories, and component-manufacturing plants were identified only after the war.

Iraq had successfully preserved much of its equipment by emptying key industrial sites and ministry buildings in a defensive campaign that began in December 1990. Most important, the research data and brain trust—the scientists and knowledge base—were intact for a future reactivation of the weapons program.[103] The same was true in Iraq's missile industry, which was hit hard at every known component but also enjoyed some protection because key components were dispersed early. In the field of general military industries, the Coalition had never caught up with the growth of Iraq's military sector, which employed 40 percent of Iraqi industrial workers and which had so surprised Western commentators with its ambition at the Baghdad arms fair in 1989. Only six of Iraq's major arms firms were identified and attacked in 1991. An additional thirty-three were identified only after the war.[104] Despite the most intense targeting effort in history, the Coalition still lacked the targeting intelligence required to not only find Iraq's fixed targets but also to track the dispersal of the vital components, the targets that caused warehouses and ministry buildings to be attacked in the first place.

At the same time that the strategic objectives of air defense, Scuds, leadership, WMDs, and military industry were under attack, an even greater challenge was unfolding for Coalition air forces, which were transitioning to fight a parallel and larger campaign to achieve the JFACC's final air-campaign objective: to "render the Iraqi army and its mechanized equipment in Kuwait ineffective, causing its collapse."[105]

4

Desert Saber
Air-Land Battle

Much to General Schwarzkopf's chagrin, the preparation of the battle-field—and particularly the destruction of the Republican Guard—did not begin with a thunderclap, as the strategic air campaign had done. Until the ground war itself, there was to be no single moment that promised to seal the fate of Iraq's ground forces with the same decisive knock-out blow that had taken down the strategic IADS. Instead, the aerial preparation of the battlefield and destruction of Iraq's ground forces was to mirror the hunt for the Scuds—it would be an attritional battle, or, as William Andrews called it, an "air-ground siege."[1]

This effort would account for approximately 30,000 of the air campaign's 42,240 strike sorties, approximately 72 percent of strike sorties.[2] However, the effort would never be sudden or heavy enough to satisfy Schwarzkopf, especially because it began with indirect attacks on Iraq's ground forces and was aimed at their air defenses, their command posts, and their logistical lifelines. These preplanned targets dominated the carefully scripted first three days of air operations, when the number of sorties flown against KTO targets steadily grew from one hundred to three hundred per day.

The interdiction of enemy logistics and lines of communication (LOCs) would prove to be an open-ended commitment. Iraq had built up massive stocks of munitions throughout the KTO, in keeping with the country's policy of massive logistical oversupply—a holdover from Saddam's experience of ammunition shortages at critical points of the Iran-Iraq War. These hundreds of bermed logistical bunkers presented an enormous target set.[3]

The vulnerable single-track rail system linking Kuwait City, Basra, and Baghdad was repeatedly cut and marshaling yards were destroyed up and down the country by PGMs, which struck critical nodes and point targets. Against Iraq's bridges, the lessons of Vietnam had to be learned all over again. Similar to the bridge at Thanh Hoa, which survived eight hundred non-PGM sorties unscathed but was finally destroyed by merely four PGM sorties, no Iraqi bridge spans were destroyed by the first two hundred Coalition sorties sent against them, thanks to a stubborn advocacy by senior officers at CENTAF of "precision delivery" of unguided munitions as opposed to PGMs.

From January 24 onward, the bridge target set was struck by precision-capable F-111Fs, A-6s, and buddy-combinations of F-15E and F/A-18 aircraft, or RAF Tornados and Buccaneers.[4] Between January 24 and 29, one bridge span was destroyed for each two sorties against the target set. On January 27 alone, eight bridges were destroyed or heavily damaged.[5]

However, as it had throughout the short history of aerial warfare, the mission of interdicting Iraq's LOCs developed into a contest of destruction and reconstitution. Bridges needed to be struck at multiple spans to prevent Iraqi reconstruction, earthen bypasses used to cross canals needed to be cratered, and easily reconstructed pontoon bridges needed to be broken at multiple points every night.[6] Aside from the short-term military benefits of striking bridges, there would also be long-term economic effects, because bridges were the linchpin of Iraq's road-based transportation system. Bridge-busting was also the pet project of the U.S. Air Force Chief of Staff General McPeak, who saw to it that not only the southern Euphrates River bridges (so-called "Republican Guard escape routes")[7] but also every other major highway bridge outside Baghdad would be attacked during the campaign, which left forty-one of Iraq's fifty-four bridges broken at one or more spans.[8]

These attacks would contribute to the aim of "isolating" the Iraqi ground forces but did not promise enough prompt damage directly to the ground forces, particularly the Republican Guard, to satisfy Schwarzkopf. Although liberating Kuwait was the CINC's primary objective and the minimum measure of victory in Desert Storm, Schwarzkopf was aware that by leaving Iraq's offensive capabilities intact, he might have to come back and fight Desert

Storm all over again one or two or five years later. If Saddam quickly folded and withdrew his forces from Kuwait, it would give the Coalition only a narrow window of opportunity to do as much damage as possible. Lieutenant General Horner suspected that Schwarzkopf had "promised Powell that he was going to annihilate the Republican Guards in the opening shot of the war."[9]

However, by taking a target-system approach, air-campaign planners had focused their initial strikes on the targets that would have indirect effects on Iraqi forces throughout the KTO. The selective attacks on the command, communications, and logistics of Iraq's ground forces would disrupt their defensive capabilities and make them more vulnerable to a Coalition ground offensive. Destroying the bridges over the Euphrates River and southern canals would create the anvil against which Iraqi forces would be clustered to await the hammer blow of the VII Corps western hook.

Without a follow-on ground campaign, however, their losses would be small, which caused Schwarzkopf to explode angrily a day before the war when he belatedly realized what air-campaign planners had planned. Schwarzkopf wanted to permanently remove Iraqi capabilities, and historically that could only mean one thing—to kill large numbers of enemy soldiers.

To assuage the irate CINC, air-campaign planners added "another thirty or forty sorties on the Republican Guard on the first day by diverting some B-52s." For the remainder of the war, the B-52 force would strike the troop concentrations of an Iraq division every three hours.[10] Even so, it would not be until January 25 that the weight of effort shifted decisively to the preparation of the battlefield and to direct attacks on the kill boxes imposed over enemy-troop concentrations.

PREPARING THE BATTLEFIELD FROM MEDIUM ALTITUDE

The takedown of Iraq's strategic IADS and its effective ceding of a high-altitude sanctuary to the Coalition put the nail in the coffin of Cold War calculations that had assessed low-altitude strike profiles to be the safest, although by no means completely safe, method of delivering ordnance. Low-altitude attack had never been a comfortable way of doing business at the best of times, as a series of training accidents during Desert Shield showed. It was even less safe in the face of strong low-level air defenses such as those that covered key areas in Iraq and almost all of the KTO.

Although the disruption of the KARI network affected Iraq's strategic air defenses and the effective cessation of radar guidance prevented accurate targeting of the strategic SAMs—the SA-2 and SA-3 missiles—or indeed almost any guidance of SAM at night or through cloud, Iraq's range of mobile electro-optically guided SAMs (the Euromissile Roland and the Soviet SA-6/8/9) was a different matter. Each could optically acquire their target and guide the missile until it was close enough to the target to activate its proximity warhead. The SA-6 would prove particularly dangerous because its missiles mounted a semiactive-radar-guidance system that activated once the missile had been fired and that would provide its own radar guidance if necessary.

Yet, although these systems meant that Coalition aircraft flying within visual range of enemy ground units during the daytime could never fully relax, the most dangerous Iraqi systems were focused on low-altitude air defense. Across Iraq and the KTO, a network of thousands of AAA guns filled the skies with "curtain" or barrage fire, not seeking to track individual targets but merely filling the sky with heavy caliber rounds. As ineffective as this seems, it proved disconcerting and highly dangerous to both Coalition pilots and Iraq's civilian populace, who quickly learned that what goes up must come down.

In addition to these weapons, Iraq maintained large stocks of SA-7 shoulder-fired MANPADS missiles, whose heat-seeking infrared guidance presented a major threat to Coalition aircraft during low-altitude daylight sorties. Most of Coalition aircraft had no warning systems to alert them to the missiles, so they could not dispense flares as decoys.[11] Because they did not rely on radar guidance, there was no easy way to locate and destroy AAA or MANPADS systems, which claimed the vast majority of the twenty-two Coalition fixed-wing aircraft proven to have been destroyed by Iraqi ground-based air defenses. Of that total, eleven aircraft were lost to MANPADS alone.[12]

As a result, the Coalition never managed to tame Iraq's low-altitude air defenses, thereby creating a "no-go" zone for Coalition aircraft. Although the U.S. military apparently had no better option than to operate at a low level during the Cold War, operating at medium and high altitudes now offered almost complete immunity to ground fire. U.S. aircraft, sensors, and weapons had been designed to operate at low altitude, but the desire to avoid losses trumped the need to strike ground targets as effectively as possible. Brigadier General Glosson, on whose shoulders the selection of altitude tactics rested, explained his quandary: "I put [the F-16s] at an altitude where they didn't have the technology to be very effective. Had I been willing to tolerate the losses, I would have let them drop from two or three thousand feet, then I'm sure they would have been significantly more effective. But I would have had to tolerate, in my own opinion, losing thirty or forty . . . F-16s. There was just no way I was going to walk down that road."[13]

Glosson imposed an eight-thousand-foot minimum ceiling for most air operations during the air-only phase of the campaign, explaining that "there's nothing worth dying for" at the lower altitudes. As Perry Jamieson noted, operating at optimal altitudes "would have been costly, and, in a war in which the American homeland was secure and CENTAF's leaders were confident of ultimate victory, risky tactics were unnecessary."[14] This was born out on the occasions when pressures for faster results drove Glosson to break his own rules. The results showed the risks of a low-altitude approach: two aircraft were shot down and fourteen had to be repaired after an attempt to breach the Tawakalna Republican Guard division's low-altitude defenses on February 15.[15]

The beginning of Desert Storm coincided with the beginning of the worst flying weather seen in the region for at least fourteen years, which complicated the move to medium and high altitude. Coalition predictions of the length of phase III (preparation of the battlefield) had assumed a 75-percent target-acquisition rate and a steady flow of six hundred dedicated sorties per day, but weather and visibility would prove to be key limiting factors in the fight against Iraq's ground forces.[16] The target-assessment rate was based on a projection of 13-percent cloud cover—the mean value for the Gulf region in the first two months of the year—but cloud cover instead averaged 38 percent throughout the war and exceeded 25-percent cover on three quarters of the forty-three days of combat operations.[17] From prewar ceilings of twenty- to twenty-five thousand feet, cloud cover dropped to as low as five thousand feet and no higher than fifteen thousand feet from the first ten days of the conflict. Weather and visibility remained spotty thereafter.

Weather is at its least predictable in the first three months of the year in the Gulf, ranging from "crystal blue sky above a thick carpet of ground fog that totally obscured targets" to "solid cloud cover and severe icing from the surface up to 35,000 feet." This presented a variety of challenges to target acquisition. In the midst of the most technology-rich military confrontation the world had seen, a great cheer went up when the CENTAF weather predictions showed the first day of relatively clear flying weather on January 28, 1991, underlining the limits of technological prowess and the basic unpredictability of war.[18]

THE CLUTTERED BATTLEFIELD

A second limiting factor on target acquisition, and thus the speed at which battlefield preparation could take place, was the cluttered and crowded topography of the battlefield. The terrain of the KTO had been characterized as "flat and open" in prewar assessments. CENTCOM stated that "cover and concealment is virtually non-existent."[19] Although this may have been true on August 2, 1990, it was not the case on January 17, 1991, thanks to the ceaseless efforts of hundreds of thousands of Iraqi troops and engineers. As a Project for Defense Alternatives report noted, "There has probably never been as much construction plant on a battlefield and such investment made in manipulating the terrain and making it suitable for military operations."[20]

Forty-three Iraqi divisions with as many as ten thousand vehicles and artillery pieces were crammed into defensive zones that covered an area of only three thousand square miles. They had spent the last six months digging in, creating "literally thousands of identical revetments" according to one Coalition pilot. There were tens of thousands of potential individual aimpoints, primarily deep horseshoe-shaped sand berms.[21] By creating more revetments than necessary, the Iraqis set the stage for an active deception campaign that would become a hallmark of their military operations in the coming years.

As Coalition pilots began the preparation of the battlefield during the preplanned first three days of Desert Storm, they were tasked to strike pinpointed targets such as headquarters, for which photographic imagery was available and which could be confidently identified as active because of their continual emission of electronic and signals signatures. As the weight of strikes shifted to artillery and armored vehicles, there was no specific imagery to guide pilots. They were instead given a rough set of coordinates in which to locate a particular Iraqi brigade or division and told to prioritize a certain type of target, such as tanks, artillery, or air defenses.

When pilots received any premission visual orientation, it came in the form of "Orient Classic" overlays for 1:50,000 and 1:12,500 maps, on which U.S. Army intelligence personnel had annotated the positions of enemy formations and sometimes individual vehicles. These maps more than sufficed for ground-combat commanders, who were grateful for any ability to see "over the hill." In contrast, this represented a retrograde step for pilots, as General Schwarzkopf noted in testimony to the U.S. House Armed Services Committee: "After the war, General Chuck Horner said to me, 'in every other war when our pilots were to go out and hit a target, they generally have an aerial photograph in their laps that was no more than twenty-four hours old of exactly what they were going to hit. We didn't have that capability.'"[22] In some cases, such as the A-10 squadrons, unofficial workarounds were developed to get photographic imagery to the unit headquarters, if not to the pilots themselves. In these cases, the squadrons got access to the raw RF-4C or U-2/TR-1 photographic reconnaissance imagery. They pasted the images together to form mosaics of the areas occupied by the Iraqi divisions they were tasked to destroy.[23]

As William Andrews noted, however, most units were handicapped from the outset: "The lack of target materials severely retarded Air Force unit learning curves. Each crew member formed individual perceptions of the battlefield, based on what he had observed. Within combat wings, there were hundreds of disjointed impressions of the battlefield, and crews had a difficult time blending these images into a coherent picture without a common framework to provide orientation. The nature of air war demands some means of maintaining continuity with the enemy. Each crew glimpses the enemy for only a few minutes each mission . . . and aircrews had to build a picture from scratch each mission."[24]

Overlays and photographic imagery two or more days old could not tell Coalition pilots the exact dispositions of Iraqi tanks, vehicles, artillery, and air defenses on the day they were overflying the enemy. From medium altitude, the battlefield appeared to offer the smorgasbord of ground targets that Coalition pilots expected, and one F-16 pilot noted: "Flying in the area of the Republican Guard was a fighter pilot's dream come true. There were revetments full of tanks, armored personnel carriers, ammunition, AAA, and artillery as far as the eye could see."[25]

Almost two weeks into the campaign, a different picture began to emerge. Coalition pilots diving down through the heavy overcast of the first ten days of the war got only the briefest glimpse of their targets before the dust of weapon impacts obscured them. Immediately thereafter, the strikers were evasively egressing from their targets, often returning with the impression that they had not located the right targets or had not succeeded in destroying them.[26] Furthermore, in the same way that the Iraqi military had played a "shell game" by continually moving its Scuds, AAA, SAMs, and aircraft before the war, Iraq's ground forces were now able to shuffle their equipment among revetments. Under the cover of night, cloud, fog, and battlefield smoke, active vehicles were moved to revetments scorched by previous kills, and pots of burning paraffin and lengths of spare tank track were planted on intact tanks to identify them as burnt-out hulks.

A-10 visual reconnaissance flights that dropped down to two thousand feet on February 1 confirmed suspicions: "The pilots noted roughly half of the revetments were filled with targets and the rest with "old farm equipment, plywood decoys, old pick-ups, and barrels of oil." From higher altitudes of four to six thousand feet, the decoys were indistinguishable from the live targets."[27] The commanders of the 23rd and 354th A-10 squadrons noted in their February 3 joint report: "It's nearly impossible to tell what's in [Iraqi revetments]. Pilots (including ourselves) describe them as deep, tarp or dirt covered, oil darkened, containing box-like containers and old trucks . . . [and] the lower we check them, the more small arms we take."[28]

The solution to the Coalition's target-acquisition problems lay in a combination of improved sensor acuity (to distinguish live targets) and what William Andrews termed the maintenance of "continuity with the enemy" (profiling activity and spotting the relocation of live vehicles). National- or theater-intelligence-collection systems could provide only limited assistance on either count. JSTARS, the linchpin of the so-called reconnaissance-strike complex that was designed to support FOFA, performed admirably whenever the enemy moved en masse, cueing night-capable airborne strikers onto Iraqi logistical columns or tactical repositioning at night and through cloud cover. JSTARS provided vital early warning and targeting guidance when Iraq had launched elements of two armored divisions and supporting amphibious forces across the Saudi border at Khafji on January 30, demonstrating the effectiveness of the FOFA suite of systems that the Cold War had created.

The Iraqis reacted by shifting to a lower rate of resupply, using small columns that, like the small Scud convoys, were difficult for JSTARS to detect.[29] Against a static and dispersed enemy, JSTARS was considerably less useful. The SAR-imaging capabilities of the experimental E-8A had insufficient acuity to discriminate live targets from hulks or Iraq's metal decoys. Although the advanced synthetic aperture radar systems (ASARS) carried by some U-2/TR-1 flights allowed the detailed near-real-time inspection of enemy revetments, the number of potential targets far outweighed the ability of this system to survey them all. Moreover, whatever could be gleaned by ASARS was not directly viewable by Coalition air crews. The SAR imagery was viewed in a specialized downlink van that was located in the parking garage outside the Coalition TACC. As a result, its image of Iraqi dispositions could be quickly outdated by enemy tactical movement.

Rather than national and theater intelligence systems, it would instead be Coalition tactical air forces that developed a solution to the need for close and persistent surveillance of the cluttered battlefield. The February 1 low-level reconnaissance by A-10 pilots showed that the Coalition had to put at least some aircraft at risk to get a low-altitude look at Iraqi ground forces. Sensor acuity would be a major problem, primarily because Cold War–aircraft sensors had been designed to serve pilots as they made high-speed, low-altitude, single-pass (or "first-look") attacks on targets.

Ironically, Coalition tactical aircraft initially had better ability to discriminate between live and dead Iraqi tanks and vehicles at night than during the day. In addition to being able to sense heat using their FLIR sensors, some Coalition tactical aircraft could also detect and target Iraqi movement at night and through cloud cover using the "look-down" moving-target indicator (MTI) modes of their radars. In the daytime, however, when Iraqi forces were stationary and there was no heat differential for FLIR to sense, Coalition aircraft were not adequately equipped with medium- or high-altitude sensors of the acuity required to tell Iraqi decoys and vehicle hulks from live vehicles.

The solution, a target-acquisition concept of operations called "Killer Scout," was developed by CENTAF between January 31 and February 3. A small cadre of forward air controllers—airborne (FAC-A) were tasked to loiter over a set of kill boxes: grids overlaid on the KTO and southern Iraq that were initially half a degree in latitude by half a degree in longitude, or roughly thirty miles square, and that were later split into four fifteen-mile-square "keypads."[30] Mounted in F-16, OA-10, F/A-18D, and OV-10 aircraft, pairs of Killer Scouts remained over the battlefield for an average of five-and-a-half hours each day, comprising three one-hour surveillance blocks over the kill boxes and refueling time. The Killer Scouts loitered at up to fifteen thousand feet and moved lower whenever ground activity required a closer look. The sensors employed by the Killer Scouts were not high-tech. They used either the "Mark-One eyeball," the twenty/twenty vision of the fighter pilot, or binoculars. Both were employed while the Killer Scout aircraft loitered in a slow-curving flight path on autopilot at medium altitude.[31] This was an uncomfortable experience for pilots trained to think of such activity as unnatural, even suicidal.[32]

Similar to the Fast FAC concept of operations in Vietnam, the Killer Scout concept allowed CENTAF to build far superior SA than otherwise possible, especially because the pilots were typically assigned to the same kill boxes day after day: "Increased familiarity and continuity with the same area led to increased perceptions and orientation on the Iraqi positions. The pilots were able to note where Iraqi units had shifted overnight and record newly-discovered assembly areas, ammunition storage bunkers, transshipment points, artillery, and communications sites."[33]

As part of the Push CAS concept of operations, Coalition strike aircraft assigned to KTO targets checked in for up-to-date target guidance upon entering the kill box they had been assigned. An AWACS or EC-130 Airborne Command and Control Center (ABCCC) aircraft would either employ the striker, handing it off to the Killer Scout, or send it on to another kill box or its secondary fixed target.[34] The Killer Scouts allowed Coalition strike aircraft to enter, attack, and leave the KTO without exhausting their fuel and without overloading the tight airspace. As the AWACS or ABCCC aircraft fed occasional targeting leads from JSTARS and other national or theater assets to the strikers, the Killer Scouts fed up-to-date targeting guidance on the sector of the battlefield below.

"PLINKING" TANKS AND OTHER TARGETS IN THE KTO

Just as the sensors designed to carry out FOFAs had been of only limited value in acquiring the dispersed and stationary Iraqi targets in the KTO, so too were many of the weapons designed specifically for low-level delivery against massed Soviet columns. The area-bombing capabilities of the B-52 fleet were an early disappointment. Forced to move from low-altitude to high-altitude tactics, inaccuracy caused by wind shearing led the long trains of munitions delivered by the bombers to deviate by six to seven hundred feet. Even when the 500-pound and 750-pound munitions hit the desired area, they appeared to have made little impact on the physical condition of the enemy, although the psychological impact of B-52 bombardment remained significant. William Andrews noted, "Quarter-mile long strings of bomb craters were observed in the vicinity of ground units, with very few direct hits on the widely dispersed revetments. Dispersed, fortified, and armored Iraqi positions were well-suited to minimize the physical effects of B-52 'area fire.' Logistical depots were so hardened that they were 'almost invulnerable to air attack.'"

As Coalition investigators explored the Kuwaiti battlefield after Desert Storm, they found "an impressive system of roads, buried communications lines, and supply depots," including "command posts buried under 25 feet of desert soil."[35] With every logistical bunker (or "igloo"), vehicle, gun, and infantry element buried, bermed, or sandbagged, the Iraqi army in Kuwait had turned itself into thousands of point targets, each requiring a direct hit to be destroyed. Yet, the move away from low altitude had reduced the effectiveness of many of the weapons that the Cold War U.S. military had planned to deploy against such targets. The fearsome 30-mm cannon on the A-10 was operated at twice its optimal slant range, forcing the A-10 community to rely heavily on the Maverick missile, which gave good service despite the travails of operating in clouds of dirty-oil smoke and fine sandy grit.

Pilots also found that the combination of higher altitudes and enemy fire made the "precision delivery" of unguided ordnance much harder than prewar analyses had suggested. One pilot noted: "When you're up there and you're in your airplane, and you're trying to drop your bombs, and all that stuff is coming up at you, and you have a 100-knot crosswind, the probability of hitting your target is pretty low."[36] This was a recipe for failure against bermed targets that each required a direct hit, especially because the most effective unguided weapons for the job, advanced CBU-87 radar-fused combined-effects munitions (cluster bombs), were husbanded until the ground war. Planners recognized that medium- or high-altitude delivery would only result in the dispersal and waste of the precious munitions.

Alongside the 5,100 Mavericks fired during Desert Storm, the key killer of point targets would prove to be the GBU-12 laser-guided 500-pound bomb. Although experience at the end of the Vietnam War had shown that relatively small LGBs could destroy tanks, their potential use against tactical targets was not widely appreciated at the end of the Cold War. In U.S. military division of labor of the late 1980s, the GBU-12-droppers (F-111Fs, F-15Es, and A-6Es) were to be used against interdiction targets, whereas F-16s, F/A-18s, AV-8 Harriers, A-10s, and attack helicopters were to be used against the vehicles and troops of the enemy tactical echelon.

However, with the pace of battlefield preparation apparently flagging, CENTAF was responsive to the proposed use of precision strikers against bermed armored vehicles. The idea emerged from the Night Camel exercises in December 1990, which sought to evaluate the F-111F's capability to locate enemy logistical movements at night using its Pave Tack FLIR system. Returning from the exercise, the F-111F crew noted that they could also see the heat emanating from Coalition armored vehicles because they radiated the day's heat longer than the desert surrounding them. Following a trial-run using a single F-111F on February 5, forty-four F-111F aircraft were moved to "tank plinking" (as the tactic became known) on the following night. Soon six of the twelve LANTIRN targeting pods in theater were also reassigned from the Scud hunt to tank plinking,[37] which allowed PGM-dropping and buddy-lasing F-15E and A-6E aircraft to carry out tank-plinking attacks. In total, tank plinking consumed 664 sorties over twenty-three days.[38]

The use of LGBs produced remarkable results. On some missions, a pair of F-15E aircraft carrying eight GBU-12s each would return from missions with FLIR video footage showing sixteen direct hits. This was a level of technical efficiency that could not be surpassed. Although the F-111F fleet was critical to a number of strategic air-campaign efforts then underway—the Scud hunt, the destruction of hardened aircraft shelters north of the Euphrates River, and bridge busting—two thirds of the valuable deployed fleet were diverted to tank plinking with relatively little ado.[39]

Beyond the technical efficiency of getting "iron on target," assessing the overall effectiveness of tank plinking was more problematic. Generally, JSTARS cued the strike aircraft onto a group of potential targets that had been identified using its rather imprecise SAR imager and handed off the targets to the F-111F, F-15E, or A-6E aircraft to examine more closely with their FLIR pods. As Michael Bodner and William Bruner noted, these FLIR pods had been designed to identify large targets (such as bridges) during low-level delivery. They were now expected to operate at well beyond their normal slant ranges against targets that were far smaller.[40]

With some practice, crews became adept at distinguishing different types of vehicles (armored versus unarmored) and telling them apart from artillery targets, but target identification by FLIR remained an imprecise art throughout Desert Storm. Furthermore, although FLIR sensors could locate heat sources, by the end of Desert Storm, the Iraqis had learned to keep their vehicle engines and electrics shut down to minimize heat emissions. At the same time, they lit small fires under wrecked vehicles and other decoys to attract attention.[41]

As a result of the imprecision of JSTARS and FLIR-imaging capability, plus Iraqi deception, it is highly likely that a proportion of the 100 to 120 kills shown each night on the FLIR videos were decoys or hulks. Even so, tank plinking had clearly hit enough live vehicles to impress the Iraqis, as the comments of a captured Iraqi suggest: "During the Iran-Iraq War, my tank was my friend, because I could sleep in it and know I was safe. . . . [In 1991] none of my troops would get near a tank at night because they kept blowing up."[42]

BOMB-DAMAGE ASSESSMENT IN DESERT STORM

From approximately February 4 onward, most of the major readjustments to Coalition air operations against Iraq's ground forces had been made. From this date until the beginning of phase IV, the commencement of ground operations and the air campaign took on an attritional character. They ground away at Iraq's operational reserve, the Republican Guard, and the frontline forces and tactical reserves of the regular Iraqi army. The attention of senior Coalition military decision makers now focused on the issue of Bomb Damage Assessment (BDA), which held the answer to the key question: how soon will preparation of the battlefield be complete?

Rightly or wrongly, the measure of success had been set at the 50-percent reduction of the key-equipment holdings of Iraqi armored and mechanized divisions in the KTO, meaning their armored vehicles and artillery. Why was this chosen as the measure of effectiveness? As previously noted, the 50-percent figure was chosen to mesh with the U.S. Army criteria for unit combat ineffectiveness, but the decision to base the assessment on equipment losses reflected the U.S. intelligence community's inability to develop the level of insight required to make a more nuanced judgment.

A comprehensive assessment of the capabilities of Iraqi divisions might have taken into account disruption of C2 nodes, interdiction of consumables (food, water), the effects of time and wear on military equipment and fortifications (many alternate Iraqi fortifications were filled with sand and minefields exposed by wind), the effects of Coalition psychological operations (21 million leaflets plus radio broadcasts), and physical strikes on Iraqi morale. Indeed, since the beginning of the war and particularly since the failed Iraqi incursion at Khafji on January 30, a trickle of EPW confirmed that morale was low in the frontline infantry divisions. Iraqis "began to realize that they had been placed in the distasteful position of an occupying force in another

Islamic country, faced with fighting their religious and cultural brothers," which caused "endemic" desertion. Reports from the Joint Debriefing Center suggest that some of these units were only 50–80 percent effective *as the war began*.[43] Less could be said about the forces Schwarzkopf and other Coalition land-forces commanders really cared about—the Republican Guard and regular army armored and mechanized forces. As Richard Lewis noted, "No matter how degraded they were, they continued to be counted as fully effective as long as they had weapons."[44]

The "bean counting" of destroyed Iraqi vehicles and artillery pieces was the responsibility of the U.S. Army and Marine components, ARCENT and MARCENT, who were given the mission by Lieutenant General Horner. Horner explained: "The Army wanted me to do BDA. I said, 'Hey, that's Army stuff. You tell me how we are doing, you write my score card.'"[45] Delegating proved a disaster because no firm rules had been agreed upon for BDA calculation. Twelve days into the air campaign, General Schwarzkopf was still awaiting his first BDA assessments on Iraqi ground forces, which had been heavily delayed because heavy cloud cover had delayed the collection of satellite imagery. On January 29, Schwarzkopf instructed ARCENT/MARCENT to include pilots' mission reports (MISREPs) to speed up the process.

When ground-forces commander Lt. Gen. John Yeostock issued the first ARCENT/MARCENT assessment, it shocked all concerned. After fifteen days of attacks, including more than two thousand sorties against the Republican Guard, Yeostock assessed the Republican Guard to be 99 percent effective and the Iraqi forces in the KTO to be 93 percent effective. He projected that it would take until D+100 (rather than the prewar projection of D+26) for all the targeted units to be reduced to 50-percent effectiveness. The assessment was based on satellite imagery, SIGINT, and MISREP from the A-10 community, whom the U.S. Army considered to be their close cousins.

In the weeks to follow, ARCENT/MARCENT loosened the rules for valid BDA data, allowing all, then some, of the FLIR video footage taken by tank-plinking aircraft. Other important sources of BDA, such as the MISREP from Killer Scout pilots who were surely the preeminent experts on BDA in the KTO, were never utilized.[46] Meanwhile, the CIA was solely dependent on overhead imagery from satellites. It issued separate assessments that downgraded ARCENT/MARCENT claims even further. Of 1,700 tanks, 900 other armored vehicles, and 1,400 artillery pieces claimed destroyed by

ARCENT/MARCENT on February 21, the CIA could only confirm a total of 500 kills. This prompted the agency to query ARCENT/MARCENT's figures in its Presidential Daily Brief although it was later forced to withdraw the query.[47]

BDA of strategic strikes had developed relatively smoothly in comparison with the evolution of a fast-track BDA system that operated alongside the more ponderous formal process. In contrast, the assessment of strikes in the KTO was a fiasco that confused decision makers precisely when they needed information about the timing of a phase IV ground campaign.[48] Schwarzkopf's understanding of the muddled BDA picture was in part informed by the 513th Military Intelligence Brigade, a unit that reported BDA directly to Schwarzkopf.[49] Mostly, however, Schwarzkopf used "farmer logic" (as Horner termed it): his own reckoning based on the sortie rates being committed against each division—information that he received on a nightly basis from Brigadier General Glosson at the daily 1900 meeting.[50] Prewar Checkmate estimates had suggested that 50-percent attrition would be achieved by D+26 (February 12, 1991), but because of the problems of target acquisition, the SPG now stated that D+33 (February 19) was the earliest possible date at which 50-percent attrition could be achieved.

Pressure was growing for the ground war to begin because Soviet Premier Mikhail Gorbachev appeared to be close to negotiating an Iraqi withdrawal from Kuwait. This would at best have ensured the near-term liberation of Kuwait while leaving the long-term threat of Iraqi capabilities intact. At worst, it would have served to give the Iraqi forces a break from the bombing in which to reorganize and regain their balance. Schwarzkopf resisted the pressure for an extended start, however, and thereafter weather became the central planning consideration in the start date of the war.

Calculating the need to fly at ten thousand feet and still be under the cloud ceiling, Glosson identified two weather windows: D+35 (February 21) and D+39 (February 25). On February 12, Schwarzkopf provisionally opted set the latter date as G-Day, the day on-ground operations would commence.

ASSESSING AND CONTROLLING THE PREPARATION OF THE BATTLEFIELD

In the lead-up to the ground war, a struggle developed over the final stages of the preparation of the battlefield as ground-forces commanders, particularly

U.S. VII Corps Commander Franks, sought to begin to shape the "deep" battlespace behind the immediate line of departure. The key forum at which these commanders sought to influence the nomination of targets in the KTO was the Joint Targeting Coordination Board (JTCB).

A primary task of the JTCB was to forge the numerous corps-level target nominations into a single, prioritized list of nominations to the KTO target list during phase III battlefield preparation.[51] Yet, at the level of nominating individual targets, U.S. ground forces proved ineffective because of a lack of targeting expertise and late staffing of the targeting sections of ground formations.[52] U.S. Army Corps commanders such as General Franks were trained to think and fight deep, but lacked the current situational awareness to sense or target deep. The intelligence reaching corps level, mostly four- to five-day-old overhead imagery, was a key limitation on effective target nomination.

Desert Storm planner Richard Lewis related how each corps was allowed to nominate forty targets per day, yet few made it onto the daily ATO. Of forty-two targets nominated by VII Corps on January 31, only six (15 percent) made it onto the ATO, and these were already scheduled to be included because of other intelligence received by the KTO Planning Cell. Of the remaining targets, fourteen (33 percent) were no longer valid or were awaiting BDA, thirteen (31 percent) were outdated SAM or AAA targets, and nine (21 percent) were infantry targets. (Infantry targets were considered off-limits according to Schwarzkopf's prioritization of the armored and mechanized formations behind the front lines.)[53]

As the last point suggests, Schwarzkopf (as de facto ground-component commander), not the corps commanders, maintained tight control over the daily weight of effort apportioned against individual enemy divisions. The JTCB wished to ensure the transfer of airpower to phase III targets, but also provided a forum at which U.S. Army, USMC, and the two Islamic corps commanders vied for relative levels of air support. Horner noted that the attitude was, "I'll get mine, and I'll get yours too if I'm smart."[54]

Regardless of the guidance issued by the JTCB, Schwarzkopf frequently shifted weight from one division to another "unilaterally, just on his own." Schwarzkopf retained personal control over JSTARS tasking, using it to spotlight whichever enemy division had caught his attention.[55] On February 15, he also directed Glosson not to attack units that were assessed at less than 50-percent strength, a decision not communicated to ground forces commanders until after the war.[56] Finally, attacks on the XVIII Corps and VII Corps front were to be minimized to prevent a tip-off concerning the left-hook attack through Iraq.[57]

Even as Coalition airpower remained under tight centralized control, a series of ground-forces activities were underway, which represented the preliminary moves of the Desert Saber ground campaign. Although often presented as distinct events, the air-only and air-land campaigns actually merged into each other during a continuum of operations in mid- to late February. Ground commanders began a process of preparing their sectors using the core firepower of Coalition ground forces—their tube artillery, MLRSs, and attack helicopters. The Coalition had been nibbling away at Iraq's frontline visual observation (VISOBS) posts since the first day of the war, when U.S. Navy SEALs called in air strikes on Iraqi VISOBS on the Saudi-Kuwaiti border.

The real commencement of the ground component's war against Iraq began on February 13, just after General Schwarzkopf had selected February 25 as G-Day. Artillery and MLRS raids and deep-attack helicopter strikes were undertaken against enemy frontline divisions and tactical reserves, aiming to disrupt logistics and communications. Above all, the strikes were to degrade enemy artillery forces that could target Coalition forces with conventional or chemical munitions as they entered Iraq through narrow breaches in the Saddam Line. In their aims and methods, the artillery raids resembled less-sophisticated versions of the takedown of the IADS. Coalition artillery barrages drew Iraqi artillery batteries into firing and thus identifying their positions.

Although the Iraqis lacked the ability to perform accurate beyond-visual-range or over-the-horizon fire, the Coalition system allowed radar and sound/light-ranging equipment to quickly locate the enemy artillery unit and dispatch devastating counterfire. MLRS systems, known by the British as the "grid-square removal system" because of their ability to fill kilometer-square areas with deadly sub-munitions, undertook the majority of this counterbattery fire. Each of their twelve air-bursting munitions delivered 644 explosive bomblets. The results on Iraqi artillery units were devastating, as the Robert Scales described: "A prisoner of war whose artillery unit opposed VII Corps revealed that his 64-gun battalion group lost seven pieces during the air phase and 46 to MLRS raids. . . . One captured battalion commander stated that his unit fired only once during the battle, and within moments, artillery bomblets devastated his position. A third of his soldiers fled the position and left most of his guns destroyed and the rest of his soldiers dead."[58]

At the same time that MLRS was reaching approximately thirty kilometers into Iraqi lines, U.S. ground commanders were seeking to send their organic air assets still deeper. In the U.S. Marine Corps sector, where the MAGTF arrangement allowed the marine commander to retain full control over the majority of marine air forces and helicopters, marine airpower ranged throughout the depth of the sectors facing the marines. In contrast, the U.S. Army Corps commanders had no control over air forces until G-Day and had to slot any deep helicopter strikes into the air component's daily ATO. On February 15, VII Corps launched a seventy-five-kilometer-deep strike using its Apaches but was restrained from launching further deep strikes and armed reconnaissance helicopter missions by Schwarzkopf, who did not want a heavy level of effort in the west to alert the Iraqis to the threatened encirclement.[59] In a series of attacks on the close battlefield, U.S. XVIII Corps helicopter operations plinked fifteen Iraqi VISOBS with antitank missiles, which caused almost five hundred Iraqis to cross over to Saudi Arabia to surrender.[60]

GROUND WAR BEGINS

The heaviest artillery raids and deep strikes were planned to occur on the three or four days preceding the planned G-Day on February 25, which was when the main Coalition ground attack was scheduled to be launched on the VII Corps front. On February 21–22 more than seven hundred MLRS munitions were fired, more than the combined total fired until that point. However, the major two-hour preliminary bombardment was scheduled to occur on the VII Corps front on G-Day, comprising two divisional artillery brigades and three corps artillery brigades, some 260 artillery pieces, sixty MLRS launchers, and brigade-sized attack-helicopter actions.

U.S. Marine Corps regimental combat teams had been probing the Kuwaiti border since February 20. The teams infiltrated strong forces into the security zone of Iraq's frontline division and capitalized on the rollback of Iraqi observation posts to "steal the march" on the enemy and close with the enemy's main defensive positions. On February 24, the marine forces and the two Islamic corps began diversionary attacks into the Saddam Line. At the same time XVIII Corps launched a deep thrust toward Highway 8, the main road paralleling the Euphrates River. By the end of February 24, the marine and Islamic forces had displayed agility in successfully breaching the Saddam Line and the air-mobile XVIII Corps forces had established forward operating base (FOB) Cobra more than 280 kilometers inside Iraq.

This unprecedented level of success led Schwarzkopf to order VII Corps to bring its February 25 attack forward by fifteen hours. This threw off the logistical, fueling, and arming preparations that were underway to unleash the massive VII Corps preliminary bombardment and instead necessitated a shorter thirty-minute artillery preparation. The first major Apache attack helicopter deep-strike operation of the war, code named Operation Boot, was scrubbed.[61]

The very rapid long-range advances undertaken by XVIII and then VII Corps on February 24–25 were new and strange experiences for the Cold War U.S. Army, despite the practice run offered by the grueling secret westward shift made in the days beforehand. In the one-hundred-hour ground war, the lead elements of XVIII and VII Corps would maneuver 416 kilometers and 240 kilometers, respectively. This degree of operational maneuverability was enabled not only by the new class of U.S. Army tracked and wheeled vehicles and helicopters, but also by careful terrain reconnaissance and new precision-navigation technologies. In the prewar period, the CIA had contributed human intelligence gained from border-crossing Bedouin to improve the U.S. Army's characterization of the terrain in southern Iraq, and a limited number of armed reconnaissance missions had confirmed these impressions during the war. GPS was another major factor underpinning the speed of the western hook, although the system was far from universally available to Coalition forces. A total of 4,492 civilian small, lightweight GPS receivers (SLGRs) were hastily purchased for Coalition forces, operating alongside the 842 U.S. military receivers, GPS-locating digital radios, and a large number of long-range navigation (LORAN) receivers. These were oil-industry instruments that triangulated the geographical bearing of the user by taking signals from towers dotted throughout the Iraqi desert. Although GPS coverage was not constant, and although LORAN devices required some minutes to provide their navigational fixes, these systems were deployed with unit and column leaders and provided substantially better daytime and nighttime navigation capabilities to Coalition forces.

Whereas Iraqi forces were limited to the traditional geographic routes used in desert warfare—roads, pipelines, wadis, and tracks—the Coalition transformed the featureless desert terrain into an almost unlimited and well-surveilled maneuver route. When combined with night-vision goggles or vehicle-borne infrared and thermal-imaging systems, the two maneuver corps were well equipped to carry out their wide outflanking missions through the featureless Iraqi desert.[62]

The two U.S. corps and their subordinate British division were also fairly well prepared in terms of operational intelligence regarding the enemy frontline forces. In terms of capabilities, military-intelligence reports and Franks' own examination of EPW had convinced him that the frontline Iraqi infantry divisions were "brittle, and would easily crack at the first hard, sustained ground attack."[63] However, according to Franks, the corps commander charged with delivering the lethal hammer-blow to the Republican Guard, a lot of unanswered questions remained about the enemy as Franks crossed the line of departure at 1500 on February 24. The condition of the enemy Republican Guard and regular-army armored and mechanized forces were harder to gauge; the enemy intentions concerning the deployment of these reserves were initially unknown. Would the Republican Guard divisions counterattack the Marine Corps' and Islamic corps' attacks in Kuwait, or retreat into Iraq, or maneuver to block the VII Corps' advance?

In short order, these questions were answered. Vital SIGINT intercepts received as early as 0200 on February 25 suggested to Franks that the Republican Guard was redeploying to face the VII Corps. This assessment was confirmed by near-real-time JSTARS imagery through its ground stations at each Coalition corps' main headquarters.[64]

At the tactical echelon of divisional commanders and below, intelligence was far more scarce, particularly for the highly mobile XVIII and VII Corps in the west. In Kuwait, where the marines and Islamic forces were engaged in more deliberate engagements throughout the depth of Iraq's prepared defenses, months of U.S. intelligence preparation of the battlefield—particularly the Orient Classic 1:50,000-scale map overlays—provided a very complete picture of Iraqi deployments: "These products plotted Iraqi positions down to the level of individual tanks and were so accurate that ground combatants remarked after the war that they were able to predict enemy contact and open fire based on the information from the charts."

The highly mobile Coalition forces on the western hook, on the other hand, were less well-served in the sphere of up-to-date tactical intelligence. The mapping of Iraqi dispositions required clear imaging weather and the Orient Classic overlays needed to be ordered forty-eight hours before an engagement took place on a specific sector of the battlefield.[65] Not only was it difficult for the maneuvering corps to know precisely where they would need to fight, but forty-eight hours gave the Iraqi forces a lot of time to reorient their defenses. As a result, the advance of the XVIII and VII Corps resembled a protracted march to contact, characterized by extreme uncertainty over enemy dispositions.

The intensity of fighting increased throughout the first forty-eight hours of the ground war. Following nerve-wracking breaching operations on the first day of the ground war, the MEF penetrated deep into the Saddam Line in southwestern Kuwait. Just prior to the beginning of the ground war, Saddam had ordered the ignition of more than seven hundred Kuwaiti oil wells, which transformed the KTO into a dark and hellish environment. The 1st Marine Division commander, Maj. Gen. James Myatt, stated that his men "had to use flashlights to be able to read maps at noon."[66]

On February 25, Iraqi tactical reserves began to harass the exposed flanks of the MEF, first by launching battalion-sized infantry attacks, and then, more seriously, a preplanned, armored counterattack by two brigades of the Iraqi 5th Mechanized Division. Emerging from the thick smoke of the burning Al-Burqan oil field, the Iraqi thrust penetrated to within three hundred meters of the 1st Marine Division tactical headquarters. It was only fought off with determined tank stalking by Marine infantrymen and daredevil flying by Marine attack helicopters. As one MEF award citation described, "The smoke from burning oil wells and bad weather had combined to reduce visibility to only a few yards. Attempts to get close air support were thwarted by this absence of visibility. Out of the darkness emerged two Marine AH-1Ws, flying at ground level. Knowing the dire need of the Marines on the ground, they had literally taxied along roads, twice passing under power lines to reach the forward units."[67]

Although the counterattack was defeated, it served its intended purpose of halting the Marine advance for the rest of the day. For the next two days, the MEF disrupted enemy counterattacks launched by remnants of the Iraqi 5th Mechanized Division and the last remaining division of the KTO tactical reserve, the Iraqi 3rd Armored Division. These two units were tasked to screen the withdrawal of Iraqi infantry divisions to a new defensive line along Mutla Pass. When these Iraqi forces massed to counterattack near Kuwait International Airport, they received a mauling by Coalition airpower. Thereafter, Iraqi forces fought in "platoon-sized pockets," defending areas of the airport and nearby quarries and junkyards.[68] After the war, 320 tanks and armored personnel-carrier hulks were recovered from within the Iraqi perimeter. Units such as the 5th Mechanized and 3rd Armored had shown that the Iraqis could and would fight.

Elsewhere, XVIII Corps secured Salman and executed a 280-kilometer helicopter insertion from FOB Cobra to insert a brigade of the 101st Air Assault division astride Highway 8 near Nasariyah. Elsewhere, the heavy armored forces of VII Corps moved into contact with significant enemy armored and mechanized forces for the first time on February 26. The third day of major ground operations would be a decisive one, bringing the destruction of Iraqi tactical reserves in Kuwait and southern Iraq and convincing the Baathist regime that the position of Iraqi forces in Kuwait was untenable. As early as the evening of February 25, the Baathist regime seemed to scent defeat in the air and had already taken steps to shore up its domestic security, initiating the withdrawal of Republican Guard units to central Iraq.

Three engagements on February 26 gave the first real indication of the relative military effectiveness of U.S. and Iraqi forces. In addition to the aforementioned Iraqi defense of Kuwait airport, two other major engagements took place late on that day. First, the 2nd U.S. Armored Cavalry Regiment (ACR) began to drive in the outposts of a hastily formed defensive line that was being erected by the Tawakalna Republican Guard Mechanized Division and elements of the 12th Iraqi Armored Division. By late afternoon, 2nd ACR had shattered this screen in a decisive engagement that would become known as the Battle of 73 Easting. This initiated a rolling destruction of the Tawakalna division as elements of the 1st and 3rd U.S. Armored Divisions enveloped and penetrated the Iraqi line.

At the same time, the 1st Brigade of the 24th U.S. Infantry Division (Mechanized) ran into a hastily assembled force composed of elements of the Iraqi 47th and 49th Infantry Divisions, plus the Nebuchadnezzar Republican Guard Infantry Division and the Iraqi 26th Commando Brigade. Dug in along a set of rocky escarpments, these forces directed "intense tank and artillery fire" at the U.S. forces to prevent the U.S. division from breaking through to the active airfields at Tallil and Jalibah.[69]

Unlike the relatively dense and cluttered terrain in southern Kuwait, where much of the fighting had been at close range, the terrain in which VII Corps and the U.S. 24th Division fought these battles was open, with unobstructed lines of fire stretching thousands of meters. The key impediment to fighting was instead the weather, although this ultimately worked in favor of the Coalition. In addition to Iraq's demolition of Kuwaiti oil wells, a low-pressure front sucked clouds into the KTO, immediately dropping the ceiling for air operations to 2,500–8,000 feet and reducing visibility to an average of one-and-a-quarter miles. Thunderstorms, soot-blackened rain, gusting winds of twenty-five to forty knots, and huge oil-smoke plumes that reached up to 10,000 feet reduced the effectiveness of air support. Although large numbers of Push CAS sorties were available, the difficulty in supporting mobile operations in such terrible flying weather meant that most of this support was diverted to deeper strikes against interdiction targets in Iraq.[70]

The MEF had requested and utilized CAS support even in poor flying conditions, but the U.S. Army divisions fought their opening battles largely using their own direct and indirect fire weapons. However, because reduced visibility made unassisted long-range targeting of ground weapons extremely difficult, the U.S. and British divisions in Iraq enjoyed considerable advantage over their Iraqi opponents.

The XVIII and VII Corps engagements on the dark and stormy afternoon of February 26 were initially characterized by long-range tank, antitank, and artillery duels in which Coalition thermal sensors and counterbattery radars provided critical advantages. Debriefs of Iraqi prisoners of war noted that they were "amazed to be attacked during a rainstorm with blowing sand," which reflected the fact that many Iraqi vehicles were destroyed by Coalition forces that remained unseen throughout the duration of the tactical combat.[71] Iraqi forces, even Republican Guard forces, were not equipped to fight under these conditions, and were reduced to firing at U.S. and British muzzle flashes that briefly appeared hundreds and often thousands of meters away through the swirling dust. The superior training of Coalition tank and infantry fighting vehicle (IFV) crews enabled long-range kills even when sandstorms rendered their laser rangefinders inoperative. Coalition antiarmor munitions were extremely lethal; U.S. tanks and even IFVs recorded catastrophic kills at ranges of more than three thousand meters. Coalition tankers often shot directly through the sand berms that their Iraqi counterparts hoped would give their vehicles "hull-down" protection, sending Iraqi tank turrets careening twenty feet away from the destroyed vehicles.

Ultimately, however, in these long-range duels it was the sensors and Coalition proficiency in using them that decided the result, both in tank/antitank combat and in the effectively one-sided artillery duels. Counterbattery radar and highly efficient Coalition crews allowed three to six accurately placed artillery rounds to be returned for every one ineffectively targeted

Iraqi shell.[72] One Iraqi tank commander recounted: "On 17 January, I started with thirty-nine tanks. After six weeks of bombardment, I had thirty-two left. After twenty minutes in action against M1s, I had none."[73]

Ground combat against Coalition armored and mechanized forces was an unforgiving environment in which to come off second best and was undeniably more deadly than the preceding weeks of counter-air-land operations. Why was this? The answer is simply that practically every U.S. and British tank and IFV in the VII Corps "armored fist" boasted a deadly combination of advanced all-weather, day/night sensors and a first-hit, first-kill antiarmor weapon. Although Coalition ground forces also sometimes failed to differentiate live targets, dead vehicles, and decoys because of the lack of acuity in their thermal imagers, the intrusive presence of Coalition ground forces prodded Iraqi tanks and artillery emplacements into undertaking tactical activities (firing, moving) that differentiated them from profitless targets. The ability of Coalition heavily armored ground forces to loiter and observe enemy positions from the one-sided sanctuary created by reduced visibility and long range subjected Iraqi ground forces to a far more intense, systematic, and deliberate campaign of destruction than air forces could inflict.

This complete superiority was the ground commander's equivalent of the aviators' supreme success in achieving the takedown of the strategic IADS. During the ground campaign, the enemy would have no opportunity for reconstitution between attacks. Coalition ground forces would put a round through any target that might still be active; there would be nowhere to run or to hide. Because Coalition commanders understood the potential of the direct-fire weaponry at their disposal, particularly in the open desert terrain, they sought wherever possible to deploy the maximum number of combat brigades abreast in line. Wherever the enemy came into contact with the buzz saw of Coalition ground forces, the enemy would get cut.

Naturally, one had to be careful where one pointed such a sharply honed cutting tool. It was apparent even before the outset of ground-combat operations that extraordinary steps needed to be taken to prevent fratricide or "friendly fire" incidents. At first friendly fire appeared to be exclusively an air-ground coordination problem; indeed, friendly fire incidents had occurred whenever ground forces had operated with CAS during Desert Storm, such as during the January 30 battle of Khafji, during probing attacks on February 17, and now again during the ground war. Although misidentification of Coalition vehicles by ground-attack aircraft caused the majority of the casualties before the ground war, 60 percent of the friendly fire incidents in Desert Storm would ultimately result from misdirected land-combat-system fire during the ground war.[74] Ground commanders anticipated that, in the absence of automated "blue-force tracking" of friendly ground units, confused, swirling armored maneuver warfare would cause "boundary and battlespace overlaps." Lieutenant General Franks admitted that tracking of friendly forces typically lagged behind tracking of enemy forces, particularly in the attack, and there was no way of differentiating friend from foe at some of the ranges and in the reduced-visibility conditions that were prevalent during the land war.[75]

Two measures were used to reduce the possibility of fratricide. The first two related specifically to friendly fire between ground units. First, GPS-equipped units ensured that they were correctly aligned with their unit boundaries and were not moving or shooting over these lines. Second, Coalition units sacrificed precious seconds to ensure positive identification of targets, sometimes deliberately elongating the six- to ten-second "detection to destruction" kill chain that had become the standard for U.S. and British tank crews.[76] Although target acquisition could thus take place at up to four thousand meters, Coalition forces might allow the enemy to get as close as eight hundred to one thousand meters to visually identify them.[77]

FAILURE TO TRAP THE REPUBLICAN GUARD

The final fire-control support measure used to reduce friendly fire would ultimately contribute to the failure to decisively destroy the Republican Guard divisions facing the VII Corps thrust. To reduce the possibility of air-to-ground fratricide, the U.S. Army and U.S. Air Force employed the fire-support coordination line (FSCL) measure to ensure that air operations near friendly troops were always cleared through ground-based forward air controllers (FAC). The FSCL would be placed by the U.S. Army Corps commander, and any air strikes within or "short" of it were conducted under the positive control of local FAC—meaning that each and every air strike would be laboriously "talked onto" the target by an FAC who described the target to a pilot overhead.

Coalition Killer Scouts sought to monitor the forward edge of friendly units to ensure that Coalition aircraft did not attack them on the occasions that they advanced beyond or "long" of the FSCL, where targets of opportunity were instead engaged under the control of the airborne FAC-A.[78] In addition to being a safety measure, the FSCL gave U.S. Army Corps commanders the ability to plan and execute deep artillery and attack helicopter attacks in a manner consistent with air-land battle doctrine.

This opportunity was seized aggressively by VII Corps Commander Franks, whose responsibility it was to close the escape routes of the Republican Guard and the Iraqi forces in Kuwait. As the initial military engagements of February 26 merged into a rolling assault on the Republican Guard positions along the Iraq-Kuwait border throughout the night of February 26–27, it was clear that the Baathist regime was preparing to undertake a major pullout. They had deftly realigned a portion of their operational reserves to hold open the escape routes from Kuwait into the Basra area of southern Iraq. Ken Pollack noted that "in a matter of hours and with great speed and efficiency, the Iraqis had six heavy brigades from at least four divisions moving west."[79]

Already, as night fell on February 26, the general Iraqi retreat from Kuwait into southern Iraq had been underway for a day. This led to the first public images from the "Highway of Death" on which thousands of Iraqi vehicles, many loaded with looted Kuwaiti infrastructure and consumer goods, were trying to escape into Iraq. Meanwhile, the regime was loading T-72 tanks of the Hammurabi Armored Division of the Republican Guard onto tank transporters and sending them further into Iraq, while Republican Guard special forces and infantry units were redeploying to provide regime security in Baghdad and Basra.[80] With the U.S. 24th Infantry Division of XVIII Corps pushing along the Euphrates River toward Basra to seal off the key road junctions in the southeastern corner of Iraq, Franks now viewed the area of land between his forward line of troops and the Gulf as his battlespace. This was an area through which he needed to thrust both to destroy the Republican Guard units directly in his way and to physically cut off all remaining Iraqi forces in the KTO. Franks gave his divisional commanders a simple directive, pointing to Iraq's slender Gulf coastline: "Attack east. Go for the blue on the map."[81]

In keeping with air-land battle's focus on fighting both close and deep, Franks sought to simultaneously smash the enemy divisions with which he was currently in contact and disrupt and degrade all the other formations between VII Corps and the Gulf coast before his ground forces met them. The close fight that had begun on February 26 continued unabated and almost without pause throughout the night. Here was modern, not futuristic, warfare at its apogee. This night looked and sounded like any of the great battles of the mechanized age, as Franks recalled: "At one point the noise was so great

I thought there was a thunderstorm, but on stepping outside the [command post], I discovered it was the sound of battle. The sky was lit up by tracers big and small, and the sparkle effect given by the MLRS as they fired off the ground into Iraqi positions. The air was filled with the constant roar of exploding artillery and the thump of tank and Bradley cannons. The ground vibrated. It was awesome."[82]

The long-range character of the daytime engagements on February 26 dissipated as the confusion of night cast the U.S. and Iraqi forces into intense close combat. Lt. Col. John Brown, commander of the 2nd Battalion, 66th Armor, recounted, "Neither side could particularly see each other. We were coaxing [shooting with the M1A1's coaxial machine gun] guys running between tanks, running between our tanks and bunkers.... It was really hairy. There were rounds flying all over the place. There were burning hulks going up like flares, infantry trying to surrender, infantry trying to hide, infantry trying to fight, infantry getting up on our tracked vehicles, either to attack or to try to surrender."[83]

In the chaos of close combat, "buttoned-down" U.S. tankers used their turret-mounted heavy machine guns to sweep Iraqis off each other's armored vehicles. U.S. foot soldiers closed with enemy armor, sometimes getting close enough to drop hand grenades into their open hatches. The Tawakalna division mounted a tenacious and well-sited reverse slope defense that won the respect of hardened critics of Arab military performance including former CIA Military Analyst Ken Pollack, who concluded that despite being outnumbered and outgunned, "the Republican Guard fought tenaciously, and many veteran US servicemen remarked afterward that the battle had been more ferocious than any they had been in before, including combat in Vietnam. Unlike the regular-army units, the Republican Guards fought and died almost to a man, and US forces captured few Tawakalna soldiers and officers. When the Iraqi tanks and armored personnel carriers [APCs] were destroyed, their infantrymen charged forward with small arms and rocket-propelled grenades. The Tawakalna maintained remarkable unit cohesion, with remnants attempting to conduct a fighting withdrawal long after the division had been virtually wiped out."[84]

The tough overnight fighting set the scene for the Battle of Medina Ridge on the following day, February 27, which Franks termed "the biggest, and, as it turned out, the fastest and most one-sided individual battle of the war."[85] The engagement was a rerun of the long-range battles of the previous day, albeit on a larger scale. Maintaining contact with the disintegrating mass of Republican

Guard forces to their front, U.S. ground forces were now grinding rather than leaping forward, like a saw whose teeth kept catching in a knotted branch. The Republican Guard were penned into a shrinking pocket of Iraq southwest of Basra, seeking to break out to the north. The rest of Iraq's regular army forces were squeezing out of the KTO like toothpaste from a tube, abandoning their vehicles, equipment, and loot to escape the interdicted highways.

While U.S. Marine Corps tanks took the southernmost end of the retreating Iraqi army in Kuwait under direct fire from the Mutla Ridge, omnipresent airpower had destoyed the bridges leading to Basra, mined the highway verges to prevent off-road dispersal, and had spent the past two days systematically destroying any vehicles moving on the road.[86] The Iraqi army was already effectively scattered like a flock of birds, and now the scene was set for a decisive battle to encircle the Republican Guard.

To prevent the Republican Guard from escaping along Highway 8 to the northwest and northeast, or falling back into Basra, VII Corps aimed to encircle the Iraqi divisions in a double pincer from the north and the south on February 28. On this day, a brigade of the 101st U.S. Air Assault division would simultaneously launch a helicopter assault on landing zones ten kilometers north of Basra that would close off the retreat routes of Iraqi forces stuck in the city. General Schwarzkopf noted a month after the war, "We had them in a rout, and we could have continued to . . . wreak great havoc among them. We could have completely closed the door on them, and made it, in fact, a battle of annihilation."[87]

This was the kind of decisive result that CJCS Powell had envisaged in August 1990. However, both military and political events on February 27 broke in Iraq's favor and allowed most of the Republican Guard's personnel and a considerable portion of its equipment to live to fight another day.

When dawn broke on February 27, attack helicopter units of XVIII Corps were scheduled to take over the interdiction of the highways running along the northern bank of the Euphrates River between Basra and Nasariyah. The FSCL was moved north of the highway to make it the exclusive hunting ground of U.S. Army deep-attack helicopters. Because of a mixture of technical, organizational, and climactic reasons, the Apache helicopters did not arrive; this caused CENTAF to petition XVIII Corps at 1100 for the FSCL to be moved back south of the river, which would enable Coalition aircraft to interdict the road. From 0700 until the movement of the FSCL at 1500, Republican Guard and other Iraqi military forces were able to withdraw from the KTO unmolested by either Coalition attack helicopters or tactical aircraft: an eight-hour daylight window of immunity.

Elsewhere in the XVIII Corps sector, large enemy traffic jams were caught short of the FSCL but beyond the twenty-five- to forty-kilometer ranges of U.S. Army divisional artillery. These were also neither attacked by XVIII helicopter forces nor by Coalition tactical air. Coalition tactical air knew (via JSTARS) that the concentrations existed but could not strike the traffic jams because of the lack of on-scene FACs.[88]

On the VII Corps front, Lieutenant General Franks had prepared for his drive to the Gulf by throwing the FSCL out to the coast at 1100 on February 27 and restricting Coalition air attacks in the entire swathe of territory between Basra and Kuwait. Following the Battle of Medina Ridge, Franks planned one final ground forces thrust on February 28 and thus needed to keep Coalition air forces under positive control in a cluttered and fast-changing battlespace.

However, safety and control would come at a cost. From 1100 onward, Iraqi forces behind the forward edge of battle enjoyed sanctuary from Coalition air attacks, which could not be kept under positive FAC control. The forward edge of VII Corps was also not moving as fast as anticipated; many of its units had reached the end of their logistical tether and its troops and equipment were fast approaching the limits of their physical endurance.[89] XVIII Corps forces, just fifty kilometers west of Basra as the war closed, were similarly overextended. Thus, instead of enabling the deep battle, the FSCL was now ensuring that Iraqi forces behind the main battle would not be on the receiving end of any Coalition firepower until XVIII and VII Corps attack helicopter units launched their planned night raids some ten hours later.

These nocturnal deep strikes, coming after so many planned helicopter operations had been cancelled because of weather and operational factors, finally displayed the devastating capabilities of the U.S. Army attack helicopter battalions. However, nothing could disguise the fact that the movement of the FSCL had denied the Coalition of hours of aerial degradation of the Republican Guard forces, which were retreating to the north.[90]

When Franks sought to move the FSCL westward to give the Coalition air forces back the autonomy to strike Iraqi retreat routes south of Basra, he found that General Schwarzkopf wanted it left where it was. The reason soon became apparent when, on the evening of February 27, CENTCOM began warning ground-forces commanders to prepare for the cessation of offensive operations at 0800 on February 28. Despite a frantic drive eastward by U.S. forces throughout the final hours of the war, VII Corps' physical encirclement of the Republican Guard would not occur, nor would the XVII Corps air assault north of Basra occur, nor would Coalition air strikes take place between Kuwait and Basra once U.S. Army attack helicopters returned from their devastating final wartime missions in the early hours of February 28. Instead, the Iraqi retreat continued unmolested.

With Kuwait City liberated on February 27 and Iraqi forces evidently in full and chaotic retreat on the "Highway of Death," pressure had grown on Washington decision makers to end the apparent slaughter of Iraq's forces. As Rick Atkinson noted, a gap had developed between Washington and the frontline commanders concerning the nature of the fighting and the extent to which the Republican Guard had been encircled. The route along the road to Basra led the public and the U.S. leadership to assume that the fighting against the Republican Guard was similarly one-sided. However, the Republican Guard at Medina Ridge were not fighting to allow buses packed with looted goods to escape; they were holding open the escape routes of mauled but intact Republican Guard divisions, which were patiently and systematically transferring their hundreds of surviving armored vehicles to the north of the Euphrates River.[91]

In the tense days between the February 28 cessation of offensive operations and the formal March 3 cease-fire at the Safwan air base, many small skirmishes took place. The largest of these occurred on the morning of March 2, 1991. Elements of the Hammurabi Republican Guard division clashed with the U.S. 24th Infantry division, resulting in the destruction of an estimated eighty Iraqi tanks, ninety-five APCs, and fifty artillery pieces or rocket launchers, plus the capture of an additional three thousand prisoners.[92] These clashes were the first indicators of an ongoing military struggle that would last not for months, or even for years, but instead for more than a decade as the Baathist regime refused to accept the chastened posture of a vanquished nation. The failure to encircle and destroy Iraq's Republican Guard had much to do with the ongoing sense of swagger that the regime displayed.

Coalition surveillance of the Iraqi withdrawal indicated that the Republican Guard forces in southern Iraq survived the war with 842 tanks and 1,412 APCs. Although the rear guard of the Republican Guard, the Tawakalna and Medina divisions, had been badly degraded, the Hammurabi Armored Division ended the war with most of its vehicles and 70 percent of its personnel intact. The elements of the three Republican Guard infantry divisions deployed to the KTO (Adnan, al-Faw, and Nebuchadnezzar) each withdrew the bulk of their personnel north of the Euphrates River.[93] Although Iraq's military had suffered a grievous reversal of fortunes since the end of the Iran-Iraq War, these personnel and, less important, their equipment, left Iraq with the cadre around which it could quickly reform its core of armored and mechanized divisions. Although they lacked some of the sophisticated equipment that they had employed in the past, they allowed the Baathist regime to retain a core deterrent force against Iranian or other external threats and maintained the "force in being" that was such a vital source of assurance to the Iraqi leadership. In time, the Iraqi government hoped, UN sanctions would be lifted, which would allow Iraq to make good on its equipment losses.

In the near-term, as the following chapter relates, these forces helped to assure the survival of the Baathist regime during postwar uprisings against the government. Ken Pollack noted: "To some extent, Baghdad's victory over the Iraqi uprisings of 1991 can be said to have been won on the battlefields of Wadi al-Batin and Medina Ridge."[94]

POSTWAR CHARACTERIZATION OF DESERT STORM

As politically unsatisfying as some features of the Desert Storm endgame had been, the operation created a sense of military reassurance that had not been felt in the United States since the outset of the Vietnam War, or perhaps even before then. The U.S. military, leading a coalition of allies, had won a major war, hands down, and at the surprisingly low cost of 148 U.S. personnel killed in action (KIA) and 458 wounded in action (WIA).[95] A U.S. Army report noted more than a decade after the war, "The speed with which the armed forces ejected the Iraqis effectively eased the painful memories of North Vietnamese tanks trundling about on the lawn of the South Vietnamese presidential palace or the charred corpses of the failed hostage rescue attempt at Desert One in the Iranian desert. Desert Storm was, in some ways, a catharsis for both the nation and its armed forces."[96]

The June 8, 1991, U.S. victory parade, the first since 1945, encapsulated this cathartic moment in which America moved toward recognizing the debt owed to its soldiers, sailors, marines, and air force personnel from wars past and present, even those as unpopular or painful to remember as the Vietnam War. In a historical and social sense, therefore, Desert Storm was an important war. Looking forward, as "Act One of the New World Order" (to borrow Bob Woodward's phrase) it was the first great struggle of the post–Cold War era.

Perhaps—it was hoped—it would provide an example of the potential strength of collective defense and international law in that new era.

At a military-technical level, the disparity in Coalition and Iraqi losses, plus the speed of the ground war, were convincing indicators that air-land battle and the broader "American way of war" had met and exceeded the expectations of Cold War planners. While achieving the mission of liberating Kuwait, Coalition forces suffered 390 personnel KIA and 776 WIA. This was an order of magnitude lower than the most conservative estimates of Iraqi personnel losses, which had been estimated at 3,500 killed, and high-end estimates, which had been estimated at 40,000 to 100,000 enemy dead.[97] Coalition estimates extrapolating from sample battlefield surveys suggest that between 2,600 and 3,800 Iraqi tanks were destroyed during Desert Storm, alongside an estimated 1,600 APCs, and 2,200 artillery pieces. On the Coalition side, 15 tanks and an additional 25 APCs were damaged or destroyed. Compared with 110 Iraqi aircraft and helicopters confirmed destroyed on the ground or in the air (plus an additional 137 permanently absorbed by Iran), 42 Coalition aircraft or helicopters were lost to hostile fire.

Just as important, Coalition losses were primarily incurred while inflicting losses on Iraqi military assets, whereas the Iraqi air force made no operational contribution to the Iraqi war-fighting effort.[98] The U.S. rapid maneuvering and the synergistic benefits of simultaneous air and ground operations had transformed Iraq's cohesive defense with tactical and operational reserves into an incohesive defense without reserves.[99] The disparity of losses would cause a major reassessment of how fighting power should be calculated; it was clear that, even if the fixing/degrading effects of airpower and the dislocating/concentrating effects of rapid maneuver were discounted, the qualitative edge of post–Cold War U.S. ground forces meant that even if they had met Iraqi forces toe-to-toe, they still would have won and won handsomely. This was a vindication of the TRADOC approach of realistic training and offensive doctrine, and of the raft of technologies that had been developed since the late 1970s to support the new U.S. military.

HIGH-TECH INFORMATION WAR?

The integration of information technology into Desert Storm was a particularly fascinating development to analysts and the general public. People speculated that Operation Desert Storm represented the first "information war." It is clear that Coalition forces enjoyed information or intelligence superiority over the Iraqi military, which lost almost all use of aerial surveillance, radar, and military communications from the outset of the war and made little use of its tactical reconnaissance capabilities.

It is also clear that the Coalition had access to an unprecedented array of intelligence-collection assets, although the war underlined the areas in which the U.S. intelligence community needed to develop more robust collection capabilities and intelligence-sharing practices. Chief among these collection shortfalls were the need for persistent, wide-area, all-weather surveillance capabilities of the type that could characterize and track individual enemy vehicles such as Scud missile launchers or armored vehicles, as well as the need for improved all-weather sensors and precision-guidance packages for strike aircraft and munitions. The Coalition also recognized the need to know itself better than it had during Desert Storm, in terms of finding a means of tracking friendly forces, monitoring the effects of friendly weapons, and generating BDA.[100] Finally, senior political and military leaders and the public had more up-to-date insight into unfolding military operations than ever before.

It is not clear, however, that Operation Desert Storm witnessed a truly new level of situational analysis at the sharp end—the tactical level of warfare at the forward corps, divisions, brigades, wings, battalions, and squadrons. Lieutenant General Franks noted, "It was the trailing edge of industrial-age warfare and the leading edge of knowledge-based, information-age warfare. Some of the old continued, and some of the new emerged."[101] One of the elements of industrial-age warfare that continued amid the unprecedented intelligence collection effort was the difficulty of moving intelligence to the tactical soldiers who needed it. Although terabytes of digital imagery, tens of thousands of hard-copy photographs, and hundreds of hours of signal intercepts were generated, they could not be freely shared by an intelligence system that was highly segregated, equipped with a mass of incompatible transmission and viewing systems, and unprepared for the automatic sharing of sensitive information among users in the United States, theater headquarters, and the front lines. The ASARS-II sensors on U-2 aircraft could pick out mines, barbed wire fences, trenches, and enemy vehicles for the six months preceding Operation Desert Storm, but these images could not reach the Coalition air and ground forces because no bulk hard-copy printing capability was established in theater until January 10, 1991. Similarly, although every Iraqi radio conversation was recorded and many hundreds decrypted and translated, National Security Director William Studeman recalled that "the key problem was getting the intelligence from the intercept operators to the code breakers to the analysts to the commanders in desert tents in time to be useful."[102]

During the ground war, the two-tier intelligence system was a disadvantage to mobile headquarters such as the corps tactical command post and divisional, brigade, and battalion headquarters. They lacked the thinly fielded, specialized equipment that allowed direct access to sensitive, national-level intelligence and JSTARS. Even if lightweight versions of these systems had been available in 1991, the forward troops lacked the reliable on-the-move digital and voice communications systems needed to maintain connectivity with the theater intelligence system.

The almost-complete communications breakdown suffered by Lieutenant General Franks at his VII Corps forward command post illustrated the divide between the "information war" of the senior leadership and the tactical soldiers. In the midst of torrential rains, Franks recalled:

> Enemy and friendly locations were posted [on the map] using one-by-two-inch pieces of acetate with adhesive on the back (cut out and posted by hand). Since they were not to scale, you had to interpolate. An enemy brigade unit sticker might cover twice the area they actually occupied on the ground. Same for our own units. Worse, the glue tended to dry out, so on occasion, the stickers fell from the map. When you picked them up, you hoped to put them back where they belonged. . . . [Now] water ran down our situation map, carrying with it to the wet ground the map stickers showing friendly and enemy situations, and streaking the markings on the map.

Franks concluded: "It was not a good situation. There was I, commanding a four-division corps. . . . Our communications were terrible. At that point, I did not have a single dependable long-haul communications line with which to talk to Third Army or my main [command post]."[103] From the headquarters of Lieutenant General Franks and his subordinate commanders, or those of the Coalition air wings who were starved of tactical intelligence and imagery, Operation Desert Storm did not seem like the first information war.

CLEAN AND EASY WAR?

In the aftermath of Operation Desert Storm, the war also appeared to have been a clean and easy war, because of the surgical nature of the high-profile air campaign, the low Coalition casualties, and the speed of the eventual one hundred-hour ground war. Indeed, the war quickly began to appear to have been the ideal mix of decisiveness and bloodlessness, with Iraq's ground forces evicted from Kuwait with fewer than four hundred Coalition fatalities. According to Iraqi prisoners of war, personnel casualties on the enemy side might also have been mercifully low. One prisoner noted, "To be honest, for the amount of ordnance that was dropped, not many of our soldiers were killed."[104]

However, behind these dry statistics, a desperate and often brutal struggle had been waged in the first months of 1991. The Iraqi military had shown that it was not bound by the same rules as its Western adversaries. They released 138 million tons of oil into the Gulf to cause an environmental disaster, torched 750 Kuwaiti oil wells and 50 other oil-related facilities, and regularly abused the laws of war by feigning surrender and carrying out other acts of perfidy.[105]

The United States, meanwhile, displayed the steely resolve that Western democracies can show when called upon to minimize risk to their own soldiers. In high-risk situations, such as the initial breaching operations at the outset of the ground war, the United States took no chances. The U.S. government justified its tactic of "using armored vehicles to crush or bury enemy soldiers" by stating that burying hundreds of entrenched enemy conscripts alive using armored bulldozers represented a "military necessity" because of the requirement for "violent, rapid action."[106] Likewise, when placed in the role of pursuing a defeated army for the first time since the Korean War, the U.S. military attacked and destroyed the retreating column of Iraqi troops with cold-blooded deliberateness. The JSTARS operator in charge of attacks on the Highway of Death recounted: "We could have hit them initially right on the outskirts of Kuwait City, but what the TACC decided was that, it would do nothing but bottle them up in Kuwait City, and we wanted them to get out of there. So we didn't hit those convoys as hard as we could have initially until we let them get out of Kuwait City and almost up to the Iraqi border, and then we stopped them."[107]

The war showed a ruthless side of the American character that had not been seen for many decades and belied the vacillating softhearted image that Americans had developed across the world.

Although the war was not easy, the Coalition enjoyed both substantial quantitative and qualitative advantages at the points when they attacked the enemy. As previously noted, postwar debriefings indicated that some Iraqi frontline units had been degraded to less than 50-percent strength *before* the war began. Almost all were gutted by desertions and casualties during the air war, when they became shadows of the hollow units they were at the beginning.

Instead of the DIA's estimated 500,000 enemy troops in the KTO, there had probably been no more than 336,000 when the war began and as few as 200,000 when the ground war commenced. The Coalition had attacked with well more than the three-to-one numerical advantage typically required by the attacker before qualitative advantage was even factored. On this count, the United States learned that so-called "state-of-the-art" or "top-of-the-line" Soviet equipment was largely a paper tiger in the hands of poorly trained opponents. Other intangible factors—Iraqi intelligence, doctrine, training, and morale shortfalls—also produced critical weaknesses in the Iraqi war machine.

As Andrew Rathmell noted, the model often used to assess Iraqi fighting capabilities—the Iran-Iraq War—was flawed. Postwar debriefings suggested the Iraqi military was war weary, not battle hardened. The Coalition was a totally different kind of opponent than Iran. Rathmell suggested that the Arab-Israeli wars were the appropriate model, not the Iran-Iraq War. The Coalition had been unstoppable: it brought to bear more than two corps of the North Atlantic Treaty Organization's (NATO's) finest forces supported by forty-five thousand strike sorties launched by the greatest air armada ever assembled.[108]

However, although anecdotes abounded about the desperation of Iraqis to surrender to Coalition forces, the Iraqi forces put up a decent fight in key portions of the war and during specific battles. In the air war, the Iraqis frustrated Coalition strike efforts through an extremely energetic campaign of deception, denial, and relocation. They maintained a guerrilla air-defense effort and a low-altitude no-go zone for Coalition forces. In the ground war, as Ken Pollack noted, tens of thousands of troops may have deserted, but equal numbers fought on against tremendous odds.

The Iraqi high command utilized years of pragmatic experience from the Iran-Iraq War to design "a strategy based on what their troops were capable of doing," according to Pollack (2002). The military sought to last the war out, preserve its assets, and use fortification and simple, local counterattacks to sap enemy strength. It successfully made one major defensive reorientation—the shift of the Republican Guard to block the VII Corps encirclement. In a host of minor counterattacks, hasty defenses, encirclements of Coalition special forces, and close-in night fighting, the Iraqi military had shown its willingness to resist.[109] Successful deception and speed of maneuver, massive precision strikes, and superior units versus unit fighting skills made the Coalition victory look easy, but as one combatant noted, "it was fast, but not easy. Do not equate swiftness with ease."[110]

PART TWO

THE WAR BETWEEN THE WARS

5
After the Storm
U.S. Responses to Ongoing Iraqi Resistance

Although Desert Storm had secured the U.S. objective of liberating Kuwait at a remarkably low cost, government and public satisfaction with the political outcome of the war quickly faded. It became clear that the Iraqi regime was not only going to survive the war but also that it was unwilling to accept the mantle of defeat and would instead continue to actively undermine U.S. objectives in the region. Barton Gellman wrote on January 16, 1992: "As an awakening of national self confidence, as a bulwark against deep cuts in military spending, as a model of post–Cold War conflict, as a spur to lasting change in the Gulf—and even as a vivid national memory—the war has not lived up to its early reviews. But nothing has done more to wilt the national mood than Saddam Hussein's persistent grip on the reins of power."[1]

FAILURE OF THE 1991 UPRISINGS
AGAINST SADDAM

The 1991 uprising, or intifada, began as masses of dispirited and traumatized Iraqi troops moved through Basra on March 1. A crowd of soldiers began to agitate against the regime, which led to the highly symbolic destruction by tank fire of one of the many gigantic pictures of Saddam Hussein in the city. In Basra, large numbers of Iraqi soldiers set themselves against the Republican

Guard, Baath Party paramilitaries, and intelligence personnel in the city. This sparked the beginning of a revolt that spread within a week to thirteen major Iraqi cities in the disadvantaged Shia south and the persecuted Kurdish north. The uprisings began with public demonstrations that became increasingly militarized as armed government militiamen of the Popular Army joined the revolt, and culminated in attacks on Baath Party headquarters and the liberation of political prisoners at regime prisons. Arms caches were seized and government facilities were looted. These features of the March 1991 uprisings were forgotten by the time scenarios for the liberation of Iraq were drawn up more than a decade later. By March 5–6, the regime faced the disintegration of Baath Party control in fourteen of Iraq's eighteen provinces.

The Bush administration hoped for, and indeed anticipated, the fall of Saddam Hussein, but the grass-roots uprisings taking place in Iraq did not conform to its preferred model of regime change—either a palace coup that would replace Saddam with a more cooperative authoritarian figure, or a Baghdad uprising that would topple the government and quickly appoint a new executive, which would have been along the same lines the events in a number of Eastern European countries after the collapse of communism in 1989. Iraq's intifada did not resemble the purposeful overthrow of the central government that President Bush had envisaged on February 15, when he offhandedly encouraged "the Iraqi military and the Iraqi people to take matters into their own hands to force Saddam Hussein, the dictator, to step aside."[2] Baghdad was under tight regime control and no uprisings were recorded in the ruling Sunni heartland.

Instead, as Rear Adm. Mike McConnell, the director for intelligence at the JSC, noted on March 5, 1991, the uprisings were "chaotic and spontaneous" and would likely fail because of their lack of central organization and leadership.[3] The southern and northern uprisings were not seen as an opportunity for regime change; instead, they were seen as a dissolving agent that could smash Iraq into a Lebanese-style mosaic of sectarian enclaves or invite Iranian dominance of Iraq's majority Shia community. As CJCS Powell recalled, "Neither uprising [Shia nor Kurdish] stood a chance. Nor, frankly, was their success a goal of our policy."[4] By March 6, 1991, as government control continued to dissolve across Iraq, U.S. State Department Spokesman Richard Boucher announced that U.S. policy was to discourage "outside powers from interfering in the internal affairs of Iraq." Maj. Gen. Martin Brandtner, the director of operations at the JSC, noted that "U.S. forces will not let any weapons slip through [to the rebels], and will not play any role whatsoever in fomenting or assisting any side."[5]

Isolated from outside interference, the internal military balance inside Iraq quickly shifted back to the government forces. Although shattered for the moment as a battlefield military force, the Iraqi armed forces proved highly adept at the form of static, positional fighting that ensued. In addition to truck-mounted, multiple-rocket launchers and tube artillery, government forces relied extensively on the attack helicopters of the IrAAC, which had been carefully dispersed and husbanded during the war. Iraq had been warned not to fly fixed-wing aircraft since the Safwan ceasefire talks, but the Iraqi delegation had secured a dispensation to fly helicopters to ostensibly allow VIP transport and the redeployment of forces away from Kuwait. In Basra, where the intifada started, the government reasserted its control the fastest: it reduced the uprising to pockets of the city by March 4 and wiped out all rebel enclaves by March 10. The government forces engaged in brutal counterinsurgency operations to clear Karbala, Nasariyah, and Najaf during March 5–15, and then turned its capabilities northward to roll back the Kurdish conquests of Tuz Kurmatu, Kirkuk, Arbil, Dohuk, and Sulaymaniyah in the weeks between March 12 and April 3.

Regime reconquest of these areas was swiftly followed by devastating mass arrests of all adult males, widespread arrests of clerics, summary executions, and the punitive demolition of residential and religious buildings. Another orgy of looting occurred, this time perpetrated by the regime forces.[6] The use of artillery and helicopter gunships was so intensive that by the time the intifada had been quelled, Iraq's counterinsurgency forces had begun to consume emergency reserves of ammunition.[7]

No part of the U.S. government watched the failure of the uprisings more closely than the U.S. military, which until early May 1991 occupied large swaths of Iraq contiguous with the areas in which government and rebel forces were fighting. U.S. forces maintained a perimeter along the Euphrates River that placed it within visual range of many of the rebel cities—Samawah, Nasariyah, and Basra—that felt the weight of the regime's counterinsurgency campaign. One U.S. Army officer, who ran a casualty-treatment center that accepted rebel casualties, stated: "We treated well over 1,000 civilians who were fighting with the resistance. They were pretty messed up. I've seen every type of combat wound that you could imagine, everything, it was there."[8] The Baathist regime quickly moved to punish the Shia and Kurdish communities for their part in what Saddam termed "the Chapter of Treason and Treachery" and used terror tactics to create an exodus.[9] One U.S. Army lieutenant recalled regime bombardments of refugee gatherings: "We were watching the Iraqis shell the [As-Samawah] train station and other small houses. This was simply designed to kill civilians or terrorize them, which it did. It did not have a military purpose, just artillery impacts on large concentrations of civilians."[10] Flour was sprinkled from helicopters to simulate chemical weapons attacks, which panicked whole communities into flight. The *Human Rights Watch* report on the 1991 intifada recounts: "During March and early April, nearly two million Iraqis escaped from strife-torn cities to the mountains along the northern borders, into the southern marshes, and into Turkey and Iran. Their exodus was sudden and chaotic, with thousands fleeing on foot, on donkeys, or crammed onto open-backed trucks and tractors. In the south, many fled into or through the maze of marshes that straddle the Iranian border. Thousands, many of them children, are thought to have died or suffered injury along the way, primarily from adverse weather, unhygienic conditions and insufficient food and medical care."[11]

As Elliot Cohen noted, it was clear that the U.S. leadership "expected Saddam's regime to collapse at the end of the Gulf War and had no plan to deal with the regime's inconvenient survival and subsequent brutality in dealing with uprisings in the north and south of the country."[12] The time for marching on Baghdad had passed, if it had ever existed. There was little inclination within the U.S. government to take on the task of garrisoning Iraq and rebuilding its political and economic infrastructure. Consequently, limited planning efforts had been put into laying out a follow-on option (or "sequel plan") to Desert Storm.

Although a short think piece called "The Road to Baghdad" had been prepared on March 6 by Maj. Gen. Steven Arnold, the U.S. Third Army operations officer, the option of a thrust toward Baghdad had been shelved on March 19, 1991, two days after the first major U.S. combat formation (the 24th Infantry Division) started to redeploy out of theater and five days before the U.S. 82nd Airborne Division began its own redeployment. Yet, the development of the Road to Baghdad plan was an early indication that the U.S. military sensed that the struggle was not yet over. Saddam's Republican Guard had escaped, the regime would survive, and there were already disturbing signs that a recalcitrant Iraq was planning to renege on its cease-fire commitments to the United States and UN.

The civilian U.S. leadership was instead focused on the more immediate need to protect the Kurdish and Shiite communities from Saddam's retribution. For a number of reasons, the Shiite south received far less attention than the Kurdish north. The U.S. military presence in southern Iraq remained extensive in April 1991. U.S. forces held an enclave whose border stretched from the Saudi border near Rafha, up the tapline road through Salman to the outskirts of Samawah, along the southern bank of the Euphrates River as far as forty kilometers west of Basra, and southeast to the Kuwaiti border. Lieutenant General Franks' VII Corps had become the de facto occupation force in this area, and, in addition to demolishing as much military infrastructure as possible within the area, would provide law and order, humanitarian support, and voluntary evacuation of willing Iraqis to Saudi Arabia until early May 1991. The U.S. zone provided some Shiite rebels with an escape route, and others traveled to Iran or into Iraq's southern marshes. Despite all this, however, the plight of the Shia was not widely appreciated in 1991. Iraq's Shia remained an unknown quantity to the United States and were regarded as potential Iranian proxies or a base for Islamic fundamentalism. The government counteroffensive in the south largely unfolded outside the field of view of the international media in tightly controlled southern Iraq and was put down in mid-March before the media latched onto the story.

The same could not be said for the Kurdish minority, whose enclaves collapsed later and whose cause was quickly adopted by now-mobilized international media, several influential U.S. politicians, and the French and British governments. With no U.S.-controlled zone in the north, the Kurds appeared to have no sanctuary save the inhospitable mountain passes, where harsh conditions caused an estimated eight hundred to one thousand deaths each day. UNSC Resolution 688 was passed on April 5, 1991 and called on Iraq to halt the persecution of its civilian population "including most recently in Kurdish-populated areas." On the same day, President Bush announced the creation of "safe havens" in northern Iraq.[13] Bush noted: "Internal conflicts have been raging in Iraq for many years, and we're helping out, and we're going to continue to help these refugees. But I do not want one single soldier or airman shoved into a civil war in Iraq that's been going on for ages. . . . We will not interfere in Iraq's civil war. The Iraqi people must decide their own political future."[14]

The creation of a safe haven for the Kurds was a post–Cold War precedent for the United States and its allies—an intervention in the internal affairs of a sovereign state for the express purpose of protecting the country's citizens from its own government. In doing so, the United States entered into a commitment that would entail rolling back Iraqi government control in a "security zone" in northern Iraq, effectively placing that area under the protection of multinational forces and the management of nongovernmental organizations and Kurdish factions. From April 7, U.S. aircraft air-dropped relief packages to the largest Kurdish camps on the Iraqi-Turkish border, which was protected by U.S. combat air patrols and A-10 ground-attack aircraft flying from Incirlik, Turkey (from which U.S. Task Force Proven Force had launched Desert Storm operations into northern Iraq). A European Command (EUCOM) operations order on April 16, 1991, established Operation Provide Comfort.

Until July 1991, a ground-forces component, including the U.S. 10th Special Forces Group and the 24th MEU, provided ground security for the new zone, and thereafter a military coordination center in Zakho maintained U.S. military ties to the nongovernmental organizations and Kurdish groups working in the area. The composite U.S., British, French, and Turkish air wing plus a small number of attached special forces soldiers and ground observers began the open-ended policing of a no-fly zone that stretching to the 36th parallel (36°N), warned Iraq against flying any aircraft *or helicopters* within the zone, and issued a further démarche that placed limits on Iraqi ground-forces movement within the specified security zone.[15] With only the occasional shot fired, 6 percent of Iraq's land mass and air space and 12 percent of its population were permanently removed from Baathist government control. Until U.S. forces left southern Iraq in May 1991, the United States and its allies briefly occupied one tenth of Iraq's territory.

POSTWAR RESISTANCE TO THE CEASE-FIRE TERMS

The immediate postwar period was filled with foreboding about the unfinished business of the U.S. struggle with Saddam's regime. The Iraqi regime clearly had plenty of fight left in it, and its postwar conduct did not indicate that it considered itself beaten or vanquished. The regime had husbanded its attack helicopters and secured the right to use them against the intifada. It had deftly slipped its military's neck from the tightening noose in the KTO by withdrawing a number of its Republican Guard divisions across the Euphrates River and using them to bolster the regular military against the rebels in Basra, then in the cities along the Euphrates and Tigris Rivers, and finally in the Kurdish north.

As soon as the Iraqi military had crushed the revolt, Saddam immediately saw the armed forces as a source of threat rather than salvation. He shuffled its key leadership and rotated the defense minister's position among his closest family loyalists for six months at a time, first to his future son-in-law Hussein Kamil and then to his cousin, "Chemical" Ali Hassan al-Majid, the notorious commander of Iraq's 1980s Anfal campaign against the Kurds. Saddam undertook a similar reshuffle among the heads of his half-dozen parallel intelligence organizations and placed his younger son Qusay in charge of the most important, the Special Security Organization (SSO).[16] Finally, following the failure of the Baath Party regional commands and their Popular Army militias to prevent the intifada, Saddam established the Tribal Chiefs Bureau to provide bodyguards, special stipends, and other honorifics to a broader base of smaller tribes dispersed across Iraq.[17] With these measures, Saddam overcame growing tensions within his family, within some of the larger Iraqi tribes, and within the Iraqi military and intelligence services. Although weakened, Saddam and his regime had survived—a victory under the circumstances.

Before 1991 had even ended, however, the Baathist regime moved from survival mode to resistance, testing the constraints being placed on its sovereignty and reneging on the very commitments with which it secured the cease-fire at Safwan. UNSC Resolution 687, passed on April 3, 1991, laid out the requirements for the lifting of economic sanctions that would otherwise remain in place, which were enforced by the multinational Maritime Intercept Operations forces in the Gulf.[18] In addition to renouncing Iraq's claim to Kuwait and accepting the country's pre-1990 debts and new responsibility for war reparations, the UN resolution required Iraq to account for 605 missing Kuwaiti citizens and third-country nationals who disappeared during the Iraqi occupation of Kuwait. Unknown to the world in 1991, most of these men had been executed by the Iraqi Mukhabarat just days after Desert Storm ended.[19]

The last key requirement of UNSC Resolution 687 called on Iraq to "accept the destruction, removal, or rendering harmless" of all NBC weapons stockpiles and research, plus any ballistic missiles with a range of more than 150 kilometers and related research and facilities.[20] To the international community and the regional countries, WMD had not been a casus belli for war, yet international consensus recognized that an embittered and isolated Saddam regime could not be allowed to maintain stocks of non-conventional weapons. To Iraq, WMD and particularly nuclear and biological weapons were linchpins of the country's potential future status as a regional hegemon. In the context of the collapse of Iraq's conventional military, chemical weapons represented a key force multiplier. However, the Iraqi government was also practical about its inability to hide large weapons systems (such as Scuds) or factory processes—most of which were already dispersed around the country or removed from their peacetime facilities—from UN inspections.

In April 1991, Iraq made its first declaration to the UN Special Commission (UNSCOM) and the International Atomic Energy Agency (IAEA), while simultaneously beginning a process of placing the entire WMD program in long-term hibernation at dispersal sites. In June 1991, U.S. satellites monitoring known Iraqi nuclear facilities spotted large industrial calutrons (used for uranium enrichment) being dispersed and managed to track these components until UNSCOM inspectors could inspect and destroy them. This proof positive of Iraqi concealment activities panicked the Iraqi regime into a process of selective destruction of its WMD programs, including bulkier items such as Scud airframes and TELs, chemical munitions, and larger industrial components. Concealable and indispensable items were dispersed, including research data, samples, and equipment; centrifuge components and valves; missile engines and guidance; tools and molds; nuclear weapon components; and select CBW samples, growth media, and precursors.

The July 1991 IAEA report overturned years of underestimation of Iraq's nuclear program using new data gathered in Iraq and pointed to the existence of an extraordinarily mature nuclear-research effort that advanced simultaneously along four parallel routes. IAEA's judgment that Iraq would have produced a nuclear bomb by 1993 if Desert Storm had not occurred was a wake-up call for the global community and suggested that if Saddam had undertaken his gamble in Kuwait two years later, the situation could have developed differently. On August 15 1991, the UNSC passed UNSC Resolution 707, which called upon Iraq to once again "provide full and complete disclosure" of its WMD.[21]

In September 1991, IAEA's suspicions were confirmed by files uncovered by UNSCOM inspectors, who had begun a paper chase in Iraq's government buildings to uncover the documentation detailing Iraqi programs and concealment. Iraq began to seriously impede inspections with methods that included holding UNSCOM personnel in a Baghdad parking lot for five days in late September and refusing to guarantee the safety of UNSCOM's fleet of five surveillance and transport helicopters.[22] President Bush threatened the use of force and offered a U.S. escort for UNSCOM aircraft if Iraq persisted in obstructing inspections. This threat, in combination with the October 11 passage of UNSC Resolution 715, which called for Iraq to comply with "the ongoing monitoring and verification" process, caused Baghdad to back down for the remainder of the year.[23] From March to July 1992 the same pattern of obstruction, threatened coercion, and grudging acquiescence emerged and became known as "cheat and retreat," which culminated in an eighteen-day siege of the Iraqi Ministry of Agriculture by UNSCOM inspectors who sought to prevent the removal of key files.[24] From July 1991 to summer 1992, U.S. military planners prepared small coercive options for use against Iraq to bring the "cheat and retreat" episodes to an end. The Iraqi government hunkered down and made initial preparations to absorb a limited series of air strikes.[25]

CREATION OF A SOUTHERN NO-FLY ZONE

Although the pattern of Iraqi provocations and U.S. threats concerning the issue of UN inspections appeared to be the most likely cause of increased U.S. military engagement in Iraq, the next military development evolved out of ongoing U.S. enforcement of UNSC Resolution 688, the UN resolution concerned with the protection of Iraq's citizens. Since April 1991, when UNSC Resolution 688 was passed, the fortunes of Iraq's Kurds and Shiites could not have contrasted more greatly. Iraq's Kurdish factions both north and south of the 36°N no-fly zone successfully kept up pressure on regime forces in northern Iraq during the summer and fall of 1991 and followed up on Iraqi withdrawals from urban areas such as Irbil and Sulaymaniyah. By October 1991, both the Iraqi military and the Kurdish groups were settling into parallel fortified lines and checkpoints, including a de facto boundary called the Green Line, which separated the adversaries by up to three miles. Cut off from government services, the Kurdish zone developed rudimentary local governance and undertook a rapid economic and infrastructural recovery, capping these achievements by electing the Kurdistan Regional Government (KRG) in local elections for the zone's 3 million inhabitants on May 16, 1992.[26]

The fortunes of the Shiite population, still held under strict martial law and whose territory was heavily occupied by government forces, could not have differed more. From mid-April 1992, the Iraqi military began an intensive series of military operations aimed at breaking the back of residual Shiite resistance groups in the south, primarily the Iranian-backed Supreme Council for Islamic Revolution in Iraq (SCIRI). Elements of ten Iraqi regular army divisions were involved in extensive counterinsurgency operations to secure the Iranian border, locate and destroy rebel camps along the border, garrison the road system in southern Iraq, and root out stubborn resistance elements from the 10,800-square-kilometer marshlands of the south. Causeways were created to provide dry roadways to bring artillery within range of key enclaves in the marshes, and new irrigation projects were designed to divert water away from the marshes, thereby drying out vast tracts of Iraq's ancient ecological treasure. By late April, the Iraqi military was systematically throwing battalion-sized cordons over suspected rebel operating areas, using leaflet drops to warn the indigenous marsh Arabs, conducting ceaseless artillery barrages and assaults during daylight hours, and repairing to mud-walled forts to protect against rebel attacks at night.[27]

What changed in summer 1992, however, was that Iraq began using its fixed-wing aircraft to launch air strikes against the rebels from 23 July 1992 onward. No Iraqi fixed-wing aircraft had flown since Desert Storm, which reflected the terms of the initial Safwan cease-fire. However, after several earlier attempts to wriggle out of the prohibition, the Iraqi government unilaterally withdrew from this understanding when twelve Iranian aircraft penetrated Iraqi airspace in April 1992 to strike an Iraqi base of an armed Iranian opposition group, the Mojaheddin-e Khalq Organization (MKO). Although one Iranian aircraft was destroyed by AAA, no IrAF interceptors were scrambled, and the incident served as both a wake-up call to the Baathist regime and a convenient excuse to restart air operations.[28] Iran announced that it was permanently keeping the 132 aircraft that Iraq had sheltered in the country in 1991, thereby forcing the shattered IrAF to recentralize aircraft sheltered across Iraq at dispersal airfields and beside archaeological monuments or mosques. In some cases these aircraft were cannibalized for spares and in others they were returned to service.

Between April and August 1992, the considerably smaller, postwar IrAF flew 350 sorties[29] and moved forty fixed-wing aircraft southward after the repair of key southern airfields such as Tallil and al-Kut. Ground-attack Su-25 and PC-7 aircraft were based at Amarah and Tallil, respectively, and Numaniyah and Basra served as key heliports.[30] Although helicopter surveillance and strikes allowed more effective hunting of the regime's human quarry, fixed-wing aircraft had an even greater psychological and physical impact.

Their use indicated Saddam's increasing freedom of action, and they delivered large quantities of napalm, white phosphorous, CS gas (tear gas), and choking or acidic agents against rebel camps.[31]

The opinion columns of major U.S. newspapers still included many contributions cautioning against supporting the Shiite rebels—citing the risks of civil war, of stimulating Iranian interference, or of reducing Iraqi willingness to compromise on inspections.[32] However, the Bush administration had decided that some form of action needed to be taken to dissuade Iraq's increasingly aggressive activities and blatant violations of UN resolutions. U.S. options included the creation of a southern no-fly zone to mirror the northern version north of 36°N, the reimposition of a full-country no-fly zone, a selective series of strikes on fielded Iraqi forces that were undertaking the counterinsurgency operations, or a series of coercive strikes against strategic targets of value to the regime. Although strikes on ground forces were threatened, the Bush administration opted for the first and most direct option to reduce Iraqi fixed-wing activity. The southern no-fly zone—Operation Southern Watch (OSW)—was formally established on August 26, 1992, by UNSC Resolution 688. The Joint Task Force—Southwest Asia (JTF-SWA), a Riyadh-based component of CENTAF that reported directly to CENTCOM, undertook OSW.

Unlike the small northern no-fly-zone task force, which numbered approximately 48 aircraft, JTF-SWA maintained a constant U.S., British, and French presence of approximately 160 aircraft. The new zone restricted Iraqi activity over an additional 47,500 square kilometers of air space. Prior to its activation, the area was surveilled by U-2 aircraft, and known SAM and IrAF interceptor bases were intensively leafleted with warnings to desist from threatening overflying Coalition aircraft.[33] Iraq moved its fixed-wing aircraft and 30 of its southern-based helicopters just north of the 32°N line to al-Jarrah and other nearby bases, leaving approximately 24 helicopters and numerous inoperable aircraft below the 32°N line.[34]

As Coalition spokespeople noted, OSW was not charged with ensuring the safety of the Shiites in the way that the security zone in the north protected Kurds within its area.[35] Instead, as CENTCOM Air Component Commander Lt. Gen. Michael Nelson explained, the mission of OSW was "to have better insight into what Saddam was doing south of 32 degrees north, and thereby be able to verify his compliance with UN Security Council Resolution 688."[36] The operation entailed "conducting presence and surveillance operations over

Iraqi territory south of 32 degrees north" and effectively forbade all Iraqi military flights in the area, including helicopters.[37] However, although OSW may have reduced aerial attacks on the Shiite rebels and marsh Arabs, it did little to protect them from artillery and ground assaults. SCIRI rebels interviewed by Bruce Nelan in late 1992 and early 1993 indicated that the subtle improvement brought by the no-fly zone was largely unappreciated by the Shia, one of whom commented: "When we saw the allied jets ignore the guns that were killing us, and only hit the missiles that were threatening their planes, we knew we had been abandoned."[38]

Even so, the opening of a second no-fly zone in the south further locked the United States into the militarized containment of Iraq and exposed up to fifty U.S. pilots each day to contact with the Iraqi air-defense system during their overflights of southern Iraq. It also created open-ended military commitments that were simple to begin but politically impossible to end without appearing to reduce U.S. commitment to regional partners and the Iraqi victims of Saddam's regime.

BUILDING TO CRISIS

Tension was already building when Iraq initiated its most overt series of postwar military challenges to date in late 1992 and early 1993. Because of the onerous concessions to which Iraq had to agree during the cease-fire period that preceded the formal end of the Gulf War on April 11, 1991, Iraq's sovereignty was heavily circumscribed. By the summer of 1992, Saddam was not only regularly pushing back on its UN commitments by seeking to run illegal imports and exports past the multinational naval blockade, obstructing UN weapons inspectors, resisting a new, permanent UN demarcation of the Iraq-Kuwait border, and providing no clues as to the whereabouts of Kuwaiti and third-country national detainees, but was also increasingly involved in a daily face-off with U.S. military forces in Iraq.

The struggle had also taken on something of a personal dynamic, often devolving into what Jeffrey Smith called "an extraordinarily personal battle between President Bush and President Saddam Hussein."[39] This dynamic came to the fore in the time between President Bush's election defeat by Senator Bill Clinton in November 1992 and the new president's formal assumption of office on January 19, 1993. During this interim, Saddam sought to mark the second anniversary of the Gulf War by "humiliating George Bush in the closing days of his administration."[40] In an example of an evolving trend, Saddam chose to time his next confrontation while the United States was heavily engaged in Somalia and the Europeans in Bosnia.

The no-fly zones provided Saddam with an excellent recurring opportunity to strike at the United States at a time and place of his choosing. Although Desert Storm had shown that Iraqi military activity could be severely dislocated by the speed, tempo, and unpredictability of Coalition air and ground operations, here was an environment that offered the Iraqi military a more balanced playing field and the ability to observe and plan at its preferred slower pace. Until December 1992, the no-fly zones were hardly contested, save for an occasional flurry of AAA fire or radar illumination in the north. Every day since April 1991 in the north and August 1992 in the south, Iraqi surveillance radar and ground observers could profile the evolving no-fly-zone patterns of activity. They noted the constant rotation of four-ship formations in and out of the zones during daylight hours, which totaled around thirty-five penetrating sorties over Iraq north of 36°N and fifty to sixty penetrating flights south of 32°N every day.[41] The Iraqi objective was to shoot down a U.S. aircraft using a mix of aerial and SAM forces: the IrAF fighters served as bait to draw the U.S. aircraft deep into the MEZ of Iraqi SAMs, a tactic that became known as a "SAMbush."

IrAF fighters had been flying since April 1992 but only began to violate the new no-fly zones after deploying to the newly repaired al-Jarrah air base just north of 32°N in late November. Incursions began on December 10, 1992.[42] The first SAMbush began with an orchestrated series of shallow incursions below 32°N on December 27, 1992. The use of aerial incursions was not new to the IrAF—it had previously performed shallow incursions of Iranian airspace in 1979[43] and Saudi airspace just after the invasion of Kuwait in 1990[44]—but what was different was the integration of SAMs into the equation. During Desert Storm, the Iraqi Republican Guard had withheld its SAM fire on a number of occasions before firing salvos at U.S. aircraft.[45] Now the two tactics were combined.

On December 27, 1992, the first indication of Iraqi intent was a MiG-25 that performed a high-speed, arcing incursion through an area patrolled by a four-ship formation of F-15C. Even though the U.S. pilots visually acquired the MiG, the pilot could not acquire permission to fire in sufficient time to engage the supersonic intruder. A flurry of MiGs then ingressed toward the 32°N line, always turning away before entering the no-fly zone. They pulled the newly arrived four F-16s east and west along the line and dared them to pursue the IrAF northward. Electronic intelligence support began to report indications of Iraqi SAMs and radar activity, which suggested an attempt to draw the F-16s into a carefully laid SAMbush. Instead, a fatal miscalculation meant that the IrAF, rather than the U.S. Air Force, ended the day one aircraft down. When a MiG-25 launched too deep of an incursion, two F-16s managed to trap it south of 32°N. The MiG attempted to launch an AAM, but the weapon suffered a malfunction. After U.S. F-16 pilots twice requested permission to engage, they destroyed the Iraqi aircraft at a range of twenty nautical miles with an AIM-120 advanced medium-range AAM (AMRAAM). F-16 pilot Lt. Col. Paul White noted that although the day had ended well, the Iraqi SAMbush had been a wake-up call: "The tactics displayed by the Iraqis in that engagement were surprisingly sophisticated, especially considering the apparent coordination between four independent aircraft and SAM missile battery operators."[46]

New incursions were launched on December 28 and 30, 1992, and January 4, 1993. At the same time, Iraq moved increasing numbers of SA-2s and SA-3s south of the 32nd parallel and north of the 36°N line, and threatened U.S. U-2 reconnaissance flights. On January 6, 1993, President Bush gave Iraq forty-eight hours to remove its SAMs from the no-fly zone, and the U.S. ultimatum was backed by a UN démarche on January 7. Iraq briefly complied, but redeployed the SAMs to the south on January 11 and broadened its resistance to other spheres, lashing out at UN activities in Iraq. On January 8, the Iraqi government announced that UNSCOM staff would not be allowed to pilot their aircraft when entering Iraq or inspecting Iraqi facilities, telling the UN that it could not otherwise guarantee the safety of the UN flights.[47] On January 10, 11, and 12, Iraq sent several hundred unarmed men into the UN zone separating Iraq and Kuwait to recover four HY-2 Silkworm antiship missiles from the former Iraqi naval base at Umm Qasr and to strip the facility (which was scheduled to be granted to Kuwait under the UN's new border-demarcation proposals) of all fixtures, fittings, valuable wiring, and valuable metals.[48] Iraq dispersed its aircraft and armored forces and braced to absorb air attacks. Although hesitant to initiate military action in the last four days of his term, President Bush consulted with the incoming administration and authorized the preparation of a military response.[49]

JANUARY 1993 STRIKES ON IRAQ

The January 13, 1993, air strikes on Iraq were the first time that the United States had initiated combat with Iraq since the end of the Gulf War, yet they bore little of the razzmatazz of the opening moments of Desert Storm. The strikes were entirely launched in the south, in large part because the Turkish government would not sanction the use of Operation Provide Comfort aircraft for strike missions.[50] Alongside its routine execution of the no-fly zones, the forward-deployed JTF-SWA headquarters in Saudi Arabia had been given the task of developing a range of options to respond to Iraqi provocations in 1992. JTF-SWA's parent formation, CENTAF, was based at Shaw Air Force Base in the United States and delegated the planning for an initial January air strike to the Saudi-based command on the grounds that it had the best appreciation of the air defenses that it was overflying on a daily basis. Maj. Gen. James Record, commander of JTF-SWA in January 1993, had developed a short list of priority Iraqi IADS targets that became the focus on the first postwar air strike on January 13. Fixed C2 facilities, communications nodes, and static radars spread among six sites were the focus of the attack. Pentagon briefers ascribed the limited objective of "disabling air defense systems south of 32°N" to the attack. SAM systems were not a major focus of the attack because of their large numbers and their mobility, which frequently made U.S. tracking efforts of these systems out of date. SAM systems were to be attacked if opportunity allowed, and a number of previously surveilled SAM sites were briefed to pilots as secondary targets or bomb dumps.[51]

Following Iraqi noncompliance with President Bush's January 6 ultimatum and the January 7 UN démarche, the outgoing president signed an execution order (EXECORD) for the strike on January 11. With U.S., British, and French aircraft already in the air, a January 12 air strike was called off because of heavy cloud cover over the target. Time was running out for the outgoing administration. Although the military requested another delay on January 13, citing continuing bad weather, the administration opted to order the strike without further delay.[52] At 2115 local time a package of 112 aircraft began the attack. The force included 32 support aircraft, 26 fighter escorts, 16 SEAD aircraft, and 38 strike aircraft, including 6 F-117A Nighthawks.[53] In contrast to Desert Storm, three quarters of the strike aircraft involved were PGM droppers.

Within twenty minutes the raid was over, and all Coalition aircraft had safely exited Iraqi airspace. Within hours, a first disappointing "cut" of mission reports and BDA imagery suggested that the strike had not performed as expected. Within days, it became clear that only sixteen of the thirty-three DMPIs had been successfully hit. Operating at nineteen thousand feet and faced with heavy cloud cover, Coalition aircraft displayed many of the same weaknesses and confronted the same challenges that had reduced bombing performances in Desert Storm. Six F/A-18 and 4 F-16 aircraft employed in the raid were equipped with FLIR night-targeting systems but employed unguided Mk. 84 2,000-pound bombs, and initial BDA suggested that none of the six radar-dish or control-van DMPIs attacked by these sorties had been destroyed. Although many of the unguided strikes had, in fact, missed their targets, the damage caused by others was merely invisible on the overhead imagery available to BDA analysts. Lt. Col. Ron Sykes recounted, "The BDA guys looked for 30 × 15 ft craters, but they had not been told that the Mk. 84s were set for airburst to kill through overpressure—there was no evidence of fire, but generally when you strike electronics with overpressure they don't burn. They could see the top of the radar antenna, but they couldn't see that all the webbing had been blown out, because the satellite picture was from nearly overhead, and later they got reports from the Bedouin that there were very small holes punched all the way through the van, but this was well after the attack.[54]

The remaining 28 strikers were PGM-capable aircraft and accounted for the sixteen assessed hits on Iraqi command posts and communications. The stealth aircraft destroyed the Amarah IOC, thereby eliminating a source of GCI guidance for Iraqi pilots in the south. Bad weather had also affected the precision strikers: two pilots were forced to abort attacks against targets that were obscured, two other attacks failed when clouds broke the laser-guidance lock and sent munitions off course, and an aircraft missed its way point and attacked a farm complex by mistake.[55]

Iraq continued to test the United States in the following days. In the south, Iraqi soldiers erected new border posts in the neutral zone that separated Kuwait and Iraq, staking a claim to certain Kuwaiti oil concessions in the area, and Iraq declared that it could not guarantee the safety of UNSCOM flights within Iraq. On January 15, President Bush gave Iraq another ultimatum to withdraw the posts and grant UN inspectors unconstrained access, or suffer further attacks. Iraq chose to ignore the ultimatum, which triggered two more large-scale military actions in January 1993. The first was a TLAM strike against an Iraqi industrial facility in the Zaafaraniyah suburb of Baghdad. According to White House Spokesman Marlin Fitzwater, the objective of the strike was "to seek Iraqi compliance with UN resolutions."[56]

At one of the last Principals Committee meetings (PCMs) of the Bush administration, senior U.S. National Security Council decision makers decided that a high-profile coercive strike should be launched and that the target should be related to Iraq's WMD program.[57] As early as August 1992, coercive strikes against civilian or dual-use infrastructure had been dropped from the menu of options; in the words of one Joint Staff official, targets needed to consist of "infrastructure that is undeniably and purely military in everybody's eyes . . . with no peaceful use."[58] The Principals Committee seized on the most concerning element of Iraq's WMD programs, the nuclear weapons program, and told the U.S. military to develop a "nuclear target." Zaafaraniyah was chosen by analysts from the Joint Staff Directorate of Intelligence and the CIA from an initial list of nine targets that included sites from which UNSCOM inspectors had been excluded or which held potential document caches, such as the Iraqi Ministry of Defense or the Ministry of Industry and Military Industrialization.[59]

Situated thirteen kilometers south of central Baghdad, the al-Rabiya factory complex at Zaafaraniyah was an unlikely target for a symbolic and preferably painful shot across the bows of the Iraqi regime. The main attraction of the site was that it was an easy target, ensconced within a large walled compound that separated it from civilian dwellings. Defector and UNSCOM reporting indicated that the site had been part of Iraq's uranium-enrichment program, one of a dozen or so plants that made components for Iraq's vital electromagnetic-isotope-separation (EMIS) calutrons and had not been identified before or during Desert Storm. Although UNSCOM had removed all EMIS components from the plant, Iraq maintained precision tools at the site—coil-winding machinery, computer-aided-design equipment, and printed circuit-board fabrication machines—that could be used to reactivate Iraq's EMIS program.[60] TLAMs were quickly identified as the safest way to penetrate the Baghdad SuperMEZ and the slab-sided buildings of the al-Rabiya factory offered prime targets for the 1,000-pound unitary warheads of the TLAM-C missile. Two or three TLAMs were considered necessary to assure the destruction of each of the sixteen DMPIs in the complex, and therefore the number of aimpoints was effectively constrained by the number of TLAMs within firing range of U.S. ships in the Gulf and Red Sea.

JTF-SWA had little to do with the Zaafaraniyah strike, except to clear the air space and stand aside. CENTAF Commander Nelson explained:

Knights: Where did the idea to use TLAM come from?

Nelson: Beats me. Better ask somebody from CENTCOM because it wasn't me. TLAM strikes were controlled entirely by CENTCOM— we were just told what was going to happen and when it was going to happen. We were just issued [time-over-targets] and targets, not that we had anything to do with executing them—all we did was watch. I didn't have an in-house capability to command and control TLAM targets anyway.[61]

The Tomahawk strike coincided with the second anniversary of the beginning of Desert Storm. At 2000 Baghdad time on January 17, forty-six TLAM-Cs were launched by four ships spread between the Gulf and Red Sea, and one missile splashed down upon take-off because of a boost failure. The remaining forty-five missiles impacted at 2115 Baghdad time, with thirty-eight of the missiles scoring direct hits. Fourteen of the sixteen DMPIs were destroyed or heavily damaged, including casting, welding, and coiling work-shops and the main and secondary fabrication and material buildings. Three missiles were close misses within the compound and three crashed harmlessly in an orchard nearby. The remaining missile, judged to have been hit by anti-aircraft fire, careened toward central Baghdad, struck the al-Rashid hotel, and caused two civilian deaths.[62] The al-Rabiya complex was gutted by fire.

On the following day, January 18, JTF-SWA launched a carefully pre-pared restrike of the IADS targets that had been attacked on January 13 and designed the attack to minimize the target acquisition, accuracy, and naviga-tional challenges that had reduced the effects of the earlier strike. CENTAF Commander Nelson had now deployed to theater, arriving on January 14, in case the crisis continued to develop and a more serious military confrontation ensued. The January 18 air strike once again did not involve Operation Pro-vide Comfort forces in the north, although these forces were heavily engaged in responding to Iraqi ground fire and a spate of IrAF incursions, one of which resulted in the January 17 destruction of an IrAF MiG-29 by a U.S. F-16.[63]

Meanwhile, JTF-SWA patiently waited to identify surviving IADS nodes and identify a good weather window. Launched in daylight and clear skies, the seventy-five-aircraft raid on January 18 left Iraqi air defenses in the south with a severe concussion. The Tallil Sector Operating Center (SOC), which had escaped attack four days earlier because of cloud cover, was destroyed, and SIGINT suggested that an Iraqi general officer and up to sixty other personnel were killed.[64] Like the Amarah IOC before them, the Tallil and Najaf IOC were destroyed. This set back Iraq's ability to control fixed-wing incursions and coordinate SAMbushes in the south. Although radars were restruck, Iraq's SAMs remained too elusive to strike, and a number of missions were scrubbed because the systems had moved since being acquired by U.S. intelligence systems. Aviation writer David Fulghum noted, "The Iraqis are apparently trying to operate inside the U.S. intelligence targeting cycle, which often requires more than twenty-four hours to locate and identify a missile site and launch a raid."[65] Two years after the Gulf War, medium-altitude, all-weather, twenty-four-hour precision strikes; BDA; and mobile-target tracking remained formidable challenges for the post–Cold War U.S. military.

Iraq's reaction to the January 17–18 strikes was swift but short-lived: it removed the border posts in the neutral zone and returned the al-Rutqa oil field to Kuwaiti control. Iraq's air defenses in the south remained stunned, displaying "moderate [IrAF] sortie rates but low radar activity" in the weeks after the strikes, according to the DoD.[66] However, the air-defense system in the north continued to engage in AAA fire, radar illumination, and attempted SAMbushes until January 19, and the southern no-fly zone would be contested frequently between April and August 1993, indicating the system's ability to regenerate. The Baathist regime set more than a thousand workers to rebuilding the al-Rabiya factory in a "round-the-clock effort" that resulted in the complex being reopened four months later, complete with gardens built over landscaped rubble and monuments forged from Tomahawk airframes. Although key industrial equipment was verified by UNSCOM inspectors as destroyed and salvaged equipment had suffered heavy wear and tear, Saddam appeared to have healed the scars left by the U.S. raid.

As every major strike on Iraq would in the years to come, the January 1993 attacks raised questions about America's interests and long-term objectives in Iraq, the Gulf, and the Middle East, and its willingness to use force to protect them. For certain U.S. commentators, the January 1993 strikes were a throwback to the "bad old days" of Vietnam when limited military force was used to send signals, and a violation of the "Powell doctrine," the CJCS's philosophy that if military force must be applied, it should be applied decisively.[67] According to CENTAF Commander Nelson, the air strikes were "message passing and trying to do something militarily useful at the same time," and administration spokesman Marlin Fitzwater stated that the Zaafaraniyah strike both "made a point" and "directly helped the process of eliminating nuclear weapons."[68] Yet, as Michael Eisenstadt argued, "military responses that are proportional and predictable, that focus strictly on the offending military activity, allow Saddam to carefully calculate outcomes and reduce risks when engaging in brinksmanship."[69] Saddam's addiction to resistance would ultimately be his undoing, but for the moment he had politically outlasted his Gulf War nemesis George Bush. Saddam now looked forward to a new U.S. presidency that appeared to offer better prospects for Iraq's international rehabilitation.

As President Bill Clinton was inaugurated, Iraq announced a "goodwill cease-fire" and withdrew SAMs from certain areas of the no-fly zones, switched off Iraq's nationwide surveillance radars, and promised full cooperation with UNSCOM and the safety of UN flights.[70] However, if Saddam hoped to enter the good graces of the Clinton administration, buoyed by Clinton's November 1992 comments about a possible rapprochement with Iraq, he had miscalculated. Within three days of Clinton taking office, the U.S. launched new strikes on Iraqi target-acquisition and rangefinder radars in the northern no-fly zone, and, a day later, a suspected AAA site was struck in the southern zone. In part, these responses were pro forma continuation of the standing rules of engagement in the zones—the first military act of the Clinton administration occurred on autopilot, as it were. A Pentagon spokesperson tersely commented that U.S. forces in the Persian Gulf region did not consult with Clinton or Defense Secretary Les Aspin before attacking the radar sites, stating "when we're threatened, we react. We inform them afterwards." The new president immediately backed the ongoing policing of the no-fly zones, stating, "We're going to adhere to our policy of attacking radar and antiaircraft sites when targeted."[71] This was more than lip service. National Security Adviser Anthony Lake commented, "We inherited policies with which we agreed. We let the military call the shots and we were happy for them to shoot back if our aircraft were targeted by radar or shot at." Although the U.S. withdrawal from Somalia occurred under the new president, Lake was quick to point out that the new president was in no hurry to change Iraq policy or begin a disengagement from Gulf security: "Clinton was not the driver in getting out of Somalia or other long-term commitments—the White House advisors and Congress pushed that. We—the national security team—thought we were in Iraq for the foreseeable future."[72]

6

"Tomahawk Diplomacy"

The stand-alone use of land-attack cruise missiles—the ship- or submarine-launched TLAMs and the air-launched CALCMs—would become synonymous with the Clinton administration's use of military force in Iraq. It was variously characterized as "Tomahawk diplomacy," "drive-by shootings," and "pinpricks"[1] and was linked in the minds of many observers with casualty aversion and in turn with perceived vacillation in the use of military force under the Clinton administration.[2] William Arkin summed up this assumed connection when he referred to cruise missile–only operations as "war without inhaling," which recalled President Clinton's half-hearted admission to experimenting with drugs.[3]

In large part, the criticism of cruise-missile-only operations came from an inherent American discomfort with the pursuit of limited objectives, even though these were commonplace features of U.S. military policy by the 1990s. During the Reagan and Bush administrations, the United States used or threatened limited strikes in Lebanon, Libya, the Philippines, Panama, Somalia, and Iraq.[4] The post–Desert Storm Iraq policy of the Bush administration set the tone and introduced the pattern of challenges and responses that would prevail throughout the Clinton era. According to Bruce Riedel, whose National Security Council–level involvement with U.S. Iraq policy spanned the Bush and Clinton administrations, "Most senior decision-makers in both adminis-trations were unanimously of the view that no military solution was possible to the Iraq problem. They knew that no application of force short of a full invasion would remove the irritant, Saddam. And neither president seriously considered the option."[5]

The Clinton administration was admittedly not primarily focused on foreign policy. Similar to many U.S. administrations, it sought from the out-set to prevent foreign-policy issues from defining the presidency or derailing its ambitious domestic political and economic programs. Just as important, however, the first Clinton administration inherited the mantle of global lead-ership in a post–Cold War security environment in which America's military had begun to downsize in anticipation of a "peace dividend." At the same time the United States faced a multiplying set of new security and humanitarian challenges. Secretary of Defense Aspin, summing up the new environment, exclaimed: "Welcome to the 1990s. You're going to find a whole series of situations in which the issue is going to be, 'should the United States act or should it not act?' And we're going to find ourselves picking and choosing because, frankly, we do not have the resources to go in everywhere and do everything."[6]

In this environment, political and military capital had to be spent thriftily. The upper echelons of the national-security elite of the first Clinton administration were seeded with cautious strategists such as National Security Adviser Lake, Secretary of State Warren Christopher, and CJCS Powell. The Clinton administration was certainly not opposed to technologically advanced, low-risk military options; however, as this chapter highlights, the weapons advice that resulted in cruise-missile-only operations originated mainly from the military and from the basing limits imposed by regional host nations. In particular, Aspin, fresh from long years of service on the Senate Armed Services Committee, had a keen appreciation of the merits of precision-strike technologies, as would his eventual successor, William Perry. Just before his appointment as secretary of defense, Aspin noted, "The limited objectives school has been strengthened as technological developments have improved our ability to achieve compellance. . . . We have stealthy aircraft and we have precision-guided munitions. We can target power grids and command and control assets. These are the kinds of targets that national leadership and military commanders hold dear."[7]

JUNE 1993 CRUISE-MISSILE STRIKE

Aspin's faith in the coercive capabilities of precision strikes would be put to the test just months into the new administration. Reports reached the U.S. government in the last days of April 1993 of a foiled assassination attempt on former President Bush that ocurred when the retired statesman had toured Kuwait in mid-April. According to the Kuwaiti Security Service, eleven Iraqis and three Kuwaitis in the pay of Iraq's General Intelligence Directorate (or Mukhabarat) had planned to detonate a car bomb as the former president's motorcade passed. The U.S. government was initially suspicious, both because of more than a week's delay between the foiled attempt and the Kuwaiti approach and because of the sheer audacity of the plan, if substantiated. Bruce Riedel recalled that the question asked was, "How could the Iraqis be so stupid or so bold? To try to assassinate a former president of the United States in the country he liberated, less than a hundred days after he left office?"[8]

Iraq certainly possessed the capability to undertake the attack; indeed it fitted with Iraq's recent modus operandi. The M-14 department of Iraq's Mukhabarat held a long and infamous record of overseas assassination. Shortly before this, it had been attributed the December 1992 assassination of an Iraqi nuclear scientist attempting to defect in Amman, Jordan.[9] The M-21 department dealt with special operations, including an active series of bombings in northern Iraq and Turkey. During the winter of 1991, as relief convoys were forced to travel through seventy kilometers of government-held territory to reach Kurdish enclaves in Irbil and Sulaymaniyah, three convoys had multiple bombs planted on their vehicles during Iraqi inspections. An additional thirty explosions within the Kurdish enclave were attributed to the Mukhabarat in the 1991–93 period.[10]

Following a laborious Federal Bureau of Investigation (FBI) and Justice Department investigation, printed circuit boards and other bomb components discovered by the Kuwaiti Security Service were forensically matched with apparently identical bomb components used in a Mukhabarat bombing in Turkey. According to Bruce Riedel, although controversy would dog the evidence for months and years to come, "the case convinced doubters in the White House and was felt to be good enough that it could be presented to the UN Security Council." President Bill Clinton was under pressure to react, and, indeed, had more reason than most new presidents to strike a firm line. Skeptically received by the military because of his antiwar stance during the Vietnam War and his policy goals concerning the controversial issue of homosexuality in the U.S. military, Clinton was perceived as being soft on security issues and had recently been criticized for not launching air strikes on Bosnian-Serb forces in the Balkans. According to Riedel, the administration recognized the need to pass the test of crafting an appropriate response and to do so before the moment for retaliation passed.[11]

The first job was to designate a target or targets to be struck. According to Leon Fuerth, national security adviser to Vice President Al Gore, "the Principals"—who included President Clinton, National Security Adviser Lake, Secretary of Defense Aspin, and Secretary of State Christopher—"met and had a meticulous discussion about the scale of the operation." The conversation focused on "establishing proportionality in the scaling of the operation, cross-checking with international lawyers, considering the political ramifications, establishing the function of the targets . . . and above all, determining the administration's intent in striking the target and how that intent could be characterized to Congress and the public."[12]

The basis for the operation would be the inherent right of self-defense enshrined in the UN Charter, building on the precedent used to strike Libyan intelligence and terrorist training facilities in 1986. This meant that the target would have to be closely connected to Iraq's ability to conduct further terrorist attacks against the United States. Target selection involved an unusual combination of actors, including the CIA, the FBI, the Secret Service (because of their role in protecting current and former presidents), and the Joint Staff. Because the planning of the assassination attempt on the former president was likely to have been carried out by certain branches of the Mukhabarat, the interagency group nominated six precise aimpoints identified by defectors— six specific offices within the General Intelligence Directorate's Baghdad headquarters.[13]

Legal vetting was a vital next step for the Clinton team, which placed strong emphasis on the legal attributes of attributability and proportionality in their military actions. Steve Coll noted, "A lawyer and advocate of international institutions, Clinton paid attention to evidence and to legal standards governing the use of military force."[14] Col. James Terry, the CJCS's legal counsel, vetted and approved the target. According to CENTCOM Deputy Judge Advocate Gen. Col. Charles Dunlap, "[Colonel Terry] and Colin Powell were very close. . . . He [Colonel Terry] was so influential that if he was associated with a target, you could go to the bank with it, you didn't even have to open the folder, it was a legal target. . . . He was very politically savvy."[15]

In a poststrike conference, Powell would reiterate the administration's focus on proportionality in their choice of target: "We selected the IIS because it is the closest thing to the provocation. . . . We wanted to make sure we had a target that was, shall we say, nexus to the provocation. . . . We designed the attack in a way that would be proportionate to the attempt on President Bush's life. . . . [The target is] located in a restricted area of downtown Baghdad, in a walled installation. . . . The headquarters section of the complex was targeted. . . . We selected parts of the complex that were of greater value to the Iraqi Intelligence Services than other parts of the complex."[16]

Deputy Secretary of State Madeleine Albright also noted that "our response was proportional and aimed at a target directly linked to the operation against President Bush. It was designed to damage the terrorist infrastructure of the Iraqi regime."[17]

The timing of the strike provided a second dimension in which the administration could finesse the proportionality of the response. Similar to the timing of any military operation, this feature of the retaliatory strike was extremely closely held and kept within the principals group, which resulted in a degree of tactical surprise even though U.S. newspapers had speculated about the strike for weeks. If the United States wished to maximize the number of Iraqi casualties, "We could have 'gone deadly' by striking during the day," recounted the then–CIA Director James Woolsey.[18] National Security Council attendee Ambassador Mark Parris recalled that the option of leaving "a smoking hole full of casualties" was supported by a stratum of more hawkish junior administration officials but did not fit with the senior decision makers' considerations about proportionality and collateral damage.[19]

On the first count, a night strike on the Iraqi headquarters was favored because it would kill fewer regime personnel—an end state that would reflect more precisely the fact that the assassination attempt on former President Bush was foiled without loss of life. According to Leon Fuerth, the U.S. National Command authorities had been deterred from "uncorking something deliberately bloody. Risks would have been high and there was concern about the delicate 'Arab street' and regional allies, as well as the French and the Russians."[20] Secretary of Defense Aspin was equally explicit at the time of the attack, stating: "It was deliberately aimed to be at a point when the number of people there would not be large."[21] A nighttime strike would also reduce the effects of collateral damage if errant munitions exploded off target. This was particularly the case because Tomahawks, which could be intercepted and shot off course, were likely to be the weapon of choice. Colonel Dunlap recounted that the timing "had to do with the weapons system used and its vulnerabilities to being shot down or intercepted in daylight."[22] Moving at merely 550 miles per hour and at a low level, TLAMs were easy targets during the daytime; the daylight arrival rates of TLAMs in the Gulf War dropped off dramatically after the first day of the war and resulted in rising collateral damage.[23] As in the January 1993 shoot, nighttime delivery was chosen, U.S. spokespeople stated, "to minimize the risks to innocent civilians."[24]

As soon as the target had been chosen, it was assumed that the strike would most likely be undertaken by Tomahawks. The civilians in the Clinton national-security team were loath to interfere in operational decisions, Leon Fuerth recalled, and "would not debate with the military concerning how they wanted to blend weapons systems."[25] Secretary of Defense Aspin noted that "for a number of reasons the TLAM was selected as the weapon of choice, and its main advantage is, of course, that it does not put U.S. pilots at risk."[26]

During and since Desert Storm, the TLAM had become the de facto weapon of choice whenever the Baghdad SuperMEZ had to be penetrated to hit an above-ground target. The military was more focused on force protection than any other element of the U.S. government, and "risk averseness was often evident in military advice" according to one senior civilian decision maker.[27] TLAMs were also used because the United States wished to display its ability to act unilaterally in what was essentially a dispute solely between the United States and Iraq. Deputy Secretary of State Albright stated at the time, "The specific incident was between Iraq and the United States directly, which is why we acted alone. Only United States forces were involved."[28] U.S. allies in the region shared this view and at "extensive consultations" held with the Saudis, the United States had not received strong backing to carry out the strike from local bases.[29] This was fine with the U.S. military, which recognized that the slab-sided target presented by the Mukhabarat headquarters represented an ideal TLAM target.

At 0200 Baghdad time on June 26, 1993, two U.S. ships initiated the launch of twenty-five TLAMs—fourteen from the USS *Peterson* in the Red Sea and nine from the USS *Chancellorsville* in the Gulf. Two missile launches failed, leaving twenty-three missiles to begin their ingress toward Baghdad. They flew over the Ar'Ar area of Saudi Arabia and southeastern Iraq at thirty meters above the ground, while a strobe light periodically provided illumination for the Tomahawk's scene-matching navigational sensors. Of these twenty-three, a total of sixteen TLAMs hit their aimpoints in a series of impacts staggered over a five-minute period. With four 1,000-pound missiles devoted to each aimpoint, the six targeted sections of the Mukhabarat building were heavily damaged. Three missiles landed in the compound but missed their specific aimpoints, and another missile was unaccounted for. Because of a target-programming error, three TLAMs detonated in a civilian neighborhood, killing eight Iraqi noncombatants, including the famed Arabic singer Layla al-Attar, and wounding twelve others.[30]

The operation had consumed a great deal more of the attention of senior civilian decision makers than most military strikes typically would. A remarkably degree of the planning took place in the Pentagon and White House. Indeed, CENTAF Commander Nelson commented that his sole involvement in the strike was to issue last-minute notice to U.S. allies in the Gulf only minutes after receiving it himself.[31] The punishment had been minutely crafted to appear proportional to the crime. Yet, the strike was not well-received in the United States because it was at once too finessed and too limited to satisfy either Congress or the public, who clearly expected a more robust and disproportionate response. Some broadcast and print media suggested that a proportional response should have directly targeted Saddam Hussein. The *Los Angeles Times* stated, "It might be recalled that when President Reagan bombed Libya in 1986 . . . he chose targets that gave us a reasonably good chance of hitting the Libyan leader Moammar Gadhafi himself. Targeting a foreign leader is difficult, of course. Indeed, it is not within the legal powers of an American president at this time. And Saddam moves around a good deal. . . . Still, perhaps some targets could be found that would suggest the possibility that his personal safety might be at risk. . . . Perhaps that could be our message to Saddam next time."[32]

In time, administration officials would offer a bevy of reasons for not targeting Saddam, ranging from philosophical and legal arguments against assassination to military-technical explanations that meticulously programmed TLAMs were unsuited to striking the time-sensitive and mobile leadership targets.[33] The truth was that Saddam could not be located with sufficient precision or timeliness to target him, which provided another example of the way that insufficient intelligence and targeting data defined the art of the possible in U.S. military operations.[34]

Congress, the media, and the U.S. public were also bemused by the care the administration took to reduce the number of regime casualties, a feature that made the strike seem feckless. Both the *Washington Post* and *Los Angeles Times* commented that the early-morning timing of the attack relegated the strike to a purely symbolic act. The latter wrote, "The twenty-three U.S. Tomahawk cruise missiles . . . were just shots across the bow for Saddam Hussein. . . . This was, in effect, an attack by unmanned missiles on an empty building."[35] This probably would have been the case whether a day or night strike was ordered, because the Baathist regime was following the public build-up to the strike very closely. Iraq had prepared for the strike by removing selected computers, files, and equipment from a range of security and industrial sites, and most Mukhabarat personnel had been sent home until further notice. Only a skeleton staff was left at the headquarters.[36] On June 19, a full week before the strike, Iraq's Foreign Minister Tariq Aziz told reporters, "Even if the Americans threaten force . . . Let me tell you, the state of Iraq is one of the most experienced in the region, maybe in the world, in terms of war. . . . Iraq knows that a couple of missiles will not win a war. We know their effectiveness, and also their limitations."[37]

"BASRA BREAKOUT"—IRAQ'S OCTOBER 1994 FEINT TOWARD KUWAIT

Aside from scattered resistance to the no-fly zones, the June 1993 Tomahawk strikes were the last military activity of the year, and Iraq quickly dropped out of the international headlines. The maintenance of UN sanctions and inspections was now the order of the day, alongside an ongoing military containment effort. The U.S. military periodically assessed the threat posed by Iraq to its neighbors, dissecting the assessment along the lines of intent and capability. As the U.S. Senate Committee on Intelligence concluded, "The issue of Saddam's *intentions* to use force against his neighbors and U.S. and Coalition forces was a high-interest matter, and, unfortunately, the main area where the intelligence community was least confident about its analysis. . . . Lack of HUMINT was the main reason for this uncertainty."[38] Lacking any reliable insight into Saddam's thinking, the intelligence community was forced to rely on Saddam's historical record, meaning that hostile intent was assumed.

Iraq's capabilities were more susceptible to U.S. technical-intelligence collection. Those efforts produced the May 1991 National Intelligence Community Memorandum, "Iraq's Ground Forces: An Assessment," which concluded that the Iraqi military "does not constitute a regional threat and is capable of only small-scale offensive operations beyond Iraq's borders. Baghdad's military could only pose a threat to Kuwait if all Coalition forces and United Nations units were withdrawn."[39] The respect accorded to the Iraqi military in assessments before the Gulf War had vanished like a mirage on the battlefields of the KTO.

Meanwhile in Iraq, the Baathist government's successful use of loyalist elements of the military to quell the intifada in 1991 was followed by an extensive reappraisal and rationalization of the Iraqi armed forces. The Gulf War and the ensuing intifada had broken many regular army and Baath Party militia units beyond repair, which caused the government to reduce the number of heavy (armored or mechanized) regular army divisions from seven to five and the number of infantry divisions from twenty to fifteen. The Baath Party's 250,000-strong Popular Army and 100,000-strong Kurdish National Defense Brigades were dissolved and reorganized.[40] Although undermanned, the six or seven divisions of the Republican Guard now represented a far larger proportion of Iraq's total armed forces than other divisions and were placed under the command of Lt. Gen. Hussein Rashid Muhammed al-Tikriti, the well-regarded commander who oversaw the expansion and increased efficiency of the Republican Guard during 1986–87. From a hollow "million-man army" a leaner military force emerged, described by Defense Minister Ali Hassan al-Majid as "a small but strongly built army to defend Iraq's security and borders from Arab reactionary forces, Israel, and Iran."[41] The 1994 U.S. military's handbook on Iraq described a more mechanized and air-mobile force that was moving toward a "quality over quantity" approach.[42]

Alongside an energetic reconstruction campaign that saw all but one of Baghdad's bridges repaired and various ministries, palaces, and public utilities returned to some level of service within a year of the end of Desert Storm, Iraq also quickly regenerated much of its military-industrial capacity. Only six of Iraq's twenty-three major military-industrial complexes had been identified and attacked effectively by the Coalition in 1991, and Iraq had busily set to fixing the war damage. By March 1992, CIA Director Robert Gates told Congress that an estimated 87 percent of Iraqi military industries had restored some level of productivity. Equipment removed from factories prior to bombing was returned, salvaged equipment from destroyed facilities was returned to service, and more than four hundred damaged buildings were repaired. Five of the six targeted industrial concerns were restored to active status, including radar, missile, electronics, and aircraft spare-parts production facilities. The key limitation on Iraq's military recovery remained the effects of sanctions on the import of raw materials and key spare parts, which Defense Minister al-Majid recognized as causing "known and important damages."[43] An updated July 1994 National Intelligence Estimate, *Iraqi Military Capabilities through 1999*, concluded: "Despite an impressive military reconstitution effort under difficult circumstances . . . Iraq's forces will be unable to engage in significant military operations outside the country as long as UN sanctions remain in place."[44]

What the 1991 and 1994 U.S. assessments failed to recognize was that, even under sanctions, Iraq had retained a high level of operational mobility. This allowed it to quickly concentrate forces on its borders *before* U.S. forces could deploy to the Gulf. Iraq had a history of long-range operational movements, from its 1948 and 1973 projection of expeditionary forces to Arab-Israeli wars and its rapid switching of up to four divisions of armored reserves along the Iran-Iraq battlefront in the 1980s.[45] In August 1990, Iraq had deployed eight divisions over distances of three hundred to four hundred miles within fourteen days, which prompted the *Conduct of the Persian Gulf War* report to note Iraq's ability to "conduct short-notice moves across considerable distances."[46] Although Iraq had lost a sizeable proportion of its tactical lift (e.g., wheeled military transport) in the KTO, it had retained most of its operational mobility through the survival of a large proportion of its 2,800 HETs and railway carriages, plus the rapid repair of its road and rail bridges and four- and six-lane north–south highways.[47] The mobility and logistical tethers of the Republican Guard divisions were meanwhile extended through the creation of northern and southern corps headquarters and depots, which put headquarters and logistical depots closer to the borders Saddam wished to threaten.[48]

On the urging of the hawkish extreme of the Iraqi elite—Defense Minister al-Majid and Saddam's sons Uday and Qusay—Saddam decided to test Iraq's ability to rapidly deploy forces to its southern border in October 1994. He hoped to catch the United States and its allies flat-footed and to derail progress on border demarcation and UN inspections.[49] Iraq's fifty-thousand-strong III Corps regular-army forces in the south had spent most of the summer conducting counterinsurgency operations in the marshes, protecting the construction of two huge canal projects intended to drain the marshes of water, and engaging in preemptive crackdowns in advance of Shiite religious festivals and other potential periods of unrest.[50]

At the same time, preparations began in late September for a major deployment of Republican Guard forces to the south. A rare HUMINT source accurately reported the mobilization of two Republican Guard divisions, cueing U.S. no-fly zone aircraft and satellite surveillance on October 5, and leading to the issuance of an intelligence warning on the following day. Iraq had stolen a vital lead on the United States. By October 9, the III Corps had been alerted, and Iraq had assembled twenty thousand troops of the Hammurabi and al-Nida Republican Guard armored divisions, complete with fifteen days' supplies, within forty kilometers of the Kuwaiti border. Aside from Kuwait's small land forces, the country lay almost undefended by ground troops, save for two thousand U.S Marines and the first advanced parties of U.S. troops, who were preparing stocks of prepositioned vehicles for use by inbound U.S. personnel from a six-company mechanized task force. A Pentagon spokesman later confirmed: "It's my view, my judgment, the 9th and the 10th [of October] constituted a critical window when Iraq had some combat strength there which I judged to be adequate for very limited military activity across the border into Kuwait, when resistance would not have been enough to stop them." The official concluded, "The time and distance factors were the most alarming of the circumstances, as well as the fact that these were their two best divisions."[51]

While JTF-SWA aircraft surged to create a presence over the Iraqi forces, and troops, ships, and additional aircraft flowed to theater, the Republican Guard forces moved away from the Kuwaiti border toward Basra. Thereafter, they moved by road and rail to the Tallil and Nasariyah areas before dispersing and digging in on October 13. Iraq had fully withdrawn by the time the United States eased back the flow of forces to the Gulf and converted its emergency deployment into the Vigilant Warrior exercise. The two Republican Guard divisions had again been entrained or loaded onto HETs and returned to their cantonments in central Iraq. They left amid "logistical chaos and monumental traffic jams" with far less aplomb than they arrived.[52]

Both sides learned a great deal from the October crisis. On the Iraqi side, Saddam appears to have been surprised that the U.S. committed so many forces—alerting a three-division ground force, 155,000 personnel, and a total of 350 aircraft for possible deployment—and managed to deploy forces and close the window of opportunity as quickly as it did. (Thirteen thousand combat troops were on the ground in Kuwait by October 20.)[53] The U.S. reaction was particularly surprising given its simultaneous military commitments in Bosnia, Haiti, and Korea. However, Saddam must also have noticed that there were few immediate or painful costs to pay for his bold maneuver. For the United States, the October crisis was as concerning as it was embarrassing. For however short a time, Kuwait had been exposed to Iraqi aggression as a result of Iraq's ability to operate inside the decision-and-deployment cycles of the United States. This prompted a new January 1995 version of the National Intelligence Estimate, *Iraqi Military Capabilities through 1999*. On intentions, the estimate stated, "Given Saddam's record of unpredictability, no agency is willing to completely rule out his attempting another high-risk military confrontation." On capabilities, the fear of another "Basra breakout" had a clear effect on the U.S. assessment, which concluded: "The military intelligence community believes Iraq has at least some chance of quickly mounting a multi-division attack that could successfully penetrate deep enough into Saudi Arabia to damage oil facilities in the Al Jubayal/Dharan area."[54]

On October 15 the United States secured the approval of UNSC Resolution 949, which ordered Iraq to move its forces back to their late-September positions and forbade any future augmentation of its military forces in the no-fly-zone areas south of 32°N. This would allow JTF-SWA forces to react forcefully to future Iraqi troops movements in the south. To enforce the new resolution, the United States accepted a Kuwaiti invitation to permanently base A-10 and F-16 ground-attack aircraft at the al-Jaber air base.[55]

STRUGGLE TO MAINTAIN CONTAINMENT

While Iraq and the Coalition mounted confrontations in the diplomatic and military spheres in the years following Desert Storm, an unseen intelligence and covert-operations war had been quietly unfolding in tandem. As early as August 3, 1990, President Bush signed a presidential "finding," which authorized the CIA to engage in hazardous foreign operations to secure regime change in Iraq. This finding had subsequently been maintained under President Clinton.[56] Saddam Hussein's intelligence agencies, for their part, had been particularly vigilant for signs of internal unrest since the Gulf War, and had uncovered an alarming series of plots during 1991–94 within areas of the Iraqi state previously considered as bastions of regime loyalists. The regime's loyalist tribes were increasingly alienated. Coup plotting had been detected even within the Republican Guard, and by 1996, well-founded suspicions would even fall on members of Saddam's own al-Tikriti tribal federation, his personal household, and the Special Republican Guard (SRG).[57]

In one sense, therefore, the power-hungry factions of the Iraqi regime offered U.S. intelligence agencies a rich menu of potential collaborators, but the CIA was simply not up to the job. Since Iraq's invasion of Kuwait, Iraq had been considered a "denied area" by the CIA and was certainly a very dangerous counterintelligence environment in which to run operatives and agents. The liberated Kurdish zone in the north, although seeded with Baathist agents, was the exception, but it was not until September 1994 that the CIA Iraq Operations Group set up a station there. It was a small one, at that, and was described by its head, Robert Baer, as "a Potemkin office."[58] CIA operatives rotated every seven weeks, rarely gaining sufficient time to settle into the environment. Most important, the CIA had no agents of worth in the senior echelons of the Iraqi government, and their potential contribution to regime change in Iraq was rated low by the U.S. administration. National Security Adviser Lake related: "Though there was no solution for regime change except covert means, these would have made the Bay of Pigs look like the six-week German conquest of France [in 1940]."[59]

Although reflective of administration disinterest in such schemes, Lake's characterization of the failure-prone coup and uprising attempts of the Iraqi opposition was an accurate one. The first major, externally planned attempt at regime change was led by Ahmed Chalabi's Iraqi National Congress (INC) émigré movement. Based near Irbil, the INC sought to generate a rolling coup by synchronizing a leadership strike by regime elements inside Baathist Iraq with a simultaneous uprising by the Kurdistan Democratic Party (KDP) and Patriotic Union of Kurdistan (PUK) militias in the north.

As CIA Operative Baer related, the plan, named "Endgame," did not receive U.S. administration backing, yet Chalabi threw the dice anyway and hoped that the United States would protect the uprising with northern no-fly-zone forces if the rebellion gathered sufficient momentum. This was an unlikely prospect considering that the Turkish government, which hosted the U.S. aircraft positioned to patrol the northern no-fly zone, was fighting a full-fledged counterinsurgency campaign against its own Kurdish guerillas in nearby eastern Turkey and remained sensitive to any Kurdish military activism. Furthermore, from the outset, the plan's delicate timing was thrown out. The coup element of the plan—a strike on Saddam launched by elements of an armored training unit stationed in Saddam's hometown of Auja and elements of three regular-army divisions—stalled because of KDP hesitation and ongoing bad blood over the miniature civil war that had smoldered between the Kurdish factions since 1994. In addition to delaying the execution of the coup attempt, which was shelved and attempted unsuccessfully in the fall of 1996, the KDP forces did not join the PUK in attacking Iraqi forces along the Green Line. This prompted the PUK to abandon the effort after three nights of successful ground operations and the overrun of two Iraqi army brigades and numerous artillery positions.[60] Controversy over the CIA role in fomenting the failed 1995 uprising, the eventual failure of the CIA-backed 1996 coup attempt, and a leadership vacuum in the agency's Iraq operations in the summer of that year left the CIA "spinning its wheels" by the fall of 1996, when Saddam chose to make his next military move.[61]

The Baathist regime had wintered many internal and external crises since the Gulf War, not least of which were the defection of Saddam's influential son-in-law Hussein Kamil in 1995 and the family rifts caused by his eventual execution when he made an ill-advised return to Iraq later that year. Although Hussein Kamil's revelations about Iraq's ongoing concealment of WMD gave a shot in the arm to UN inspections and sanctions just as they appeared to be winding down, Saddam still had reason to maintain a relatively optimistic and, as ever, aggressive outlook. There were signs that containment was loosening, if not failing, which was a subject of heated debate within the Clinton administration's interagency group of Iraq specialists in the spring and summer of 1996. Recognizing that his attempt to wait out the end of UN inspections had failed with Hussein Kamil's defection, Saddam instead turned his attention to how sanctions could be manipulated to his advantage. For five years, Saddam had resisted a UN scheme called the "Oil-for-Food Program" (OFP), which would allow Iraq to legally sell oil. The funds would enter a UN escrow account and be spent on food and humanitarian support ordered for the Iraqi people by the Baathist government, and assistance to the Kurdish zone, as well as reparations to Kuwait and other international claimants. Baghdad had instead assumed that the global oil markets could not do without Iraqi oil and that Iraq would eventually have to be given unconstrained permission to sell its oil. However, the international oil markets quickly made up the Iraqi shortfall and Saddam belatedly accepted the arrangement in 1996, recognizing that there were two key diplomatic benefits promised by the program.

First, the commencement of the OFP appeared to mark the beginning of Iraq's return to the international community, a development that a number of Arab nations had been calling for throughout the mid-1990s. More important, OFP gave Iraq a means to curry favor in the international community, through its distribution of contracts (called OFP "vouchers") to different countries, and on a regional level, where certain neighboring countries stood to gain from the increased oil exports. Until 1996, the Baathist regime had used the trickle of illegal trucked-oil exports to win influence in Amman, Ankara, and the KDP territories bordering Turkey. Oil transportation was now big business, and as early as February 1996, Saddam's envoys entered into financial and political discussions with the KDP to ensure the Kurdish faction's role in protecting northern export pipe lines from the Kirkuk oil fields. The newly elected Turkish government likewise drew closer to Saddam, looking forward to increased transit revenues and welcoming closer Iraq-KDP-Turkish relations.

The PUK remained the "odd man out" in this arrangement. Although Ankara had grown relatively comfortable with Masoud Barzani's pragmatic KDP, it remained "daggers drawn" with Jalal Talabani's more pan-Kurdish PUK, which was suspected of harboring Kurdish militants from Turkey. The PUK was engaged in internecine warfare with the KDP that claimed approximately three thousand lives by December 1995. It had also earned the intractable hostility of Baghdad because of its close relations with Iran, as well as its hosting of opposition figures and its overt involvement in the March 1995 attempt to topple the regime. Destruction of the PUK enclave and an Iraq-KDP power-sharing arrangement in northern Iraq thus formed the base of what veteran Iraq-watcher Amatzia Baram termed "the Ankara-KDP-Iraq triangle."[62]

SADDAM'S INVASION OF KURDISTAN

Iraq could not have chosen a better place or time to confront the United States than the Kurdish north in the fall of 1996. Washington's attention to Iraqi issues was distracted by a potential crisis brewing between China and Taiwan, and the hiatus of CIA activities in northern Iraq reduced the information flow emerging from the area. The annual summer slowdown was underway within the Washington beltway, and the impending U.S. presidential elections dominated schedules. Few on-the-shelf plans existed for the political complexity of the situation in northern Iraq that precluded preparatory military planning and made Turkish host-nation support for the operation an uncertain prospect. As late summer came, the U.S.-brokered cease-fire agreements between the Kurdish factions were disintegrating as quickly as Saddam's ties to the KDP were blossoming. Always a melting pot of interest and identity groups, the Kurdish north had become a considerably more violent and complicated scene since the heyday of the KRG elections in May 1992.

The latest crisis began in June 1996 when the KDP murdered the head of a subordinate Kurdish tribe within its territories, the Sourchi, who threw their 1,200 fighters in with the PUK. Sensing the PUK's impending economic and perhaps military isolation, Jalal Talabani launched an offensive in early August against the KDP headquarters at Salaheddin and the nearby city of Irbil. After securing Tehran's permission to skirt through Iranian territory to bypass KDP forces, the PUK and Sourchi forces experienced complete tactical success: they routed the KDP and captured both Salaheddin and Irbil. Masoud Barzani, faced with a catastrophic defeat, sent envoys to Saddam Hussein on August 18 to secure the assistance of Iraqi forces in rolling back the PUK gains.[63] U.S. officials were dismayed. The KDP, a "client" of the United States, had chosen to appeal to Saddam rather than the United States for assistance. Bruce Riedel, who was then the assistant secretary of defense for Near East, recounted: "The Kurdish infighting was something of a surprise. We knew they were feuding but we never guessed one would go so far as to invite Saddam in. It was remarkable even by Middle Eastern standards— like inviting the fox into the chicken coop. Overall, the administration was positively disgusted with the Kurds. How could you be so stupid as to ask in the neighbors, who you know do not have your best interests at stake? It caused a very distinct frost in relations."[64]

Although a Baathist military operation in the Kurdish zone carried some risk of upsetting Iraq's apparent international rehabilitation, strong strategic incentives offset these factors and Saddam did not hesitate to seize the opportunity. From a security viewpoint, an incursion into the north offered an opportunity to evict the CIA toehold in Iraq, strike powerfully at the INC and other external opposition groups, erase Iran's increasingly overt presence in the north, and deal a series of blows to the PUK. According to Amatzia Baram, a northern expedition also provided "an easy military victory as a way to stamp out growing discontent" within the Republican Guard.[65] As evidenced by the vast quantities of booty in their possession when Iraqi forces attempted to retreat from Kuwait in 1991, Iraq's authorities perpetuated a long and thriving tradition of encouraging its military forces to loot. This resulted in the Iraqi officer's customary adage, "The heads of the people are for me; their property is for you."[66] For the Republican Guard, an invasion of Kurdistan promised a professional and economic windfall. At the political level, the invasion aimed to show the Iraqi people and the world that Saddam was a powerful military leader. The trick, Saddam knew from his October 1994 experience, would be to use surprise and rapid deployment to enter and leave the Kurdish north before international opinion mobilized.

Iraq's armed forces were well-configured and well-deployed to undertake this mission. Since the Kurdish militias became organized fighting forces in the 1960s, the Iraqi state had traditionally kept two thirds of its military divisions in the north. This remained true in 1996.[67] There was no "no-drive zone" circumscribing military deployments in the north, and U.S. intelligence assets were instead primarily focused on detecting indicators of military mobilization facing Kuwait.[68] In the north, the first vague reports of Iraqi preparations were detected by the residual CIA presence on August 20. Discernable indicators and specific warnings of a major military effort only became evident to the CIA chief of station in Saleheddin on August 27–28, and this was the impetus for the beginning of the CIA evacuation. In the ten days since the KDP requested Iraqi help, Baghdad assembled elements of four Republican Guard divisions—the Medina armored division, the Abed mechanized division, and the Adnan and Baghdad infantry divisions—and alerted six regular-army divisions along the Green Line south of Irbil. On August 29, DIA detected these large tank movements using satellite imagery, which confirmed the CIA's HUMINT reports.[69] The PUK reported that Irbil was being shelled by Iraqi long-range artillery on August 30, which was the beginning of the operation.

On the night of August 31, an Iraqi armored spearhead thrust northward across the Green Line and up the four-lane highway linking al-Kuwayr to Irbil. The multidivision force overcame a rear guard of PUK and INC fighters south of Irbil and was safely ensconced within the city within hours, having suffered around two hundred casualties. KDP forces attacked the city from the west, north, and east, and linked up with the regime's forces at the governor's palace to hold a liaison.[70] The Iraqi security and intelligence services quickly and efficiently moved into exploitation mode. Iraq's military-intelligence service (al-Istikhabarat al-Askariya) summarily executed ninety-six INC fighters captured on the road to Irbil, while the Mukhabarat scoured Irbil and Salaheddin for opposition figures named on their target lists. The hastily evacuated INC offices in Saleheddin and the KRG parliament building in Irbil were ransacked and all documentation removed for analysis at intelligence centers in Mosul.[71] Saddam mobilized an additional four regular-army divisions cantoned at Chamchamel, fifty kilometers away from the PUK capital at Sulaymaniyah, which began shelling PUK positions across the Green Line. South of 36°N, Sulaymaniyah was outside the protective umbrella of the northern no-fly zone and thus vulnerable to Iraqi helicopter-gunship attacks of the sort that had rolled back PUK gains in March 1995.[72] Saddam waited to see what manner of U.S. response would be forthcoming before proceeding against the city.

OPERATION DESERT STRIKE

Thus began the story of Operation Desert Strike, the U.S. military response to Saddam's incursion and one of the most revealing and simultaneously least-analyzed military operations in modern U.S. military history. Friday, September 1, 1996, marked the beginning of the Labor Day weekend in Washington, D.C., and the Deputy Principals Committee meeting held that morning to formulate a response to Saddam's actions was sparsely attended. Seeking re-election, President Clinton was appearing at campaign rallies in Maine, and Secretary of State Christopher was traveling. CJCS Gen. John Shalikashvili was in Saudi Arabia along with CINCCENT Gen. Binneford Peay. Although National Security Adviser Lake was present, the operational planning of Desert Strike would be largely shaped by the new secretary of defense, William Perry; the vice chairman of the JSC, Gen. Joseph Ralston; and the head of the U.S. government interagency working group on Iraq, the senior director for Near East and South Asia and special assistant to the president, Ambassador Mark Parris. Once the meeting had ascertained the broad lines of the confused situation in northern Iraq, it was agreed that the United States had to launch a military response.

As it entered its final months, the first Clinton administration was at the end of its tether with Iraq, frustrated by periodic Iraqi resistance to UN inspectors and the no-fly zones, by the failure of its efforts to bring regime change in Iraq or peace between the Kurds, and by the onset of "sanctions fatigue" in many of America's former Coalition partners. As former National Security Council Iraq specialist Ken Pollack recounted: "Saddam was pushing on his box. This was a clear threat to his containment and to the Kurds. It could have made containment come apart faster. The Kurds might draw a negative conclusion if there was no consequence to Saddam's action."[73] At the same time, however, the White House was not interested in bringing Iraq to the center of public attention or escalating a military confrontation as the election campaign unfolded, and the Kurds had only themselves to blame for the consequences of their internecine struggles. As Mark Parris related, "Our response had to serve the requirements of honor and plausibility."[74]

The most directly proportional or symmetric use of force that the United States could employ would surely have been air strikes on the Iraqi forces that had invaded Kurdistan, but it became apparent from the very outset of the September 1 morning meeting that this was not a credible option. General Ralston briefed the meeting and explained that no plans existed concerning the use of air strikes directly against an Iraqi incursion in the north. He told the group that the protective umbrella extended by Operation Provide Comfort strictly applied to Iraqi air attacks and, consistent with the limited authorization granted by the Turkish host nation, no defensive plans for the Kurdish zone had been developed.[75] It was unlikely that Ankara's assent could be secured for air strikes launched from Turkish air bases. Every time the new Turkish parliament had been asked to approve Operation Provide Comfort in 1996, it had shortened the term agreed, from six months to two months and finally to thirty days. It had taken a visit from a U.S. military delegation, headed by Ralston, to persuade the government to gather enough support to once again authorize a six-month extension of the no-fly zone during the August–December 1996 period.

In addition to Ankara's interest in seeing the PUK reduced, the Turkish government remained sensitive about a U.S. Congressional block on key arms sales that was enacted in March 1996 in response to Turkey's human-rights record. Reflecting the impressions gained during Ralston's August 14–16 visit to Ankara and exploratory phone calls made by Secretary of Defense Perry to his Turkish counterpart, Operation Provide Comfort Commander Maj. Gen. Donald Lamontagne was not called upon to formally request the use of Turkish bases to strike Iraqi forces.[76]

Even if Turkish bases had been available, however, U.S. decision makers were hesitant to set unrealistic objectives or thrust forces into a confused factional struggle involving Iraqi, Kurdish, and Iranian forces. Operation Provide Comfort's small forty-eight aircraft force was not configured to launch a sustained series of strikes against enemy ground forces, nor could it count on acquiring enemy ground targets or discriminating them from friendly or neutral units. Even successful strikes offered little strategic payoff. Anthony Lake recalled "We didn't want to create an all-out fight, with the Kurds rising, that we could not win."[77] The Iraqi military had already completed its conquest of Irbil by the time the deputies' meeting convened, and, as Bruce Riedel noted, "If we destroyed another Iraqi regular army division, so what?"[78] The United States needed to land a visible strategic blow against the Baathist government for consumption by audiences at home, in foreign governments, and in Baghdad.

Because a northern option was blocked, JTF-SWA became the military command charged with executing a strike. Ralston briefed the meeting on the strike options that the Saudi-based command updated on a quarterly basis. According to Capt. Jamie Navarro, then an officer in CENTCOM J-2, the main plan was a TLAM-only strike on a handful of Iraqi leaders, suspected WMD, and military targets. A variant was an enlarged option that incorporated one hundred to two hundred sorties by tactical aircraft on forty IADS targets within the southern no-fly zone south of 32°N.[79] This option proved too expansive and was considered to represent too escalatory a step for the administration to take, especially because of "substantial" concerns that Iraq might seize hostages from among the multinational aid workers or weapons inspectors in Iraq.[80] An attack limited to the IADS fell much more squarely within the comfort zone of the administration and promised to directly benefit the United States as it faced Iraq's regenerating air defenses in the southern no-fly zone. Secretary of Defense Perry tasked General Ralston and Ambassador Parris with the development of an IADS-focused option that was "doable yet meaningful and costly to Saddam."[81]

The solution that emerged on September 1 involved the expansion of the southern no-fly zone, a coercive measure that had been under consideration by the administration and think-tank analysts for some time. Ralston and Parris consulted a JTF-SWA feasibility study on the issue that laid out the advantages and disadvantages of different variants. The report strongly discouraged the establishment of a full-country no-fly zone. If policed in the same way as the existing no-fly zones, the option would require the use of new bases in Turkey and Saudi Arabia or Jordan, and would consume half the U.S. tanker fleet as well as necessitate aerial refueling over Iraq. Furthermore, the Baghdad SuperMEZ could not be patrolled.[82] A western no-fly zone was also considered, boxing off the area west of 41° or 42° latitude, but this also relied on new Saudi or Jordanian bases that, as with the full-country option, were not offered for use.[83]

The creation of a northern no-drive zone or the southward extension of the northern no-fly zone to 35°N (encompassing Sulaymaniyah) or 34°N (encompassing all of Kurdistan) had been mentioned in Washington think-tank pieces but were not covered in the JTF-SWA paper. Considering the dismal failure of the northern no-fly zone to protect the Kurds, it is unsurprising that these were not considered by the U.S. government. Instead, the choice came down to a northward extension of the Operation Southern Watch area to either 34°N (encompassing Baghdad) or 33°N (ending in Baghdad's southern suburbs). The former option would require U.S. KC-135 tankers to refuel U.S. patrols inside Iraq and was quickly discounted because of the strain it would place on tankers and combat search-and-rescue capabilities. As JTF-SWA Commander Maj. Gen. Kurt Anderson noted, "33N stretched it; 34N would have broken it."[84]

As chair of the Iraq interagency working group, Ambassador Parris recommended that the no-fly zone be extended sixty-nine miles northward from 32°N to 33°N. The justification would be that the United States intended to impose a strategic cost on Saddam at a time and place of Washington's choosing and in a way that directly benefited the United States. From a military-technical point of view, the swath of territory between 32°N and 33°N contained key IrAF training ranges and some of Iraq's most important air-defense headquarters Reflecting on Parris' ability to make a virtue out of a necessity, Ken Pollack remarked, "He could make a silk purse out of a sow's ear."[85]

The new concept of operations—to degrade Iraqi IADS capabilities between 32°N and 33°N in anticipation of an immediate expansion of no-fly-zone policing—was accepted. Perry ordered the JSC to assemble a list of significant IADS targets in the planned no-fly zone south of 33°N, using the newly established targeting office at the Joint Staff Directorate of Intelligence, known as J-2T. Normally, senior decision makers would set the objectives and target sets, and leave the combatant command (CENTCOM) and its air component (CENTAF or JTF-SWA) to plan the targets, but Perry concentrated these functions within the Deputy Principals Committee during Desert Strike. The committee got "pretty in the weeds ... down to a pretty elaborate level of detail," according to Bruce Riedel.[86] This was possible because of both the small size of the operation and the increased availability of targeting information in Washington, D.C. Maj. Gen. Glen Shaffer, former director of intelligence to the Joint Chiefs, explained:

> In those kinds of operations—where there are such a small number of targets—you are always going to get more interest from senior decision-makers, because they can actually comprehend the whole target set. They have access to all the details. When we first developed digital image libraries and moved imagery onto file servers, from around 1993, we went through a period, an era, where people in many places felt open to building target lists, so you'd get target lists come at you from CIA, and target lists come at you from DIA, and from components. There was no reason why people anywhere couldn't build a target list. It was enabled largely by information technology that allows people anywhere, including inside the beltway, to be able to see what's going on anywhere in the world, to get imagery from anywhere in the world, to learn targets systems and do target systems analysis. . . . Any level of command anywhere can get access to target quality information.[87]

CENTCOM planners were ordered to strike as many of the IADS targets south of 33°N as possible to clear the way for expanded no-fly-zone policing.

The use of tactical aircraft was an integral part of the plan to strip air defenses out of the new zone, which would allow simultaneous strikes against relatively large numbers of IADS targets. Recall that JTF-SWA identified forty high-value IADS targets south of 32°N before it even began to look in the target-rich areas between 32°N and 33°N. In 1996, the United States did not maintain constant (or "1.0") aircraft-carrier coverage in the Gulf, and the nearest carrier, the USS *Carl Vinson* (CVN 70), could not move to the necessary location to launch air strikes until September 4. The United States was instead relying on the one hundred or so Saudi- and Kuwaiti-based aircraft of JTF-SWA. However, for the first and only time since the end of the Cold War, the United States experienced a total lock-out of all its local basing options because of host-nation opposition to the strike. CENTCOM's original TLAM-only plan had been designed with such a scenario in mind, recognizing the growing discomfort felt by regional allies over the U.S. use of force against Iraq.

By Saturday, September 2, it was clear that the attack would have to be planned as a cruise-missile-only operation. In low-profile discussions, the United States learned that the Sunni elites of Jordan and the Gulf nations were unwilling to host strikes on Iraq's Sunni government merely to support the country's Kurdish separatists. Kuwait, Jordan, and Qatar made their unwillingness clear by Saturday, September 2, at which time Saudi Arabia also formally declined to take part in the strikes. In addition to the sectarian aspect, Riyadh's decision was also symptomatic of a broader cooling of relations between the U.S. and Saudi militaries. One cause was Saudi Arabia's discomfort with the ongoing costs of U.S. military presence in the Gulf, which the kingdom shared with the United States and Kuwait. According to Col. David Frazee, the CENTAF political adviser in 1994, the Saudi military had viewed the October 1994 Vigilant Warrior deployment of U.S. forces as "a disaster, costing them a non-trivial amount of money, tens of millions of dollars, at a time when their defense budget was tightening and they faced cuts."[88] Following the June 24, 1996, Khobar Towers bombing of U.S. facilities in Dharan, which killed 19 U.S. personnel and injured 270, the movement of JTF-SWA to the remote Prince Sultan Air Base (PSAB) at al-Kharj was another factor that reduced U.S. liaisons with the Saudis and allowed a more distant relationship to develop.[89]

As former CENTAF Commander Horner noted, "The 1996 Iraqi crisis demonstrated that foreign base access cannot be taken for granted. Once Jordan, Saudi Arabia, and Turkey opted out, the entire land-based fighter force was effectively neutralized, leaving U.S. military capabilities seriously circumscribed."[90] One JTF-SWA pilot remarked, "We had guys in theater who had been running in every day on the targets that got hit in Desert Strike, but they had to sit out the attack because of host nation problems."[91]

Because U.S. B-52 and B-1B bombers did not yet possess robust precision-bombing capabilities, and because the new B-2 stealth bomber was not operationally available for CENTCOM tasking, the sole remaining alternative-delivery means available to the U.S. was ship-, submarine-, and air-launched land-attack cruise missiles. Task Force 50 (TF-50), a small flotilla of two TLAM-capable vessels, was present in the Gulf when the United States adopted the cruise-missile-only option, and three other TLAM-capable vessels from the USS *Vinson* carrier battle group were inbound and able to contribute to any strike.

The U.S. Air Force, meanwhile, did not have B-52s stationed at either RAF Fairford in the United Kingdom or the British-owned Indian Ocean air base of Diego Garcia, nor did it have time to secure overflight and foreign-basing permissions for a deployment of CALCM-armed bombers. Instead, it welcomed the chance to deploy a pair of B-52s on the longest "global strike" mission to date, which would be launched directly from the continental United States (CONUS) via the U.S. air base at Guam.[92] The readjustment of the evolving IADS target set to suit the characteristics of a cruise-missile-only operation entailed extra work and precluded Perry's ordered execution date of September 2, which was initially preferred to maintain the closest linkage between Saddam's crime and the admittedly disconnected punishment. Nonetheless, the extra effort was considered worthwhile because confidence had grown in the technical capabilities of conventionally armed cruise missiles since their debut in Desert Storm. Furthermore, the secretary of defense was an aficionado of their capabilities. Bruce Riedel commented, "Bill Perry was the father of the Tomahawk missile; whatever doubts others had about the cost-effectiveness of TLAM, he didn't."[93]

Sunday, September 2, was a grueling day for U.S. military planners as they attempted to stretch the vastly reduced number of weapons at their disposal to meet the secretary of defense's requirements. Perry's guidance to CENTCOM had been unusual, because instead of stating a military objective (say, "reduce air defenses in the area 32°N to 33°N"), he had provided a target list and a list of weapons to be used. Late on September 1, CENTCOM planners pushed back, arguing that to make the new no-fly zone safe, the United States would also need to hit SAMs and radar threats that were physically located north of 33°N but that could ellipse the new zone. CENTCOM also requested that the State Department issue a poststrike démarche warning Iraq against firing or illuminating from "across the line."[94] However, Washington decision makers stuck to their guidance on targets south of 33°N to maintain the "conceptual clarity" of the strike.[95] Mathew McKeon wrote, "The Iraqi IADS, in other words, had to be targeted functionally, not geographically. . . . The National Command Authorities chose a targeting strategy that ignored hostile air defense threats just north of the 33rd parallel, leaving large sections of the new no-fly zone still exposed to some very capable threats."[96]

Perry's guidance was a throwback to the days before Lieutenant Colonel Deptula's use of effects-based targeting in Desert Storm. The 1996 strikes focused on *quantitative* strikes on every node of a system rather than *qualitative* degradation of the system as a whole: they stressed physical destruction over functional degradation. Additional concerns over the likely effectiveness of the attack were raised during the frantic September 2 preparations for the strike, when a CIA operative recalled, "There was a debate taking place on the issue of effect."[97] The numbers of TLAMs and CALCMs available were a key limiting factor, and CENTCOM calculated that they could reliably launch fourteen TLAMs and sixteen CALCMs in the September 3 strike.

Previous cruise-missile strikes had assigned three or even four missiles to each DMPI and allowed the number of missiles available to dictate the size of the target set. The opposite occurred in Desert Strike, and the number of targets designated in the Washington EXECORD did not allow anywhere near this level of redundancy. According to CENTCOM J-2 Colonel Cochran, CENTCOM whittled Washington's target list down from more than thirty to eighteen and finally to fifteen DMPIs, allowing two missiles and a projected 70-percent kill rate per aimpoint.[98] JTF-SWA Commander Major General Anderson recalled: "There was a lot of guidance coming down from on-high. Weapons effects were less important than the political goal of responding in a timely fashion. My folks told me that we weren't going to achieve the levels of destruction that were needed to shut those targets down. There was an emphasis on hitting more targets but the limiting factor was the number of cruise missiles we had available. We would have liked to wait for more missile shooters to arrive or hit less targets and concentrate the available missiles on the C2 targets."[99]

As Anderson noted, the types of targets being attacked were also a complicating factor that did not bode well for the success of the mission. The IADS targets on CENTCOM's initial strike option had mostly been assigned to tactical aircraft because of the ability of manned aircraft to make minor targeting corrections against targets than had slightly shifted positions. Manned strikes could also drop munitions capable of destroying hardened or buried targets such as SOCs, IOCs, and buried communications cables. When planning the January 1993 strikes, CENTCOM had previously rejected a TLAM-only option "because of the mobile systems that move about and the command bunkers," which alluded to the unsuitability of cruise missiles for these purposes. In September 1996, however, a wide range of targets needed to be hit to make the new no-fly zone safe, which meant that TLAMs or CALCMs had to be used against targets for which they were not designed. Seven hardened or buried command, control, or communications (C3) aimpoints were slated for attack by cruise missiles. The remaining targets consisted of eight soft but relocateable SA-2 and SA-3 batteries, and radar sites, which were typically spread out over a kilometer or so of ground. Launchers and radar equipment were dispersed and rotated among large numbers of Iraq's ubiquitous horseshoe-shaped protective sand berms. The CIA representative on the Deputies Committee stated that, in the agency's view, Iraq's increasingly frequent shuffling of these systems made it unlikely that they would still be in the same berms by the time U.S. missiles reach their aimpoints. This prompted an increased effort to regularly revalidate these targets until H-Hour.[100]

Throughout Sunday, September 2, specialist cruise-missile planners in Virginia, Hawaii, Nebraska, and Bahrain struggled to program the missiles on time. TLAM planners aimed to compete and lock down their targeting process eight hours before launch. The two B-52Hs began their nineteen-hour approach from Guam long before their mission planning had been completed and their CALCMs received their targeting and mission profiles "on the pylon" via satellite communications, which provided dynamic targeting updates throughout the flight. Although only thirty missiles needed to be programmed against fifteen targets in the September 3 attacks, the effort consumed the entire U.S. cruise-missile planning community and would not have been possible without post–Desert Storm upgrades to the cruise-missile inventory and planning systems. All the missiles used on September 3 were GPS-guided versions. Although CALCMs had always relied on satellite guidance, TLAMs planners benefited greatly from their ability to make the first use of Block III GPS-guided Tomahawks against Iraq. This meant that the specialist Tomahawk mission-planning cells did not have to undertake the time-consuming process of updating the terrain contour matching (TERCOM) maps that older missiles used to navigate to the approximate vicinity (within six hundred feet) of their target because they had switched to the very accurate digital scene-matching area correlator (DSMAC) for terminal guidance. The main workload came from the need to generate DSMAC images for the mobile-target sites, many of which were new targets. This involved the rendering of overhead multispectral satellite imagery into a three-dimensional "Tomahawk-eye view" of the target.[101] Once completed, the mission packages were transmitted directly to the missiles using new digital mission-distribution upgrades rather than the Desert Storm–era hand-delivered mission packages.[102]

At approximately 0800 Baghdad time on September 3, the USS *Laboon* (DDG 58) and USS *Shiloh* (CG 67) successfully executed their fourteen planned TLAM launches. The two 96th Bombardment Squadron B-52Hs began launching their CALCMs from a launch box off the coast of Kuwait, and sent thirteen missiles toward their targets. Three malfunctioned and were not fired. At 0925, air-raid sirens began to blare across southern Iraq as the twenty-seven cruise missiles struck their targets almost simultaneously. GPS guidance had been faultless throughout the mission, with each of the GOS-guided missiles drawing simultaneous guidance from at least seven Navstar satellites throughout their flights.[103]

The small strike was supported by a bevy of BDA assets, including tethered monitoring of the strike by a U.S. Air Force/CIA Lacrosse SAR satellite, a CIA Keyhole-11 electro-optical imagery satellite, and ELINT-collection assets. Although cloud cover obscured many targets, the cloud-penetrating SAR and ELINT gave the United States an early "cut" with which to judge the mission's performance. Aside from the three failed CALCM launches, the arrival rate and accuracy of U.S. cruise missiles was impressive. None crashed or were intercepted. GPS guidance freed mission planners of the need to follow the TERCOM-friendly routes that had in earlier years seen the United States send missiles along mountain ranges fifty miles inside Iran or predictably drive them down Iraqi pipelines and major roads or wadis on their way to Baghdad, where they were occasionally intercepted. GPS and enhanced DSMAC guidance delivered most of the missiles to within thirty-nine feet of their aimpoints. The problems instead started when they got there.

In some cases, the strikes were ineffective because of avoidable planning oversights caused by the compressed timeframe of the operation. An incorrectly programmed CALCM ignored its aimpoint and automatically flew to its secondary target, while the other missile assigned to that original aimpoint missed, leaving that target unscathed. Despite last-minute efforts of stateside planners to get the missile reprogrammed before flight, a TLAM needlessly struck an empty berm where Iraqi radar had been observed leaving shortly before the launch. Other cruise missiles struck a disused IOC that had not been operational since 1991, again despite the efforts of Pentagon analysts to cancel the target.[104] A CALCM variant loaded with a type of cluster-bomb submunitions was used against a slab-sided hardened building—an ideal target for the standard CALCM.[105] Some missiles simply could not penetrate their underground targets.

The problem had been that CENTCOM—lacking strong in-house expertise in cruise-missile targeting—had parceled targets out to the separate CALCM and TLAM planning communities that did not suit the characteristics and explosive packages of each type of missile. Lacking any means to communicate or reassign targets, each community had done the best it could in the short time available to it. Although cloud cover had concealed some successes, particularly from hard-to-spot submunitions damage against radars, the attacks were not particularly successful and the initial BDA assessment of "moderate overall damage" put a brave face on the outcome. Only five of eight SAM and radar sites had been hit, and individual systems had survived at these sites thanks to the protection offered by sand berming and constant movement. Of the C3 aimpoints, only one was destroyed, four were damaged, and two escaped damage.[106] Military and lower-level civilian participants in Washington were not surprised by the results, but the administration was disappointed.[107]

An immediate restrike launched on the morning of September 4 hit four aimpoints with a heavy spread of seventeen TLAMs that were fired from arriving U.S. Navy ships. Up to fifteen of the missiles hit the three existing and one new target with pinpoint accuracy, although, again, military commanders observers that the match of weapons to targets was suboptimal. The strike phase of the operation was a means to an end, however. Although it already had the whiff of military-technical failure about it, the real test of its effectiveness would come when the United States asserted its presence in the newly expanded no-fly zone. Had the Iraqi air defenses been suppressed?

JTF-SWA was formally ordered to prepare for operations in the new slice of no-fly zone on September 3 and received the final clearance after the September 4 re-strike. By this time, the USS *Carl Vinson* had arrived in the Gulf, and a mixture of land-based and carrier-based tactical aircraft was inserted into the new zone. Initial indicators looked encouraging as Iraq responded to President Clinton's September 3 announcement of the enlarged zone by relocating northward twenty-three of the forty-six fixed-wing aircraft that had been based south of 33°N. This total probably represented the only aircraft that could be suddenly made airworthy for the short flight.[108] The initial Coalition package (minus French aircraft, which were not authorized by Paris to fly north of 32°N) was heavy on air-to-air assets, and quickly spotted two Iraqi MiG-29 aircraft that scrambled and attempted to lure the Coalition package into a SAMbush near the 33°N line. Postured for combat and expecting a fight, Coalition aircraft held the new line and avoided the SAMbush, patrolling airspace that no Coalition aircraft had entered since 1991.

It would not be long, however, before Iraq demonstrated its intent to mount more dangerous SAMbushes at times and places of its choosing. For example, it targeted a two-ship formation of F-16s northwest of Mosul on September 11, 1996 and mounted a no-notice SA-6 missile attack. Briefly bursting its radar to generate initial target acquisition, the SA-6 was ballistically fired toward its target until its integral semiactive radar-homing warhead activated and locked on to the F-16s. This necessitated that the F-16s take an evasive maneuver so extreme that one of them suffered structural damage and needed to be respined,[109] (i.e., the aircraft's structural backbone needed to be replaced). Imagery and ELINT suggested that Iraq had reactivated all the C2 nodes attacked in Desert Strike less than a month after the attack. Although the new zone did degrade IrAF capabilities and enhance U.S. ability to reconnoiter Iraq up to the suburbs of Baghdad, the military effects of Desert Strike were paltry.[110]

Although Saddam had already withdrawn most of his forces back behind the Green Line within days of the invasion and had pulled all of them out by September 14, the United States maintained a strong military presence in the Gulf throughout the remainder of 1996. The USS *Enterprise* (CVN 65) made a high-speed transit of the Suez Canal to join the USS *Carl Vinson* in the Gulf on September 6, and the latter carrier's rotation out of theater was delayed until October 6. Secretary of Defense Perry toured U.S. regional allies, garnering support for further military action should it become necessary, and issued a planning order for a mixed tactical-air and cruise-missile operation along the lines of CENTCOM's initial option under the working title, "Desert Strike II."[111] Four B-52Hs were maintained at Diego Garcia until October 28, and land-based reinforcements to JTF-SWA—F-117A Nighthawks and F-16s—remained until December 1.[112]

FALLOUT FROM THE ERA OF "TOMAHAWK DIPLOMACY"

The U.S. response to Saddam's incursion into the north met the administration's minimum requirement to "do something," and a military response was regarded by a bipartisan two-thirds majority of the U.S. public as the right thing to do, according to U.S. polls.[113] The administration stressed that the marginally successful air strikes were merely a means to an end and that the successfully expanded no-fly zones were the real focus of the operation. However, attention was inevitably drawn to the more dramatic September 3–4 air strikes. The problem, it would emerge, was that cruise-missile-only operations bore a stigma. Days after Desert Strike, CIA Director John Deutsch told the Senate Intelligence Committee that the strikes created "a perception of weakened determination of the U.S. to deter Iraqi aggression." In part, this was due to the apparently dislocated response to actions in the north by attacking enemy targets in the south, but the key reason was the exclusive use of cruise missiles. As Michael Rip and James Hasik noted, "The apparent unwillingness of the United States to send its troops in harm's way, but instead dispatch robotic munitions to do its bidding, did little to convince Saddam Hussein of a commitment to defend the Kurds."[114] In short, it was difficult to serve Parris' "requirements of honor and plausibility" with cruise missiles alone.

Even accounting for the difficult circumstances, Desert Strike had been a clumsy political-military performance by the administration. Saddam had hit on a lucky moment to meddle in Kurdistan, a moment propitious to cause the lock-out of U.S. combat forces already present in the Gulf. Building on his experience in October 1994, Saddam had expertly judged his ability to work within Washington's reaction cycle, and, as Lieutenant General Horner noted, "Saddam knew from these exercises that we could not deploy our short-range forces quickly enough to stop him from accomplishing his Irbil objectives."[115] The United States, meanwhile, limited its options by seeking to link the punishment to the crime in time rather than space. Although the administration would ill-advisedly state in public that the use of cruise missiles "was a choice of convenience, not necessity," reliance on TLAMs and CALCMs were, in fact, caused by the fragility of America's military coalition in the Gulf and Washington's unwillingness to wait until stronger afloat and global strike forces could be assembled. The resulting strike communicated weakness and vacillation, and reflected badly on the military power, particularly the airpower, of the United States. As Elliot Cohen had foreseen in 1994, the coin that airpower had earned in Desert Storm could be quickly spent if frittered away in small and inconsequential strikes: "Air power is an unusually seductive form of military strength, in part because, like modern courtship, it appears to offer gratification without commitment.... American air power has a mystique that it is in America's interest to retain. When Presidents use it, they should either hurl it with devastating lethality against a few targets or extensively enough to cause sharp and lasting pain to a military and a society."[116]

In addition to the military-technical fallout, the September 1996 crisis and the general course of military events since Desert Storm had important political ramifications for Iraq's containment. While the United States was building up its forces in the Gulf in a show of force after Desert Strike, less-visible retrograde movements were underway within Iraq. When Saddam's forces left, they left as victors, piled high with loot, intelligence, and prisoners, the latter of which would often never be seen again. The CIA's exit from Iraq had been ignominious in comparison, and in the weeks and months after the crisis, more than a thousand opposition figures would be quietly evacuated from the Kurdish zone and flown to Guam in an operation code named Quick Transit. Although the PUK bounced back as quickly as ever, reclaiming its lost territory by mid-October 1996, U.S. relations with the Kurdish factions had been soured. White House Spokesman Michael McCurry stated that defending the Kurds from Saddam and themselves had been "a difficult and, obviously somewhat tragically, impossible process."[117] On September 4, the multinational Military Coordination Committee (MCC) at Zakho disbanded. Alan Makovsky noted at the time, "The MCC had been a statement of U.S. and allied support and resolve in the area. For the first time since 1991, there is no U.S. ground presence in Iraq."[118] The United States and its allies had been chased out of the north, and it would be six years before they returned in force.

Saddam's apparent military strength on the ground and in the north compared favorably to the United States'. National Security Council Analyst Ken Pollack stated that "Desert Strike and earlier crises showed that when Saddam pushed, we couldn't push back."[119] The trimmed-down Iraqi military performed efficiently and emerged well-exercised and content, and Saddam "reasserted his ability to use military force, bolstering his stature amongst his troops, and further fracturing the Gulf coalition."[120]

Although the speed of America's reaction may have surprised Saddam and even thrown off a possible follow-on attack on Sulaymaniyah, there would be few negative consequences to deter him from future resistance. Saddam's regional profile appeared to be reviving and it was notable that the KDP turned to Baghdad rather than Washington when the PUK threatened it. Conversely, as the Clinton administration hawks had warned in spring and summer 1996, containment appeared to be weakening. Former State Department Director for Persian Gulf Affairs Steve Grummon recalled: "It was impossible to keep Iraq off the front pages. Saddam seemed to have the initiative, and time proved to be the great destroyer of policy. We couldn't just hold the line." In recognition of the darkening picture, the December 1996 Intelligence Community Brief, *Iraq Regime Prospects for 1997*, concluded:

> Some governments interpret the return of Iraqi oil to the world market as a signal that Iraq is emerging from its isolation and that a crack in sanctions is emerging. . . . Some Arab states such as Syria and Oman are beginning to call for Iraq's reintegration into the Arab fold. Baghdad's relations with Ankara have improved considerably, with border traffic up to the highest level since 1990. . . . Baghdad has utilized [Oil-for-Food] contracts to boost influence with Jordan and Turkey, especially useful as Saddam attempts to rebuild relations with Amman following the Hussein Kamil debacle and to secure Ankara's support on northern Iraq.[121]

7

"Cheat and Retreat"
Iraq's Resistance to UN Inspections

After staving off coups, uprisings, and a handful of U.S. military actions, Saddam Hussein's regime had regained its balance by 1997 and now initiated a slow-burning program aimed at weakening economic sanctions and hamstringing the UNSCOM inspections effort.[1] "Sanctions fatigue" had become increasingly evident among America's UNSC partners and its Arab allies. However, the end of sanctions could only follow a clean bill of health issued by UNSCOM that stated that Iraq had accounted for all missing WMD and had curtailed all its proscribed scientific programs. Building on the partial normalization in Iraq's commercial relations with many countries as the UN-administered OFP began generating funds and contracts, Saddam aimed to wear down international resolve to maintain sanctions by drawing the United States into a series of military standoffs. As usual, Saddam demonstrated a faith in the road of resistance and defiance rather than accommodation, and his "cheat-and-retreat" tactics were simple but effective: the United States would be drawn into expending political capital at the UNSC and carrying out costly military deployments to the Gulf, but Saddam would back down shortly before the United States resorted to the use of force.

Saddam had come as close as he ever would to a relaxation of UN inspections toward the end of the 1991–94 period, when the UNSCOM effort had delivered appreciable results and Iraq's unconventional-weapons threat appeared to many nations to be fading. As the post–Cold War era

developed, early fears of "loose nukes" or nuclear materials for sale, or nuclear scientists for hire, receded to some extent. Baghdad's advanced indigenous nuclear-weapons program had been razed down to its roots in a dynamic
intelligence-led campaign of inspections, with all known highly enriched uranium or plutonium materials having been removed and all identified industrial
elements having been destroyed. In the sphere of biological weapons, Iraq's
planned custom-built biological-weapons factory complex at al-Hakim had
been converted into a nonmilitary facility, its specialized equipment removed,
and its premises placed under regular inspection. Reflecting Anglo-American
assessments, the classified September 8, 1994, estimate by the British Joint
Intelligence Committee (JIC) claimed that Iraq had no stocks of biological
agents suitable for weaponization, although it could quickly regenerate its
program if inspections on potential dual-use civilian pharmaceutical facilities ceased.

From possessing the developing world's most advanced chemical-
weapons program, Iraq had been drawn back down to the level of aspiring
chemical-weapons proliferator. UNSCOM inspectors destroyed or verified
the destruction of twenty-eight thousand chemical-weapons munitions, almost half a million liters of chemical-weapons agents, and almost two million
liters of precursors or chemicals. Iraq's well-known chemical-weapons factories had been heavily damaged in the Gulf War and many of their surviving
factory components were later destroyed by UNSCOM. Although the JIC
assessed Iraq to have some residual stocks of high-quality chemical agents,
Iraq lacked the tens of thousands of filled and maintained chemical munitions
required for effective battlefield use. Iraq could not account for all of the materials it claimed to have destroyed, but UNSCOM's search for incriminating
materials, evidence of weapons programs, or a concealment program explic-
itly tied to WMD had drawn a blank. This created the impression that Iraq
was being asked to prove a negative—that WMDs *did not exist*. The central
pillar on which sanctions, and thereby the containment of Iraq, rested was
weakening.[2]

The August 9, 1995, defection of Saddam's influential son-in-law,
Hussein Kamil, charged this dynamic and breathed new life into inspections and containment. Hussein Kamil's most important revelations concerned
the existence of a sophisticated concealment effort that protected a number
of WMD programs that were in temporary stasis rather than long-term re-
mission. His testimony reinforced Western suspicions that hard-to-replace

components and computer disks containing research and engineering data had been secreted in elaborately dispersed stashes across Iraq. Most important, he seemed to validate that Saddam intended to reactivate his "break-out" CBW capabilities as soon as inspections were relaxed.

The August 24 JIC estimate issued by the British indicated a subtle change in Coalition thinking. Although nuclear weapons remained Saddam's ultimate goal and the linchpin of Iraq's future status as a regional hegemon, the nuclear program could not be concealed or reconstituted while inspections lasted and now existed only in the human capital of Iraq's closely guarded nuclear scientists and technicians. Hussein Kamil's testimony had a dramatic effect on Western assessments of Iraq's biological-weapons ambitions and led the JIC to conclude that Iraq not only had the strong intent to reactivate its break-out capability but also possibly maintained small stocks of easily stored agents—such as dried anthrax spores—and mobile drying, grinding, and fermenting laboratories. In the field of the less-easily concealed chemical weapons and missiles, Hussein Kamil highlighted Iraq's concealment of rapid break-out capabilities behind industries operating in plain sight by claiming that Iraq planned to use hidden components and precursor stocks to convert pesticide, petrochemical, and fertilizer factories into chemical-agent production lines.

Using its existing missile-design bureaus (which conducted research into permitted systems with ranges of less than 150 kilometers), Iraq was producing missile fuel and engine components to reintegrate with components and missiles systems currently in hibernation. Two years after the end of effective inspections, the JIC announced that missiles with ranges of three hundred or five hundred kilometers, such as the Scud or al-Hussein, could be produced, whereas missiles with ranges of one thousand kilometers could be developed three to five years after UN oversight ended.[3] Whatever blend of concoction, exaggeration, obsolescence, and faithful retelling it represented, Hussein Kamil's testimony spoke to the need for an open-ended and effective program of inspections that was needed not only to find Iraq's residual WMDs but also to prevent Iraqi break-out production of new WMD and long-range delivery systems.

After Hussein Kamil's defection, Iraq released 1.5 million previously undeclared documents on its WMD programs to swamp the UNSCOM system while appearing to be cooperating. UNSCOM's focus was not be diverted by this paper chase, however, nor was it directed solely at the onerous task of searching directly for the residual components purportedly being concealed by Iraq. As a British government report on Iraqi WMD noted, "The volume of biological and chemical agents unaccounted for, even if they were all held together, would fit into a petrol tanker. If they were dispersed and hidden in small quantities, they would be even harder to discover."[4] Iraq's residual WMD components and materials were likely to be much smaller than the volume of a petrol tanker and the location of each piece was likely known only to a tiny circle. Thus, they would be impossible to locate in the absence of the most precise intelligence, which even Hussein Kamil claimed not to possess.

The loose thread that might unravel the fabric of Iraq's hibernating programs and highlight Iraqi noncompliance appeared to be the concealment mechanism itself. Composed of cells within the OPP, the Military Industrial Commission, each of the major Iraqi intelligence organizations, and the SRG, the concealment mechanism had been the subject of UNSCOM profiling since 1994 under UNSCOM Inspector Ritter. Following Hussein Kamil's revelations, the effort was increased in March 1996 with the initiation of Ritter's "Shake the Tree" strategy—a series of inspections that were specifically designed to trigger the activation of the concealment effort, which would allow UN inspectors to observe and record its activities.[5] When Australian diplomat Richard Butler replaced Rolf Ekeus as UNSCOM's chairman in July 1997, he quickly gave his backing for continuation of Ritter's provocative approach and placed Ritter at the head of the UNSCOM Special Investments Unit.[6]

Shake the Tree was the cutting edge of an intelligence war in which the Coalition military and intelligence agencies had a major part to play. UNSCOM had developed its own intelligence cell, the Information Assessment Unit, headed up by Rachel Davies, a former member of Britain's Defence Intelligence Staff (DIS). Between September 1996 and early 1998, the unit forged close working relationships with the CIA, Britain's Secret Intelligence Service (SIS), Israeli military intelligence (Aman), the German national intelligence service (Bundesnachrichtendienst), and Iraqi opposition groups.[7] Inspectors were briefed and debriefed in Bahrain before each deployment to Iraq and received intelligence on Iraq's overseas procurement efforts or satellite or U-2 imagery of potential WMD-related buildings or suspected underground hides.

Iraq's Mukhabarat also had eyes and ears in Bahrain. As Charles Duelfer, the long-time deputy head of UNSCOM, noted, "The Iraqis were amazing systems analysts" who kept files on individual inspectors. These noted their specialist roles, profiled their movements, and were used to predict the locations that would be visited on so-called "surprise inspections."[8] Potential target destinations received preemptive visits from Iraqi intelligence teams, who moved files, installed shredding machines, intimidated scientists and other staff, and slowed down inspection teams. As Ritter's unit probed the inner sanctums of the Iraqi security state, shadowed by Iraqi concealment teams, the inspectors received support from allied intelligence services. Fixed SIGINT monitoring stations and a dozen Mi-8 helicopters with SIGINT equipment from Iraq's Project 858 monitoring organization sought to intercept UNSCOM communications.[9] At the same time, SIGINT support from Britain's Government Communications Headquarters (GCHQ) listened in on the listeners and the concealment teams they supported, which were later supplemented by eavesdropping equipment planted by CIA Special Activities Staff personnel working on the UNSCOM teams.[10] UNSCOM's small fleet of helicopters and U.S. military U-2 aircraft that were loaned to UNSCOM provided near-real-time IMINT to inspectors via encrypted wireless data and voice communications. The IMINT was used to identify routes around Iraqi checkpoints and expose Iraqi attempts to destroy or evacuate document stashes.[11]

Although it offered the best chance of uncovering Iraqi deception, the aggressive intelligence-led inspections of Shake the Tree were sure to elicit a response from the Baathist government because they probed into the regime's most sensitive security organs. Between June and September 1997, Iraq obstructed Special Investigation Unit visits to several regime security sites and palaces. After months of relative quiet, Iraq's confrontation with UNSCOM flared into life again in June 1997. An Iraqi minder almost caused the crash of an UNSCOM helicopter by trying to wrest the controls away from the pilot as he flew toward a regime site. Ritter's team was blocked from entering a compound on June 21, which prompted the UNC to pass Resolution 1115. Resolution 1115 demanded that Iraq grant UNSCOM "immediate and unrestricted access" to Iraqi facilities. On September 13, Iraqi minders again almost caused the crash of an UNSCOM helicopter while trying to prevent inspectors from taking photographs while airborne, and on September 17, Ritter's team videotaped Iraqi concealment teams attempting to sanitize a facility while UN inspectors were being held outside.

A dangerous time of year was approaching. Rear Adm. John Sigler, the director of plans at CENTCOM, recalled that "every fall, near Ramadan, Saddam would provoke the U.S. This was about the time that he traditionally carried out military exercises, because it's cooler in Iraq. He'd use these exercises to move troops to his borders, bring SAM and aircraft into the no-fly zones, and threaten to shoot down our U-2s."[12]

PROTECTING THE U-2 FLIGHTS OVER IRAQ

Encouraged to develop aggressive response options by a more militarist second-term Clinton administration, it was the threat to the U-2 that galvanized CENTCOM planners in late summer 1997. Although President Bill Clinton was still determined to prevent Iraq from becoming the centerpiece of administration policy, or even its foreign policy, the administration increasingly recognized that if it wished to keep Saddam off the front pages and firmly "in his box," it would have to reestablish the administration's credibility in the region with a greater readiness to meet Iraqi resistance with an impressive show of force.

Important cabinet changes made likely a more militarist U.S. policy in Iraq. The replacement of cautious strategists such as Secretary of State Christopher and National Security Adviser Lake with the more activist Madeleine Albright and Sandy Berger, respectively, were key changes.[13] The hawkish Secretary Albright laid out an uncompromising administration position on Iraq in a landmark speech at Georgetown University on March 26, 1997. Although the address did not lay out the detailed agenda for loosening Saddam's grip on Iraq that some administration activists sought, it made clear that the United States would not permit the lifting of sanctions while Saddam remained in power and appealed to a future "successor government."[14]

Sandy Berger, meanwhile, had been much more willing to advocate military activism in Iraq than his former boss, former National Security Adviser Lake. Completing the new line-up of policy makers was Secretary of Defense William Cohen and the new CINCCENT, Marine Corps Gen. Anthony Zinni.

The new CINCCENT was pleased to prepare a new, more aggressive series of response options to punish an Iraqi attempt to shoot down the U-2 aircraft that supported UNSCOM operations. As Deputy CINCCENT, Zinni had worked closely with UNSCOM to coordinate U-2 flights and was on record as favoring military strikes on Iraq if Baghdad threatened, let alone attacked, the U-2s.[15] Cruising at approximately sixty-five thousand feet, unescorted and deep within central Iraq, the unmaneuverable U-2 was one of the only U.S. assets still highly vulnerable to interception by either an Iraqi fighter aircraft or Baghdad's SA-2 and SA-3 missiles, which made CENTCOM particularly protective of the flights.

Despite their vulnerability and repeated Iraqi threats against them since 1992, the U-2s were a vital resource for UNSCOM, which necessitated that they fly both as an exercise of UN freedom of movement in Iraq and to perform the important intelligence-gathering function. UNSCOM Chairman Rolf Ekeus recalled: "The U-2 is the workhorse. The data it provides is fundamental to UNSCOM planning. The images provide details of the hiding of production equipment and the movement of such equipment. It can systematically cover large areas of Iraq, revealing new facilities and production sites.... We need more night missions. We know the Iraqis engage in [concealment] activity when the U-2 is not flying."[16]

For starters, U.S. aircraft patrolling the no-fly zones were given special dispensation in their ROE to cross into Iraq's remaining sovereign airspace north of 33°N and south of 36°N to protect the U-2 if they were close enough to intervene. Initially, the ROE used by U.S. fighter pilots were designed by military lawyers and were overly complex: they only allowed U.S. aircraft to engage Iraqi interceptors if the Iraqis signaled hostile intent to the U-2s by moving within AAM range of the aircraft—that is, within seventy-five miles if the Iraqis were above thirty thousand feet or within forty-five miles if they were below thirty thousand feet. JTF-SWA Commander Maj. Gen. Roger Radcliff scrapped this guidance in 1997 to allow any enemy aircraft within seventy-five miles of the U-2s to be engaged, effectively creating a new seventy-five-mile wide moving "bubble" of no-fly zone that could be imposed over central Iraq up to four times a week at UNSCOM's request.[17]

Meanwhile, the threat from SAMs could only be deterred rather than intercepted. To achieve a level of deterrence, the U-2 response options designed by CENTCOM and approved by the administration would break the mold of previous Iraq operations developed under the Clinton national-security team, moving away from the first term's focus on proportionality and deliberately promising to inflict a *disproportional* level of damage on the Iraqis. Rear Admiral Sigler recalled, "The U.S. had been accused of becoming reactive, responding with pinpricks.... The U-2 response options were designed to address the shortcomings of previous strikes. Washington was saying, 'let's make this more than a pinprick, let's use lots of airplanes and TLAM, and appear to be more proactive, both for Saddam's consumption, and for the consumption of our allies in the Gulf.'"[18] On August 18, 1997, five days after taking command, CINCCENT Zinni visited UNSCOM Chairman Richard Butler to discuss Iraqi threats against the U-2s. By September 1997 five variants of a punitive strike were on the shelf at JTF-SWA, each focusing on a massive, disproportional response that would stun Iraq's leadership if it chose to strike out at America via the symbolic and vulnerable U-2s, regardless of whether the attack succeeded or failed.

According to Col. Gary Crowder, who headed the JTF-SWA Long-Range Plans section, these "super-secret" response options were merged into a single strike plan—Operation Desert Thunder I—at video-teleconferences (VTC) in September 1997. Such VTCs were to become a regular feature of the planning process over the next sixteen months. Each lasted around three or four hours and involved ten to fifteen different executive branch, military, and intelligence agencies.[19]

Desert Thunder I had been designed to punish Iraq by launching up to 250 ship- or submarine-launched TLAMs at IADS nodes in the center and south of the country. Since Operation Desert Strike, the U.S. Navy had moved to 1.0 carrier coverage in the region—meaning that a carrier battle group was constantly in the Gulf—vastly boosting the number of TLAMs available at any time for surge attacks. Desert Thunder would unleash this barrage in a single wave and would not require the use of manned aircraft. Other elements of the option satisfied the classic Clinton-era requirements for the use of force. The punishment was directly linked to the crime. If aircraft or missiles under the control of the Iraqi IADS struck a blow against the U-2s, retaliation would fall directly on the air defense system. The connection between cause and effect would be made doubly clear by the timing of the strike, which the national command authorities stipulated should be no more than six hours after an Iraqi provocation. According to Colonel Crowder, "We specifically built in approval timelines so that on the east coast [of the United States], they knew by when they had to make a decision to attack."

An effort was made to keep at least two of the "principals"—key NSC decision makers including the president, the secretary of defense, and the national security adviser—on hand in the case of an Iraqi provocation. Throughout the high-tension period of Iraqi threats in October and November 1997, UNSCOM and the United States kept up U-2 surveillance flights and often flew provocative profiles purely to defy Iraqi threats.[20] Although Baghdad had been warned through the UN not to interfere with U-2 flights, the Baathist leadership was oblivious to the scale of the proverbial sword of Damocles hanging over its head.

DEVELOPMENT OF ENLARGED COERCIVE OPTIONS

A range of U.S. military-planning shops now began to use Desert Thunder I as the basis for a new set of employment plans. The secret effort was extremely closely held, involving only a handful of planners on a day-to-day basis, but a number of organizations fed the process with guidance and intelligence at the regular VTCs. JTF-SWA's small Long-Range Plans cell and CENTCOM's Directorates of Intelligence (J-2) and Operations (J-3) were the principal planning agencies. The former, based at the remote PSAB, was principally staffed by U.S. Air Force and, to a lesser extent, U.S. Navy planners. JTF-SWA executed the constant but low-intensity day-to-day policing of the no-fly zones and represented the primary repository of air-campaign planning expertise in CENTCOM. CENTCOM J-2 and J-3, on the other hand, were dominated by U.S. Army officers and were based at MacDill Air Force Base in Tampa, Florida, collocated with CINCCENT Zinni. This arrangement made VTC the principal means of coordinating planning between CENTCOM and JTF-SWA. From around September 1997, such conferences were held at least every three weeks and often more frequently as possible execution dates drew close. The CIA, NSA, DIA, and JCS frequently attended such VTCs to input guidance and targeting intelligence.

During September and October, military planners began to receive feedback from the principals on how Desert Thunder I should be modified to punish Iraqi noncompliance with UNSCOM and a more overt attempt to shoot down the U-2s. James Steinberg, deputy national security adviser to President Clinton, explained that the principal guidance coming from the national command authorities was for larger options and noted that "to the extent that there was a targeting review, it was always 'aren't there any more, can't we do more,' we wanted to hit as many strategic targets as possible. . . . The initial options presented by the military were very light."[21]

Although the Clinton administration required more targets to be hit, it was ill-equipped to give detailed guidance to military planners on what those targets should be. As usual, the administration's civilian decision makers deferred such matters to the military. JTF-SWA's Colonel Crowder noted that the effect was to begin a scramble to find targets, without much guidance on what the targets should be. "The problem in air contingency planning—and this happens every single time—is that ... you're usually told, 'the President wants to do something,' you're not told what he wants to do, you're told 'we need to do something with airpower, so we need some targets,' so everyone and their brother starts filing in targets."[22]

The results of planning during this period were the operational plans (OPLANs) Desert Thunder II and Desert Thunder III. Anticipating the Clinton administration's need to link the central issue of the crisis—WMD—to any military response, Desert Thunder II consisted of a range of targets related to Iraq's *potential* or *suspected* development of CBWs, principally through a large single-wave TLAM strike and a single night of limited manned aircraft strikes. The target list was not impressive, consisting largely of suspected CBW-related locations identified before or during the 1991 Gulf War—dual-use industrial targets from the pharmaceuticals, chemicals, and food industries—or buildings identified by UNSCOM inspections and U.S. intelligence-collection operations as potential hides for undeclared materials or documents.[23]

When civilian decision makers sought a longer-lasting option, Desert Thunder III (also known as Desert Night) was developed, which incorporated Desert Thunder II into a broader range of targets that included heavier strikes on the IADS and some C2 targets. The planned duration of Desert Thunder III—some two to three days—opened the possibility that a coercive dynamic could be incorporated into the operation. Unlike in the earlier single-wave options, Desert Thunder III strikes could, if required, be suspended after the first or second day to allow Saddam a chance to acquiesce to whatever demands the United States might make.[24] The option of such "bombing halts" was an anathema to U.S. Air Force officers, who recalled the use of such tactics in North Vietnam, but it remained an option at the political level, although not a popular one. Mindful of its doubtful record of success, James Steinberg noted "there was never a lot of juice behind the bombing halt thing."[25]

"CHEAT-AND-RETREAT" CRISES

In October 1997, Iraq initiated the first of its major "cheat-and-retreat" episodes by banning Ritter's teams from any location designated a "presidential site" and ratcheting up pressure for any U.S. presence to be expunged from the UNSCOM effort—including the U-2 flights. From October 12 to 23, the United States began to ramp up its military presence in the Gulf by deploying two aircraft carriers, another 28 aircraft in addition to Operation Southern Watch's 160 aircraft, plus the customary 6 F-117A Nighthawks in Kuwait and 6 B-52Hs in Diego Garcia.[26] The United States pushed UNSC Resolution 1134 through the Security Council on October 23, 1997, which imposed an international travel ban on most senior Iraqi leaders. However, five abstentions, including France, China, and Russia, sent the message that the international community remained fractured over the issue of Iraq.

On November 3, Iraq again upped the ante by demanding that U.S. members of UNSCOM leave the country and again threatened U-2 flights over Iraq. The three existing options—Desert Thunder I, II, and III—were briefed to President Clinton on November 8 by CJCS Gen. Henry Shelton. When the U-2 next flew on November 10, the entire U.S. military machine in the Gulf was on a hair trigger. Although the danger passed, the principals in Washington authorized the development of even heavier strike options on that day.[27] On November 12, 1997, the UNSC unanimously passed Resolution 1137, again condemning Iraq for restricting UNSCOM access, and most UN inspectors left the country on November 13. James Steinberg recalled, "November 1997 was when the administration got really serious about military options."[28] Yet, tensions began to slowly dissipate. By November 20, Russian Foreign Minister Yevgeny Primakov succeeded in negotiating Iraq's agreement to comply fully with existing UN resolutions, and UNSCOM inspectors were back in Iraq and operational within two days. U.S. forces stood down for the time being.

The lull was predictably short. By December 17, UNSCOM Chairman Butler reported that Iraq was again refusing to grant Ritter's Special Investigations Unit access to presidential palaces. In late December, CJCS Shelton briefed President Clinton on the range of military options now available. Desert Thunder V was the principal option. It represented a fusion of all the IADS, CBW, and C2 targets covered by Desert Thunder II and III, and—three plus two making five—was thus given the numeral V. Manned air strikes played a more advanced role than in previous iterations of the plan.

For completeness, Shelton briefed the president on options involving ground forces, although these were not seriously on the table. Desert Scorpion—no relation to the unofficial option to occupy Iraq's western desert developed before Desert Storm—offered a limited land option aimed at pinching off the strategic port and oil fields of Basra, thereby robbing the regime of its primary source of revenue, and building a southern protected enclave to mirror the KRG zone in the Kurdish north. Desert Fury built on this option but included further plans for exploitation if the regime appeared to be faltering. Then, there was the main OPLAN 1003, the 250,000-man march to Baghdad that CENTCOM planners had periodically updated since it was first conceived as the "Road to Baghdad" think piece at the end of Operation Desert Storm in March 1991.[29] Secretary of Defense Cohen argued vainly for the execution of Desert Strike V before the onset of the Muslim holy month of Ramadan around December 31.

However, Iraq was to escape military action once again. Iraq entered 1998 apparently having decided that it would be the year when UN inspections and related sanctions would be decisively broken. On January 2, 1998, a rocket attack was launched against UN offices in Baghdad, part of an intimidation effort in which Iraq's government maintained plausible deniability. On January 13, 1998, Iraq again withdrew cooperation with UNSCOM, citing the presence of U.S. and British inspectors as the reason. On January 17, Saddam personally delivered a speech in which he claimed that unless sanctions were lifted by May 20, Iraq would permanently expel UNSCOM. Indications began to surface in early February that VX nerve-gas traces had been found on Iraqi warheads destroyed by UNSCOM. However, above all, the central issue remained Iraq's opposition to the Shake the Tree program, which was encapsulated in its unwillingness to allow Ritter's team to enter eight key presidential palace compounds.

Between January 20 and February 20, Butler and UN Secretary General Kofi Annan sought to resolve the issue, first by sending a team to Iraq to carry out an external survey of the eight sites and followed by Annan's own visit to Baghdad to meet the Iraqi leadership. Between February 20 and 23, Annan secured new assurances from Iraq that it would guarantee "immediate, unrestricted, and unconditional" access to facilities . . . on certain conditions. The Baathist regime managed to secure dispensations on conditional access to facilities deemed sensitive to Iraq's sovereignty and national security, which complicated the work of the Special Investigations Unit.

Although the CENTCOM crisis action-planning team stood down on February 27, the United States remained postured to strike, once again hedged in by Muslim holidays. This time it was the annual Hajj pilgrimage to Saudi Arabia, which prompted Secretary of Defense Cohen to seek a test of Iraq's purported willingness to cooperate. The United States pressured UNSCOM to test Iraq in early March 1998, which left a strike window of six to eight days to bomb before the March 15 beginning of the Hajj festival.[30] Sensing the threat,

Iraq fully complied with an intrusive series of inspections by Ritter's teams on March 9 and the crisis subsided. The UNSC and America's European and Arab allies were not firmly behind a strike, which would have antagonized them at precisely the moment when international solidarity was required to maintain the ailing sanctions effort. The United States had maintained two aircraft carriers in the Gulf since October 1997, added a third in early 1998, amassed three hundred to four hundred aircraft in the region for months at end, and cost the U.S. taxpayers an estimated $1.2 billion in additional costs.[31] Cheat and retreat had forestalled military action again. As Ralph Peters would later note, despite America's ability to fight more cleanly and precisely than ever before, "ironically it was Saddam who won the first bloodless military victory of our time."[32]

DISARMING IRAQ

The "cheat-and-retreat" crises were the beginning of a fundamental shift in Clinton administration policy, and indeed broader and longer-term U.S. policy on Iraq. They lay the seeds that would eventually germinate into regime change in Baghdad. Until the crises, the U.S. government still retained faith that despite its declining international acceptability, the open-ended containment of Iraq was working and was an economical way of dealing with Saddam. As long as UNSCOM inspections and sanctions functioned, Saddam would stay "in his box."

However, as Scott Ritter himself admitted, by 1998, the perception was that UN inspections "were rapidly being reduced to the mere illusion of arms control."[33] UNSCOM still maintained a system of live-feed cameras at key Iraqi industrial facilities and would yet make important WMD finds, but its public inability to launch surprise inspections was a constant humiliation for the United States and UN, neither of which wanted to continue sinking political capital into the issue for the foreseeable future. The Clinton administration had effectively given up on UNSCOM inspections, perceiving little benefit from further attempts to gain Iraqi compliance on the issue of UN inspectors. As former Clinton administration Iraq analyst Ken Pollack recalled, an early summer 1998 review resulted in a new outlook: "It was felt that there could be no happy solution involving UNSCOM. Military action stopped being about coercing Saddam into letting the inspectors back in. Now it was viewed as an opportunity to cease this game, to impose a cost, and not to even seek the return of inspectors. We were looking for a way to end 'cheat and retreat' with a bang. From now on, we were going to rely on means other than inspections to roll back Iraq's WMD."[34]

Since the November 1997 crisis, civilian decision makers had guided Zinni to focus his targeting effort on Iraq's suspected WMD effort. James Steinberg noted two main reasons for this. The first followed the Clinton national security team's long-standing preference for targets that were clearly derived from the nature of the provocation and could be rationalized to Congress and the public. Steinberg noted that the emerging options were "increasingly built around WMD to link the casus belli to the attack." Equally important, however, was the administration's changed appreciation of what UNSCOM could achieve. Steinberg recalled, "We were no longer thinking of force as a coercive measure. In the 1997 through early 1998 period, the idea was to use force in conjunction with diplomacy to get UNSCOM back in." Yet, as the planning effort progressed in 1998, the Clinton national-security team "had decided that force could not be used coercively. There was no set of circumstances in which the use of force was going to get Saddam to accept UNSCOM and therefore force was used to degrade and damage his capabilities... to provide an alternative to inspections."[35]

This posed a number of problems for CENTCOM military planners. The WMD targets used in options such as Desert Thunder II through V primarily encompassed suspected CBW facilities and related industries; as James Steinberg noted, "We did not have any intelligence on nuclear programs." When planners looked closely at their existing CBW-related target sets, the result was a major rethink. In early 1998 the U.S. military simply could not say where any proscribed Iraqi CBW research documentation, components, agents, or munitions were stored with any degree of certainty. CENTAF Commander Gen. Hal Hornburg recalled: "I don't think it was our plan to go directly after weapons of mass destruction. First of all, we didn't know where they were.... We hadn't even had full inspections on the ground for months."[36] JTF-SWA Commander Lt. Gen. Stephen Plummer concurred: "All the CBW targets were suspected rather than proven."[37]

Civilian decision makers were dismayed to slowly realize that far from providing the clues that UNSCOM then investigated, Western intelligence agencies were almost wholly reliant on UNSCOM for intelligence on Iraq's WMD. As Britain's Butler Report on intelligence on Iraq noted regarding the operations of Western intelligence agencies, "Between 1991 and 1998, the bulk of information used in assessing the state of Iraq's biological, chemical, and ballistic missile programs was derived from UNSCOM records." A trickle of defectors, most notably Hussein Kamil, provided further information, but no one could locate WMD stashes.

On this issue, the U.S. Senate Intelligence Committee noted: "The CIA had no dedicated WMD sources on the ground in Iraq until the late 1990s . . . [and] did not have any WMD sources in Iraq after 1998. . . . We were never able to directly access Iraq's WMD programs." The Senate committee noted that the U.S. intelligence community used UNSCOM as a budget-free resource and came to "rely too heavily" on its intelligence-gathering efforts.[38] David Wood related, "UNSCOM was an intelligence officer's dream, with its regular access to factories and laboratories; video cameras monitoring suspicious sites 24 hours a day; chemical sniffers sampling the air around laboratories; over 2,000 industrial machine parts tagged with bar codes; teams of scientists flying in to pour over documents and interview Iraqi scientists."[39]

Because CBW agents could not be located and directly attacked, CENTCOM's initial targeting focused on two sets of targets that could be plausibly related to CBW, namely the "presidential sites" made off limits to UNSCOM and various dual-use industries in Iraq's pharmaceutical, agricultural chemicals, and food-processing sectors. The former category of targets included regime palaces and ministries linked to Iraqi obstruction of UNSCOM activities. As a result of six years of U-2 overflights in support of UNSCOM, hundreds of UNSCOM helicopter sorties, and permanent U.S. overhead imagery from satellites, CENTCOM had an encyclopedic knowledge of the external (and often internal) layout of Iraq's palaces and government buildings. The UN technical report requested by Annan in February 1998 had highlighted the elements of eight palace complexes to which Iraq had repeatedly denied access, which narrowed the possible hiding places of WMD-related equipment and files still further. Ritter's Shake the Tree program had provided additional targeting intelligence and had captured low-power VHF communications among Iraqi concealment units as they sought to guide UN inspectors away from sensitive parts of target complexes.[40]

This overlapping coverage allowed CENTCOM to identify five key palace targets that appeared central to the concealment effort—Abu Rajash, Jabul Makhul, Radwaniyah, the Republican palace (Baghdad), and Sijood. Brigadier General Dunlap, then chief judge advocate general (JAG) to CENTAF, recalled that "all those types of targets needed to be linked to specific intelligence about specific types of things that were supposed to be at those palaces." The same criteria extended to other types of government buildings that UNSCOM had been blocked from investigating or that had supported the obstruction effort. The Iraqi Intelligence Service headquarters, the Ministry of Industry, the Ministry of Labor and Social Affairs, and the OPP (known as the Secretariat) were to be struck. The Baghdad University office of Dr. Rihad Taha al-Azawi al-Tikriti—the head of Iraq's biological weapons program, known as Dr. Germ—was selected for destruction, as were specific rooms within the Baghdad Museum of Natural History. The Baath Party headquarters was also on the target list from an early point in 1998. A WMD-related rationale supported each target and Dunlap recalled, "There was a conscious effort to make all the targets bullet-proof.... If a friendly government asked, 'Why did you bomb that palace?', we could go and give them material and they would be satisfied. That was the criteria."[41]

Iraq's pharmaceutical, agricultural chemicals, and food-processing industries had represented the second potential set of WMD targets in U.S. strike plans since 1991, but strong reservations had incrementally grown against their inclusion as targets. On the one hand, there was the slender risk that agents in production might be released into the atmosphere, but this risk was considered academic because the targeted sites were under UNSCOM inspection and did not appear to be actively producing WMD. Although journalists attributed unwillingness to hit factories to the U.S. military's lack of specialized "agent-defeat" incendiary munitions, this was never a major factor in planning.[42] On the other hand, even without the presence of WMDs, striking petrochemical, fertilizer, or pesticide factories was not without risk, and these targets were judged to be unattractive from a safety perspective.[43]

What made them even less attractive was the potential for Iraqi exploitation of their dual-use nature. CJCS Shelton outlined the sensitivities of striking such sites: "You don't know where the storage sites are, and the dual-use facilities—well, you're not going to hit hospitals. So, he's got things that can be converted in a fairly rapid period of time, ranging from one-week to about six-weeks, depending on whether it's chemical or biological."[44] Zinni was also opposed to striking dual-use targets if they could be avoided: "I think in this case when we looked at facilities that we would strike, a number of factors came into play: obviously, things like collateral damage, our ability to get to these facilities, how much we knew about them. I think also in terms of what the dual use might be, and how assured we were that the second part of the dual use was in play. You can make the case that almost any kind of, maybe a milk factory, again, could be a chemical factory or whatever. So I think we tried to be very selective. We tried to make the point on this, we tried to hit targets that we were very certain of."[45] Between February and August 1998, targeting policy changed to make dual-use targets a restricted class of targets that required political authorization by Washington decision makers.

Zinni's concerns about dual-use targets were soon to be confirmed, although in Sudan rather than Iraq. On August 20, 1998, the United States retaliated against Al Qaeda attacks on U.S. embassies in Kenya and Tanzania by firing thirteen submarine-launched TLAMs at the El Shifa pharmaceutical plant in Khartoum, and an additional sixty-six submarine-launched missiles were fired at terrorist training camps in Afghanistan. Although technically a brilliant strike that caused enormous damage to the facilities and little collateral damage, the Khartoum strike sparked a political fiasco. Zinni recalled: "That target was a surprise to me. The Chairman gave me the target after the final Principals meeting when the attack was authorized. We were not only given the mission, but also the specific target. That was very rare—in fact, it never happened either before or after while I was CINC. I was told to shoot the target, so I did."[46]

The CIA had injected the target into the strike very late in the week-long planning process, claiming that the site had been credibly identified as an Al Qaeda biological-weapons production facility. Whether this was true or not, there was simply no way of convincing skeptical global opinion that biological-weapons research had taken place at El Shifa. The twisted factory ruins and melted rows of pharmaceutical bottles were silent witnesses, and the episode reinforced CENTCOM's determination to eschew dual-use targeting and find a better way to degrade Iraq's WMD programs.

Between November 1997 and August 1998, both civilian and military decision makers came to terms with the limitations of U.S. military power in the new sphere of counterproliferation. Barton Gellman noted that the military saw counterproliferation as "a new mission with inherent obstacles."[47] General Shelton recalled, "As time went on, more and more people, I think, began to understand that you can't destroy his capability, but you can certainly diminish his capability, you can degrade it, you can set it back. This is not something that a lot of civilian or military people had a lot of

experience with."[48] Zinni was the principal agent of change in the administration's thinking on the issue:

> First they [civilian NSC] came to us and asked us about the ability of
> military strikes to eliminate WMD. They wanted to know what we could
> accomplish with a strike. You see, there were not a lot of targets—there
> was no smoking gun. I think we can see now that he [Saddam] had
> made a decision to stay within the rules—running short-range missile
> programs that could quickly give Iraq a long-range missile capability—
> and to leave no smoking gun around for someone to find. The program
> was in the heads of scientists not in weapons; that's why he was so
> unwilling to expose scientists to interrogation outside the country. I
> told them we could strike at the delivery systems and some industrial
> elements—the extended-range missile programs, the rocket fuel, the
> Special Republican Guard units that protected the programs, and the
> high-tolerance machinery. We calculated that we could set the program
> back two years. So, they [civilian NSC] gave us what they would like
> to accomplish, and we gave them what was possible.[49]

If Iraq's missile-, aircraft-, and helicopter-delivery systems, rather than
its WMD agents and related industries, were targeted, then quite a lot could
be achieved because of the greater visibility of these systems. Iraq's pursuit
of short-range missile systems such as the 150-kilometer Abadil 100 had
been allowed by the United States during cease-fire talks at Safwan in March
1991. Iraq could use these programs to research many elements of missile
design that would be directly applicable to longer-range designs, such as
gyroscopic guidance, telemetry, and missile fabrication. Since 1991, they
had been intensively inspected by UNSCOM, both through inspector visits
and through remote monitoring of facilities by UNSCOM television cameras
and electricity-usage logs. By exploiting UNSCOM privileges, the United
States had built a complete picture of Iraq's missile industry by 1998, which
allowed Zinni to identify the targets that would cause the longest setbacks to
Iraq's delivery capabilities.

This form of "bottleneck targeting" utilized a number of intelligence
sensors.[50] With regard to Iraq's missile industry, the key ones were UNSCOM
surveillance cameras, part of a system of three hundred cameras operating
throughout Iraq's industrial sectors since May 1993, and 159 pieces of tagged

missile equipment at sixty-three sites.[51] Providing near-real-time surveillance of Iraqi missile facilities, the cameras ensured that once high-value
pieces of machinery had been identified, they could be precisely targeted.
The CENTCOM J-2 directorate's targeting section (J-2T) used this highly
classified and sensitive data to identify hard-to-replace elements for destruction. These included specialized precision-folding presses that could be used
to fabricate missile casings and steering fins. In addition to allowing Iraq to re-
calibrate or realign its SAMs when they were due for maintenance, the presses
allowed Iraq to create new bodies to accommodate the Scud guidance and
motor sections that Iraq was assumed to be hiding.[52] Missile-fuel-production
facilities were designated. U.S. intelligence-collection assets designated two
air fields—al-Sahra and Tallil—where Iraq was believed to be converting aged
Czech L-29 training aircraft into remote-controlled drones that were capable
of delivering CBW attacks. Four Iraq Army Aviation Corps helicopter bases
and three other air fields were also targeted. Not for the first time, if the United
States could not find what it wanted to hit, it would hit what it could find.

STRIKING THE CONCEALMENT MECHANISM

The bottleneck targeting that Zinni planned had only one significant drawback
from the administration's point of view—the small scale of the operation. As
conceived, even with air-defense targets included, the strike could be undertaken in a single wave. This reduced the sense that the United States had
imposed a cost on Saddam and invited accusations that another "pinprick"
had been administered. Strikes on government ministries would be highly
visible, perhaps even impressive, but the majority of strikes in the operation
would be unobservable and would take place at remote air-defense sites, air
fields, factory complexes, and palaces situated deep within expansive walled
compounds. When the administration pressed for more targets, the obvious
choice was to open the category of regime security forces. Although the most
elusive components of Iraq's dispersed and hibernating WMD effort could
not be found, intelligence from Hussein Kamil and UNSCOM had given the
United States a very good idea of which Iraqi organizations were involved
in the concealment effort, which made these organizations some of the only
visible parts of the WMD system.

The headquarters of Iraq's internal security forces had been subjected
to a sprinkling of strikes in 1991 and had been attacked highly selectively in

1993, but the targeting effort against regime forces in 1998 was of a scale and comprehensiveness never before seen. The difference came from the improved understanding of Saddam Hussein's regime that had developed in the seven years of Iraq's containment. Before 1990, Western intelligence agencies had few dealings with Iraq's shadowy regime security organs, which was part of a deliberate Iraqi approach to counterintelligence. From 1990 onward a trickle of defectors filled out Coalition knowledge on the personalities, institutions, and facilities involved. This accelerated as Iraqi officers' movements such as the Syrian-based and CIA-backed Iraqi National Accord began attracting defectors from 1994 and culminated in the defection of Hussein Kamil in 1995. Saddam's son-in-law, a former head of the SSO and Iraq's Military Industrial Commission, gave the United States a complete rundown on Iraq's intelligence services, national-security bureaucracy, and concealment regime.

This historical and operational context was supplemented with fresh intelligence provided by UNSCOM's Shake the Tree missions, which produced inspection target folders containing high-resolution photography and maps that showed the layout of Iraqi security establishments down to the level of individual offices.[53] As William Arkin noted, UNSCOM had given the United States a "diagrammatic" understanding of the concealment mechanism, and "the same mission folders that UNSCOM put together to inspect specific buildings and offices in its search for concealed Iraqi WMD became the basis for the targeting folders that missile launchers and pilots later used."[54]

The new understanding of the Baathist regime exposed a new center of gravity that had not been targeted in 1991—Saddam's personal secretary, Abid Hamid Mahmoud, who was installed at the Presidential Secretariat Building. A distant Tikriti cousin of Saddam's, Mahmoud was assessed by Hussein Kamil to be the second or at least third most influential figure in the regime because of his position as an information broker who provided Saddam with intelligence on his lieutenants. His office also served as the central node in passing Saddam's directions concerning Iraq's concealment effort to a joint board of concealment organizations. The Ministry of Internal Affairs, the General Recruitment Office, and other obscure offices that once would have avoided U.S. notice were slated for destruction. In addition to the SSO headquarters, the United States now targeted its joint operations room—which performed real-time management of concealment operations during inspections—and computer archives, where microfilmed files were believed to be kept. SSO barracks and garages were targeted, as were WMD-related elements of Iraq's other intelligence services, including the Mukhabarat's M-4 (covert operations) and M-19 (covert procurement) directorates, the Istikhabarat's Strategic Concealment cell, and the Amn al'Amn's Concealment Security group. Four battalions of the SRG, the only military force allowed within the Iraqi capital, were targeted as a result of their involvement in concealment activities. Finally, UNSCOM's electronic and eavesdropping opponents, Project 858 listening and jamming stations, were placed on the target list.[55]

BULKING OUT THE TARGET SETS

Regime security forces were not to be the last addition to the rapidly expanding target-development effort. The national command authorities continued to request an option that could last two to five days, which necessitated the development of a yet broader range of target sets. CINCCENT Zinni successfully proposed that the operation focus not only on the degradation of Iraq's WMD but also the reduction of Iraq's threat to its neighbors. Iraq's conventional land and naval forces were opened as new target sets and prompted the predominantly U.S. Army targeteers at J-2T to develop a range of new aimpoints. The threat of Iraqi incursions into Kuwait or Saudi Arabia had markedly decreased by 1998 as shown by the post-1994 development of strong indicators and warnings from modeling Iraqi logistics and rail movements.[56] However, Gen. Tommy Franks, who then commanded the Army component of CENTCOM, known as ARCENT, spent much of the first half of 1998 polishing plans to halt potential Republican Guard thrusts with heavy use of the permanently deployed U.S. air forces engaged in policing the no-fly zone. This so-called Halt Phase strategy involved kill-box interdiction on the Kuwaiti border and deep interdiction strikes on the Hammurabi Republican Guard division headquarters and logistics targets at Kut.[57] If the national command authorities wanted a larger option with more targets, Franks argued, it would be useful to take the opportunity to strike at these and other deep interdiction targets. The Republican Guard, furthermore, was closely tied to the regime, and would be the most likely military units to employ WMDs if the regime decided to use them. As a result, the headquarters of each Republican Guard division and the northern and southern Republican Guard corps, plus valuable regular-army tank-transporter units, were slated for destruction.

CENTCOM's attitude to the rest of the regular Iraqi army differed markedly from its treatment of the Republican Guard. U.S. Air Force officers at JTF-SWA and CENTAF were initially keen to strike regular Iraqi armored units based in the south of the country.[58] These formations were closer to the Kuwaiti border than the Republican Guard divisions, which were routinely cantoned further to the north where they could cover the approaches to Baghdad. However, Zinni vetoed all attempts to place regular-army targets on the target list, which reflected his intuitive belief that these units could and should be treated in a different manner than the Republican Guard. His motivation was twofold. First, he considered the army to be a "victim of the regime"—an assertion that JTF-SWA disagreed with, based on their front-seat view of the regular army's role in suppressing Iraq's southern tribes.[59] Just as important, however, Zinni considered the regular army to be a potential ally. If the Baathist regime collapsed, Zinni looked to the army to maintain stability and centralized control in Iraq and prevent the country's disintegration into ethnic enclaves. This would require it to retain some capabilities. The army could also swing the balance against the regime were it to be gravely weakened by internal upheaval and its Republican Guard divisions somehow degraded. Following Desert Fox, Zinni commented that he hoped "seeing the effect [of air strikes] on the Republican Guard might even be encouraging to the regular army."[60]

Thus, although the Republican Guard would be prevented from launching incursions to the south by disabling strikes to its C2 and logistics networks, the regular army—much closer to Kuwait—was instead warned by 2.4 million leaflets and radio broadcasts to remain in barracks or suffer the same fate as the Republican Guard formations. The psychological operations (PSYOPs) effort was an extension of CENTCOM's periodic leafleting of air-defense gunners and SAM operators and its longstanding covert broadcast of sinister voice communications that directly addressed enemy air-defense personnel.[61] Although not novel, it did mark another step in CENTCOM's evolving stratification of Iraq's armed forces, who could now switch their status from combatants to noncombatants according to their behavior. This laid the groundwork for future information-operations approaches to be used in the no-fly zones and Operation Iraqi Freedom.

ON REGIME CHANGE

As the target lists grew, it took close personal focus by Zinni to maintain the connection between the targets chosen and their contribution to the missions of degrading Iraq's WMDs and reducing the threat to neighboring states. Zinni noted "on a virtual daily basis I would ask about targets when I visited my J-2, not to get down in the weeds, but to understand how targets were connected to commander's intent."

The concept of commander's intent was at that time being incorporated into U.S. planning doctrine and aimed to ensure that U.S. commanders included a section in every plan that described the strategic and operational effects that the commander sought to achieve through military operations. "Whereas previous commanders had briefed target lists and [DMPIs], I made sure that the commander's intent was well articulated," Zinni explained. However, Zinni could not control every element of the targeting process, especially because the planning of the operation was undertaken using "a federated targeting system" that netted all the non-CENTCOM targeting agencies to create a "virtual targeting staff" that included JTF-SWA, Checkmate, the intelligence agencies, and the Joint Warfare Analysis Center (JWAC).[62]

Seven thousand miles away and linked to CENTCOM J-2 by periodic VTC sessions, JTF-SWA, for instance, had developed a very different conception of the CINC's strategic intent. JTF-SWA was aware that the various targeting shops had been authorized to develop and nominate targets from almost all of the potential target sets—regime targets, air defenses, land and naval forces, WMD—but had not been briefed on Zinni's commander's intent vis-à-vis WMD and the reduction of Iraq's external threat. Instead, JTF-SWA was forced to extrapolate strategic guidance from administration statements. Colonel Crowder recalled, "No-one from CENTCOM ever articulated anything approaching commander's intent. The political objective was basically to hit a bunch of targets. But airmen had a tradition of briefing the crews about the objective of the mission and the significance of the target to it, partly because air targeting is more complicated than the capture of terrain or the destruction of enemy forces, the significance of which is pretty obvious. But we weren't given those answers by CENTCOM, so we made it up, because airmen need to know why they are flying in harm's way."[63]

Lacking communicated objectives, Colonel Crowder's Long-Range Plans cell brainstormed objectives based on public statements issued by the U.S. government. "Clear [objectives included] weapons of mass destruction, eliminate these capabilities ... but we did a lousy job of that in the Gulf war and we really only did that effectively with the [UN] inspectors, and so I knew, that's clearly not what we want to do, so we kind of read between the lines and came up with our own objectives."[64] Instead, Crowder focused on regime change as the political objective:

> We basically listened to what the senior leadership was saying, there was a lot of rhetoric about Saddam being a bad guy or whatever, so that unofficial objectives were to 'set the conditions for regime replacement.' . . . This was a meaningless term, really what they're trying to say is 'we want to overthrow the regime, force the collapse of Saddam Hussein,' so we wrote those objectives down on a piece of paper. I'm not sure whether my objectives ever got to be the CINC's objectives or were approved by the national command authorities. What I can say is that my [JTF-SWA] commander approved them. Now the fact that our plan of action, our objectives, may not have been universally understood, probably contributed to a lack of understanding and full buy-in on the target set that we were proposing.

Given the lack of clear U.S. political objectives vis-à-vis Iraq, JTF-SWA planners can be forgiven for focusing on regime change. The Clinton national-security team was undoubtedly growing more hawkish on Iraq with each passing year. A majority of its members were in favor of toppling the Baghdad regime, yet it did not seek regime change at any cost or regardless of the consequences. Having seen one uprising and one coup fail spectacularly and bloodily during its first administration, the issue of *when* and *how* regime change should be supported to enhance its chance of success was a key consideration. Following Secretary of State Albright's speech in March 1997, the Republican demands for regime change had become a drumfire. Foreshadowing future events, a letter calling for the overthrow of Saddam Hussein was presented to President Clinton on January 26, 1998, by the Project for the New American Century. It was signed by notables such as Richard Perle, Donald Rumsfeld, Paul Wolfowitz, and eight other members of the future Bush administration.

Neither the Clinton team nor CENTCOM had clear ideas about the desirability of near-term regime change. For the moment, the administration was *content to threaten or risk regime change, but not to specifically seek it.* Ken Pollack noted that senior national-security decision makers such as Bruce Riedel and Martin Indyk wanted to shape military options "not to be punitive, but coercive—a lengthy, punishing air campaign directed at his

[Saddam's] internal security forces, which would weaken his grip on the country."[65] For maximum effect, this concept of operations needed to be effectively open-ended, thus giving the enemy no idea how long he might suffer—the very situation that the Clinton administration inadvertently stumbled into during the seventy-day Kosovo air campaign a year later. Others in the NSC, such as Deputy National Security Adviser Steinberg, were less focused on an open-ended coercive campaign and instead sought to deny Iraq as much of its WMD infrastructure as possible, while also getting a coercive effect over a number of days. "There was no expectation of a coup," Steinberg recalled, "but we did want to hit those around Saddam to let them know that his policies were putting things of value to them at risk." As a result, Steinberg observed, "We were trying to maximize the target set, consistent with any plausible rationale we could give."[66] CINCCENT Zinni's attitudes toward the desirability of regime change in Iraq were complex but can be broadly characterized as hesitant, perhaps even unconvinced. Between 1998 and 2000, Zinni would speak out against U.S.-sponsored regime change on the grounds that the Iraqi opposition groups that some U.S. activists pinned their hoped on were unreliable. He argued that the risk of a collapsing, fragmented Iraq outweighed any potential gains that regime change might bring.[67]

Largely unbeknown to the NSC or CENTCOM but with the support of JTF-SWA Commander Plummer, Crowder's team at JTF-SWA spent the first months of 1998 developing two target sets, C2 and economic, specifically aimed at loosening the Baathist regime's grasp on Iraq. Crowder developed these two largely because his team lacked the necessary clearances to handle the national intelligence used to build a leadership target set. Crowder recalled, "Their [CENTCOM] target list was almost exclusively weapons of mass destruction targets, so we say, 'Well, that's not going to help us here, clearly we're not going to do anything to threaten the regime if we take down those WMD targets.'"[68] Both IADS and WMDs were used for external purposes only, Crowder noted, and thus were not of central interest to his concept of operations: "So we said, 'What are the types and classifications of targets that are going to enable us . . . to threaten his ability to control the country?'"[69]

The thrust of Crowder's effort was to sever Baathist control of southern Iraq. Crowder's Navy TLAM specialist, Lieutenant Dorbecker, utilized nodal analysis from the JWAC at Dahlgren, Virginia, to "build an architecture of the communications infrastructure in southern Iraq all by himself." After that, Crowder recalled, "We sent our plan out to JWAC [and it] validated our plan." JTF-SWA's analytical knowledge of the system came from its ongoing intelligence collection and its familiarity with the communications used by the IADS to threaten Coalition aircraft in the no-fly zones. Both the Kut-Mosul and the Nasariyah-Basra lines would be cut. The JWAC and JTF-SWA analysis identified the nodes with high risk of collateral damage, which would need to be skirted. Four forms of communications were targeted, including radio relay, tropospheric scatter, microwave, and landline, although the public-telephone network was classified as a dual-use economic target and therefore remained off-limits. In theory, Crowder sought to "eliminate the whole military command and control architecture in the south, because if he lost physical control of the south. . . . Well, he just can't afford to lose control of the south, then he's got a real problem."[70]

Strikes on C2 appealed to senior U.S. and British civilian and military decision makers, because they promised to give Saddam a major fright while also damaging air defenses and military C2 in the south. Zinni noted, "We saw how much loss of control in the south concerned him—he created four zones and placed his cousin, Chemical Ali, in the south. He was paranoid. We worked on this."[71]

Crowder's cell had a harder time when the communications target set overlapped with the off-limits category of dual-use or economic targets, which had to be authorized on a case-by-case basis by the CINC and later by Washington. Neither was willing to sanction strikes on the public switching network (PSN), even though this remained a vital pillar of Saddam's military C2 system. Zinni explained, "Well, you have to understand that we wanted to send the message as clearly as possible, that we were only targeting the regime. We didn't want to create any humanitarian or collateral damage counter-effect. We were concerned that someone would say we had caused civilian deaths because the public telephone lines went down."[72] In addition, Crowder was blocked from striking the PSN and a number of other two-way communications systems because they were providing valuable SIGINT to covert CIA operations inside Iraq and to satellite and airborne military assets.

JTF-SWA managed to get one regime-related target authorized: a Basra refinery distribution manifold that U.S. intelligence had linked to regime-sanctioned oil smuggling. To overcome NSC and CENTCOM resistance, Crowder identified the refinery as one of the regime's economic choke points. He showed that the oil it produced was sold illegally outside the UN OFP and the proceeds were siphoned off to the Baathist elite. To overcome objections about environmental damage, JTF-SWA Long Range Plans worked in partnership with JWAC to develop an effects-based weaponeering (weapons engineering) solution that would close the refinery for three to six months and prevent serious ecological damage. This solution included three sets of 1,000-pound laser-guided GBU-12s delivered to three bundles of piping in the manifold's pumping stations. Although three to six months was a shorter interruption than Crowder had hoped, the solution satisfied the target's opponents and met the CINC's requirements. In late December 1998, Zinni commented, "The oil facility we struck in the south was one that was used for illegal gas [and] oil smuggling. We intentionally did it in such a way to disrupt the flow, but not cause any environmental damage. We did not want to do what Saddam did. You're not going to see burning oil fields. You're not going to see oil spills into the water. We very selectively and very precisely went after a point in that target that accomplished our goal."[73]

However, Crowder learned the limits to the senior leadership's interest in coercing or humiliating the Iraqi regime when, in a cheeky nod to the 1991 air-campaign planners, Crowder requested to strike the Hands of Victory monuments that tower over Baghdad's Festivities Square. Built from the melted steel of Iranian tanks, the monument was one of the statues that had been unsuccessfully nominated as targets in 1990–91. The statue's historic immunity from U.S. air attack was "one of the reasons I tried to explore that possibility," Crowder recalled, but the cultural significance of the monument was too great and it remained off the target list. Zinni commented that such symbolic targeting would make the United States seem "impotent and childish."[74] Crowder noted, "We didn't explore it very hard because we got such a tremendous amount of pushback. . . . Nobody was willing to even play that game."[75]

LAST "CHEAT-AND-RETREAT" EPISODE

Instead, the only game played in the summer of 1998 was a final hand of "cheat and retreat" that began with UNSCOM discoveries of stores of Scud-specific missile fuel and further evidence of undeclared production of advanced VX nerve gas in the pre-1991 period. On August 5, Iraq once more ejected UN inspectors, called for the reform of UNSCOM, and demanded that the UN both certify Iraq as free of WMD and repeal sanctions. Relations between UNSCOM Chairman Butler and Iraqi Deputy Prime

Minister Tariq Aziz degraded during a series of summits. By early September, Washington began to seriously prepare for military action once more, now "anticipating and even welcoming" a chance to bring Iraq's ability to generate UNSCOM-related crises to an end.[76] National Security Adviser Berger directed CENTCOM to begin building a new coalition in the Gulf; in the UNSC, the United States succeeded in unanimously passing Resolution 1134, which strongly criticized Iraq's activities and led Iraq to back down. However, on November 1, Iraq announced once again that it would halt cooperation with UNSCOM. Exactly a year had passed since the first cheat-and-retreat episode and again the United States found itself on the verge of military action.

On November 7–8, General Zinni briefed U.S. military and civilian decision makers on the military options available. The latest iterations were named Desert Viper and Desert Viper Plus; the latter was a larger option that required a longer buildup time. Members of the Principals Committee, at a meeting at Camp David on November 8, opted to start with Desert Viper and transition into Desert Viper Plus if more prolonged strikes were required. This compromise indicated the ongoing lack of consensus between those who sought to punish Iraq with a short, sharp thunderclap and those who sought to coerce Iraq with a more drawn-out series of strikes.

Although Saudi bases were not made available for Coalition strike aircraft, Arab support for military action had coalesced, with eight regional states warning Iraq to comply, and both Russia and France stood aside as the United States readied to attack.[77] By November 11, the United States had augmented Operation Southern Watch forces (most of which could not contribute because they were based in Saudi Arabia) with fifty-four additional U.S. and British combat aircraft, plus a heavy-hitting strike package of twelve F-117A Nighthawks, twelve B-52Hs, and six B-1B bombers.

The attack was scheduled to be kicked off by the launch of ninety-six CALCMs from the dozen B-52Hs based at Diego Garcia. These aircraft were inbound and eight minutes away from launching their missiles when the order came to recall the bombers and stand down the three hundred TLAMs being readied for launch on nine U.S. ships and submarines in the Gulf. Iraqi Deputy Prime Minister and Foreign Minister Aziz had appeared on Iraqi television to announce Baghdad's agreement to unconditionally accept UN inspections, therefore removing the near-term casus belli at literally the last minute. With UN inspectors withdrawn from Iraq and U.S. Patriot missiles deployed to screen Israel, Iraq was alert to the incoming attack and had somehow detected it. A breach of operational security had tipped the Anglo-American Coalition's hand, but how? Every U.S. civilian and military leader from the time has a different opinion. Some say the Russians tipped off Iraq to prevent the crisis. Other says that the Saudi Arabian government used its inside knowledge of the ATO prepared at JTF-SWA's PSAB headquarters to warn Baghdad, or that the Omani or UAE governments detected the B-52s on their inbound journey and used the information to force Iraq's hand. Still others suggest that Iraq developed overseas agents who detected U.S. preparations, or picked up the B-52s on long-range surveillance radar.[78]

Whether one, some, or none of these theories are true, the administration vowed never again to cede tactical surprise to Baghdad. Iraq had once again neutralized the trillion-dollar-a-year military with a simple ruse. Ken Pollack recalled, "We wanted to get inside his decision loop, but on this occasion, he inside ours. We were quite disillusioned. We had put a lot of work into creating a harmonious moment with the Brits, the Saudis, and the others. Sandy Berger held a meeting the next day, November 15th, and told us to do it all again."[79]

The U.S. government planned on an execution date just after the December 15, 1998, release of UNSCOM's latest report on Iraq, which was expected to reflect new revelations from the summer and declare Iraq in breach of its commitments to the UN. The United States and Britain would have approximately a five-day strike window before the onset of Ramadan. International support was holding for the moment and Arab and UNSC states were exasperated by Saddam's brinksmanship. Sandy Berger described it as a "favorable constellation of forces" that would probably not hold after Ramadan in the new year.[80]

The new operation, code named Desert Fox, originated from a determined effort to avoid the loss of tactical surprise that would give Iraq the chance to make a diplomatic appeal and rob the operation of its military fruits. The November 14–15 cancellation had one important beneficial effect—it had given the United States a dry run and exposed Iraqi patterns of dispersal. As soon as UN inspectors had left Iraq in mid-November, Iraq had begun to disperse assets and personnel, and sped the process as U.S. military preparations unfolded. "Professional cruise missile recipients" by 1998,[81] Saddam's Fedayeen and other internal security forces had flooded areas of potential dissent, while intelligence, SRG, and Republican Guard units had relocated and spread out.[82] Immediately after that crisis, CJCS Shelton relayed the national-security team's questions about tactical surprise, asking, "Can we do the strike with the forces we have in theater and with the maximum operational security and limited numbers of people in on the planning?" The aim, Gen. Shelton exclaimed, was to "outfox 'em."[83]

The United States sent home the F-117As but kept the B-52s, B-1Bs, and TLAM shooters in theater and also left Patriot missiles in Israel. As mid-December drew close, the United States did not deploy the stealth fighters. JTF-SWA Commander Plummer explained, "Every time we deploy F-117s, it's a very visible statement, we give up any tactical surprise. . . . The CINC was very clear that he wanted to conduct whatever operation we did using the stuff we had in-theater at the time."[84] Just as significant, to reduce the risk that leaks would occur at air bases or involving host nations, the first night of strikes would not include any land-based airpower and would be controlled from the aircraft-carrier strike cells rather than from the Combined Air Operations Center at PSAB. After one night of ship- and submarine-launched TLAM strikes followed by naval aviation, manned land-based strikes would begin on night two.

As CENTCOM prepared to execute on December 16, many elements of U.S. military and political posture combined to deceive the Iraqis. A second U.S. aircraft carrier was not expected to join the USS *Enterprise* (CVN 65) in the region until December 18, only two days before the onset of Ramadan. CINCENT Zinni remained at CENTCOM's headquarters in Tampa, Florida, apparently undertaking routine duties, while a U.S. presidential visit to Israel put the Iraqis at ease. On December 13, the principals held a secure VTC with Secretary of State Albright and Sandy Berger, who had accompanied President Clinton on the visit to Jerusalem. On December 14 at the Hilton Hotel in Jerusalem, Clinton signed the EXECORD. The president could thereafter opt out of the attack at any point until 1400 hours EST on December 16.[85] Butler delivered his report on December 15 and, after citing a raft of Iraqi violations of its commitments to UNSCOM, concluded, "Iraq did not provide the full cooperation it promised on 14 November 1998."[86]

OPERATION DESERT FOX

The last UN inspectors left Baghdad on the afternoon of December 16, destined not to return until the last months of 2002. At 2306 Baghdad time that day, ten U.S. ships and submarines in the Gulf launched the first wave of

TLAMs; thirty-nine minutes later, U.S. naval-carrier aviation launched from the USS *Enterprise*.[87] Curtains of AAA filled the sky above Baghdad, and TLAMs began to impact fifty minutes after they launched. At 1711 EST, White House spokespeople announced that Operation Desert Fox had begun, and at 2000 hours EST, President Clinton had made a televised announcement while Secretary of Defense Cohen briefed Congress.

Fifty of the one hundred targets struck in Desert Fox were attacked on this first night. The first wave of attacks involved approximately 250 TLAMs and focused on many of the most important and time-sensitive targets. SRG barracks were targeted in the first minutes of the attack to maximize the number of potential personnel casualties. Other mobile targets included locations believed to hold computer and laboratory equipment and files, such as the Presidential Secretariat and the SSO headquarters, computer archives, and joint operations room, which were attacked early in the first night. Iraq's intelligence agencies and a presidential palace complex on Lake Tharthar also received Tomahawk strikes in the opening minutes. Another time-critical target set attacked in the initial massive TLAM strike was the IADS, which was attacked in a purely functional manner to achieve suppression of enemy air defenses (SEAD) during the operation.[88] The SEAD part of the attack was designed to consume as few assets as possible, to allow the weight of the attack to fall on the target sets that planners presumed would cause Saddam the most pain. Other targets included the ring of twenty-four sites used by Iraqi SA-2 SAMs and the high-power, low-frequency surveillance radars protecting Baghdad, which were the teeth of the SuperMEZ surrounding the Iraqi capital. The U.S. Navy fired two TLAM-Bs on each SAM aimpoint and one TLAM-D, carrying a submunitions warhead, on each radar.[89]

Tactical surprise had been maximized by CENTCOM's deception plan, which arguably allowed the United States to operate inside Iraq's decision cycle for the first time since 1991. General Zinni noted that "by using in-theatre assets only, we achieved tactical surprise. We caught a lot of stuff that would normally have been moved, and we were remarkably lucky."[90] Although the UNSCOM pull-out some hours before had initiated an Iraq dispersal effort, the lack of other indicators of impending attack had encouraged sluggishness, as Zinni later noted: "Somebody had put out the word to move the equipment and documents, the way they normally did, but they were not in a hurry to do it."[91] As a result, some regime security forces were literally caught napping. General Shelton noted some days later, "There were quite a few the first night in the housing, barracks, and headquarters."[92] Sean Boyne wrote, "One of the unstated aims of the offensive was to kill thousands of Republican Guard soldiers in their beds," which was an indication of how far the Clinton administration had come since its deliberate attempt in 1993 to reduce casualties by striking the empty Mukhabarat building in the dead of night.[93] Shortly before the operation commenced, IrAAC helicopters were observed by tethered satellite coverage to be relocating, which caused U.S. planners to withhold some planned TLAM strikes.

Although the SEAD effort did not include the sort of complex electronic warfare plan used in 1991, advanced intelligence support had combined with the elements of surprise and simultaneity to land a crippling blow. Iraq's air-defense operators had become very proficient in moving SAM systems every twelve to twenty-four hours. In emergencies, even bulky, older strategic SAMs—Soviet SA-2s and SA-3s—could be moved from one berm to another within forty-five minutes. Despite this, Crowder and the JTF-SWA team had managed to get inside the decision cycle of Iraq's air-defense operators. The key was to create what Crowder called "a number one priority sensor collection deck," in which a large number of intelligence-collection sensors were dedicated to tracking the ring of twenty-four sites, which were imaged every twenty-four hours. This allowed JTF-SWA to monitor and profile the movement of the systems. TLAM targeting solutions for each potential dispersal berm were generated and each site was checked for the presence or absence of SAM elements as late as four hours before the missiles launched. Building on the tethering of satellites to cruise-missile attacks in Desert Strike, Operation Desert Fox enjoyed unprecedented satellite support from the new National Reconnaissance Office's Operational Support Office, including three advanced versions of the KH-11 electro-optical and infrared imaging satellite, two Lacrosse SAR cloud-penetrating imagers, and a collection of other signals- and multispectral-collection assets.[94] Twenty-four of the thirty-four targeted IADS nodes were in their reported or predicted locations when attacked, which resulted in the destruction or crippling of nine SAMs or radar systems and damage to an additional thirteen.[95]

On the first night, manned aircraft sorties launched by USS *Enterprise* were limited to targets in southern Iraq because of the lack of land-based tanker, command, and defensive counterair support. Despite this, naval-carrier aviation played a key role by following the TLAM wave with strikes on SA-3 sites at Basra and Nasariyah. F-14B "Bombcats" carried the LANTIRN targeting pod for first time, and each went into battle carrying four GBU-24 2,000-pound LGBs. In addition to SA-3 sites, the Bombcats destroyed possible storage sites of Silkworm missiles that might have threatened USS *Enterprise* battle group. They also joined U.S. Navy and Marine F/A-18 Hornets in striking enemy radio-relay and military landline cable-repeater communications links. Lt. Kendra Williams and 1st Lt. Cherry Lamoureux, America's first female pilots to engage in bomb-dropping combat missions, took part in these two hundred sorties.

Following the first night of strikes, C2 of Desert Fox reverted to JTF-SWA at PSAB in Saudi Arabia. At 2203 Iraq time on December 17, the next wave of cruise-missile attacks were launched. B-52 bombers flying from Diego Garcia launched ninety CALCMs. The missiles were new Block I variants (only Block 0 had been used previously) that incorporated larger, 3,000-pound warheads, half again as heavy as the 2,000-pound charges carried by Block 0 CALCMs and packing three times the throw-weight of 1,000-pound Tomahawk warheads.[96]

The primary targets engaged by the CALCM wave were the missile-related industries identified in CENTCOM bottleneck targeting models. Crowder noted that machinery related to WMD delivery systems was large and well surveilled, which allowed it to be struck on the second day: "The WMD stuff could go anytime, it wasn't going anywhere."[97] Days later, televised BDA imagery would show selected individual buildings blackened and reduced to rubble within Iraq's missile complexes: the SAM recalibration equipment at the Taji missile-fabrication facility, the two main hangers containing specialized folding presses and computer-modeling equipment at the Ibn al-Haytham missile research and design center, and the facility that produced Shahiyat liquid rocket-motor fuel. The Baath Party headquarters received twelve of the massive warheads; the first five arrived at precisely the same aimpoint in five-second intervals to burrow their way deep within the structure's thirteen floors, and were followed twenty-five minutes later by another salvo.[98]

At 0034 Iraq time on December 18, air-raid sirens sounded in Iraq, indicating the approach of the first of two waves of manned aircraft strikes, which would total 213 sorties. A range of land-based aircraft now joined U.S. Navy Bombcats and Hornets, providing tanker, C2, and fighter support necessary to extend operations farther north. A broad range of IADS, communications, and barracks sites were targeted by U.S. and British aircraft. On their first bombing missions, B-1B bombers walked sticks of 500-pound dumb bombs across now-empty Republican Guard barracks and headquarters at al-Kut. RAF Tornados joined U.S. aircraft in striking communications sites, IADS nodes, and maintenance hangers used to convert L-29 trainers into suspected CBW carriers. Interspersed between manned strikes, a second cruise-missile salvo of around one hundred TLAMs was launched at 0504 Iraq time on December 18. That ended the second night of strikes, during which twenty-five targets were engaged.

The first and only piece of dynamic targeting in the operation was used on the third night of Desert Fox, spanning December 18–19. Following the withheld attack on one of the four Iraqi helicopter bases identified on the target list, the helicopters had been reacquired by overhead assets at a new dispersal location near K-2 airfield, Tikrit. One of the small number of TLAM strikes on night three was tasked with the destruction of the helicopters, using TLAM-D to dispense cluster bombs and destroyed twelve of fifteen helicopters located in a forested area.[99] Other than that, the strikes on the third night focused on the least time-sensitive targets of all: principally the fixed infrastructure, such as barracks, offices, tank-maintenance workshops, missile-test stands, the Habbaniyah castor-oil plant (a suspected ricin biotoxin production site), and the oil refinery.

Beginning at 0404 local time, a wide range of targets were struck during 150 manned aircraft sorties, including the Tikrit radio-jamming facility and other television and radio transmitters. Despite these strikes, the regime successfully got a taped speech of President Saddam Hussein to the Al-Jazira network in Qatar, which aired the defiant statement at 0730 local time. The tape indicated not only that Iraqi broadcasting capabilities had been hit hard, but also that the regime was desperate to show that its remained in charge and that the leadership had survived the attack.

Early on December 19, NSC decision makers in Washington and CENTCOM in Florida faced the issue of whether to continue bombing into Ramadan, which was to begin within twelve hours. BDA provided by the National Reconnaissance Office satellite constellation tethered to the strikes had produced enough BDA to convince military decision makers to advise suspending operations after a final fourth night of strikes. By the end of the second night of attacks, CENTAF Commander Hornburg had already recommended that four nights of bombing would be enough.[100] Based on the early BDA he was seeing, Zinni agreed. The targets that met Zinni's strategic concept—the missile-delivery sites, palaces, and concealment personnel—had been hit by the end of the second night. The third night had primarily seen attacks on the targets that had been added to bulk out the target list. Zinni was concerned that these strikes, and any further attacks, would cause a countereffect and make "Saddam appear a victim for no good reason." Zinni concluded, "I felt the U.S. should either take him down or specifically target for specific reasons."[101]

The NSC had mixed feelings, reflecting its complex mélange of hopes and motives for launching the attack. Steinberg reflected, "If we'd have had more good targets, we might have kept going." This was true; were Desert Fox to be extended using elements from other larger variants such as the comically named Desert Badger and Desert Lion, the United States would have to scrape the barrel for targets, as it was forced to do in Kosovo months later. The target list would quickly lose its WMD rationale, which could (at a stretch) still be maintained after the first three nights of Desert Fox. Yet, it achieved its degradation mission against the WMD target set and punished Saddam in a manner that might deter future defiance. Therefore, the administration felt it had done enough. Ken Pollack noted, "This was about ending a commitment. There was no rationale for extending the bombing because we weren't trying to coerce Saddam and bombing would only have perpetuated the crisis."[102]

After so many episodes of cheat and retreat, no Iraqi concession could hold any weight. Pollack summarized the feeling in the NSC: "Washington convinced itself that Saddam would not be persuaded by any amount of military force, and therefore had set no political goals for the operation." Under these circumstances, the NSC seized on Ramadan as a good excuse for ending the operation.[103] On the morning of December 19 EST, Saudi diplomats warned the United States that the Saudi religious establishment had sighted the new moon, meaning Ramadan had begun. The beginning of the religious month would be announced at sunrise in Saudi Arabia on December 20 around 0400 local time. President Clinton left the final decision to suspend strikes to Zinni, who recalled that "the president said, 'It's your call,' so I ended the operation." However, Desert Fox was allowed to end with a bang rather than a whimper. Eighty-seven final sorties flew at 2108 local time on December 19, supporting a small number of strike aircraft undertaking restrikes guided by crude early BDA. At 2200 local time, JTF-SWA received guidance from CENTCOM J-3 to "recall everyone out of the box, we're terminating operations," according to JTF-SWA Commander Plummer.[104]

REFLECTIONS ON DESERT FOX

Operation Desert Fox was the largest single U.S. military action against Iraq since Desert Storm, although it only employed a tenth of the aircraft used in 1991 and only struck one hundred targets over its four days. The operation was a stunning success from a military-technical point of view, underlining how far twenty-four-hour U.S. precision-strike capabilities had traveled since the liberation of Kuwait: 211 of 275 planned DMPIs were struck.[105] There were no well-publicized collateral-damage incidents in Desert Fox, a first for a post–Cold War U.S. air campaign, and the targeting was so selective that life went on as normal for many Iraqis. General Zinni recalled that U.S. imagery from Baghdad showed a wedding procession calmly walking through the streets while bombs were falling elsewhere in the city.[106] The fidelity of the target list was apparent in the first satellite BDA images to be paraded by the Pentagon as the operation unfolded, which showed large sprawling presidential complexes in which innocuous-looking annexes had been destroyed or government buildings in which a handful of individual offices had been "plinked."[107]

U.S. weapons systems had performed almost flawlessly, particularly land-attack cruise missiles, of which 325 TLAMs and 90 CALCMs were fired. This made Desert Fox the largest cruise-missile salvo yet. The permanent presence of a U.S. carrier battle group in the Gulf had given the United States a powerful ability to "sucker punch" Iraq with little warning, and the missiles had registered historically unprecedented launch and arrival rates. Aside from the precision saturation bombing of large complexes with the B-1Bs, all the weapons used in Desert Fox were precision guided, which resulted in an 85-percent hit rate.[108] Roughly two thirds of the C2, WMD concealment, and WMD-production facilities targeted were destroyed or severely damaged and thirty-seven helicopters and aircraft were destroyed.[109]

More critical analysis was to follow, however, as the international community, Congress, and the public tried to unravel what the administration's expectations had been at the outset of Desert Fox. Given the nature of many of the targets, there was an understandable assumption that one of the U.S. government objectives had been to destabilize the Iraqi government and increase its vulnerability to coup or uprising. In Desert Fox, nonmilitary (e.g., regime) leadership and C2 targets accounted for 20 percent of the aimpoints, compared with 9 percent in Desert Storm, and the individual targets seemed chosen to destabilize the Iraqi government. Although involved extensively in concealment, the SSO Joint Operations Room and computer center directed the regime's countercoup capabilities. The targeted intelligence services and eavesdropping stations were likewise nodes in the regime's self-protection suite. When asked how targets such as oil refineries and television or radio stations were connected to WMD, many military and civilian decision makers were at a loss to explain. Their answers seemed to point to a U.S. government effort to unseat the regime. General Shelton, for instance, explained that regime security forces were targeted because they "protected the center of gravity," and television and radio transmitters were hit because they could be used to "jam incoming radio and television signals, for example, Voice of Iraq," a U.S.-sponsored propaganda station. British spokespeople announced that C2 strikes in the south "had made it harder to control [Saddam's] military and internal security forces," and Zinni postulated that the preferential treatment given to the army over the Republican Guard "might give encouragement to the regular army."[110]

Although regime change had neither been considered an aim of the operation nor a likely outcome, U.S. military and civilian decision makers were surprised by indicators of internal unrest that emerged from Iraq after the strikes. Ken Pollack observed that in terms of loosening Saddam's grip on Iraq, "Desert Fox actually exceeded expectations. Saddam panicked during the strikes."[111] The south remained restive and under periodic marshal law. Government forces maintained a heavy presence in Karbala, Najaf, and Nasariyah throughout Desert Fox. In the wake of the bombings, a purge was launched in certain divisions of the regular army in the south, which led to the execution of its commander and senior staff. Tensions continued to grow between the regime and a key Shia cleric, Ayatollah Mohammed Sadiq al-Sadr, the cousin of another great Shia cleric murdered by the regime in 1980, Ayatollah Mohammed Bakr al-Sadr.[112] Apparently unbalanced by Desert Fox and various security threats, the regime had Mohammed Sadiq al-Sadr and two of his sons murdered on February 19, 1999. This cast the south into open warfare against the regime on a scale not seen since the 1991 intifada. The Shiite Saddam City area of Baghdad was isolated and all roads into the Karbala-Najaf-Nasariyah area closed, which drew drive-by shootings and other retribution killings, riots, and protests. Saddam's troubleshooter in the center-south, longtime loyalist Izzat Ibrahim al-Douri, survived an assassination attempt in Karbala.[113]

General Zinni recalled being surprised to hear from Arab diplomats that the regime was "badly shaken" by Desert Fox. Desert Fox prompted the regime to lash out at its Gulf neighbors, whom Saddam dubbed "throne dwarves" in an angry, ranting Army Day speech. That speech restored U.S. standing in the Gulf just as problems appeared to be arriving that might have threatened the very nature of U.S. military presence in the area.[114] The regime's apparent vulnerability also promoted Zinni to commission a simulation for late 1999, run by Booz Allen and called Desert Crossing, which sought to forge an interagency plan for the stabilization of Iraq on the off chance that internal fighting or U.S. military action resulted in regime collapse.[115]

Although the effect of Desert Fox on the regime's stability was an important side issue, the key measure of effectiveness for the operation was its effect on Iraq's ability to launch production of WMD. As a starting point, it was clear that whatever the technical effectiveness of strikes on delivery systems and the concealment mechanism, the U.S. military had been limited to striking what it could find rather than what the national command authorities initially sought to destroy: Iraq's residual WMD research documentation, components, and agents or materials. "Effective *maskirova*," wrote Michael Rip and James Hasik on the Russian concept of deception, "can fatally compound precision weapons campaign planning." As with the Scud hunt in 1991, the United States was forced to hit what it could find. Surprise meant that the opening attacks of Desert Fox were unusually effective, yet many of the second and third night strikes in Desert Fox were simply new manifestations of the "empty-building syndrome," where "war planners seek unimportant fixed sites to turn to rubble."[116] Although perfectly surveilled by UNSCOM video cameras, some WMD sites were not struck until the second night, which allowed the Iraqis to strip components from the sites in plain view of the UN cameras hours before the same cameras faithfully recorded munitions crashing through the buildings. Other targets were well chosen but poorly targeted, such as an SRG barracks highlighted by Scott Ritter:

> I knew that site almost as well as the back of my hand. I was sure it was unoccupied at the time it was bombed, their battalion staff safely ensconced in their operational bunker located several hundred yards away. I looked in wonderment at those barracks, trying to fathom why those structures had been chosen for destruction. Why weren't the armories

and ammunition bunkers hit? Why wasn't the vehicle park destroyed? What about the fighting positions along the perimeter, which would be fully manned and therefore susceptible to crippling casualties. None of this, just an empty headquarters and barracks. How did this strike advance the U.S. goal of containing Saddam Hussein? How did it diminish Iraq's ability to threaten its neighbors with weapons of mass destruction? What had been achieved by destroying this empty building? If bomb damage assessment teams were interpreting these photographs as examples of mission success, then there was something fundamentally wrong about the entire effort. . . . Precision bombardment with cruise missiles made many walls crumble. They fell as precisely as targeted, but few today will argue that there was anything of substance behind those walls, and cement, even in Iraq, is cheap. UNSCOM crumbled with those buildings in Baghdad. Weapons inspections ceased. And a once-mighty coalition of our allies disintegrated.[117]

Iraq would never again allow UNSCOM inspectors to enter Iraq and would only readmit its successor—the UN Monitoring and Verification Commission (UNMOVIC)—on the eve of another war in four years' time. In the meantime, UNSCOM would be a hard act to follow, even taking into account the restrictions placed on its inspections by Iraq. Even UNSCOM Chairman Butler underestimated the organization's effectiveness, failing to appreciate that UNSCOM gave more than it received from the Western intelligence agencies: "U.S. satellites can practically read license plates from fifty miles up; they can take heat-sensitive photos that show, as if by magic, whether a factory is in operation or not. Anyone who thinks that a military with tools like these would rely on information from an operation like UNSCOM, equipped with a thirty-year old U-2 and a fleet of thirty-year old helicopters rattling around the countryside of Iraq, is not dealing with reality. If anything, we at UNSCOM coveted the highly advanced intelligence data the Americans owned, which could have been very useful to our disarmament mission."

However, UNSCOM truly was "an intelligence officer's dream," as David Wood noted.[118] General Zinni estimated that Desert Fox set back Iraq's delivery capabilities by one to two years, but stripped of UN inspections, Iraq was now theoretically free to quickly restart its hibernating WMD programs if, in fact, that was its strategic intent. The long-standing logic of containment—that it could work as long as UN inspections *and* sanctions were effectively maintained—had suffered a grievous blow. Veteran Washington analyst Patrick Clawson reflected the prevailing wisdom of the time when he noted, "Without the inspections, the WMD problem will only grow worse so long as Saddam is in power. Without UNSCOM, there is more reason to concentrate on efforts to replace Saddam's regime."[119] Immediately after Desert Fox, U.S. National Security Adviser Berger commissioned a review of options aimed at toppling the Baathist regime and put in place a new formal policy of containment until regime change.[120]

8

Prelude to War
The No-Fly Zones after Desert Fox

T he Baathist regime's passivity during Operation Desert Fox only added to the anticlimactic impression left by the bombings. However, as ever, Saddam was readying a new phase of resistance to follow the four days of strikes. Resistance, defiance, and regular crises were ingrained features of the regime's raison d'être by now. Although UN inspections could no longer provide a global stage on which to confront the United States, the ongoing aerial policing of the no-fly zones offered a last theater in which the regime could regularly strike out directly at its Anglo-American adversaries. The pattern was well established by late 1998: Iraq would weather the storm of a planned U.S. strike, declining to challenge the Pentagon while U.S. forces were on maximum alert and postured to strike back hard. Then, once the U.S. military operation was over, Iraq would attempt an intricate SAMbush in the no-fly zones, hoping to destroy a U.S. or British aircraft. As Paul White noted, "The real threat to pilots tended to occur in the weeks after airstrikes, rather than during the attacks themselves."[1]

Iraq's air defenses had been narrowly targeted in Desert Fox; the strikes primarily fell in the "free-fly zone" between 33°N and 36°N. This targeting temporarily suppressed the IADS in the Baghdad SuperMEZ but had not been optimized to produce long-term beneficial effects in the no-fly zones. Indeed, the outlying MEZ at Tallil in the south, H-3 air base in the West, and Kirkuk and Mosul in the north had not been effectively targeted since 1993.

As a result, the Iraqi IADS was relatively well positioned when it initiated a new phase of military resistance against U.S. and British aircraft patrolling the no-fly zones on December 23, 1998. Five days later, Iraq launched three SA-3s against Operation Northern Watch (ONW) patrols near Mosul and then launched six SA-6 missiles two days later against OSW aircraft near Tallil.[2] On January 5, the IrAF initiated its most serious incursion into the no-fly zones since its first SAMbush attempt on December 27, 1992; two pairs of MiG-25 aircraft drew U.S. F-15C and F-14A fighters into hot pursuit and evaded six unsuccessful AAMs launched by the JTF-SWA combat air patrols, the first U.S. AAM shots since 1993. Between December 20 and January 28, the IrAF launched seventy penetrations of the no-fly zones involving one or more aircraft, unsuccessfully attempted to draw the United States into a series of SAMbushes, and offered bounties of $14,000 for the successful downing of a U.S. or British aircraft and $2,500 for the capture of a pilot.[3]

JTF-SWA Commander Plummer began canvassing CENTAF Commander Hornburg, the CENTCOM staff, and CINCCENT Zinni about expanding U.S. ability to commence retaliatory strikes to deter further Iraqi resistance to patrols. He argued, "We've got to have a way to show them some retribution."[4] There had been so little Iraqi antiaircraft fire in the 1994–98 period that existing JTF-SWA response options were limited to either immediate HARM shots against radar emitters or immediate air-to-ground strikes against the AAA site or SAM unit that attacked the aircraft. The latter option, code named Iron Hand, was unpopular, both because of the difficulty of visually acquiring AAA or SAM shooters from fifteen thousand feet and because it surrendered the initiative to the Iraqis. Plummer recalled, "I never liked Iron Hand because it was predictable and so encouraged higher risk operations." Likewise, Iraq's shallow, high-speed aerial incursions were almost impossible to intercept. This suggested the need for an indirect response to aerial incursions, which one U.S. government official termed "going after the trap rather than going after the bait."[5] Plummer stated, "I told General Zinni, 'I want to be able to go and find the targets that are militarily significant to us and that will do the most damage to him. I want to punish him for violating the no-fly zone and shooting at us.'"[6] Zinni was receptive to a broadening of the response options open to JTF-SWA and believed firmly that Iraq needed to be shown there was a consequence to its actions.[7]

On January 8, 1999, Zinni's request for a broadening of the ROEs was presented to the PCM by CJCS Shelton, whose presentation detailed Iraq's recent pattern of incursions, SAM deployments, and SAMbushes.[8] Following Desert Fox, which failed to create the sense of heavy punishment for which it was purportedly developed, the Clinton national-security team was still seeking to impose a military cost on Saddam for his ongoing defiance and was thus highly receptive to the request. As Ken Pollack recalled, "Everyone on the National Security Council was thinking of regime change, and, intellectually, the Principals all understood that containment was failing and we needed to go on the offensive. We decided to use the no-fly zone violations to ratchet up the pressure by allowing pilots a broader interpretation of self-defense."[9]

In keeping with its general policy on military affairs, the Clinton team left the details to the military, giving them a blank slate on which to design an expanded set of ROEs. If desired, the military could broaden the types of Iraqi action that would trigger a U.S. military response against ground targets—the so-called "ROE trip." Since the no-fly zones began, ROE trips had been strictly limited to enemy firing of AAA guns, illumination of an aircraft with acquisition or tracking radar, or the launching of SAMs. Now, if desired, the military could launch air strikes to respond to aerial incursions, the deployment of radars and SAMs, the use of general-surveillance radar, or the augmentation of military forces in the south. Furthermore, when it responded, it could strike back indirectly at almost any element of the air-defense system (and even naval systems) within the no-fly zones. As Patrick Clawson wrote, "Under the old system, a plane could be authorized to hit an Iraqi radar site only if the site's target acquisition radar illuminated a specific plane—a clear indication that the Iraqis were about to fire. Now, if the Iraqis simply turn on the [surveillance] radar used to monitor whatever traffic might be in the air, U.S. planes may respond by hitting Iraqi communications centers scores of miles away. That's a pretty expansive definition of defense."[10] The national command authorities had written a blank check.

CENTRALIZED EXECUTION IN OPERATION SOUTHERN WATCH

To the surprise of some members of the civilian national-security team, the military were hesitant to cash the blank check; Ken Polack recalled that "they saw it as political pressure to use more force."[11] CINCCENT Zinni immediately recognized the potential for uncontrolled escalation inherent in the administration's proffered loosening of the ROEs and sought to develop a more structured set of rules that kept the national command authorities and CENTCOM in the loop. A range of considerations influenced this cautious approach to what he termed "the very liberal ROE" offered by the administration, one of which was the concerns of the principal OSW host nations, Saudi Arabia and Kuwait.[12] Although the house of Saud and to a lesser extent the Al-Sabah dynasty in Kuwait were concerned by the prospect of escalating confrontation in Iraq, Saddam dispelled any sympathy that Desert Fox might have generated when he lashed out at the Gulf monarchies in his January 5 Army Day speech. In that speech, he accused them of "pandering to Western interests" and called on their citizens to "release your anger and rebel."[13] The Saudis had become increasingly sullen and distant in their dealings with the U.S. military from 1992 onward, especially since JTF-SWA moved to the remote PSAB in 1996. However, the changed ROEs affected Saudis minimally because the only aircraft based in the kingdom were support aircraft or F-16CJs, which were permitted to carry only HARMs for direct defense against the proven threat of an enemy radar.[14]

The strike aircraft most affected by the new ROEs would instead be carrier-based or would fly from Kuwait, whose leadership strongly supported the U.S. military containment of Iraq. Even so, as one of only two Arab states that provided basing for bomb-dropping aircraft in Desert Fox (the other was Oman, which based the B-1Bs), Kuwait was feeling the heat. It had a spotlight shone on its involvement in Operation Desert Fox by an insensitive British decision to fly a contingent of its press corps to Ali Al-Salem Air Base during the operation. Although Britain had sweated over a withdrawal of Kuwaiti basing and went so far as to deploy the carrier HMS *Victorious* to the Gulf in January to "gap" the potential loss of its ground-based aircraft, any Kuwaiti unease faded after Saddam began issuing his thundering threats toward his southerly neighbors. Then-Colonel Dunlap, the CENTAF JAG, recalled, "Though the host nations put few restrictions on us, there was a lot of self-censorship on our part, and there was a lot of sensitivity about avoiding upsetting the Saudis or the Kuwaitis."[15]

Just as important, CENTCOM and JTF-SWA had developed a conservative operational style over the preceding seventy-seven months of OSW operations. CENTCOM Deputy Political Advisor Frazee recalled, "By that time in the no-fly zones, the furrows had been ploughed and there was a certain routineness [sic] to everything."[16] At the outset of OSW, CENTAF Commander Nelson had focused on "avoiding embarrassment to the U.S. by shooting down the wrong aircraft or losing an aircraft." He commented, "We were very risk averse—I could see very little advantage in being highly aggressive under those circumstances."[17] CENTAF and JTF-SWA commanders ever since had tended to be fundamentally conservative in their execution of the mission. Nothing could be won no matter how aggressive the zones were policed yet everything could be lost in a moment if they became the first commander to lose an aircraft on their watch. JTF-SWA Commander Maj. Gen. Randall Schmidt recalled, "Part of that effect is that you don't want to incur losses in an operation where you're not out to win. . . . This is a commander's nightmare. If you don't have the option of going offensive, as we didn't, you have your hands tied. We had the mandate of defending ourselves and the perfect tour would be not to lose anyone and to maintain the status quo. That was a recipe for disaster, people got the mentality that I'm not going to war to win, I'm going there to just not lose."[18] This primary focus on force protection was reinforced by the dismissal of the JTF-SWA Wing Commander Brig. Gen. Terry Schwalier following the terrorists bombing of U.S. Air Force facilities in Saudi Arabia in 1996.

For his part, General Zinni did not want the purpose of the no-fly zone to be blurred to include general degradation of Iraqi military capabilities, and he did not want JTF-SWA pilots being lured into SAMbushes in pursuit of lucrative ground targets.[19] CENTCOM maintained centralized control and centralized execution of no-fly-zone responses through the mechanism of "banked" responses that could be executed on the next occasion that JTF-SWA launched patrols into Iraq. This method had been used in 1993, principally to allow the JTF-SWA commander to validate the provocation using cockpit footage and to allow the target to be vetted for collateral damage or Law of Armed Conflict risks.[20] The next-day response also gave commanders the ability to plan a response option at their leisure: decide on a suitable response and vet the target at the daily Target Review Board, an early evening VTC attended by senior representatives from JTF-SWA, CENTAF, CENTCOM, and other organizations. Any Iraqi provocations from the day's patrols were considered at the meeting, which focused on the "quality and quantity" of the offending air-defense activity and resulted in a decision to either launch a punitive strike the next day or to ignore the action. Even at its most aggressive, the provocation-to-response ratio in OSW would often be 3:1 or higher.

If a strike was authorized, the board would select one of a menu of response options (RO) from a deck of targets that had been vetted for collateral damage and validated as legitimate targets with hard-copy imagery and two pieces of collaborating evidence (such as cockpit footage and SIGINT or ELINT).[21] RO-1 authorized a strike on an active radar. RO-2 authorized a strike on one or more elements of an AAA site, and RO-3 directed a strike on one or more elements of a known SAM battery. Although these three response options did not require permission from Washington decision makers, they were carefully scrutinized for proportionality by military lawyers. JTF-SWA Commander Schmidt noted, "I would never sanction or nominate a target unless I had my Judge Advocate General sitting on my shoulder."[22]

The last category, RO-4, encompassed all other potential retaliatory strikes, including attacks on targets outside the IADS (including air fields), targets within the free-fly zone, or targets with a high risk of collateral damage. To ensure political buy-in for any such attacks, Zinni decided that these targets required approval by the secretary of defense. Iraqi communications facilities were a common RO-4 target and were struck on twenty-seven occasions in 1999.[23] On two occasions, the U.S. naval component commander (NAVCENT) successfully nominated Silkworm antiship missiles and their associated Rice Pad radars as RO-4 targets by citing their deployment as violations of the October 1994 "no-drive" zone moratorium on military augmentation south of 32°N. As long as they were not located too close to the Iranian border, antiship missile targets were generally approved. However, the national command authorities rejected other naval nominations, such as refurbished Iraqi missile boats, on the grounds that "it was too hard to connect a no-fly zone violation three hundred miles north with the sinking of a boat in the Al-Faw area."[24]

With this system in place, JTF-SWA's execution of the new ROEs unfolded with strong restraining pressures on the escalation of violence in the southern no-fly zone. The next-day targeting capability kept the commander in the loop and kept a lid on the response ratio, and prevented Iraqi air-defense operators and U.S. pilots from driving the operational tempo of the no-fly zone. Even when the acquisition of lucrative fleeting targets required a rare time-sensitive strike against a target not vetted for collateral damage, a quick authorization system was put in place to secure JTF-SWA approval (for RO-1 to RO-3) or national-level approval (for RO-4). Major General Schmidt noted that he "could expedite the system very quickly, getting a decision back in the minutes it took to regroup the package on a tanker and go back into the box to execute."[25] New wide-bandwidth communications were beginning to allow CENTCOM and other stateside organizations to monitor cockpit or Predator UAV feedback in real time, which increased the potential for centralized control.[26] VTCs, meanwhile, had ushered in the period of committee management of the southern no-fly zone, reducing the autonomy of individual commanders and further strengthening the conservative impulses governing the conduct of the zone.

DECENTRALIZED ROLLBACK IN OPERATION NORTHERN WATCH

The setup and outlook at Operation Northern Watch could not have been more different; it prompted a far more aggressive exploitation of the ROE parameters offered by the national command authorities. In its ninety-four months of operations, the Incirlik-based mission was always semiautonomous; it first played an adjunct and often overlooked role in the Gulf War (as JTF Proven Force) and then ran operations Provide Comfort (1991–97) and Northern Watch (1997–). Combined Task Force (CTF) Northern Watch was a subunified command reporting to U.S. EUCOM and theoretically was organizationally a slice of U.S. Air Forces in Europe (USAFE) and the U.S. 12th Air Force, but it was left well alone by its parent organizations. General Wesley Clark, the CINC at EUCOM (or CINCEUR), initially had little to do with the operation in 1998 and very rarely got involved in operational details; the CTF typically liaised with Deputy CINCEUR Adm. Abbot, who also granted the Incirlik headquarters a lot of autonomy. Iraq was within CENTCOM's area of responsibility, which made EUCOM's role there a secondary consideration for U.S. planners in Europe. EUCOM and USAFE's primary focus was the Balkans, and as 1999 began, they were heading into the seventy-day Kosovo air campaign, which commenced on March 23 and consumed the full attention of both organizations throughout most of the year.

In another contrast to JTF-SWA, the small size of CTF Northern Watch meant that it had never developed the large bureaucracy or management by committee that governed Southern Watch. Compared with the 160 aircraft of JTF-SWA, the Incirlik force employed merely 48 aircraft. The relationships among commanders, staff, and pilots was that much more intimate, and it was usual for Northern Watch commanders to fly occasional combat missions in northern Iraq and accompany packages entering the no-fly zone by flying on their supporting tankers.[27] In late 1998, the character of Northern Watch was very much defined by its commander, then–Brigadier General Deptula, the key planner in the Desert Storm air campaign and a bright light of the new generation of post-Vietnam fighter pilots.

Deptula was very different from the Southern Watch commanders in experience and outlook. First, Deptula saw the strategic role of the no-fly zones very clearly and welcomed the mission, writing: "When we set up a no-fly zone we are seizing an element of sovereign authority (the right to control airspace) on behalf of the world. We are declaring the subjected state to be less than a full member of the family of nations, unfit to govern in at least this one aspect, and under interdiction of sorts. This is a surrogate of war that clearly established the rogue status of the subject state."[28]

Second, Deptula's preoccupation was air strategy—the targeting, timing, and weaponeering of air strikes to achieve strategic objectives and operational effects—and his instinctive reaction to Iraq's increased resistance was to develop an approach that would defeat, not accommodate, the enemy actions. Ambassador Parris, former U.S. ambassador to Turkey, recalled, "Deptula was a warrior and a strategist."[29] This approach translated into a far more aggressive policing of the northern no-fly zones than the battened-down operations in the south and reinforced Richard Grunawalt's view that the personality of the commander is particularly important in limited war environments controlled by ROEs:

> As ROE are actually implemented by the operational commander, they may very well be a function of the "mind-set" of that individual. In the compressed time equation of a hostile act or demonstration of hostile intent encounter, when a potentially fateful decision may have to be taken on literally a moment's notice, the mind-set that the commander awoke with that morning may be decisive. If that mind-set is one of safety over security, of 'try not to hurt anyone,' that commander's response may be quite different than of the commander with a mind-set of 'don't take the first hit.'...There is more to the business of ROE than promulgating written guidance. It is also important to understand how that guidance is being inculcated in the thought processes of the commander—the mind-set.[30]

In an inversion of the south, where host-nation considerations were secondary and the CINC's strategic intent was king, Deptula would face little opposition from EUCOM to broadening his ROEs but needed to get any new rules approved by the traditionally querulous Turkish government. The U.S. mission at Incirlik had never been a comfortable arrangement for Ankara, one of America's most important but simultaneously most prickly strategic allies. Turkey had committed to host the small Joint Task Force (JTF) Proven Force only days before Desert Storm began. The timing reflected its ongoing fears about an Islamist backlash to basing forces involved in bombing a Muslim country and about long-term effects on its relationship with Iraq. By early 1999, Turkey's Prime Minister Bulent Ecevit remained critical of U.S. policy on Iraq, which he blamed for drawing new threats from Baghdad aimed at Turkey and other nations that hosted no-fly-zone forces. The Turkish government and military also held deep-seated fears that a Western military mission protecting the KRG zone in Iraq would interfere with Ankara's very active counterinsurgency campaign in southeastern Turkey and northern Iraq, which pursued Kurdistan Worker's Party (PKK) guerrillas into their mountain retreats. Turkey feared that this might result in an international recognition of the Kurdish claim to an autonomous homeland.[31]

These strategic concerns resulted in major operational restrictions on almost every sphere of Northern Watch activities. To assuage Turkish concerns about Islamist backlash and Iraqi relations, Ankara wanted the no-fly zone presented as a defensive operation. ONW Combined Forces Air Component Commander (CFACC) Col. Steve Callicutt recalled, "The Turks were very sensitive to any perceived offensive capabilities coming out of Turkey." In addition to limiting the size of the operation and the types of aircraft, Turkish sensitivity led to close scrutiny of the types of munitions used (missile systems and cluster bombs had to be authorized by the Turkish General Staff (TGS) from August 1996 onward) and meant that a formal system of next-day responses was out of the question—responses had to appear to be closely linked to the provocation. To prevent interference in the counterinsurgency against the PKK, the TGS limited ONW flying days and prevented all nighttime flying. This kept the air space clear for their own daytime and nocturnal strike missions and helicopter insertions; Turkish staff regularly canceled or pulled ONW patrols out of northern Iraq to make way for "Turkish Special Missions," the U.S. terminology for strikes on the PKK.[32]

Although relationships with the Turkish officers at Incirlik ranged from generally friendly to periodically frosty, the Turkish military were under orders to closely watch U.S. operations to ensure that restrictions were being followed and that Turkish interests were not being harmed. A Turkish officer flew on board the U.S. AWACS supporting every ONW mission and provided the Turkish Air Force regional command at Diyarbakir and his fellow officer monitoring the Incirlik command center with real-time coverage of U.S. activity. If the datalink broke between the Turkish officer on the AWACS and his ground stations—as it often did in its early days—the day's patrolling had to immediately cease and all U.S. and British aircraft return to Incirlik. This actually happened on a number of occasions.[33] The Turks highly valued this insight into U.S. operations and the real-time monitoring of U.S. aerial ISR activities over northern Iraq, including SIGINT cues, tactical imagery, and look-down radar coverage that Turkey frequently used to investigate or target potential PKK activities. In this sensitive environment, any new ROEs would require careful presentation, because, as Deptula recalled, "They would object to all kinds of things for no good reason, just because they could." CFACC Callicutt added, "It was the strangest strategic relationship I ever saw."[34]

When Deptula's deputy, Col. Callicutt, received word that the JCS were preparing a new and radically broader set of ROEs for use in the no-fly zones in early January, he immediately recognized the need to guide the process so that the result would be acceptable to the Turks. He initiated direct interaction with the Pentagon: "I called some friends of mine up [on the Joint Staff] and we nailed down what we were going to get, and they ended up giving us broader authority than we had actually requested. . . . The Secretary of Defense decided he didn't want any limiting restrictions upon our response options. . . . When we first read the ROE we saw there were now no restrictions and we knew that probably wouldn't go over too well from a Turkish viewpoint, to be able to strike anywhere we wanted at any time of our choosing, so we decided we would like to try and build a set of coalition ROE."[35]

Deptula was naturally receptive to a new set of ROEs and had already probed the issue with his Turkish counterpart at Incirlik. Deptula's needs were modest; he didn't want to hit a much broader range of targets (e.g., ground forces) or respond to a broader range of ROE trips. He was satisfied with enemy hostile acts (firing AAA or launching SAMs) and hostile intent (illumination with height-finding, acquisition, or tracking radar). Aerial incursions, relatively rare in the north, need not be punished with ground strikes. His priority was merely "to make sure our ability to respond was not limited just to the guns and missiles who [sic] were firing at us at the time."[36]

The U.S. response would not be instantaneous but would occur during the same mission (e.g., within minutes, not hours). Deptula was sensitive to

Turkish concern about any perception of overtly offensive activity involving Turkish-based forces, which ran high after Northern Watch aircraft destroyed the three offending SA-3 units in the December 28 SAMbush.[37] The December 28, 1998, responses against SA-3s had exposed Turkish sensitivity, as demonstrated when the chief of staff of the Turkish Air Force visited Incirlik to express concerns raised by the Turkish prime minister that the multiple SA-3 launches and the U.S. response were separated by seventeen minutes. On that occasion, Deptula "showed him camera footage and demonstrated to him in every single case the timelines between [SAM] shot and response, the sequence, [which left him] very comfortable that we were doing this by the book."[38] Deptula was willing to closely link the timing of Iraqi provocation and U.S. response if it meant keeping his ability to strike back at any part of the IADS and noted, "I needed to operate within the parameters of keeping the Turks on board, so I didn't want to push things to the degree where it would cause them to withdraw [from the new ROEs]."[39]

The formal ROE-generation process should have involved the Joint Staff and EUCOM, yet Callicutt explained that both these bodies soon dropped out of the drafting stage of the process: "At first the US was of the opinion that we had to approve this document in Washington.... The Joint Staff said for about two weeks that we had to send it to them for approval, then all of a sudden they decided, 'You can do it at your level if you don't change the intent of our document,' which we actually were going to be more restrictive than, so at that point they didn't care. Then the European Command decided they would become the approving authority for it, but that became unworkable because they came to one meeting and they sent one person who wasn't actually an expert on rules of engagement. Finally we decided that if we had the three senior officers sign it, I guess you would call it a fait accompli."[40]

Callicutt and his staff then entered into initial negotiations with the TGS concerning the new ROEs: "We drafted the language probably thirty times trying to satisfy the TGS.... Finally we told the Turkish General at Incirlik, 'Pick a set of words that you think are the correct English words and we'll see if we agree.'... It turned out they picked a less restrictive set of words than we had.... We had been getting more and more precise."[41] The highly detailed twenty-five-page draft ROEs was then marked up by Deptula and Callicutt, who outlined their minimum requirements (ability to strike back at any element of the IADS, not just the offending unit) and the issues open to compromise. According to Deptula, Callicutt and his staff had already identified the main areas of Turkish "pushback"[42]—which Callicutt confirmed could typically be skirted by couching language in defensive terms.[43] Deptula then took the draft ROEs to a meeting with the TGS in Ankara, which was also attended by Deputy CINCEUR Abbot and a EUCOM JAG. To Deptula's surprise, perhaps in reaction to ongoing Iraqi threats against Ankara and in response to a U.S. offer to deploy Patriot missiles, the Turkish four-star general confirmed that his delegation was ready to sign the ROEs the same day and Admiral Abbot confirmed that once Turkish approval was granted, U.S. Joint Staff approval of the ROEs would be a formality. Both senior officers then left. Deptula and a Turkish two-star general rapidly negotiated the approval, agreeing that U.S. forces could "strike any part of the IADS when threatened or fired upon" by any other part. Although the EUCOM JAG who was present throughout was nervous about the brevity of the discussion, Admiral Abbot accepted the new ROEs.[44] They were in place by January 14, 1999, more than a month ahead of the formal signing ceremony on February 22.[45] Ambassador Parris recalled, "Deptula was a real asset—very smooth and very smart— as he showed when he access to a wider range of targets than we thought possible. The issue had been hanging over the northern no-fly zone for nearly ten years, and the Ecevit government was no friend to the U.S., but he got the ROE in two days and built a wonderful relationship with the Turks."[46]

Decentralized execution—the delegation of response decisions and interpretation of ROEs by mission commanders in the cockpit—would be the hallmark of ONW under Deptula. The relatively uncontroversial nature of the IADS target set meant that, with very few exceptions, the Incirlik command center did not need to ask CINCEUR for permission to strike targets. There were no senior commanders in the loop, particularly during Kosovo, and although the CTF headquarters maintained live datalinks to the AWACS during patrolling periods in Iraq (known as "vul-time"), the pilots called the shots. Deptula explained: "When the 28 December missions were executed, our consolidated operating procedure said that the mission commander, before he employs any ordnance, will call back to and get approval from the commander before he can release ordnance. I went in and I changed that. And I told them, 'Look, you are the execution authority, I'll always hold the veto . . . but you're the first one on the scene, you're the closest to knowing what's going on. . . . Now I would brief them every day in the mission brief on the ROE, telling them, 'If you act in accord with these then you're cleared to engage.' So I would delegate default authority to the mission commander to release, which is a clear example of decentralizing execution to the lowest possible level."[47]

Northern Watch strike aircraft took off carrying preset response options, essentially a list of targets that had been validated the previous day by satellite imagery or SIGINT (provided by the Joint Analysis Center in Molesworth, U.K., or U.S. Strategic Command during the Kosovo conflict) or by ONW's British Jaguar or Tornado photoreconnaissance aircraft or other airborne sensors. On the morning of the patrol, the tactical reconnaissance aircraft would again verify the targets, return to Incirlik, and brief strike-aircraft crews before they took off. These pilots would also revisit their preset targets to validate their positions.[48] In the course of these activities, the air defenses would probably target or fire on the reconnaissance or patrolling aircraft, which tripped the ROEs. Iraq chose to actively resist the no-fly zone and the small size of the northern zone made the targeting of coalition aircraft inevitable. "Fifteen minutes deep and thirty minutes wide," in Callicutt's words, the zone was a shooting gallery. Although Deptula would be criticized for apparently goading Iraqi air defenses, simple geography meant that OSW practice of skirting known MEZs and gun positions was not an option for CTF Northern Watch, nor was it an acceptable course of action for Deptula: "If you impose any limits, then you're not complying with the strategic intent of the no-fly zone, placing restrictions on yourself as opposed to restrictions on the adversary. My view on reducing threat to U.S. aircraft or coalition aircraft is to take away the threat not cede segments of the airspace to the enemy . . . and have him establish a no-fly zone to us. . . . You eliminate the missile engagement zone, you don't avoid it."[49]

Upon detecting an ROE trip, the airborne mission commander would attempt to directly target the attacking element. This happened on only ten occasions under Deptula, according to Callicutt, and represented roughly 4 percent of strikes performed during Deptula's command. Eight years after Desert Storm, the problem remained target acquisition in cluttered terrain, a problem that was simultaneously stymieing the targeting of Serb ground forces and air defenses in the Kosovo campaign. Flying at twenty thousand feet, safely but not comfortably three to five thousand feet above bursting AAA fire, the shooters were rarely spotted except through F-15E imaging pods. However, as later ONW Commander Maj. Gen. Edward Ellis explained, "The pods give a soda straw view. If you're in someone's pod, woe betides you, but the chances of that happening are low. Finding an AAA piece is like finding a needle in a haystack."[50]

More often, therefore, the mission commander could select one or more targets from his onboard ROs to strike and ask for higher guidance if need be. As Callicutt explained, the number of responses was informally calculated: "It was a combination of judgment among the package commander, the senior officer on the AWACS, myself, or maybe even the General depending on how big a response we thought was appropriate. If a single gun got shot at you, it might be a single bomb or maybe two or three [in response] but it would never be many. What we viewed as more serious was when they started shooting missiles at us. . . . That tended to [draw] a bigger response. There was never a set response; it was more, 'What have they been doing over the past few weeks?'"[51]

The result was a major spike in the number of responses as CTF Northern Watch stepped up to Iraqi provocations rather than backing away from them. The amount of Iraqi fire or illumination set the pace of strikes, which sometimes resembled a miniature war. On January 30, 1999, six AAA aimpoints, one SAM unit, and various radars were struck, and on March 1, thirty 500-pound and 2,000-pound LGBs were delivered against a range of targets near Mosul.[52]

The air-defense rollback underway in the north saw CTF Northern Watch bring real sustained pressure to bear on the Iraqis. In a series of determined search-and-destroy sweeps, CTF Northern Watch taught the Iraqis that their radars and SAMs needed to be fully mobile to survive. The time lag between the morning reconnaissance sweep and the afternoon patrols had been used by the Iraqis to relocate their IADS elements, so ONW reduced the period by downloading reconnaissance data on the runway and digitally transferring the updates to strike aircraft already inbound for Iraq.[53] The radar elements of the IADS were subjected to advanced electronic-warfare efforts by the Northern Watch EA-6B aircraft, which decoyed radar-guided SAMs into empty areas or alternately attracted the SAM toward them, making it zigzag through the area until its fuel was expended. Using improved datalink architectures, the EA-6Bs and other sources of SIGINT and ELINT boosted the emissions-locating capabilities of Northern Watch F-16CJ HARM shooters, whose advanced HARM targeting systems complicated Iraqi attempts to avoid attracting HARM by simply switching off their radars momentarily.[54]

When the EA-6Bs were withdrawn in March 1999 to operate in the Kosovo campaign, the Northern Watch team adapted new tactics to keep up the pressure despite the relative lack of jamming and targeting support against enemy radar-guided SAMs. The use of AGM-130 rocket-assisted 2,000-pound guided bombs was a key element of the effort. Rushed to Incirlik following the December 28 SAM shots, the AGM-130s arrived on December 31 and saw their first operational use by the United States on January 11, 1999, when two SAMs were destroyed by a pair of the munitions delivered by F-15Es. An AGM-130 was useful because of its ability to be launched from a range of forty miles and guided from approximately one hundred miles away. This meant that it could be launched from outside the MEZ of Iraq's longest-ranged missile, the SA-2, while the controlling F-15E retired to a safer position. Once the GPS-guided missile was within three miles of its target, the F-15E could then perform terminal guidance using the munition's television-guidance system.[55]

In addition to increasing pilot safety, the weapon caused massive, unrepairable damage and was excellent at catching Iraqi IADS elements by surprise because its impact had little relation to the location of the F-15E; this earned it the nickname "the holy hand grenade."[56] With such a weapon at hand, it was tempting for U.S. commanders to fire it or guide it from within Turkey's safe air space or to reach south of 36°N and strike the Iraqi radars and long-range SAMs that could and frequently did ellipse the northern no-fly zones. As Callicutt recalled, "That was where the Turks got even more sensitive. An air-to-air weapon going across the line was one thing, a HARM going across to find a radar was another, but an air-to-ground weapon was well outside what they allowed."[57] As noted, the Turks had to approve all munitions used in the no-fly zone, and they remained very skeptical about allowing stand-off weapons or indeed any offensive-sounding munitions. One Northern Watch officer explained, "The Turks didn't like the AGM nomenclature—they'd previously banned the AGM-65 Mavericks and generally didn't like things that fired off of aircraft, they had to drop off of aircraft. . . . We never did quite get round to explaining that [AGM-130] had a [rocket] motor on it, we figured that's going to really upset them, we just said it was a 2,000-pound bomb with television guidance and changed its nomenclature on the ATO to LGB-130."[58]

Reflecting on the lack of Turkish responses after some strikes south of 36°N, another ONW officer recalled, "I think the Turks really knew this thing was powered but they didn't want to officially acknowledge it. If something blew up ten miles south of the line, it was obvious that gravity didn't get it there. Its like 'we know what you're doing; we just don't want to tell people we know what you're doing.'"[59]

To maintain pressure on the air defenses, the Incirlik planners also had to learn to react to collateral-damage incidents. The first of these occurred on February 28, 1999, when a microwave-relay tower was deliberately targeted and its destruction isolated pipeline-monitoring equipment, thereby shutting down a pipeline that delivered Iraqi oil to Turkey. Turkish reaction was quick and fiery. President Sulayman Demirel criticized the strike while the Foreign Ministry spokesperson focused on the broader issue of the military containment of Iraq, stating: "This latest event is an opportunity for us to underline our sensitivity. No, it is not acceptable. There should be a solution to this tension, which has been a bleeding wound since 1991." In the United States, the strike attracted strong comments at the UNSC and drew statements from U.S. Secretary of Defense Cohen and from U.S. State Department spokespeople.[60] Following Deptula's explanation of the rationale behind the strike, the TGS placed a moratorium on all targets within one mile of the pipeline but took no further action.[61]

On the next occasion, the mistaken bombing of a group of shepherds on May 12, 1999, civilian deaths were involved. Satellite-imagery analysts at U.S. Strategic Command had identified a metal water trough surrounded by farming equipment, vehicles, and shepherd tents as a SAM plus support vehicles and camouflage netting, and passed on the GPS coordinates of the site (rather than imagery) to CTF Northern Watch. It conducted an AGM-130 strike on the site, followed up by further attacks. In total, the attacks killed nineteen Iraqi civilians and injured forty-six. In response, Deptula quickly briefed the TGS with U.S. imagery and put in place a new system that required printable imagery to be validated at Incirlik before any future strikes were authorized, once again defusing any potential Turkish restrictions on the mission.[62]

In addition to postincident damage mitigation, CTF Northern Watch developed new tactics to allow it to attack Iraqi targets that were deliberately exploiting civilian neighborhoods or religious and cultural locations. One measure of the effectiveness of Deptula's aggressive approach was the effect it had on the Iraqi adversary, who had not only got more mobile but had also readopted the Gulf War tactics of collocating military equipment at sites on the no-target list. By the end of Deptula's term as CTF commander in late October 1999, Iraq's air defenses had been physically rolled back to some extent, redeployed from the countryside to the urban sprawls around Tall Afar and Mosul.[63]

Iraqi SAMs and AAA pieces were showing up in the center of hamlets, so the Incirlik command group responded by deploying "inert" weapons—LGBs filled with concrete rather than explosives—and counted on their kinetic impact to destroy targets without the risk of tiers of collateral damage from fragmentation and blast effects. Unpopular with conventional military thinkers at USAFE and EUCOM, the highly accurate inert weapons (concrete-filled 1,000-pound GBU-12 LGBs) proved effective against solid buildings and vehicles (e.g., radar vans) but needed a lucky dead-on hit to cause damage to spindly targets such as AAA pieces and SAMs. Deptula also sought to use a concrete-filled 2,000-pound GBU-27 to attack the Iraqi Northern SOC, which had relocated to the archaeological ruins at Nineveh after the Mosul SOC had been destroyed by two explosive-filled GBU-27s on February 23, 1999. Although the inert payload offered less collateral damage, the request was turned down by EUCOM JAGs concerned about Turkish and international reaction to any damage to the ancient site.[64]

In the year since Deptula had taken command of ONW in November 1998, the CTF had met the Iraqi air-defense system blow-for-blow by responding at almost a 1:1 ratio to the Iraqi attacks it had detected. A comparison of OSW and ONW statistics gives an illustration of the relative aggressiveness of the northern zone. In the south, 16,000 sorties were flown by 160 aircraft from December 1998 to November 1999, compared with 7,500 sorties flown by the 48 aircraft of ONW. The larger OSW used 550 munitions and engaged 135 targets, whereas Northern Watch used 1,100 munitions and engaged 250 targets, yet Northern Watch had suffered only one major fatal collateral-damage incident, the same total as OSW.[65] In the north, at least, the immovable object of Iraq's will to resist had been met by the unstoppable force of U.S. warriors given free rein, resulting in an almighty clash.

PUTTING THE BRAKES ON NORTHERN WATCH

A new era began when Deptula handed over command of CTF Northern Watch to Brig. Gen. Robert Dulaney in late October 1999, which signaled the beginning of CTF Northern Watch's "normalization" under a series of less aggressive and more force protection-oriented commanders. Under Deptula's command, the formulaic no-fly zones had become dynamic and controversial and their political profile had grown: both Russia and France tied their support of U.S.-supported sanctions-reform efforts to a quieting of the no-fly zones.[66]

When Dulaney met with CINCEUR Clark just before taking command, the instructions he received illustrated the change of attitude toward Northern Watch. Dulaney recalled, "Up to that point, there had been a lot of noise from ONW. News was slow and a U.S. election was coming, and Clark was tight with the political cycle. I was told to get the no-fly zone stuff off the front page." The "don't ask, don't tell" elements of the U.S.–Turkish military relationship were also going to end and there was to be no bending, stretching, or breaking the ROEs. Dulaney was ordered "to start picking up broken glass and work on improving relations with the Turkish General Staff." Dulaney's mission was couched in terms of negative conditions; "don't lose a pilot, don't cause collateral damage you can't justify." Above all, Clark stressed, primarily enforce the no-fly zone, meaning prevent Iraqi aircraft from flying within the zone, an event that had not taken place since the mid-1990s. Clark's successor, Gen. Ralston, continued in the same vein, and told the Incirlik commander, "We're not looking for a fight." The message Dulaney took away from these briefings was that "this was a no-fly zone, not a war. The driving factor was not to annihilate the Iraqi military, or even the IADS, in fact we wanted the Iraqi military to be strong in the region, and no-one told me to take them down."[67]

Dulaney and his successor, Brigadier General Ellis, translated these objectives into a sequence of operational decisions that made the northern no-fly zone a quieter and safer place for CTF Northern Watch pilots and Iraq air-defense operators alike. First, Dulaney stopped posting operational details on the command's website, instituted a news crackdown, and maintained a far lower media profile than Deptula.[68] Second, he approached the Turks and tackled the issue of U.S. actions outside the ROEs head-on by apologizing for the historical use of the AGM-130 and even the inert munitions in Northern Watch. He stated, "My pledge to you is that I will honor the ROE you have signed. I will stick to it, I will never lie to you, or I will resign."

The bemused Turks thereafter vetoed the use of AGM-130 and later EUCOM banned the reactive use of HARMs, removing the two most effective arrows from Northern Watch's limited quiver. Dulaney immediately briefed the pilots to lower the response rate and made Iraqi provocations less likely by skirting known AAA sites and MEZ. Because antiaircraft fire could not reach the Northern Watch aircraft, AAA fire ceased to be an automatic ROE trip, which vastly reduced the number of Iraqi "violations" of the no-fly zone. Response options also tightened under Dulaney and Ellis, with EUCOM

playing a far greater role in vetting out-of-the-ordinary targets such as ammunition dumps or SAM sites south of 36°N. Communications nodes dropped
off the menu because they ran coaxial to roads and pipelines and therefore
represented too much of a risk of collateral damage to the Turks.[69] They were,
Ellis recalled, "way out there from what the host nation would accept."[70] Far
from using inert munitions to reach into the urban hiding places of Iraq's air
defenses, CTF Northern Watch skirted all potential high-collateral-damage
targets that could not be comprehensively vetted by EUCOM and Incirlik-
based JAGs. Dulaney recalled that "Nineveh and all those other targets of that
kind were just not worth the pain."[71]

Little by little, the northern no-fly zone was returning to its roots, a
tightly constrained operation focused on preventing air and, to a lesser extent,
ground attacks on the Kurds. This was much to the relief of the many advocates of the slow collapse of at least one of the no-fly zones. By May 2001,
when CINCEUR Ralston addressed the Senate Armed Services Committee
about the no-fly zone, EUCOM was openly advocating replacing patrols over
northern Iraq with ad hoc retaliatory strikes as and when Iraq violated the
no-fly zone. An unnamed U.S. defense official told *Aviation Week and Space
Technology* that "we've been periodically planning to do away with Northern
Watch for ages," which reflected widespread exasperation about overstrain and
readiness in the U.S. military after a decade of post–Cold War expeditionary
deployments.[72] The U.S. military had been called upon to launch an average of 10 contingency operations a year under President Clinton compared
with 1.75 contingency deployments per year under Reagan and 3.5 under
President George H. W. Bush.[73] Following ten years of no-fly zones and the
grueling Kosovo campaign, U.S. airpower was particularly fatigued, which
resulted in the lowest tactical fighter-fleet readiness in a decade, a nadir
in spare parts and flying days, and plummeting retention. U.S. Air Force
Chief of Staff Ryan and ACC Chief Gen. Richard Hawley commented that
when viewed on a global level, the U.S. Air Force had been operating at a
higher operational tempo during Kosovo than during either the Vietnam or
Gulf Wars.[74]

Although OSW would also be under pressure to reduce its operational
tempo and move to a more sustainable model of patrolling and retaliating, the
United States had fewer strategic interests in the north and less cooperative
hosts. This marked Northern Watch for a slow fade out. Eternally skeptical
about the no-fly zones, Dulaney's approach had merely encouraged greater

Turkish interference in the ONW mission, both in terms of weaponeering restrictions and further reductions in the flying time allowed to the mission. As Ellis added, "By 2000, our job was to make sure that no-one thrust a microphone in the president or prime minister's face because of us, and to make sure that one of us didn't end up being dragged through the streets of Baghdad, alive or worse."[75] Force protection and the avoidance of controversial activity was the focus. ONW aircraft only spent 5 percent of each week over Iraq, spread across a maximum of eighteen flying days. Compared to 105 responses in the first half of 1999, reduced patrolling and response rates meant that only 3 armed responses occurred in the northern no-fly in the first six months of 2002.[76] Iraq's ongoing resistance would hereafter be concentrated in the southern no-fly zones, where potentially lucrative targets and opportunities for ongoing confrontation remained in steady supply.

DEVOLUTION AND EVOLUTION OF IRAQI AIR DEFENSES BY 2001

Although it may sound counterintuitive, a U.S. pilot overflying Iraq at medium altitude in January 2001 was no safer than a pilot flying at the close of the Gulf War in 1991. As Desert Storm finished, the Iraqi air-defense system was in ruins and in deep shock—it had been pounded relentlessly for forty-three days by radar-chasing HARMs and bunker-penetrating LGBs. Postwar Coalition patrols over Iraq as late as December 1992 were primarily composed of four-plane formations of fighter bombers. Yet, in January 2001, after ten years of sanctions and no-fly-zone patrolling, no Coalition commander would think of sending a four-plane unit into Iraq alone. Instead, balanced packages of specialized fighter combat air patrols, HARM shooters, jammers, and reconnaissance aircraft alongside the multirole aircraft would be dispatched.[77] The story of what happened to Iraqi air defenses and Western tolerance toward aircraft losses is a tale that says much about the Iraqi military's capacity not only to resist but to adapt and evolve to meet any level of threat.

As previous chapters note, the postwar awakening of Iraq's air defenses began in April 1992 and accelerated into meaningful armed resistance with the December 27 SAMbush of that year. Following the air strikes of January 1993, the air defenses were largely quiescent until 1996, when another series of SAMbushes were launched after Desert Strike. These actions made clear to the U.S. intelligence community that in the intervening years, Iraq's air defenses had recovered considerably and displayed "a high level of redundancy and the first signs of partial and selective reintegration." Between 1996 and 1998, the number of active C2 nodes increased; the mobility of radar, SAMs, and guns increased; and communications intercepts decreased as more voice and digital data passed through fiber-optic cables.[78] Although Desert Fox had struck at some valuable radar, engineering plants, and air-defense reserve-equipment depots, the IADS was simply big enough to roll with the blow and come out of its corner fighting within days. The really critical fixed infrastructure—SOCs and IOCs—had not been effectively hit since 1993, or 1996 in a limited number of cases. The fully mobile or relocatable elements of the system—the SAMs, radar, and AAAs—were easily repaired and retained in large stocks. Because Iraq only needed to fire small numbers of SAMs to defy and even present some threat to the United States, under conditions short of war the system could only be momentarily suppressed, never defeated.

Likewise, although sanctions could prevent any leap in improvement of the Iraqi IADS (such as the procurement of cutting-edge Russian SAMs or AAMs) and prevent large-scale redevelopment of the IrAF, it could only delay the incremental reconstitution of ground-based air defenses. By 1994, Iraq had transitioned from its prewar reliance on overseas overhaul of aircraft and in-country, expatriate technicians to largely indigenous missile and aircraft repair and upgrade industries that employed selective outreach programs to access foreign technology and technicians. Iraq was relatively well postured to undertake a clandestine rearmament program through its extensive prewar, covert procurement infrastructure.

The Mukhabarat M-19 directorate and a range of other government departments continued to manage a host of front companies in China, India, Pakistan, Malaysia, Singapore, and Thailand. Baghdad stationed M-19 representatives at Iraq's embassies in every major procurement hub in the former Soviet bloc, from Ukraine to Belarus, to the Russian Federation, to the Czech Republic, Bulgaria, Romania, and Hungary. Eritrea, Nigeria, Greece, and Yemen were favored transshipping nodes, and Jordan, the UAE, Turkey, and Iran all served as entry points for land and sea deliveries throughout the 1990s. Spare parts, chemicals, and explosives arrived within second-hand kitchen appliances or under forged UN documentation. In the late 1990s, Syria emerged as a new and significant import artery because of its combination of both an unsupervised payment mechanism—the 150,000 to 200,000 barrels per day of oil flowing through the Iraq-Syria pipeline—and a secure transport mechanism for large items: the Aleppo-Baghdad railway and road systems. By February 2001, Germany's Bundesnachrichtendienst assessed that Iraq's covert procurement network was highly active, outperforming even Iran's well-recognized clandestine acquisition capability.[79]

The majority of Iraq's exposed covert acquisitions efforts appeared to be aimed at improving IADS. Spare parts were acquired for Iraq's dwindling numbers of aircraft, which allowed the small fleet of IrAF aircraft used to violate the no-fly zones (principally MiG-25 and MiG-23 variants) to be maintained in relatively good condition. Tires, engines, and other parts were procured from foreign vendors, including many spare parts cannibalized from IrAF aircraft stored in Hungary, Serbia, Sudan, and Belarus prior to the Gulf War, where they were awaiting refurbishment when UN sanctions began.[80] Since the mid-1990s, Iraq had also imported solid-fuel packs for certain SAMs, guidance and spare parts, and vehicles adapted to give static SAMs (such as the SA-2s and SA-3s) or radar arrays greater mobility. Iraq appears also to have sought out former Soviet Bloc assistance with range and mobility improvements to its SA-3 missiles. It tried—unsuccessfully—to procure passive radio-reconnaissance early-warning systems from the Czech Republic (the Tamara system in 1997) and Ukraine (the Kolchuga system in 2002). Furthermore, Iraq either developed or bought a small number of GPS jammers.[81]

The air defenses received priority treatment in the covert acquisition effort because they represented Iraq's main theater of resistance against Anglo-American military containment from Desert Fox onward. Ten years of continuous U.S. suppression of enemy air defenses built an up impressive body of experience. In addition, contrary to other arms of the military, purges had been few and far between in the Air Defense Command (ADC), which allowed such experience to accrue at all levels of the leadership. Similar to the ADC, the IrAF maintained close links with the regime, although its commander, Lt. Gen. Hamid Reja Shilah, and the ADC commander, Lt. Gen. Yaseen Shaheen Mohammed, were professional officers, not political appointees. Monthly meetings between Saddam and these commanders were highly publicized, as were meetings with teams from air defense and air-force research centers. Although the Iraqi military's size dropped from approximately 1 million personnel to fewer than seven hundred thousand, the ADC maintained its staffing levels despite repeated cutbacks to other services.[82]

The ADC represented a mixture of token and effective elements, as did the rest of the Iraqi military more generally. Some research and design efforts were undoubtedly dreamed up purely for Saddam's delectation and many were hyped to "maintain the illusion of progress," as David Fulghum surmised.[83] One Iraqi air-defense engineer noted in a 2003 interview that many air-defense projects had been "lies, all lies."[84] At the sharp end, likewise, much of the air-defense effort comprised token efforts to show fealty to the regime, to perform the bare minimum required by military duty, and to signal defiance—however feckless—to the overflying forces. The classic anecdotal example is the footage captured by a Predator UAV that shows an air-defense gunner running from a distant foxhole to his AAA piece, hurriedly pulling the lanyard to fire the piece, and dashing back to his hole without a second thought for military effectiveness.[85] As ineffective as this was, the majority of Iraq's air defenses operated in this mode or at a slightly higher level of motivation and skill. It formed a pattern of token resistance wherever allied aircraft flew and successfully deterred low-altitude operations throughout Iraq.

The key mid- and high-altitude threat from the ADC instead came from Iraq's SAMs and radar operators, plus the cadre of its residual air force. Operational losses in this community were a steady trickle throughout the 1990s but do not appear to have greatly affected its ability to maintain active and relatively formally structured MEZs around key hubs at the H-3 air base (west), the Tallil air base and Basra (south), and Mosul (north), plus the Baghdad SuperMEZ that covered the so-called "presidential security triangle encompassing Tikrit-Baghdad/Taji-Kirkuk. Within these MEZs, a number of normal and extended-range SA-3 and SA-3 systems constantly rotated on average a half mile every twelve to thirty hours among a large number of sand berms and camouflaged hides connected to the IADS by landlines.[86] Where the effective defenses offered by relocation, concealment, and berming failed, Iraq could quickly draw on its large stocks of SA-3s and SA-3s to replace lost missiles and likewise maintained repair workshops and depot reserves of radars and control vans.[87]

Even more dangerous than the relatively fixed radii of the known MEZs were the groups of mobile SAMs that Iraq had increasingly deployed to the no-fly zones since Desert Storm. These expeditionary SAM groups would deploy from their depots within the free-fly zone and disperse within the no-fly zones, moving eighty to a hundred kilometers south or north, stay a couple of days, and then return to the center for maintenance and rearmament.[88] In their operations, they acted much like roaming nuclear submarines or the ground-launched cruise missiles of the Cold War. The SA-6 was the most feared of these weapons—its three missiles were nicknamed "the three fingers of death"—but converted BM-21 "Ringback" truck-mounted, surface-to-surface, multiple-rocket launchers were also used. Previously cumbersome SA-2 and SA-3 missiles were made mobile using ingeniously engineered, commercial articulated six- and eight-wheel trucks. Dump trucks with hydraulic arms functioned as SAM transporters, as well as TELs for Iraq's in-plain-sight post–Desert Fox Al-Samoud missile program.[89] As U.S. or British aircraft sought to skirt known MEZs, the expeditionary SAM groups lay in wait. Depending on the level of preparation, the missiles might be employed with a range of tactical support. At the least ambitious level, the missiles would simply ambush any overflying aircraft by maintaining emission control (EMCON, that is, giving off no radar or signals emissions) and firing at the last moment. SAMs would typically be optically guided, and the SA-6 enjoyed the strong advantage of having a "late lock-on" semiactive radar seeker in the missile that could guide the missile once in flight. This occurred on September 11, 1996, when an SA-6 narrowly missed a Northern Watch F-16. The Ringbacks, meanwhile, simply filled a box of air space with their forty 122-mm rockets, which Dulaney recalled "was really scary for pilots because you might have to pull a high-g maneuver at no notice to get out of that box when the missiles started coming up at you."[90]

However, the United States was more worried about the digitization and integration of the threat than hardware at the sharp end. The integration of the expeditionary SAM groups into the Iraqi air-defense effort could get much more complex and more deadly, starting with the relatively simple coordination of radar illumination by nearby MEZ to distract overflying aircraft or alternately the integration of an IrAF incursion to draw U.S. aircraft into the classic SAMbush. Mobile SAMs were also able to maintain EMCON by receiving early-warning data from a range of Iraqi sensors. One source of information about the bearing, direction, speed, and altitude on inbound aircraft was the large French Volex III and Soviet P-14 Tall King surveillance radar near Baghdad. These were ensconced safely within the free-fly zones and passed early-warning data to any elements of the IADS connected to Iraq's growing fiber-optic landline network.

To provide the SAM batteries with more detailed targeting data, a range of smaller target-acquisition radar (such as Soviet P-15 Flat Face and the radar elements of the Roland mobile SAMs) was increasingly networked; each radar tracked the target for approximately eight seconds before another radar took over, which mimicked the Serbian tactics of "time-shared illuminating."[91] Expeditionary SAM groups plugged into the network at so-called "planned drops," temporary firing points where they could receive voice cues through mobile or landline phone conversations or even receive digital targeting data through Iraq's fiber-optic network. This made the expeditionary SAM groups harder to track, target, and jam.[92] Iraq's use of mobility and sensor networks threatened to negate many of the assumed post–Desert Storm advantages that airpower was presumed to hold over air defenses, which Carlo Kopp summed up thus: "The air battle is a battle of attrition. As such, it is a battle where mobility confers a major advantage in allowing the choice of entering an engagement or not, and that mobility is an attribute of the attacking air force, weighing heavily in its favor."[93]

In the no-fly zones, where the aircraft were tied to patrolling terrain and the expeditionary SAM groups could choose when and how to engage, the equation had slowly been turned on its head. It seemed only a matter of time before Iraq got lucky.

FEBRUARY 2001 STRIKE

CENTAF's new commander, Lt. Gen. Charles Wald, was not willing to let the Iraqis land the first blow if preventative action could reduce the chances of a U.S. pilot being shot down. Wald explained:

> When I became the commander at CENTAF I was not interested in just doing the status quo, my feeling was that we needed to do something different.... This thing was all getting out of hand politically and militarily and the objectives seemed to be clouded, Saddam's ability had increased to creep in and take out ability to police the no-fly zone away from us. My feeling was that with the turn of the new Millennium, with the new [Bush] administration, it would be the perfect time to change how we were doing things, so we built a briefing for CENTCOM and gave it to the CINC and the chief of staff, and in that briefing we recommended a change in how we did business—either we push it up, or we do the status quo, or we do hardly anything, we quit. We needed to get out of this middle road that was really dangerous ... this cynical status quo approach to the no-fly zones and to Iraq. You can't do this tit for tat thing. Our recommendation was that we do something more aggressive.[94]

Wald's planners at CENTAF, who coordinated their efforts with the JTF-SWA planners in Saudi Arabia, developed an RO-4 option that sought to dismantle the increasingly integrated air-defense system. CENTAF sought to "change the rules" by striking at the static surveillance radar and fiber-optic nodes in the free-fly zone that had been feeding early-warning data to the southern air defenses. By destroying these radars and degrading Iraq's means of high-speed, secure data communications among elements of the IADS, CENTAF hoped to force Iraq to rely primarily on its vulnerable shorter-ranged radars south of 33°N and sought to "put the Iraqi decision-maker back in the system." CENTAF hoped KARI could again become an antiquated and easily jammed or mapped fire-control system. As soon as it was once again reliant on voice communications to cue SAM operators onto their targets.[95]

General Franks, who became the new CINCENT in July 2000, agreed to send up the requested RO-4 to the Joint Staff for presentation to the new national command authorities under recently inaugurated President George Walker Bush, son of the Desert Storm president. Although the strike would be the first military act of the new administration, CJCS Shelton had strong grounds on which to rationalize the action when he presented in at a weekly National Security Council meeting on February 14. Since January 1, 2001, Iraq had fired AAA on fifty-one occasions and, more important, had fired fourteen SAMs. Saddam had been up to his old tricks, giving the outgoing president a send-off and testing the new administration. Lt. Gen. Gregory Newbold, director of operations at the JCS, recalled, "It was not the number of systems that posed the threat, it was that the systems in place were firing more frequently, and they were more accurate because they were coordinated."[96] In a *Washington Post* Op-Ed on February 10, 2001, titled "A Risky No-Fly Zone over Iraq," Jim Hoagland wrote, "For the first time since the Persian Gulf War ended a decade ago, Iraqi anti-aircraft units seriously endanger the lives of American and British pilots enforcing the no-fly zones."[97]

However, although the description of Iraq's threat was convincingly laid out to the new administration and clearly understood, there was confusion about CENTAF's proposed response. On the surface, the strike looked relatively routine; although it would strike targets north of 33°N, it could be launched from south of the line and from outside the risky Baghdad SuperMEZ because of the overwhelming use of aircraft-delivered stand-off munitions (the powered AGM-130 and the glide-bomb JSOW, rather than the high-profile TLAM). Furthermore, the rationale for striking them was clear, the targets were unarguably military and assessed as low collateral-damage risks, and the decision to strike on the Muslim Sabbath was made to reduce the number of construction workers, including Chinese contractors, who would be working on fiber-optic development.[98] What had been not been conveyed was that some of the targets were so close to Baghdad—within five miles of the center of the city—that the attack would look and sound like an attack on the city itself, a significant action for a new president to sanction.

Patrolling levels had been increased since February 11 to desensitize the Iraqis to the blow that was coming, and no out-of-theater assets (such as the B-2 Spirit stealth bomber or the B-52/CALCM combination) had been incorporated into planning. By 1920 Baghdad time on February 16, strike aircraft were inbound from Kuwaiti air bases and the carrier USS *Harry S. Truman*. Thirty minutes later impacts began to register. Two RAF Tornados plinked the An-Numaniyah IOC with 2,000-pound Paveway III bombs, both to stun the air defenses and to wreck one of the locations where Baghdad's fiber-optic lines emerged and fed data into the southern IADS. U.S. Navy F/A-18s hit another southern command center at As-Suwayrah with stand-off land-attack missiles—extended range (SLAM-ER). U.S. Air Force F-15Es carried out the most northerly strike against the central node of Iraq's coaxial fiber-optic network at the Al-Taji SOC, just north of Baghdad, and launched five 2,000-pound AGM-130s at communications and radar aimpoints. The remaining targets—surveillance radar at Baghdad and Taqaddum—were attacked with twenty-eight GPS-guided AGM-154 JSOWs (joint stand-off weapon) delivered by U.S. Navy F/A-18s. By 2140 local time, all strike aircraft had safely exited Iraq.[99]

With tethered-satellite and airborne surveillance monitoring the strikes in real time (by RAF Nimrod ELINT/SIGINT aircraft and U.S. RQ-1B Predators), BDA was quick in coming, but political reaction came faster. The strike on radars and communications nodes just north, west, and south of Baghdad had tripped off reflexive AAA firing over the Iraqi capital—a potent image of crisis that recalled the beginning of the Gulf War almost exactly ten years earlier. Any shift in the enforcement of the no-fly zones had long been scoured for policy significance and the zones became the center stage of the U.S.–Iraqi confrontation. Therefore, the bombing seemed doubly significant as the first act of a new president. Because of the weaknesses of the initial February 14 briefing and subsequent communication failures, at a high-profile press conference with Mexican President Vicente Fox, President Bush was surprised to be asked why he was bombing Baghdad. Lieutenant General Wald recalled, "On the day of the attack, the President was in Mexico and the NSC thought the attack was going to be at a certain time and we had to change the time of the attack a little bit for various reasons and I'm not sure the NSC staff were notified, I'm not sure if the Joint Chiefs actually went over to the NSC and said, 'we're changing our Time-over-Target.' In the meantime, Bush's press conference coincided with the [new] TOT. . . . The press conference got out of whack and became focused on bombing Iraq."

Aside from embarrassing the president, the strikes did not appear to have been optimally effective either. Although the vital Al-Taji fiber-optic aimpoints had been hit hard by the AGM-130s and the An-Numaniyah and As-Suwayrah strikes had also been successful, the takedown of Iraq's surveillance radar appeared to have gone badly wrong. It was typical for submunitions damage to radar dishes to be difficult for satellite imagery to detect, but tethered-satellite and Predator footage clearly showed that all but two of the twenty-eight JSOWs had uniformly veered to away from their targets by thirty feet or so, a problem that was later attributed to unanticipated wind sheer. Wald stated, "That pissed off the National Security Council even worse because, not only did you embarrass the President, but you didn't hit shit."[100]

TRYING TO BACK OFF IN OPERATION SOUTHERN WATCH

The February 16 strike had been a political setback for the administration, underlining growing international sensitivity to the no-fly zones. This occurred just as Secretary of State Colin Powell was seeking to deactivate growing international opposition to UN sanctions on Iraq by building a coalition to support a new program of "smart sanctions" that promised to bring less hardship to the Iraqi people. Following the strike, the United States was accused by Russia and China of exacerbating tension in the region, where a new intifada had broken out between the Palestinians and Israelis in October 2000. France and a number of other European countries criticized the United States and Britain for acting without consulting them, as did close U.S. allies in the Middle East such as Jordan and Egypt.[101]

The no-fly zones were also not popular in the U.S. Congress or the U.S. military, where concern was growing about the possibility that the United States might lose a pilot while undertaking the wearying and apparently endless burden of patrolling Iraqi air space. The Iraqis had not missed a beat after the February 16 strike and sat out the strike as usual—as much because of its rapid execution as of any Iraqi intent—then quickly repaired damaged radars and ramped up their resistance. Between February 16 and May 9, 2001, Thomas Ricks reported that slightly more than a hundred SAM launches had been observed by U.S. aircraft, which was "an unusually determined effort to shoot down an aircraft."[102] At a May hearing of the Senate Armed Services Committee, CINCCENT Franks was candid about his fears of losing a pilot. In 1995, Capt. Scott O'Grady had been shot down in Bosnia and recovered after escaping and evading pursuit for a week. In 1999, an F-117A Nighthawk and an F-16CJ had been shot down by Serbian air defenses. These incidents showed it could happen.

Franks told Congress that risks could be reduced by limiting the extent of OSW patrolling, which is exactly what began to happen in summer 2001. JTF-SWA Commander Maj. Gen. Gene Renuart recalled that CENTCOM directed "a modified employment pattern," which involved a lower rate of response, albeit against more valuable Iraqi C2 targets, and a decrease in the number of days on which U.S. aircraft would fly. OSW patrols began to skirt known MEZs and even AAA pieces, which eventually resulted in an almost complete cessation of flights north of the Euphrates River.[103] The United States had ceded air space before; in summer 1996, for instance, U.S. patrols raised their minimum altitude by four thousand feet to invalidate certain types of Iraqi threats, which forced them to accept an incremental degradation of monitoring and retaliatory capability. Reacting to the growing political critiques and operational risks, OSW was beginning to move down the same path that had caused ONW to adopt minimalist objectives and sink into obscurity. Unlike in the north, however, Iraq's southern air defenses represented the last major theater in which Baghdad could maintain its military resistance to Anglo-American containment, and Baghdad was unwilling to allow the zone to slip into inactivity. In the first six months of 2001, Iraq fired on or tracked allied aircraft on 370 occasions, compared with 110 in a similar period in 2000. The OSW response rate, meanwhile, had dropped from a ratio of 1:7 in 2000 (meaning roughly one response per seven provocations) to 1:40 in 2001.

However, the United States now had the tiger by the tail, and it proved difficult to convince Iraq to enter into the one-sided cease-fire. Baghdad took advantage of reduced U.S. aerial presence over Iraq to increase its violations of the no-fly zones, as it had done the previous summer and autumn when key elements of the OSW package were grounded and the patrols were ceased for occasional "maintenance days." On September 4, 2000, for instance, Iraqi MiG-25RBTs had made a carefully planned incursion clean through the undefended southern no-fly zone and into Saudi Arabia, the first Iraqi violation of Saudi air space since the IrAF probed it in August 1990. Iraq's prior dispersal of IADS and military elements suggested that Baghdad's aim in the September 2000 incursion had been to draw a U.S. response during the UN Millennium Summit in New York.[104]

In 2001, the residual IrAF was gearing up for further confrontations. The IrAF now boasted between 30 and 130 usable airframes, according to various estimates, and low serviceability made it likely that the real total of active aircraft was at the lower end of the scale.[105] The primary fixed-wing types in service appeared to be the MiG-23 fighter/ground-attack aircraft, which was flown by a number of Iraqi squadrons.[106] In June 2001, Iraq had deployed a number of MiG-23 units to two reopened air bases in western Iraq as part of a series of four major deployments carried out since the beginning of the intifada in October 2000, apparently to show support for the Palestinian cause. Elements of six Iraqi Republican Guard and army divisions, plus air defenses and the MiG-23 units, had shuffled back and forth across the western Anbar province. These drew Israeli protests to the United States, but presented little danger to anyone, even Jordan, whose air space was penetrated as far as the capital, Amman, by Iraqi MiG-25RBT aircraft on July 30 and 31.[107]

Although the bulk of Iraq's remaining air fleet was for show—its pilot training consisted of taking off, circling the airfield, and landing—the MiG-25 community in Iraq was a different story. Composed of the remaining half dozen or so aircraft, the MiG-25 and its small cadre of highly experienced pilots represented a strategic asset to the Baghdad regime and provided the Baathist government with a means of continually signaling its defiance by violating the no-fly zones or the territory of its neighbors. MiG-25s could do this without suffering attrition through interception, and indeed, the inability to intercept the Mach 2.4 incursions of Iraq's MiG-25s was one of the issues that had prompted the loosened ROEs in January 1999. Since the Iran-Iraq War, the MiG-25 was considered the most capable Iraqi interceptor and proved to be the hardest to shoot down. They achieved twenty kills in the 1980-88 war and one unconfirmed kill in Desert Storm (the downing of Lt. Cdr. Scott Speicher's F/A-18C on the first night of the war). Since Desert Storm, the

MiG-25 fleet had become the Baathist regime's remaining showcase aerial capability; it was feted at annual military parades in Baghdad and performed all deep incursions beyond the free-fly zone.

In addition to the raw speed of the MiG-25 variants used by Iraq, the quality of its pilots kept the MiG-25 dangerous. U.S. monitoring of the IrAF had shown that although some flight training continued as late as 2002, U.S. intelligence analysts concluded, "We believe the limited flight training hours go to senior people rather than attempting to maintain any sort of pipeline for new pilots."[108] In fact, as Col. Jim Moschgat, the U.S. Air Force wing commander at PSAB, recalled, by 2001 "the really deep incursions were carried out by just two Iraqi Air Force colonels." The limited roster of other pilots were well known to U.S. SIGINT officers.[109] These long-serving IrAF pilots were among the most experienced combat aviators in the world. On the offensive, they were highly experienced in performing high-speed merges and swift single-pass slash attacks, and indeed, since 1997 they had trained to make high-altitude interceptions, which U.S. analysts interpreted as a threat to the U-2 flights. U.S. SIGINT showed that they were understandably "scared shitless" during their hair-raising incursions into the no-fly zones or neighboring countries, but the MiG-25 pilots were uniquely well trained to survive these episodes.

As Tom Cooper and Farhad Bishop noted, the IrAF was a uniquely experienced force by 1990 because it had been involved in approximately a thousand AAM engagements, including the world's first widespread use of active and semiactive radar homing missiles and "beyond visual range" engagements. Desert Storm and incursions since 1991 had also given the narrowing cadre of Iraqi pilots unparalleled experience at evading U.S. missiles.[110] F-16 pilot Col. Paul White highlighted Iraq's ability to time its incursions when U.S. aircraft were egressing the no-fly zones or were low on fuel, and praised Iraqi pilots for their fine judgment of U.S. missile-engagement ranges and well-executed escape maneuvers.[111] Indeed, as late as early 2003, IrAF MiG-25s were able to launch an incursion that penetrated sixty kilometers into Saudi Arabian air space before U.S. fighters could scramble to intercept, by which time the MiG had safely recovered to the central Iraq free-fly zone.[112]

Alongside incursions of the no-fly zones, Iraq also began to aggressively target U.S. airborne C2ISR assets in summer 2001. In mid-July, a U.S. Navy E-2C Hawkeye visually acquired the trail of an Iraqi extended-range SA-3 that had been fired into Kuwaiti air space in an attempt to hit the aircraft. In late July, a U.S. Air Force AWACS reported a similar visual sighting along the Saudi-Iraqi border. Then, on July 25, an Iraqi SA-2 missile targeted a U-2 aircraft cruising over Iraq at seventy thousand feet, and the SAM exploded close enough to the aircraft to catch the U-2 in its shock wave. Although the SA-2 attempt did not employ radar guidance, it was clear that surveillance radars near Baghdad had tracked the U-2 and predicted its path based on previous sorties and basic predictive mathematics of the same type used to "lead" AAA fire ahead of fast-moving aircraft. With its radar guidance removed, the SA-2 could achieve the necessary lift required to reach the operating altitude of the U-2.[113] In previous years, the targeting of a U-2, let alone a near miss, would have triggered a massive U.S. response, yet CENTCOM launched no response until August 7 and further U-2 flights were curtailed.

Next, the Iraqis began to target RQ-1B Predator UAVs, which had remained in Kuwait since the February 16 strike. On August 8, an Iraqi MiG buzzed an OSW Predator, but because it was traveling four times faster than the UAV it failed to hit the drone with its cannon. Following the incident, CENTCOM began experimentally mounting Stinger AAMs on the Predator, which resulted in the first air-to-air duel between manned and unmanned aircraft on December 27, 2002. In that incident the Iraqi MiG-25PD won the joust by shooting down the Predator and escaping the no-fly zone intact.[114] With enough time, CENTCOM Analyst Greg Hooker recalled, Iraq's air-defense operators could perfect their intercept geometries.[115]

The first Predator downings had been achieved using SAMs in late summer and early fall of 2001. On August 27, 2001, the first Predator was shot down during a night mission near Basra, probably by an aging Roland SAM. This incident caused mirth and some embarrassment at JTF-SWA.[116] The next Predator was lost while flying a routine reconnaissance mission on September 11, 2001, a day that had begun like any other. That Predator was lost at 0730 Baghdad time, nine hours before the first plane hit the north tower of the World Trade Center. While reeling from the sight of the destruction of the Twin Towers, CINCCENT Franks recalled ordering the retaliation for the lost Predator: "I said, 'Prepare a kinetic response.' No matter what was happening in New York, Saddam Hussein and his military had to understand that they would not be permitted to take advantage of the situation."[117] Thus, the first U.S. military action after the 9/11 attacks would not fall against the Taliban but rather against Iraq air-defense operators.

Although Iraq had not sponsored the 9/11 attacks, the stage was now set for conflict between Washington and Baghdad on a scale not seen since 1991. The increased post-9/11 focus on security and preemption of threats provided the backdrop to a final acceleration in the U.S. struggle with the Baathist regime. Endgame was in sight. The no-fly zones would soon land the first blows of the new phase of conflict, and less than two years after 9/11, the no-fly zones would be collapsed as the invasion of Iraq ended. Through the no-fly zones, the United States and Iraq had remained locked in direct and daily military confrontation since the Gulf War. They allowed Baghdad and Washington to signal to each other their defiance and their resolve, respectively. By the time Operation Southern Focus began, the United States and Britain had flown 265,000 sorties in the southern no-fly zone and 122,500 in northern Iraq—an average of 34,000 sorties each year, the equivalent of refighting Desert Storm every three years. During the twelve years of no-fly-zone operations, Iraq had never backed off, even under the sustained campaigns of 1999 and 2002. It used the no-fly zones to underline the regime's unflinching opposition to foreign containment.

On the American side of the balance sheet, the no-fly zones would offer a means of escalating the conflict with Iraq when war approached in 2002–3. When that war began, the United States would greatly benefit from the long-term heritage of combat experience that the zones had developed throughout the U.S. aviator community. CENTAF Commander Lt. Gen. Michael Moseley related, "I was particularly lucky because I've got probably the highest level of combat experienced pilots and crews.... There's not too many captains and majors and lieutenant colonels out there in the Air Force and in the flying Navy that haven't been in this theater multiple times. Thanks to countless Red Flags, Blue Flags, and Cope Thunder [exercises], plus twelve years of real-world training in Northern Watch and Southern Watch . . . this is the most experienced force in the history of aviation."[118]

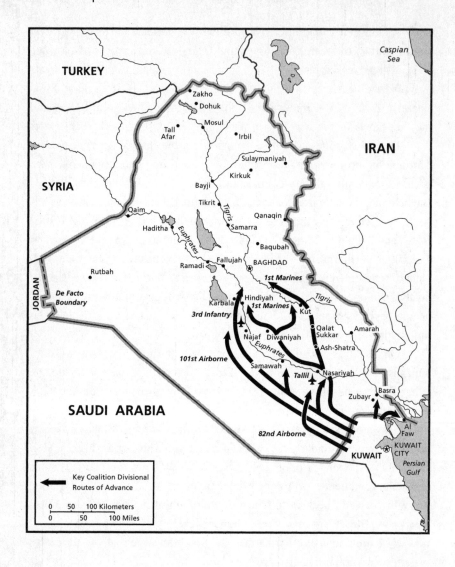

TURKEY

Caspian Sea

Zakho
Dohuk
Tall Afar
Mosul
Irbil

SYRIA

Sulaymaniyah
Kirkuk
Bayji
Qaim
Tikrit
Tigris
Qanaqin
Haditha
Samarra
Euphrates
Baqubah
Ramadi
Fallujah
BAGHDAD

IRAN

JORDAN
De Facto Boundary
Rutbah
Karbala
Hindiyah
1st Marines
1st Marines
Tigris
Kut
3rd Infantry
Najaf
Diwaniyah
Qalat Sukkar
Amarah
101st Airborne
Euphrates
Ash-Shatra
Samawah
Tallil
Nasariyah
SAUDI ARABIA
82nd Airborne
Zubayr
Basra
Al Faw
KUWAIT CITY
KUWAIT
Persian Gulf

Key Coalition Divisional Routes of Advance

0   50   100 Kilometers
0   50   100 Miles

PART THREE
ENDING RESISTANCE

9
Transitioning to War

F or the first time since its establishment, CENTCOM's main war-fighting focus shifted outside the Gulf, necessitating a virtual cessation of combat operations in the no-fly zone. General Franks promulgated a new set of instructions aimed at limiting Iraq's opportunities to provoke the United States. CENTCOM recognized that if the United States did not have to respond to as many provocations, resources would be freed up for Operation Enduring Freedom in Afghanistan. JTF-SWA began an intensive program of leaflet drops to convince Iraqi air-defense operators that the United States would not attack them unless they undertook a hostile act. This policy required U.S. pilots to return to the pre-1999 ROE ROs, which called for direct response to only observed hostile acts.[1] U-2 flights within Iraq stopped and other patrolling was greatly curtailed. Despite increasing air-defense activity in the Tallil and Basra MEZs and the movement of expeditionary SAM groups into the south, only one next-day response was launched in the five months after 9/11.[2]

During that time, the Taliban were toppled in Operation Enduring Freedom and Al-Qaeda remnants were driven from enclaves in Tora Bora and the Shahikot Valley. Beyond these near-term actions, an open-ended war against terrorism beckoned. However, far from slipping into the hiatus that Saddam Hussein had long awaited, the military containment of Iraq was entering a new and decisive phase. The no-fly zones would return, forged into a weapon of war and integrated into an endgame: the military overthrow of Saddam Hussein's regime.

There was nothing new about the aim of regime change in Iraq—it had been covert U.S. policy since President George H. W. Bush signed a CIA finding in August 1990 and overt U.S. policy since Clinton administration statements and the enactment of the Iraq Liberation Act in 1998. What was new, however, was the unprecedented injection of energy that the policy received under President George W. Bush. When the new administration received its brief on Iraq policy from the outgoing Clinton administration on January 10, 2001, Secretary of Defense Cohen told the Bush team that little support existed within the region for aggressive regime change in Iraq, and the CIA briefing to the new president made hardly any mention of the Baathist regime in Baghdad.[3]

According to the Senate committee on prewar intelligence, the U.S. intelligence community broadly agreed that the Baathist hierarchy knew that any aggressive act would hasten, not delay, the end of the regime—in short, Iraq was contained. The one exception to this assessment was the issue of WMD in Iraq, about which little could be said with certainty since the cessation of UN inspections in December 1998. The one feature on which most analysts agreed was that eventual ownership of WMD remained a central goal of the regime and therefore the Baathist regime would always be a threat to regional and U.S. security interests.[4] On June 12, 2000, Saddam Hussein had stated in a televised address, "If the world tells us to abandon all our weapons and only keep the sword, we will do that. . . . But if they keep a rifle and then tell me that I only have the right to possess a sword, then we would say no."[5] U.S. intelligence analysts believed that Iraq had been concealing WMD break-out capabilities since 1991 and that it had ample opportunity to begin a reconstitution of its weapons programs since 1998. Consistent with its former behavior, the regime's *intent* to possess WMD was assumed. This state of affairs required constant and open-ended vigilance and military containment on the part of the United States and its regional allies.

What the new Bush administration brought to U.S. Iraq policy was a sense of impatience vis-à-vis the eventual collapse of Baathist rule and a willingness to actively bring about the fall of the regime. The failure of U.S.-backed coup and uprisings in the mid-1990s had left the policy of regime change in the doldrums. The Baathist regime appeared increasingly feeble in the late 1990s, its defiant gestures robbed of much of their international profile since the platform of obstructing UN inspections was removed. The dictatorial regime, increasingly an anachronism in the new millennium, was compared to a rundown house that would someday collapse under its own weight. The Bush administration believed that the structure would collapse far sooner given a well-placed kick, and the sooner, the better. Administration decision makers such as Secretary of Defense Donald Rumsfeld believed that the open-ended containment of Iraq was an unwanted distraction that required increasing amounts of political capital to maintain. In early 2001, Rumsfeld told CINCCENT Franks: "We need concrete goals. The current policy is open-ended. . . . Containment has not changed the regime's behavior. We still see Saddam shooting at our aircrews. . . . The sanctions are collapsing."[6]

Between February and June 2001 the administration held an unusually busy schedule of five Deputy Principals Committee meetings about Iraq. The meetings gave birth to a vague strategy document titled "Iraq: A Liberation Strategy," which proposed that Iraqi opposition forces backed by U.S. military assistance could spark an uprising in southern Iraq and liberate a new enclave to mirror the KRG enclave in the north. From this base, the opposition would declare a provisional government. The United States would seek to win international recognition for it and encourage further defections until eventually the Baathist government could be ousted from Baghdad. This strategy had been supported by Rumsfeld and his subordinate, Deputy Secretary of Defense Paul Wolfowitz, since the early-1990s, and was one of the proposals made in the February 19, 1998, "Open Letter to the President" written by Washington notables about regime change in Iraq. Contrary to the coup options preferred by the CIA and U.S. State Department—which stressed the "centrist" maintenance of power within the existing Sunni-dominated political system—the new plan was instead "peripheral" in nature. It started in the north and south, empowered opposition actors, and promised to radically change the sectarian power balance of the Iraqi state. The enclave strategy sought to plan regime change rather than simply exploit an opportunity thrown up by internal splits within the regime, and thus involved a far higher degree of U.S. military support, both in the training and equipping of five thousand opposition forces and in the likely use of U.S. air assets and special forces to protect and expand the opposition enclaves.[7]

If left to rely on the ponderous capabilities of the external opposition groups, this endgame strategy for Iraq might have floundered like previous regime change plans, but 9/11 and the successful execution of Operation

Enduring Freedom in Afghanistan opened the door for a far more direct U.S. role in the destruction of the Iraqi regime. Although Iraqi air-defense operators were the first victims of U.S. military action in the post-9/11 period, an Iraqi role in 9/11 and a knee-jerk U.S. response against Iraq were discounted at an early stage during the September 15, 2001, PCM at Camp David. However, the longer-term outlook of the Baathist regime had disastrously turned on 9/11.

President Bush noted, "Prior to 9/11, a president could see a threat and contain it," whereas after 9/11 "Saddam Hussein's capacity to create harm, all his terrible features, became much more threatening. Keeping Saddam in a box looked less and less feasible to me."[8] British Prime Minister Tony Blair likewise noted, "What changed for me with September 11th was that I thought then you have to change your mindset. . . . You have to deal with this right away or the threat will grow. . . . You have to take a stand, you have to say 'Right, we are not going to allow the development of WMD in breach of the will of the international community to continue.'" The British Butler report on prewar intelligence remarked, "What changed was not the pace of Saddam Hussein's WMD programs, but our tolerance of them post-11th September."[9] Thus, as opposed to being the savior of Saddam Hussein's regime, WMD were now the greatest threat to the Baathist regime, even though there was little possibility that their existence could be proved. With neither the UN nor Western intelligence agencies able to judge Saddam's capabilities or intentions regarding WMD worst-case assumptions substituted for facts. There would no longer be any need for half measures vis-à-vis Iraq, Bush administration hawks reasoned.

Bruce Riedel, a senior DoD and National Security Council decision maker on Iraq in the every administration since 1990, recalled that a page had been turned in U.S. policy: "Most senior decision-makers in both [the first Bush and Clinton] administrations were unanimously of the view that no military solution was possible to the Iraq problem. They knew that no application of force, short of a full invasion, would remove the irritant, Saddam. And neither president seriously considered the option. This was for three reasons: 1) Allied countries would not support an invasion; 2) the US public would not support one either; and 3) there was the fear of a quagmire. There was no clear endgame or exit strategy. After 9/11, only one of these seemed to have changed—US public support for a more aggressive foreign policy."[10]

Against the backdrop of a global war of terrorism, a full-scale invasion and occupation of Iraq was both a major gamble and a controversial project of epic proportions, as former DIA Analyst Jeffrey White noted when he wrote, "For the first time since World War II, the United States and its allies sought to invade a large and well-armed country with the express intention of toppling its government, disarming it, and reconstructing it."[11]

PLANNING OPERATION IRAQI FREEDOM

The planning of Operation Iraqi Freedom began on November 21, 2001, amid ongoing combat operations in Afghanistan and only seventy-two days after 9/11. On that day, President Bush enquired about the status of U.S. war plans vis-à-vis Iraq, which initiated a rapid update of the existing defensive OPLAN, 1003-98, undertaken against the backdrop of a routine review of all the U.S. military's on-the-shelf war plans.[12]

There was nothing routine about the planning process that took place between November 21 and December 28, however, when an updated offensive version of OPLAN 1003-98 was briefed to President Bush. Secretary of Defense Rumsfeld had communicated a very clear set of strategic objectives to CINCCENT Franks. The core mission was unequivocal and a complete departure from prior U.S. policy in Iraq: to militarily remove the regime of Saddam Hussein. Ancillary strategic objectives included the prevention of attacks on Israel and other neighboring states and the prevention of "scorched-earth" actions by the regime and avoidable collateral damage by the Coalition. The "strategic flank" of the conflict—the public relations and public-support challenge—was to be protected by keeping the war short: "fast and final" as one planner recalled General Franks commenting.[13]

By December 28, 2001, Franks had developed a set of military objectives to achieve the strategic missions proposed by Rumsfeld. Planners at CENTCOM identified a range of centers of gravity that the United States planned to attack. The leadership—Saddam, his sons, and his key lieutenants, family, and tribe—were a target set. Other regime elements including security forces and C2 were second. WMD delivery mechanisms and industry was a third. The regime's military core—the SRG and Republican Guard—were targeted. Iraqi intelligence and terrorist operatives were identified as a center of gravity. The regular army was a target, as was the perceptions and loyalties of the population. Using a method that had proven useful in

Afghanistan, Franks then plotted these centers of gravity against a type of action that the U.S. might utilize, termed "lines of operation." These included "kinetic operations"—the use of airpower, missiles, and other firepower—special operations, maneuvering forces, influence or information operations, support for the Iraqi opposition, and postwar humanitarian assistance. The matrix of centers of gravity and lines of operation formed sixty-three boxes that encompassed the full range of military, diplomatic, and economic tools that the United States could bring to bear during an operation to liberate Iraq.[14]

To CENTCOM, the most important line of operation was the maneuver of ground forces, which would have to be launched primarily from Kuwait, the only regional state willing to provide basing for the multidivision ground force required. The military objective given to the Combined Forces Land Component Commander (CFLCC), Lt. Gen. David McKiernan, was to re-move Saddam Hussein's "ability to control and direct the country"; to U.S. military commanders, this meant seizing Baghdad.[15] In contrast with the pe-ripheral nature of the enclave strategies of the past, a common feature of planning for Operation Iraqi Freedom would be a singular focus on the isola-tion of Baghdad. The cities of the south and the north were to be by-passed, as were any enemy forces that did not threaten the drive on Baghdad. Once Baghdad was isolated and ringed with U.S. military bases, the city would be methodically cleared by infantry-heavy U.S. forces under a concept of op-erations developed by CENTCOM's "Operational Planning Team—Fortress Baghdad." Only then, with the regime ousted, would the other cities and con-centrations of Iraqi forces be intensively assaulted if they failed to capitulate. CENTCOM analysts predicted no major redeployment of Iraqi ground forces from their peacetime barracks, and thus this operational model would stress the importance of fixing in position the Iraqi regular-army corps guarding the Iranian border and the fourteen Iraqi divisions guarding the Green Line in the north.[16]

Two other areas of key terrain were identified by CENTCOM planners as priority military objectives. The first was Iraq's western desert, where it was feared the Baathist regime would once again fire Scud missiles toward Israel, seeking again to draw Israel into the war to shatter the fragile and much-diminished Coalition. Both U.S. and British intelligence assessments credited Iraq with maintaining a residual Scud force of up to twenty al-Hussein missiles in various stages of readiness, and the two intelligence communities agreed that there would be few disincentives to deter Saddam Hussein from ordering an attack on Israel, perhaps even a strike involving CBWs.[17] In response, according to air planner Lt. Col. David Hathaway, CENTCOM planned an early and comprehensive blanketing of the western Scud launch areas with special forces and airpower to ensure that at best not a single missile round could be fired at Israel and at worst that any missile launcher would be destroyed after firing its single missile (thus reducing Iraq's ability to fire future salvos).[18] Shortly after Iraq's western desert was to be blanketed, Iraq's southern oil fields were also to be secured by special forces to prevent any demolition of the vital economic assets in the south of the country.

From early January 2002 until the next presidential briefing on February 7, 2002, CENTCOM planners stitched together components of existing operational and contingency plans. The defensive OPLAN 1003-98 provided many of the necessary deployment schedules required to undertake the complex deployment of forces to theater, whereas a number of employment plans provided tactical and operational-employment concepts. Operation Plan Vigilant Guardian and Contingency Plan Wood provided air-land options for seizing the southern oil fields and securing an enclave in southern Iraq that included the capture of bridges over the Euphrates River at Nasariyah, which was a necessary precursor underpinning any attempt to move further north toward Baghdad. A large range of existing ROs from no-fly zone operations and the cheat-and-retreat crises of the late 1990s provided airpower employment options against a range of target sets, including southern Iraqi ground forces.[19] However, although many technical details could be lifted from earlier plans, the design of Operation Iraqi Freedom would involve a fundamental revision of the assumptions about the scale of the forces required, the speed with which they would be built up, and the conditions under which combat would begin.

As early as November 2001, Secretary of Defense Rumsfeld had called on CINCCENT Franks to reduce the scale of the U.S. military commitment required to remove the regime in Baghdad. Conventional thinking about the relative importance of quality and quantity on the battlefield had been under attack throughout the 1990s. The Gulf War and the subsequent revolution in military affairs—the marriage of sensors, advanced processing power, and precision-strike technologies—provided strong indications that qualitatively superior training and equipment could offset considerable quantitative disadvantages in modern warfare. Throughout the 1990s, the U.S. military had maintained and even increased its "training and doctrine superiority" and continued to hone its late–Cold War ability to fight outnumbered and win.[20]

Furthermore, CENTCOM planners had long been mentored by former XVIII Airborne Corps Commander Gen. Gary Luck, who had stressed the importance of "overmatching power, not overwhelming forces" and "precision engagement": massing U.S. combat power precisely where it was required to ensure decisive local supremacy.[21]

Operation Iraqi Freedom would stress speed and simultaneity, focusing on the very principles that had made air-land battle so successful in 1991. Offensive maneuver and seizure of the initiative would set the terms of battle. The ability to think and act faster than the enemy, and to think and fight deep, would win the battle. Just as Desert Storm represented the first test of the late–Cold war military and its concepts of operations, so Operation Iraqi Freedom would represent the first test of the concepts that were intended to shape the post–Cold War transformation of the U.S. military.

The dilapidated state of the Iraqi military further increased the military differential that was predicted before Operation Iraqi Freedom began. U.S. intelligence-community assessments of Iraq's conventional military power had consistently downgraded Iraqi military potential for a decade. Iraq's air force had literally disappeared on the eve of war; its navy consisted of a ragtag fleet of dhows and coastal patrol boats. Of Iraq's twenty-one land-forces combat divisions and seven special-forces or commando brigades, merely half were assessed as combat ready in the lead-up to the war, all were under strength and armed with archaic and poorly maintained Cold War equipment, and merely a third of serving personnel were assessed to be regulars or long-term reservists.[22] The Iraqi regular army had lost most of its credibility in 1991 and during various uprisings since. Aside from half a dozen armored or mechanized divisions, the regular army comprised almost no combat power. Recalling the physical deterioration of these forces, Scott Ritter wrote, "The Iraqi Army is in total disarray, capable of manning little more than security pickets along the Iran-Iraq border, in northern Iraq, and in southern Iraq. I have visited numerous Iraqi barracks and I have seen soldiers in tattered uniforms and bare feet. Military training is without substance, barely sufficient to convert recruits into simple soldiers, let alone provide skills in the intricacies of modern combined-arms combat."[23] Only the SRG division and the four remaining Republican Guard armored or mechanized divisions were rated as serious threats by CENTCOM.

Both Rumsfeld and Franks considered Iraqi military deterioration to be symptomatic of the broader fragility of the Baathist regime. As CENTCOM

Intelligence analyst Greg Hooker recalled, Rumsfeld and those advocating near-term regime change had argued since the mid-1990s that Saddam's house would collapse with the first good kick. Now, as war approached, plans were laid in case of what Franks termed "catastrophic success"—the collapse of the regime in the opening hours of a war. Elements of the U.S. 82nd Airborne Division were placed on notice to fly into Saddam International Airport to secure the city in this event.[24] Considering the predicted military differential between the U.S. and Iraqi forces, plus the war plan's emphasis on avoiding all the major urban areas except for Baghdad and selectively engaging Iraqi army units based on their ability to interfere, the U.S. leadership sought to reduce the number of U.S. forces deployed in Iraqi Freedom. OPLAN 1003-98 suggested 400,000 troops, but U.S. leadership wanted the number reduced to a maximum of 250,000–350,000, with the option of starting combat with as few forces as 105,000.[25] Whereas Gen. Norman Schwarzkopf had built up a 4.8 to 1 numerical superiority at the point of impact for his decisive left hook in 1991, the U.S. military were now preparing to drive to Baghdad with a 2 to 1 advantage, at best, over the Iraqi forces that might offer resistance along the route of advance. [26]

OPERATION SOUTHERN FOCUS AND THE SLIDE TO WAR

Operation Iraqi Freedom was also designed to give the president the ability to execute the invasion on relatively short notice. Rumsfeld pressed Franks to shorten the time between the visible beginning of a military buildup (Notification Day or N-Day) and the beginning of ground combat (G-Day). This feature of Operation Iraqi Freedom was driven by the political and military lessons of the years of cheat-and-retreat crises in the mid- and late 1990s. Franks and the CENTCOM staff were well aware of Iraq's proven ability to sense the U.S. transitioning from political to military means. On a number of occasions, Iraq had been able to use this warning to carry out diplomatic countermeasures that enabled it to dissuade the United States from military action or to enact military preparations that reduced the value of Coalition strikes.[27]

At the military level, Franks wanted to achieve maximum tactical surprise and to reduce the exposure of U.S. troop concentrations in Kuwait to preemptive Iraqi attacks with conventional weapons or CBWs. At the political level, the civilian leadership wanted to reduce the period of diplomatic and

political wrangling that might immediately precede a war and could potentially disrupt the operation. For a government that had internally decided that
only regime change and U.S. military occupation in Iraq could deactivate the
threat posed by the country, a compressed execution timeline represented a
prudent step, considering Iraq's proven ability to succeed in cheat-and-retreat
episodes.

The apparent telescoping of U.S. deployment schedules owed more to
an effective campaign of deception than a streamlined U.S. logistical effort.
The period between N-Day and G-Day had been 114 days in OPLAN 1003-
98, meaning that the United States needed to begin deploying forces to the
Gulf in November 2002 to be able to execute in late March 2003. The United
States began a covert deployment of low-profile logistics, communications,
and personnel as early as the spring of 2002, followed by a "shadow N-Day"
on December 6, 2002, when larger numbers of U.S. forces began a low-profile
103-day buildup in the Gulf.[28] The periodic deployments of new groups of
forces to the Gulf were termed "spikes" or "sine waves" by Franks, which he
described as "spurts of activity, followed by periods of inactivity. We want
the Iraqis to become accustomed to military expansion and then apparent
contraction."[29]

CENTCOM Director of Operations Renuart recalled, "The UN process raised the noise level and we could move forces and still stay within
that context, ostensibly using the deployment to show resolve. Instead of a
sixteen-day intensive build up, we spread that out between November and
February, nibbling away at the deployment process all the way through the
UN diplomacy."[30]

A final covert feature of the transition between peace and war occurred
in the relative beginning of ground and air operations. Although various iterations of the new operations plan—code named OPLAN 1003V—involved
either a short period of air operations before G-Day or a simultaneous air and
land commencement, in reality the air war began months, arguably years, before ground forces crossed the line of departure in Operation Iraqi Freedom.
As far back as 2001, Franks had described the objectives of the no-fly zone as
"ensuring that Iraq cannot easily repair its anti-aircraft activities in the no-fly
zone … [and] ensuring that ingress and egress routes that would be necessary to prosecute an expanded war against Iraq remain sufficiently clear of
sophisticated air defense systems."[31] At the December 28, 2001, presidential
briefing, Franks had suggested that the no-fly zones could serve as a means

of carrying out battlefield preparation in the prewar period.[32] Then, in March
2002, CENTAF officers held a post-Afghanistan meeting at the U.S. Air Force
base at Ramstein, Germany, to discuss the near past and the future of air operations in the CENTCOM area of responsibility. It was at this conference that
CENTAF Commander Moseley formally proposed a revitalization of the no-
fly zones. For all intents and purposes, this meant OSW, because the Turkish
government would never again allow ONW to reach the operating tempos of
the Deptula era, particularly in support of a future war against Iraq.[33] Moseley had previously been the CJCS's representative on the U.S. government
Deputy Principals Committee and had dealt extensively with no-fly zone issues at that level. Moseley suggested that planners begin considering how
OSW could be used to reduce the time between A-Day (the beginning of
wartime air operations against Iraq) and G-Day, in keeping with Secretary
of Defense Rumsfeld's avowed preference for speed and simultaneity in any
future operation.

The concept of operations was next fleshed out at a meeting or "huddle"
of CENTAF, USAFE, and JTF-SWA planners at Camp Doha, Kuwait, on
April 24, 2002. The group proposed that OSW soon return to full patrolling,
including flights north of the Euphrates and even the Tigris Rivers, and restart
U-2 flights, which would provide vital ISR support in the lead-in to war.
As Major General Renuart, now director of operations at CENTCOM, noted,
"Our thinking was, 'If the Iraqis keep giving us [ROE] triggers, we'll keep
degrading them.'"[34] The United States would henceforth respond to a high
proportion of provocations, requiring a larger roster of prepared ROs. This
process would be more deliberately calculated than ever before, because OSW
finally had an end goal: the aerial preparation of the battlefield for a full-scale
invasion of Iraq. At Ramstein, the U.S. planners set out a series of operational objectives that would complement a future invasion of Iraq. They were
"(1) Gain and maintain air superiority; (2) Degrade tactical communications;
(3) Cause strategic and tactical surprise and capitulation through Information
Operations; (4) Eliminate Iraq's anti-access capabilities, such as surface-to-
surface missiles and anti-shipping missiles."[35] OSW ROs were structured to
meet this set of objectives in a program scheduled to commence in June 2002,
code named Operation Southern Focus. The coordinating mechanism was a
target list that was derived from a "systems approach to targeting" that had
ranked the most vital C3 components of Iraq's IADS south of 33°N. Operation
Southern Focus planner Lieutenant Colonel Hathaway recalled that the target

list was completed at a meeting of targeteers at CENTCOM between May 8 and 10, 2002: "The list was put together using nodal analysis, fused from two separate efforts, one done by the CENTAF Information Operations flight, and the other built at [the JWAC]. It aimed to achieve the most effect with the least damage. It also had 'revisit' windows built in, allowing re-strikes to be regularly undertaken if our leaflets hadn't persuaded the Iraqis to desist from repairing the sites."[36]

The Iraqis could be counted on to play ball, and throughout the spring and early summer of 2002, Baghdad gave the United States all the ROE trips it required to undertake Southern Focus. Large numbers of Coalition aircraft were still returning to their bases in Saudi Arabia and Kuwait with their drop tanks ejected, a sure sign that evasive action had needed to be taken. One no-fly zone commander recalled, "We were shot at once an hour in summer 2002, and that's just what we noticed."[37] The attacks on communications came first: OSW strikes concentrated on Baghdad's expanding fiber-optic network, which had recently been boosted by a loosening of sanctions that allowed French and Chinese firms to undertake a total of $133.5 million worth of telecommunications upgrades, including fiber-optic cable development and other digital upgrades that could be used to relay air-defense data.[38] Fiber-optic vaults, where the piped signals were periodically boosted, were about the size of manhole covers and needed to be very precisely plinked, but U.S. laser-guided munitions were equal to the task. Throughout the summer of 2002 a relentless series of strikes forced Iraq's air defenses to rely on high-frequency radio communications, which aided the task of monitoring, jamming, and targeting the communications network.[39]

Southern Focus accelerated again in September 2002, when Moseley gained authorization from the national command authorities to routinely strike C2 targets. This marked what Lieutenant General Renuart termed "the real start of Southern Focus." On September 5, 2002, a heavy attack was launched against the H-3 SOC, the C2 linchpin of Iraq's western air defenses. Renuart recalled, "That strike was a long time in coming. Since Fall 2000, Saddam had deployed forces out there, re-established command and control facilities, and caused a constant risk of Israeli reaction."[40] The strike also marked the opening of a campaign to blind the Iraqi IADS and keep its C2 centers constantly suppressed. Within weeks, all the other Iraqi active SOCs and IOCs south of 33°N had also been hit with heavy 2,000-pound GBU-27 ground-penetrating bombs.

Alongside these "kinetic" strikes, the United States accelerated its information operations campaign in late 2002. More than 4.2 million PSYOPs leaflets were dropped between the beginning of Operation Southern Focus and the start of Operation Iraqi Freedom, first simply telling air-defense operators to desist from firing and warning maintenance crews and civilians to stay away from destroyed fiber-optic vaults. These were backed by the threat of overflying OSW aircraft and loitering Predators, which were now armed with AGM-114 Hellfire missiles.[41] Regime security forces assiduously collected and destroyed as many leaflets as possible.[42] Finally, on December 12, the EC-130 Commando Solo aircraft of the 193rd Special Operations Wing began transmitting PSYOPs radio broadcasts into Iraq, which complemented other programming generated by ground stations in Kuwait. Broadcasts not only told air-defense operators and ground forces how to act to avoid attack, so-called "surrender terms," but also began to condition the Iraqi people to stay away from military installations and to sit out any future conflict.[43]

Southern Focus flights also played a part in the program of force buildups (the spikes or sine waves mentioned previously) that were being used to deceive, desensitize, and probe the Iraqi military. From the latter months of 2002 until February 2003, no-fly-zone aircraft periodically undertook surge operations, particularly whenever rotating U.S. aircraft carriers would overlap. In February 2003, the United States began to fly six hundred to one thousand sorties per day on selected days, increased mission lengths from four to twelve hours, incorporated twenty-four hour missions, and tested new weapons, sensor pods, and C2 procedures. Whenever Southern Focus would surge, U.S. and British intelligence platforms monitored Iraqi air bases, air defenses, and communications to profile their dispersal patterns and to assess whether the Iraqi air force was preparing to scramble interceptors or the Air Defense Commander was laying SAMbushes.[44]

During the final weeks before Operation Iraqi Freedom, the no-fly zone provided cover for an intelligence-collection effort of unparalleled intensity. Air crews involved in no-fly-zone strikes were told to meticulously catalog targets spotted during their patrols. Pioneer and Predator UAVs monitored Iraqi activity in the oil fields and scouted priority targets such as artillery units, airfields, and potential SSM hides.[45] The single Global Hawk assigned to Iraq operations began flying during Southern Focus; it provided persistent surveillance of the enemy ORBAT and profiled the movements of Iraqi SAMs and SSMs.[46] U-2 aircraft flew north of 33°N to gather SIGINT data from central Iraq as part of an expanded effort to make SIGINT more useful to tactical users. U.S. Air Force officers were seconded to the National Reconnaissance Office's Operational Support Office to assess the tactical value of SIGINT data from airborne and satellite surveillance, and a web-based chat room, Zircon-chat, was established to give tactical military intelligence users at division and brigade levels access to national intelligence. IMINT from airborne assets was fused with twelve direct and twenty-four indirect passes by U.S. KH-11 electro-optical and Lacrosse SAR imaging satellites.[47] Although Iraq's tactical forces continued to relocate until the very beginning of the war, the U.S. intelligence community finally enjoyed sufficient sensor coverage to track and profile many of the military movements being made by the adversary.

FAILURE OF "CHEAT AND RETREAT" IN 2003

Although regime removal was the strategic and military objective of Operation Iraqi Freedom, there was no legal standing to underpin such a mission, and the Anglo-American Coalition (joined now by a third major military partner, Australia) instead looked to the raft of UN resolutions concerning WMD to provide a legal casus belli for a military intervention. The Coalition required Iraq to be shown to be in material breach of UNSC Resolution 687, which called on Iraq to "accept the destruction, removal, or rendering harmless" of all NBC stockpiles and research, plus any ballistic missiles with a range of more than 150 kilometers and related research facilities.[48] Failure to meet this requirement would theoretically allow the United States and its allies to revoke the cease-fire of 1991 and continue with military operations mandated by UNSC Resolution 678, which authorized the use of "any necessary means."

To secure evidence of a material breach, the Coalition would once again require the initiation of UN inspectors, a matter that consumed U.S. and British diplomatic efforts throughout much of 2002. On September 12, 2002, President Bush addressed the General Assembly of the UN and gave the UN a last chance to pass a new resolution calling on Iraq to readmit UN inspectors and account for the destruction of its WMDs. UNSC Resolution 1441 was passed unanimously on November 8, 2002, and within weeks UN inspector team—now called UNMOVIC—was once again on the ground in Iraq.

For the Iraqi regime, the internationalization of the Iraq issue represented a last slender life line to survival, yet the Baathist regime had arguably lost its diplomatic deftness during the preceding three years. Deprived of the forum of UN inspections, Iraq had languished on the diplomatic sidelines since 1998. Obscurity was the one indignity that Saddam Hussein could not endure, and throughout the period after Desert Fox, the regime sought to maintain its international profile by noisily supporting the Palestinian cause following the eruption of the new intifada in the fall of 2000. Even after moving elements of military divisions to the Jordanian border and threatening the destruction of Israel, Iraq's global profile had continued to recede.[49] Although it continued to maintain common economic and anti-Kurdish interests with Turkey, attempts to court better relations with its southern neighbors had failed: Uday Hussein had called on a number of occasions for the reannexation of Kuwait and Foreign Minister Mohammed Said al-Sahhaf bungled attempts to smooth relations at the Arab League summit in March 2002.

Iraq had also not done much to please France or Russia, the permanent members of the UNSC that had previously done the most to shield Baghdad from the unrestrained censure directed at it by Washington and London. Iraqi intransigence on issues ranging from WMD to "smart sanctions" reduced France's ability to propose alternative solutions to the hawkish options proposed by the Bush administration, and Iraq and Russia had begun to disagree over the very issue that maintained relations between Baghdad and Moscow—Russia's oil-exploration contracts in Iraq—from which the Baathist government now appeared to be distancing itself.[50] A U.S.-led campaign to unseat the Baghdad government had little international backing, but the Baathist regime had lesser still and had failed in the years since 1998 to adequately prepare itself for a critical diplomatic showdown.

Iraq also faced a U.S. administration that was prepared to press on with the military option even if given the most slender political mandate to do so. In the years since Operation Desert Fox, the U.S. and British intelligence communities had developed little reliable intelligence on the issue. Iraqi missile- and WMD-delivery capabilities were the best surveilled of the WMD-related industries because they relied on satellite imagery of open-air Iraqi missile test facilities and suspected cruise-missile tests, but no other element of the WMD industry could be as reliably or intensively surveilled. Assessments of Iraqi CBW programs were based on satellite imagery of the reconstitution of Iraqi civil chemical and pharmaceutical industries and on the reporting of a handful of human agents within Iraq, with two-thirds of the data originated from a single source. Assessments of potential Iraqi reactivation of its nuclear program were even more inferential and unreliable; they rested only on an image of the rebuilt Iraq's Atomic Energy Committee building and unsubstantiated HUMINT about the procurement of uranium and aluminum tubes. A new alarmist outlook may have been influenced by emerging intelligence about Pakistani nuclear scientist Abdul Qader Khan's decade-long trade in uranium enrichment and bomb-making technology.[51]

When UNMOVIC and the IAEA commenced inspections in late 2002, the U.S. intelligence community provided a list of 148 suspect sites to add to those identified by the inspectors, including 37 high-priority sites. UNMOVIC undertook 731 inspections and visited 411 sites, including 88 that had not been inspected prior to 1998. As inspectors traversed Iraq, U.S. and British intelligence collection focused on detecting Iraqi concealment operations that could help cement the case for war. The results were ultimately inconclusive, providing indicators of Iraqi concealment and ongoing WMD ambitions but falling short of finding the "smoking gun" that most members of the global public would recognize as evidence of threatening WMD programs.

Although neither UNMOVIC nor the IAEA uncovered evidence of a reactivated Iraqi nuclear program, the former organization uncovered some evidence of undeclared prohibited activities in the chemical-, biological-, and missile-delivery sectors—apparently misplaced unfilled chemical-weapons munitions, indications of previously underreported VX nerve-gas production, and incontrovertible proof that Iraq was using its highly advanced short-range missile industry to create missiles with ranges of greater than 150 kilometers, primarily using improved Scud components.[52] As a result of the latter discovery, UNMOVIC destroyed seventy Al-Samoud II missiles and fifty warheads, plus incomplete missile components and illegally imported engines, before the beginning of Operation Iraqi Freedom.[53]

In an attempt to situate UNMOVIC's findings within a broader framework of Iraqi concealment, U.S. Secretary of State Powell made a seventy-six-minute address to the UNSC on February 5, 2003, in which he presented U.S. and British intelligence findings gathered during the preceding months and years. Powell displayed evidence of purported "housecleaning" at thirty sites in advance of UNMOVIC inspections and displayed satellite imagery of the alleged sanitization of chemical-weapons bunkers at Republican Guard facilities in al-Musayyib and Taji, which showed what appeared to be de-contamination trucks scraping off the top layer of soil. SIGINT intercepts provided inferential evidence of security-service personnel discussing the removal of phrases such as "nerve gas" from documents and the movement of "modified vehicles" believed to be biological-weapons laboratories. Satellite imagery showed Iraqi UAVs flying 500-kilometer nonstop racetrack patterns over Iraqi air bases, more than double the range permitted by the Missile Technology Control Regime.[54] Again, however, the evidence fell short of the smoking gun required to convince many doubters, and inconclusive reports by UNMOVIC Chairman Hans Blix on February 14, 2003, and IAEA Chairman Mohammed El-Baradei on March 7, 2003, muddied the waters still further.

START OF OPERATION IRAQI FREEDOM

With antiwar demonstrations and diplomatic pressure mounting on all fronts, on March 17 the U.S. administration withdrew a new U.S.- and British-backed UN resolution that sought explicit backing for new military action but which now looked unlikely to pass the UNSC. After consultation with the British, Australian, and Israeli governments, President Bush issued an ultimatum to Saddam Hussein: leave Iraq with his sons within forty-eight hours or face military action. Franks was told to prepare to execute Operation Iraqi Freedom within seventy-two hours; if Saddam ignored the ultimatum, the opening insertion of special forces would take place on the night of March 19–20, Baghdad time.[55] UNMOVIC staff left Iraq on March 17, and the world waited for the latest and possibly the final round of the long-running confrontation between the United States and Iraq.

Behind the scenes, military preparation had been accelerating for several weeks; the number of sorties in the no-fly zones reached a thousand per day by February 9. The United States and Britain initiated the last and most aggressive phase of Southern Focus. In mid-February the Coalition responded to Iraqi antiaircraft fire, which had been documented on 170 occasions since the start of 2003, by striking Iraqi SSMs and other potential WMD-delivery systems. Simultaneously, Coalition troops from three divisions prepared for the ground war from the tight confines of the Kuwait desert. By late February a range of Abadil-100, FRoG-7, and Astros-2 missile launchers had been struck; on March 17 the Coalition began striking long-range tube artillery just over the border in Az-Zubayr and on the Al-Faw Peninsula. From March 14 onward, no-fly-zone strikes began to blind Iraqi border radars, including those along the Jordanian border and those facing Kuwait. These included the Basra airport's air-traffic-control radar, which was a dual-use facility that U.S. aviators had not been allowed to target until now. Last-minute strikes peppered southern communication nodes.[56] By the time President Bush signed the EXECORD initiating Operation Iraqi Freedom in Washington on the morning of March 19, the preparations for war were well advanced and the last pretence of peace was rapidly falling away.

In the late afternoon of that day, U.S. SOFs began designating Iraqi VISOBs for destruction by U.S. AH-6 Little Bird and MH-60 defensive armed penetrator helicopters. Tactical air patrollers, ostensibly undertaking no-fly-zone patrols, could also attack these targets. During the night, nine VISOBs on Iraq's Jordanian border and twenty-four facing the Saudi Arabian border were plinked; each disappeared in a cloud of dust and smoke as LGBs and thermobaric Hellfire missiles tore apart the squat bunkers and skeletal observation towers. At 2100 local time, thirty-one special-operations teams began entering Iraq. These teams were the vanguard of an estimated nine thousand special or elite forces involved in the war. The Combined Joint Special Operations Task Force—West (CJSOTF-West), which combined teams from the U.S. 5th and 19th Special Forces Groups, the U.S. Rangers and 82nd Airborne division, and the British and Australian SAS, represented four thousand of this total. Striking across the borders from Jordan and Saudi Arabia, these heliborne and vehicle-mounted forces quickly isolated the H-1, H-2, and H-3 air fields in western Iraq, interdicted the Amman-Ramadi-Baghdad highway that had been vital to Scud convoys in 1991, and moved to secure or reconnoiter key terrain. This terrain included the Haditha Dam and the Karbala Gap, the narrow channel of land between Karbala and Lake Rezazza that provided the best approach for ground forces to attack Baghdad from the south.

Meanwhile in the southeast and the Kurdish north, other forces from the U.S. 10th Special Forces Group, the CIA, and the "black" special-operations community (which included the U.S. Army 1st Special Operations Detachment—Delta; the Naval Special Warfare Development Group, formerly SEAL Team Six; and the U.S. Air Force 24th Special Tactics Squadron) worked alongside U.S. Army and Marine Corps reconnaissance forces and British or Polish special forces to link up with Iraqi opposition groups, isolate terrorist camps, and secure key economic and transportation infrastructure.[57] Within a few short hours, decades of Baathist control had been rolled back across large swaths of Iraq. Although the numerically inferior special-forces teams would face sharp fights and some reverses throughout the coming days and weeks, the balance between them and the Iraq forces had transformed since 1991. With support from reliable communications and near-ubiquitous airpower and heavy weapons, the SOFs were now able to dominate the terrain and to pen Iraqi forces into ever-shrinking pockets of regime control—a far cry from being cut off deep behind enemy lines as Western SOF were in the first Gulf War in 1991.

Although everything was going according to plan at the start of the night of March 19–20, a host of developments would unfold to radically alter the opening move of Operation Iraqi Freedom before the sun would rise on March 20. In contrast to the beginning of Operation Desert Storm, which had been a triumph of orchestration, the opening of Operation Iraqi Freedom would prove to be a triumph of improvisation. The first indications of potential adjustments to the operation emerged that night when two CIA operatives within Iraq reported that the Saddam Hussein and his two sons were going to meet at a house owned by Saddam's wife, Sajida, which was known as the Dora farm. More than a year of development of human sources within Iraq appeared to have finally paid off.

Since 1996, Iraq had been a "denied environment," and as such had lacked any CIA ground presence. As late as 9/11, there were only four members of the agency's clandestine directorate of operations working on Iraq from the United States; a mere four agents were within the country and they produced merely ninety reports in the whole of 2001. The CIA had returned to northern Iraq within days of a February 16, 2002, presidential directive to reconstitute its field presence in the country. Despite intense harassment by the sensitive Turkish military and intelligence establishment, the CIA had managed to find Kurdish partners. This allowed them to develop a network of eighty-seven human agents sprinkled throughout the Baathist security architecture, who were collectively code named the Rockstars. As the military conflict drew close, two Rockstars began to provide intelligence that hinted at Saddam's movements. The first, an SSO communications officer, provided tips about the frequency and imminence of Saddam's movements based on changes to Saddam's access to secure communications. The second, a bodyguard or hanger-on attached to Qusay Hussein's entourage, provided details of a forthcoming meeting between Saddam and his sons at the Dora farm. The location had been geolocated through his Thuraya satellite phone.[58]

By 0100 local time on March 20, SOFs were beginning what was planned to be two days' worth of local preparation before the main U.S. air attack would fall. The Bush administration now faced a tantalizing possibility: that a quick and clean aerial strike could decapitate the regime and potentially collapse Baathist resistance before the maneuver phase of the war would begin. Military and civilian decision makers quickly supported the strike. While the principals discussed the issue, CENTCOM readied the strike by adding two F-117A Nighthawks to a TLAM-only option prepared the day before. The F-117As were tasked with the destruction of a suspected leadership bunker beneath the farm. In anticipation of such a mission, the U.S. Air Force had expedited the clearance of new GPS/laser-guided penetrating munitions (EGBU-27s) for carriage on the F-117As, had rushed them to theater, and even had one pair of bombs mounted on an F-117A for local trials.

To allow the stealth aircraft to strike the Dora farm and exit Iraqi air space before they became visible to electro-optical targeting at sunrise, the principals needed to approve the strike by 0315 Baghdad time, which was 1700 in Washington.[59] The strike was authorized ahead of schedule at 0230 Baghdad time, 1830 in Washington, despite some decision makers' concerns about the possibility of killing civilians along with the regime leadership.

That the decision to strike was almost automatic was testament to how far the United States had traveled during the prior decade vis-à-vis the issue of lethally targeting Iraq's leadership. Although leadership facilities had been targeted in major U.S. air strikes on Iraq in 1991 and 1998, the death of senior Iraqi leaders would have been coincidental rather than intentional, because reliable data concerning the movements of key national leadership figures had never before been available. Furthermore, in 1991 and 1998 residual discomfort about lethally targeting a national leader such as Saddam Hussein still existed. This was reflected in the existing moratorium on assassination that was embedded in successive presidential EXECORDs since the 1970s. No such hesitation existed in 2003. Legitimization of the targeted killing of terrorists had evolved in the U.S. government between 1996 and 1998, culminating in the unsuccessful attempt to kill Osama bin Laden with a cruise-missile strike on terrorist camps in Khost, Afghanistan, on August 20, 1998. Since the strike, the CIA had been practicing four-hour kill-chain exercises that sought to prepare the agency to have weapons on target within four hours after receipt of at least two corroborating reports on an enemy-leadership location.

Since 9/11, the bar had dropped even further. Enemy leaders were increasingly seen as fair game, as evidenced by a *Newsweek* poll showing that two thirds of polled Americans accepted the necessity of targeted killings of enemy leaders.[60] As Operation Iraqi Freedom began, Saddam, Uday, and Qusay Hussein were high-value targets (HVTs). Major General Renuart noted, "There was always provision for time-sensitive targeting on those three and a couple of other senior leaders if executable or actionable targeting intelligence emerged. If we got the chance to cut the head off the snake, we couldn't afford to hesitate because we might never get another chance."[61] Everyone involved in the chain of command recognized the unique opportunity that was unfolding. If anything, Saddam had been becoming harder to target in recent years. He was reducing the length of meetings to single sessions and avoiding predictable locations, including his own birthday parties.[62] Finally, Saddam Hussein—a man guided by his own instincts as a former assassin, who had been described as "a kind of refugee in the country he rules" because of his constant and unpredictable movements[63]—appeared vulnerable to direct attack.

The two F-117As began their inbound journey from Qatar to Baghdad at 0038 local time, twenty-five minutes after the supposed cutoff point for the strike. The no-frills mission had been thrown together so rapidly that the aircraft had to find airborne refueling on the way in and out of Iraq by merging in with the no-fly-zone aircraft that were performing night missions over southern Iraq. These night missions sought to draw the attention of Iraqi air defenses away from the stealth aircraft. Two F-16CJs closely shadowed the stealth aircraft to 33°N in order to provide radar returns that would over-shadow the stealth aircraft's minimal radar signature. Hastily launched EA-6B jammers from the USS *Constellation* provided jamming support, creating the illusion that they were protecting the visible F-16s.[64] At 0439 the stealth air-craft were followed by a salvo of forty TLAMs launched by four surface ships and two submarines in the northern Gulf.

As the F-117As reached their target at 0530, the aircraft were faintly visible in the twilight, yet Iraq's air defenses remained unaware of the coming blow. The four EGBU-27s drilled into the ground at four GPS aimpoints that U.S. guesswork suggested would bracket a number of the chambers of the suspected leadership bunker. They fell in a square roughly fifteen meters wide on each side. By the time air-raid sirens began blaring across Iraq, the incoming salvo of Tomahawks caved in three above-ground buildings at the Dora farm. To muddy the waters and confuse the Iraqis about the origin of the precision intelligence guiding the strike, a handful of other targets in

Baghdad—SSO and Republican Guard offices—were also struck by TLAMs. Although CENTAF planners requested follow-on TLAM strikes to complicate any rescue effort and to inflict further personnel casualties, military lawyers rejected the additional strikes because of the risk of killing medical staff and civilians.[65] After the stealth aircraft were safely recovered outside Iraq as the sun rose, President Bush addressed the American people at 0616 Baghdad time (2216 in Washington) to announce the dramatic assassination attempt and the beginning of Operation Iraqi Freedom.

GROUND BEFORE AIR—REORDERING OPERATION IRAQI FREEDOM

Over the course of the twelve hours that followed the assassination attempt, expectations of success rose and fell. It would be a week before the CIA managed to get human operatives to the Dora farm to discover that the suspected bunker did not actually exist and that no positive proof of Saddam's demise (or indeed presence) could be gathered. In the meantime, however, as the first full day of Operation Iraqi Freedom began, the operation continued to develop in a fluid and unpredictable manner. Uncertainty over the fate of Saddam Hussein complicated preparations for the beginning of decisive combat operations.

Throughout the daylight hours of March 20, little visible military activity took place, which created a misleading sense of suspended operations. In fact, Coalition SOFs had been fighting hard throughout the day, engaging mechanized and motorized columns of Iraqi counter-SOF forces that had emerged on the morning of March 20 to root out the Coalition intruders. These battles pitted mobile columns against each other across the length and breadth of the western desert. They were swung decisively against the Iraqi defenders by the overwhelming firepower of the so-called "desert air force": rotating stacks of A-10, F-16, and Tornado aircraft, plus loitering AC-130 gunships and B-1B bombers that augmented the direct-fire weapons and truck-mounted, multiple-launch rocket systems of the special-forces columns. Before nightfall on March 20, the SOFs had secured or isolated each of the key Iraqi air bases in the west and prepared their local battlespace by carrying out direct-action missions against air defenses and communications nodes in the area.[66] Far from being confined to operating at night and laying up during the day, as they were forced to in 1991, major SOF formations were now operating around the clock. Reliable communications and fire support enabled them, at any time of day, to join battle with any Iraqi military formations that interfered with their counter-Scud mission.

As the special forces secured western Iraq early on March 20, CINCCENT Franks succumbed to a growing sense of unease over the time lag before offensive ground operations were scheduled to begin in the south. The main air attack (set for 2100 Baghdad time on March 21) was scheduled to be executed a full thirty hours after the insertion of SOFs, with major ground operations commencing five hours later at 0600 on March 22.[67] In this war plan, the insertion of special forces represented just another incremental step in the slide to war. However, war in the western desert had been interpreted as the beginning of major hostilities, particularly following the assassination attempt. Regardless of whether Saddam Hussein or either of his sons was alive, the regime had not immediately folded and could be counted on to begin implementing counterstrategies. In the south, these could include the "scorched-earth" destruction of Iraq's southern oil fields or conventional or WMD attacks on the tightly massed Coalition-assembly areas in Kuwait.

On the afternoon of 20 March, the trigger for expedited ground operations was what a specialized CENTCOM intelligence cell believed to be the beginnings of oil-field demolitions in southern Iraq. HUMINT gleaned from Shia opposition forces had previously reported that demolitions explosives were moved by rail into the massive Rumailah oil fields, but the key pretext for the seizure of the southern oil fields were unusually large flames—between 18 and 90 meters tall—issuing from two oil wells that were detected by U.S. satellite and Predator surveillance. Before the war, U.S. imagery analysts in the Joint Analysis and Control Element of the CENTCOM Joint Fusion Cell had been trained to discriminate between the normal burn-off flares seen in oil fields as opposed to signs of wellhead fires or demolitions. They reported to General Franks that demolitions had begun, which jump-started ground operations.[68] At 1700 on March 20, CENTCOM began extensive aerial and ground reconnaissance of the southern oil fields; between 1900 and 2200, U.S., British, and Polish SOFs seized a number of vital offshore gas and oil platforms and export manifolds.

This triggered the first Iraqi SSM launches of the war, at 2009 hours, when two Iraqi ballistic missiles arced southward from the date groves north of Basra and just north of the Kuwait border at Az-Zubayr. Although British Royal Marines achieved a landing on the Al-Faw Peninsula under cover of a heavy naval and aerial bombardment, a modified Iraqi antiship missile was fired into Kuwait from the marshy peninsula. By 0300 on March 21, the Coalition probes increased to brigade- and eventually division-strength reconnaissance into the Rumaliah oil field. U.S. Marine Corps attack helicopters and U.S. Army artillery raids targeted Iraqi defensive positions nestled in the oil field and destroyed the remaining VISOBs along the Kuwaiti border. U.S. Marine forces of the 15th MEU, backed by other Marine and British forces would secure the vital Az-Zubayr pumping turbines by first light and clear the Rumaliah oil fields and port of Umm Qasr of organized enemy resistance by 1800 on March 21.[69]

As March 21 unfolded, six more Iraqi missiles streaked southward to strike the U.S. assembly areas in Kuwait. The missiles were extraordinarily ineffective military weapons, and an estimated two-thirds appear to have been intercepted by the dense protective screen of satellite and airborne early-warning sensors and Patriot advanced capability (PAC)-III missiles. Their significance was also reduced by the improvements in targeting the launchers.

As part of the effort to prevent a wave of Scud launches against Israel, the U.S. military extensively prepared a combination of U.S. DSP satellites and RC-135S Cobra Ball and RC-135V/W Rivet Joint aircraft that could pinpoint the heat signatures of missile launches far more precisely than had been possible in 1991. This allowed the United States to locate missile launches within a square mile in any weather or light conditions. Heat cues were rapidly fused with moving-target indicators and SAR coverage by JSTARS, which could direct Predator and other UAVs to visually track the missile launcher as it sought to relocate.[70]

This sensor-to-shooter kill chain was a quantum leap in U.S. military effectiveness against mobile launchers as compared with the capability demonstrated in the Scud hunt in 1991. The result was that although Abadil-100, FRoG, and Al-Samoud launchers often managed to launch a first missile against U.S. forces or facilities in Kuwait and Iraq, they rarely survived to return to their forward depots and reload. Of the eighty-five Iraqi missile launchers of these types believed to be in Iraq at the outset of Operation Iraqi Freedom, forty-six were conformed destroyed by Coalition air or artillery strikes.[71]

However, even with the various degrees of antimissile protection afforded by preemptive and reactive counterforce attacks, airborne interception, and passive defenses (chemical sensors and suits), General Franks could not endure the prospect of leaving the U.S. divisions grouped in a close geographic area while chemical or biological attacks were possible. At 0600 on March 21, the 3rd Infantry Division and the 101st Air Assault Divisions launched north-westward into Iraq.

"Shock and awe?"—Neutering the strategic air campaign

Instead of a five-hour head start on the ground operations, as originally planned, the beginning of intense U.S. air operations in Operation Iraqi Freedom would unfold a full fifteen hours after the beginning of the V Corps ground attack. Throughout the rollercoaster ride of the first days of Operation Iraqi Freedom, the air campaign had remained inextricably tied to its original execution time—2100 on March 21—in large part to maintain the intricate and inflexible scheduling of the opening strikes by aircraft as far afield as the continental United States. However, changes to the strategic and operational context of the war would wreak havoc with the best-laid plans of Coalition aviators and considerably reduce the effects of what media commentators had expectantly dubbed the "shock-and-awe" air campaign. The phrase, initially intended to describe the rapid dominance that could be achieved through sudden and overwhelming air and land operations, had come to sum up popular expectations of air operations in Operation Iraqi Freedom.[72] In essence, the world expected a rerun of the dramatic opening minutes of Desert Storm—a highly visible thunderclap that would mark the transition from peace to war. Instead, the air campaign followed two days of special-forces and ground operations and underwhelmed many observers with what appeared to be a truncated and stammering series of air strikes.

When initially planned, however, the air campaign had promised to deliver exactly what "shock and awe" suggested: an extremely violent and sudden release of precisely targeted strikes timed to coincide with the beginning of ground operations. As early as late January 2002, air-campaign planners had translated CINCENT Franks' "centers of gravity" into a circular, twelve-ring model that encompassed the target sets that airpower would strike.[73] In contrast to Colonel Warden's concentric ring model, used in 1991, the new targeting model reflected more than a decade of U.S. experience at dissecting and examining the Iraqi regime as a target system. The "enabling rings"—Iraq's air, air-defense, and naval forces—were on the outside, like the bark of a tree trunk. These systems would require far less effort to suppress than they had in 1991 because of a decade of degradation. The next rings of the model encompassed the Iraqi population (targeted for influence, not physical attack) and the regular army, which planners hoped could be persuaded not to resist. To reduce the risk of WMD use or removal from the country during the war, air planners focused on the destruction of delivery platforms: missiles, aircraft, helicopters, and UAVs. Seven key Iraqi air fields were slated to receive a rolling series of multiple strikes throughout the war. Col. David Minster, the JCS head of targeting, recalled that the air-component commander, Lt. Gen. Moseley, "had been told by Franks, 'Your responsibility is to ensure that no air attacks are launched against my troops.' Moseley knew that U.S. troops had not been attacked from the air since the Korean War, and he wasn't going to let it happen on his shift."[74] To destroy or immobilize suspected agents in transit, special agent-defeat weapons were developed that used nonexplosive munitions to rupture containers and phosphorous incendiaries to incinerate agents.

Although these elements were important, the heart of the planned air campaign, code named Velocity, was the innermost rings of the targeting model. These were the hardcore elements of the regime including the SRG and Republican Guard, government C3, the regime's security services and bodyguards, and Saddam's family and tribe.[75] The military objective for striking these target sets was termed "disruption of government control," and a large share of the planning effort went into developing the targeting intelligence and the concept of operations that would be required to kill large numbers of regime loyalists. This took attempts at regime-targeting in Operation Desert Fox a step further.

In addition to developing the HUMINT, SIGINT, and IMINT sources required to undertake a persistent campaign of assassinations of a dozen of the most senior Baathist leaders, the Velocity plan also called for a massive surprise strike at the outset of the war against the regime security forces. Well-placed HUMINT sources developed by the CIA station in northern Iraq, plus new means of eavesdropping on the regime security establishment, created an even deeper understanding of the habits and locations of Iraq's security and intelligence personnel. This allowed the United States not only to build a highly detailed map of possible targets, but also identified the optimal time to carry out strikes.[76] The ACC head of strategy and plan, Colonel Crowder, recalled, "Every single security apparatus was slated to be struck. It practically read like the chapter on Iraq's security forces in Ken Pollack's book [*The Coming Storm*]. They wanted to kill the guys in those offices. Detailed analysis was undertaken showing when those guys were in the building. It showed that after a leisurely breakfast, they tended to be at the offices around nine on the morning, so that was when the time-on-target was set for. If it had been undertaken simultaneously with the beginning of ground operations, it would have gutted the regime's loyal manpower."[77]

Alongside the lethal targeting of regime personnel, Velocity also laid out extensive plans for the nationwide takedown of Iraq's C2 network. Instead of the overambitious Desert Storm objective of "isolating" the Iraqi leadership, the objective was now to disrupt Iraqi C2 and to direct Iraqi signals onto communications channels that could more easily be intercepted or jammed.[78] CENTCOM and the national intelligence providers spent the final nine months of 2002 profiling the Iraqi military- and civilian-communications infrastructure, including Iraq's frequent modifications and additions to the system (such as cell phones and satellite phones). Air-defense, regular-army, and Republican Guard military headquarters, switchboards, and other communications nodes were mapped and posted for planners to dissect on the U.S. National Ground Intelligence Center classified website.[79] At the strategic level, the NSA and the JWAC profiled the Iraqi PSN and identified thirty key nodes that could be selectively attacked if necessary. Major General Shaffer, the director of intelligence at the JCS, recalled that "they were routing military command and control through the commercial network, and it was understood by everyone that if C3 went down, you have to take down elements of the [PSN], no matter how hesitant we were to attack dual-use targets."[80]

The resistance to hitting the public telephone system, even though it represented a glaring chink in the communications takedown, was symptomatic of the flip side of the "effects-based" targeting that had taken hold since Desert Storm. The precision demonstrated during Desert Storm combined with the unintended consequences of dual-use targeting from that war had considerably raised the bar for acceptable conduct in subsequent air operations. As defined by RAND corporation analysts, effects-based operations (EBO) consisted of military actions that were "conceived and planned in a systems framework that considers the full range of direct, indirect, and cascading effects."[81] Precision warfare now meant it was as important to pick the right targets as it was to hit them precisely. In the Operation Iraqi Freedom air campaign, this would translate into a drive to create the desired military effects with the least possible physical destruction: knocking out power, communications, or fuel at the precise node where they were diverted to military use rather than by attacking their national infrastructures. The short-term benefits of attacks against dual-use infrastructures such as the electrical grid or phone system were carefully weighed against the long-term effects on the Iraqi economy. In addition, because this war was thought likely to last merely weeks, an aimpoint was no longer a valid target if its destruction could not affect the near-term conduct of the war.[82]

Every target in Iraqi Freedom was vetted to preclude both prompt and long-term suffering to noncombatants and to maximize the prospects of Iraqi national recovery. The ability to characterize and minimize the risk of collateral damage represented a facet of U.S. military operations that had experienced the most radical change since 1991. Of the four thousand targets and eleven thousand DMPIs the military reviewed at the start of Operation Iraqi Freedom, advanced weaponeering and tactical solutions (including axis and angle, timing variation, fusing and size of weapon tweaks) were able to reduce the collateral-damage risk until merely twenty-four carried a collateral-damage estimate of thirty or more probable civilian deaths.[83]

Human Rights Watch conceded, "For the most part, the collateral damage assessment process for the air war in Iraq worked well, especially with respect to preplanned targets. Similarly, Human Rights Watch's month-long investigation in Iraq found that, in most cases, aerial bombardment resulted in minimal adverse effects to the civilian population. . . . [Coalition forces] employed other methods to help minimize civilian casualties, such as bombing at night when civilians were less likely to be on the streets, using penetrator munitions and delayed fuses to ensure that most blast and fragmentation damage was kept within the impact area, and using attack angles that took into account the locations of civilian facilities such as schools and hospitals."[84]

To enable this form of targeting, the United States had cataloged a "no-target list" of several thousand civilian facilities. Major General Shaffer remarked, "This list was the longest we had, many times longer than the target list itself. We had people looking at Iraq every day of every year, constantly generating new no-strike locations that they had identified as cultural, religious, or archaeological sites, schools or hospitals, or foreign embassies and non-governmental organizations." Such information could be difficult to find. Shaffer stated, "Our knowledge of embassies and ambassadorial residences or international facilities was not as good as we would have liked. This intelligence came together at the last minute and took a considerable effort. We could take photography and know which block they were in, but where in each block? This kind of information was surprisingly difficult to find out."[85] After the misidentification of the Chinese Embassy in Belgrade during Operation Allied Force, which had been mistakenly located in the old premises of the Federal Directorate of Supply and Procurement, nobody wanted to be "the next Chinese Embassy guy," according to air-campaign planner Major Mike Downs.[86] In the buildup to war, the U.S. military both tracked the location of volunteer "human shields" and asked foreign governments and international organizations to use a phone line and website to nominate no-strike locations that the U.S. intelligence community may have missed.[87]

However, the planned violent, sudden, and discriminating aerial assault would be gradually worn down until the strategic air campaign was a shadow of its former self by the time it was executed on March 21. First, prewar planners abandoned the vital 0900 time-on-target opening to the assault. Its extensive reliance on Tomahawk missiles to breach the Baghdad SuperMEZ during daylight hours did not meet the approval of the influential U.S. Air Force advocates of stealth aircraft such as the F-117A and the B-2. By changing the time of the assault, the only chance of effectively targeting regime forces was lost because only a daylight surprise strike could catch meaningful numbers of intelligence and security officers at key installations. The planned launch of the main air strike forty-eight hours after the insertion of special operations further reduced the likelihood that Iraq's regime security forces would be exposed to aerial targeting. As CENTCOM Intelligence Analyst Greg Hooker noted, "The new levels of precision achieved by the first mass use of TLAM Block III missiles during Desert Fox in 1998 helped the Iraqis refine techniques for the rapid dispersal of military, industrial and government facilities in periods of heightened tension."[88] In all likelihood, the bombs would strike empty buildings with unerring accuracy as they had so often in the past.

In the hours following the assassination attempt, the air campaign was further censured, according to air-campaign planner Maj. Anthony Roberson:

The original first strike was very, very thorough. There wasn't a target we hadn't accounted for, but due to the supposed success of the decapitation strike, General Franks placed a call to Moseley and told him that they didn't want to appear to be powering on. At the four-star and political level, they hoped it was enough and that we had proved our offensive capability was way beyond the regime's ability to protect themselves. At that point, the fear in Washington was that we would launch our main blow just as the Iraqis surrendered..... Within 6 hours we had removed 300 DMPIs from the target list—it felt like we had stripped out half the ATO. We took off secondary and tertiary leadership targets—fixed headquarters and Baath Party or Fedayeen buildings.[89]

All twenty-four high-collateral-damage leadership targets were removed from the target list scheduled to be struck at A-Hour, 2100 on March 21. Other regime C2 targets were considered high-collateral-damage targets because "civilians" worked at them as laborers or support staff and thus were removed from the target lists—an inexplicable decision considering the nature of the institutions.[90] Ultimately, only 39 percent of the regime targets nominated for attack were struck throughout the campaign.[91]

As planners raced to incorporate the new limitations into the first ATO, the air campaign suffered another blow when Franks sought to move up the start of ground operations by twenty hours. With only hours to go before the main body of Coalition ground forces entered Iraq, Moseley could not move up the timing of the intricately orchestrated strategic air campaign because the bomber aircraft would take fifteen hours to arrive from bases in the United States.[92] As a result, the major air attack would fall a full twenty-eight hours after the main Coalition ground forces entered Iraq. Put another way, it would begin twenty-five hours after Iraq recognized the beginning of full-blown hostilities with the launch of its own SSM. Experience had shown that to be effective against strategic targets in Iraq, airpower had to strike like a bolt from the blue. Instead, this was the complete opposite of tactical surprise—the regime was fully awake, and none of its servants were sipping tea in their peacetime headquarters.

A second major effect of the reversal of the ordering of air and ground operations was the removal of targets from the ATO if they were short of the fire-control support line (FCSL), which was an area up to 130 kilometers in front of the advancing ground troops. As in 1991, striking any targets within this area required permission from "eyes-on" ground observers through time-consuming terminal-control procedures communicated by voice. Many of the targets slated for destruction were physically overrun in the fifteen hours that separated the beginning of ground operations and A-Hour, and thus were legitimately scrubbed from the target list, but the movement of the FSCL invalidated many other profitable targets simply because they were located well behind enemy lines, and could not be kept under "eyes-on" positive control. As a result, enemy C2 in the south were effectively scrubbed from the target list. As one air-campaign planner put it, "Bad guy command and control got a free pass."[93]

As senior Coalition commanders gathered to watch the opening of the strategic air campaign, attention focused on the blows that could still be struck against the Baathist war effort. Moseley, the air-component commander, paced in his "battle-cab"—a "glassed-in church balcony" looking out over the dim, cavernous Combined Air Operations Center at PSAB in Saudi Arabia. At exactly 2100 Baghdad time, hundreds of simultaneous explosions rocked the Iraqi capital and other areas in central and northern Iraq. Utilizing the pro-filing techniques from Desert Fox and new geolocated coordinates supplied by CIA assets in Iraq, a heavy salvo of cruise missiles struck the ring of SA-2 and SA-3 sites that formed the Baghdad and Tikrit SuperMEZs. Other missiles struck Iraqi surveillance radar or gutted air-defense maintenance hangers and SAM or radar depots. Most of those were empty, their contents dispersed days or weeks earlier. The remainder of the 320 Tomahawks and 80 CALCMs fired on the first night impacted at regime palaces and build-ings throughout central Iraq. Television coverage showed rows of mushroom clouds lit by the orange flames of burning government buildings along the Tigris River.

In the minutes after the blinding and stunning of the Baghdad Super-MEZ, five U.S. Air Force Firebee drones flew circuits over Baghdad, dis-pensing radar-reflective chaff to interfere with any surviving radar-guided SAMs. At 2146 the first manned strikes were delivered against Baghdad tar-gets by U.S. stealth aircraft. Although two thirds of the twelve F-117A aircraft were forced to return to base with their weapons onboard because of a lack of refuellers, the remaining Nighthawks struck five bunkers with EGB-27 deep-penetrating munitions. Nine B-2 Spirit stealth bombers then delivering their heavy payloads of satellite-guided bombs. Those bombs had a circular error of probability of merely two meters, despite being dropped from alti-tudes of 26,000 feet. By 2300 nonstealthy tactical aircraft had delivered their munitions, bringing the total number of DMPIs struck in the first night of operations to approximately a thousand. The Coalition had demonstrated the incredible throw-weight that it could muster: in the first seventy-two hours of strategic air operations, a total of 2,500 munitions would be delivered against targets in central and northern Iraq.[94] Yet, for all the technical brilliance of the strikes, the regime rode them out, as it had ridden out every aerial bombardment it had faced beforehand.

It would be easy to overlook the intangible effects of the bombing campaign on the ability of the Iraqi regime to organize the war effort, but it is fair to say that the opening strike of the neutered air campaign left the Iraqis and the world, to quote Robert Pape, "unshocked and unawed."[95] The administration and the military had played it safe, and the result was underwhelming to friend and foe alike. There would be no major collateral-damage incidents directly attributable to the air campaign—a notable first for the post–Cold War U.S. military—nor would there be an appreciable effect on the enemy war effort. The primary reliance on nocturnal strikes allowed Iraqis to go about business as usual. During the war, Jeffrey White wrote, "The coalition's precision attacks on a limited set of regime-associated targets in Baghdad have allowed the regime to portray a resilient population standing behind its government without having the morale of that population suffer from attacks on power, transportation, and other services vital to everyday life."[96] However, Greg Hooker argued, shock and awe might well have been impossible to impose on an enemy inured to U.S. military strikes during more than a decade of confrontation: "Given the high levels of continuous military pressure, the Iraqi military and populace were inured, to a degree, to Coalition capabilities, making it difficult to create Shock and Awe. Even new capabilities in the U.S. inventory would be 'previewed' in operations against Iraq, gradually acquainting Iraq's military in a way that allowed them to adjust their expectations, and even attempt to develop countervailing tactics and equipment to mitigate the effects of new Coalition weapons."[97]

Critics of the air campaign would derisively refer to the strikes as "impressive fireworks displays" or "pyrotechnics." Although this had not been the intent when the strikes were planned, their gradual neutering may justify the claim that the strategic air campaign involved more style than substance. CINCENT Franks recalled, "The scene was incredible. I had dreamed of such an Olympian view of the battlefield. Now I watched in real-time as Predator UAVs transmitted night-vision video of TLAMs and JDAMs silently blasting air defense sites and C2 buildings."[98] Although the opening strike had a sense of occasion, it could never match the suspense of the initial strikes of Desert Storm. The opening of air operations in 1991 had been a thunderclap, the first shots fired in anger between the United States and Iraq, but the commencement of the strategic air campaign in Operation Iraqi Freedom felt like an afterthought coming days after the beginning of hostilities when Coalition ground forces were lodged scores, even hundreds, of kilometers inside Iraq.

10

The March on Baghdad

After the 3rd U.S. Infantry Division's AH-64D Apaches and artillery shoots had eliminated the eleven Iraqi VISOBs along Kuwait's northeastern border with Iraq in the predawn hours of March 21, their first brush with the enemy proved to be ghosts from an earlier conflict—wrecked T-55s that had been destroyed by the wheeling V Corps armored fist in 1991.[1] In 2003, the U.S. Army's V Corps was now making the journey in reverse: the 3rd Infantry Division (Mechanized) was striking northwesterly into Iraq, like a spear pointed directly at Baghdad, and the 101st U.S. Air Assault Division was leapfrogging its helicopter battalions and truck convoys on a parallel arcing course through the open desert to the south of the mechanized forces.

The 3rd Infantry Division scheme of maneuver was initially to thrust deep into Iraq and seize key points along the Euphrates River. First the 1st and 3rd Brigade Combat Teams (BCT) would seize crossings at Nasariyah, then the 2nd BCT would isolate the city of Samawah, and finally the division's 7th ACR would seize a potential helicopter forward-area rearming and refueling point (FARRP) near Najaf, entering virgin territory never before occupied by the United States.

As the spearhead unit, the 3rd Infantry Division would be the hardest worked and most eagerly watched formation in the war. The post 9/11 stop-loss order had ensured personnel retention, and the division had been deployed to Kuwait since November 2002, which increased local acclimatization and training opportunities. Fifty embedded reporters had been with the troops throughout the deployment and would stay with them throughout the campaign. Although it was less digitized than the showcase 4th U.S. Infantry Division (Mechanized), the 3rd Infantry Division had received priority assignment of new sensors, weapons, and digitized C3 equipment in the months before the war, making it a jury-rigged digitized formation. More than any other formation, the division would need to be able to maintain C3 and direct its organic and supporting fires while moving across great distances. This would be particularly important during the opening days of the campaign, when the air component was in catch-up mode.[2]

The division's first major combat action unfolded on the morning of March 21 at the Tallil air base, near Nasariyah, where elements of the Iraqi 11th Infantry Division and twenty-five attached armored vehicles were entrenched. As the 1st and 3rd BCTs prepared to clear the airfield and head toward their ultimate objective—two bridges on the outskirts of Nasariyah— they did not adopt a "shoot first, ask questions later" approach. Prewar intelligence assessments suggested that most Iraqi regular-army formations would make a show of resistance but would quickly fold, their already depleted personnel melting away into the civilian community. Indeed there had been remarkably little resistance during the seizure of the Rumailah oil fields.[3] The 11th Infantry Division and its supporting 10th Armored Division were considered particularly likely to capitulate en masse after CIA operations yielded indications that Iraqi commanders were receptive to Coalition invitations to surrender.[4]

As the U.S. brigades approached, they assumed an assertive and threatening posture with armor and scouts to the fore and Apaches offering "over-the-shoulder" fire support. In the Rumaliah oil fields, Iraqis had neatly lined up beside their tanks and "held out wads of cash" to the advancing Marines.[5] Closing on Tallil airfield, U.S. tankers searched for signs of Iraqi intent and saw Iraqi troops surprised by the deep U.S. penetration but ready to fight from their prepared defensive positions.

The fight was reminiscent of the initial meeting engagements of Desert Storm: the United States transformed the clear advantage of its sensors and weapons into a killing edge. Although the majority of the 3rd Infantry Division air and ground platforms were Desert Storm vehicles with Desert Storm sensors—first generation FLIR and optical sights with ranges of three thousand meters—there had been some advances in the ability of U.S. ground forces to "out see" their opponents by even greater distances. Finally, U.S. forces could see as far as they could shoot. The new long-range scout surveillance system provided zoomable daylight television and third-generation thermal imaging that allowed the division to look seven to eight thousand meters beyond its forward line of troops.[6] However, it was only selectively deployed to 3rd Infantry Division scouts in lead units. This system, alongside the division's Bradley fighting vehicle–mounted fire-support team (FIST) and combat observation and lasing teams (COLT), increased the already impressive number of vehicles and squads within the unit that were able to geolocate enemy units and call down precise artillery or air strikes. In 1991, for instance, only four Bradley FISTs in an entire armored battalion were connected to the Coalition artillery network. In 2003, there were seventy-four vehicles with the digital and voice connectivity to spot for artillery,[7] which led General Franks to comment, "A 3rd Infantry Division sergeant in a Bradley controlled more firepower than a Desert Storm armored battalion."[8]

The one-sided fights at Tallil (Objective Firebird) and Nasariyah (Objective Liberty) unfolded in fits and spurts until all objectives were secured by 0551 on March 22. Iraqi armored vehicles and bunkers were precisely dispatched by M1A1 and Bradley direct fire and by fire-support Apaches. Amid the range of fired artillery munitions, the new SADARM round was extensively used. The SADARM round was the U.S. Army's first fully automated fire-and-forget multisensor munition: each artillery round opened to dispense two parachute-delivered submunitions over the target area, whereupon each bomblet would determine its altitude, scan the area for threats, use its millimetric wave radar and infrared sensors to verify the signature of Iraqi tanks, and destroy them with a top-down penetrating attack.[9] Equipped with advanced safety features to prevent unexploded munitions from causing civilian casualties, SADARM represented the beginning of a late but welcome transition to truly smart weapons in the U.S. Army. Overarching the fight on the forward line of troops, U.S. and Iraqi artillery dueled throughout the day and repeated the unequal struggle witnessed in Desert Storm: ineffective Iraqi artillery fell haphazardly while U.S. counterbattery fire systematically destroyed Iraqi artillery units.

Although the victories of the 1st and 3rd BCTs provided reassurance that the skill differential between the U.S. and Iraqi forces had grown wider since the last time their ground forces clashed, the engagements at Nasariyah had a disturbing element to them. The Iraqi 11th Infantry division had been deployed in poorly prepared fighting positions and its marksmanship and tactical leadership had been deeply flawed, but it had not immediately surrendered. In the fight for the Tallil air base and in Objective Liberty in Nasariyah, U.S. forces had fought off advancing enemy "dismounts"—infantrymen advancing on foot—and an "accurate sand table of U.S. positions" had been found near Objective Liberty.[10] Some combination of professionalism, nationalism, and regime coercion had held the 11th Infantry Division together, a unit that had been considered by U.S. planners to be one of the weaker Iraqi regular-army divisions. One planner irreverently noted, "It had its ass handed to it by the Kurdish militias in [the brief uprising of March] 1995. It was one of the worse, piece of garbage units in the Iraqi Army. But it fought."[11] Reflecting a growing sense of unease about the level of Iraqi resistance in those opening days on Operation Iraqi Freedom, embedded writer Rick Atkinson pondered, "What did an eight-digit coordinate tell you about your enemy's willingness to die for his cause?"[12]

THE LUNGE NORTHWARD

The development of an accurate assessment of enemy capabilities and course of action would continue to be a vital and sometimes flawed element of the V Corps thrust into central Iraq. To prepare the ground for rapid-maneuver operations, CENTCOM had closely investigated whether Saddam would manipulate local hydrology to swamp the Coalition's approach to Baghdad by opening sluices or destroying dams. CENTCOM concluded that even though Iraq had created water obstacles to slow and channel Iranian offensives in the past, conditions did not favor the use of such tactics: although Operation Iraqi Freedom was launched in Iraq's wet season, years of drought had drained Iraqi reservoirs. As insurance, a range of U.S., Australian, and Polish SOFs had taken direct actions at three key Iraqi dams. These resulted in prolonged combat actions that would last until early April and confirming that Iraq had not, in fact, planned to flood the Tigris and Euphrates valleys.[13]

More important, however, the Coalition planned its lightning thrust to Baghdad by skirting and "masking" all the major cities on the Euphrates valley and by relying on ISR assets to function as its flank guard. This latter feature of the plan reflected the U.S. military goal of fighting increasingly information-enabled operations or "network-centric warfare" (NCW), described by the

U.S. Army as the development of "a self-adapting system of thinking participants who are able to act rapidly on the basis of understanding both the commander's intent and the situation around them."[14] According to the plan, situational awareness created by the network of ISR assets overflying and surrounding the V Corps—combined with the effects of shock, deception, and information deprivation on Iraqi decision makers—would allow the U.S. Army to penetrate deep into Iraq without systematically defeating the threats that they were by-passing. As the 3rd BCT of the 3rd Infantry Division moved to secure bridges at Nasariyah in anticipation of handing off the area to U.S. Marine Division units on March 23, the rest of the U.S. V Corps plunged northwest toward objectives at Samawah and Najaf, some five hundred kilometers inside Iraq.

The ISR constellation assembled by the Coalition was centrally controlled by the CENTCOM J-2, although some assets were apportioned to V Corps control. It provided unparalleled coverage of the battlefield surrounding the U.S. thrust. National intelligence platforms were carefully integrated into the common operational picture (COP) developed in the Pentagon, at CENTCOM and land-component forward headquarters in Qatar, the Combined Air Operations Center (CAOC) in Saudi Arabia, and the V Corps and MEF headquarters in Kuwait. Stateside analysts scrutinized the fruits of the dozen direct and two dozen indirect overhead passes by imaging satellites. ELINT and SIGINT spacecraft communicated with operational headquarters through classified online chat rooms. These combined in the closest integration yet of the national and operational intelligence systems. The U.S. Army 714th Military Intelligence Brigade enjoyed a close link with the NSA and fed SIGINT into the operational intelligence picture. The National Ground Intelligence Center and NIMA were linked to the CENTCOM J-2, bringing the real experts on the Iraqi ORBAT into direct communications with operational planners. JCS J-2 Major General Shaffer stated that it was like "taking a guy who might have watched Iraqi ground forces in southern Iraq every day for five years and putting him in the loop."[15]

Eighty dedicated ISR aircraft added theater-level intelligence to this picture: every U.S. service and the British military combined to provide twenty-four-hour multispectral imagery, thermal imagery, moving target indicators (MTI) cues, EMINT, and SIGINT. The large Global Hawk, Predator, and Hunter UAVs carried out missions lasting between ten and thirty-five hours, which further bolstered persistent twenty-four-hour all-weather surveillance.[16]

In addition to these dedicated ISR assets, the Coalition had effectively turned a range of strike aircraft and helicopters into ISR sensors by integrating data from their onboard targeting systems via the range of datalinks that had been installed on U.S. and British aircraft since Desert Storm. The MTI capability of the radar on the B-1B bomber, which loitered over Iraq for up to fifteen hours at a time, was exploited as an ISR sensor, as were the look-down radars and targeting pods carried by a range of tactical strike aircraft.[17] Other intelligence also streamed upward from the tactical level, including time-delayed information on the "red forces" (the enemy), arriving through regular reporting channels, and near-real-time information on "blue forces" (Coalition troops), reported by the so-called blue-force trackers (BFT) distributed to company level in the combat brigades of the Coalition divisions. Commanders in 1991 had only the vaguest idea of where the advanced elements of Coalition forces were located, but commanders could now locate any company-sized maneuver element to within a ten-digit GPS coordinate at all times.[18] Here, then, was the "Olympian" view that General Franks had described—a view of the battlefield where any major movement of enemy military vehicles and any use of artillery or air-defense weapons could be probably detected and located.

Down at the plebian level, however, things looked decidedly different and far more old-fashioned. Whereas the national, theater, component, and Corps headquarters were stationary and settled, the combat divisions were constantly moving, which made it difficult to flow intelligence via the short-range, line-of-sight voice and data communications backbones that fighting units still depended on. To augment FM (frequency modulation) voice communications and the U.S. Army mobile subscriber equipment (MSE) data-communications systems, the 3rd Infantry Division and other spearhead units received military tactical satellite (TACSAT) and commercial international maritime (INMARSAT) satellite phones, and Iridium pagers. Their BFT systems also had limited satellite-based text-messaging capabilities. These workarounds required bandwidth, the measurement of simultaneous voice- and data-transmission capacity, and lots of it. However, although CENTCOM's bandwidth had been boosted from the peacetime 113 megabytes to a wartime 783 megabytes—forty times that available in Desert Storm—it would never keep up with demand. Frequency and bandwidth became an important battlespace and a commodity that corps- and divisional-level staff fought over throughout the war.[19] For those headquarters with sufficient bandwidth, appropriate equipment, and the ability to remain stationary, there was one intelligence picture that had live streaming images from ISR platforms and web-chat with U.S.-based intelligence analysts accessed through the classified SIPRNET (Secret Internet Protocol Router Network). The rest, the majority, were on the wrong side of the so-called "digital divide."[20]

It might be more useful to imagine the "digital divide" as a downward slope rather than a sudden drop-off, because the ability of tactical units to receive intelligence fell off gradually the further down the chain of command the units were positioned. At the top of the digital slope were the rear headquarters of the combat divisions, complex circus-type convoys of vehicles and collapsible structures known as Division Main (DMAIN). The 3rd Infantry Division DMAIN moved eight times during Operation Iraqi Freedom; each time it was moving, DMAIN slid right down the digital slope, effectively cutting itself off from the fight. When set up, however, the DMAIN sat astride the digital divide: it was able to access national-level intelligence and receive "oven-fresh" imagery and other intelligence through its embedded national intelligence providers and specialized ground stations that were capable of directly receiving footage from airborne ISR platforms.[21] The division's forward tactical headquarters, known as the (DTAC) sat on the other side of the digital divide, further down the slope because of its constant movements and less-advanced equipment. Although it was mostly able to maintain voice communications at all ranges because of its various satellite phones, the DTAC had patchy data connectivity because its ability to surf the SIPRNET relied on the terrestrial MSE system, which could not effectively be maintained on the move despite the ingenuity and best efforts of U.S. signalers. Maj. Gen. Buford Blount, the 3rd Infantry Division commander, would not enjoy an Olympian view because he could neither task UAVs (only the Marines and the British fielded divisional-level UAVs) nor could he watch the footage from his DTAC. He watched the war with his own eyes, and read or heard about UAV reports whenever voice and data communications were available.

The digital slope got a lot steeper at brigade level and below. In theory, the brigade intelligence officers could connect to the DMAIN and DTAC through the all-source intelligence system (ASAS), one of twelve types of battlefield intelligence or operating systems used in the division. *Wired* magazine referred to this setup as the "cobbling together" of "a remarkable system from a hodgepodge of military-built networking technology, off-the-shelf gear, miles of Ethernet cable, and commercial software."[22] Yet, with each

BCT headquarters constantly on the move and stopping for a maximum of four hours in any day, the MSE-reliant ASAS system would quickly become outdated. Brigade staff became reliant on the time-honored sources of tactical intelligence, namely the optics and naked eyes of their own forward platoons, companies, and battalions. These tactical units lay at the base of a veritable digital cliff. FM and MSE networks were frequently unavailable because of the massive distances being traversed: the 3rd Infantry Division traveled 350 kilometers in an eighty-hour lunge, a period during which the BCTs were sometimes separated by 270 kilometers and the lead and tail elements of logistical columns were sometimes out of FM range.[23] Because upward communication was often maintained by the single TACSAT phone or Iridium pager at each battalion headquarters, and downward communication was often reliant on the limited-bandwidth texting capabilities of the BFT systems, the SA of "red force" activities developed by the tactical units at the forefront of the advance would typically be earned the hard way: by meeting the enemy at close hand.

RUNNING INTO QUICKSAND

By the end of March 22, 3rd Infantry Division forces were in position to secure their initial objectives: seizing key bridges at Nasariyah, setting up masking-position objectives at Samawah, and securing the future 101st Air Assault FARRP outside Najaf. According to military analyst Michael Eisenstadt, their average advance of 120 kilometers per day outdistanced similar armored advances by the Germans in Russia (1941) and North Africa (1942), the Russians in the Ukraine (1944) and Manchuria (1945), Israel in the Sinai (1967), and the United States during Desert Storm.[24] Most of the fighting formations had spent all day moving, and the 3rd BCT of the 3rd Infantry Division at Nasariyah had completed its handshake with its relief force, the Marines of Task Force Tarawa. The enemy appeared immobile; the ISR constellation registered no major movements of ground forces that could threaten the flank of the V Corps thrust to Baghdad. The isolation of Baghdad looked to be a foregone conclusion, with little prospect of resistance in the outlying provinces. However, within twenty-four hours a different and darker picture would emerge.

The first hints of the asymmetric strategy being employed by the Baathist regime had emerged in the preceding forty or so hours of ground operations.

Mirroring the tactics used by Iraq's air defenses to resist the no-fly zones, Iraqi artillery pieces had been dispersed into small platoon-sized concentrations and placed next to schools, mosques, housing, and, most notoriously, a children's hospital in Nasariyah—locations that were marked as restricted target areas on the Controlled Image Base at the divisional artillery headquarters. Because U.S. artillery units lacked weapons precise enough to be used in close proximity to civilians, the highly effective target-acquisition and strike combination of the U.S. Army's Q-36/G-37 Firefinder radars was instantly negated. This forced the 3rd Infantry Division to rely on the cumbersome process of using its attached U.S. Air Force enlisted tactical air controllers (ETACs) to describe the targets to precision-armed fighter-bomber pilots using the uncertain combination of map readings and voice communications. A number of smaller Iraqi artillery pieces were able to relocate in the five to thirty minutes required to call in air support.[25]

Teams of regime watchers dressed in civilian clothes, mounted on motorcycles or in civilian cars and linked to the Iraqi batteries and to local military and Baath Party officials by cell phones, satellite phones, and even by the public telephone network, allowed Iraqi batteries to target Coalition forces as soon as they entered certain areas of Nasariyah or the outskirts of Samawah. Although Iraq had also made use of Bedouin and other border crossers to glean information about U.S. deployments in Saudi Arabia before Desert Storm, the enemy vedettes that then formed the outer lip of their divisional "security zones" had at least been recognizably uniformed and mounted in Eastern Bloc reconnaissance vehicles.[26] Now, they looked exactly like the thousands of bewildered, friendly, or sullen civilians that were mixing freely with Coalition forces as they closed on the outskirts of Nasariyah, Samawah, and Najaf. These urban sprawls had not been correctly characterized on Coalition maps, and thus Coalition forces were placed inside the fringes of the very urban areas they were attempting to seal off.

In fact, the United States was not so much at the edge of the Iraqi security zone as it was sitting astride a rapidly pooling sea of enemy that did not look or fight like the Iraqi divisions that CENTCOM had expected to meet. The first major clash between the U.S. troops and the plain-clothes irregular troops deployed to the south occurred at Samawah on the morning of March 23. U.S. forces had arrived outside the town twenty-four hours earlier and linked up with U.S. SOFs mounted in "white pick-ups, rubbed down and painted up crazy, the way the Iraqis do," to borrow Rick Atkinson's description.[27] The SOFs were primarily concerned with whether the Iraqis had rigged the town's bridges with explosives and whether enemy forces were present. One of the special operators' local contacts—a taxi driver equipped with a cell phone—had reported that paramilitary barracks were positioned astride the entrance to the town, were flanked by trenches, and were lightly fortified. The 3rd Infantry Division's helicopter-mounted scouts had reported no major enemy forces were anywhere near the city, and nobody was particularly worried by the paramilitaries, who had made no aggressive moves for the whole day and were not expected to come out of their urban sanctuary.[28]

As CENTCOM Intelligence Analyst Hooker noted, "Security forces were believed to have little or no capability to fight the Coalition military directly. Their main mission was to keep the population in check; they were not equipped and trained to engage in attacks against conventional forces. They did not practice fighting as organized units against another military force. Some of the security forces, particularly the Saddam Fedayeen, were not regarded as having a very high degree of professionalism. Created as a 'vanity' force by Saddam's unstable eldest son, Uday Hussein, the Fedayeen had suffered in changes in recent years to its personnel, equipment, leadership and mission."[29]

The prognosis would prove to be an underestimation of the recklessness, if not the tactical ineptness, of the irregulars. Most of the fighters were too young to remember a time before Desert Storm and a time before the twelve-year war with America. They greeted the 3rd Infantry Division probe into the suburbs of Samawah with fierce counterattacks. General Franks recalled watching the unorthodox forces on live footage gathered by a UAV and describing "five dusty white pickups each mounting a heavy machine-gun—crammed with men in civilian clothes armed with Kalashnikovs and RPGs—speeding through rutted alleys. . . . A motorcycle with a sidecar carrying what looked like a 75mm recoilless rifle bounced out of a walled compound and joined the attack force."[30]

One U.S. Army trooper, Staff Sgt. Dillard Johnson, recounted, "Total mayhem broke out! We began to receive a huge volume of fire. . . . Between 150-200 guys then began to pour out of the buildings. They engaged us with small arms and a few RPGs. They were so close that my M240 coax [machine gun] was destroyed by small-arms fire. Also, literally dozens of RPGs were bouncing off the vehicle because the Iraqis were too close! The RPGs did not have enough range to arm so were just non-explosive projectiles. . . . I engaged enemy dismounts with my M9 [9-mm pistol] and M4 [5.56-mm assault rifle]."[31]

Moments later, Johnson was blown from his tank by an AK-47 burst in his chest plate, and, like the rest of his unit, spent the next four hours beating back the frenzied attacks.

From his vantage point, Franks watched as the irregulars spent themselves, wave after furious wave:

We couldn't hear the blast of gunfire, but we saw the first pick-up stagger and wobble under the impact of .50 caliber machine-gun rounds. Dead fighters flipped over the sides of the truck, but the man at the technical's machine-gun continued to fire. A survivor beside him in the cargo bay launched an RPG, but the back-blast from the rocket tube set on fire a wounded man slumped near the tailgate. The RPG did not fly far enough to arm itself before it bounced harmlessly off the thick armor of one of the Abrams tanks. When a Bradley opened fire with its 25mm chain gun, the technical and its crew disappeared in a cloud of smoking chunks. . . . Still the enemy attacked. Halfway down the column, another technical managed to slam into a Bradley. Five enemy fighters scrambled onto the Bradley's hull and fired their assault rifles at the armored glass observation blocks in the buttoned down hatches. The trooper commanding the Bradley swung his turret, knocking off two of the enemy with the barrel of the chain gun. Then the tank behind the Bradley swept the hull with 7.62mm rounds fired from its remotely operated external machine-gun."[32]

As March 23 wore on, similar scenes were unfolding in Najaf and Nasariyah, where U.S. forces were seizing a series of bridgeheads on the far side of the Euphrates River. There, elements of the 3rd Infantry Division's cavalry regiment were caught in the midst of an Iraqi ambush, trapped on three sides, forced to salvage Iraqi small arms to fight off dismounts, and fought so close "that Iraqi soldiers were being killed by ricochets of their own rocket-propelled grenades."[33] At Nasariyah, meanwhile, a host of setbacks inflicted the heaviest sequence of U.S. casualties suffered in the war. In addition to a friendly fire incident that claimed the lives of six Marines, two U.S. convoys were heavily ambushed in Nasariyah's streets. The 507th Maintenance Company, a U.S Army Patriot missile–support unit, mistakenly drove straight into the thronging urban defensive zone: eleven were killed and six captured of its thirty-three personnel. Soldiers from Task Force Tarawa were trapped in Ambush Alley, a stretch of road on the enemy side of the

Euphrates River, with three of their armored vehicles destroyed. Throughout a long afternoon and night, the Marines moved their armored vehicles back to back and needed constant air support to hold off the massed attacks of the regime irregulars and soldiers. Major James Cox, a Marine Corps AH-1W Cobra pilot, recalled, "We were so low over them that the firing from machine guns made your teeth rattle. Every couple of minutes, a [FAC] would give me a rollout heading, and I'd either ripple a pod of rockets, or blast away with cannons. Everything was danger-close."[34]

Although tactically reckless, the irregular forces had been gathered and unleashed as part of a deliberate and operationally sophisticated military effort by the regime, one that had passed entirely undetected by the ISR architecture designed to guard the Coalition flanks. Before the war, Iraq positioned masses of weaponry and armed civilian vehicles at hospitals, schools, nurseries, mosques, and the ubiquitous walled compounds throughout the Euphrates River valley. The Baath Party Emergency Battalion and Qods (Jerusalem) forces were placed under former Republican Guard generals to develop their military capabilities.[35] During the war, Baath Party officials and Republican Guard military officers escorted small groups of irregular fighters and paid or ideologically motivated foreign fighters to the south; they moved them at night in "nontactical vehicles" (NTV)—U.S. military parlance for the taxis, trucks, buses, and even ambulances used by the regime.

General Franks stated, "We had anticipated there might be up to forty thousand of these Fedayeen-type irregulars recruited to conduct urban warfare in Baghdad. But at no point had I thought these forces would be moved south to fight as guerrillas. Our lack of reliable HUMINT had given us a nasty surprise: We'd had no warnings that Saddam had dispatched these paramilitary forces from Baghdad. Our analysts had seen reconnaissance pictures of pick-up trucks, their cargo bays covered by tarps, and civilian buses loaded with passengers heading south, but this raised no concern. The traffic was taken to be normal commerce."[36]

Using couriers or low-power communications such as cell phones, the regime escorts matched the fighters with weapons and vehicles, sent them out to press gang civilians and to defend key locations, and then returned to Baghdad to retrieve a new group to escort. According to postwar U.S. investigations, during the war as many as ten thousand irregulars may have linked up with those already stationed in the south.[37] The neutered air campaign, particularly after the scrubbing of all the Baath Party offices and other C2 sites in central and southern Iraq, had done little to shake the faith of Saddam's party faithful, who were now playing their part. Iraq had found a way to carry out hidden operational movements under conditions of complete enemy air supremacy.

The irregulars had to be neutralized because they were proactive enough to sally forth from the urban sprawl of the Euphrates River valley to threaten Coalition lines of supply. The V Corps commander, Lt. Gen. William Wallace, recalled, "I make no apologies for these comments. . . . The enemy we fought . . . was much more aggressive than what we expected him to be, or at least, what I expected him to be. He was willing to attack out of those towns towards our formations, when my expectation was that they would be defending those towns and not be as aggressive. There was also a presence of foreign fighters that we subsequently discovered to be seeded within and cooperating with Saddam's Fedayeen, which were at least fanatical, if not suicidal."[38]

In contrast to the relative quiet soldiers anticipated of the march north, during which Iraqi conscript units were expected to surrender en masse, the path instead was drenched in blood. The irregulars performed even more acts of perfidy than the Iraqi Republican Guard had in 1991: they regularly violated flags of truce, habitually wore civilian clothing, and played dead or pretended to surrender only to take up arms again the moment Coalition forces passed. The regime forces left the U.S. military no recourse but the complete and ruthless destruction of Fedayeen personnel and equipment. Vehicles and weapons would be demolished in their thousands. Enemy troops that "surrendered" to Coalition helicopters only to immediately take up arms again would be given no second chances. Corpses near weapons would be "double tapped" to make sure they were dead. And civilians would no longer be able to approach Coalition forces without risking life and limb.[39]

At the strategic level, a picture was beginning to form of the Iraqi regime's capabilities and intentions and the effect that Coalition military operations had thus far had on them. The Iraqi regime was neither shocked nor awed, although there are strong indications that it did not expect the Coalition to attack as soon as it did and may have been led by Coalition deception efforts to expect some form of direct airborne assault in central Iraq. It possessed more than enough asymmetric means of C3 to enact its simple defensive plan for Iraq. As the U.S. Army's *On Point* review of the war noted, "Early in OIF, the U.S. employed tactical fires to neutralize much of Iraq's strategic and operational communications infrastructure and to neutralize Iraq's integrated air defense system. Yet, defending Iraqi forces continued to fight fiercely. Primarily using simple instructions, they continued to maneuver and continued to fight."[40] Jeffrey White added, "The first surprise of this war has been the resiliency of the regime. . . . Saddam's regime has not proven to be as brittle as many originally believed: when the coalition kicked in the front door, the rotten edifice did not collapse. The Iraqis are still in the fight, which may be their greatest achievement to date. . . . Saddam and the Baath Party are facing their most comprehensive crisis, but they have not collapsed and are resisting in creative ways."[41]

According to White, who wrote one of the most cogent analyses to appear during the war, the Iraqi regime continued to defend at as many points as possible and utilized all loyalist elements and capabilities, however militarily ineffective. Trading space for time and the dissipation of Coalition forces, the regime sought "to stay in the fight as long as possible." In addition to Iraq's ongoing smattering of SSM attacks, which "keep the Iraqis in the fight in a highly visible way," Iraq continued to exploit tactical victories using its well-orchestrated media effort. White concluded, "The drawing out of fighting at Umm Qasr, Basra, and Nasiriyah has allowed the regime to cite these cities as examples of heroic national resistance. Moreover, the U.S. combat losses at Nasiriyah have been broadcast widely as examples of Iraq's ability to inflict damage on the coalition. The losses themselves are small, but the images are large, and they are playing well on the Arab street."[42]

In addition to exploiting tactical victories, the regime had also held off committing any damaging scorched-earth actions that could have hastened its own demise. Although nine oil wells had apparently been subjected to demolitions, with two of the hastily rigged wells failing to ignite, only twenty of the thousands of other oil wells, platforms, separation plants, and pumping stations in the Rumailah oil fields and in the regime controlled oil fields near Kirkuk were prepared for demolitions. This led U.S. Army analysts to conclude that the threat of destroying Iraq's oil wells, like many other threats, had been maintained precisely to deter an attack. Likewise, although all but one bridge along the Euphrates River had been rigged, only four were destroyed, and no dams or other infrastructure were demolished by the regime.

Instead of conducting such suicidal actions, Jeff White noted, "At least outwardly, the central government appears to be operating, whether or not Saddam is dead, wounded, or in hiding. There have been no significant breakdowns of civil order or uprisings by the population. Press conferences and briefings are being held, the government's handling of the first U.S. prisoners of war was rapid and coordinated, and the ability of the Baghdad security services to operate effectively was displayed in the recent hunt for reportedly downed coalition aviators. The regime was also able to send its foreign minister to the Arab summit in Cairo."[43] Chillingly, the regime was acting as if it would live to fight another day. Michael Eisenstadt argued:

> Saddam has survived numerous close calls and crises (including the most recent known attempt to kill him at the outset of the current invasion), and he seems optimistic that this war is not only survivable, but winnable. This may explain the regime's apparent decision to avoid torching Iraq's oil fields, destroying its infrastructure, gassing civilians, producing massive refugee flows, or launching Scud missiles against Israel. The regime intends to remain in power, and it is therefore unwilling to destroy the country—at least for now. Moreover, it may believe that such actions would dramatically weaken its relatively favorable international position, which will be a vital asset in the coming phase of the war. And if Iraq's leaders are removed from power, the prospects for a comeback would be significantly harmed if they were to raze the country in the process.[44]

March 23 had been a sobering day for the United States and its allies. In a war where Coalition soldiers had previously died at an average rate of fewer than three per day, twenty-nine Americans had been killed in less than twenty-four hours. Two British aviators had also been killed in a friendly fire incident at the outset of the day when their Tornado was shot down in error by a U.S. Patriot system. As night fell the weather turned, and a sandstorm, a shamal, of frightening intensity descended like a cloak over the battlefield, stripping the spread-out Coalition forces of much of their space-based and airborne ISR and airborne-strike capability for an unknown period. For the troops trapped inside enemy-held territory across the Euphrates River, long hours of uncertainty beckoned. The U.S. Army commented, "By any definition, 23 March 2003 proved a dark day for coalition forces fighting in Iraq" and caused "a palpable effect on the morale of higher-echelon headquarters" as the sun set.[45] Yet, before the night was out, there was one final asymmetric sucker punch to come.

FAILED DEEP STRIKE AGAINST
THE MEDINA DIVISION

Coalition ground-forces commanders at V Corps headquarters remained focused on Baghdad and the Republican Guard divisions ringing the city, which
were still regarded as the enemy's main forces, even as the other setbacks were
occurring and as the sandstorm swept over Iraq. Operation Iraqi Freedom was
a joint operation, yet the thrust on Baghdad was planned by U.S. Army generals, from CINCCENT Franks to the ground-forces component commander,
Lieutenant General McKiernan, down to the V Corps commander, Lieutenant
General Wallace.

These officers had reached high command under the air-land battle
doctrine, which stressed the role of the U.S. Army corps commander as the
ultimate manager of the "deep fight" against enemy forces beyond the forward
line of troops (FLOT), one or two engagements down the line. Although the
U.S. Air Force–dominated air component believed that enemy ground forces
should be degraded to the maximum extent possible before the Coalition
ground forces ever reached them, the U.S. Army instinctively felt that the role
of their army was to destroy the enemy army. This is how it had worked at the
divisional level at Tallil on March 21: the attack relied almost exclusively on
the attack-helicopter and artillery assets of the 3rd Infantry Division. However,
the real test of air-land battle's corps-level deep-battle doctrine was yet to
come with the long-awaited deep strike on the Republican Guard defenses
surrounding Baghdad.

Controlling the deep battle relied on the ownership of battlespace, which
according to U.S. doctrine is "a geographical area, including the airspace
above it, usually defined by lateral, forward, and rear boundaries assigned
to a commander."[46] Similar to bandwidth, battlespace is a jealously hoarded
commodity in modern warfare. When it has to be shared by both friendly
ground and air forces, the real trick is to ensure that the battlespace is safe for
your own side but still dangerous for the enemy. If the battlespace is not clearly
owned, it is dangerous for either everybody or nobody. The primary fire-
control support measure used to define the ownership of battlespace remained
the FCSL. This had changed little since 1991, when the difficulty of rapidly
shifting its position contributed to the escape of the very Republican Guard
units that were now entering the U.S. cross hairs once again. This time, every
part of Iraq had been gridded into "kill boxes" roughly 48 kilometers on

a side, and each box was further subdivided into nine "key pads" roughly 16 kilometers on a side. The FSCL could now be "digitized"—more precisely drawn along the forward edges of any outline of kill boxes or even key pads—but otherwise the concept stayed the same.

Every night, the CFLCC would nominate the FSCL, the CINC would approve it, and it would be enacted the next day. Beyond or "long" of the FSCL was the hunting ground of the air component, which could either strike prearranged targets on that day's ATO or assign a number of aircraft to kill boxes, where they would be given targets of opportunity by airborne FAC-As. Whereas all kill boxes long of the FSCL were open to air attack, all those within or "short" of the FSCL were closed unless the air support controllers at the ground-component or V Corps headquarters otherwise specified. The area short of the FSCL was instead the hunting ground of V Corps. The V Corps used either its divisional weapons (in the area up to thirty to forty kilometers beyond the FLOT) or its deep-strike assets: the three Apache battalions of the 11th Attack Helicopter Regiment and the ATACMS shooters of the 41st and 214th Field Artillery Battalions. If tactical air support was required within the FSCL, either the ground component had to open a kill box short of the FSCL and allow air attacks under the control of FAC-As,[47] or air support had to be carried out under the Corps CAS methodology. Corps CAS methodology meant that the entire air strike had to be carried out under terminal-attack procedures (the cumbersome voice-communications cueing process that involved ground observers and reduced the possibility of high-volume air support).

If used judiciously, the digitized FSCL could reduce friendly fire while at the same time exposing enemy forces to the maximum U.S. combat power. The precise placement of the line allowed air power to hunt in certain areas short of the FSCL where ground troops were not present and kill boxes could be opened to air attack. Instead, however, the FSCL was wielded like a blunt instrument. According to Maj. Gen. Dan Leaf, the senior U.S. Air Force air-liaison officer in the ground component, at the precipitate beginning of ground operations the FSCL was thrown forward more than 130 kilometers. This scrubbed preplanned targeting in the massive area short of the FSCL and stretched U.S. aerial refueling capacity by pushing U.S. air support further north.[48]

Even so, during the massive initial lunge, U.S. ground forces nearly overran the FSCL twice. On March 22 and 23, the FSCL was again thrown forward 130 kilometers to keep U.S. airpower away from the advancing columns. Most of the tactical battlespace thus became off limits to protect forces occupying pencil-thin routes of advance. Col. Steve Seroka, an assistant to Leaf at the ground component, recalled, "Every day, Gen. Leaf would arrange for the FSCL to be pulled a little back, but every night the Army majors would throw it far out again. Majors really run the military, but they haven't generally been trained at joint schools—that comes at a later stage in their careers—and at the intermediate service schools where they had studied, the FSCL was always thrown as far as it could go to let the army exercise its corps battles."[49]

To offset the loss of airpower, V Corps planned to tightly control all joint fires—meaning direct fire, artillery, helicopter and air support that occurred in its enormous battlespace. In some instances, this meant that V Corps deep-strike systems were launched in unsettling proximity to the FLOT of U.S. troops to engage high-value targets spotted by corps-level intelligence-collection systems. The 3rd Infantry Division after-action report complained: "Instead of passing intelligence information down to the division and allowing 3rd Infantry Division elements to engage targets, higher headquarters insisted upon engaging the targets themselves. On several occasions no known coordination was attempted. Corps does not have the situational awareness [SA] to engage targets within battlespace that they do not own. There is a large possibility for fratricide. . . . [For instance,] 3rd Infantry Division ETACs reported explosions within their battlespace 4 km from their position. Several minutes later, corps contacted division, wanting to use that area to strike, control, and reconnaissance [SCAR] for enemy artillery and surface-to-surface SSMs."[50]

Although the ubiquitous BFTs allowed them to strike opportunity targets with some certainty that areas were clear of *most* U.S. ground troops, V Corps' SA of the enemy fell far short of that needed to launch deep strikes, as the 3rd Infantry Division report noted:

The FCSL was 100 km beyond the range of standard munitions from our M109A6s and M270s. This created a dead space between the area that the army could influence and the area shaped by the CFACC. The placement of the FSCL was so far in front of the forward edge of the battlefield [FEBA] that neither divisional nor corps assets could effectively manage the battlespace. . . . The argument seems to be that CFACC would not adequately address V Corps targeting requirements; 3ID (M) violently disagrees. CFACC is a component, manned and equipped to effectively manage this battlespace forward of the FSCL; V Corps is not and has demonstrated their inability to manage said battlespace. 3ID

(M) believes CFACC is better prepared to engage targets to effectively shape the battlefield versus V Corps' use of corps CAS.[51]

In fact, working independently, neither the ground nor the air component probably had enough ISR assets or SA to effectively target enemy ground forces that were bermed and awaiting the aerial onslaught. Nonetheless, V Corps readied its deep strike, despite its lack of SA about the enemy threat and target systems—a classic case of the modern U.S. military's ability to shoot farther than it could see.

The large Apache helicopter deep strike planned for the night of March 23 had been a long time coming: the Apache battalions had seen little action since Desert Storm. They had been excluded from use in Operation Allied Force because of the threat environment and had provided an important but quantitatively small force in Afghanistan. V Corps planners had been straining at the leash to use the four Apache battalions of the reinforced 11th Attack Helicopter Regiment from the very outset of Operation Iraqi Freedom. On the first expedited night of ground operations, V Corps planners had hoped to launch a seventy-Apache deep strike on the paltry defenses of the 11th Infantry Division at Tallil, but the mission had been scrubbed because the regiment's C2 and fuel-carrying helicopters could not navigate the Iraqi desert at night. A full regimental helicopter assault would also throw up heavy dust clouds, further impeding navigation. A U.S. Army report concluded, "After the aborted mission, morale sunk. Some pilots had compared this attack to the 101st Aviation Brigade's legendary deep-attack operation in Operation Desert Storm; they too were going to be heroes. Their frustration continued to build, adding to the 11th AHR's collective desire to get into the fight."[52]

Two days into the war, V Corps would finally get the chance to use the regiment in the deep-strike mission as they leapfrogged the all-important FARRPs to areas as far west as Najaf. The mission had been in planning even as the V Corps crossed the line of departure into Iraq and involved a three-battalion attack by forty-eight Apaches against two brigades of the Medina Republican Guard division. Ascribing each Hellfire missile carried by the Apaches a 60-percent chance of killing an enemy target, V Corps projections suggested that the Medina would be destroyed after two nights of deep strikes. One officer noted, "When we attack the 14th Brigade of the Medina Division, we expect to see a hundred burning vehicles within an hour."[53]

Visualization software took planners on "magic-carpet-ride" simulations across relatively open terrain toward the enemy forces. Serious enemy antiaircraft threats such as mobile SAM launchers and heavy AAA pieces were profiled and their positioned bracketed for a preemptive barrage of thirty-two ATACMS. Tactical aircraft would overfly the attack, prepared to attack enemy radars or air defenses with HARM missiles and bombs. Enemy company-sized positions were located down to an eight-digit location, that is, within ten meters, and targeting updates were planned once the attack-helicopter battalions reached Objective RAMS, their forward FARRP outside Najaf.[54]

However, as the old adage says, no plan survives contact with the enemy, and the mission quickly began to unravel as night fell on March 23. As the three Apache battalions reached Objective RAMS, the sandstorm was in full swing, causing "brown-out" conditions that led one Apache to crash. Because of the weather and threats to the lines of supply, insufficient fuel made it to the FARRP. The attack would now be limited to two battalions, thirty-two Apaches, with strikes concentrated on the Medina division's 14th Mechanized Brigade only. Poor weather and communications further disrupted the intelligence preparation of the mission, grounding the UAVs that would have provided up-to-date enemy target coordinates and limiting the 11th Attack Helicopter Regiment's intelligence officer to receiving "give-or-take-a-kilometer" locations of the enemy company-sized clusters of targets.[55] Because of poor communications, the strike's tactical air support was not aware that the mission was launched more than two hours behind schedule, and the air support left the target area just as the Apaches arrived. The thirty-two Apaches making the inbound journey were flying using night-vision goggles (NVG) in a heavy sandstorm, a dangerous prospect even in relatively open terrain but doubly so because the routes were far more suburban and cluttered than anticipated. Where the visualization software had showed open fields and occasional towers or power lines, there were farmhouses, adobe sheds, walled compounds, and masses of date groves and palm trees. As Rick Atkinson noted, "I wondered how a nation could spend more than $30 billion annually on intelligence and still be unsure where there are towns and where there are not towns."[56]

Similarly, although the rescheduled thirty-two ATACMS strikes pounded identified air-defense targets, the bulk of Iraq's antihelicopter air defenses had been missed by the radar of the Coalition's ISR constellation.

The Iraqis had been savaged by Apache raids in 1991 and had experienced the Coalition air-defense rollback tactics in the no-fly zones, which gave them plenty of time and relevant experience to develop a response. Similar to any network-centric or information-enabled military activity, the Iraqis started with sensors and gathered information by using their network of plain-clothes observers to report the arrival, departure, and heading of U.S. helicopters from Objective RAMS. U.S. SIGINT sensors picked up a local signals spike of reverse-encrypted cell-phone activity, including fifty calls to an Iraqi general coordinating the effort from Najaf.

One of the inbound Apache battalions aborted the mission after receiving increasingly intense antiaircraft fire from the sprawl of hamlets below, while the other continued. As the remaining battalion began searching for its targets from their "attack by fire" positions, thousands of meters away from the "engagement areas" where the enemy companies were supposed to be, the enemy trap was sprung. It had been triggered by the switching off and on of city power grids in Hasway and Iskandariyah. Rather than being thousands of meters distant from the enemy, heavy small-arms, rocket propelled grenade (RPG), and AAA fire came from directly around the Apaches, indicating an unassessed threat—that hundreds or thousands of soldiers and civilians were firing personal and crew-served weapons from houses and garages.[57]

Unable to fly their preferred nap-of-the-earth profiles because of power lines and other obstructions, the Apaches were exposed to AAA fire. The street lights of the mischaracterized urban sprawl lit up the sky, uncovering the Apaches and maxing-out their pilots' NVGs and the thermal sights of their gunners. The benefits of stand-off weaponry and technological superiority had been stood on their heads. Contrary to the Longbow radar's factory performance of simultaneously finding and characterizing 256 targets at ranges of up to twelve thousand meters, the scattered and hidden Republican Guard artillery and vehicles could not be seen. Instead, a mosquito swarm of thousands of individual targets were firing from behind and underneath the Apaches and from civilian buildings that were restricted targets under the rules of engagement. The Hellfire missiles that could accurately plink out these targets required a steady laser-lock that was impossible to maintain under the volume of fire.[58] As the U.S. Army's *On Point* report conceded, "After 12 years of experience with the Americans targeting their air defense systems, the Iraqis had adapted. They developed a simple, yet sophisticated air defense system that was virtually impossible to detect or suppress" and had "decentralized command and control that could not be disrupted."[59]

In addition to the Apache lost in the crash at Objective RAMS, another Apache did not return from the mission; its pilots were captured and the helicopter paraded on Iraqi and international media as a symbol of resistance. The regime quickly moved to create one of the iconic images of the war— an aged Iraqi farmer with an old rifle, purported by the regime to be the slayer of the much-vaunted Western war machine. Every other Apache that had pressed the attack was also damaged, as Rick Atkinson's eyewitness account emphatically communicated: "The sun came up and it was eerie. You have never seen helicopters so muddy, so many canopies with holes in them. . . . Stunned pilots sat slumped in cockpits or on the Apache's stubby wings. On average, each helicopter had fifteen to twenty bullet holes; one took twenty-nine hits. The regiment had been shot to pieces in exchange for less than half a dozen Iraqi vehicles. Two $20 million helicopters had been lost; on one squadron, only a single helicopter was still considered mission-capable, and a month would pass before the entire regiment was fully ready to fight."[60]

The ambush was reminiscent of the heavy losses suffered by the A-10 community on February 5, 1991, when they had been pushed too deep against the Tawakalna Republican Guard division: they had lost two aircraft and twenty-seven others needed serious repairs. Put simply, by getting under the Coalition's radar, the Iraqis had won their first and possibly only battle against the United States in Operation Iraqi Freedom.

"SMACKDOWN": BOMBING THROUGH THE SANDSTORM

V Corps Commander Wallace would later confide, "Personally, the period during the dust storm was the low point of the entire campaign for me."[61] The sandstorm grounded almost all UAVs, blinded airborne and space-based electro-optical and infrared imagers, and prevented the use of laser guidance for precision munitions. Moreover, it made life miserable for the troops and infinitely more complicated for commanders and logisticians, especially as rainstorms combined with the shamal to "turn the air into mud."[62]

However, the fighting continued in this surreal environment. Zero visibility and zero ceiling became the norm, and the sun was a "golden lozenge" somewhere beyond the "relentless brown."[63] Neither the Coalition nor the Iraqis used the sandstorm to snatch anything approaching an operational pause. Although the global media seized on the setbacks of March 23 and the subsequent sandstorm to suggest a general bogging down of the operation, the embedded media with the Coalition forces had a more accurate picture of events. Wallace recalled, "The period of the dust storm was also tough because we were fighting our tails off. There was all this discussion about a lack of progress, but in actual fact, we were still maintaining a high operational tempo. We just weren't gaining ground. What we were doing was setting conditions for a decisive fight to follow."[64]

The most pressing task facing the Coalition was the defense of the bridgeheads over the Euphrates River and the LOCs. Each of these were particularly threatened now that the irregulars swamping the Euphrates River valley were masked from Coalition airborne sensors and stand-off weaponry by the sandstorm. Between March 24 and 26, massed Iraqi irregulars repeatedly attacked all the toeholds over the Euphrates River and the LOCs running from Samawah to Najaf. U.S. combat and support troops became used to hunkering down during the long hours of zero visibility, erecting ground-surveillance radar masts to peer into the dimness, turning every vehicle and handheld thermal or optical sensor outward to search for stalking Fedayeen and militiamen, and keeping their personal weapons at the ready to fend off close-range encounters.

At the other end of the spectrum of available firepower, satellite-guided munitions had become a vital tool, as demonstrated dramatically by the case of the 3-7 Cavalry scouts of the 3rd Infantry Division. Trapped on the enemy side of the Euphrates River for two days, the unit's ETAC was its lifeline. He was a young U.S. Air Force staff sergeant who earned a Silver Star by bringing down hundreds of Joint Direct Attack Munitions (JDAMs) all around the Coalition unit, which was later found to be surrounded by the bodies of hundreds of Iraqi irregulars. As the bridgeheads were relieved in more than one hundred hours of nonstop, zero-visibility fighting, more than 182 CAS sorties rolled back the enemy. As the 3rd Infantry Division report remarked, supporting firepower had to impact danger-close because of the near-zero visibility. The unit held out only because of its ability to button up within its vehicles in order to survive the close-in detonations, to geolocate itself, and to bring down JDAMs.[65]

The Coalition's ability to employ satellite-guided weaponry would remain critical as it shifted to the offensive once again. Throughout the

sandstorm, Coalition and Iraqi forces had been busily repositioning and reor-
ganizing. While V Corps closed on the area around Najaf, the MEF opened up
a second line of advance toward Baghdad between the Euphrates and Tigris
Rivers following the capture of bridges north of Nasariyah. Meanwhile, the
Iraqis had been restlessly shifting Republican Guard forces from as far north
as the Green Line or the north and west of Baghdad to locations south and
southeast of the city. Elements of Iraqi regular-army divisions from the south
were also slowly moving northward, shadowing the advance on the other side
of the Euphrates River or simply falling back on the capital. What the Coalition
needed was a way to fix the Iraqi forces in place, to degrade them before the
main attack on Baghdad commenced, and to maintain the momentum of the
attack. When asked what needed to happen next, Maj. Gen. David Petraeus,
commander of the 101st Air Assault Division, quipped "a thirty-five day air
campaign," referring to the preassault aerial preparation in Desert Storm.[66]
And that was exactly what satellite-guided munitions allowed the Coalition
to do, albeit in an abridged and more intense form, during a miniature air
campaign known to the aviators who planned it as "Smackdown."[67]

Following the neutralization of V Corps' deep-strike capability and
the temporary slowdown of the Coalition's front line, the ground component
reined in the FSCL to just past the Euphrates River and opened up as many
kill boxes and key pads as it could to create a permissive environment for air
support. What transpired in the U.S. Army's V Corps sector was something
akin to the arrangement that had been in place in the MEF sector throughout the war. The MAGTF concept underpinned the difference, allowing U.S.
Marines (and their subordinate British division) to fight as a true air-land
partnership rather than as a ground and an air component trying to get out of
each other's way. The Marines created the battlefield coordination line (BCL),
a form of divisional forward boundary that extended to the maximum range
of the division's own artillery. Short of the BCL, all kill boxes were closed
unless otherwise stated, whereas long of the BCL but within the FSCL all
kill boxes were open to MAGTF air forces unless otherwise stated. The battlespace was controlled by an airspace control authority made up of ground
and air personnel. The 3rd Infantry Division had wanted an arrangement of
this kind from the start, and now that the advance had slowed, there was more
of a chance to use this approach.[68]

The Smackdown concept of operations was simple: it used new all-
weather sensors and strike capabilities to carry out battlefield preparation

against the Republican Guard right through the sandstorm, so that the renewed offensive could hit the ground running. The key driving force behind
Smackdown was Maj. Roberson, one of Lieutenant General Moseley's key
air-campaign planners. As the events of March 23 sunk in and the sandstorm
promised to make traditional CAS impossible, the air-campaign planners designed an alternative targeting scheme. Roberson recalled, "We went straight
to the Battlefield Coordination Detachment, the land liaison officers sat the
CAOC, and said, 'Give us all the targets you want us to hit in the next few
days,' and they handed over 3,000 DMPIs. They were just the coordinates of
every known revetment, every defensive area, every ammo storage dump. We
didn't have any imagery to validate them by, so we just grabbed the Global
Hawk liaison community and sent them all 3,000 DMPIs. We said 'image
these.' This broke all the rules regarding tasking of ISR, but it worked."[69]
The objective, air-campaign planner Lt. Col. David Hathaway recalled, was
to leave the Republican Guard physically and psychologically shattered, unable to sleep or eat or feel safe at any time before the ground-forces attack
commenced.[70]

The effort relied on a range of airborne ISR platforms equipped with
sensors capable of penetrating the sandstorm, such as SIGINT packages,
SAR, and MTI radar. To make it possible to keep these aircraft on-station for
prolonged periods of time, the Coalition air-component commander, Lieutenant General Moseley, moved the vulnerable tanker aircraft forward and to
begin undertaking air-to-air refueling as far north as one hundred miles south
of Baghdad. Even with the ongoing suppression of enemy air fields and air
defenses, the move represented a risk, one which Moseley shared by riding
on one of the first tankers to make the trip further north.[71]

The Iraqi frontline divisions deployed in a crescent to the south of
Baghdad thought that they were safe within the sandstorm; in fact, they were
little safer than they would have been under open skies thanks to a massive
increase since 1991 in the Coalition's ability to sense through bad weather.
Although SIGINT satellites and aircraft (the U-2S, RC-135 Rivet Joint, and a
host of smaller SIGINT aircraft) had been around in 1991, they were now able
to locate emitters with far greater precision than before. Similarly, whereas
the JSTARS contribution to Desert Storm had been the experimental fielding
of two prototype aircraft, nine fully operational systems were deployed in
Operation Iraqi Freedom that provided wide-area coverage of ground movement. JSTARS also contributed to Coalition SAR imaging capability, which

was the key sensor type used in Smackdown. In addition to Lacrosse SAR satellites, U-2S, and JSTARS, the Coalition made extensive use of a single long-loitering Global Hawk UAV for SAR imaging. The drone was kept aloft for twenty-six-hour missions on every other day, imaging two to three hundred sites per sortie.[72]

The data from these systems were analyzed at three direct ground stations (DGS)—DGS-1 in Langley, Virginia; DGS-2 in Beale, California; and DGS-4 in Ramstein, Germany—plus the 152nd Intelligence Squadron in Reno, Nevada. Each DGS maintained sixty-four SIPRNET chat rooms frequented by end users at the CAOC, which allowed the intelligence analysts in Iraq to talk directly with the air-campaign planners who were arranging strikes one, two, and three days out. Extensive reliance on SIGINT, SAR, and MTI had its drawbacks: the Iraqis maintained fairly good communications security and used landlines, SAR imagery could not often differentiate between real targets and decoys, and MTI still found it difficult to operate against small numbers of enemy vehicles amid extensive ground clutter. However, the ability to merge the inputs of the sensors negated many of these drawbacks. Plus, the air-campaign planners were not looking for perfect SA; all they needed to know was whether a revetment or a tactical assembly area was empty or full. Anything that resembled a threat was going to get bombed.

Although U.S. ability to see through the weather had improved markedly since 1991, the real revolution in strike warfare was the Coalition's ability to strike with precision right through the sandstorm. The integration of JDAM satellite-guided bombs and onboard datalinks were the keys. The low-cost JDAM satellite-guidance kits' development began in reaction to the U.S. Air Force's inability to bomb through cloud cover during Desert Storm, and they had first been operationally tested in Operation Allied Force seven years later. An unprecedented level of integration between space and air operations ensured that the GPS constellation gave maximum coverage throughout the war. The increased fielding of digital radios and datalink systems allowed strike aircraft to retarget JDAM "on the pylon."

On March 24 and 25, the air component concentrated on low-collateral-damage targets. "Bomb trucks"—B-1B and B-52H bombers—dropped hundreds of 2,000-pound GBU-31 JDAMs and even sticks of unguided bombs onto positions well away from civilian dwellings and no-target sites. As the result of "last-look" surveillance by airborne ISR, communicated to the CAOC via chat rooms, inbound bombers received minutes-old updates on which positions were full and which were empty.[73] Any significant Iraqi tactical movement was spotted by JSTARS and passed down to B-1B aircraft that interdicted the columns, using their own MTI radar to confirm the targets. After forty-eight hours on nonstop, round-the-clock surge air operations against the Republican Guard, almost every identified target had been struck and restruck as necessary. As the sandstorm receded on March 26, the air component went after the higher collateral-damage targets: it sent F-15E and other tactical aircraft to supplement the bombers, sometimes dipping them under the cloud cover to lase targets for 500-pound GBU-12s and to explode airburst munitions over enemy trenches.[74]

Colonel Crowder noted, "Operation Iraqi Freedom showed that we've got the capability to destroy single enemy vehicles and weapons in a really systematic way, which is a new capability and one that has changed our way of thinking."[75] Neither tightly integrated with ground troops nor in close proximity to them, the targeting model used in Smackdown was not CAS. Neither was it air interdiction, which typically sought to destroy massed enemy forces on the move or fixed military installations. This was the mauling of the tactical elements of a field army with no use of ground observers: what Major General Deptula, Colonel Crowder, and Col. George Stamper termed "direct attack."[76]

The effect on the Republican Guard was devastating, although the lack of embedded reporters with the air component and the secrecy surrounding Smackdown hid its effectiveness from the public and from the ground component. Postwar interrogations showed that Smackdown had achieved its purpose of physically and psychologically shattering many Republican Guard units. Personnel had been badly shocked by the intensity and precision of the attacks, which intensified the oppressive and disorienting atmosphere during the sandstorm. One Republican Guard colonel explained, "I'm sorry, but I can't remember what day events occurred. We didn't sleep for days on end, we were constantly moving. There were constant attacks. It still seems crazy to me."[77] An Iraqi SSM commander reinforced the impression that precision bombing through the sandstorm had left a deep impression on the enemy:

"We were surprised when [U.S. pilots] discovered us," said Khalidi, 28, a Republican Guard captain from a military family. "It was late at night, a strong sandstorm was blowing, the vehicles were hidden under the trees, and the soldiers thought they were safe," he said. But two enormous bombs and a load of cluster bombs hit their targets on a tract of agricultural land in the Sabaa Abkar (Seven Virgins) area of northern Baghdad, killing six members of Khalidi's unit and destroying much of their equipment. "This affected the morale of the soldiers, because they were hiding and thought nobody could find them," he said. "Some soldiers left their positions and ran away. When the big bombs hit their target, some of the vehicles just melted. And the effect of the cluster bombs was even greater, because they covered a larger area." How did U.S. forces know to bomb the tree-studded tract between the Qanat al Jaysh (Army Canal) and the Tigris River? "Most of the commanders were sure it was through spies, because it was impossible to find through satellite or aircraft," Khalidi said. "Even if you drove by it, you couldn't find it."[78]

In reaction to the constant threat of destruction, Iraqi Republican Guard soldiers abandoned their equipment wholesale, paving the way for what was known as the turkey shoot—the destruction of scores of abandoned Republican Guard vehicles by advancing U.S. forces in early April.[79] It was only at that point, some days after Smackdown, that ground-forces commanders recognized the effectiveness of the air campaign that had worked on their behalf through the sandstorm. CINCCENT Franks stated, "The bombardment that lasted from the night of 25 March through the morning of 27 March was one of the fiercest and most effective in the history of warfare."[80] The Chief of Staff of the U.S. Air Force, Gen. John Jumper, concluded, "I'd like to ask the commander of the Medina division when he thought the pause was."[81] After trailing the ground forces by two days, air power had finally caught up.

ENTERING THE CITIES

While the air component was degrading Baghdad's defensive ring, the ground forces of V Corps were moving to address the unforeseen threat posed by the irregular forces. Instead of the clear flanks shown by the conventionally focused ISR collection effort, in reality the V Corps sat astride a series of hornets nests placed along its path by the regime. Luckily for the Coalition, the irregulars had not waited for the Coalition's main forces to pass by before falling on the logistical tail—an alternative course of action that might have made for a considerably more costly war—but had spent much of their strength on vainglorious but suicidal attacks on the spearhead of the Coalition war machine. As the main forces pressed on to Baghdad, however, the irregulars would present a key threat to LOCs, which CENTCOM assessed were vulnerable to attack at 170 key points.[82] A major readjustment had to be made to protect the open flank at Najaf and Samawah, as V Corps Commander Wallace recalled, "We never had any intention of fighting in those southern cities, because we felt that would put us at a disadvantage; so we intended to bypass them. As it turned out, the enemy was so aggressive in coming out of the cities and attacking us that we had to counterattack, first to secure our lines of communication, and second because the enemy was going to keep coming at us until we went into the cities and whacked him. So we had to make an adjustment to our battle plan and tactics to compensate for that aggressive tactic by the enemy."

At a meeting of the senior ground-forces commanders on March 26, the decision was made to commit the theater reserve, elements of the 82nd Airborne Division, to contain Samawah. The 101st Air Assault Division would free up the three major units of the 3rd Infantry Division bogged down in Najaf. As Wallace noted, "That decision may very well represent the single most significant adjustment we made in this entire war."[83]

The decision to not simply mask but to comprehensively isolate and reduce the resistance in urban centers was indeed a major step away from the initial concept of operations. Rick Atkinson noted that "the political imperative of waging a short decisive campaign increasingly conflicted with the military necessity of girding for a longer, more violent and costly war of attrition."[84] Indeed, this statement accurately summed up U.S. military involvement in Iraq ever since 1990 and foreshadowed years of U.S. military occupation to come.

In late March 2003, however, the challenge was the immediate and near-term need to take on the irregulars in the cities of the Euphrates valley. The infantry-heavy forces of the 82nd Airborne and 101st Air Assault divisions had been intended to carry out exactly this form of combat in Baghdad, albeit with the support of 3rd Infantry Division armor and an extensive planning and mapping effort of the Baghdad area. Now they were required to operate without armored support in other, less-surveilled cities, which necessitated an innovative and opportunistic approach akin to that being executed by the British 7th Armored Division at Basra.[85]

The first step involved close surveillance of the terrain and the enemy. Although the whole country had been gridded, certain areas had received priority surveillance and had been mapped down to extremely fine levels of detail. For instance, Baghdad had been divided into sixty zones or objectives, with every building numbered to give air and ground commanders a common reference for every significant location.[86] Other Iraqi cities had received a far lower level of intelligence preparation on the assumption that they would not need to be assaulted but would instead be isolated until after the removal of the Baathist regime. Therefore, the first task facing the U.S. airborne or air-mobile divisions was to update their maps with information gleaned by SOFs and CIA teams in the area. As the British were finding in the Basra area, it was quite possible to run human agents and infiltrate SOFs into regime-occupied towns. Plus, there were an increasing number of "walk-ins"—Iraqis who voluntarily gave information on regime locations either for money or personal reasons.

In addition to these forms of intelligence, the U.S. divisions made up for their lack of organic UAVs by tasking hand-launched SOFs' mini-UAVs and using their own scout helicopters as ISR platforms. In this capacity, the small OH-58D Kiowa Warriors and U.S. Marine Corps AH-1W Cobras did sterling work, staying 15 meters or less from the ground at all times, moving and firing at sixty to seventy knots, hovering only at night, and employing strict separation and overwatch tactics to defeat enemy ground fire.[87]

At the outset of the containment of the Euphrates cities, including ongoing Marine Corps operations in Nasariyah, the irregulars continued to initiate most combats by either covertly infiltrating or overtly sallying out of the cities to strike at LOCs or the checkpoints ringing the conurbations. Sometimes these fights were clean, but increasingly they involved ugly acts of perfidy that placed civilians at risk. On March 29, the Coalition was struck by the first confirmed suicide car bomb at a roadside checkpoint, which put all Coalition troops on edge. The irregulars made any movement by civilians extremely hazardous, yet despite Coalition entreaties to remain in their homes, Iraqi families trying to escape the war zone continued to take to the roads and even tried to run Coalition checkpoints, with horrific consequences. In addition to giving warning of some irregular sorties, intelligence gathering also pointed to the lack of prepared defenses in regime-held towns. This invited a number of raids using mixes of heavily and lightly armored Coalition vehicles to gather local intelligence, demolish statues of Saddam and other Baathist symbols, and strike at known Baathist locations to capture or kill resistance leaders.[88]

Detailed profiling of enemy movements also allowed urban air strikes to lethally target irregular leaders and troops. Although fiercely aggressive, the irregulars were neither disciplined nor able to adapt to precision attacks, in part because strikes were so lethal that few survivors remained to pass on the lessons learned. For instance, daily surveillance showed that the irregulars worked office hours—gathering to begin their day of fighting at almost exactly 0800 and finishing at 1800, "like they were punching the clock."[89] Coalition intelligence analysts soon recognized their gathering places—the anonymous walled compounds or Baath Party headquarters where they "puddled" at various points every day. When the puddle "filled," loitering Coalition aircraft would obliterate the area.[90] Between March 26 and April 5, at least fourteen Baath Party headquarters were destroyed in precision air strikes when meetings were observed to be underway.[91]

Close observation and responsive fire support were the keys to this form of highly lethal targeting. The main problem facing the U.S. forces was that the most responsive sources of firepower were also the least useful in the sensitive environment of military operations in urban terrain. Snipers were excellent for engaging point targets within four hundred to one thousand meters, but were limited to certain locations and could not engage massed targets. Divisional artillery could typically place artillery fire on a target within two to ten minutes of a request, which included clearing the target against the no-strike list and judgment calls by the divisional JAG, but the munitions available were either too large or too inaccurate to use.

Air support provided a more accurate and scaleable range of destructive effects. At one end lay the projectiles fired by AC-130 gunships, A-10 aircraft, and armed helicopters. In the middle lay the helicopter or aircraft-launched Hellfire and Maverick missiles, the former capable of plinking out individual rooms thanks to its fusing and shaped warhead. A range of concrete-filled or unfused 500-pound and 1,000-pound guided bombs were used as inert munitions with mixed results. The most reliable means of engaging point targets with no risk of breaking the laser-lock at the last minute were 1,000-pound and 2,000-pound JDAMs.[92] The downside of airpower remained the slow speed of processing it under the corps CAS system, which could only handle six or so weapon releases an hour. This resulted in typical waits of five to thirty minutes for air strikes, with most tactical aircraft having to leave the CAS stack for lack of fuel before they had an opportunity to drop their munitions.[93] Despite these limitations, the containment and rollback of the irregular forces proved remarkably effective: killing and bottling-up large numbers of enemy fighters, increasingly dominating their urban havens, and considerably reducing the threat to the LOCs as the final assault on Baghdad began.

SHAPING THE COMING BATTLE FOR BAGHDAD

The campaign to remove the Baathist regime moved into its second and decisive phase on April 28, when ground-component commanders held their second conference within a week to initiate the assault on Baghdad. The concept of operations required four precursors to be in place before the assault was launched. First, air superiority had to be maintained over the city. Second, Baghdad needed to be isolated from outside reinforcement from the north or the south. Third, the Republican Guard and army formations ringing the city had to be prevented from falling back inside the city as organized units and instead had to be destroyed in their present locations. Fourth and finally, the enemy had to be tricked into believing that the Coalition was going to attack the city from the south or southeast, between the Tigris and Euphrates Rivers. This would necessitate feints to draw attention away from the real point of penetration—the Karbala Gap, a narrow strip of land between Karbala and Lake Rezazza, which would allow the Coalition to cross the Euphrates River at an unexpected point and enter Baghdad from the west. Coalition intelligence assessments uniformly agreed that if Saddam Hussein was going to unleash CBW anywhere, it would be there.[94]

Air superiority was the simplest of the four preconditions to secure thanks to the preceding twelve years of aerial preparation and the intensive IADS takedown on March 21. Because the Coalition had pushed vulnerable tanker and ISR aircraft forward, the air component had maintained a close watch over Iraqi air fields and sometimes dedicated up to a fifth of the Coalition's daily sorties to plinking aircraft in the open and cratering runways. However, although such an elaborate effort was prudent, it was not necessary: the IrAF had enacted an even more elaborate and draconian hunkering-down strategy than it had in 1991. Its remaining operational sixty or so aircraft were dispersed in date groves or even buried in carelessly prepared covered trenches.[95]

The rest of the Iraqi strategic IADS had suffered a similar demise during Operation Iraqi Freedom under the unblinking stare of Coalition ISR and the

Coalition's unrestricted ability to strike that followed as the no-fly zones gave way to full aerial warfare. After the first three days of full air operations, Moseley moved from suppressing the enemy air defenses to destroying them wherever they could be found; his aircraft switched from HARM missiles to cluster munitions and bombs. Moseley recalled that the Coalition initiated "a discerned, specific mission to go hunt them down and kill them. Kill the antennas, kill the launchers, kill the support vans, the comm vans, break up their command and control and force them to move. And as they're moving they're not setting up and plugging in and getting their systems up. And every time they move one of those things they have a tendency to break something on them, and so by forcing them up and by individually hunting them down and keeping them on the run you begin to be able to control the airspace."[96]

The Coalition brought to bear a level of "staring ISR" coverage that had never been available in the no-fly zones. Time-sensitive targeting (TST) cues were provided by twenty-four-hour chat-room connections to analysts monitoring the loitering ISR constellation. Tactical aircraft became deadly hunters thanks to their ability to datalink sensors such as the HARM targeting system (which geolocated enemy emitters) and advanced targeting pods on Coalition strike aircraft.[97] The result was the rapid collapse of the Iraqi IADS and the dissolution of the much-vaunted Baghdad SuperMEZ. Similar to the IrAF, the ground-based IADS had dispersed for long-term survival prior to the war, and hundreds of SAM and radar would be found dispersed or half-buried in caches across Iraq in the months to come.

The isolation of Baghdad was similarly successful, both because of successful deception operations and because of pressure maintained on enemy concentrations in the north and south since the outset of the war. In the north, a deliberate Coalition deception effort involving the use of a double-cross system to exploit enemy agents had successfully given the Iraqis the impression that a major effort was being withheld to open a northern front in the KRG zone or through airborne action near Tikrit or elsewhere north of Baghdad.[98] To bolster this impression and to fix in place the fourteen or so divisions along the Green Line, the Coalition had supported Kurdish militiamen or *peshmerga* with Coalition SOFs. This reproduced the unconventional warfare formula used successfully in partnership with the Afghan mujaheddin in Operation Enduring Freedom. The three northern corps— 1st Corps at Kirkuk, 2nd Corps at Diyala, and 5th Corps at Mosul—plus the southern 4th Corps at Amarah were held in place by a combination of existing fears of Kurdish and Iranian intervention and Coalition air and special-forces activities. Here, if anywhere, was evidence that quality and technological edge could trump the weight of numbers in the post–Cold War world.

The Republican Guard divisions and army elements that made up the remaining battered screen around Baghdad were made of sterner stuff, however, and would require ongoing intensive bombardment and ground attacks to keep them out of the fight for Baghdad. It was during this period of shaping the battle for Baghdad that the U.S. military arguably first began to fight effectively as a joint team. For the first ten days of Operation Iraqi Freedom, the U.S. ground and air components, dominated by the U.S. Army and Air Force respectively, were thinking different wars, focusing on proving different operational concepts or theories, and were competing for the battlespace required to test them. The U.S. Army had focused on deep battle and corps CAS, whereas the U.S. Air Force had followed its dual instincts to create shock in the enemy leadership and to kill the enemy army before the ground forces could close with them. Both the ground and air components had given the Iraqi regime their best shots, and it was still standing.

Now a new period began, one in which the components truly acted as a team. CJCS Gen. Richard Myers called this going "beyond deconfliction mode," meaning that they worked together and shared battlespace instead of merely staying out of each other's way.[99] The ongoing bombardment that hit the ground running after the sandstorm was a case in point. Lieutenant General Moseley summed up the new focus on by stating, "I'm not sure it matters who kills the tank as long as we kill the tanks."[100]

As the Coalition approached the task of destroying the Republican Guard, it had key advantages over the force that had attempted the same feat in 1991. Unlike the Desert Storm Coalition, the current force maintained truly intensive twenty-four-hour surveillance over the battlefield. Global Hawk, multiple JSTARSs, and other ISR satellites and platforms provided omnipresent wide-area surveillance of the Iraqi defenders. With the lifting of the sandstorm, the ISR constellation regained its electro-optical and infrared sensors coverage. In addition to the many dedicated ISR platforms, this increased the number of sensors watching the enemy by an order of magnitude because of the massive increase in the proportion of strike aircraft carrying targeting pods, which were capable of carrying out high-acuity ground surveillance from altitudes of up to 25,000 feet. In every kill box, FAC-As perpetuated the

"Killer Scout" tradition began in 1991, but now each FAC-A also controlled a number of SCAR assets—strike aircraft with high-resolution targeting pods and laser-designation capabilities. Instead of one FAC-A scouring the desert in each kill box, there were now up to ten airborne scouts maintaining rolling SA over the key pads inside the kill box who were spotting Iraqi tactical repositioning and discriminating between decoys and live targets.[101] Coalition analysts could better discriminate valid targets because of the range of multispectral sensors mounted on UAVs and strike aircraft, from color television cameras able to spot unrealistic decoys to SAR able to tell visually indistinguishable wooden decoys from real metal targets.[102] From the FLOT to enemy rear areas, the Coalition had the ability to precisely target a fielded enemy army in cluttered terrain.

The killing edge was provided by a synergistic combination of ground- and air-combat power that shared the battlespace as never before. A series of major feints were launched from the south and southeast of Baghdad from March 31 onward, beginning with a 3rd Infantry Division attack into the Republican Guard at Hindayah. This was followed by 101st Airborne Assault Division attacks into the strongly held regime bastion of Hillah and Marine Division threats toward Diwaniyah and Kut. During these tough fights, divisional and corps artillery laid down extremely heavy fire to complement the direct fire from combat battalions closing with the enemy. A Marine Division fire controller remarked that so many rounds were simultaneously in the air that "it's like being an air traffic controller in Los Angeles."[103] Above the crisscrossing streams of artillery shells and rockets at 10,000 feet and above, Coalition airpower was loitering in omnipresent CAS stacks, each loaded with a rotating smorgasbord of precision and unguided munitions.

Real synergies were developing between the ground and air forces during these fights. The first Apache deep strike since the repulsion of the large V Corps helicopter attack was launched on March 28 and demonstrated the difference in approach. Twenty-one of the remaining serviceable helicopters of the 11th Attack Helicopter Regiment were assigned to the 101st Air Assault Division's attack-helicopter battalion. These forces were sent once again against the Medina Division, after having absorbed the lessons of the strike in the five days following the abortive attack. This time one half of the Apaches took unpredictable routes to "attack-by-fire boxes," flying defensively all the way and skirting the kind of urban sprawl from which heavy ground fire had radiated on March 23. Wherever they met resistance, the Apaches pulled back and requested CAS against the points of resistance. They only fired off their own weapons when their fuel was expended and it was time to egress. Meanwhile, the second half of the attack helicopters took a long circuitous route over Lake Rezazzah. Eighteen ATACMS munitions created a rolling barrage four minutes in front of the helicopters as they made landfall. The results of the strike were modest—forty AAA, artillery, radar, and armored vehicles destroyed—but the mission ended with only two helicopters damaged in noncombat accidents.[104]

Meanwhile, the feints launched by Coalition ground forces were prompting Republican Guard units to maneuver to meet the threats in-between the Euphrates and the Tigris Rivers, which further exposed them to Coalition airpower. Lieutenant General Wallace recalled, "I'm about 95 percent convinced that when we crossed the Euphrates in a series of feints just after the dust storm hit, it forced the Medina to start repositioning its forces to counter an advance between the rivers that was never our main intent. We had beautiful weather with clear skies at that point, and we started getting reports of enemy armor moving on trucks, of Iraqi artillery forces repositioning, and of attempts by Medina brigades to occupy what they believed would be optimum defensive positions. All that happened in the full view of the U.S. Air Force, and they started whacking the hell out of the Medina."[105]

The air component was now pumping on all cylinders to service the mass of targets it was faced with. It operated fixed-wing aircraft from captured forward air strips in Iraq or topped off their fuel tanks with "gas-and-go" touchdowns in Kuwait and aerial refueling.[106] Every conceivable type of munition from the 6,800-kilogram BLU-82 Big Blue (or "Daisy Cutter") to Hellfire munitions was being dropped on the Republican Guard according to the sensitivity of the target areas. Roughly three quarters of every day's eight hundred strike sorties were assigned to the defensive ring around Baghdad. The Killer Scout and SCAR systems, combined with the new permissive placement of the FSCL, were allowing record numbers of strikes to rain down on the enemy. "Tank plinking" was now the rule, not the exception, and seventy F-15Es alone delivered 673 GBU-12 500-pound munitions in a single day.[107] On a single sortie, one pair of F-15Es SCARs delivered their own eighteen GBU-12s and then lased another fifty munitions dropped by other aircraft.[108] Using existing BDA systems, it was impossible to keep up with assessing this level of destruction. Although the destructive capacity of the Coalition air forces and their ability to gather BDA data had increased massively since 1991, their ability to process and analyze BDA data had not. Basic BDA needed to be self-reporting, pro forma, automated, and primarily machine to machine, but it was still a manual and laborious process. Air-campaign planner Lieutenant Colonel Hathaway recalled, "We were so much more effective than we were in Desert Storm that we just did not prepare for that amount of information. When each morning General Franks asked Moseley, 'How we doing?,' he was forced to say 'I don't know.' In the end, we had to send an officer out to the bomb dumps to count how many bombs were missing."[109]

Although the Desert Storm air campaign had sought to create precise numerical BDA so that it could initiate of ground operations once the enemy was degraded by 50 percent, the planners in Operation Iraqi Freedom used a less exact but more effective system. JCS Director of Intelligence Shaffer remembered that it was "really effective": a simple thermometer-like mea-surement bar showed the fighting capacity of enemy units down to brigade level, factoring in destruction of equipment, isolation from resupply, and psychological impact. Seven straight days of round-the-clock joint fires and probing by ground forces had put the nail in the coffin of the organized de-fense of Baghdad's suburbs. The defensive crust was brittle now and could be pierced easily. Reflecting on the status of enemy ground forces as the battle for Baghdad began, Moseley concluded:

> Our sensors show that the preponderance of the Republican Guard di-visions that were outside of Baghdad are now dead. We've laid on these people. I find it interesting when folks say we're softening them up. We're not softening them up, we're killing them. I'll tell you what we're seeing is we're seeing elements in much smaller combat formations that have been cut off from their central command and control. As far as large fighting formations, we haven't seen any of that lately because again, we've been attacking steady for about six or seven days now. I would suggest that they're probably attempting to get away from the withering fire from Apaches and from ATACMS and from A-10s and F-16s and F-15s and F-18s and Cobras, and I think they're trying to find a place that they can get away from this and attempt to reconstitute. The fact that we've got the Marine Expeditionary Force and the 3rd ID moving onto the city is beginning to take that sanctuary away from them also.[110]

THE END OF SADDAM HUSSEIN'S REGIME

The road to Baghdad ran through the Karbala Gap, which Tom Donnelly referred to as "one of the most intensely studied pieces of terrain in the world of U.S. military planners—the Iraqi version of the Fulda Gap of the Cold War central German plain."[111] The gap provided access to a single-lane road and a bridge just west of Iskandariyah that Iraqi defenders had largely overlooked and which represented the unguarded back door through which the 3rd Infantry Division would enter the city. At the same time, using the Karbala Gap was risky because it was traversable on only two single-lane roads bordered by irrigated farmlands and quarries, and because it was narrow. The U.S. Army described it as "a chemical [weapons] target from hell, with a choke point 1,800 meters wide."[112] The possibility that Saddam might order a release of CBWs seemed to be increasing following the detection and interdiction of tanker trucks traveling to the battle front from the Latifah phosgene plant, the discovery of new CBW suits and antidotes, and a stream of menacing SIGINT interceptions.[113] V Corps planned to squeeze through the Karbala Gap as rapidly as possible. Its commander, Lieutenant General Wallace, recalled, "For nearly a year, we had recognized collectively that once we were through the Karbala Gap, the fight would not be over until we seized the international airport in Baghdad. The entire fight from Karbala to the airport was considered as one continuous assault, because once we crossed through the gap, we were inside the range of all the artillery that was in support of Baghdad and all the Republican Guard divisions around Baghdad. Once we crossed through the gap, we would be within Saddam's red zone in terms of defenses, and we had damn sure better be ready to continue the fight all the way to the encirclement of Baghdad."[114]

Following a grinding advance in which 3rd Infantry Division forces flowed around and to the north of Karbala, the thrust into Baghdad began in the early hours of April 2. Following a heavy preparatory barrage, a U.S. armored task force pierced the gap and penetrated as far as the bridge over the Euphrates River. In a scene reminiscent of the U.S. effort to "bounce the Rhine" at the end of World War II, the bridge was blown by Iraqi engineers, yet the structure remained standing and allowed U.S. forces to establish a bridgehead on the eastern bank. Through this slender aperture, U.S. forces began to move into Baghdad; one troop of the divisional cavalry regiment reached Saddam International Airport, where a handful of U.S.

armored vehicles began a two-day fight against a reinforced SRG battalion nestled within the sprawling complex. From the capture of the bridge until first light on April 3, Republican Guard forces from the Medina Division fired heavy artillery "stonks" at the bridgehead and made determined nighttime assaults, but the 3rd Infantry Division bridgehead could not be dislodged. The 3rd Infantry Division forces flowed through the bridgehead like water through a breached seawall. To the east, the division encountered and destroyed masses of abandoned Republican Guard equipment and vehicles in what became known as the "turkey shoot," the first tangible proof of the fury and effects of the air and artillery bombardment that was delivered since March 24.[115] By 1030 on April 4, the 3rd Infantry Division had secured the city's main airport, now renamed Baghdad International Airport (BIAP).

With the airport secure and with U.S. Army and Marine forces simultaneously closing on the northwestern and southeastern suburbs of Baghdad, the United States was now in a position to implement the plan designed to isolate and seize Baghdad. The so-called FOB strategy envisioned the encirclement of the capital, followed by the methodical domination of the city's most vital areas once Coalition forces were freed up from destroying the defensive ring.[116] Although the media and the "TV generals"—retired officers serving as on-screen consultants—talked up the possibility of a tenacious and systematic Iraqi defense of Baghdad as a modern-day Stalingrad or Grozny (the Chechen city that had become a graveyard for Russian armored vehicles), CENTCOM's assessment had always been more muted. Historical precedent suggested that the regime would mount its main defense on the outskirts of the city, as it had done in Basra during the Iran-Iraq War, and that it would resist the temptation to allow regular-army or Republican Guard units in the city for fear of a military coup.[117] The SRG and irregular forces allowed inside the city represented the core of the urban defense, CENTCOM believed, but their capabilities and intentions were unknown. This promoted a cautious and methodical plan to clear the city as and when sufficient U.S. infantry forces closed the ring surrounding the city.

Now, at the gates of Baghdad, U.S. commanders felt justified in assuming a more aggressive and dynamic approach. In part, this instinct was born from a better understanding of the relative capabilities of U.S. forces and the enemy. Lieutenant General Wallace explained, "You have to go back to the battle of Najaf to understand our actions at that point, because that's where we learned we could do better. We learned that armor could fight in a city and survive, and that if you took heavy armored forces into a city—given the way that Saddam was defending with technical vehicles and bunker positions—we could knock out all those defenses and survive. As a result of Najaf, I think out soldiers also gained an extraordinary appreciation for the survivability of their equipment."[118]

Aside from these calculations, however, the 3rd Infantry Division commanders wanted to keep pushing because they were on a roll, the enemy was folding, victory scented the air, and that most precious of all commodities in attack, momentum, had been generated and needed to be maintained. The solution was to mount a "thunder run"—an armored drive-through—along twenty kilometers of Iraqi highway, with an armored battalion and attendant air support entering the city from the south and arcing northwest to the safe harbor of BIAP. Despite the focus of powerful space-based and airborne ISR assets on the city, at the tactical level the troopers were once again going in virtually blind; they lacked even the highway maps needed to confidently navigate the freeways. As usual, for those at the spearhead it was a movement toward contact. There would be little intelligence preparation for the thunder run; instead, the thunder run *was* intelligence preparation.

The twenty-nine M1A1 Abrams tanks and fourteen Bradley or M113 armored vehicles set out early on April 5. The firepower of the column was boosted by the addition of up to six machine guns on each infantry carrier. Bristling with armaments and flanked by A-10 aircraft that provided reports of enemy movements and interdicted targets out of sight in neighborhoods on either side of the highway, the column entered Baghdad. Certain that the Americans could not be so near and that Baghdad could not be so vulnerable to attack, Iraqi sentries were cooking breakfast as the column pierced the city.[119] Normal traffic was moving throughout the city.

Despite total surprise, the enemy quickly mustered its forces. Enemy troops began to appear in civilian vehicles at points along the convoy's route, and the militiamen fell in on their assigned defensive positions: trenches and bunkers positioned at major "cloverleaf" intersections or parks. These forces were a blend of the uniformed SRG—Saddam's praetorian, recruited from smaller tribes owing their social elevation to the regime—and the various irregular forces raised by the regime, and were roughly commanded by Baathist enforcers carrying Motorola mobile phones. Sometimes they were killed en masse as their buses and taxis stopped in plain sight of U.S. forces to disgorge troops or as they tried to close with the U.S. armor on foot, carrying little more than small arms. Their bunkers and trenches became deathtraps as they were crushed and collapsed by U.S. tanks and Bradley guns. Sometimes they rammed their sedan cars and trucks into U.S. armored vehicles or closed alongside the convoy to deliver short-lived broadsides. They died in droves, yet they kept coming.

Meanwhile, the U.S. column received heavy fire, which created a steady drumbeat of small-arms fire against U.S. vehicles. One tank commander was killed and other troopers who were standing exposed in their cupolas and hatches were injured. Every vehicle in the convoy was struck at least once by RPGs and other antitank weapons. Irregulars lobbed RPGs at the convoy from highway overpasses while SRG recoilless rifle and antitank gun teams and BMP infantry-fighting vehicles sniped at the flanks and rear of U.S. vehicles from alleys and highway verges. Despite the hail of fire, only one U.S. vehicle was destroyed to stop it from being captured: an M1A1 suffered a serious fire in one of its external stowage bins and was subsequently destroyed by U.S. forces. Even the United States had to try multiple times to destroy an M1A1, using thermite grenades, a point-blank-range M1A1 tank gun round into the damaged tank's ammunition bin, and two Maverick missiles delivered by an A-10 aircraft. The episode that underlined the hardiness of U.S. armored vehicles. They were struck many hundreds of times by antitank munitions and penetrated on twenty-three occasions during Operation Iraqi Freedom but only suffered catastrophic destruction by enemy fire on one occasion.[120] William Hawkins dubbed this "the heavy advantage" and it was a deciding factor in the running fight. Williamson Murray and Robert Scales agreed: "Older weapons systems such as the Abrams and Bradley, with their advantages in protection, mass, and explosive power proved to be particularly effective."[121]

Murray and Scales take the point too far when they add that "speed and information superiority became less decisive" than "traditional machine-age equipment" in the urban fighting. In fact, the thunder run offered more proof that in modern combat, speed literally kills. Time and again the Iraqi defenders had superior tactical placement and the opportunity to fire the shot, yet they ended up taking the first and decisive blow. In an age when TST had become a military buzzword, here was a reminder that the tank crewman has hardly ever known a target that was not time sensitive. The gunners, crew, and infantrymen in the convoy engaged hundreds of TSTs during the thunder run and typically encountered new threats at a range of two hundred meters. Speed as well as armor plate brought the column through.

Two-and-a-half hours after crossing into enemy territory, the column battered its way through enemy roadblocks and roared back through U.S. lines into the BIAP complex. David Zucchino described the scene: "Every vehicle was shot up with dents and holes and jagged scrapes that peeled the tanned paint back. They were leaking oil and hydraulic fluid and trailing smoke from burning bustle racks. A couple of tracks were streaked with blood. There was shattered glass from the cars that had rammed the tanks and thousands of expended brass casings that sparkled in the morning sunlight."[122]

A 3rd Infantry Division officer recalled that the troopers had also been sorely tested when he remarked, "You would have thought there would be a lot of high fives, but there were a lot of soldiers in shock. There were a lot of guys crying; they were just emotionally spent. I was emotionally spent. One of my tank commanders had been killed. I had a soldier shot in the eye, shot in the forehead, shot in the shoulder, shot in the back, shot in the face."[123] The thunder run had shown two things: that Baghdad could be penetrated by armored spearheads and that the United States would have to fight every inch of the way.

While heavy fighting raged between encircling U.S. forces and Iraqi defenders northwest and east of Baghdad on April 6, the 3rd Infantry Division was absorbing the lessons and evaluating the effects of the previous day's thunder run. Much had been learned at a tactical level, but the strategic effect had been minimal because U.S. forces had not penetrated to the center of the Iraqi capital or stayed in the city.

Iraqi Information Minister Mohammed Said al-Sahhaf, who had performed so poorly as Iraq's Foreign Minister in 2002, had found his niche as the regime's propaganda spokesman and was dubbed "Comical Ali" by Western media. However, Comical Ali was no laughing matter in Washington and London, where senior decision makers were increasingly frustrated by Iraq's ongoing propaganda capability. Crowing over footage of the abandoned and destroyed Abrams, the minister denied that U.S. forces were at the airport or in the city. The thunder run had shown that Iraqi civilians were shocked to see Western forces in the city—an indication that regime propaganda was having the desired effect. Although the few Iraqi air-defense and headquarters units equipped with radios were genuinely spooked by the U.S. PSYOPs broadcasts that blocked out their own tactical frequencies, most Iraqi fighters and civilians were tuning in to Iraqi and Arab television and radio or to the BBC, or knew someone who was.[124] As Colonel Crowder put it, "The bad guys were just eating us up, maintaining a semblance of civilian command and control, acting like a government and holding the defense together. They had rumor on their side."[125]

Civilian decision makers at the Pentagon and CINCCENT Franks began to weigh in and demand that something be done. Although a smattering of strikes had been carried out against government media in Iraq, impetus was growing for a more robust actions against that target set. Colonel Minster, the head of targeting intelligence at the JCS, stated, "The main factor restraining us was the collateral damage issue—most of these places were downtown and not surrounded by walled compounds like the other regime targets were. After the first few strikes, they stayed on the air and frustration was growing. This guy was still talking and all the low collateral damage targets had been hit. What we needed to do, in a network attack situation like this, was to attack all the nodes simultaneously instead of piecemeal. National-level agencies looked at how we could shut the Iraqi media effort down. There were three options—direct attacks on the stations, taking out the power, and attacks on their transmission capabilities—the broadcasting antennae."[126]

In Operation Allied Force (1999), the Radio Serbia building had been destroyed and a number of journalists had been killed. After the outcry over that attack, direct attacks on media buildings had been ruled out. As Colonel Crowder remarked, "Killing a twenty year-old broadcast girl is not going to win us any friends." This meant the media infrastructure enjoyed protected status as a necessity for postwar stabilization.[127] Likewise, attacks on electricity infrastructure were banned, and, in any case, the Information Ministry was well prepared to move to generator power: in fact, they did so when the Baghdad grid collapsed late in the war from lack of maintenance and the unintended secondary effects of the conflict.

Instead, the focus fell on enemy broadcast capabilities. Armed Predator UAVs were used to plink antennae on the Information Ministry roof, and submunition Tomahawks were exploded over other buildings to scour the roofs of aerials and dishes. To prevent the Arabic-language station Al-Jazira from broadcasting regime interviews and tapes—a means the regime used to disseminate its message since Operation Desert Fox—a Predator destroyed Al-Jazira's transmission dish with a Hellfire missile.[128] However, as the United States had found during years of no-fly-zone activities against Iraq's radar dishes and communications towers, the regime and Al-Jazira quickly jury-rigged new transmission antennae and moved to mobile satellite transmission vans. Nothing could be done to stop the transmissions. There was also little that could be done to pressure the network, even though CENTCOM's forward headquarters were based in Qatar, the home of Al-Jazira.

Instead, a less prosaic and more kinetic solution emerged to deal with the regime's propaganda. Smarting over the thunder run's lack of strategic effect and the fact that major media outlets such as the BBC did not report the incursion, Col. David Perkins of the 2nd BCT of 3rd Infantry Division devised a tactical scheme to launch a new brigade-sized thunder run that would strike at the most symbolic areas of regime control in Baghdad and, if possible, stay there. This would be the apogee of inside-out warfare—"a mission of persuasion as well as force," as David Zucchino wrote. Colonel Perkins planned to bring a Fox television news crew with him to the heart of Baghdad. He told his troops, "We have set the conditions to create the collapse of the Iraqi regime. Now we're transitioning from a tactical battle to a psychological and informational battle."[129]

The entire 2nd BCT was going downtown on April 7 to strike the regime in its heart. David Zucchino described it: "It was like planning a third world coup: you take the presidential palace, the top ministries, a TV station, the security headquarters . . . and boom, the government falls. In the case of Baghdad, these nodes were conveniently centralized in or around Saddam's palace complex, a walled city within a city about three kilometers long and a kilometer and a half wide." One battalion-sized task force was assigned Objective Diane, which consisted of the main presidential palaces and the Baath Party headquarters. A second was tasked with securing Objective Woody, the parade grounds, crossed-swords statue, zoo, and parks within the government sector of Baghdad along the Tigris River. The third task force was charged with holding open the line of supply at three intersections on Highway 8—Objectives Curley, Larry, and Moe.

During the early hours of April 7, a minefield three hundred meters deep was covertly cleared to allow the seventy M1A1 and sixty Bradleys passage. The attack began at 0620. Kicking off once again into hostile territory, the convoy was overflown by a U.S. Army Hunter UAV, which relayed images directly to V Corps headquarters that reminded Lieutenant General Wallace of televised police pursuits. Airborne ISR and strike aircraft relayed information on enemy movements to the 2nd Brigade Tactical Operations Center, located eighteen kilometers south of Baghdad, and to Colonel Perkins and other commanders with the column. After the first thunder run, the brigade had learned not to slow down and to clear overpasses of enemy troops before passing under them. As this column fought its way through the city, a wave of air-bursting artillery exploded over each overpass just ahead of the column, killing or wounding any enemy fighters on the bridges. Stacks of tactical aircraft and bombers circled above in the CAS stack, and A-10 aircraft flanked the column at a low level. The column experienced lighter incoming fire than the previous thunder run, although it was resisted at every turn. This was a result of the heavy attrition of the forces assigned to the affected areas of highway. Within two hours, U.S. troops had arrived at their objectives, sweeping through palaces and driving under the crossed swords, and established security cordons.

The relatively unobstructed passage into Baghdad proved to be the calm before the storm. It came before most Iraqi irregulars had showed up for work, another reflection of the "office hours" approach of the regime forces. With the U.S. forces located, the enemy forces once again massed and emerged to attack the highway intersections and avenues occupied by the 2nd BCT. The Iraqis seemed to be adopting "Somali tactics," described by David Zucchino as "move, harass, circle, and close." On the first thunder run, the Iraqis closed up the gaps behind the column in an attempt to trap and eliminate the force. Now they moved to isolate and overrun the company-sized units at Objectives Curley, Larry, and Moe. Hundreds of Iraqis started to show up at the cloverleaf traffic intersections, debussing from civilian vehicles or making futile suicide runs in taxis, sedans, and luxury cars toward the U.S. positions. U.S. forces likened the scene to that of a disturbed ant colony.[130] The enemy's disregard for self-preservation was disturbing to U.S. troops, and the appearances of Iraqi fighters was thoroughly inconsonant with the field of battle: almost all enemy combatants had shed their uniforms and taken the field wearing jeans, polo shirts, cologne, and sunglasses, even at night. As hundreds of Iraqis threw themselves in the way of U.S. firepower in hour after hour of desperate but one-sided combat, Iraqi families watched from distant rooftops.

In the midst of this insanity, U.S. troops fought a "one meter to one hundred meter fight" with dismounted Iraqi loyalists. The brigade commander, Colonel Perkins, had to kill Iraqi attackers with his own 9-mm pistol. Quick reactions and superior armor were deciding factors as much in the hundreds of personal engagements as they were in mounted combat. Medical officers at the besieged intersections could sense the powerful combat advantage conferred by the U.S. body armor . One surgeon noted, "Remarkably, there were no head wounds, no sucking chest wounds, no wounds to vital organs. [The medic] was impressed by how thoroughly the soldiers' body armor and helmets had protected them. He had never fully appreciated their value, but he did now—especially after getting a look at the ghastly wounds suffered by one of the poorly outfitted enemy troops dragged in for treatment." Dressed for dinner rather than for battle, "the Iraqis were easy to kill," wrote David Zucchino. "They didn't wear helmets or flak vests. Just one round through the helmet or torso put them down."[131]

The all-day fight to resupply the U.S. positions and allow the forces to stay in the city overnight was the penultimate act of the war, although the Iraqi and U.S. forces continued to trade blows throughout the day. Both sides were still striking blows with their missile and air forces even though the high-tech war had now mostly given way to close-quarter battle. In the midst of the crises at Objectives Curley, Larry, and Moe, the 2nd BCT main headquarters was struck by an Iraqi SSM launch, one of six missiles fired from the Baghdad area since April 1. Although no Scuds had been fired at Israel, the Iraqis continued to fire SSMs from the Basra and Baghdad areas and many stashes of missiles would be discovered only after the war.

As the headquarters gathered up its two dozen wounded soldiers and five dead, an equally dramatic leadership-decapitation attempt was unfolding high above Baghdad. The United States had not let up on Iraq's leadership at any stage of the war: it launched fifty strikes against thirteen Iraqi leaders on the basis of time-sensitive intelligence and often risked serious collateral damage to strike directly at the Baathist leadership in a committed effort to kill them.[132] As midday passed on April 7, the Coalition received new intelligence on the alleged whereabouts of Saddam Hussein. A HUMINT report was received about a leadership meeting in the Mansour district of Baghdad and there was Thuraya satellite phone activity in the area. The meeting and phone signals appeared to be taking place at a restaurant frequented by regime figures. Within merely thirty-five minutes the target had been authorized, plotted, and geolocated. In the following twelve minutes, a loitering B-1B bomber proceeded to the area, validated the aimpoints, and dropped four satellite-guided GBU-31 2,000-pound bombs—one penetrator followed by a delayed fuse bomb. The two bombs hit aimpoints 30 meters apart, gutting the restaurant.[133] For all the technical proficiency the raid displayed, in the coming weeks U.S. investigators concluded that Saddam probably had not been present when the bombs landed.

However, for all intents and purposes the regime had been removed and the Iraqi capital surrounded and occupied by the night of April 7. Now all that remained was to convince the Iraqis of that fact. The mission had subtly shifted to the suppression of resistance. The 1st BCT of the 3rd Infantry Division entered the city overnight, while 2nd BCT prepared for ongoing operations on April 8. The final large-scale showdown between Coalition and regime forces took place at the Jumhuriya Bridge, one of three Tigris River bridges used by regime loyalists to launch a final counterattack from east of the river. Technicals—jeeps with gun mounts in the flat bed—and civilian vehicles crossed westward loaded with fighters flocking to this last stand, and retuned eastward loaded with the deeply stacked bodies of freshly killed fighters. The irregulars shocked the U.S. forces that were holding Objectives Diane and Woody with their recklessness and the volume of fire they could bring to bear. In addition to their small arms, RPGs, and vehicle-mounted heavy machine guns and recoilless rifles, the loyalists appeared to be using observers with cell phones in a high-rise building to direct mortar fire against Coalition troops. A-10 aircraft strafed both sides of the main road leading to the bridge and one aircraft was lost to a shoulder-launched missile. Using this cover, U.S. armored forces made one last determined push to reach the bridge and block the enemy advance. Their capture of the western bridge approaches was followed by an air strike against the multistory building used by the Iraqi artillery observers. This blinded the enemy mortars, but not before U.S. forces mistakenly fired on journalists filming them from the Palestine Hotel thousands of meters away.[134]

After the capture of the Jumhuriya Bridge, the last vestiges of the old regime began to dissolve. Already endemic desertion gave way to complete dissolution. Senior Iraqi military officers changed into civilian clothing and toured the city to tell their troops to do the same and return to their families. On April 9, as U.S. Army and Marine forces linked up north of Baghdad, a huge statue of Saddam Hussein in Firdos Square was toppled by a U.S. armored recovery vehicle and left for Iraqis to dismember and drag through the streets in pieces.

Twelve years after the end of Desert Storm, the Baathist regime had been toppled in less than a month of military operations. The narrow military objectives of the campaign—to capture Baghdad and depose the regime—had undeniably been achieved, and the costs had been mercifully light. Merely 108 U.S. personnel were killed and 399 were wounded, even fewer than the 146 killed and 467 wounded in the liberation of Kuwait. On the Iraqi side, casualty estimates of military fatalities ranged from 5,000 to 20,000, with civilian fatalities estimated to be at least 4,000 and probably higher.[135] Nonetheless, these figures were considerably lower than the wildly unrealistic suggestions of prewar assessments such as the Oxford Research Group's prediction of 53,000–135,000 civilian deaths or MEDACT's prediction of 48,000-201,000 civilian fatalities.[136]

Speed and the use of minimum force were thus the defining and essential elements of the military formula trialed in Operation Iraqi Freedom. These features enabled the rapid march to Baghdad, but arguably carried a strategic cost. Military analyst Michael Eisenstadt wrote as early as March 26, 2003, that the lack of scorched-earth actions of the Baathist regime suggested a long-term view that would make Baghdad a "way point rather than the end point" for Saddam Hussein and his followers. Eisenstadt suggested that although the battle for Baghdad would be the "decisive phase of the current campaign," a new phase would begin thereafter and would continue as long as U.S. forces remained in Iraq. In this "protracted struggle," Eisenstadt wrote:

> Iraqi leaders will simply go to ground and fade away. In either case, there is a good chance that some members of the current regime—most likely individuals affiliated with the its security apparatus—will manage to slip out of Baghdad and return to their home regions (for most, this means the Sunni triangle region north and northwest of Baghdad). Believing that they have not really been defeated—as many are likely to survive the war—they may try to organize a protracted, low-intensity insurgency against the U.S. presence, drawing support from the Sunni Arab community and Shi'a tribes that have supported the regime in the past. Their goal would be to obstruct U.S. efforts to set up a transitional administration and thereby prevent the United States from "winning the peace" and implementing its exit strategy. Their tactics would likely include stoking anti-American sentiment, intimidating or assassinating Iraqis who deal with the United States, and discouraging potential members of a "coalition of the willing" whom Washington might try to enlist in efforts to create a stability force or a transitional administration. The bottom line is that a definitive end to the current conflict is unlikely.[137]

11

Ending Resistance

The toppling of Saddam Hussein's statue in Firdos Square marked the beginning of the end of major combat operations but did not signal an end to U.S. military involvement in Iraq or an end to Iraqi resistance. On April 10, 2003, a day after the statue fell, it was still unclear whether the regime would try to make a last stand north of Baghdad in Saddam's home province of Salaheddin, either at his favored city, Tikrit, or his nearby birthplace, the village of Auja. Although Republican Guard and other loyalist elements still fought north of Baghdad, the Iraqi military had vanished into thin air in the days after Baghdad's fall. To the southeast, the Iraqi IV Corps had abandoned its positions on the staircase of defensive positions between Basra and Kut. To the north, the Iraqi V Corps surrendered at Mosul, the I Corps at Kirkuk, and the II Corps melted away near the Iranian border northeast of Baghdad.

Minor skirmishes with formed bodies of Iraqi troops continued for more than a week, but the U.S. DoD proclaimed the end of major combat operations on April 14, the last day that aircraft from all five of the deployed U.S. carrier battle groups flew over Iraq. Akin to bringing a great juggernaut to a sudden stop, the end of major combat operations was a jarring and disorienting experience for the U.S. forces in Iraq. Interviews with deployed soldiers vividly captured the fleeting sense of loss, clarity, and fulfillment that soldiers felt as the rollercoaster ride of Operation Iraqi Freedom drew to a sudden end. It was replaced by what David Zucchino called "the vague, amorphous business of stabilization and rebuilding."[1]

The end of major combat operations—the third phase of Operation Iraqi Freedom—signaled the commencement of the fourth and final phase, known as stabilization and support operations (SASO). Whereas the U.S. military and its allies had occupied one tenth of Iraq in 1991, the Coalition now accepted the legal rights and responsibilities of the occupying force throughout the entire country. The U.S. Office of Reconstruction and Humanitarian Assistance (ORHA) deployed to Baghdad, and humanitarian assistance began to enter the country through reopened airports and shipping ports.

Meanwhile, exploitation teams scoured the country for the WMD and missile technology that had played such a prominent role in the public debate about the necessity of military action. For the next twenty months, a variety of U.S.-led inspection efforts interviewed Iraqi government figures and perused surviving documents, operating with the freedom and unconstrained access that UN inspectors lacked. What they found was consistent with the more cautious passages of many prewar assessments of Iraq's WMD and missile ambitions. The Iraq Survey Group (ISG) concluded from interviews that Saddam Hussein urged his cabinet to give full cooperation to UNMOVIC in the closing months of 2002. Senior Baathist interviewees disclosed that Iraq had no weaponized WMD capability save for its advanced missile-design program. Undeclared (perhaps misplaced) WMDs were present in Iraq, as evidenced by the apparently accidental use of an artillery shell filled with four liters of Sarin nerve agent in an insurgent roadside bomb in May 2004, but it is likely that the regime did not knowingly hold any stocks under its control.[2] According to ISG interviews, however, the regime continued to work on WMD research, in anticipation of the day when sanctions would be lifted. It undertook scientific research on the synthesis of VX nerve gas, the dry storage and delivery of biological agents, and scattered nuclear-weapons-related topics. According to the CIA documentation of interview materials, "Saddam felt that any country that had the technical ability to develop WMD had an intrinsic right to do so. He saw WMD as both a symbol and a normal process of modernity. Saddam's national security policy demanded victory in war, deterrence of hostile neighbors, and prestige and strategic influence throughout the Arab world. These concerns led Iraq to develop and maintain WMD programs."[3]

330 | ENDING RESISTANCE

THE CHALLENGE PROJECT

Although Iraq did not rely on WMD to deter the invasion or ensure victory in war, the deposed regime did have a fallback option and a means of continuing its resistance to the United States beyond the fall of Baghdad. There would no decisive showdown in Tikrit, which fell meekly under Coalition control on April 14. Instead, when the newly arrived U.S. 4th Infantry Division pushed into the Baathist heartland, it encountered scattered groups of Fedayeen and paramilitaries loading weapons and munitions into trucks amid the widespread looting that broke out after the regime's fall. Rather than witnessing the end of the regime, the U.S. troops were witnessing the birth of something new, as the regime's defensive effort moved into a new phase. According to ISG interviews, the plan was known within the Baathist top echelon as "the Challenge Project" and involved the creation of a two-stage guerrilla campaign: the first would take place in tandem with the conventional defense of Baghdad and the second was intended to take effect after the fall of Iraq's capital. In essence, the plan sought to inflict attritional losses on the U.S. military to deter it from advancing all the way to Baghdad or to shorten the period of postwar occupation. In other words, it was an updated version of Saddam's defensive strategy in Kuwait in 1990 that reflected the experiences of the decade that followed. In particular, Saddam focused on the U.S. withdrawal from Somalia and distributed copies of the book *Black Hawk Down* to senior officers to instruct them on how to wear down the U.S. military.[4]

The first phase, executed before and during Operation Iraq Freedom, involved setting the conditions for prolonged guerrilla warfare. The regime's longstanding fear of ammunition shortages during wartime led to the establishment of ammunition supply points (ASP) throughout Iraq and was taken to new extremes before Operation Iraqi Freedom. An estimated 650,000 to 1 million tons of weapons and explosives were distributed throughout the country in a deliberate attempt to sustain local resistance during and after the war. In addition to Iraq's well-known arms depots—some of which covered more than a hundred square kilometers—more than ten thousand forward ASPs were created in schools, hospitals, mosques, fields, and warehouses. Finally, an unknown number of small, dispersed weapons caches were sown throughout the Euphrates and Tigris River valleys along likely Coalition routes of advance and throughout the Sunni triangle. The ISG calculated the average size of Iraqi arms dumps to be forty tons, although the presence of some superdepots indicate that statistically the vast majority of arms caches were small stores consisting of less than a ton of small arms, RPGs, artillery shells, and land mines. With an eye to the future, the regime marked the GPS coordinates of many smaller or remote caches.[5]

The parallel security structure was charged with undertaking the postwar resistance effort already in operation during the war, directing the effort or the Fedayeen and other irregular groups. It was built around four key sets of individuals. The first was a command element composed of a narrow slice of the regime leadership (e.g., Saddam and a few close advisors). According to U.S. intelligence reports, the second set was made of specialist cells formed from elements of the Baathist intelligence services, particularly the M-14 (assassinations) and M-21 (bomb-making) branches of the Mukhabarat. In addition to distributing large numbers of suicide vests at caches throughout Iraq, one of the fifteen- to twenty- person "Tiger Groups" formed by these Mukhabarat organizations carried out a suicide attack on April 3: a pregnant Mukhabarat member exploded her explosives vest, killing three U.S. special operations forces at Haditha Dam. The third and fourth sets of resistance actors were the "minders" sent by the intelligence services, SRG, and Republican Guard to facilitate and liaise with resistance cells out in the provinces, and the local Baath Party officials in each province. These groups played key roles in the plain-clothes-resistance effort undertaken in parallel with the Iraqi military's campaign throughout Operation Iraqi Freedom.

The sudden cessation of regime communications and the citywide disappearance of the Baathist leadership in Baghdad on April 10 signaled the activation of the postwar phase of this resistance effort. It had been preceded by a regime advisory to senior officials to don civilian clothes, go to their homes or hiding places, and await further instructions. The regime also sent large quantities of hard currency into hiding, adding $1 billion to the estimated $3 billion stashed away in banks outside Iraq. This nest egg prepared the ground for a prolonged resistance effort in which former regime elements would continue to employ their prewar combination of financial patronage and nationalist or religious propaganda. Just as Iraqi air-defense gunners were offered rewards to shoot down U.S. aircraft and deliver pilots, Iraqi resisters would be paid to carry out attacks on occupation forces, with bonuses for successful attacks. The release of tens of thousands of criminals in late 2002 created a demographic base from which the resistance effort could draw even if the broader Iraqi populace could not be drawn into resistance.

The Baathist regime had also developed close prewar ties with radical Salafist militants in Iraq and local terrorist groups such as Ansar al-Islam, thereby creating temporary local alliances of mutual convenience in the post-war period. Since 1999, the Baathist government's Return to Faith campaign (*al-Hamlah al-Imaniyyah*) encouraged a resurgence of Sunni Islamist activity throughout Iraq, which cracked down on drinking and gambling establishments not patronized by the regime and boosted the status of religious education and media. As long as they criticized the United States and other Western supporters of Iraq's isolation, Sunni Arab clerics and radical Salafist militants were free to act with increasing swagger throughout the twilight years of the Baathist regime.[6]

Throughout 2001 and 2002, Mukhabarat officers liaised with terrorists in the Ansar al-Islam enclave in northern Iraq and facilitated the supply of funding, explosives, and vehicles.[7] The Mukhabarat and Ansar al-Islam both brought foreign militants to Iraq, a practice that the Baathist regime had carried out since the 1970s. They trained a range of Arab extremists at the Mukhabarat compound at Salman Pak. Small numbers of foreign volunteers fought the Coalition advance during Operation Iraqi Freedom, including a stream of fighters bussed in from Syria during the war itself, just as in 1991 when a tiny cadre of Yemeni and Sudanese volunteers fought on Iraq's side.[8] After the war, this flow continued, encouraged by Baathist elements in Syria and by transnational Salafist groups such as Ansar al-Islam and cells associated with Jordanian terrorist Abu Musab al-Zarqawi. The presence of these latter two groups ensured that even if the Baathist cause failed, Iraq would have a prolonged violent struggle.

BROADER INSURGENCY

As Baghdad fell, the former regime had a workable plan to continue resistance in the postwar period and work toward the intermediate aim of ending foreign military occupation and the long-term aim of regaining power. Even if the Baathist leadership's attempt to create a broad-based nationalist and Islamist insurgency failed, the regime had enough money, connections, and expertise in assassinations and bomb-making to undertake a sustained terrorist campaign. The potential weakness of the project lay in the Coalition's ability to decapitate the Baathist leadership, cut off its access to funding and armaments, and convince active and potential resisters that their future interests were best served by cooperating with a new Iraqi government rather than the ousted regime. If these weaknesses could be exploited, the insurgency would fizzle in a manner similar to the Nazi regime's postoccupation resistance project (known as Werewolf).

Through decades of authoritarianism, Iraqis learned to display passivity during periods of conflict until a clear winner could be discerned, unless they were operating under the protection of their own individual power or the power of a patron. The initial postwar period presented a critical window of opportunity for the occupation forces to claim the mantle of a security guarantor by showing that they were in charge and that they could improve upon the lives of Iraqis. In addition to the difficulty inherent in making post-Saddam Iraqis trust a government of any hue, the Coalition faced specific challenges in garrisoning a country that had become increasingly Islamicized and anti-Western following a decade of Western sanctions and Baathist indoctrination. On this note, counterinsurgency expert Steven Metz wrote, "An insurgency is born when a power fails to address social or regional polarization, sectarianism, endemic corruption, crime, various forms of radicalism, or rising expectations. The margin of error is narrower for an outside occupying power than for an inept or repressive national regime as people tend to find mistakes or bad behaviour by one of their own more tolerable than that of an outsider."[9] If this list sounds applicable to Iraq, it is because Metz penned these words as a critique of Coalition policy after Operation Iraqi Freedom.

Put simply, the postwar phase in Iraq was badly botched by a combination of planning and bureaucratic shortfalls. The military had put some thought into the stabilization of Iraq during the 1999 Desert Crossing war game and in the subsequent addition of a peace support-operations branch to OPLAN 1003-98, but its prewar interest in the stabilization of Iraq was low; it was limited to a 58-person cell with a $2,000 research budget. The SASO phase of Operation Iraqi Freedom was instead largely planned by ORHA, an interagency body with 2,500 staff members, a $50-million operating budget, and access to $700 million of U.S. aid funding. With little effective prewar integration between the military and ORHA, the military's stabilization effort was effectively limited to preparations to counter Baathist scorched-earth policies (WMD, oil fields, dams, bridges, and other infrastructure) and to meet immediate humanitarian needs. Other contingencies—such as widespread looting or dispersal of armaments—were not prioritized, and the military blithely assumed that Iraqi army elements could be redeployed to keep internal order.

In execution, a number of factors reduced the capability of the U.S. military to take charge and provide basic services. The lack of a northern entry point and the lightweight force package used in Operation Iraqi Freedom meant that battalion-sized U.S. forces reached many Iraqi cities eleven to sixteen days after the fall of Baghdad and only began to patrol Iraq's northern and western borders another week later. The Coalition needed to deploy approximately 1.4 million troops to Iraq to achieve the troop to civilian ratio (1:50) often required by peace support operations alone, let alone that necessary to cope with the explosion of looting that followed the fall of the regime. This ratio was impossible because of the U.S. military's lean force structure and because no formed Iraqi security forces were immediately available to assist the Coalition. Looting only stopped when all unsecured goods and fittings were stripped from public buildings and redistributed, which initiated a period of endemic lawlessness. The collapse of the national electrical grid exacerbated cascading critical infrastructure failures throughout the country. The Coalition had failed its first postwar test in the eyes of the Iraqi people.

The provision of basic services and security were stubborn challenges, but they need not have resulted in a prolonged insurgency—and indeed they did not spur such an insurgency in the Shia areas of Iraq. The embedded and persistent Sunni Arab insurgency developed because Sunni Arabs feared they would be excluded from sharing power in the new Iraq. The exacerbation of this fear was the second key failure of Coalition policy. Tensions already existed between the U.S. forces and the Sunni Arab communities in the postwar period because of wartime deaths (such as the accidental killing of tribal sheikhs during leadership-decapitation attempts), postwar deaths (among others, the April 28 killing of fifteen locals during violent protests in Fallujah), and the general friction caused by occupation forces. The U.S. military quickly learned that blood-money payments could limit the damage caused by some of these incidents, but emerging Coalition policies had far more counterproductive and long-lasting impacts.

When the underperforming ORHA was restaffed and recast as a new agency, the Coalition Provisional Authority (CPA), a raft of policies were introduced to make sure that the Baathist regime could not stage a return to power. On May 16, 2003, CPA Directive 1 ("De-Baathification of Iraqi Society") struck a death blow to the hopes of reintegration held by tens of thousands of former Baathists, from lowly schoolteachers to the senior party officials earmarked for linchpin roles in the insurgency. On May 23, 2003, CPA Directive 2 ("Dissolution of Entities") dissolved the country's security apparatus, including the Ministry of Defense and armed forces. Hundreds of thousands of military personnel became unemployed at a time when the only people hiring were the leaders of the nascent insurgency. These two postwar failures combined to breathe life into the insurgency, elevating it from the last gasp of so-called "regime dead-enders" to a multifaceted resistance phenomenon with long-term potential.

Some of the violent factions refused to work with the former regime elements, regardless of what secular, political, or criminal guise these chameleons took. Even so, former regime facilitators of the ousted regime found many willing collaborators in its effort to expel foreign forces; the scattered attacks that followed Operation Iraqi Freedom became a recognizable pattern of resistance operations. Combined Joint Task Force (CJTF) 7, the newly constituted theater command in Iraq, reported that in the month after the end of major combat operations there were at least 112 incidents in which lethal force was employed against the Coalition, primarily in the Sunni triangle.[10] According to CJTF-7, approximately three quarters of captured assailants had been paid to carry out attacks. This highlighted the former regime element's role in these attacks, although many attackers also espoused other motivations based in national, sectarian, local, or tribal grievances toward the Coalition presence in Iraq.[11] Added motivation came from the religious edicts issued by radical Salafist mosques throughout the Sunni triangle, which ferociously criticized the Coalition presence in Iraq and its policies vis-à-vis the Sunni. In an increasingly radicalized state such as Iraq, which was cut off from the West for more than a decade and stripped of its secular middle class and educational system, the mosques were influential.

The scope of targets attacked by insurgents after April 2003 was very broad, but violence unfolded at two distinct levels. At one end of the scale, small numbers of carefully targeted terrorist-type attacks (e.g., mass-casualty car bombings, assassinations, and infrastructure sabotage) cast doubts on the Coalition's ability to provide security, build new institutions, attract international assistance, or provide basic government services. Both the core former regime elements and Salafist terrorists had a strong interest in undermining the stabilization and reconstruction of Iraq. The rationale for this kind of approach is explained by the so-called "focoist" model of insurgency, which is the preferred strategy of insurgent groups that lack the popular support to launch decisive urban seizures of power or enlarge rural "no-go zones" until the ruling elite are hemmed into isolated urban areas. The focoist model instead seeks to prevent the occupying power from stabilizing the country and politically integrating local communities by using its dedicated vanguard of terrorists to carry out antioccupation actions. These actions awaken the sympathies of the population by generating what might be termed "myths of resistance" and simultaneously luring the occupying power into heavy-handed tactics that upset the local population.[12] Both the Baathist and Salafist cadres also shared an interest in fomenting sectarian strife between Iraq's Sunni Arab minority and the Shiite and Kurdish communities. The result of these shared aims was a series of car bombings and assassinations throughout the summer of 2003 and beyond that targeted the UN presence in Iraq, various aid and reconstruction efforts, and a range of Iraqi politicians, technocrats, and intellectuals.

Alongside these tightly focused attacks, the broader mass of Iraqi insurgents—who were either paid by the former regime elements or acting autonomously—carried out actions that directly targeted Coalition forces. At a tactical level, the competition between insurgent and multinational forces mirrored the rapid evolutionary cut and thrust observed between Baathist and multinational forces seen in the no-fly zones. In attacks in April and early June, insurgents attacked U.S. military outposts and convoys with small arms and RPGs in a continuation of the irregular tactics used during the war. In some cases, Iraqi fighters employed increasingly complex ambushes throughout the summer, shadowing convoys, avoiding armored vehicles, and integrating mortars into their tactical actions. Every class of vehicle suffered attacks; numerous "soft skins" (un-armored trucks) and even one M1 Abrams were disabled.[13] Ten Coalition troops were KIA and thirty-seven, WIA within the first month after the end of major combat operations. In combination with body and head armor, extant and jury-rigged armor added onto vehicles saved huge numbers of lives and made casualty figures alone a poor indicator of the intensity of such combats.[14] As a result, in almost every case, insurgent losses outweighed those of Coalition forces, yet attackers were not difficult to replace. Instead of a slackening number of attacks, effective defensive measures merely pushed the price of attacks up. Each attacker was paid between $75 and $500 per attack depending on the risk and on market conditions. The comparison between this price and the Saddam-era bounty of $14,000 for the successful downing of a U.S. or British aircraft and $2,500 for the capture of a pilot says much about the increased vulnerability of the U.S. military in Iraq.[15] Where once only a small cadre of Iraqis enjoyed even the slimmest chance of killing an American, now anyone could have a shot. Although still a risky and difficult exercise, killing Americans had never been this easy.

DEFENSIVE AND OFFENSIVE COALITION RESPONSES

The U.S. military had been able to hunker down when facing previous, lower-intensity terrorist threats in the Gulf, for example, by moving to the remote PSAB in Saudi Arabia following the Khobar Towers bombing. However, the broader mission of stabilizing Iraq did not allow for a defensive lockdown. On a typical day, each of the U.S. divisions garrisoning Iraq would conduct approximately 200–250 patrols, man approximately 20 checkpoints, secure up to 400 individual infrastructure sites or ASPs, escort a number of resupply and deployment convoys, and carry out civil affairs and training missions.[16] Faced by the need to adopt offensive measures and lacking doctrinal guidance or training in counterinsurgency operations, the initial instinct of U.S. divisional commanders was to focus on aggressive actions to apprehend the remaining Baathist leaders at large: the familiar HVTs that included Saddam Hussein, his sons, and nineteen other missing members of the "deck of cards." According to Steven Metz, this instinct reflected a conviction commonly held by military men facing an insurgency, which Metz described as "a tendency to deny or underestimate the threat, to believe that killing or capturing only a few of the most obvious rebel leaders will solve the problem." This tendency conceals the need to "identify and rectify the structural problems that spawned them."[17]

Operation Planet X was the first such operation, launched on May 15, 2003, against a village near Tikrit. The 2nd BCT of the U.S. 4th Infantry Division cordoned off the village from landward and river approaches and then engaged in a nocturnal search of the two hundred houses in the village that netted 260 prisoners. Although the raid captured 1 of the HVTs from the deck of cards and 29 other legitimate captives, the remaining 230 villagers were released. This underlined the imprecision of the HUMINT used to cue the operation.

A string of cordon and search operations (Peninsula Strike, Desert Scorpion, Sidewinder, Soda Mountain) involving one or more brigades were mounted in the Sunni areas throughout June and July by the 101st Air Assault

Division, the 4th Infantry Division, and the newly arrived U.S. 1st Armored Division. Some of these operations took place against clearly defined targets in remote areas, notably the long-range heliborne assaults by entire BCTs of 101st Division. More often, these operations simultaneously targeted large numbers of villages throughout the Sunni-triangle areas north of Baghdad. The final large-scale operation in early summer, Operation Ivy Serpent, was launched on July 12, 2003, to preempt the holiday marking the anniversary of the Baath Party's seizure of power.[18] The proliferation of multidivisional operations throughout the Sunni triangle, complete with armor, artillery, and air support, gave the Sunni Arab population an insight into the war, which most of them had not witnessed firsthand. Soldiers searched hundreds of houses and detained thousands of Iraqis on each occasion, which engendered greater resentment and fear among local communities.

As Operation Ivy Serpent was concluding, a different type of operation was unfolding in the Baathist stronghold of Mosul. On July 22, 2003, exactly twenty-four hours after a "walk-in" informer provided information to a tactical HUMINT team (THT) at 101st Division headquarters and passed a polygraph test, U.S. special forces and 101st Division troops surrounded a house containing Uday and Qusay Hussein. Following a three-and-a-half-hour standoff and two unsuccessful assaults, the building was secured in the third attempt and the bodies of both sons (plus one of Saddam's grandsons and a bodyguard) were removed.[19] The quality of the HUMINT supporting the operation facilitated the deaths of HVT 2 and 3; the operation used less than a battalion of U.S. troops and a range of heavier assets (armor and air support), most of which were not required, thereby minimizing the disruptive footprint of the operation. Although the intelligence lead that doomed Uday and Qusay was an unexpected windfall, the sort of high-quality intelligence needed to undertake such pinpoint raids typically took time to develop. A number of the existing HVTs were still on the run, and mapping the hydra-headed resistance effort represented an intense and dynamic challenge for the U.S. intelligence community. After twelve years of militarily containing Iraq, the U.S. military knew the enemy inside out, including its ORBAT, operational habits, and capabilities; the day after Baghdad fell, the U.S. intelligence community had to tear up the book and start again.

Technical-intelligence collection (e-mail and mobile phone intercepts and aerial tracking) provided some pointers to insurgent activity, but the initial cuing of most counterinsurgency operations in Iraq came from slowly developed insights gleaned from multiple human sources or captured written materials and files. Maj. Gen. Raymond Odierno, commander of the most digitized division in the U.S. military (4th Infantry Division) reflected this view in an interview in fall 2003, when he stated that "we need to work towards developing the HUMINT structure, because we believe that was what worked best against the postwar threat."[20] As Odierno intimated, the most advanced division of the world's most advanced military found this requirement difficult to fulfill. Although the technical sensors fielded by the U.S. military had increased in density and acuity, the same could not be said for its ability to collect HUMINT.

The best results came from the range of specialist intelligence-gathering human assets available to division commanders, including attached special forces, organic THT, and long-range surveillance detachments. Every U.S. foot soldier is theoretically a sensor, but the types of information each is capable of collecting remain very limited. As Operation Iraqi Freedom ended, few U.S. soldiers had any "social intelligence" on the Arab world, a fancy way of saying that they understood very little about Arabic culture or customs. Still fewer understood the language, with an average of 1 fluent linguist per battalion of 800 troops.[21] As U.S. Army officer and counterinsurgency expert Maj. John Nagl noted, only the cross-attachment of reliable Iraqis can partially make up for this shortfall. He explained, "They know who is supposed to be where and what they are supposed to be doing. They can see patterns of behaviour that are irregular in a way that our untrained eye cannot. They can talk to everybody in a way that we cannot."[22]

Difficult though it is to collect, the patient, workmanlike build-up and validation of HUMINT proved the key to launching successful operations with small disruptive footprints. Knowledge management at a divisional and later national level took time to develop because the shortages of translators and analysts slowed the development of databases that cataloged agent reliability and cross-referenced activities and associations to produce patterns of insurgent behavior. Such analysis reduced the incidence of false indicators of insurgent activity, which led to fewer misdirected raids and unnecessary detentions. Maturing HUMINT allowed a more detailed understanding of the enemy to emerge, resulting in a HVT list that now included hundreds of individuals.

By the fall 2003, Coalition intelligence analysts had already begun to piece together the rough topography of the resistance effort. In particular, the level of facilitators between the few Iraqi and Syrian-located leaders—the "board of governors" primarily responsible for dispensing funding—and the foot soldiers became more clear. This middle level of former regime facilitators provided all-important "staff-type functions" including national and international liaison, planning, financing, logistics, bomb-making, intelligence collection, counterintelligence, recruitment, and training.[23] Similar schematics developed for the Salafist networks operating in Iraq, which allowed the Coalition to target both the secular and religious resistance networks at their most important nodes. Working from these target lists, digital-mapping and covert HUMINT operations generated mission-support packages that ensured each raid used a 10-digit GPS coordinate and a detailed photograph of the target premises. Detailed and precise intelligence support eventually allowed highly effective raids such as Operation Reindeer Games on December 10, 2003, in which the 101st Division launched simultaneous raids on thirty-four locations and detained twenty of thirty-four targets, as compared with merely twenty-three unnecessarily detained Iraqis.[24]

CALIBRATING FORCE

This patient, workmanlike approach to intelligence-gathering showed results from the outset, but such patience was hard for U.S. divisional commanders to muster in the face of increasingly frequent and deadly insurgent attacks throughout early winter 2003. Neither the U.S. Army nor the U.S. Marine Corps went to war with up-to-date or exercised counterinsurgency doctrine—a shortfall that would not be recognized until eighteen months into the insurgency.[25] In the meantime, the divisional commanders had a rough grasp of the tools and concepts, falling back on the crude lessons of Vietnam. In the absence of a theater-wide concept of operations, each divisional commander made efforts to win the fabled "hearts and minds" of the population.

Tasked with controlling Anbar province black spots Fallujah and Ramadi, the U.S. 82nd Airborne Division designated the "popular support of the Iraqi people" as its new center of gravity. It sought to win such support by providing security, essential services, employment, and governance.[26] In the Baathist heartland of Nineva province, an early and sustained application of this approach by the 101st Division yielded very positive results by the time the division rotated out in January 2004. The Commander's Emergency Repair Program (CERP), a constantly replenished fund of two hundred thousand dollars held by U.S. brigade commanders, proved to be the most useful civil affairs tool available to local units and prompted the adoption of the maxim, "money is ammunition."[27] Compared to the cumbersome bureaucracy involved in disbursing U.S. aid through the CPA and the tendency for resultant jobs to go to foreign contractors, the U.S. military proved to be an excellent conduit for rapidly disbursed aid that immediately improved the quality of life for Iraqis and injected money into the local economy. As an example, by the end of 2003 the 101st Air Assault Division was the biggest employer in northern Iraq. U.S. divisional commanders found that they spent a huge proportion of their time reopening businesses, fixing bridges, reversing cooking fuel shortages, averting industrial strikes, and helping Iraqis to bring in the harvest. As well as calculating how to weave kinetic and information-operations activities to serve the operational objective, the "Effects Coordination Cells" at occupying divisions brought together CERP and civil-affairs programs. Blood-money payments, postraid reconstruction, and sit-downs with the local tribal leaders offset some of the friction caused by the occupation. The Coalition also took steps to address the concerns of Iraqis, such as agreeing to target criminal as well as insurgent groups and limit searches of mosques and women.

The problem remained, however, that such local efforts were damage-control measures that could temporarily slow but not curb the development of the insurgency, which would continue to develop as long as Sunni Arab communities perceived themselves to be suffering political exclusion and foreign occupation. In mid-November 2003, a national long-term strategy for the transition to Iraqi self-rule emerged. The timeline envisaged a handover of power to an appointed interim government in June 2004, the election of a transitional government in December 2004, and the drafting of a new constitution and election of a constitutional government by the end of 2005. In early winter 2003, however, this timeline offered scant comfort to frontline commanders, who wrestled with the immediate and pressing problem of force protection and stabilization in the face of a rapidly developing insurgency. At a quantitative level, the national total of anti-Coalition attacks jumped from a declining figure of approximately twenty per day in late summer to new highs of fifty per day in November.

At a qualitative level, attacks carried out during Ramadan (October and November) in 2003 pointed to a maturing of insurgent capabilities. Former regime elements displayed the ability to penetrate agents within the nascent

Iraqi security forces, Coalition bases, and government and economic infrastructures by building on their prewar network of neighborhood informers retained by the Mukhabarat, each of which would still be susceptible to either ongoing payment or blackmail. The insurgents displayed an intimate understanding of Iraq's oil, electrical, and transport infrastructures and struck with insight and precision that the nodal analysts at the JWAC would have appreciated.[28] In stark contrast to the Coalition, the resistance had a functioning HUMINT network from day one of the conflict and remained a number of steps ahead of the occupation forces in term of intelligence. Iraqi insurgents gained unprecedented insight into U.S. military routines, even profiling average response times by U.S. heliborne quick-reaction forces in order to lay traps for these reinforcements.[29] Indeed, in November 2003, the United States lost both a CH-47D Chinook (killing sixteen troops) and a UH-60 Blackhawk (killing six), and a DHL courier plane joined the growing list of fixed-wing military aircraft to be forced down over Iraq as a result of missile or small-arms strikes.

In addition to improved intelligence, Iraqi insurgents displayed boosted attack capabilities. After months of witnessing attacks by groups tied strictly to their local areas, the Coalition intercepted a resistance cell in November that appeared to be relocating within the Sunni triangle, complete with weapons and large quantities of cash. Other cells seemed to be moving closer to their financial lines of supply on the Syrian border. In addition to "fielding" armed forces in this way, the resistance also showed increasing ambition during its November 30 attack on two convoys in Samarra: it massed between thirty and one hundred fighters to simultaneously attack the convoys after warning civilians to clear the streets. Its most significant tactical adaptation was increasingly deadly "stand-off" modes of attack, including long-range mortar and rocket attacks and roadside bombs.

Although both these modes of attack developed in midsummer in response to deadly Coalition return-fire capabilities in direct fire engagements, they increased in quantity and sophistication throughout the year. By November, insurgents were firing an average of more than mortar or rocket attacks a week, employing weapons as varied as eight- to fifteen-kilometer rockets of 107-mm and 122-mm calibers to short-range missiles. One of these missiles was concealed within a donkey cart and fired at the Rashid Hotel during Deputy Secretary of State Wolfowitz's visit to Baghdad in October 2003. Meanwhile, truck-borne mortars offered a means for insurgents to "shoot and scoot." Mortar crews valued preserving their forces more than shooting accurately, and maintained local sympathy by firing from locations well away from civilian structures.[30]

Long-range attacks provided the insurgency with a low-risk way of staying in the fight, reflecting the Baathist tradition favoring the preservation of forces, even if military action became largely ineffective. However, roadside bombs and car bombs were far more lethal means in the hands of insurgents, responsible for fully half of the casualties caused by resistance actions. With good reason, an officer at the U.S. Marine Corps Lessons Learned Center in Fallujah told reporters, "We certainly respect their ability to make bombs." This ability initially developed from the Mukhabarat personnel involved in the insurgency, specifically from the experts of the M-21 section. Utilizing the massive stocks of explosives cached all over Iraq, insurgent roadside and car bombs employed payloads ranging from professionally packaged plastic explosives to piles of artillery shells. In the months after the end of Operation Iraqi Freedom, experts from the M-21 electronics and mechanical departments taught Iraqi bomb makers to produce shaped charges, timers, wiring, and fuses, and incorporate command lines, encrypted mobile phones, pagers, garage door openers, and other remote controls into devices. Other M-21 specialists instructed Iraqi bombers on bomb concealment: elevating them in parked truck cabs or highway barriers, and placing them in refilled craters or even inside dead animal carcasses.[31]

Although U.S. electronic jammers prematurely detonated or prevented the detonation of some bombs, and other bombs were detected and disarmed by combat engineers and robotic vehicles (as many as 35 percent, according to U.S. military estimates), the primary means of defense remained vehicle hardening. Jury-rigging floor plates and steel doors saved hundreds of lives. However, when an M1 Abrams had its turret blown off by a roadside bomb in October 2003, it was proof positive that hardening was a necessary but not sufficient defensive measure for U.S. forces in Iraq.[32]

The two response options with the greatest long-term potential, which Steven Metz termed "the two key battlespaces of intelligence and Iraqi perception," were quickly accepted by U.S. commanders by the fall of 2003. The value of intelligence was apparent to U.S. commanders, but little consensus existed concerning the best method to achieve the second half of the equation—controlling Iraqi perceptions. The slow workmanlike approach of civil affairs and reconstruction assistance required tremendous patience, and

CPA's attempts to set up local media operations were ineffective. The "hearts and minds" of Iraqis needed to be won and rewon, one day at a time. Even the best-case results, which 82nd Airborne Division commander Maj. Gen. Chuck Swanneck termed the "toleration" of Coalition forces, were invisible to the eye. Toleration consisted attacks that did not occur and produced no apparent metrics to report or to judge the success or failure of the mission. All the time, a different set of metrics was constantly accumulating in the form of the U.S. KIA and WIA.[33]

When interviewed while serving with his unit in Iraq, counterinsurgency expert John Nagl gave insight into the dilemma facing U.S. commanders and troops: "I'm not really all that concerned about their hearts right now. . . . We're into the behavior-modification phase. I want their minds right now. Maybe we'll get their hearts later, as we spend $100,000 on their schools and health clinics this week and another $100,000 on their schools and health clinics next week and $100,000 on their schools and health clinics the week after that. Over time I'll start winning some hearts. Right now I just want them to stop shooting at us, stop planting [improvised explosive devices]. If they're not involved in these activities, they should start turning in the people who are. Whatever techniques that are legal and moral that I have to use to accomplish that, I will. Counterinsurgency is not always a pretty thing."[34]

To U.S. commanders versed in the centrality of shock and psychological dominance in successful operations, the temptation was to reply to the environment with equally warlike countermeasures. As Major General Swanneck noted, "This is war. And we're not going to prosecute war holding one hand behind our back. When we identify positively an enemy target, we're going to go ahead and take them out with every means we have available."[35]

The spike in attacks in November and the attendant frustration resulted in a series of violent displays of U.S. military power in the areas north and west of Baghdad controlled by the 1st Armored Division, the 4th Infantry Division, and the 82nd Airborne Division. In two of the largest actions, Operation Iron Hammer and Operation Ivy Cyclone, the U.S. military married precision intelligence with overwhelming firepower in a manner not seen since major combat operations ended in April 2003. Intelligence preparation of the battlefield fused technical intelligence and HUMINT; the former provided cues from the counterbattery radar coverage at U.S. bases and increasing numbers of smaller brigade-level UAVs. Patterns of enemy activity became clear as incident data from mortar and rocket attacks and roadside bombings was analyzed, just as patterns became clear when Iraq was resisting the no-fly zones. The U.S. intelligence community identified repeatedly used firing positions, safe houses, and ambush sites, which were termed "anti-Coalition structures." Area-limitation analysis used photographs and three-dimensional computer modeling to identify areas with sight lines on targeted outposts or roads.[36] The U.S. military increasingly moved from current to predictive intelligence preparation.

Alongside large-scale series of raids and aggressive patrolling, Operations Iron Hammer and Ivy Cyclone used widespread artillery and air strikes against so-called anti-Coalition structures in Baghdad, Tikrit, Baqubah, Fallujah, Kirkuk, and Balad. Uninhabited structures regularly used by insurgents were destroyed with precise and scalable direct fire from Apache helicopters and A-10 and AC-130 aircraft pulled down from the overhead CAS stacks. Targets were vetted through Bugsplat, a computer modeling system that predicted collateral damage from planned strikes. Satellite-guided, 2,000-pound JDAMs were used for the first time since the end of major combat operations. Numerous other air strikes were launched from F-16 and F/A-18 aircraft that flew from the Al-Udeid air base in Qatar or, for the first time since the end of major combat operations, from a carrier in the Gulf, the USS *Enterprise*. In Operation Ivy Cyclone, the 4th Infantry Division launched 36 ATACMS rounds at a range of safe houses, launch sites, and training grounds. The high-velocity missiles allowed near-instantaneous surprise strikes to be launched during daylight hours. Counterbattery fire was permitted where it did not endanger civilians. Major General Swanneck recalled that counterfire could be automatically cued onto launch locations as quickly as one minute and forty-two seconds after launch, which occasionally resulted in blood trails and other evidence of successful strikes. Where such counterfire was impractical and where locally posted snipers and ambushes could not engage enemy shooters, Coalition air support and UAVs were sometimes able to maintain "eyes-on" contact with insurgent mortar teams or groups placing roadside bomb, thereby tracking them back to safe houses and cuing further Coalition action.[37]

Deliberate intimidation of the insurgent population and the civilian communities that sheltered them was an aspect of such operations and those that followed throughout the winter months of 2003–4. This process had begun in early summer with the deliberate destruction of abandoned Iraqi armored vehicles by U.S. tank fire in regime strongholds near Tikrit. The intention was to display U.S. military power and make the valleys of the Baathist heartland rumble to the sound of U.S. guns. Following Saddam Hussein's capture in an intelligence-driven raid on December 13, the 1st Armored Division and 4th Infantry Division launched more raids throughout December and January, searching hundreds of homes and detaining large numbers of Iraqis. As John Nagl noted, counterinsurgency was not always a pretty sight.

During this period the U.S. divisions around Baghdad utilized a number of hard-hearted measures to gather intelligence and engage in behavior modification. Some were American in origin, such as the curious social-control experiment undertaken at Saddam's hometown of Auja. The town was encircled by a ring of concertina wire and the residents inventoried and issued with identification cards by the 4th Infantry Division. The local battalion commander told reporters, "The insurgents should not be allowed to swim among the population as a whole. What we elected to do was make Auja a fishbowl, so we could see who has swimming inside."[38]

Other measures were typically tried-and-true techniques that regional governments, including the Baathist government, had used on their own people. These included the detention of relatives until wanted suspects turned themselves in—a form of hostage taking, although relatively benign when undertaken by the United States—and the punitive demolition of the houses of suspected insurgents, a tactic widely used by Israel and other governments throughout the Middle East.[39] The use of such tactics emerged from a deep uncertainty concerning the best approach to modifying the behavior of Iraqis. By the end of 2003, it had become apparent—as Nagl noted—that the hearts of Iraqis were not up for grabs. Instead, U.S. divisional commanders increasingly noted a toughness about Iraqis and a grudging respect for strong authority. A common proverb tells of an Iraqi father who cements his leadership of the family by taking a cat and cutting its head off on the kitchen table one day in front of his assembled relatives. The hard-hearted actions of winter 2003–4 were the U.S. military's attempt to "cut the head off the cat."

The U.S. approach was undercut by the willingness of populations to accept certain types of behavior from their own people but to hold others to a different standard, as Steven Metz noted. Furthermore, only instinctive understanding of Iraq's tribal system, a huge network of informers, and an unconstrained capacity for brutality allowed the Baathist regime to patiently and precisely bring pressure to bear on its internal opponents. Some U.S. officers, notably U.S. Marine Corps Lt. Gen. James Conway, were highly skeptical that cutting the head off the cat would yield results. Conway told the *New York Times* in January 2004: "I don't want to condemn what people are doing. I'll simply say that I think until we can win the population over and they can give us those indigenous intelligence reports, that we're prolonging the process. I do not envision using that tactic. It would have to be a rare incident that transcends anything that we have seen in the country to make that happen."[40] Exactly one year later, following the deployment of the MEF to Anbar province, Conway was forced to concede that "our vision to win hearts and minds was met squarely with a 300% increase in the number of attacks in our sector."[41]

As it had been ever since 1990, the challenge was to deter Iraqi resistance, but something had changed in the intervening years. When the conflict began, the Iraqi military effort was centralized and U.S. efforts at coercion correctly identified Saddam Hussein as the only actor capable of ending resistance. Throughout the latter years of policing the no-fly zones and the invasion of Iraq, the United States recognized that Iraqi air-defense operators and soldiers could be deterred from engaging in aberrant behavior on a unit-by-unit basis, perhaps even on an individual basis. By the start of 2004, the decentralized web of Iraqi leaders and fighters needed to be deterred on an individual basis, day after day, but there was little consensus on whether sticks (force) or carrots (civility) or some unfamiliar hybrid of the two represented the best way for the U.S. military to deter Iraqi insurgents. In the meantime, the U.S. military focused on killing and detaining them, seeking to undertake what the 101st Air Assault Division commander Major General Petraeus termed "operations that get more bad guys off the streets than they create."[42]

"NO-GO" ZONES AND IRAQ'S SEASON OF BATTLES

Resistance and occupation became a settled routine in the early months of 2004, but the apparent lull was actually the calm before the storm. A major escalation in the intensity of the conflict in Iraq was soon to come. The risk of a Baathist return appeared to be receding, with Saddam Hussein, his sons, and most of his senior associates either captured or dead. At the same time the force-protection environment remained unsatisfactory and no good solution existed to reduce the number of attacks suffered by the Coalition and its Iraqi partners in the government ministries and the Iraq Governing Council.

Although resistance appeared to be an inevitable corollary of occupation in Iraq, the slow transfer of political and security roles to Iraqis seemed to offer an end to occupation in 2004. The successful multisectarian negotiation of a temporary constitution known as the Transitional Administrative Law was completed in March 2004. Political power would be transferred to an appointed Iraqi interim government (IIG) in June, pending elections in January 2005. A range of Iraqi security forces had been hastily developed from the mass of unemployed men and promised to replace foreign Coalition forces in a range of static defense and patrolling roles.

U.S. divisional commanders began to prepare for the relocation of most of their troops to remote and easily defended camps outside Iraq's heavily populated areas; the number of U.S. troops was slated to fall from seventeen brigades to thirteen in May 2004. In the meantime, U.S. forces scaled back their presence in certain insurgent hot spots, creating effective "no-go zones." As one Marine officer in Anbar province noted, "We'll protect the government and keep travel routes open, but . . . we've reduced our presence." Commenting on hot spots within Fallujah and Ramadi, the officer explained that "we've lost a lot of Marines there and we don't go there anymore. If they want it that bad, they can have it."[43] As was the case in the no-fly zones, there were some areas that were apparently not worth the effort and the risk to patrol.

As the spring of 2004 began, pockets of Iraq were subtly slipping out of Coalition control, where Coalition forces were being successfully deterred from entry. The former regime elements of the resistance had been rocked by Saddam's capture, which ended the prospect of a much-feared literal return of the Iraqi dictator and signaled the failure of the Challenge Project. Yet, almost without missing a beat, the resistance continued its operations, driven by a range of factors that continued to motivate resisters. Ambitious former regime or community leaders maintained the view that the Sunni Arabs would once again rule Iraq, refusing to accept the demographic minority status of Sunni Arabs. They drove countercollaboration attacks that sought to isolate the Sunni Arabs from the transitional process and aimed to make any emergent Coalition-supported government as weak and infiltrated as possible. At a local level, both secular and Salafist resistance leaders saw the potential to ossify the effective no-go zones into permanent "liberated zones," areas of local autonomy and weak central government control similar to the KRG zone in the north. Armed with the same funding and connections as before, such leadership elements continued to exploit the street- and mosque-level Sunni

Arab sense of disentitlement. They emerged, in the words of Ken Gause, as a "tribal-based mafia."[44]

The most prominent example of a liberated zone within the Sunni triangle emerged in the radicalized religious center and regime stronghold of Fallujah, a city of three hundred thousand just west of Baghdad. Known as the "city of mosques," Fallujah was an extremely poor and radicalized city that relied on regime largesse for its economic livelihood and religious foundations. Also strongly traditional, the families of the area were vested in tribal law, which required that they seek revenge for the deaths of family members killed by the Coalition in the wartime bombings and postwar shooting incidents.

The 82nd Airborne Division had only carried out pinpoint raids within the city and had never saturated the area in shows of force, because the province was lightly garrisoned and the Fallujah area was extreme hostile. The division searched only a thousand homes in almost a year of occupation and managed to effectively penetrate the city's arms bazaar only once. As a result, the area became an effective sanctuary for insurgents, including both local former regime elements and powerful local and foreign Salafist elements associated with Abu Musab al-Zarqawi.[45]

A second, and in many ways stronger, liberated zone emerged in the predominantly Shiite Thawra district of Baghdad. It was an area colloquially known as Sadr City, named after the revered Shia cleric Mohammed Sadiq al-Sadr, who was assassinated by the Baathist regime along with two of his sons on February 17, 1999, in the instability following Operation Desert Fox. A remaining son of the cleric, the young firebrand Moqtada al-Sadr, now operated as the focal figure of a group of clerics loyal to the memory of his father.

Moqtada al-Sadr took steps from the earliest stage of the occupation to resist inroads into his maneuverings on what Jeff White termed "the violent edge of Iraqi politics." He arranged the death of a U.S.-favored Shia cleric Abdel Majid al-Khoei on April 11, 2003. Denied a position on the Iraq Governing Council, Sadr's social movement developed a military wing, the Jaish al-Mahdi, in August 2003, that had the potential to tax and control Shiite shrines throughout the south. The movement soon became involved in armed clashes with U.S. military forces, killing two 1st Armored Division soldiers in Karbala in October 2003 and undertaking actions to deter U.S. activities in Sadr City. Reporting from Sadr City, Michael Schwarz noted: "Once the Americans enter Sadr City, the [Jaish al-Mahdi] usually resist ferociously. They are determined to carve out areas into which Americans are at least hesitant to come, and, over time, make these areas more-or-less immune to American incursions. This goal may be unreachable in the sense that US military superiority will always allow it to mount an attack from the air or to march through the community by massing a force of sufficient size; but if the end result is that Americans come to Sadr City infrequently and stay briefly, then the guerrillas will have won a sufficient victory to proceed with their broader plans." The broader plan involved the creation of counters to government institutions, including locally controlled law enforcement and governance (including a legislature made up of community figures).[46]

At the end of March 2004, a series of events precipitated the beginning of Iraq's season of battles, an almost nonstop period of counterinsurgency offensives that lasted throughout the remainder of the year. After tolerating the murder of Abdel Majid al-Khoei and later attacks on U.S. servicemen, the Coalition was set on a collision course with Moqtada al-Sadr in March 2004, when the Jaish al-Mahdi engaged in what amounted to the ethnic cleansing of a gypsy village near Diwaniyah. The Coalition response was to close al-Sadr's newspaper and arrest a number of his key associates in late March and early April.

As this showdown developed, a second crisis erupted in Fallujah, where four U.S. security contractors were ambushed and their bodies dismembered, burnt, and dragged through the streets in a manner reminiscent of the treatment of the bodies of U.S. servicemen after the battle of Mogadishu in October 1993. The Coalition pressed ahead against both sets of enemies, arresting another Sadr associate and preparing a U.S. Marine assault on Fallujah. In a repeat of the Sadr loyalists' response to the 1999 assassinations, Coalition action against Sadr immediately sparked an uprising by Jaish al-Mahdi groups throughout the Shiite south. These groups overran police stations and key transport nodes along Coalition lines of supply before U.S. forces reinforced faltering multinational and Iraqi troops in the Shiite cities between Baghdad and Nasariyah a week later. Although Sadrist forces were beaten back from many locations, the truce that was arranged by Iraqi political figures left the Jaish al-Mahdi intact. Meanwhile, the brigade-strength Marine assault on Fallujah was halted amid dramatic heavy fighting in the suburbs; pressure from Iraqi politicians and citizens had pushed Coalition decision makers to negotiate with the insurgent groups for the handover of the March 31 attackers. By mid-April, the setback at Fallujah looked more and more like an insurgent victory, carrying heavy political costs and resulting in thirty-nine Marine fatalities. Although the Marines had heavily blooded the enemy in the heavy fighting, it was apparent that many local civilians had joined the hard-core former regime and Salafist insurgents in an effort to defend the city.[47]

These crises of April 2004 yielded lessons that profoundly changed the Coalition's military strategy and operations in Iraq. The impression that the Coalition was on a smooth path to withdrawal was shattered by the collapse of Iraq's fledgling security forces in April, which prompted a reevaluation of expectations. Coalition leaders realized that increases in funding and a focus on qualitative improvement through elongated training schedules would eventually produce more durable forces, but only when Iraqis were able to fight under their own leaders and their own flag.

It was also clear that the freedom of action enjoyed by Coalition security forces up to that point had significantly eroded. Iraqis played major roles in crafting the political deals that reduced the level of violence in Fallujah and undercut regional support for Moqtada al-Sadr. Coalition military operations during the uprisings succeeded where they were integrated with Iraqi political initiatives (e.g., against Sadr's militia) and failed where they were attempted in the face of Iraqi objections (e.g., in Fallujah). Contracting local Sunni Arab proxies in Fallujah did little to stop violent attacks in the city, but it did indicate the potential value of negotiations as a way of splitting the intractable resisters—senior former regime elements and Salafist terrorists— from the broader mass of Iraqis who were more amenable to deal-making and political reintegration. As opposed to the military-technical approach that had previously characterized the counterinsurgency effort, these insights led to the development of a truly political-military approach that shaped the offensive operations undertaken throughout the rest of the year to prevent the maintenance or formation of no-go zones.

From May to August 2004, the U.S. military undertook a range of unilateral and joint U.S.–Iraqi operations to roll back insurgent gains across the country. The military returned to no-go zones such as "RPG alley" in Samarra and Haifa Street in Baghdad, and opened up previously denied areas to Coalition civil-affairs and intelligence-collection elements. The United States also prepared for a larger and conclusive rollback operation at Fallujah. But first, it was given an early chance to incorporate the military and political lessons learned in the spring during the second round of major combat operations against Moqtada al-Sadr's Jaish al-Mahdi militia in August. Sadr's new challenge came merely weeks after the establishment of the new IIG. It involved weeks of cease-fire violations, reoccupation of the Imam Ali shrine in Najaf, and another widespread uprising throughout the south.

The first serious crisis since the transition of power to the IIG, the second Sadrist uprising represented a test of the Coalition's ability to work in partnership with the new government. Although the IIG limited some Coalition freedom of action, it also assisted in the development of consent for military operations within the Shiite community and guided U.S. forces in their calibration of violence and their selection of operational aims. Whereas Brig. Gen. Mark Kimmitt, the deputy head of U.S. military operations in Iraq, had threatened in April to "hunt down and destroy" Sadr, by May the 1st Armored Division commander Maj. Gen. Martin Dempsey was able to enunciate a subtler aim. Dempsey stated, "Essentially we want to eliminate Muqtada Sadr's ability to intimidate."

When U.S. 1st Cavalry Division and Marine forces turned on Jaish al-Mahdi forces in Najaf and elsewhere, they were operating on a battlefield that had been fought over extensively during Operation Iraqi Freedom (when Fedayeen resisted from Najaf's old city and graveyards) and the April uprising. After civilians were largely evacuated from the battlefield, the U.S. operation in Najaf penned the Jaish al-Mahdi into an ever-smaller and better-surveilled pocket. Inside this pocket, the United States scrupulously vetted fire requests in the direction of the Imam Ali shrine, yet still managed to use stand-off firepower wherever militiamen gathered. For example, it dropped one 2,000-pound bomb merely 130 meters from the southwest wall of the shrine.[48] Although the Old City of Najaf suffered heavy damage, the shrines remained almost untouched by the fighting that raged around them. This allowed the Coalition's IIG partners to maintain the consent required to allow the U.S. military to fight Sadr to a standstill and threaten to keep inflicting dissimilar losses on his forces until they backed down.

Following the battle of Najaf and the defeat of the second Sadrist uprising, the Coalition continued to roll back insurgent havens throughout the country. It focused its efforts on eighteen major cities considered crucial to the success of the January elections. By expediting the deployment of certain formations and deploying the outward rotation of others, U.S. commanders amassed close to 185,000 U.S. troops in Iraq as the fall began. Reducing the number of static defensive positions guarded by U.S. forces, which had previously consumed an estimated 56 percent of U.S. troop strength, freed up higher proportions of these forces for offensive operations. In

September and October, the Coalition and Iraqi security forces launched large-scale, intelligence-led joint operations to reestablish military presence in key cities such as Tall Afar, Samarra, Ramadi, Baqubah, and Tikrit. At the same time, U.S. commanders utilized new flows of targeting intelligence provided by the IIG to launch weeks of preparatory air strikes on identified insurgent safe houses and bomb-making workshops in Fallujah. The rising drumfire of air strikes, which reached approximately fifty a day in the lead-up to the assault on Fallujah, evoked little negative public reaction in Iraq or the international community because of both the Coalition's careful restriction of media access to Fallujah and the political cover offered by its new partnership with a sovereign Iraqi government.[49]

When the long-awaited battle of Fallujah commenced on November 8, 2004, the Coalition put into play the lessons that it had learned throughout the year. Comparisons with Operation Vigilant Resolve, the foiled assault on Fallujah in April, are fruitful. On the first count, although the November assault had an English-language code name, it was also given an Arabic-language code name, al-Fajr or "dawn," to reflect joint U.S.–Iraqi involvement. Similar to the August Sadrist revolt, the operation was given political cover by the IIG, which built the political consensus needed to mandate the operation. The April operation had taken place in a city full of civilians and media, whereas the November assault went in only after approximately 90 percent of the city's occupants and all of its media had been evacuated, which allowed an extensive artillery and aerial preparation of the battlefield. U.S. Marine Corps doctrine called for a divisional-size effort to take on a city of Fallujah's size—roughly twenty kilometers square, with a thousand city blocks and fifty thousand buildings—but the April assault had gone in with only two Marine battalions and no Iraqi forces. In contrast, the November assault used six battalions of U.S. forces and two battalions of reliable Iraqi special forces, the latter of which were used to secure Fallujah's hundred mosques and other sensitive sites.

The ten-day battle that followed was arguably the fiercest seen in the history of the U.S.–Iraq conflict in terms of the risks faced by combatants on both sides. Insurgents had dug tunnels and trenches throughout the approaches to the city center and placed mines and booby traps throughout the deserted urban landscape. Sixty of Fallujah's hundred mosques contained arms or had been converted into strongpoints, and many other arms caches were lodged throughout the city. More than 2,000 defenders were dug in, typically in mobile groups of fewer than 10 men operating according to a basic defensive plan. In the sixteen hours required to capture the Muhammadia mosque, U.S. and Iraqi forces were subjected to heavy RPG and small arms fire, counter-attacks, and suicide bombs developed at the eleven bomb-making workshops found in Fallujah after the battle. Fifty-one U.S. troops were killed in Fallujah during the operation and another 20 in clearance operations afterward. Approximately 1,200 U.S. forces were wounded—roughly a fifth of all assault troops—including 425 seriously injured. In terms of the fruits of the city's reduction as an insurgent base, approximately 1,200 enemy fighters were killed and 1,000 captured.

The city ceased to be a threat to nearby LOCs or the forthcoming elections, and was instead rebuilt under the tightest surveillance as a model Iraqi city. The high levels of destruction required to root out diehard fighters rendered the city uninhabitable and, in any case, the U.S. Marines bermed off all approaches to the city. Small numbers of returnees were carefully screened, fingerprinted, retinal scanned, and given identification badges to wear at all times. Private vehicles were banned in the city to prevent car bombings. Despite the destruction, depopulation, and draconian social engineering of Fallujah, criticism from the Sunni Arab community was minimal, which sent a clear message to the hard core of insurgents about the willingness and capability of the new government and the Iraqi nation to act against them.[50]

The reduction of the insurgent stronghold in Fallujah was the centerpiece of the strategy developed in summer to build the population's confidence in the Coalition's ability to secure Iraq in time for the January elections. If Fallujah could be secured, the logic ran, any area could be secured. Although no Iraqi city enjoyed as permanent or as traumatic a transformation as Fallujah, all but a few (e.g., Mosul and Ramadi) emerged from the fall months more firmly under Coalition control than they had previously been during 2004.

In the final weeks before the elections, Coalition security operations consisted of a rolling program of small, intelligence-led raids against bomb-making workshops and other targets. Alongside these raids, a specialized security scheme to protect the January 30 elections was put into effect throughout the country. The identities of election workers and candidates, plus the location of voting facilities, were concealed as long as possible. Increased security measures during January 29–31 included the closure of borders and a ban on the movement of private vehicles between provinces, which aimed to disrupt the movement of car bombs between bomb-making workshops and their target areas. Layered checkpoints and pedestrian areas were set up around 5,776 voting stations (reduced from 9,000 to allow tighter security at each). Coalition rapid-reaction forces handled outer-tier security and approximately one hundred thousand Iraqi security forces undertook personnel searches inside the cordon. To maximize the number of Coalition forces available in this final period, U.S. forces in Iraq stockpiled supplies for weeks beforehand, which reduced the need escort convoys during the final run-in to elections.

SECURING THE ELECTIONS

Both the Coalition and its enemies had long recognized that the transitional process was a fulcrum on which their efforts to control Iraq pivoted. Whereas the Coalition had previously identified the military dismantling of the insurgent movements and then briefly the hearts and minds of Iraqis as centers of gravity, it had been clear since summer that the transitional process and elections offered a means of striking at the root causes of the insurgency by reintegrating the Sunni and clearing a path for the withdrawal of foreign troops. Likewise, the former regime element and Salafist hard core of the insurgency were certain to seek to undermine the elections because, in the words found in a captured Salafist communiqué, the development of local security forces and democracy in Iraq threatened the insurgency with "suffocation." The communiqué further noted, "There is no doubt that the space in which we can move has begun to shrink and that the grip around the throats of the mujahidin has begun to tighten. With the deployment of soldiers and police, the future has become frightening." The letter warns "the gap ... will emerge between us and the people of the land. How can we fight their cousins and their sons and under what pretext after the Americans, who hold the reins of power from their rear bases, pull back? Democracy is coming, and there will be no excuse thereafter."[51]

On polling day itself, insurgents launched almost 200 attacks, including 108 attacks on election infrastructure, yet fewer spectacular bombings occurred than were expected. Eight suicide bombers carrying explosive vests accounted for the majority of the twenty-five Iraqi voters and eight Iraqi security personnel killed on election day, a remarkably low death toll given the circumstances surrounding Iraq's first post-Saddam election. Considering that an average of thirty-one car bombs had been detonated in Iraq since the transition of power in June 2004, it was a triumph that no car bombs were detonated on elections day.[52] Weeks of boosted security conditions and Multinational Forces (MNF) offensive operations, and the three-day special security procedures, forced insurgents to use stand-off means of attack such as mortar fire. In the face of robust Coalition patrolling and counterfire capabilities, these attacks had a minimal effect on turnout.

Preelection violence had a far greater negative effect on turnout. Even under intense Coalition pressure, the insurgency excelled at intimidation in the Sunni triangle towns. Before election day, insurgents and terrorists launched dozens of bombings and assassinations against Iraqi security forces, government officials, and electoral workers. Intimidated electoral staff and Iraqi security forces failed to open polling stations in smaller areas that lacked priority support from the Coalition. Many eligible voters were deterred from going to the polls, afraid to leave their homes or risk bearing the indelible ink marks used for voter identification.

As a result of security shortfalls combined with clerical calls for a Sunni boycott and a lack of local candidates, turnout in the core provinces of the Sunni triangle was low. In Anbar province, home of resistance hotspots Fallujah (which had only a quarter of its population resettled) and Ramadi, less than 2 percent turnout was recorded. In Nineva, which includes populous centers such as Mosul and Tall Afar, turnout was only 17 percent and only 93 of the province's 330 polling stations were opened. A similar turnout was registered in Salahuddin province cities such as Samarra, Tikrit, and Balad. The highest levels of Sunni turnout occurred in Baquba and the rest of Diyala province (an estimated 50 percent) and predominantly Sunni Arab West Baghdad (estimated 65 percent). The low Sunni Arab turnout reduced the overall success of the elections: insurgent political and military action put off the decisive struggle for the political heart of the Sunni Arab community to a future date.

This temporary disruption could not disguise the negative effect that the elections were likely to have on the insurgency in the mid- to long-term future. The elections marked a new milestone that had been imperfectly but successfully reached in Iraq's transition to representative government. The unbroken chain of transitional steps slowly built confidence in the cautious Iraqi public. Although the January polls were the twentieth set of national elections to be held in Iraq since 1921, they were the first to accurately reflect the cluttered political landscape of the country. In every one of the previous nineteen elections or plebiscites, the polls resulted in a clear majority of at least 70 percent of parliamentary seats for the winning Sunni Arab faction. The Iraqi transitional government (ITG), brought in following the January elections, broke this mold. It was a broad-based institution and the first Iraqi government to rise and fall on the success of the cross-sectarian Coalition politics. Although prone to be slow-moving, consensus-based government, prone to deadlock, inertia, and procrastination, it represented a true demography of the nation and thus stood a chance of moving Iraq toward a realistic and sustainable political balance of power.

The disenfranchisement of the Sunni Arab community led to the beginning of efforts to integrate the political wings of insurgent groups based in Iraq, Jordan, and Syria into the development of the new constitution. These initiatives were the first step in the long process of fracturing the insurgency, separating out the strands that could not accommodate themselves to the new Iraq—such as Salafist terrorist factions—from those who could. For instance, when a huge car bomb killed 125 Iraqis and injured another 130 at Hillah on February 28, 2005, condemnation came from both the government and Sunni religious leaders usually associated with the resistance.

By offering to bring the Sunni Arab community back into the political fold, hopes of a slow normalization of the security environment were raised. The rejectionist elements would continue to plant car bombs and carry out internecine assassinations against so-called collaborators within their own community, but many former regime elements or nationalist insurgent groups would mobilize on a less-frequent basis when their vital interests were challenged at the local level. In time, Sunni areas are likely to develop threat profiles more akin to the areas in which Sadr's Jaish al-Mahdi militia were active, where the widespread use of violence was threatened more frequently than it was used. In other words, the Coalition had clawed its way back to where it started in April 2003, before it failed the first two great tests of the occupation period and breathed life into the regime's planned resistance effort.

Epilogue
America's Fifteen-Year War in Iraq

T he elections of January 2005 did not mark the end of U.S. military
involvement in Iraq. Instead, the events of 2004 showed that the U.S.
and Coalition military presence was the glue holding a fragile transitional
process together. Nevertheless, by the time the polls closed on January 31,
2005, the record of U.S. military involvement in Iraq had encompassed the full
gamut of military missions that the Pentagon could be expected to undertake
in the post–Cold War era.

The U.S. military confrontation in Iraq started as an attempt to check
Iraq's expansionist military policies at a time when the cream of Iraq's million-
man military stood on the Kuwaiti border with little to stop it from seizing
the heart of the global economy—the oil fields of Saudi Arabia. Fifteen years
later, the U.S. military was securing Iraq's first post-Baathist elections. In
the interim period, U.S. military forces fought large-scale mechanized warfare, carried out the first major post–Cold War humanitarian effort in Iraqi
Kurdistan, christened and maintained a set of no-fly zones and maritime intercept operations for more than a decade, engaged in stand-off coercive
strikes, provided intelligence support to UN inspection teams, fought another
conventional war, and occupied and partially rebuilt a fractious and violent
country.

The unparalleled post–Cold War commitment of the U.S. military to
contain and recast Iraq made the Pentagon's efforts in that country the defining

experience of the modern U.S. military. It was a make-or-break experience that tested the endurance of an entire generation of soldiers, sailors, and aviators. The constant maritime and aerial patrolling stretched the personnel and equipment of the U.S. Navy, U.S. Marine Corps, and, above all, the U.S. Air Force to breaking point during more than a decade of containment. Following Operation Iraqi Freedom, the U.S. Army bore the burden along with the other services; tremendous pressure was placed on the all-volunteer force and the reserve component. For this armed service, the experience of postwar Iraq was the beginning of a new era, which Thomas Ricks identified as a new "training revolution" that echoed the post-Vietnam revitalization of the U.S. Army.[1] Iraq was the anvil on which the modern 21st-century U.S. military was forged and sharpened.

At the same time, the story of America's military struggle with Iraq is a cautionary tale. It chronicles the means that an aspiring regional hegemon developed to resist U.S. military power. From an American perspective, the struggle with Iraq highlighted the difficulties encountered by the world's pre-eminent military power in modifying the behavior of a determined regional adversary. This dynamic struggle is replete with lessons about the strengths and limitations of U.S. military power at the dawn of the 21st-century.

A net assessment of U.S. military performance must recognize that CENTCOM met its minimum strategic objectives of containing Iraq's large-scale military activism for more than a decade, reversed Baghdad's annexation of Kuwait, and neutered the overland invasion threat that the Iraqi military posed to its neighbors. There is no question that the U.S. military could have successfully continued its offensive toward Baghdad in March 1991 or at any time thereafter if U.S. politicians had asked it to do so. Instead, the United States engaged in a limited war of militarized containment, spanning the administrations of three U.S. presidents. During this period, CENTCOM prevented Iraqi expansionism but frequently failed to achieve the more difficult political objective of compelling Iraq to cease active resistance to the cease-fire terms of the 1991 war. Coercion failed time and time again. Invasion was finally necessary to effect regime removal, although what it actually achieved was regime dispersal and thus necessitated additional years of conflict to root out resistance.

Is this an unnecessarily harsh judgment to place at the feet of the world's greatest military, an institution more used to being feted? This book argues that U.S. national interests are best served by developing a more sober understanding of the modern U.S. military that recognizes its weaknesses as well as strengths. The very fact that regime removal in Operation Iraqi Freedom was necessary is an indicator of the paucity of U.S. military capability to compel the Iraqi state to quit its resistance during the preceding decade. Put simply, despite its overwhelming ability to destroy symmetrical fielded armed forces, the U.S. military rarely enjoyed a good chance of achieving its overarching strategic objective—that is, to decisively end resistance. Why was this?

The many myths surrounding U.S. militarized containment of Iraq have served to obfuscate the real reasons for the strategic frustration felt by three American governments. It is a myth, for instance, that President Bill Clinton was "softer" on Iraq than his predecessor or successor. Limited pinprick strikes were initiated by President George H. W. Bush. The Clinton regime inherited the containment of Iraq. Clinton's successor, President George W. Bush, continued limited strikes and planned to undertake limited and gradual dismembering of Baathist control until 9/11 changed the strategic equation.

It would be a mischaracterization to paint the Clinton team as uniquely concerned with political blowback from military actions; for example, although Clinton sought to minimize regime casualties in the 1993 strike on Iraq's intelligence services, the administration of George W. Bush undertook a similar vetting of intelligence targets to prevent the deaths of civilians working at regime strongholds in 2003. Equally, however, it is also a myth that the Clinton administration was any wiser on Iraq or its WMDs than the George W. Bush administration or that it was any less committed to a unilateral policy of regime change. Throughout the second Clinton term, the White House authorized increasingly vigorous military actions and fully believed that Iraq owned and planned to reconstitute its WMD capabilities, eventually precipitating the crisis that would end UN inspections. The common thread running through all three presidencies was U.S. military hesitance concerning increased military commitments in Iraq.

ANALYZING IRAQI RESISTANCE

The most significant factors explaining the decade of frustrated U.S. strategic objectives in Iraq were the intransigent nature of the Iraqi regime, its self-destructive addiction to resistance, and the Iraqi security establishment's ingenuity. In America's fifteen-year war in Iraq, the enemy had a vote and cast it regularly. The Iraqis displayed three characteristics that may represent a template for the types of adversary the United States will increasingly face in the 21st-century: They were highly adaptive. They fought for (and sometimes maintained) intelligence superiority. And they maintained the types of forces that were most useful for resistance.

ASYMMETRIC RESISTANCE AS ADAPTATION

Above all, the story of the U.S. military confrontation with Iraq was one of resistance and asymmetry. Although the word resistance is now synonymous with the postwar insurgency in Iraq, the broader phenomenon of resistance characterizes the entire period of the U.S. military confrontation with Iraq. At the political level, there was an underlying asymmetry in the levels of commitment shown by the United States and Iraq. Until the administration of President George W. Bush, the United States viewed Iraq's resistance through the prism of the limited threat that Saddam posed to America's vital interests. This sharply contrasted with the life-or-death struggle for political and physical survival waged by the Baathist regime in Iraq.

Baghdad's resistance to the United States began from the moment that the Baathist regime refused to evacuate Kuwait in August 1990, although Saddam had hoped that the confrontation would be limited to the administration of George H. W. Bush. When the Clinton administration continued to support the postwar restrictions on Iraq, the Baathist regime committed to a long-term policy of resistance against the U.S.-led effort. Ongoing resistance became the raison d'être of the regime, a means of turning internal anger outward and displaying regional leadership and an ongoing role on the global stage. As long as the U.S. government was prepared to contain the Iraqi regime but not to develop a reliable mechanism to unseat it, Baghdad's cheat-and-retreat strategy of resistance did not harm the regime's chances for survival. As soon as a U.S. government decided to unseat Saddam, the situation reversed. By late 2002, the regime belatedly recognized that the time for resistance had passed and that confrontation had become a greater threat to the regime than acquiescence, but by then the regime was addicted to resistance and too set in its ways to give up its compulsive intransigence.

When Operation Iraqi Freedom began, the regime apparently had nothing to lose as it set in motion its final resistance effort. However, it believed it still had something to gain and launched a nationalist and Islamic-based resistance effort instead of taking the fatalistic "Samson option" of scorched-earth sabotage. The blend of nationalistic, Islamic, and sectarian motifs employed by the remnants of the Baathist regime drew on a deep well of sentiment that were used to foster an indigenous Sunni Arab resistance. All through the era of Baathist rule, various Sunni Arab tribes and interest groups had feuded with the regime to maintain their autonomy over tribal territories and access to resources and awards. Unless their interests were taken into account, the Sunni Arab minority would likewise resist foreign invaders and occupiers. The Baathist resistance took advantage of the Coalition's failure to manage Sunni Arab political reintegration and tapped into this well of discontent and fear to raise a new army of resisters under the very noses of the occupation forces. The proclivity of Iraqis to resist was greater than any one man or group of henchmen, as evidenced by the continuation of the insurgency after the capture of almost the entire pantheon of high-ranking Baathists.

The story of the regime's fifteen-year resistance to the United States also chronicles the adaptation of a regional adversary to overwhelming U.S. military power. The Baathist regime's million-man army may have ebbed away during the militarized containment of Iraq, but its intention and capability to resist U.S. pressure survived throughout and beyond the life span of the dictatorship. Under Saddam, Iraq resisted the U.S. role as policeman of the Gulf and its military continued to mount armed challenges in the face of apparently insurmountable Iraqi military inferiority. In terms of Iraq's ability to invade and overthrow a neighboring country, Baghdad largely ceased to be an existential threat to its neighbors during the 1991 Gulf War; this would have continued to be the case as long as sanctions and UN inspections were effectively maintained.

This somewhat misses the point, however, because although Iraq's military had become a third-rate force, the Baathist regime was determined to continue to play a disruptive role on the regional and global stage using whatever military means it could continue to muster. First, Saddam attempted to retain Kuwait as the 19th province of Iraq, hoping to at least retreat with some of his forces intact and claim the honorific of having stood up to the last remaining superpower and survived. Although the Iraqi nation and armed forces were mauled in the unsuccessful annexation of Kuwait, the regime was able to put a brave face on the so-called "mother of all battles" and direct some blame onto the Shiite and Kurdish rebels, whose intifada was termed the "chapter of treason and treachery."

As this book outlines, the Baathist regime ramped up its resistance to the United States and United Nations as soon as the Safwan cease-fire was signed. Weapons inspections and the no-fly zones were the first platforms Saddam used to display his defiance and seek to preserve his future military capability and sovereign control over Iraq. By 1993 the conflict had become fully militarized again, following Saddam's attempts to chase President George H. W. Bush out of office with aggressive military action in January of that year and to assassinate him in Kuwait less than a hundred days later. In both 1994 and 1996, Saddam demonstrated his ability to launch limited but profile-raising military expeditions to the southern and northern borders of Baathist-controlled Iraq. With the global Coalition facing the Baathist government fragmenting and with Iraq's conventional military falling apart, Saddam used the UN weapons inspectors as a platform to resist the Coalition and to renege on his international obligations. When the Clinton administration collapsed this platform in December 1998, Saddam turned to the only remaining area where he could militarily resist the United States and its allies: the no-fly zones.

Iraq's military challenge to the United States says much about the way regional adversaries cope in the face of crushing conventional military disparity. Conventional wisdom states that regional militaries will increasingly adopt asymmetric tactics and organization to offset their inability to maintain symmetric parity with advanced Western militaries. Many existing analyses of this coevolutionary dynamic are unconvincing because of their assumption that war-fighting institutions function as "rational systems" that learn and adapt automatically. This simplification has spawned mechanistic and abstract models of adversary adaptation. For example, depiction of military-technical adaptation as self-canceling or "paradoxical" assumes that adversaries have the intellectual and material capital, and the cultural and organizational flexibility, to automatically adapt to technological advances by the enemy.[2] Likewise, analysts of asymmetric warfare have often presumed that adversaries possess very high levels of organizational learning capacity and that each will develop rather similar asymmetric styles of warfare based on an accurate appreciation and imaginative exploitation of their opponents' vulnerabilities. The literature of asymmetric warfare thus often assumes that asymmetric adaptation will be undertaken in an extreme form, with conventional military efforts being replaced by WMDs and cyber-terrorism.

The case study of Iraq illustrates that asymmetric adaptation is more varied and less predictable than anticipated and is rooted in the strategic culture and circumstances of the disadvantaged adversary. Throughout their fifteen-year record of military activism against the United States, Saddam Hussein and other Iraqis utilized a broad range of military capabilities to challenge and frustrate the U.S. military.

FOCUS ON COUNTERINTELLIGENCE

The cornerstones of Iraq's ability to mount a credible defense and resist U.S. military pressure were the regime's largely successful counterintelligence efforts combined with a deliberate preservation of Iraqi conventional military assets and the ambiguity surrounding Iraq's suspected WMD arsenal. Locked in a militarized struggle, the United States could never generate strategic surprise in its dealings with Iraq, nor could it generate tactical surprise because of Iraq's exhaustive watch for signs of U.S. military preparation. Many U.S. military strikes on strategic targets fell days after Iraqi evacuation efforts had cleared vital personnel and equipment out of key facilities, resulting in the "empty building syndrome" described in earlier chapters. Technology rarely delivered tactical surprise. For instance, although U.S. stealth aircraft could evade most Iraqi radars, their well-publicized deployment to theater was a clear sign of an impending attack. Long-range global-strike capabilities were similarly signposted whenever Western press reported that the B-52s were in the air. U.S. land forces and attack helicopter strikes were detected by a low-tech network of spotters with cell phones. Whether it was the U.S. military or the UN inspection teams that were tracked, Iraq's intelligence apparatus often remained one step ahead of Western attempts to develop the levels of tactical surprise necessary to achieve decisive military or political effects.

Working on the principle that U.S. forces could not destroy what they could not find, Iraq demonstrated a strong ability to negate U.S. military power by breaking down or operating within CENTCOM's targeting cycle or hiding its most precious strategic assets. Iraq frequently denied the U.S. military the information dominance it needed to achieve its complex political and military objectives. The Iraqi military fought from within the population as another means of preserving its assets and complicating the targeting challenge faced by its adversaries. Iraq's use of mobility, concealment, and deception frequently frustrated the cutting-edge strike capabilities of the post–Cold War U.S. military; for example, cheap and simple wooden decoys and scrap-metal hulks soaked up hundreds of expensive PGMs. Moreover, the United States could only find, fix, target, and track the targets of least value to the Baathist hierarchy—numerous or easily repaired weapons systems and empty buildings.

Preservation and deception were therefore adeptly used by the Baathist regime. The West cautiously assessed the continuing threat posed by Iraq's conventional forces and its suspected WMD programs because of this. The regime deliberately preserved the best elements of the former and maintained ambiguity concerning the latter. Baghdad's "Fabian strategy"—referring to the Roman general who frustrated Hannibal's conquest of Italy by refusing decisive battle—consistently confounded U.S. military planners by foregoing the use of key military capabilities in clashes with the United States in order to vouchsafe them for future conflicts where they might be used more decisively against regional adversaries. This reflected the regime's unshakeable belief that it would survive its confrontation with the United States and return to the regional stage. Iraq accepted war-fighting penalties by eschewing the use of advanced fixed C2 sites in Operation Desert Storm and quickly abandoned use of its acquisition radar and aircraft in the face of heavy attrition. Throughout the remainder of the military conflict, Iraq continually husbanded its air defenses and the Iraqi Air Force took no part in Operation Iraqi Freedom. Eschewing the use of such assets turned them into "nonemitters"—equipment that no longer gave off a distinctive electronic or visual signature—and rendered them largely invisible to a U.S. military reliant on technical intelligence-collection tools.

Even as Baathist control of Baghdad ended, the regime was planning its next stage of resistance and encouraging its loyalists to shed their uniforms, go home, await contact, and thereby survive to fight another day. The regime favored deliberate ambiguity concerning its nonconventional capabilities while simultaneously preserving the scientific base necessary to resurrect the deeply hibernated programs as soon as UN sanctions and inspections were lifted. Preservation and deterrence through deception were linchpins of Iraq's asymmetric adaptation to U.S. military power, although, in actuality, preservation often became terminal decay and each element of the Baathist system habitually deceived each other as well as the United States.

PRESERVING ELITE FORCES

Iraq's preservation of its military forces was successful because the Baathist government quickly realized that the regime's true armed capabilities lay within smaller and smaller cadres of forces. The acme of skill in conventional warfare may be the creation of disciplined large-scale forces that enjoy training and technological advantages, but such forces are not necessary for resistance. Most of Iraq's hollow military represented mere window dressing, functioning largely to keep hundreds of thousands of Iraqis on the government payroll. Large-scale Iraqi formations still operated in an offensive capacity until 1996 and retained internal security functions thereafter, but Iraq's military challenge was increasingly built on elite cadres. The resistance capability of the air-defense system rested with the roaming expeditionary SAM groups. Iraq's ability to penetrate Saudi and Jordanian air space was the responsibility of the tiny MiG-25 community. Although the Republican Guard represented the regime's remaining conventional military force, it was left exposed to Coalition air operations in 2003 and frittered away on Baghdad's outskirts. The real territorial defense system was built around Baathist enforcers, each of whom controlled networks of young loyalist paramilitaries such as the Fedayeen.

U.S. V Corps Commander Wallace described the enemy ORBAT as "incomprehensible" and declared that he found it unsettling to fight an enemy that did not appear to have a plan.[3] In fact, the asymmetric ORBAT and defensive plan were a valid and deliberate Iraqi counterpoise to overwhelming U.S. military power in the conventional sphere of armored and aerial operations. U.S. occupation forces sifting through the wreckage of the Iraqi military were struck by the many contradictory characteristics of Iraq's armed forces. Large-scale formations had atrophied completely, beset by lack of resources, corruption, and mismanagement. Yet, many of the most important niche capabilities had been lovingly maintained and even modernized using smuggled spare parts, local research and development, and elite operators. As Colonel Crowder noted, Iraq could not build large disciplined armed forces, but it could "maintain and create discipline within groups of twenty—the very smart and innovative air defense operators who fought us day in and day out for over a decade, the individual platoons who fought during the war or in the insurgency."[4] These "groups of twenty" arguably represent a template of the kinds of small but capable enemies that will face America in the 21st century.

The decay of Iraq's military affected these cadres less than its other elements, allowing the regime to maintain a surprising capacity to resist. Although the Iraqi security establishment was boiled down to an ever-smaller core, that core became harder and more effective. The ultimate expression of this trend is the relative effectiveness of Iraq's million-man army in 1991 and its insurgents since 2003. Iraq inflicted 184 U.S. fatalities in 1991, whereas Iraqi militants inflicted almost 1,300 U.S. combat deaths between March 2003 and the time of writing in June 2005. At closer range, over a longer time-frame, the United States is now engaged toe-to-toe with the last remnants of the Baathist regime's elite cadres—the bomb makers and assassins of the Mukhabarat's M-14 and M-21 sections. Viewed over the continuum of the U.S. conflict with Iraq, the Baathist regime's key military attribute was adaptability, evident in the fluid transition from conventional military resistance by fielded land forces, to guerrilla air defense, and finally to irregular warfare and terrorism.

EXPOSURE OF U.S. MILITARY WEAKNESSES

Iraqi resistance may have used conventional military and guerilla tools, eschewing exotic asymmetric means such as cyberattacks, but it was truly asymmetric because it focused on exploiting the weaknesses of its principal opponent, the U.S. military. Although it is the preeminent military power of the early 21st century, the United States displayed a range of military strengths and weaknesses in its confrontation with Iraq. Some of these features have been highlighted in dozens of reports and books concerning individual U.S. military operations in Iraq, particularly the large-scale operations in 1991 and 2003.

Such analyses tend to focus on the tactical or operational levels of war, particularly their military-technical components. In contrast, the long view of the continuum of operations between 1990 and 2005 highlights the way in which the pursuit of political-military objectives at the strategic level of the conflict interacted with military-technical aspects of the operational and tactical levels. For example, it is impossible to judge the political and military effectiveness of Operation Desert Storm in 1991 without examining the postwar survival of the Baathist government and the decade of Iraqi intransigence that followed. Likewise, it is impossible to understand the apparent ease with which Baghdad was captured during Operation Iraqi Freedom without understanding the continual military operations being undertaken against Iraq since 1991. Finally, the political and military effectiveness of Operation Iraqi Freedom can only be assessed in the light of the postwar insurgency. Using the superior vantage point of long-term study of the Iraq conflict, one key question needs to be addressed: how could the United States military have been more successful in Iraq?

At the military-technical level, the long view of America's highly varied military operations in Iraq suggests that no single military formula, no single combination of force structures or technologies, could have served the U.S. military in all the wide variety of operations that it undertook in Iraq (and thus will be required to undertake in the future). Analyses originating from Operation Iraqi Freedom have stressed the factors that allowed rapid penetration to the Baathist interior and the scattering of Iraq's armed forces, such as technological and training superiority, high tempo and precision warfare, and joint action. These are all worthy characteristics of the U.S. military that have frequently reduced the losses and increased the per-unit efficiency of U.S. formations. Improvements can and should continue to be made in each dimension. Technological and training superiority are edges that require constant sharpening, ongoing maintenance through investment. True precision warfare requires increased numbers and varieties of networked sensors capable of locating stationary or nonemitting targets, identifying decoys and noncombatants, and tracking all friendly units in the battlespace. Joint action must mean more than deconfliction or "staying out of each other's way"; it must mean seamless shared understanding of the battlespace. Such sensible recommendations are by now platitudes.

The long view of CENTCOM's fifteen-year cycle of coadaptation with Iraq's armed forces suggests that adaptability, rather than any single military formula, needs to be the key attribute of the future U.S. military. Iraq's movement toward its style of asymmetric warfare was a direct result of the qualitative explosion of U.S. military power in the 1990s and validated the technologically advanced Western way of war utilized by the U.S. military in the post–Cold War era. The overarching lesson to emerge from the American military's highly varied missions in Iraq is that the technologically driven revolution in military affairs is necessary but not sufficient to transform America into the dominant military power of the 21st century. It is not enough to shift from being configured to fight the mechanized foe that Iraq was in 1990 to being ready to fight the terrorist foe that Iraqi adversaries became by 2005.

Instead, there is a real and pressing need for true "full spectrum dominance," which means the ability to generate decisive military effects at all intensities of conflict and the suppleness to track and shadow the changing requirements of fighting an adaptive enemy. The first step on this path is an honest recognition that the United States did not win every battle in its fifteen-year struggle with Iraq and cannot win every tactical engagement in the future. What America's military can do is to learn from the lessons of such setbacks at a faster pace than its adversaries.

In general, the United States will not be able to choose the types of adversaries that it will fight or the durations of its wars, even if such conflicts are fought preemptively. The finessed economization of force—using lighter forces and causing less destruction—is a laudable goal but may not always be possible. As an example, whereas Operation Iraqi Freedom captured Iraq's capital with unprecedented economy of forces by using high-tempo operations to dislocate some of the regime's defensive plans, future nation-building operations stress the need for different force structures. U.S. organizational learning capabilities were markedly superior in short, intense clashes where Iraqi reaction was sluggish. In longer engagements such as the no-fly zones and the post–regime change insurgency, Iraqis proved far more effective at learning strategic, operational, and tactical lessons.

Does this mean that America should anchor its military superiority on fighting short, sharp wars and leaving others to do the rebuilding? On the contrary, a key lesson from Iraq is that not all wars can be short; some may take years, some may span decades. No one else may be willing to rebuild nations. And there may be stubborn resistance to U.S. presence, because it is intrinsically easier to resist than it is to snuff out resistance. As Tom Donnelly noted, although Operation Iraqi Freedom stressed the need for a "sprinter," other operations to suppress resistance (such as no-fly zone and maritime intercept policing or postwar nation building) require the attributes of a "marathon runner": larger forces that can remain deployed for longer periods. Developing this line of logic, Donnelly rightly argued that a larger U.S. Army should be built if further nation-building projects are to be undertaken almost unilaterally by the United States.[5] A right-sized force—meaning a larger force than currently exists—will ultimately be more adaptable than a smaller, over-committed force. Such a force can partially negate the asymmetric tactic of "waiting out" the United States.

INTELLIGENCE AND ADAPTATION

Many episodes of U.S. military weakness and slowness to adapt flowed from a limited understanding of the enemy and the environment in which the confrontation took place—in other words, weaknesses in the sphere of intelligence. The lack of timely and complete intelligence narrowed the strategic and tactical options of U.S. political and military decision makers throughout the struggle with Iraq. At the strategic level, the United States never truly gained an accurate appreciation of Iraqi public opinion or internal regime dynamics and intentions. It is true that U.S. intelligence assessments often intuitively guessed right, but policy makers were often left without firm evidence to back the informed hunches of the intelligence community. As a result, Iraq's capabilities were often poorly assessed, particularly in the realms of WMDs and defensive strategy. At the close of a fifteen-year process of trial and error, the United States was still unsure of the best way to win their hearts and minds of Iraqis, and alternately how to find and coerce or kill Iraqi resisters. U.S. analysts could only guess at how to shock and awe Iraqis, and later how to win their hearts and minds. The incomplete level of expertise gathered by the United States on Iraq took fifteen years of observation to develop; the next war could emerge without warning in a new and immature theater of operations.

At the operational and tactical levels, the U.S. intelligence community engaged in a dynamic intelligence and counterintelligence battle with their Iraqi counterparts. Indeed, in this dimension of the conflict, the two sides were far more evenly matched than in any other sphere. Strategic and tactical surprise was extremely difficult for the United States to generate. The U.S. military only infrequently gained information dominance. In the crassest sense, U.S. military commanders knew more than their adversaries did, particularly considering the endemic dishonesty that existed throughout the Iraqi reporting structure. However, the United States frequently lacked the kinds of intelligence—the current location of leadership figures and high-value military assets—that would have allowed it to achieve the operational effects it sought. When stand-off actions were launched, operational effects were extremely difficult to gauge. Limited intelligence was the bottleneck through which the behemoth of U.S. military power was forced to pass, and it constricted the options and the credibility of the U.S. military.

Intelligence failures meant that it frequently proved impossible to achieve the kind of psychological dominance over the enemy that is sought in warfare and has proven fundamental to successful coercive operations. Despite its manifest superiority, the U.S. military very rarely achieved the levels of "shock and awe" or "rapid dominance" it aimed to inflict. The real centers of gravity of the Baathist state were moving targets and were either only correctly identified at a late stage in the conflict or never located with sufficient precision to be effectively targeted. Coercive air strikes were often reduced to feckless destruction of empty buildings. Purportedly decisive ground operations mistakenly identified Baghdad as the regime's center of gravity, whereas in fact it was the key regime facilitators and bomb makers, the money, and the hearts and minds of the Sunni Arab population. By the time a U.S. military boot pinned Saddam's head to the ground, the former dictator was no longer the center of gravity that he had once been.

PROPER USES OF U.S. MILITARY POWER

One of the most important lessons to emerge from America's struggle with the Baathist regime is that the U.S. military may have been the preeminent military power at the dawn of the 21st century but it was far from invincible. A dangerous myth of invincibility had built up around the post–Cold War U.S. military, creating unrealistic expectations about the capabilities of the Pentagon. In terms of assuring America's defense, this was never more cruelly demonstrated than on 9/11, when the most sophisticated air-defense system in the world was sidestepped by a cunning and despicable adversary. In Iraq, the fallibility of the U.S. military was more subtle. The emergence of attritional warfare, clearly visible in the no-fly zones and the postwar insurgency, is the clearest indicator of an inability to shock the adversary, which resulted in periods of military deadlock and even partial withdrawal.

If the U.S. military is not invincible and if its success relies on suitable conditions, then it needs to be selectively and carefully employed. It should never be used to undertake hollow or cosmetic military operations that stand little chance of achieving political objectives. Although such actions might not result in the loss of blood or treasure, the deterrent effect of U.S. military power is degraded every time the U.S. military falls short of inflicting real pain on an adversary or fails to meet its objective.

Hollow U.S. military actions took place in Iraq when the United States perceived itself to be fighting for limited objectives with no vital interests at stake. Iraq's threat to Saudi Arabia deteriorated in 1991, after which the regime in Baghdad arguably no longer posed a threat to U.S. vital interests. From this point onward, realist calculations of U.S. national interests complicated the White House's ability to commit military force in Iraq throughout the 1990s. The disparity between Washington's limited objectives in Iraq versus the Baathist regime's internal war of survival placed the U.S. military at an inherent disadvantage, reducing its ability to employ decisive force or to risk major losses even though it was faced by a determined and cornered opponent. As early as 1991, senior U.S. officers recognized that the key impediment to a military resolution in Iraq lay not in the Baghdad regime's ability to defend itself but in the fear of overcommitment by U.S. political and military decision makers. It is notable that military decision makers were consistently more cautious than the politicians.

Following the failure of the United States to topple the regime in 1991, the Baathist leadership correctly gauged that it could survive endless cheat-and-retreat episodes throughout the 1990s. Why was this? The answer is simply that the United States failed to develop the political and technical credibility needed to deter a regional resister. At the political level, it was clear from the moment that Kuwait was liberated until late 2002 that no U.S. government was willing to commit ground troops to topple the regime of Saddam Hussein. Most other forms of military sanction inflicted so little real pain on the regime that there was no disincentive to carry out acts of resistance. Under President George H. W. Bush, the cycle of limited air and missile strikes began. Under President Bill Clinton, they increased in frequency but never secured dominance because they imposed such minimal costs on the regime. Only through Operation Desert Fox's partially intended focus on regime targets did the U.S. military give Saddam a shock, although even then the regime did not signal its willingness to scale back resistance until war clouds gathered in late 2002. Even at this point, however, Saddam was attempting to initiate a new episode of cheat and retreat, banking on his ability to outlast U.S. commitment to a new war or ride out what he imagined would be simply a larger version of Desert Fox. Here was a regime that had grown so confident—or perhaps overconfident—in its ability to sidestep U.S. military power that it could not be militarily compelled to conclusively cease its resistance. Either such resistance had to be tolerated—and it would surely have grown in time—or the regime had to be removed.

Did the conflict between the United States and Saddam's regime have to unfold like this? It took more than a decade of Saddam's intransigence and the increasing degradation of containment to lead the United States to embark on military regime change and occupation. Covert regime change through a coup or uprising had always been under consideration from August 1990 onward but was never pursued with sufficient vigor or willingness to accept risk, leaving the containment of Iraq to become the almost exclusive purview of the U.S. military.

Certain moments stand out as pivotal points in the U.S. conflict with the Baathist regime. Saddam's invasion of Kuwait in August 1990 is obviously one of them, and his decision to fight in January 1991 is another. The decision not to take the road to Baghdad in March 1991 was another fateful moment. Less obviously, a crucial remilitarization of the conflict occurred in late 1992 and early 1993. The search for WMD in Iraq was reinvigorated by Kamil Hussein's defection in 1995. Operation Desert Strike in September 1996 represents perhaps the lowest ebb of U.S. military performance versus Iraq. The year 1998 stands out as a pivotal year, which the Clinton administration recognized, perhaps belatedly, that Saddam could not be deterred from stirring up crises. Finally, in 2001 Saddam's fate was sealed by the 9/11 attacks and their galvanizing effect on the advocates of regime change. In sum, until 2001 the United States adopted a wait-and-see approach with Saddam, hoping against hope that he might fall from power through illness or internal challenge, or that he might at least relent in his resistance. Was there an alternative to this approach?

IRAQ AND DETERRENCE

Hindsight is 20/20, and the past fifteen years have granted key insights into the costs and benefits of both containment and regime change. Neither are cheap or easy options. Some might argue that Saddam had ceased to pose a threat to his neighbors and should have been contained until he and his odious regime dropped off the map completely. There are some merits to this argument. It would be disingenuous, however, to fail to recognize the costs inherent in a long-term strategy of containment. The post–Cold War world can not be equated with the Cold War world. The containment of Iraq did not enjoy the same unity of purpose that sustained the long-term containment of Communism, and neither will future containment efforts launched by the United States. Opposed by an intractable and ingenious foe such as Iraq, a strategy of containment required the constant injection of political, diplomatic, economic, and military capital, and even with that, Iraq's containment began to unravel uncontrollably. With hindsight, one might naturally conclude that we should have either taken the road to Baghdad in March 1991, when the regime lay wide open, or that we should have developed a truly effective effort to unseat Saddam using covert means in the years that followed.

The alternative—launching a military campaign to effect regime change years after the invasion of Kuwait—was always seen as controversial. No single act of resistance by the Baathist regime seemed to merit the invasion and occupation of a country. Knowing this, the U.S. administrations of President George H. W. Bush and President Bill Clinton felt they lacked the political credibility to threaten the military invasion and occupation of Iraq.

This is arguably the wrong way to view the strategic calculus of the U.S. government vis-à-vis the Baathist regime. Lack of political credibility will remain a key weakness of the U.S. grand strategy and strategic deterrence as long as the United States views the world in terms of direct threats to narrowly defined national interests. An alternative way of viewing the world would be to look upon regimes such as Saddam Hussein's Baathist government as intolerable beacons of resistance against U.S. global power. As Saddam's distribution of the book *Blackhawk Down* to his officer corps indicates, resistance to U.S. military power in one corner of the world (Somalia in that case) can encourage and bolster further resistance elsewhere. Now, resistance tactics from Iraq are replicated in the handbooks of Islamic terrorist organizations seeking to fight the United States in other theaters. In this unipolar age, when resistance to the hegemonic and globalizing power of the United States is likely to proliferate, resistance should not be viewed as an isolated phenomenon but should instead be diagnosed and treated as a global contagion.

The U.S. military has demonstrated determination in its decades-long commitment to Iraq—one of the most vital characteristics for a hegemonic power to display. Yet, a modern-day empire must demonstrate other characteristics such as foresight and flexibility if it is to maintain its freedom to act as a force for good. The Pentagon's record in Iraq between 1992 and 2005 stripped away some of the aura of invincibility that foreign countries had accorded to the U.S. military after Operation Desert Storm in 1991. If the United States moves toward a strategy of preempting threats and changing regimes, it must recognize that its military prowess is under review by potential adversaries on each and every one of these occasions. Such operations need to be considered and undertaken as exemplary deterrent engagements if they are to bolster the deterrent effect of U.S. military power.

America's war in Iraq provides key insights into the principles that such exemplary deterrent engagements should always seek to replicate. In military-technical terms, the United States needs to enter conflicts with a greater understanding of the true centers of gravity of targeted nations or groups. It is imperative to integrate military operations into a broader concatenation of pressures that include all the other instruments of national power from the intelligence, diplomatic, and economic spheres. In the recent case of Operation Iraqi Freedom, such a balanced political-military policy might have secured the fruits of the wartime blitz on Baghdad by developing a credible postwar plan to neutralize Iraq's Sunni Arab community as a source of resistance. A broader deterrence-based view of U.S. national interests need not be a prescription for perpetual war as long as exemplary deterrent engagements are integrated with other instruments of national power, are chosen with care, and are executed effectively and efficiently.

Notes

CHAPTER 1. RAISING THE SHIELD

1. Joyce Battle, ed., *Shaking Hands with Saddam Hussein: The U.S. Tilts toward Iraq, 1980–1984* (National Security Archive, 2004), http://www.gwu.edu/~nsarchive/NSAEBB/NSAEBB82/.
2. Ibid.
3. Douglas Borer, "Inverse Engagement: Lessons from US–Iraq Relations, 1982–1990," *Parameters* (Summer 2003), 54–55.
4. Brian G. Shellum, *Defense Intelligence Crisis Response Procedures and the Gulf War* (2002), http://www.dia.mil/History.Histories/response.html, 9–11.
5. Anthony H. Cordesman, *Kuwait: Recovery and Security after the Gulf War* (Boulder, Colo.: Westview, 1997), 66.
6. Bob Woodward, *The Commanders* (New York: Simon & Schuster, 1991), 184–86.
7. U.S. Department of Defense, *Conduct of the Persian Gulf War. Final Report to Congress* (Washington, D.C.: U.S. Department of Defense, 1992), 46.
8. Woodward, *Commanders*, 195.
9. Shellum, *Defense Intelligence Crisis*, 10.
10. Woodward, *Commanders*, 197.
11. Bruce Jentleson, *With Friends Like These: Reagan, Bush, and Saddam, 1982–90* (New York: Norton, 1994), 139.
12. Quoted in Woodward, *Commanders*, 184–86.
13. U.S. Department of Defense, *Conduct of the Persian Gulf War*, 42.

14. Kenneth Pollack. *Arabs at War: Military Effectiveness, 1948–1991* (London: University of Nebraska Press, 2002), 236–38.
15. Quoted in Woodward, *Commanders*, 211. All oil production and reserves figures are from from the U.S. Energy Information Administration website, http://www.eia.doe.gov/emeu/international/petroleu.htm#IntlProduction
16. U.S. Department of Defense, *Conduct of the Persian Gulf War*, 58.
17. Woodward, *Commanders*, 211.
18. Ibid., 246.
19. Ibid., 211.
20. U.S. Department of Defense, *Conduct of the Persian Gulf War*, 58.
21. Woodward, *Commanders*, 331.
22. Ibid., 225, 247.
23. Suzanna Gehri, Richard Reynolds, and Edward Mann, *Interview with Buster Glosson (Part One)*(Maxwell, Ala.: AFHRA, 1991), 23.
24. Perry D. Jamieson, *Lucrative Targets: The U.S. Air Force in the Kuwaiti Theater of Operations* (Washington, D.C.: Air Force History Support Office, 2001), 2.
25. U.S. Department of Defense, *Conduct of the Persian Gulf War*, 89.
26. Jamieson, *Lucrative Targets*, 2.
27. Suzanna Gehri, Richard Reynolds, and Edward Mann, *Interview with Steve Wilson* (Maxwell, Ala.: AFHRA, 1991), 19.
28. Charles Horner, "What We Should Have Learned from Desert Storm, but Didn't," *Air Force Magazine* (1996): 2.
29. Tom Clancy, *Into the Storm: A Study in Command* (New York: Putnam, 1997), 190.
30. Jamieson, *Lucrative Targets*, 33.
31. Michael W. Boardman, *Leashing the Hydra: Control of Joint Intelligence Architectures* (Naval War College, 1997), 5.
32. Robert Estvanik, *Intelligence and the Commander: Desert Shield/Desert Storm Case Study* (Naval War College, 1992), p. 30.
33. U.S. Department of Defense, *Conduct of the Persian Gulf War*, 388.
34. Ibid., 388.
35. Suzanna Gehri and Richard Reynolds, *Interview with General Michael Ryan* (Maxwell, Ala.: AFHRA, 1992), 18.
36. U.S. Department of Defense, *Conduct of the Persian Gulf War*, 257. Also see Coy Cross, *The Dragon Lady Meets the Challenge: The U-2 in Desert Storm* (Washington, D.C.: U.S. Department of Defense, 1991), 2.
37. John Stewart, *Operation Desert Storm: The Military Intelligence Story: A View from the G-2, US Third Army* (Washington, D.C.: U.S. Department of Defense,1991), 38.
38. Ibid., 4.
39. Ibid., 28.
40. U.S. Department of Defense, *Conduct of the Persian Gulf War*, 652.

41. Stewart, *Operation Desert Storm*, 28.
42. Ibid., 30.
43. U.S. Department of Defense, *Conduct of the Persian Gulf War*, 304. Also see Clancy, *Into the Storm*, 8.
44. Shellum, *Defense Intelligence Crisis*, 9–11.
45. U.S. Department of Defense, *Conduct of the Persian Gulf War*, 388.
46. IISS, *The Military Balance 1990–1991* (London: Oxford University Press, 1990), 35–36.
47. Pollack, *Arabs at War*, 149–267, with special focus on pp. 208–9.
48. Ibid., 192, 203, 206.
49. *Gulf War Airpower Study,* vol. 1, *Planning and Command and Control* (Washington, D.C.: U.S. Government, 1993), 73.
50. U.S. Department of Defense, *Conduct of the Persian Gulf War*, 306.
51. Ibid., 307. Also see Pollack. *Arabs at War*, 206.
52. U.S. Department of Defense, *Conduct of the Persian Gulf War*, 115, 257. Also see Marvin Pokrant, *Desert Storm at Sea: What the Navy Really Did* (Westport, Conn.: Greenwood, 1999), 36.
53. Anthony H. Cordesman and Abraham R. Wagner, *The Lessons of Modern War*, vol. 1, *The Iran-Iraq War* (Boulder, Colo.: Westview, 1990), 414. Cordesman remarks on Iraq's use of remote-piloted vehicles in 1988 but concedes that they suffered from sensor and datalink problems.
54. U.S. Department of Defense, *Conduct of the Persian Gulf War*, 54.
55. Stewart, *Operation Desert Storm*, 31.
56. Tom Cooper, interview by Michael Knights, 2004.
57. Battle, *Shaking Hands with Saddam Hussein.*
58. Pollack, *Arabs at War*, 206–7.
59. William Andrews, *Airpower against an Army: CENTAF's Duel with the Republican Guard* (Air University, 1995), 3.
60. Ibid., 3.
61. U.S. Department of Defense, *Conduct of the Persian Gulf War*, 48.
62. Tom Cooper and Farhad Bishop, *Iran-Iraq War in the Air, 1980–88* (Atglen: Schiffer, 2003), 273, 287.
63. Jamieson, *Lucrative Targets*, 11–12.
64. Cooper and Bishop, *Iran-Iraq War*, 280–81.
65. U.S. Department of Defense, *Conduct of the Persian Gulf War*, 51.
66. Cooper, interview by Knights.
67. U.S. Department of Defense, *Conduct of the Persian Gulf War*, 51.
68. Cooper and Bishop, *Iran-Iraq War*, 244. Also see Cordesman and Wagner, *Lessons:Iran-Iraq War*, 417.
69. Chris Bowie, Robert Haffa, and Robert Mullins, *Future War: What Trends in America's Post–Cold War Military Conflicts Tell Us about Early 21st Century Warfare* (Washington, D.C.: Northrop Grumman Analysis Center, 2003); Andrew Krepinevich, Barry Watts, and Robert Work, *Meeting the*

Anti-Access and Area-Denial Challenge (Washington, D.C.: Center for Strategic and Budgetary Assessments, 2003).

70. Cooper and Bishop, *Iran-Iraq War*, 285–86.
71. U.S. Defense Intelligence Agency, *Point Paper on BDA: Day Six— Operator's Outlook* (Washington, D.C.: Defense Intelligence Agency, 1991).
72. U.S. Department of Defense, *Conduct of the Persian Gulf War*, 55.
73. William Rosenau, *Special Operations Forces and Elusive Enemy Ground Targets: Lessons from Vietnam and the Persian Gulf War* (Santa Monica, Calif.: RAND, 2001), 30–33, 41.
74. Michael Eisenstadt, *Iranian Military Power: Capabilities and Intentions* (Washington, D.C.: Washington Institute for Near East Policy, 1996), 44.
75. Jentleson, *With Friends Like These*, 155.
76. U.S. Department of Defense, *Conduct of the Persian Gulf War*, 52.
77. William Arkin, "Cheney's Private Scud War," *Stars and Stripes*, p. 15, October 23, 2000.
78. Barry Jamison and Rich Davis, *Interview with General Charles A. Horner*, ed. Oral History Interview (Maxwell, Ala. AFHRA, 1992), 42. Also see Suzanne Gehri and Richard Reynolds, *Interview with General Charles A. Horner*, ed. Desert Story (Maxwell, Ala.: AFHRA, 1991), 56–60.
79. Quoted in Tim Ripley, *Scud Hunting: Counter-Force Operations against Theater Ballisitc Missiles* (Center for Defense and International Security Studies, 1996), http://www.cdiss.org/scednt3.htm,3.
80. Woodward, *Commanders*, 231.
81. Quoted from an assessment by Col. Wallace Franz in Andrews, *Airpower against an Army*, 3.
82. Stewart, Operation Desert Storm, 31.
83. Bob Woodward, *Veil: The Secret Wars of the CIA 1981–87* (New York: Simon & Schuster, 1988), 556.
84. Pollack, *Arabs at War*, 211–12.
85. Cordesman and Wagner, *Lessons: Iran-Iraq War*, 414.
86. Woodward, *Commanders*, 231.
87. Clancy, *Into the Storm*, 7.

CHAPTER 2. FORGING THE SWORD

1. Suzanna Gehri, Richard Reynolds, and Edward Mann, *Interview with Colonel Dave Deptula and Major Buck Rogers*, ed. Desert Story (Maxwell, Ala.: AFHRA, 1991), 53.
2. Diane T. Putney, "From Instant Thunder to Desert Storm: Developing the Gulf War Air Campaign's Phases," *Air Power History* 41, no. 3 (1994): 42.
3. Jamison and Davis, *Charles Horner*, 62.

4. U.S. Department of Defense, *Conduct of the Persian Gulf War*, 119.
5. Clancy, *Into the Storm*, 92.
6. U.S. Department of Defense, *Conduct of the Persian Gulf War*, 291.
7. James R. Locher, "Taking Stock of Goldwater Nicholls," *Joint Forces Quarterly* (Autumn 1996): 12.
8. Gehri and Reynolds, *Charles A. Horner*, 66.
9. U.S. Department of Defense, *Conduct of the Persian Gulf War*, 419.
10. *Gulf War Airpower Study*, 421.
11. *Iraqi Ground Forces,* (U.S. Department of Defense: Washington, DC, 1991), p. 35.
12. Trevor Dupuy, "Combat Data and the 3:1 Rule," *International Security* 14, no. 1 (1989); Joshua Epstein, *Force Reductions: A Dynamic Assessment* (Washington, D.C.: Brookings Institute, 1990); John Mearsheimer, "Assessing the Conventional Balance: The 3:1 Rule and Its Critics," *International Security* 13, no. 4 (1989).
13. U.S. Department of Defense, *Conduct of the Persian Gulf War*, 18.
14. Ibid., 114.
15. Ibid., 134.
16. Ibid., 277.
17. Ibid., 8.
18. Diane T. Putney, *Telephone Interview: General Norman H. Schwarzkopf* (Maxwell, Ala.: AFHRA, 1992), 1.
19. Diane Putney and Richard Reynolds, *Interview with Lieutenant Colonel Sam Baptiste*, ed. Oral History Interview (Maxwell, Ala.: AFHRA, 1992), 25, 56. Colonel Sam Baptiste, CENTAF director of combat operations, twice remarked that Checkmate products were better than their CENTAF equivalents during this period.
20. Marvin Pokrant, *Desert Shield at Sea: What the Navy Really Did* (Westport, Conn.: Greenwood, 1999), 73. Richard Reynolds, *Interview with Lt. Commander Mike Casey*, ed. Desert Story (Maxwell, Ala.: AFHRA, 1991), 4, 14.
21. Richard T. Reynolds, *Heart of the Storm: The Genesis of the Air Campaign against Iraq* (Maxwell Air Force Base, Ala.: Air University Press, 1995), 39–46. Reynolds summarizes this period comprehensively.
22. Putney and Reynolds, *Sam Baptiste*, 15–18, and Putney, "Instant Thunder," 43.
23. Suzanna Gehri, *Interview with Colonel John A. Warden (Part One)*, ed. Desert Story (Maxwell, Ala." AFHRA, 1991), 63. This summary of Instant Thunder relies heavily on Warden's own 1991 interview, although none of the points raised here are contradicted by the accounts of the other attendees at the Schwarzkopf and Powell briefings: General Alexander, General Moore, Col. Ben Harvey, and Col. Ronnie Stanfill of Checkmate.

24. Two main accounts chronicle the meeting. Dave Deptula took notes throughout, as did Ben Harvey, and these are stored at Maxwell Air Force Base or reflected in the transcripts stored there. See Gehri, Reynolds, and Mann, *Dave Deptula and Buck Rogers*, 1994. Many other accounts touch on the meeting and differ largely in flavor only.

25. Edward Mann, *Thunder and Lightning: Desert Storm and the Airpower Debates* (Maxwell Air Force Base, Ala.: Air University Press, 1995), 27.

26. Richard G. Davis, *On Target* (Washington, D.C.: Air Force History Support Office, 2002), 42.

27. Mann, *Thunder and Lightning*, 66.

28. Gehri, Reynolds, and Mann, *Dave Deptula and Buck Rogers*, 132–40.

29. Suzanna Gehri, Richard Reynolds, and Edward Mann, *Interview with Colonel Dave Deptula* (Maxwell, Ala.: AFHRA, 1991), 24, 34, 146, and Gehri, Reynolds, and Mann, *Buster Glosson (Part One)*, 1.

30. Deptula quoted in Mann, *Thunder and Lightning*, 100.

31. Ibid., 37–41, 45.

32. Dave Deptula, interview by Michael Knights, 2002.

33. Ibid.

34. Gehri, Reynolds, and Mann, *Dave Deptula and Buck Rogers*, 23, 26.

35. Suzanna Gehri, Richard Reynolds, and Edward Mann, *Interview with Lt. Gen. Robert M. Alexander*, ed. Desert Story (Maxwell, Ala.: AFHRA, 1991), 39. Also see Suzanna Gehri and Edward Mann, *Interview with Lt. Col. Ronnie A. Stanfill*, ed. Desert Story (Maxwell, Ala.: AFHRA, 1991) and John Warden, interview by Michael Knights, 2002.

36. U.S. General Accounting Office, *Operation Desert Storm: Operation Desert Storm Air War* (Washington, D.C.: U.S. General Accounting Office, 1996), 5.

37. From a Powerpoint briefing given to the author by Major General Deptula on June 7, 2002.

38. *Gulf War Airpower Study*, 91, and Woodward, *Commanders*, 250–51.

39. On the latter point, both Horner and, to a lesser degree, Glosson believed that some strikes had to be launched during the day to keep pressure on the Iraqi populace and the attacked target systems. See Gehri, Reynolds, and Mann, *Buster Glosson (Part One)*, 94, and Gehri, Reynolds, and Mann, *Dave Deptula and Buck Rogers*, 135.

40. Suzanna Gehri, Richard Reynolds, and Edward Mann, *Interview with Buster Glosson (Part Two)*, ed. Desert Story (Maxwell, Ala.: AFHRA, 1992), 94.

41. William Arkin, interview by Michael Knights, 2002.

42. Gehri, Reynolds, and Mann, *Buster Glosson (Part One)*, 76.

43. Jamieson, *Lucrative Targets*, 45.

44. Andrews, *Airpower against an Army*, 9–11.

45. Shellum, *Defense Intelligence Crisis*, 25.
46. For a listing of air campaign objectives, see *Gulf War Airpower Study*, 147.

CHAPTER 3. DESERT STORM: STRATEGIC ATTACK

1. Woodward, *Commanders*, 225, 352.
2. Jamison and Davis, *Charles A. Horner*, 50.
3. U.S. Department of Defense, *Conduct of the Persian Gulf War*, 1, 765.
4. Ibid., 1.
5. Lee A. Downer, "The Composite Wing in Combat," *Air Power Journal* 6, no. 1 (1991), and George Eichelberger, interview by Michael Knights, 2002.
6. U.S. Department of Defense, *Conduct of the Persian Gulf War*, 244.
7. Williamson Murray and Robert Scales, *The Iraq War: A Military History* (Cambridge, Mass.: Belknap, 2003), 1–4.
8. Carlo Kopp, "Desert Storm: The Electronic Battle," *Australian Aviation* (June/July 1993): 2.
9. Ibid., 2.
10. Ibid., 2–3.
11. U.S. Department of Defense, *Conduct of the Persian Gulf War*, 150.
12. Kopp, "Desert Storm," 2.
13. Pollack, *Arabs at War*, 243–44.
14. U.S. Department of Defense, *Conduct of the Persian Gulf War*, 96, 127.
15. Kopp, "Desert Storm," 8.
16. Andrews, *Airpower against an Army*, 54.
17. Ibid., 54.
18. Kopp, "Desert Storm," 3.
19. U.S. Defense Intelligence Agency, *Point Paper on BDA*. Also see Christopher Centner, "Ignorance Is Risk: The Big Lesson from Desert Storm Air Base Attacks," *Airpower Journal* (1992): 4, 18.
20. U.S. Department of Defense, *Conduct of the Persian Gulf War*, 179.
21. Edward Mann, *Interview with Major Dave Karns*, ed. Desert Story (Maxwell, Ala.: AFHRA, 1991), 24.
22. Jamieson, *Lucrative Targets*, 42.
23. U.S. Defense Intelligence Agency, *Point Paper on BDA*.
24. U.S. Department of Defense, *Conduct of the Persian Gulf War*, 182.
25. Warden, interview by Knights, 2002.
26. Centner, "Ignorance Is Risk," 2.
27. Roy Sykes, interview by Michael Knights, 2002, and Deptuala, interview by Knights, 2002.
28. U.S. Department of Defense, *Conduct of the Persian Gulf War*, 227.
29. Ibid., 204.
30. Ibid., 181–82.

31. Ibid., 244.
32. Not all were PGM droppers—some used "buddy-lasing" techniques to partner PGM droppers with nondesignating aircraft carrying PGMs.
33. Rick Atkinson, *Crusade: The Untold Story of the Gulf War* (London: Harper Collins, 1993), 156–57.
34. U.S. Department of Defense, *Conduct of the Persian Gulf War*, 217.
35. Mann, *David Karns*, 24.
36. Ripley, *Scud Hunting*, 3.
37. Davis, *On Target*, 85.
38. Suzanna Gehri and Richard Reynolds, *Interview with Col. Trexler*, ed. Desert Storm (Maxwell, Ala.: AFHRA, 1992), 55.
39. Suzanna Gehri and Richard Reynolds, *Interview with Major General John A. Corder*, ed. Desert Story (Maxwell, Ala.: AFHRA, 1992), 191.
40. Ibid., 201.
41. Rosenau, *Special Operations Forces*, 33–36.
42. Deptula, interview by Knights.
43. Michael Rip and James Hasik, *The Precision Revolution: GPS and the Future of Aerial Warfare* (Annapolis, Md.: Naval Institute, 2002), 181. Reading between the lines of the memoirs of Iraq's missile forces commander, it would appear that fourteen is the most likely number. See Hazim Abdul-Razzaq Al-Ayyubi, *Forty-Three Missiles on the Zionist Entity* (Washington, D.C.: Foreign Broadcast Information Service, 1998).
44. U.S. Department of Defense, *Conduct of the Persian Gulf War*, 391.
45. Cross, *Dragon Lady*.
46. Thomas Hunter, *The Role and Effect of Special Operations Forces in Theater Ballistic Missile Counterforce Operations During Operation Desert Storm* (Special Operations, 1998), http://www.specialoperations.com/Focus/SCUD'Hunt/default.htm.
47. Rosenau, *Special Operations Forces*, 36.
48. Scott Ritter, *Endgame: Solving the Iraq Problem—Once and for All* (New York: Simon & Schuster, 1999), 43.
49. James Bamford, *Body of Secrets* (New York: Anchor Books, 2002), 545.
50. Al-Ayyubi, *Forty-Three Missiles*, 19.
51. Rosenau, *Special Operations Forces*, 33–36.
52. Rip and Hasik, *Precision Revolution*, 311.
53. Hunter, *Role and Effect*.
54. Al-Ayyubi, *Forty-Three Missiles*, 24.
55. An excellent source on time-sensitive targeting and the kill chain is Chris Bowie, *Destroying Mobile Ground Targets in an Anti-access Environment* (Washington, D.C.: Northrop Grumman Analysis Center, 2001).
56. U.S. Department of Defense, *Conduct of the Persian Gulf War*, 244, 272.
57. Ibid., 244.
58. Ibid., 214.

59. Rosenau, *Special Operations Forces*, 11–17.
60. U.S. Department of Defense, *Conduct of the Persian Gulf War*, 218.
61. Hunter, *Role and Effect*.
62. Mark Kipphut, *Crossbow and Gulf War Counter-Scud Efforts: Lessons from History* (Air University, 1996), 50.
63. Rip and Hasik, *Precision Revolution*, 319.
64. Ibid., 181.
65. Shellum, *Defense Intelligence Crisis*, 23–33.
66. Al-Ayyubi, *Forty-Three Missiles*, 60.
67. Ibid., pp. 16, 60.
68. Ibid., pp. 42, 48–49, 54.
69. Hunter, *Role and Effect*.
70. Edward N. Luttwak, "Air Power in US Military Strategy," in *The Future of Air Power in the Aftermath of the Gulf War*, ed. Richard Shultz and Robert Pfalzgraff (Maxwell Air Force Base, Ala.: Air University Press, 1992), 19.
71. U.S. Department of Defense, *Conduct of the Persian Gulf War*, 207.
72. U.S. Defense Intelligence Agency. *Point Paper on BDA*.
73. Luttwak, "Air Power," 19.
74. Anthony H. Cordesman, *The Lessons of Desert Fox: A Preliminary Analysis* (Washington, D.C.: Center for Strategic and International Studies, 1999), 6. Also see William Arkin, Baghdad: The Urban Sanctuary in Desert Storm," *Air Power Journal* (1997).
75. Gehri, Reynolds, and Mann, *Dave Deptula*, 28
76. Ibid., pp. 29–30, 42–43. Deptula confirms McKeon's assertions in detail on p. 5.
77. Matt McKeon, *Joint Targeting: What's Still Broke?* (Air University, 1999), 29–30.
78. Deptula, interview by Knights.
79. Robin Holliday, interview by Michael Knights, 2002.
80. U.S. Air Force, *Air Force Doctrine Document 2–1.2: Strategic Attack* (Washinton, D.C.: Department of the Air Force, 1998), 26.
81. Human Rights Watch, *Needless Deaths in the Gulf War: Civilian Casualties during the Air Campaign and Violations of the Laws of War* (New York: Human Rights Watch, 1991), 9.
82. Cordesman, *Lessons of Desert Fox*, 6.
83. U.S. Defense Intelligence Agency, *Point Paper on BDA*.
84. Bruce Riedel, interview by Michael Knights, 2004.
85. Robert Baer, *See No Evil: The True Story of a Ground Soldier in the CIA's War of Terrorism* (New York: Crown, 2002), 180.
86. Mann, *Thunder and Lightning*, 104–5.
87. Atkinson, *Crusade*, 295.
88. U.S. Department of Defense, *Conduct of the Persian Gulf War*.

89. U.S. Defense Intelligence Agency, *Point Paper on BDA*.
90. Gehri, Reynolds, and Mann, *Buster Glosson (Part Two)*, 94.
91. U.S. Department of Defense, *Conduct of the Persian Gulf War*, 700.
92. Gehri, Reynolds, and Mann, *Buster Glosson (Part Two)*, 291.
93. Harry L. Heintzelman and Edmund S. Bloom, "A Planning Primer: How to Provide Effective Legal Input into the War Planning and Combat Execution Process," *Air Force Law Review* 37 (1994): 5.
94. John G. Humphries, "Operations Law and the Rules of Engagement in Operations Desert Shield and Storm," *Air Power Journal* 6, no. 2 (1992): 34. The bad weather that descended from day three of the air campaign had a major effect on no-strike sortie rates.
95. Ibid., 32.
96. Ibid., 33.
97. Heintzelman and Bloom, "Planning Primer," 21, and Scott L. Silliman, "JAG Goes to War: The Desert Shield Deployment," *Air Force Law Review* 37 (1994): 85.
98. Humphries, "Operations Law."
99. Donald B. Rice, "Air Power in the New Security Environment," in *The Future of Air Power in the Aftermath of the Gulf War*, ed. Richard Shultz and Robert Pfalzgraff (Maxwell Air Force Base, Ala.: Air University Press, 1992), 11.
100. Ritter, *Endgame*, 75.
101. William Arkin, "Q&A with Lieutenant General Charles Horner," *Washington Post*, August 1, 1991, http://www.washingtonpost.com.
102. John A. Warden, "Employing Air Power in the 21st Century," in *The Future of Air Power in the Aftermath of the Gulf War*, ed. Richard Shultz and Robert Pfalzgraff (Maxwell Air Force Base, Ala.: Air University Press, 1992),70–72.
103. McKeon, "Joint Targeting," 34. Also see *Gulf War Airpower Study*, 216–47.
104. Timothy Hoyt, "Iraq's Military Industry: A Crucial Military Target," *National Security Studies Quarterly* (1998): 1, and Michael Eisenstadt, *Like a Phoenix from the Ashes? The Future of Iraqi Military Power* (Washington, D.C.: Washington Institute for Near East Policy, 1993), 27.
105. U.S. Department of Defense, *Conduct of the Persian Gulf War*, 148.

CHAPTER 4. DESERT SABER: AIR-LAND BATTLE

1. Andrews, *Airpower against an Army*, 25.
2. Cordesman, *Lessons of Desert Fox*, 6.
3. Hoyt, "Iraq's Military Industry," 3.
4. Atkinson, *Crusade*, 311.

5. Jamieson, *Lucrative Targets*, 184.
6. Ibid., 36–27, 68–71.
7. Ibid., 68.
8. Suzanna Gehri, Richard Reynolds, and Edward Mann, *Interview with Colonel Jim Blackburn*, ed. Desert Story (Maxwell, Ala.: AFHRA, 1993), 133. Blackburn provides other examples of McPeak's involvement in operational detail on p. 133. My interviews with both Warden and Deptula produced very strong evidence that McPeak drove the expansion of bridge bombing throughout the war.
9. Jamison and Davis, *Charles A. Horner*, 62.
10. Gehri and Reynolds, *John A. Corder*, 186.
11. Kopp, "Desert Storm," 10.
12. Ibid., pp. 8–9.
13. Jamieson, *Lucrative Targets*, 91.
14. Ibid., 91.
15. Ibid., 93.
16. Putney, "Instant Thunder," 45.
17. Rip and Hasik, *Precision Revolution*, 216.
18. U.S. Department of Defense, *Conduct of the Persian Gulf War*, 219.
19. Jamieson, *Lucrative Targets*, 8.
20. Carl Conetta, Charles Knight, and Lutz Unterseher, *Toward Defensive Restructuring in the Middle East*, Project on Defense Alternatives Research Monograph 1 (Cambridge, Mass.: Project on Defense Alternatives, 1991).
21. Jamieson, *Lucrative Targets*, 93.
22. Cross, *Dragon Lady*.
23. Jamieson, *Lucrative Targets*, 27.
24. Andrews, *Airpower against an Army*, 14.
25. U.S. Department of Defense, *Conduct of the Persian Gulf War*, 127.
26. Mark Welsh, "Day of the Killer Scouts," *Air Force Magazine* 75, no. 4 (April 1992).
27. Andrews, *Airpower against an Army*, 27.
28. Jamieson, *Lucrative Targets*, 93.
29. Andrews, *Airpower against an Army*, 51.
30. Jamieson, *Lucrative Targets*, 77.
31. Ibid., 77.
32. Michael J. Bodner and William W. Bruner, "Tank Plinking," *Air Force Magazine Online* (March 9, 2004) http://www.afa.org/magazine/perspectives/desert_storm/1093tank.asp.
33. Andrews, *Airpower against an Army*, 33.
34. Gehri and Reynolds, *John A. Corder*, 41.
35. U.S. Department of Defense, *Conduct of the Persian Gulf War*, 115.
36. Jamieson, *Lucrative Targets*, 91.

37. James Winnefield, Preston Niblack, and Dana Johnson, *A League of Airmen: U.S. Air Power in the Gulf War* (Santa Monica, Calif.: RAND, 1994), 113.
38. Atkinson, *Crusade*, 263.
39. Deptula, interview by Knights.
40. Bodner and Bruner, "Tank Plinking."
41. Clancy, *Into the Storm*, 354, 396.
42. Andrews, *Airpower against an Army*, 55.
43. U.S. Department of Defense, *Conduct of the Persian Gulf War*, 135.
44. Richard B. H. Lewis, "JFACC Problems Associated with Battlefield Preparation in Desert Storm," *Air Power Journal* (Spring 1995).
45. Gehri and Reynolds, *Charles A. Horner*, 62.
46. Lewis, "JFACC Problems," 38. Also see Jamison and Davis, *Charles A. Horner*, 44.
47. Atkinson, *Crusade*, 238; Lewis, "JFACC Problems," 39; and Gehri and Reynolds, *John A. Corder*, 30–31.
48. For a discussion of these pressures, see Jamison and Davis, *Charles A. Horner*, 22, and Gehri and Reynolds, *John A. Corder*, 30–31, 143.
49. Ibid., 143.
50. Jamison and Davis, *Charles A. Horner*, 44.
51. McKeon, *Joint Targeting*, 25, and John W. Schmidt and Clinton L. Williams, "Disjointed or Joint Targeting?" *Marine Corps Gazette* 76, no. 9 (1992): 68.
52. Paul E. Bowen, "Create a Fighting Staff," *Marine Corps Gazette* 75, no. 11 (1991), 52–53.
53. Lewis, "JFACC Problems," 34, and Michael R. Moeller, *The Sum of Their Fears: The Relationship between the Joint Targeting Coordination Board and the Joint Force Commander* (Air University, 1995): 15.
54. Jamison and Davis, *Charles A. Horner*, 52, 55
55. Davis, *On Target*, 80
56. Lewis, "JFACC Problems," 36.
57. Ibid., 37.
58. Robert Scales, "Accuracy Defeated Range in Artillery Duel," *Jane's International Defense Review* 24, no. 5 (May 1991): 473.
59. Clancy, *Into the Storm*, 259.
60. U.S. Department of Defense, *Conduct of the Persian Gulf War*, 304.
61. Ibid., 277, and Clancy, *Into the Storm*, 243–45.
62. Clancy, *Into the Storm*, 9, 239, and U.S. Department of Defense, *Conduct of the Persian Gulf War*, 314, 678, 875.
63. Clancy, *Into the Storm*, 7.
64. Ibid., 285. Also see Stewart, *Operation Desert Storm*, 36–37.
65. Andrews, *Airpower against an Army*, 13.
66. Jamieson, *Lucrative Targets*, 156.

67. U.S. Department of Defense, *Conduct of the Persian Gulf War*, 331.
68. Pollack, *Arabs at War*, 252.
69. U.S. Department of Defense, *Conduct of the Persian Gulf War*, 426.
70. Jamieson, *Lucrative Targets*, 143.
71. Clancy, *Into the Storm*, 404.
72. U.S. Department of Defense, *Conduct of the Persian Gulf War*, 322, 326, 329.
73. Clancy, *Into the Storm*, 107.
74. John McDaniel, *C2 Case Study: The FSCL in Desert Storm* (Vienna, Va.: Evidence Based Research, 2001), 4.
75. Clancy, *Into the Storm*, 390.
76. U.S. Department of Defense, *Conduct of the Persian Gulf War*, 674.
77. Rip and Hasik, *Precision Revolution*, 274.
78. Andrews, *Airpower against an Army*, 36.
79. Pollack, *Arabs at War*, 262.
80. Ibid., 251. Also see Clancy, *Into the Storm*, 369.
81. Clancy, *Into the Storm*, 407.
82. Ibid., 386.
83. Ibid., pp. 396–97.
84. Pollack, *Arabs at War*, 253–54.
85. Clancy, *Into the Storm*, 421.
86. Jamieson, *Lucrative Targets*, 152–53.
87. Ibid., 163.
88. McDaniel, *C2 Case Study*, 10.
89. Lewis, "JFACC Problems."
90. U.S. Department of Defense, *Conduct of the Persian Gulf War*, 319, 335.
91. Atkinson, *Crusade*, 469–80.
92. Jamieson, *Lucrative Targets*, 162.
93. McDaniel, *C2 Case Study*, 13.
94. Pollack, *Arabs at War*, 263.
95. Jamieson, *Lucrative Targets*, 168.
96. U.S. Army Center for Lessons Learned, *On Point: The United States Army in Operation Iraqi Freedom* (August 23, 2004), http://onpoint. leavenworth.army.mil.
97. Eisenstadt, *Like a Phoenix*, 44.
98. U.S. Department of Defense, *Conduct of the Persian Gulf War*, 19.
99. David Ockmanek, "The Air Force: The Next Round," in *Transforming America's Military*, ed. Has Binnedndijk (Washington, D.C.: National Defense University, 2002), 259.
100. U.S. General Accounting Office, *Operation Desert Storm*, 1.
101. U.S. Army Center for Lessons Learned, *On Point*.
102. Bamford, *Body of Secrets*, 545.
103. Clancy, *Into the Storm*, 11, 320.

104. John Heidenrich, "The Gulf War: How Many Iraqis Died?" *Foreign Affairs*, no. 90 (1993): 116.

105. Michael Knights, "Bringing Down The Temple: Would a Beleaguered Saddam Deploy the 'Samson Option'?" *Gulf States Newsletter*, October 23, 2002, 10. Also see Michael Knights, "Weighing the Cost of a War on Infrastructure," *Gulf States Newsletter*, January 10, 2003, 2. On perfidy, see U.S. Department of Defense, *Conduct of the Persian Gulf War*, 327.

106. U.S. Department of Defense, *Conduct of the Persian Gulf War*, 721.

107. Jamieson, *Lucrative Targets*, 152–53.

108. Andrew Rathmell, "Iraq's Military: Waiting for Change," *Jane's Intelligence Review* 7, no. 2 (1995): 2, and Jamieson, *Lucrative Targets*, 171.

109. Pollack, *Arabs at War*, 260.

110. Clancy, *Into the Storm*, 397.

CHAPTER 5. AFTER THE STORM: U.S. RESPONSES TO ONGOING IRAQI RESISTANCE

1. Barton Gellman, "One Year Later: War's Faded Triumph," *Washington Post*, January 16, 1992.

2. Ibid.

3. Human Rights Watch, *Endless Torment: The 1991 Uprising in Iraq and Its Aftermath*, 1992, http://www.hrw.org/reports/1992/Iraq926.htm.

4. Colin Powell, *My American Journey* (New York: Random House, 1995), 531.

5. Human Rights Watch, *Endless Torment*.

6. Ibid.

7. Hoyt, "Iraq's Military Industry," 3.

8. U.S. Department of Defense, *Conduct of the Persian Gulf War*, 321.

9. Eisenstadt, *Like a Phoenix*, 7.

10. Human Rights Watch, *Endless Torment*.

11. Ibid.

12. Eliot Cohen, "Sound and Fury," *Washington Post*, December 19, 1998, A25.

13. United Nations, *Resolution 688: Iraq* (1991), http://ods-dds-ny.un.org/doc/RESOLUTION/GEN/NR0/596/24/IMG/NR059624.pdf?OpenElement.

14. Human Rights Watch, *Endless Torment*.

15. David E. Clary, *Operation Provide Comfort: A Strategic Perspective* (Alexandria, Va.: Defense Technical Information Center, 1994), 2, 8.

16. Sean Boyne, "Saddam Reasserts Control," *Jane's Intelligence Review* 5, no. 3 (1993): 121–23.

17. Eisenstadt, *Like a Phoenix*, 7.

18. United Nations, *Resolution 687: Iraq-Kuwait* (1991), http://ods-dds-ny. un.org/doc/RESOLUTION/GEN/NR0/596/23/IMG/NR059623.pdf? OpenElement.
19. John Powers, "Mass Graves Testify to Saddam's Evil," *Insight Magazine* (March 16, 2004): 1.
20. United Nations, *Resolution 687.*
21. United Nations, *Resolution 707: Iraq* (1991), http://ods-dds-ny.un. org/doc/RESOLUTION/GEN/NR0/596/43/IMG/NR059643.pdf? OpenElement.
22. Ritter, *Endgame*, 34–35.
23. United Nations, *Resolution 715: Iraq* (1991), http://ods-dds-ny.un. org/doc/RESOLUTION/GEN/NR0/596/51/IMG/NR059651.pdf? OpenElement.
24. U.S. Congress, Senate Committee on Armed Services, *The "Threat and Forget" Approach Is No Answer* (July 30, 1992).
25. Gehri, Reynolds, and Mann, *Steve Wilson*, 44. Also see Bill Gertz, "Saddam 'On a War Footing,'" *Washington Times*, August 19, 1992, A1, and David Fulghum, "Pentagon Halts Planned Attack on Iraqi Sites," *Aviation Week and Space Technology* (August 10, 1992): 23.
26. Human Rights Watch, *Endless Torment.*
27. Gerald Seib, "Iraq Restores Air Network, US Sources Say," *Wall Street Journal*, August 19, 1992, A3; Associated Press, "With No-Fly Zone in Effect, Iraq Hits Shiites on the Ground," *Washington Times*, December 29, 1992, A1; and Bruce Nelan, "Saddam, Still," Time (March 29, 1993): 33–34.
28. Eisenstadt, *Like a Phoenix*, 57.
29. Gertz, "Saddam 'On a War Footing,'" A1.
30. U.S. Department of Defense, *Defense Department Briefer: Iraq*, 1992.
31. Associated Press, "Iraqis Drop Napalm on Shiite Towns," *Washington Times*, August 16, 1992.
32. Anthony Cordesman, "How to Hit Iraq," *New York Times*, August 19, 1992; *New York Times* Editorial, "Don't Shoot the Helicopters," August 19, 1992; Michael Gordon, "Leave Iraq Alone, US Tells Iranians," *New York Times*, August 25, 1992.
33. Gerald Seib, "Iraq is Warned Not to Employ Ground Forces," *Wall Street Journal*, August 31, 1992, A17.
34. Bill Gertz, "Iraqis Move Aircraft out of Forbidden Zone," *Washington Times*, August 26, 1992, and Gordon, "Leave Iraq Alone."
35. John Lancaster, "Allies Declare 'No-Fly Zone' in Iraq," *Washington Post*, August 27, 1992.
36. Robyn A. Chumley, "Southern Watch," *Airman* (January 1993): 2.
37. U.S. Congress, Senate Committee on Armed Services, *Joint Chiefs of Staff Briefing on Current Military Operations in Somalia, Iraq and Yugoslavia*, 1st sess., January 29, 1993, 56–63.

38. Nelan, "Saddam, Still," 33–34.

39. Jeffrey Smith, "'Cheat and Retreat' Familiar by Now," *Washington Post*, January 9, 1993.

40. Laurie Mylroie, *Saddam Defiant* (Washington, D.C.: Washington Institute for Near East Policy, 1993): 1.

41. *January 1993 briefing on Iraq*, 56–63. U.S. Congress, Senate Committee on Armed Services, Joint Chiefs of Staff Meeting on Current Military Operations in Somalia, Iraq, and Yugoslavia, First Session, January 29, 1993.

42. Ibid., 46–71.

43. Tom Cooper and Farhad Bishop, *Iran-Iraq War*, 63.

44. *Gulf War Airpower Study*, 79.

45. Jamieson, *Lucrative Targets*, 93.

46. Paul White, *Crises after the Storm: An Appraisal of U.S. Air Operations in Iraq since the Persian Gulf War* (Washington, D.C.: Washington Institute for Near East Policy, 1999), 17, 25.

47. John Morocco, "Raids Highlight Pitfalls of Limited Use of Force," Aviation Week and Space Technology, January 25, 1993, 49.

48. Gerald Seib, "Saddam Hussein Seen Trying to Boost Posture of Iraq in Dealing with Clinton Administration," *Wall Street Journal*, January 12, 1993.

49. Riedel, interview by Knights.

50. White, *Crises after the Storm*, 26.

51. *January 1993 briefing on Iraq*, 65.

52. Julie Bird, "U.S. Allies Threaten to Strike Iraq Again," *Air Force Times* 53, no. 4 (1993): 3.

53. John Boatman and Paul Beaver, "Coalition Draws New Line in the Sand," *Jane's Defense Weekly*, January 23, 1993, 6.

54. Sykes, interview by Knights.

55. David Fulghum, "Pentagon Criticizes Air Strike on Iraq," *Aviation Week and Space Technology*, January 25, 1993, 47.

56. Morocco, "Raids Highlight Pitfalls," 3.

57. Riedel, interview by Knights.

58. Fulghum, "Pentagon Halts Planned Attack," 6.

59. Patrick Tyler, "U.S. Said to Plan Raids on Baghdad over Inspections," *New York Times*, August 16, 1992, A1.

60. David Fulghum, "Clashes with Iraq Continue after Week of Heavy Strikes, *Aviation Week and Space Technology*, January 25, 1993, 42.

61. Mike Nelson, interview by Michael Knights, 2002.

62. Fulghum, "Clashes with Iraq," 42.

63. *January 1993 briefing on Iraq*, 65.

64. Boatman and Beaver, "Coalition Draws New Line," 6.

65. Fulghum, "Clashes with Iraq," 38.

66. *January 1993 briefing on Iraq*, 46–71.
67. Michael Eisenstadt, *Blunder over Baghdad: Assessing US Military Action against Iraq* (Washington, D.C.: Washington Institute for Near East Policy, 1993), and Morocco, "Raids Highlight Pitfalls."
68. Mike Nelson, interview by Knights. Also see Morocco, "Raids Highlight Pitfalls," 49.
69. Eisenstadt, *Blunder over Baghdad*, 3.
70. Nora Boustany, "Iraq Said to Shut Down Radar to Prevent New Confrontations," *Washington Post*, February 1, 1993, A14.
71. William Matthews, "Brief Cease-Fire in Iraq Ends with U.S. Bombs," *Air Force Times* 53, no. 5 (February 1993): 5.
72. Anthony Lake, interview by Michael Knights, 2004.

CHAPTER 6. "TOMAHAWK DIPLOMACY"

1. For a description of this characterization, see Michael Ignatieff, "To Fight but not to Die," *World Today,* 2000.
2. Mark J. Conversino, "Sawdust Superpower: Perceptions of US Casualty Tolerance," *Strategic Review* 15, no. 1 (1997); Eric V Larson, *Casualties and Consensus* (Santa Monica, Calif.: RAND, 1996).
3. Arkin, interview by Knights.
4. Stephen E. Anno and William E. Einspahr, *Command, Control and Communications Lessons Learned: Iranian Rescue, Falklands Conflict, Grenada Invasion, Libya Raid* (Maxwell Air Force Base, Ala.: Air War College Air University,1988), 52–56. See Woodward, *Commanders*, 123, 153.
5. Riedel, interview by Knights.
6. Quoted in Thomas Friedman, "The Missiles' Message," *New York Times*, June 28, 1993, 1.
7. Morocco, "Raids Highlight Pitfalls," 49.
8. Riedel, interview by Knights.
9. Eisenstadt, *Like a Phoenix*, 12, 14.
10. Laurie Mylroie, *Saddam's Deadly Game of Cat-and-Mouse* (Washington, D.C.: Washington Institute for Near East Policy, 1993, 1. Also see Ritter, *Endgame*, 9.
11. Riedel, interview by Knights.
12. Leon Fuerth, interview by Michael Knights, 2002.
13. Rip and Hasik, *Precision Revolution*, 364–65.
14. Steve Coll, *Ghost Wars* (New York: Penguin, 2003), 410.
15. Charles Dunlap, interview by Michael Knights, 2002.
16. U.S. Department of Defense, News Briefing, June 26, 1993. http://www.fas.org/man/dod-101/ops/docs/dod_930626.htm
17. Madeleine Albright, "For the Record," *Congressional Questions*, July 3, 1993.

18. James Woolsey, interview by Michael Knights, 2004.
19. Mark Parris, interview by Michael Knights, 2004.
20. Fuerth, interview by Knights.
21. Cite the source from FN 16 above. These were the same.
22. Charles Dunlap, interview by Michael Knights, 2002.
23. Pokrant, *Desert Storm*, 251–52.
24. Federation of American Scientists, *Cruise Missile Strike: 26 June 1993 Operation Southern Watch,* 1993, http://www.fas.org/man/dod-101/ops/strike_930626.htm.
25. Fuerth, interview by Knights.
26. U.S. Department of Defense, News Briefing, June 26, 1993.
27. Fuerth, interview by Knights.
28. Albright, "For the Record."
29. U.S. Department of Defense, News Briefing, June 26, 1993; Fuerth, interview by Knights.
30. Rip and Hasik, *Precision Revolution*, 363–64.
31. Nelson, interview by Knights.
32. Federation of American Scientists, *U.S. Opinion Round-Up: Strike on Iraq*, 1993, http://www.fas.org/man/dod-101/ops/strike_930626.htm; A CIA Analyst, interview by Michael Knights, 2002.
33. CNN, "Most Missiles Hit Their Target in U.S. Air Strike,"January 9, 1993, http://www.fas.org/man/dod-101/ops/strike_930626.htm; CIA Analyst, interview by Knights.
34. Riedel, interview by Knights.
35. Federation of American Scientists, *U.S. Opinion Round-Up*; CIA Analyst, interview by Knights.
36. Eisenstadt, *Like a Phoenix*, 27.
37. Rip and Hasik, *Precision Revolution*, 361.
38. U.S. Congress, Senate Committee on Intelligence, *US Intelligence Community's Pre-War Intelligence Assessments on Iraq*, 2004, 373.
39. Ibid., 378
40. Eisenstadt, *Like a Phoenix*; Rathmell, "Iraq's Military," 6.
41. Quoted in Eisenstadt, *Like a Phoenix*, 44.
42. U.S. Department of Defense, *Iraq: Country Handbook* (Washington, D.C.: U.S. Department of Defense, 1994), 53–54.
43. Hoyt, "Iraq's Military Industry," 5; Eisenstadt, *Like a Phoenix*, xv, 63.
44. U.S. Congress, Senate Committee on Intelligence, *US Intelligence Community's Pre-War Intelligence*, 381.
45. Pollack, *Arabs at War*, 178, 192, 206, 207.
46. U.S. Department of Defense, *Conduct of the Persian Gulf War*, 46.
47. Eisenstadt, *Like a Phoenix*, 48.
48. Ritter, *Endgame*, 201.

49. "Power Strugle Behind Iraq's Policy Muddle?" *Middle East Mirror*, October 21, 1994, 19.

50. Sean Boyne, "Saddam Intensifies Campaign in the Marshes," *Jane's Intelligence Review* 6, no. 9 (1994): 1.

51. U.S. Department of Defense, *Defense Department Briefer: Iraq*, October 11, 1994, 1, http://www.defenselink.mil/transcripts/1994/t101194_t1011asd.html.

52. Rathmell, "Iraq's Military," 6.

53. White, *Crises after the Storm*, 33.

54. U.S. Congress, Senate Committee on Intelligence, *US Intelligence Community's Pre-War Intelligence*, 381–84.

55. Michael Gordon, "US Continuing Build Up, Sees Sign of Iraqi Retreat," *New York Times*, October 12, 1994, 1.

56. Woodward, *Commanders*, 219.

57. Boyne, "Saddam Reasserts Control"; Eisenstadt, *Like a Phoenix from the Ashes*; Sean Boyne, "Feuds Cut Deeper into Saddam's Power Base," *Jane's Intelligence Review* 7, no. 7 (1995); Sean Boyne, "Iraq's Military Purge," *Jane's Intelligence Review* 8, no. 10 (1996); Sean Boyne, "Saddam Purges his Inner Circle," *Jane's Intelligence Review* 9, no. 12 (1996).

58. Baer, *See No Evil*, 180, 213, 234–35.

59. Lake, interview by Knights.

60. Baer, *See No Evil*, 201–5. Also see Jerome Socolovsky, "Iraq Reports Fresh Clashes with Kurds, Blames US," Associated Press, March 7, 1995.

61. Kenneth Pollack, interview by Michael Knights, 2004; Parris, interview by Knights.

62. Amatzia Baram, *Saddam Husayn Conquers Irbil: Causes and Implications* (Washington, D.C.: Washington Institute for Near East Policu, 1996), 2.

63. Sean Boyne, "Saddam's Alliance with Kurdish Faction," *Jane's Intelligence Review* 7, no. 11 (1996): 2.

64. Riedel, interview by Knights.

65. Baram, *Saddam Husayn Conquers Irbil*, 1.

66. Human Rights Watch, *Endless Torment*.

67. Hoyt, "Iraq's Military Industry," 1–2.

68. U.S. Congress, Senate Committee on Intelligence, *US Intelligence Community's Pre-War Intelligence*, 375, 388.

69. A CIA Operative, interview by Michael Knights, 2002. Also see Sean Boyne, "Qusay Considers a Reshuffle for Iraq's Command Structure," *Jane's Intelligence Review* 9, no. 9 (1997), 2.

70. "Iraqi Kurdistan Risks Being Turned into Regional Battleground, KDP Warns," *Middle East Mirror*, September 6, 1996, 13.

71. Sean Boyne, "Saddam's Move to Exorcise the Enclaves," *Jane's Intelligence Review* 9, no. 10 (1997), 1.
72. Pollack, interview by Knights; Bill Gertz and Warren Strobel, "Iraqi Jets Challenge Bigger No-Fly Zone," *Washington Times*, September 4, 1996, 1.
73. Pollack, interview by Knights.
74. Parris, interview by Knights.
75. Ibid.
76. Donald A. Lamontagne, interview by Michael Knights, 2002. For details of Turkish attitudes toward the United States over arms sales, see Phillip Finnegan, "US Must Rebuild Coalition against Saddam," *Defense News*, September 9, 1996, 5.
77. Lake, interview by Knights.
78. Riedel, interview by Knights.
79. Many of these details are not discussed in any secondary literature. They were gleaned from my interviews with the following: CIA Operative, Bruce Riedel, Kenneth Pollack, and Kurt Anderson. Also see Captain Navarro quoted in McKeon, *Joint Targeting*, 71.
80. Fuerth, interview by Knights.
81. Joseph Ralston, interview by Michael Knights, 2003.
82. Parris, interview by Knights.
83. Riedel, interview by Knights.
84. Anderson, interview by Knights. Also see Rip and Hasik, *Precision Revolution*, 159.
85. Pollack, interview by Knights.
86. Riedel, interview by Knights.
87. Glen Shaffer, interview by Michael Knights, 2002.
88. David Frazee, interview by Michael Knights, 2002.
89. White, *Crises after the Storm*, 36.
90. Horner, "Learned from Desert Storm," 5.
91. Miquel Peko, interview by Michael Knights, 2002.
92. Julie Bird, "Desert Strike: The Mission in the Gulf Widens," *Air Force Times* 53, no. 4 (1996): 4.
93. Riedel, interview by Knights.
94. Ralston, interview by Knights.
95. Parris, interview by Knights.
96. McKeon, *Joint Targeting*, 79.
97. CIA Analyst, interview by Knights; CIA Operative, interview by Knights.
98. Quoted in McKeon, *Joint Targeting*, 71.
99. Anderson, interview by Knights.
100. CIA Analyst, interview by Knights.
101. Rip and Hasik, *Precision Revolution*, 163–64.
102. Holliday, interview by Knights.

103. David Fulghum, "Hard Lesson in Iraq: Lead to New Attack Plan," Aviation Week and Space Technology, September 16, 1996, 24.

104. McKeon, *Joint Targeting*, 84.

105. Fulghum, "Hard Lesson in Iraq," 24.

106. Ibid., 24. Confirmed by Anderson, interview by Knights.

107. Riedel, interview by Knights; Parris, interview by Knights.

108. Gertz and Strobel, "Iraqi Jets Challenge Bigger No-Fly Zone"; Eric Schmitt, "Clinton, Claiming Success, Asserts Most Iraqi Troops Have Left Kurds' Enclave," *New York Times*, September 5, 1996.

109. Lamontagne, interview by Knights. Also see Boyne, "Saddam's Alliance"; David Fulghum, "Iraq's Mobile SAMs Stay on the Move," Aviation Week and Space Technology, September 16, 1996.

110. Carla Ann Robbins and John Fialka, "Iraq Repairs Air Defenses, Defying Clinton," *Wall Street Journal*, September 11, 1996, 1; White, *Crises after the Storm*, 44. Fine

111. CIA Analyst, interview by Knights,.

112. White, *Crises after the Storm*, 44. Also see Fulghum, "Hard Lesson in Iraq," 24.

113. Gertz and Strobel, "Iraqi Jets Challenge Bigger No-Fly Zone," 1.

114. Deutch quoted in Rip and Hasik, *Precision Revolution*, 13.

115. Horner, "Learned from Desert Storm," 6.

116. Eliot A. Cohen, "The Mystique of US Air Power," *Foreign Affairs* 71, no. 1 (1994), 121, 124.

117. Steven Lee Myers, "A Failed Race against Time: US Tried to Head Off Iraq," *New York Times*, September 5, 1996, 1.

118. Alan Makovsky, Amatzia Baram, and Michael Eisenstadt, *Crisis in Iraq: Saddam Hussein, the Kurds, and US Policy* (Washington, D.C.: Washington Institute for Near East Policy, 1996), 1.

119. Pollack, interview by Knights.

120. Baram, *Saddam Husayn Conquers Irbil*, 3.

121. U.S. Congress, Senate Committee on Intelligence, *US Intelligence Community's Pre-War Intelligence*, 383–85.

CHAPTER 7. "CHEAT AND RETREAT": IRAQ'S RESISTANCE TO UN INSPECTIONS

1. Ken Pollack, *The Threatening Storm: The Case for Invading Iraq* (New York: Random House, 2002, 88–95.

2. For facts and figures on UNSCOM's record, see Madeleine Albright, "SecState Albright Policy Speech on Iraq," *Global Security, August 8, 1997*, http://www.globalsecurity.org/wmd/library/news/iraq/1997/bmd970327b.htm. For British intelligence reports, see United Kingdom House of Commons, *Review of Intelligence on Weapons of Mass*

Destruction (London: House of Commons, 2004), 48–50. Also see Ritter, *Endgame*, 103, 201, for discussion of missiles, launchers, and chemical weapons stocks.

3. United Kingdom House of Commons, *Weapons of Mass Destruction*, 48.
4. Ibid., 97.
5. Barton Gellman, "Arms Inspectors 'Shake the Tree'," *Washington Post*, October 12, 1998.
6. Ritter, *Endgame*, 154–56.
7. Ibid. For details of the British role, see United Kingdom House of Commons, *Weapons of Mass Destruction*, 90.
8. Charles Duelfer, interview by Michael Knights, 2002. Also see Ritter, *Endgame*.
9. Sean Boyne, "Iraqis Perfect the Art of Evading," *Jane's Intelligence Review* 10, no. 2 (1998): 2.
10. Dana Priest and Bradley Graham, "Airstrikes Took a Toll on Saddam, U.S. Says Iraqi Army's Loyalty, Size Appear Changed," *Washington Post*, March 7, 1999.
11. Ritter, *Endgame*, 18–21, 90. Also see Duefler, interview by Knights.
12. John Sigler, interview by Michael Knights, 2003.
13. Pollack, *Threatening Storm*, 95.
14. Albright, "SecState Albright Policy Speech on Iraq."
15. Tom Clancy, Tony Zinni, and Tony Koltz, *Battle Ready* (London: Putnam, 2004), 4, 7.
16. Charles Wilson, *Strategic and Tactical Aerial Reconnaissance in the Near East* (Washington, D.C.: Washington Institute for Near East Policy, 1999), 84.
17. Gary Crowder, interview by Michael Knights, 2002.
18. Sigler, interview by Knights.
19. Crowder, interview by Knights, 2002.
20. Ibid.
21. James Steinberg, interview by Michael Knights, 2002.
22. Crowder, interview by Knights, 2002.
23. Ibid.
24. Ibid.
25. Steinberg, interview by Knights.
26. White, *Crises after the Storm*, 50.
27. Barton Gellman, Dana Priest, and Bradley Graham, "US Threat of Force on Iraq Masked Doubts: Deep Foreboding about Lasting Effects of Attack Propels Furious Diplomatic Efforts," Washington Post, March 1, 1998.
28. Steinberg, interview by Knights.
29. Gellman, Priest, and Graham, "US Threat of Force."
30. Ritter, *Endgame*, 17.
31. Paul White and Daniel Byman, *Air Power and US Policy towards Iraq* (Washington, D.C.: Washington Institute for Near East Policy, 1999), 51.

32. Ralph Peters, "How Saddam Won this Round," *Newsweek*, November 30, 1998, 39.
33. Ritter, *Endgame*, 20.
34. Pollack, interview by Knights.
35. Steinberg, interview by Knights.
36. Hal Hornburg, interview by Michael Knights, 2002.
37. Stephen Plummer, interview by Michael Knights, 2002.
38. United Kingdom House of Commons, *Weapons of Mass Destruction*, 107; U.S. Congress, Senate Committee on Intelligence, *US Intelligence Community's Pre-War Intelligence*, 260, 289.
39. David Wood, "US Will Miss Having Its Nose Inside Iraq," Cleveland Plain Dealer, January 6, 1999, 1.
40. Priest and Graham, "Airstrikes Took a Toll."
41. Dunlap, interview by Knights.
42. For suggestions about agent-defeat munitions, see Eliot Cohen and Michael Eisenstadt, *Air Power against Iraq: An Assessment* (Washington, D.C.: Washington Institute for Near East Policy, 1998); Robert Wall, "New Weapons Debut in Attacks on Iraq," *Aviation Week and Space Technology*, December 21, 1998. My interviews with all the U.S. military personnel referenced in this chapter conclusively refuted the theory that CBW targets were avoided for fear of agent release.
43. Gellman, Priest, and Graham, "US Threat of Force."
44. Ibid.
45. Cordesman, *Lessons of Desert Fox*, 85.
46. Anthony Zinni, interview by Michael Knights, 2003.
47. Gellman, Priest, and Graham, "US Threat of Force."
48. Ibid.
49. Zinni, interview by Knights.
50. See an explanation of 1930s U.S. targeting of key economic nodes in Philip S. Meilinger, "Air Targeting Strategies: An Overview," in *Air Power Confronts an Unstable World*, ed. Richard P. Hallion (London: Brasseys, 1997), 56–63.
51. Barton Gellman, "U.S. Spied on Iraqi Military via U.N. but Arms Control Team Had No Knowledge of Eavesdropping," Washington Post, March 2, 1998.
52. Plummer, interview by Knights.
53. Ritter, *Endgame*, 21.
54. William Arkin, "The Difference Was in the Details," *Washington Post*, July 29, 1999, http://www.washingtonpost.com/wp-srv/inatl/longterm/iraq/analysis.htm.
55. Ibid.
56. Sigler, interview by Knights.
57. Plummer, interview by Knights.

58. Dunlap, interview by Knights; Crowder, interview by Knights, 2002.
59. Crowder, interview by Knights, 2002.
60. Cordesman, *Lessons of Desert Fox*, 81–83.
61. Zinni, interview by Knights.
62. Ibid.
63. Gary Crowder, interview by Michael Knights, 2004.
64. Crowder, interview by Knights, 2004.
65. Pollack, *Threatening Storm*, 92.
66. Steinberg, interview by Knights.
67. Jim Mannion, "Zinni, Gulf Forces Commander, Pounces after Long Game of Cat-and-Mouse," *Washington Post*, December 19, 1998.
68. Crowder, interview by Knights, 2002.
69. Ibid.
70. Ibid.
71. Zinni, interview by Knights.
72. Ibid.
73. Cordesman, *Lessons of Desert Fox*, 49.
74. Zinni, interview by Knights.
75. Crowder, interview by Knights, 2002.
76. Pollack, interview by Knights.
77. Sigler, interview by Knights.
78. Because of the sensitivity of this subject, the multiple interviewees who commented on this issue would prefer to remain anonymous.
79. Pollack, interview by Knights.
80. Quoted in Dana Priest et al., "Albright: U.S. May Attack Iraq Again," Washington Post, December 20, 1998.
81. Rip and Hasik, *Precision Revolution*, 395.
82. Iraq Broadcasting Corporation, "War Preparations in Iraq," (Irbil: Iraq Broadcasting Corporation, 1998), 1.
83. Clancy, Zinni, and Koltz, *Battle Ready*, 16.
84. Plummer, interview by Knights.
85. Priest and Graham, "Airstrikes Took a Toll."
86. Federation of American Scientists, *UNSCOM Chairman Butler's Report to UN Secretary General*, http://www.fas.org/news/un/iraq/s/butla216.htm
87. Ross Roberts, "Desert Fox: The Third Night," *U.S. Naval Institute Proceedings* 125, no. 4 (April 1999), 36.
88. Cordesman, *Lessons of Desert Fox*; Department of Defense News Briefing, 19 December 1998, http://www.defenselink.mil/news/Dec1998/t12191998_t1219fox.html; Crowder, interview by Knights, 2002.
89. Crowder, interview by Knights, 2002.
90. Zinni, interview by Knights.
91. Clancy, Zinni, and Koltz, *Battle Ready*.
92. Cordesman, *Lessons of Desert Fox*, 46.

93. Sean Boyne, "In the Wake of Desert Fox, Saddam Moves to Tighten His Grip," *Jane's Intelligence Review* 11, no. 1 (1999): 30.

94. Craig Covault, "New Intelligence Ops Debut in Iraq Strikes," *Aviation Week and Space Technology*, December 21, 1998, 125.

95. Wall, "New Weapons Debut," 15.

96. Ronald Lewis, "Saddam Outfoxed," *Air Force's Monthly* (1999).

97. Crowder, interview by Knights. 2002

98. Rip and Hasik, *Precision Revolution*, 374.

99. Crowder, interview by Knights, 2002.

100. Hornburg, interview by Knights.

101. Zinni, interview by Knights.

102. Pollack, interview by Knights.

103. Pollack, *Threatening Storm*, 93

104. Plummer, interview by Knights.

105. Robert Wall, "US to Replenish Missile Stocks, Steps Up Strikes against SAMs," *Aviation Week and Space Technology*, January 18, 1999, 24.

106. Zinni, interview by Knights.

107. For satellite BDA from Desert Fox, go to *Operation DESERT FOX— December 1998—Bomb Damage Assessment Imagery,* Global Security, January 3, 1999, http://www.globalsecurity.org/intell/library/imint/desert_fox.htm.

108. Cordesman, *Lessons of Desert Fox*, 97–98.

109. Wall, "New Weapons Debut," p. 15. Also see Iraq Broadcasting Corporation, "Details of Some Losses Inflicted on Saddam's Regime during Operation Desert Fox" (Sulaymaniyah: Iraq Broadcasting Corporation, 1999).

110. Cordesman, *Lessons of Desert Fox*, 35, 46, 103.

111. Pollack, *Threatening Storm*, 93.

112. Steven Lee Myers, "Iraq Damage More Severe than Expected," *Washington Post*, January 9, 1999.

113. Howard Schneider, "Clashes Reported in Iraq," *Washington Post*, February 24, 1999; Daniel Williams, "Cleric's Killing Arouses Shiites: Iraqi Officials Nervous about Turmoil in the South," *Washington Post*, March 16, 1999.

114. Zinni, interview by Knights.

115. Clancy, Zinni, and Koltz, *Battle Ready*; Zinni, interview by Knights; Sigler, interview by Knights.

116. Rip and Hasik, *Precision Revolution*, 420–23.

117. Ritter, *Endgame*, 29, 196–97.

118. Wood, "US Will Miss," 1.

119. Patrick Clawson, *The Implications of Bombing Iraq* (Washington, D.C.: Washington Institute for Near East Policy, 1998), 1.

120. Pollack, interview by Knights.

CHAPTER 8. PRELUDE TO WAR: THE NO-FLY ZONES AFTER DESERT FOX

1. White, *Crises after the Storm*, 27.
2. Steven Lee Myers, "Iraq Vows to Defy US Ban and Fly in 'No-Flight' Zones," *New York Times*, December 30, 1998, 6; John T. Correll, "Northern Watch," *Air Force* (February 2000): 34.
3. White, *Crises after the Storm*, 62–63.
4. Plummer, interview by Knights.
5. White, *Crises after the Storm*, 63.
6. Plummer, interview by Knights.
7. Zinni, interview by Knights.
8. Dana Priest and Howard Schneider, "Over Iraq, US Fights a Quiet War," *Washington Post*, March 7, 1999.
9. Pollack, interview by Knights.
10. Patrick Clawson, "Stealth Bombing: Our Silent War in Iraq," *New Republic*, September 6, 1999, 18.
11. Pollack, interview by Knights.
12. Zinni, interview by Knights.
13. Amatzia Baram, *Saddam Husayn's Rage and Fury* (Washington, D.C.: Washington Institute for Near East Policy, 1999), 1.
14. Frazee, interview by Knights.
15. Dunlap, interview by Knights.
16. Frazee, interview by Knights.
17. Nelson, interview by Knights.
18. Mark Schmidt, interview by Michael Knights, 2002.
19. Zinni, interview by Knights.
20. Nelson, interview by Knights.
21. Plummer, interview by Knights.
22. Schmidt, interview by Knights.
23. Steven Lee Myers, "Something New in the Iraqi Conflict: Concrete Bombs," *New York Times*, October 7, 1999.
24. Plummer, interview by Knights. Also see Charles Moore, interview by Michael Knights, 2002.
25. Schmidt, interview by Knights.
26. David Fulghum and Robert Wall, "Iraqi Air Defenses Broken but Dangerous," Aviation Week and Space Technology, February 15, 1999, 30–31.
27. Edward Ellis, interview by Michael Knights, 2004; Deptula, interview by Knights, part 1.
28. White, *Crises after the Storm*, 84.
29. Parris, interview by Knights.
30. Richard Grunawalt, "The JCS Standing Rules of Engagement: A Judge Advocate's Primer," *Air Force Law Review* 42 (1997): 257.

31. For sketches of these issues, see Clary, *Operation Provide Comfort*; Bruce A. Weber, *Combined Task Force Provide Comfort: A New Model for "Lead Nation" Command?* (Naval War College, 1994) Newport, RI; and Timothy Warnock, *Short of War: Major USAF Contingency Operations* (Maxwell, Ala.: Air Force Historical Research Agency, 2000).

32. Steve Callicutt, interview by Michael Knights, 2002. Also see Myers, "Something New."

33. Mark Waite, interview by Michael Knights, 2002. Waite was the "Duke"—the mission controller—on AWACS flying in Northern Watch.

34. Callicutt, interview by Knights; Deptula, interview by Knights, part 1.

35. Callicutt, interview by Knights.

36. David Deptuala, interview by Michael Knights, 2002, part 3.

37. Ibid.

38. Ibid.

39. Ibid.

40. Callicutt, interview by Knights.

41. Ibid. Deptula confirmed that he staffed the drafting of ROEs to Callicutt in Deptula, interview by Knights, part 3.

42. Ibid.

43. Callicutt, interview by Knights.

44. Deptula, interview by Knights, part 3.

45. Ibid. The new ROEs were publicly acknowledged on February 23. See Sarah Graham-Brown, "No-Fly Zones: Rhetoric and Real Intentions," *Middle East Report* (2001).

46. Parris, interview by Knights.

47. Deptula, interview by Knights, part 3.

48. Callicutt, interview by Knights.

49. Deptula, interview by Knights, part 3.

50. Ellis, interview by Knights.

51. Callicutt, interview by Knights.

52. See the chronology, beginning on p. 8, in Anthony H. Cordesman, *The Air Defense War since Desert Fox: A Short History* (Washington, D.C.: Center for Strategic and International Studies, 1999).

53. Callicutt, interview by Knights.

54. Wall, "US to Replenish," 24; Fulghum and Wall, "Iraqi Air Defenses," 31.

55. Rip and Hasik, *Precision Revolution*, 251, 255. Rip and Hasik discuss the use of AGM-130s in the no-fly zones in depth.

56. Ellis, interview by Knights.

57. Callicutt, interview by Knights.

58. Because of the sensitive nature of this issue, the U.S. officer asked to remain anonymous.

59. As above.

60. Cordesman, *Air Defense War*, 3, 14.
61. Callicutt, interview by Knights.
62. Parris, interview by Knights.
63. Myers, "Something New."
64. Callicutt, interview by Knights; Deptula, interview by Knights, part 3.
65. Myers, "Something New"; Correll, "Northern Watch," 34.
66. Myers, "Something New."
67. Robert DuLaney, interview by Michael Knights, 2004.
68. Terry Boyd, "Northern Watch Keeps Tight Reins on Iraq," *European Stars and Stripes*, May 8, 2000.
69. DuLaney, interview by Knights.
70. Ellis, interview by Knights.
71. DuLaney, interview by Knights.
72. David Fulghum, "U.S. May Suspend Northern Watch Patrol," *Aviation Week and Space Technology*, May 14, 2001, 31.
73. White, *Crises after the Storm*, 53.
74. Michael Knights, "Time May Be up for Iraq's Northern No-Fly Zone," *Gulf States Newsletter*, September 25, 2001, 1.
75. Ellis, interview by Knights.
76. Ibid.
77. White, *Crises after the Storm*, xiii.
78. CIA Operative, interview by Knights.
79. Michael Knights, "Iraq: New Tensions, Ukrainian Complications in the No-Fly Zones," *Gulf States Newsletter*, May 1, 2002; Michael Knights, "Yugoslav Connection Suggests Business as Usual for Iraq's Arms Suppliers," *Gulf States Newsletter*, September 12, 2002.
80. Michael Knights, "Iraq's Military Options: Blunting the Air Assault," Gulf States Newsletter, September 27, 2002; Knights, "Iraq: New Tensions."
81. Knights, "Iraq: New Tensions," 1.
82. Michael Knights, "Iraq Raises the Heat in a War of Diplomatic Attrition," Gulf States Newsletter, September 6, 2001.
83. David Fulghum, "Central Iraq's Air Defenses Remain as Dense as in 1991," *Aviation Week and Space Technology*, October 21, 2002, p. 27.
84. William Branigin, "A Brief, Bitter War for Iraq's Military Officers: Self-Deception a Factor in Defeat," *Washington Post*, April 27, 2003.
85. Jim Moschgat, interview by Michael Knights, 2004.
86. Callicutt, interview by Knights.
87. Fulghum, "Central Iraq's Air Defenses"; Fulghum and Wall, "Iraqi Air Defenses Broken."
88. Fulghum, "Central Iraq's Air Defenses," 27.
89. Richard Speier, *Iraq's Al-Samoud: A Missile with Great Possibilities* (Washington, D.C.: Washington Institute for Near East Policy, 2002), 2.

90. DuLaney, interview by Knights.
91. Gene Renuart, interview by Michael Knights, 2003.
92. David Fulghum and John Morocco, "Strike Hits Old Targets, Reveals New Problems," *Aviation Week and Space Technology*, February 26, 2001, 1.
93. Kopp, "Desert Storm," 3.
94. Charles Wald, interview by Michael Knights, 2002.
95. Fulghum and Morocco, "Strike Hits Old Targets," 1.
96. Ibid., 1.
97. Jim Hoagland, "A Risky No-Fly Zone over Iraq," *Washington Post*, February 10, 2001, B07.
98. Thomas Ricks, "Bombs in Iraq Fell Wide of Targets: New Navy Weapon Blamed for Misses," *Washington Post*, February 22, 2001.
99. Ibid. Also see Rip and Hasik, *Precision Revolution*, 250, and Fulghum and Morocco, "Strike Hits Old Targets," 30.
100. Wald, interview by Knights.
101. CNN, "Iraq Air Patrols Resume after Raid," August 15, 2001, http://www.cnn.com/2001/WORLD/meast/02/18/iraq.airstrike/index.html.
102. Thomas Ricks and Alan Sipress, "Cuts Urged in Patrols over Iraq," *Washington Post*, May 9, 2001.
103. Renuart, interview by Knights.
104. Michael Knights, "Tensions Rise over Air Incursion Claims," *Gulf States Newsletter*, September 25, 2000, 1.
105. Sean Boyne, "How Saddam Rebuilt His Forces," *Jane's Intelligence Review* 8, no. 11 (1996); Criag Hoyle and James O'Halloran, "Iraqi Air Defense: Fortress Iraq," *Jane's Defense Weekly* (2002); Cooper, interview by Knights.
106. I am thankful for the many enlightening conservations I have had with Tom Cooper, an Austrian aviation journalist who remains the world's leading expert on the Iraqi air force.
107. Knights, "Iraq Raises the Heat," 1.
108. Fulghum, "Central Iraq's Air Defenses," 29.
109. Moschgat, interview by Knights.
110. Cooper and Bishop, *Iran-Iraq War*, 280–83.
111. White, *Crises after the Storm*, 62.
112. Tom Cooper, *Exhumating the Dead Iraqi Air Force,* Air Combat Information Group, 2003, http://www.acig.org/artman/publish/article_247.shtml.
113. Knights, "Iraq Raises the Heat," 2.
114. David Fulghum and Robert Wall, "North Korea Nuke Crisis Complicates Iraq Build-Up," *Aviation Week and Space Technology*, January 6, 2003, 21.
115. Gregory Hooker, *Military Intelligence Assessments Shaping the Plan for*

Operation Iraqi Freedom (Tampa, Fl.: U.S. Central Command, 2004), pp. 19–20.

116. Tom Erhardt, interview by Michael Knights, 2002.
117. Tommy Franks, *American Soldier* (New York: Regan Books, 2004), 241.
118. U.S. Department of Defense, "Coalition Forces Air Component Command Briefing April 5, 2003," News Transcript, April 5, 2003, http://www.defenselink.mil/news/Apr2003/t04052003_t405mose.html.

CHAPTER 9. TRANSITIONING TO WAR

1. Renuart, interview by Knights.
2. Knights, "Iraq: New Tensions," 1.
3. Bob Woodward, *Plan of Attack* (New York: Simon & Schuster, 2004), 11, 25.
4. U.S. Congress, Senate Committee on Intelligence, *US Intelligence Community's Pre-War Intelligence*, 388.
5. Quoted in Charles Duelfer, "Why Iraq Will Never Give Up Its Worst Weapons," *Aviation Week and Space Technology*, March 11, 2002, 73.
6. Woodward, *Plan of Attack*, 231, 233.
7. Ibid., 25; Michael Knights, "New Endgames," *Gulf States Newsletter*, August 9, 2002, 1.
8. Woodward, *Plan of Attack*, 11, 25.
9. Quotes from United Kingdom House of Commons, *Weapons of Mass Destruction*, 63, 70.
10. Riedel, interview by Knights.
11. Jeffrey White, *War in Iraq: A Preliminary Assessment* (Washington, D.C.: Washington Institute for Near East Policy, 2003), 1.
12. Woodward, *Plan of Attack*, 25.
13. Mason "Mase" Carpenter, interview by Michael Knights, 2003.
14. Franks, *American Soldier*, 339. Also see Woodward, *Plan of Attack*, 54, 56.
15. U.S. Army Center for Lessons Learned, *On Point*.
16. Hooker, *Military Intelligence Assessments*, 19.
17. See Greg Hooker, a senior analyst at CENTCOM, in Ibid., 40. Also see United Kingdom House of Commons, *Weapons of Mass Destruction*, 71.
18. Hathaway, interview by Knights.
19. Thomas Donnelly, *Operation Iraqi Freedom: A Strategic Assessment* (Washington, D.C.: American Enterprise Institute, 2003); Hooker, *Military Intelligence Assessments*; U.S. Army Center for Lessons Learned, *On Point*.
20. U.S. Army Center for Lessons Learned, *On Point*.

21. Murray and Scales, *Iraq War*, 93.
22. Michael Knights, "Strategies for Repelling a Ground Assault," *Gulf States Newsletter*, October 9, 2002, 9.
23. Ritter, *Endgame*, 199–200.
24. Franks, *American Soldier*, 392.
25. Hooker, *Military Intelligence Assessments*, 13.
26. Carl Conetta, *Catastrophic Interdiction: Air Power and the Collapse of the Iraqi Field Army in the 2003 War* (Cambridge, Mass.: Project on Defense Alternatives, 2003), 2.
27. Hooker, *Military Intelligence Assessments*, 51.
28. Ibid., 24.
29. Franks, *American Soldier*, 342.
30. Renuart, interview by Knights.
31. Phillip Gibbons, *US No-Fly Zones in Iraq: To What End?* (Washington, D.C.: Washington Institute for Near East Policy, 2002), 2.
32. Franks, *American Soldier*, 352.
33. Mark Cline, interview by Michael Knights, 2003.
34. Renuart, interview by Knights.
35. Because of the sensitivity of this information, the officers interviewed asked for their comments to be made off the record.
36. Hathaway, interview by Knights.
37. Ellis, interview by Knights.
38. Knights, "Weighing the Cost," 1.
39. Renuart, interview by Knights.
40. Ibid.
41. Ronald O'Rourke, *Iraq War: Defense Program Implications for Congress* (Washington, D.C.: Congressional Research Service, 2003), 61.
42. U.S. Army Center for Lessons Learned, *On Point*.
43. Michael Knights, "PSYOPS Comes into Play against Saddam," *Jane's Intelligence Review* (2003): 3–4.
44. Moschgat, interview by Knights; Renuart, interview by Knights.
45. Robert Wall, "Time Runs Short," *Aviation Week and Space Technology*, March 17, 2003, 28.
46. Rebecca Grant, "Eyes Wide Open," *Air Force* (November 2003): 1.
47. David Fulghum and Robert Wall, "Deployment of New Technology Continues," *Aviation Week and Space Technology*, January 27, 2003, 37. Also see Craig Covault, "Secret NRO Recons Eye Iraq Threat," *Aviation Week and Space Technology*, February 16, 2002, 23. For Zircon chat and other SIGINT issues, see Woodward, *Plan of Attack*, 217, 305.
48. United Nations, *UN Resolution 687*.
49. Michael Eisenstadt, *Iraq's Weapons of Mass Destruction: An Emerging Challenge for the Bush Administration* (Washington, D.C.: Washington Institute for Near East Policy, 2001), 1.

50. Jon Marks, "Is Saddam, No Longer the Immortal, Preparing for the Après Saddam?" *Gulf States Newsletter,* February 6, 2002; Jon Marks, "Saddam's Reshuffle Points to Policy Shift, but Iraq Remains Intransigent," *Gulf States Newsletter*, April 30, 2001.

51. U.S. Congress, Senate Committee on Intelligence, *US Intelligence Community's Pre-War Intelligence*, 86, 148, 196, 217–222. Also see United Kingdom House of Commons, *Weapons of Mass Destruction*, 54–58, 59–60, 63.

52. United Kingdom House of Commons, *Weapons of Mass Destruction*, 91.

53. Speier, *Iraq's Al-Samoud*, 1.

54. David Fulghum, "Powell Details List of Iraqi Violations," *Aviation Week and Space Technology*, January 25, 2003, 43–45.

55. Woodward, *Plan of Attack*, 367.

56. For a good round-up of these strikes, see Anthony Cordesman, *The Lessons of the Iraq War* (Washington, D.C.: Center for Strategic and International Studies, 2003), 54.

57. This section draws on various works as well as interview material with special-forces personnel who wished to make their remarks off the record. A key text is Robin Moore, *The Hunt for Saddam Hussein* (New York: Penguin, 2003), 10, 112–15. Other useful information is contained in the following texts: Franks, *American Soldier*, 434; Woodward, *Plan of Attack*, 379; Murray and Scales, *Iraq War*, 69, 185.

58. Most of this information is derived from Woodward, *Plan of Attack*, 108, 142–44, 209, 306.

59. Adam Hebert, "The Baghdad Strikes," *Air Force* (July 2003); 1.

60. Coll, *Ghost Wars*, 417–423.

61. Renuart, interview by Knights.

62. Marks, "No Longer the Immortal," 1.

63. See Pape on Saddam's assassin instinct: Robert Pape, *Bombing to Win: Airpower and Coercion in War* (Ithaca, N.Y.: Cornell University Press, 1996), 231, 233.

64. Anthony Roberson, interview by Michael Knights, 2003.

65. Carpenter, interview by Knights.

66. Moore, *Hunt for Saddam Hussein*, 115, 117, 120. Also see David Fulghum, "Fast Forward," *Aviation Week and Space Technology*, April 28, 2003, 32.

67. Woodward, *Plan of Attack*, 401–2.

68. Franks, *American Soldier*, 437–39.

69. Murray and Scales, *Iraq War*, 116, 129–53.

70. David Fulghum and Douglas Barrie, "War Preparations Reveal Problems," Aviation Week and Space Technology, December 9, 2002, 29–31. Also see Tim Ripley, "Iraqi Missile Forces Failed to Impact on Iraqi Freedom," *Jane's Intelligence Review* 14, no. 4 (April 2003): 1.

71. Ripley, "Iraqi Missile Forces," 1.

72. The original concept was described by Harlan Ullman and Jim Wade in *Shock and Awe: Achieving Rapid Dominance* (1996).

73. Cline, interview by Knights.

74. David G. Minister, interview by Michael Knights, 2003.

75. Hooker, *Military Intelligence Assessments*, 20.

76. Woodward, *Plan of Attack*, 108.

77. Crowder, interview by Knights, 2004.

78. Franks, *American Soldier*, 471.

79. Third Infantry Division (Mechanized), *After-Action Report: Operation Iraqi Freedom*, February 18, 2004, 74.

80. Shaffer, interview by Knights, 2002.

81. Quoted in Joris Lok, "Communication Weaknesses Endanger Allied Integration in U.S.-Led Air Campaigns," *Jane's International Defense Review* 37, no. 3 (March 2004), 4.

82. Cordesman, *Lessons of the Iraq War*, 194.

83. Bradley Graham, "Military Turns to Software to Cut Civillian Casualties," *Washington Post*, February 21, 2003. Also see Woodward, *Plan of Attack*, 110–11.

84. Human Rights Watch, *Off Target: The Conduct of the War and Civilian Casualties in Iraq*, February 6, 2003.

85. Shaffer, interview by Knights, 2002.

86. Mike Downs, interview by Michael Knights, 2003.

87. Woodward, *Plan of Attack*, 277.

88. Hooker, *Military Intelligence Assessments*, 19–20.

89. Roberson, interview by Knights.

90. Woodward, *Plan of Attack*, 331.

91. Crowder, interview by Knights, 2004.

92. Hathaway, interview by Knights.

93. Crowder, interview by Knights, 2004.

94. Cordesman, *Lessons of the Iraq War*, 28. Murray and Scales, *Iraq War*, 168–70.

95. Robert Pape, "The True Worth of Air Power," *Foreign Affairs* 83, no. 2 (2004): 127.

96. Jeffrey White, *Iraq Fights Its War 'Outside-In'* (Washington, D.C.: Washington Institute for Near East Policy 2003), 1.

97. Hooker, *Military Intelligence Assessments*, 19–20.

98. Franks, *American Soldier*, 287.

CHAPTER 10. THE MARCH ON BAGHDAD

1. U.S. Army Center for Lessons Learned, *On Point*.

2. Ibid. Also see Third Infantry Division (Mechanized), *After-Action Report*, 35, 95–96.

3. Hooker, *Military Intelligence Assessments*, 47.
4. Robert Wall, "Lessons Emerge," *Aviation Week and Space Technology*, April 14, 2003, 27. Also see Patrick Warren and Keith Barclay, "Operation Airborne Dragon, Northern Iraq," Military Review (November/December 2003): 2.
5. MEF, "Commanding General, 1st Marine Division, 'Operation Iraqi Freedom: Lessons Learned'" (Washington, D.C.: Department of Defense, 2003).
6. Third Infantry Division (Mechanized), *After-Action Report*, 53, 114, 127. Also see Mark Hewish, "Battlefield Air Operations: Weight and Time Are the Main Targets," *Jane's International Defense Review* 37, no. 5 (May 2004): 50.
7. U.S. Army Center for Lessons Learned, *On Point*.
8. Franks, *American Soldier*, 477.
9. Cordesman, *Lessons of the Iraq War*, 263.
10. Biddle et al., *Iraq and the Future of Warfare: Implications for Army and Defense Policy* (Carlisle, Penn.: Strategic Studies Institute, 2003), 5.
11. Crowder, interview by Knights, 2004.
12. Rick Atkinson, *In the Company of Soldiers* (New York: Penguin, 2003): 106.
13. Hooker, *Military Intelligence Assessments*, 33, 35. For details of some of these actions, see Cordesman, *Lessons of the Iraq War*, 73, 78, 90.
14. U.S. Center for Lessons Learned, *On Point*.
15. Glenn Shaffer, interview by Michael Knights, 2003.
16. U.S. Congress, House Armed Services Committee, *Operational Lessons Learned from Operation Iraqi Freedom*, October 2, 2003.
17. For extensive discussion of this issue, see the following articles: Robert Wall, "Super Hornets at Sea," *Aviation Week and Space Technology*, March 17, 2003, 57; Robert Wall, "Cobras in Urban Combat," *Aviation Week and Space Technology*, April 14, 2003, 74.
18. Cordesman, *Lessons of the Iraq War*, 160, 188.
19. Third Infantry Division (Mechanized), *After-Action Report*, 183.
20. U.S. Army Center for Lessons Learned, *On Point*.
21. Ibid.
22. Quoted in Cordesman, *Lessons of the Iraq War*, 175.
23. Communications limitations are the central theme of the 3rd Infantry Division lessons learned report. See Third Infantry Division (Mechanized), *After-Action Report*, 114, 139, 177, 255–56.
24. Michael Eisenstadt, *Iraqi Strategy and the Battle for Baghdad* (Washington, D.C.: Washington Institute for Near East Policy, 2003), 1.
25. Third Infantry Division (Mechanized), *After-Action Report*, 17, 134; "U.S. Artillery Demonstrates Flexible Fires in Iraq," *Jane's International Defense Review* 37, no. 3 (March 2004): 30.

26. Biddle et al., *Iraq and the Future of Warfare*, 5. For Iraqi reconnaissance in 1991, see *Gulf War Airpower Study*, 71.

27. Atkinson, *In the Company of Soldiers*, 173.

28. U.S. Army Center for Lessons Learned, *On Point*.

29. Hooker, *Military Intelligence Assessments*, 51.

30. Franks, *American Soldier*, 485.

31. U.S. Army Center for Lessons Learned, *On Point*.

32. Franks, *American Soldier*, 487–88.

33. Rebecca Grant, "Saddam's Elite in the Meat Grinder," *Air Force* (November 2003): 1.

34. Quoted in Murray and Scales, *Iraq War*, 123.

35. Michael Knights, "Saddam's Vulnerability to 'Inside Out' Warfare," *Gulf States Newsletter*, September 27, 2002, 7.

36. Franks, *American Soldier*, 486.

37. Biddle et al., *Iraq and the Future of Warfare*.

38. Quoted in Cordesman, *Lessons of the Iraq War*, 130, 156.

39. Franks, *American Soldier*, 489. For "double tapping," see the chapter of the same name in Zucchino, *Thunder Run*: The Armored Strike to Capture Baghdad (New York: Atlantic Monthly Press, 2004), 31–46. For details on U.S. helicopters and fake surrenders, see Wall, "Cobras in Urban Combat," 74.

40. U.S. Army Center for Lessons Learned, *On Point*.

41. White, *War in Iraq*, 1.

42. White, *Iraq Fights Its War 'Outside-In'*, 1.

43. Ibid., 2.

44. Eisenstadt, *Iraqi Strategy*, 1.

45. U.S. Army Center for Lessons Learned, *On Point*.

46. Third Infantry Division (Mechanized), *After-Action Report*, 108.

47. Ibid., 98, 108.

48. Daniel Leaf, interview by Michael Knights, 2003.

49. Steve Seroka, Michael Knights, 2004.

50. Third Infantry Division (Mechanized), *After-Action Report*, 139.

51. Ibid., 98, 104.

52. U.S. Army Center for Lessons Learned, *On Point*.

53. Atkinson, *In the Company of Soldiers*, 114, 124.

54. Ibid., 105, 119, 148, 155.

55. Ibid., 119, 147–50. Also see Murray and Scales, *Iraq War*, 104–7.

56. Atkinson, *In the Company of Soldiers*, 155. Also see Franks, *American Soldier*, 496.

57. Wall, "Cobras in Urban Combat," 74.

58. Atkinson, *In the Company of Soldiers*, 152, 188.

59. U.S. Army Center for Lessons Learned, *On Point*.

60. Atkinson, *In the Company of Soldiers*, 153.

61. Quoted in Cordesman, *Lessons of the Iraq War*, 129–30.

62. Franks, *American Soldier*, 502.

63. Atkinson, *In the Company of Soldiers*, 142.

64. Quoted in Cordesman, *Lessons of the Iraq War*, 129–30.

65. Third Infantry Division (Mechanized), *After-Action Report*, 108, 139. Also see U.S. Army Center for Lessons Learned, *On Point*.

66. Atkinson, *In the Company of Soldiers*, 184.

67. Hathaway, interview by Knights; Cline, interview by Knights; Roberson, interview by Knights.

68. Third Infantry Division (Mechanized), *After-Action Report*, 105.

69. Roberson, interview by Knights.

70. Hathaway, interview by Knights.

71. Roberson, interview by Knights.

72. Eric Schmitt, "In the Skies over Iraq, Silent Observers," *New York Times*, April 18, 2003, 8. Also see "Joint STARS: Backbone of Joint Warfare," *Defense News*, February 12, 2004.

73. Grant, "Eyes Wide Open," 1. Also see David Fulghum and Robert Wall, "Baghdad Confidential," *Aviation Week and Space Technology*, April 28, 2003, 32.

74. Roberson, interview with Knights.

75. Crowder, interview with Knights, 2004.

76. David Deptula, Gary Crowder, and George Stamper, "Direct Attack: Enhancing Counterland Doctrine and Joint Air-Ground Operations," *Air & Space Power Journal* (2003): 1.

77. Quoted in Robert Collier, "Behind Baghdad's Fall: Hussein Son's Wild Orders Led to Iraq Military Collapse," *San Francisco Chronicle*, May 25, 2003.

78. Branigin, "Brief, Bitter War."

79. Zucchino, *Thunder Run*, 5.

80. Franks, *American Soldier*, 503.

81. Adam Hebert, "The Long Reach of the Heavy Bombers," *Air Force* (November 2003): 1.

82. Donnelly, *Operation Iraqi Freedom*, 42.

83. Quoted in Cordesman, *Lessons of the Iraq War*, 130.

84. Atkinson, *In the Company of Soldiers*, 187.

85. Murray and Scales, *Iraq War*, 145, 200.

86. U.S. Army Center for Lessons Learned, *On Point*.

87. Murray and Scales, *Iraq War*, 200. Also see Atkinson, *In the Company of Soldiers*, 142, and Third Infantry Division (Mechanized), *After-Action Report*, 26, 130.

88. U.S. Army Center for Lessons Learned, *On Point*.

89. Ibid.

90. Franks, *American Soldier*, 489.

91. Cordesman, *Lessons of the Iraq War*, 71.
92. Third Infantry Division (Mechanized), *After-Action Report*, 25–26, 108, 130.
93. *Coalition Forces Air Component Command Briefing April 5, 2003*.
94. Hooker, *Military Intelligence Assessments*, p. 42. Review of Intelligence on Weapons of Mass Destruction, pp. 71, 73.
95. Cooper, *Exhumating the Dead Iraqi Air Force*.
96. U.S. Department of Defense, "Coalition Forces Air Component."
97. Roberson, interview by Knights.
98. Franks, *American Soldier*, 435. Also see Hooker, *Military Intelligence Assessments*, 29.
99. Quoted in Cordesman, *Lessons of the Iraq War*, 52.
100. U.S. Department of Defense, "Coalition Forces Air Component."
101. Crowder, interview by Knights, 2004.
102. Robert Wall, "Fight Control," *Aviation Week and Space Technology*, April 14, 2003, 26.
103. MEF, "Lessons Learned."
104. Atkinson, *In the Company of Soldiers*, 184. Also see Robert Cassidy, "Renaissance of the Attack Helicopter in the Close Fight," *Military Review* (July/August 2003): 5.
105. Quoted in Cordesman, *Lessons of the Iraq War*, 131.
106. Seroka, interview by Knights.
107. Roberson, interview by Knights.
108. Crowder, interview by Knights, 2004.
109. Hathaway, interview by Knights.
110. U.S. Department of Defense, *"Coalition Forces Air Component."*
111. Donnelly, *Operation Iraqi Freedom*, 63.
112. U.S. Army Center for Lessons Learned, *On Point.*
113. Franks, *American Soldier*, 513–15.
114. Quoted in Cordesman, *Lessons of the Iraq War*, 131.
115. Zucchino, *Thunder Run*, 5. Also see Murray and Scales, *Iraq War*, 197.
116. Zucchino, *Thunder Run*, 71.
117. Hooker, *Military Intelligence Assessments*, 42, 47.
118. Quoted in Cordesman, *Lessons of the Iraq War*, 131.
119. Collier, "Behind Baghdad's Fall."
120. "U.S. Armor in Combat: The Iraqi Lessons," *Military Technology* 27, no. 11 (2003): 54.
121. William Hawkins, "Iraq: Heavy Forces and Decisive Warfare," *Parameters* (Autumn 2003): 61. Also see Murray and Scales, *Iraq War*, 244.
122. Zucchino, *Thunder Run*, 62.
123. U.S. Army Center for Lessons Learned, *On Point.*
124. Robert Fisk, "How US Demoralised Iraq's Army," *Independent*, May 28, 2003.

125. Crowder, interview by Knights, 2004.
126. Minister, interview by Knights.
127. Crowder, interview by Knights, 2004.
128. Minister, interview by Knights.
129. Zucchino, *Thunder Run*, 72, 80.
130. Ibid., 173, 293.
131. Ibid., 183, 188.
132. Michael Moseley, *Operation Iraqi Freedom: By the Numbers* (Shaw Air Force Base: CENTAF Analysis and Assessments Division, 2003), 9.
133. Human Rights Watch, *Off Target.* Also see Hebert, "Baghdad Strikes," 3, and Douglas Jehl and Eric Schmitt, "Errors Are Seen in Early Attacks on Iraqi Leaders," *Washington Post*, June 13, 2004.
134. Zucchino, *Thunder Run*, 273–95, 305.
135. Cordesman, *Lessons of the Iraq War*, 90.
136. Knights, "Weighing the Cost," 1.
137. Eisenstadt, *Iraqi Strategy*, 2.

CHAPTER 11. ENDING RESISTANCE

1. Zucchino, *Thunder Run*, 323.
2. Franks, *American Soldier*, 548.
3. U.S. Central Intelligence Agency, *Comprehensive Report of the Special Advisor to the DCI on Iraqi WMD,* 2004, http://www.cia.gov/cia/reports/iraq_wmd_2004/chap1.html.
4. Alex Berenson and John Burns, "Eight Day Battle for Najaf: From Attack to Stalemate," *New York Times*, August 18, 2004.
5. Michael Knights, *Proliferation Presents a Long-Term Challenge*, Oxford Analytica, 2004, http://www.oxan.com/display.aspx?ItemID=DB114074.
6. Ryan Phillips and Jeffrey White, "Sadrist Revolt Provides Lessons for Counterinsurgency in Iraq," *Jane's Intelligence Review* 16, no. 8 (2004). Also see Ahmed Hashim, *The Sunni Insurgency In Iraq*, Middle East Institute, 2003, http://www.mideasti.org/articles/doc89.html.
7. Michael Knights, "Proxy War and Political Shifts in Northern Iraq," *Gulf States Newsletter*, May 1, 2002.
8. U.S. Department of Defense, *Conduct of the Persian Gulf War*, 66.
9. Steven Metz, "Insurgency and Counterinsurgency in Iraq," *Washington Quarterly* 27, no. 1 (2004): 27
10. U.S. Army Center for Lessons Learned, *On Point.*
11. Anthony Cordesman, *The Current Military Situation in Iraq*, Center for Strategic and International Studies, 2003, http://www.csis.org/features/031114current.pdf, 26.

12. Willian Miller, "Insurgency Theory and the Conflict in Algeria: A Theoretical Analysis," *Terrorism and Political Violence* 12, no. 1 (2000): 66.
13. Megan Scully, "U.S. Army Rushes Helo Defense Systems to Iraq," *Defense News*, March 17, 2003, 10.
14. U.S. Army Center for Lessons Learned, *On Point*.
15. White, *Crises after the Storm*, 62–63.
16. David Petraeus, interview by Michael Knights, 2004.
17. Metz, "Insurgency and Counterinsurgency," 32.
18. Petraeus, interview by Knights. Also see the listing of operations at http://www.globalsecurity.org/military/ops/iraq_ongoing_mil_ops.htm.
19. Ibid. Also see Murray and Scales, *Iraq War*, 224.
20. David Fulghum, "Terror vs Intelligence," *Aviation Week and Space Technology*, November 3, 2003, 20.
21. U.S. Army Center for Lessons Learned, *On Point*. Also see Scully, "U.S. Army Rushes."
22. Berenson and Burns, "Eight Day Battle."
23. Jeffrey White, interview by Michael Knights, 2004.
24. Petraeus, interview by Knights.
25. Berenson and Burns, "Eight Day Battle."
26. Chuck Swanneck, interview by Michael Knights, 2004.
27. Petraeus, interview by Knights.
28. Berenson and Burns, "Eight Day Battle."
29. Scully, "U.S. Army Rushes."
30. United Kingdom House of Commons, *Weapons of Mass Destruction*.
31. Nick Wadhams, "Iraq Car Bombings up under Interim Gov't," Associated Press, 2005, http://www.cleveland.com/lake/plaindealer/index.ssf?/base/iswar/110561733925420.xml. Also see Stephen Hedges, "Roadside Bombs: U.S. Battles Low-Tech Threat," *Chicago Tribune*, October 23, 2004.
32. William Matthews, "Boom Time for Bomb Jammers," *Defense News*, March 22, 2004. Fulghum, "Terror vs Intelligence," 21.
33. Swanneck, interview by Knights.
34. Berenson and Burns, "Eight Day Battle."
35. Rajiv Chandrasekaran and Daniel Williams, "U.S. Military Returns to Use of Heavy Munitions in Iraq," *Washington Post*, November 23, 2003.
36. Cordesman, *Current Military Situation*, 10.
37. Swanneck, interview by Knights; James Janega, "In Ramadi, GIs Fight an Elusive Foe," *Chicago Tribune*, November 1, 2004.
38. Donnelly, *Operation Iraqi Freedom*, 89.
39. Chandrasekaran and Williams, "U.S. Military Returns."
40. Quoted in Berenson and Burns, "Eight Day Battle."
41. James Conway, "'Farther and Faster' in Iraq," *U.S. Naval Institute Proceedings* 131, no. 1 (January 2005).

42. Petraeus, interview by Knights.
43. Tom Lasseter, "In the Face of Stubborn Insurgency, Troops Scale Back Anbar Patrols," *Knight Ridder*, 2004, http://www.realcities.com/mld/krwashington/9200682.htm?template=contentModules/printstory.jsp.
44. Miller, "Insurgency Theory," 64–69. Also see Michael Schwartz, "The Taming of Sadr City," *Asia Times*, January 12, 2005. Ken Gause, "Can the Iraqi Security Apparatus Save Saddam?" *Jane's Intelligence Review* 14, no. 11 (2002): 9.
45. Swanneck, interview by Knights.
46. Phillips and White, "Sadrist Revolt."
47. Ibid.
48. Berenson and Burns, "Eight Day Battle." Also see Tom Engelhardt, "Icarus over Iraq: The Miracle of a Single Haasen Hand Grenade," *Antiwar.com*, 2004, http://www.tomdispatch.com/index.mhtml?pid=2047.
49. Cordesman, *Current Military Situation*, 14; also see Engelhardt, "Icarus over Iraq."
50. Jeffrey White, *Faces of Battle: The Insurgents at Fallujah* (Washington, D.C.: Washington Institute for Near East Policy, 2004); Schwartz, "Taming of Sadr City"; Jonathan Keiler, "Who Won the Battle of Fallujah?" *U.S. Naval Institute Proceedings* 131, no. 1 (January 2005).
51. International Policy Institute for Counter-Terrorism, *Full Text of "Al-Zarqawi Letter,"* 2005, http://www.ict.org.il/documents/documentdet.cfm?docid=62.
52. Wadhams, "Iraq Car Bombings."

EPILOGUE: AMERICA'S FIFTEEN-YEAR WAR IN IRAQ

1. Thomas Ricks, "U.S. Army Changed by Iraq, but for Better or Worse?" *Washington Post*, July 6, 2004.
2. Luttwak, *Strategy, the Logic of War and Peace*, 3–17, 73–117.
3. Quoted in Atkinson, *In the Company of Soldiers*, 168.
4. Crowder, interview by Knights, 2004.
5. Donnelly, *Operation Iraqi Freedom*, 89.

Bibliography

Al-Ayyubi, Hazim Abdul-Razzaq. *Forty-Three Missiles on the Zionist Entity*. Washington, D.C.: Foreign Broadcast Information Service, 1998.

Albright, Madeleine. "For the Record." *Congressional Questions*, July 3, 1993, p. 1766.

———. "SecState Albright Policy Speech on Iraq," *Global Security*, August 8, 2004, http://www.globalsecurity.org/wmd/library/news/iraq/1997/bmd970327b.htm.

Anderson, Kurt. 2004. Interview by Michael Knights. *Telephone interview,* Jan 20. Washington D.C.

Andrews, William. *Airpower against an Army: CENTAF's Duel with the Republican Guard*. Maxwell Air Force Base, Ala.: Air University, 1995.

Anno, Stephen E., and William E. Einspahr. *Command, Control and Communications Lessons Learned: Iranian Rescue, Falklands Conflict, Grenada Invasion, Libya Raid*. Maxwell Air Force Base, Ala.: Air War College, Air University, 1988.

Associated Press. "Iraqis Drop Napalm on Shiite Towns," *Washington Times*, August 16, 1992.

———. "With No-Fly Zone in Effect, Iraq Hits Shiites on the Ground," *Washington Times*, December 29, 1992.

Arkin, William. 2002. Interview by Michael Knights. March 12. Washington, D.C.

———. "Baghdad: The Urban Sanctuary in Desert Storm." *AirPower Journal* *XII*, no. 1 (1997): pp. 6–22.

———. "Cheney's Private Scud War," *Stars and Stripes*, October 23, 2000.

———. "The Difference Was in the Details," *Washington Post*, July 29, 1999, http://www.washingtonpost.com/wp-srv/inatl/longterm/iraq/analysis.htm.

———. "Q & A with Lieutenant General Charles Horner," *Washington Post*, August 1, 2004, http://www.washingtonpost.com.

Atkinson, Rick. *Crusade: The Untold Story of the Gulf War*. London: Harper Collins, 1993.

———. *In the Company of Soldiers*. New York: Penguin, 2003.

Baer, Robert. *See No Evil: The True Story of a Ground Soldier in the CIA's War of Terrorism*. New York: Crown, 2002.

Bamford, James. *Body of Secrets*. New York: Anchor Books, 2002.

Baram, Amatzia. *Saddam Husayn Conquers Irbil: Causes and Implications*. Washington, D.C.: Washington Institute for Near East Policy, 1996.

———. *Saddam Husayn's Rage and Fury*. Washington, D.C.: Washington Institute for Near East Policy, 1999.

Battle, Joyce, ed. "Shaking Hands with Saddam Hussein: The U.S. Tilts toward Iraq, 1980–1984." *National Security Archive Electronic Briefing Book No. 82*, June 11, 2004, February 25, 2003 http://www.gwu.edu/~nsarchiv/NSAEBB/NSAEBB82/.

Berenson, Alex, and John Burns. "Eight Day Battle for Najaf: From Attack to Stalemate," *New York Times*, August 18, 2004.

Biddle, Stephen, James Ebrey, Edward Filiberti, Stephen Kidder, Steven Metz, Ivan Oelrich, and Richard Shelton. *Iraq and the Future of Warfare: Implications for Army and Defense Policy*. Carlisle, Penn.: Strategic Studies Institute, 2003.

Bird, Julie. "Desert Strike: The Mission in the Gulf Widens." *Air Force Times* 57, no. 7 (1996): pp. 3–4.

———. "U.S., Allies Threaten to Strike Iraq Again." *Air Force Times* 53, no. 4 (1993): p. 3.

Boardman, Michael W. *Leashing the Hydra: Control of Joint Intelligence Architectures.* Naval War College, 1997. Final Report, no. A171823, 19 May 1997. Newport, R.I.: Naval War College.

Boatman, John, and Paul Beaver. "Coalition Draws New Line in the Sand." *Jane's Defense Weekly*, January 23, 1993.

Bodner, Michael J., and William W. Bruner. "Tank Plinking," *Air Force Magazine Online*, March 9, 2004, http://www.afa.org/magazine/perspectives/desert_storm/1093tank.asp.

Borer, Douglas. "Inverse Engagement: Lessons from US–Iraq Relations, 1982–1990." *Parameters* (Summer 2003): pp. 51–65.

Boustany, Nora. "Iraq Said to Shut Down Radar to Prevent New Confrontations," *Washington Post*, February 1, 1993.

Bowen, Paul E. "Create a Fighting Staff." *Marine Corps Gazette* 75, no. 11 (1991): pp. 52–53.

Bowie, Chris. *Destroying Mobile Ground Targets in an Anti-access Environment.* Washington, D.C.: Northrop Grumman Analysis Center, 2001.

Bowie, Chris, Robert Haffa, and Robert Mullins. *Future War: What Trends in America's Post–Cold War Military Conflicts Tell Us about Early 21st Century Warfare.* Washington, D.C.: Northrop Grumman Analysis Center, 2003.

Boyd, Terry. "Northern Watch Keeps Tight Reins on Iraq," *European Stars and Stripes*, May 8, 2000.

Boyne, Sean. "Feuds Cut Deeper into Saddam's Power Base." *Jane's Intelligence Review* 7, no. 7 (1995): p. 206.

———. "How Saddam Rebuilt His Forces." *Jane's Intelligence Review* 8, no. 11 (1996): pp. 506–7.

———. "In the Wake of Desert Fox, Saddam Moves to Tighten His Grip." *Jane's Intelligence Review* 11, no. 1 (1999): pp. 402.

———. "Iraq's Military Purge." *Jane's Intelligence Review* 8, no. 10 (1996): pp. 465.

———. "Iraqis Perfect the Art of Evading." *Jane's Intelligence Review* 10, no. 2 (1998): p. 65.

———. "Qusay Considers a Reshuffle for Iraq's Command Structure." *Jane's Intelligence Review* 9, no. 9 (1997): p. 278.

————. "Saddam Intensifies Campaign in the Marshes." *Jane's Intelligence Review* 6, no. 9 (1994): p. 301.

————. "Saddam Purges His Inner Circle." *Jane's Intelligence Review* 9, no. 12 (1996): pp. 565–66.

————. "Saddam Reasserts Control." *Jane's Intelligence Review* 5, no. 3 (1993): p. 176.

————. "Saddam's Alliance with Kurdish Faction." *Jane's Intelligence Review* 8, no. 11 (1996): p. 508.

————. "Saddam's Move to Exorcise the Enclaves." *Jane's Intelligence Review* 9, no. 10 (1997): p. 301.

Branigin, William. "A Brief, Bitter War for Iraq's Military Officers: Self-Deception a Factor in Defeat," *Washington Post*, April 27, 2003.

Callicutt, Steve. 2002. Interview by Michael Knights. Tape recording (author's collection). June 5. Langley Air Force Base, Va.

Carpenter, Mason. 2003. Interview by Michael Knights. August 6. Washington, D.C.

Cassidy, Robert. "Renaissance of the Attack Helicopter in the Close Fight." *Military Review* LXXXIII, no. 4, (July/August 2003): pp. 5–7.

Centner, Christopher. "Ignorance Is Risk: The Big Lesson from Desert Storm Air Base Attacks." *Airpower Journal* 6, no. 4 (Winter 1992): pp. 25–35.

Chandrasekaran, Rajiv, and Daniel Williams. "U.S. Military Returns to Use of Heavy Munitions in Iraq," *Washington Post*, November 23, 2003.

Chumley, Robyn A. "Southern Watch." *Airman* 37, no. 1 (January 1993): pp. 2–7.

CIA Analyst [anon.]. 2002. Interview by Michael Knights. No further details here to protect confidentiality.

CIA Operative [anon.]. 2002. Interview by Michael Knights. No further details here to protect confidentiality.

Clancy, Tom. *Into the Storm: A Study in Command.* New York: Putnam, 1997.

Clancy, Tom, Tony Zinni, and Tony Koltz. *Battle Ready.* London: Putnam, 2004.

Clary, David E. *Operation Provide Comfort: A Strategic Perspective.* Alexandria, Va.: Defense Technical Information Center, 1994.

Clawson, Patrick. *The Implications of Bombing Iraq.* Washington, D.C.: Washington Institute for Near East Policy, 1998.

———. "Stealth Bombing: Our Silent War in Iraq," *New Republic*, September 6, 1999.

Cline, Mark. 2003. Interview by Michael Knights. *Telephone interview,* August 12. Washington, D.C.

CNN. "Iraq Air Patrols Resume after Raid," August 15, 2004, http://www.cnn.com/2001/WORLD/meast/02/18/iraq.airstrike/index.html.

———. "Most Missiles Hit Their Target in U.S. Air Strike," June 26, 1993. http://www.fas.org/man/dod-101/ops/strike_930626.htm.

Cohen, Eliot A. "Sound and Fury," *Washington Post*, December 19, 1998.

———. "The Mystique of US AirPower." *Foreign Affairs* 73, no. 1 (1994): pp. 109–124.

Cohen, Eliot, and Michael Eisenstadt. *Air Power against Iraq: An Assessment*. Washington, D.C.: Washington Institute for Near East Policy, 1998.

Coll, Steve. *Ghost Wars*. New York: Penguin, 2003.

Collier, Robert. "Behind Baghdad's Fall: Hussein Son's Wild Orders Led to Iraq Military Collapse," *San Francisco Chronicle*, May 25, 2003.

Conetta, Carl. *Catastrophic Interdiction: Air Power and the Collapse of the Iraqi Field Army in the 2003 War.* Cambridge, Mass.: Project on Defense Alternatives, 2003.

Conetta, Carl, Charles Knights, and Lutz Unterseher. *Toward Defensive Restructuring in the Middle East.* Project on Defense Alternatives Research Monograph 1. Cambridge, Mass.: Project on Defense Alternatives, 2004.

Conversino, Mark J. "Sawdust Superpower: Perceptions of US Casualty Tolerance." *Strategic Review* 15, no. 1 (1997): pp. 19–20.

Conway, James. " 'Farther and Faster' in Iraq." *US Naval Institute Proceedings* 131, no. 1 (January 2005): pp. 25–30.

Cooper, Tom. 2004. Interview by Michael Knights. 12 July, 2004. Washington, D.C.

———. *Exhumating the Dead Iraqi Air Force.* Air Combat Information Group, August 16, 2004, http://www.acig.org/artman/publish/article_247.shtml.

Cooper, Tom, and Farhad Bishop. *Iran-Iraq War in the Air, 1980–88*. Atglen, Pa.: Schiffer, 2003.

Cordesman, Anthony H. *The Air Defense War since Desert Fox: A Short History.* Washington, D.C.: Center for Strategic and International Studies, 1999.

———. *The Current Military Situation in Iraq.* Center for Strategic and International Studies, February 28, 2005, http://www.csis.org/features/031114current.pdf.

———. "How to Hit Iraq," *New York Times*, August 19, 1992.

———. *Kuwait: Recovery and Security after the Gulf War.* Boulder, Colo.: Westview, 1997.

———. *The Lessons of Desert Fox: A Preliminary Analysis.* Washington, D.C.: Center for Strategic and International Studies, 1999.

———. *The Lessons of the Iraq War.* Washington, D.C.: Center for Strategic and International Studies, 2003.

Cordesman, Anthony H., and Abraham R. Wagner. *The Lessons of Modern War,* vol. 1, *The Iran-Iraq War.* Boulder, Colo.: Westview, 1990.

Correll, John T. "Northern Watch," *Air Force* 83, no. 2 (February 2000): pp. 4.

Covault, Craig. "New Intelligence Ops Debut in Iraq Strikes," *Aviation Week and Space Technology*, December 21, 1998.

———. "Secret NRO Recons Eye Iraq Threat," *Aviation Week and Space Technology*, February 16, 2002.

Cross, Coy. *The Dragon Lady Meets the Challenge: The U-2 in Desert Storm.* Washington, D.C.: U.S. Department of Defense, 1991.

Crowder, Gary. 2002. Interview by Michael Knights. Tape recording (author's collection). June 6. Langley Air Force Base, Va.

———. 2004. Interview by Michael Knights. *Telephone interview,* August 23. Washington, D.C.

Davis, Richard G. *On Target.* Washington, D.C.: Air Force History Support Office, 2002.

Deptula, Dave. 2002. Interview by Michael Knights, part 1. Tape recording (author's collection). June 10. Langley Air Force Base, Va.

———. 2002. Interview by Michael Knights, part 2. Tape recording (author's collection). June 11. Langley Air Force Base, Va.

———. 2002. Interview by Michael Knights, part 3. Tape recording (author's collection). June 13. Langley Air Force Base, Va.

Deptula, David, Gary Crowder, and George Stamper. "Direct Attack: Enhancing Counterland Doctrine and Joint Air-Ground Operations." *Air & Space Power Journal* XVIII, no. 4 (Winter 2003): pp. 20–23.

Donnelly, Thomas. *Operation Iraqi Freedom: A Strategic Assessment*, vol. 2003. Washington, D.C.: American Enterprise Institute, 2003.

"Don't Shoot the Helicopters," *New York Times*, August 19, 1992.

Downer, Lee A. "The Composite Wing in Combat." *Airpower Journal* VI, no. 4 (Winter 1991): pp. 4–16.

Downs, Mike. 2003. Interview by Michael Knights, July 10. Washington, D.C.

Duefler, Charles. 2002. Interview by Michael Knights, March 6. Washington, D.C.

Duelfer, Charles. "Why Iraq Will Never Give Up Its Worst Weapons," *Aviation Week and Space Technology*, March 11, 2002.

Dulaney, Robert. 2004. Interview by Michael Knights.

Dunlap, Charles. 2002. Interview by Michael Knights. Tape recording (author's collection). June 6. Langley Air Force Base, VA.

Dupuy, Trevor. "Combat Data and the 3:1 Rule." *International Security* 14, no. 1 (1989): pp. 12–28.

Eichelberger, George. 2002. Interview by Michael Knights. February 12. Maxwell Air Force Base, Ala.

Eisenstadt, Michael. *Blunder over Baghdad: Assessing US Military Action against Iraq*. Washington, D.C.: Washington Institute for Near East Policy, 1993.

———. *Iranian Military Power: Capabilities and Intentions*. Washington, D.C.: Washington Institute for Near East Policy, 1996.

———. *Iraq's Weapons of Mass Destruction: An Emerging Challenge for the Bush Administration*. Washington, D.C.: Washington Institute for Near East Policy, 2001.

———. *Iraqi Strategy and the Battle for Baghdad*. Washington, D.C.: Washington Institute for Near East Policy, 2003.

———. *Like a Phoenix from the Ashes? The Future of Iraqi Military Power*. Washington, D.C.: Washington Institute for Near East Policy, 1993.

Ellis, Edward. 2004. Interview by Michael Knights. *Telephone Interview*, August 20. Washington, D.C.

Engelhardt, Tom. "Icarus over Iraq: The Miracle of a Single Haasen Hand Grenade," *Antiwar.com*, December 6, 2004, http://www.tomdispatch.com/index.mhtml?pid=2047.

Epstein, Joshua. *Force Reductions: A Dynamic Assessment*. Washington, D.C.: Brookings Institute, 1990.

Erhardt, Tom. 2002. Interview by Michael Knights. Tape recording (author's collection). February 21. Maxwell Air Force Base, Ala.

Estvanik, Robert. *Intelligence and the Commander: Desert Shield/Desert Storm Case Study.* Naval War College, 1992. Newport, R.I. Thesis. No. M-U 41662 E82i.

Federation of American Scientists. *Cruise Missile Strike: 26 June 1993 Operation Southern Watch*, http://www.fas.org/man/dod-101/ops/strike_930626.htm.

———. *U.S. Opinion Round-Up: Strike on Iraq,* http://www.fas.org/man/dod-101/ops/strike_930626.htm.

———. *UNSCOM Chairman Butler's Report to UN Secretary General*, http://www.fas.org/news/un/iraq/s/butla216.htm.

Finnegan, Phillip. "US Must Rebuild Coalition against Saddam," *Defense News*, September 9, 1996.

Fisk, Robert. "How US Demoralised Iraq's Army," *Independent*, May 28, 2003.

Franks, Tommy. *American Soldier*. New York: Regan Books, 2004.

Frazee, David. 2002. Interview by Michael Knights. Tape recording (author's collection). June 11. Langley Air Force Base, Va.

Friedman, Thomas. "The Missiles' Message," *New York Times*, June 28, 1993.

Fuerth, Leon. 2002. Interview by Michael Knights. March 10. Washington, D.C.

Fulghum, David. "Central Iraq's Air Defenses Remain as Dense as in 1991," *Aviation Week and Space Technology*, October 21, 2002.

———. "Clashes with Iraq Continue after Week of Heavy Strikes," *Aviation Week and Space Technology*, January 25, 1993.

———. "Fast Forward," *Aviation Week and Space Technology*, April 28, 2003.

———. "Hard Lesson in Iraq: Lead to New Attack Plan," *Aviation Week and Space Technology*, September 16, 1996.

———. "Iraq's Mobile SAMs Stay on the Move," *Aviation Week and Space Technology*, September 16, 1996.

———. "Pentagon Criticizes Air Strike on Iraq," *Aviation Week and Space Technology*, January 25, 1993.

———. "Pentagon Halts Planned Attack on Iraqi Sites," *Aviation Week and Space Technology*, August 10, 1992.

———. "Powell Details List of Iraqi Violations," *Aviation Week and Space Technology*, February 10, 2003.

———. "Terror vs Intelligence," *Aviation Week and Space Technology*, November 3, 2003.

———. "U.S. May Suspend Northern Watch Patrol," *Aviation Week and Space Technology*, May 14, 2001.

Fulghum, David, and Douglas Barrie. "War Preparations Reveal Problems," *Aviation Week and Space Technology*, December 9, 2002.

Fulghum, David, and John Morocco. "Strike Hits Old Targets, Reveals New Problems," *Aviation Week and Space Technology*, February 26, 2001.

Fulghum, David, and Robert Wall. "Baghdad Confidential," *Aviation Week and Space Technology*, April 28, 2003.

———. "Deployment of New Technology Continues," *Aviation Week and Space Technology*, January 27, 2003.

———. "Iraqi Air Defenses Broken but Dangerous," *Aviation Week and Space Technology*, February 15, 1999.

———. "North Korea Nuke Crisis Complicates Iraq Build-Up," *Aviation Week and Space Technology*, January 6, 2003.

Gause, Ken. "Can the Iraqi Security Apparatus Save Saddam?" *Jane's Intelligence Review* 14, no. 11 (2002): 8–13.

Gehri, Suzanna. *Interview with Colonel John A. Warden (Part One)*. Edited by Desert Story. Maxwell, Ala.: AFHRA, 1991.

Gehri, Suzanna, and Edward Mann. *Interview with Lt. Col. Ronnie A. Stanfill*. Edited by Desert Story. Maxwell, Ala.: AFHRA, 1991.

Gehri, Suzanna, and Richard Reynolds. *Interview with Col. Trexler*. Edited by Desert Story. Maxwell, Ala.: AFHRA, 1992.

———. *Interview with General Charles A. Horner*. Edited by Desert Story. Maxwell, Ala.: AFHRA, 1991.

———. *Interview with General Michael Ryan*. Edited by Desert Story. Maxwell, Ala.: AFHRA, 1992.

———. *Interview with Major General John A. Corder*. Edited by Desert Story. Maxwell, Ala: AFHRA, 1992.

Gehri, Suzanna, Richard Reynolds, and Edward Mann. *Interview with Buster Glosson (Part One)*. Edited by Desert Story. Maxwell, Ala.: AFHRA, 1991.

———. *Interview with Buster Glosson (Part Two)*. Edited by Desert Story. Maxwell, Ala.: AFHRA, 1992.

———. *Interview with Colonel Dave Deptula*. Edited by Desert Story. Maxwell, Ala.: AFHRA, 1991.

———. *Interview with Colonel Dave Deptula and Major Buck Rogers*. Edited by Desert Story. Maxwell, Ala.: AFHRA, 1991.

———. *Interview with Colonel Jim Blackburn*. Edited by Desert Story. Maxwell, Ala.: AFHRA, 1993.

———. *Interview with Lt. Gen. Robert M. Alexander*. Edited by Desert Story. Maxwell, Ala.: AFHRA, 1991.

———. *Interview with Steve Wilson*. Edited by Desert Story. Maxwell, Ala.: AFHRA, 1991.

Gellman, Barton. "Arms Inspectors 'Shake the Tree'," *Washington Post*, October 12, 1998.

———. "One Year Later: War's Faded Triumph," *Washington Post*, January 16, 1992.

———. "U.S. Spied on Iraqi Military via U.N. but Arms Control Team Had No Knowledge of Eavesdropping," *Washington Post*, March 2, 1999.

Gellman, Barton, Dana Priest, and Bradley Graham. "US Threat of Force on Iraq Masked Doubts: Deep Foreboding about Lasting Effects of Attack Propels Furious Diplomatic Efforts," *Washington Post*, March 1, 1998.

Gertz, Bill. "Iraqis Move Aircraft out of Forbidden Zone," *Washington Times*, August 26, 1992.

———. "Saddam 'on a War Footing'," *Washington Times*, August 19, 1992.

Gertz, Bill, and Warren Strobel. "Iraqi Jets Challenge Bigger No-Fly Zone," *Washington Times*, September 4, 1996.

Gibbons, Phillip. *US No-Fly Zones in Iraq: To What End?* Washington, D.C.: Washington Institute for Near East Policy, 2002.

Gordon, Michael. "Leave Iraq Alone, US Tells Iranians," *New York Times*, August 25, 1992.

———. "US Continuing Build Up, Sees Sign of Iraqi Retreat," *New York Times*, October 12, 1994.

Graham-Brown, Sarah. "No-Fly Zones: Rhetoric and Real Intentions." *Middle East Research and Information Project, Press Information Note 49* (20 February 2001).

Graham, Bradley. "Military Turns to Software to Cut Civillian Casualties," *Washington Post*, February 21, 2003.

Grant, Rebecca. "Eyes Wide Open." *Air Force 86*, no. 11 (November 2003): pp. 2–3.

———. "Saddam's Elite in the Meat Grinder." *Air Force*, September 2003.

Ground Forces 1991, Global Security, June 27, 2004, http://www.globalsecurity.org/military/world/iraq/ground-91.htm.

Grunawalt, Richard. "The JCS Standing Rules of Engagement: A Judge Advocate's Primer." *Air Force Law Review* 42 (1997): pp. 12–45.

Gulf War Airpower Study, vol. 1, *Planning and Command and Control*. U.S. Department of Defense. Washington, D.C.: U.S. Government, 1993.

Hashim, Ahmed. *The Sunni Insurgency in Iraq,* Middle East Institute, February 28, 2005, http://www.mideasti.org/articles/doc89.html.

Hathaway, David. 2003. Interview by Michael Knights. *Telephone interview*. September 14. Washington, D.C.

Hawkins, William. "Iraq: Heavy Forces and Decisive Warfare." *Parameters*, Autumn 2003. pp. 61–67.

Hebert, Adam. "The Baghdad Strikes." *Air Force 86*, no. 7 (July 2003): pp. 1–2.

———. "The Long Reach of the Heavy Bombers." *Air Force 86*, no. 11 (November 2003): pp. 2–3.

Hedges, Stephen. "Roadside Bombs: U.S. Battles Low-Tech Threat," *Chicago Tribune*, October 23, 2004.

Heidenrich, John. "The Gulf War: How Many Iraqis Died?" *Foreign Affairs*, no. 90 (1993): pp. 108–25.

Heintzelman, Harry L., and Edmund S. Bloom. "A Planning Primer: How to Provide Effective Legal Input into the War Planning and Combat Execution Process." *Air Force Law Review* 37 (1994): pp. 17–34.

Hewish, Mark. "Battlefield Air Operations: Weight and Time Are the Main Targets." *Jane's International Defense Review* 37, no. 5 (May 2004): pp. 44–50.

Hoagland, Jim. "A Risky No-Fly Zone over Iraq," *Washington Post*, February 10, 2001.

Holliday, Robin. 2002. Interview by Michael Knights. March 16. Washington, D.C.

Hooker, Gregory. *Shaping the Plan for Operation Iraqi Freedom: The Role of Military Intelligence Assessments.* Washington, D.C.: Washington Institute for Near East Policy, 2005.

Hornburg, Hal. 2002. Interview by Michael Knights. Tape recording (author's collection). June 6. Langley Air Force Base, Va.

Horner, Charles. "What We Should Have Learned from Desert Storm, but Didn't." *Air Force Magazine* 79, no. 12 (1996): pp. 3–6.

Hoyle, Criag, and James O'Halloran. "Iraqi Air Defense: Fortress Iraq," *Jane's Defense Weekly,* May 29, 2002.

Hoyt, Timothy. "Iraq's Military Industry: A Crucial Military Target." *National Security Studies Quarterly* 4, no. 1 (Spring 1998): pp. 1–6.

Human Rights Watch. *Endless Torment: The 1991 Uprising in Iraq and Its Aftermath,* http://www.hrw.org/reports/1992/Iraq926.htm

———. *Needless Deaths in the Gulf War: Civilian Casualties during the Air Campaign and Violations of the Laws of War*. New York: Human Rights Watch, 1991.

———. *Off Target: The Conduct of the War and Civilian Casualties in Iraq.* New York: Human Rights Watch, 2004.

Humphries, John G. "Operations Law and the Rules of Engagement in Operations Desert Shield and Storm." *Air Power Journal* VI, no. 2 (Fall 1992): pp. 25–41.

Hunter, Thomas. *The Role and Effect of Special Operations Forces in Theater Ballistic Missile Counterforce Operations During Operation Desert Storm,* Special Operations, July 2, 2004, http://www.specialoperations.com/Focus/SCUD_Hunt/default.htm

Ignatieff, Michael. "To Fight but not to Die," *World Today*, February 2000, pp. 7–12.

International Institute for Strategic Studies (IISS). *The Military Balance 1990–1991*. London: Oxford University Press, 1990.

International Policy Institute for Counter-Terrorism. *Full Text of 'Al-Zarqawi Letter.'* March 7, 2005, http://www.ict.org.il/documents/documentdet.cfm?docid=62.

Iraq Broadcasting Corporation. "Details of Some Losses Inflicted on Saddam's Regime During Operation Desert Fox." Sulaymaniyah: Iraq Broadcasting Corporation, 1999.

———. "War Preparations in Iraq." Irbil: Iraq Broadcasting Corporation, 1998.

"Iraqi Kurdistan Risks Being Turned into Regional Battleground, KDP Warns," *Middle East Mirror*, September 6, 1996.

Jamieson, Perry D. *Lucrative Targets: The U.S. Air Force in the Kuwaiti Theater of Operations*. Washington, D.C.: Air Force History Support Office, 2001.

Jamison, Barry, and Rich Davis. *Interview with General Charles A. Horner*. Edited by Oral History Interview. Maxwell, Ala.: AFHRA, 1992.

Janega, James. "In Ramadi, GIs Fight an Elusive Foe," *Chicago Tribune*, November 1, 2004.

Jehl, Douglas, and Eric Schmitt. "Errors Are Seen in Early Attacks on Iraqi Leaders," *Washington Post*, June 13, 2004.

Jentleson, Bruce. *With Friends Like These: Reagan, Bush, and Saddam, 1982–90*. New York: Norton, 1994.

"Joint STARS: Backbone of Joint Warfare." *Defense News*, February 12, 2004.

Keiler, Jonathan. "Who Won the Battle of Fallujah?" *US Naval Institute Proceedings* 131, no. 1 (January 2005): pp. 31–34.

Kipphut, Mark. *Crossbow and Gulf War Counter-Scud Efforts: Lessons from History*. Maxwell Air Force Base, Ala.: Air University, 1996.

Knights, Michael. "Bringing Down the Temple: Would a Beleaguered Saddam Deploy the 'Samson Option'?" *Gulf States Newsletter*, October 23, 2002.

———. "Iraq: New Tensions, Ukrainian Complications in the No-Fly Zones," *Gulf States Newsletter*, May 1, 2002.

———. "Iraq Raises the Heat in a War of Diplomatic Attrition," *Gulf States Newsletter*, September 6, 2001.

———. "Iraq's Military Options: Blunting the Air Assault," *Gulf States Newsletter*, September 27, 2002.

———. "New Endgames," *Gulf States Newsletter*, January 9, 2002.

————. *Proliferation Presents a Long-Term Challenge,* Oxford Analytica, November 23, 2004, http://www.oxan.com/display.aspx?ItemID= DB114074.

————. "Proxy War and Political Shifts in Northern Iraq," *Gulf States Newsletter*, May 1, 2002.

————. "PSYOPs Comes into Play against Saddam." *Jane's Intelligence Review* 15, no. 3 (March 2003): pp. 1–4.

————. "Saddam's Vulnerability to 'Inside Out' Warfare," *Gulf States Newsletter*, September 27, 2002.

————. "Strategies for Repelling a Ground Assault," *Gulf States Newsletter*, October 9, 2002.

————. "Tensions Rise over Air Incursion Claims," *Gulf States Newsletter*, September 25, 2000.

————. "Time May Be up for Iraq's Northern No-Fly Zone," *Gulf States Newsletter*, June 11, 2001.

————. "Weighing the Cost of a War on Infrastructure," *Gulf States Newsletter*, January 10, 2003.

————. "Yugoslav Connection Suggests Business as Usual for Iraq's Arms Suppliers," *Gulf States Newsletter*, September 12, 2002.

Kopp, Carlo. "Desert Storm: The Electronic Battle, Part One." *Australian Aviation*, June 1993, pp. 23–45.

————. "Desert Storm: The Electronic Battle, Part Two." *Australian Aviation*, July 1993, pp. 30–38.

————. "Desert Storm: The Electronic Battle, Part One." *Australian Aviation*, August 1993, pp. 23–28.

Krepinevich, Andrew, Barry Watts, and Robert Work. *Meeting the Anti-access and Area-Denial Challenge.* Washington, D.C.: Center for Strategic and Budgetary Assessments, 2003.

Lake, Anthony. 2004. Interview by Michael Knights. June 5. Washington, D.C.

Lamontagne, Donald A. 2002. Interview by Michael Knights. Tape recording (author's collection). February 10. Maxwell Air Force Base, Ala.

Lancaster, John. "Allies Declare 'No-Fly Zone' in Iraq," *Washington Post*, August 27, 1992.

Larson, Eric V. *Casualties and Consensus*. Santa Monica, Calif.: RAND, 1996.

Lasseter, Tom. "In the Face of Stubborn Insurgency, Troops Scale Back Anbar Patrols," Knights Ridder, July 20, 2004, http://www.realcities.com/mld/krwashington/9200682.htm?template=contentModules/printstory.jsp.

Leaf, Daniel. 2003. Interview by Michael Knights. Tape recording (author's collection). March 8. Washington, D.C.

———. 2003. Interview by Michael Knights. Tape recording (author's collection). March 12. Washington, D.C.

———. 2004. Interview by Michael Knights. June 10. Washington, D.C.

Lewis, Richard B. H. "JFACC Problems Associated with Battlefield Preparation in Desert Storm." *Air Power Journal* X, no. 2 (Spring 1995): pp. 4–21.

Lewis, Ronald. "Saddam Outfoxed." *Air Force's Monthly* (March 1999): pp. 6–9.

Locher, James R. "Taking Stock of Goldwater Nicholls." *Joint Forces Quarterly 13* (Autumn 1996): pp. 10–16.

Lok, Joris. "Communication Weaknesses Endanger Allied Integration in U.S.-Led Air Campaigns." *Jane's International Defense Review* 37, no. 3 (March 2004): p. 4.

Luttwak, Edward N. "Air Power in US Military Strategy." In *The Future of Air Power in the Aftermath of the Gulf War*, edited by Richard Shultz and Robert Pfalzgraff. Maxwell Air Force Base, Ala.: Air University Press, 1992, pp. 19–38.

———. *Strategy, the Logic of War and Peace*. Cambridge, Mass.: Belknap Press of Harvard University Press, 1987.

Makovsky, Alan, Amatzia Baram, and Michael Eisenstadt. *Crisis in Iraq: Saddam Hussein, the Kurds, and US Policy*. Washington, D.C.: Washington Institute for Near East Policy, 1996.

Mann, Edward. *Interview with Major Dave Karns*. Edited by Desert Story. Maxwell, Ala.: AFHRA, 1991.

———. *Thunder and Lightning: Desert Storm and the Airpower Debates*. 2 vols. Maxwell Air Force Base, Ala.: Air University Press, 1995.

Mannion, Jim. "Zinni, Gulf Forces Commander, Pounces after Long Game of Cat-and-Mouse," *Washington Post*, December 19, 1998.

Marks, Jon. "Is Saddam, No Longer the Immortal: Preparing for the Après Saddam?" *Gulf States Newsletter*, February 6, 2002.

————. "Saddam's Reshuffle Points to Policy Shift, but Iraq Remains Intransigent," *Gulf States Newsletter*, April 30, 2001.

Matthews, William. "Boom Time for Bomb Jammers," *Defense News*, March 22, 2004.

————. "Brief Cease-Fire in Iraq Ends with U.S. Bombs." *Air Force Times* 53, no. 5 (February 1993): p. 1.

McDaniel, John. *C2 Case Study: The FSCL in Desert Storm*. Vienna, Va.: Evidence Based Research, 2001.

McKeon, Matt. *Joint Targeting: What's Still Broke?* Maxwell Air Force Base, Ala: Air University, 1999.

Mearsheimer, John. "Assessing the Conventional Balance: The 3:1 Rule and Its Critics." *International Security* 13, no. 4 (1989): pp. 54–89.

MEF. "Commanding General, 1st Marine Division, 'Operation Iraqi Freedom: Lessons Learned'." Washington, D.C.: Department of Defense, 2003. Marine Expeditionary Force.

Meilinger, Philip S. "Air Targeting Strategies: An Overview." In *Air Power Confronts an Unstable World*, edited by Richard P. Hallion. London: Brasseys, 1997, pp. 51–73.

Metz, Steven. "Insurgency and Counterinsurgency in Iraq." *Washington Quarterly* 27, no. 1 (2004): pp. 12–24.

Miller, William. "Insurgency Theory and the Conflict in Algeria: A Theoretical Analysis." *Terrorism and Political Violence* 12, no. 1 (2000): pp. 13–35.

Minister, David G. 2003. Interview by Michael Knights. June 22. Washington, D.C.

Moeller, Michael R. *The Sum of Their Fears: The Relationship between the Joint Targeting Coordination Board and the Joint Force Commander.* Maxwell Air Force Base, Ala: Air University, 1995.

Moore, Charles. 2002. Interview by Michael Knights. March 18. Washington, D.C.

Moore, Robin. *The Hunt for Saddam Hussein*. New York: Penguin, 2003.

Morocco, John. "Raids Highlight Pitfalls of Limited Use of Force," *Aviation Week and Space Technology*, January 25, 1993.

Moschgat, Jim. 2004. Interview by Michael Knights. August 17. Washington, D.C.

Moseley, Michael. *Operation Iraqi Freedom: By the Numbers.* Shaw
Air Force Base, SC: CENTAF Analysis and Assessments Division,
2003.

Murray, Williamson, and Robert Scales. *The Iraq War: A Military History.*
Cambridge, Mass.: Belknap, 2003.

Myers, Steven Lee. "A Failed Race against Time: US Tried to Head Off Iraq,"
New York Times, September 5, 1996.

———. "Iraq Damage More Severe than Expected," *Washington Post*,
January 9, 1999.

———. "Iraq Vows to Defy US Ban and Fly in "No-Flight" Zones," *New York
Times*, December 30, 1998.

———. "Something New in the Iraqi Conflict: Concrete Bombs," *New York
Times*, October 7, 1999.

Mylroie, Laurie. *Saddam Defiant.* Washington, D.C.: Washington Institute for
Near East Policy, 1993.

———. *Saddam's Deadly Game of Cat-and-Mouse.* Washington, D.C.:
Washington Institute for Near East Policy, 1993.

Nelan, Bruce. "Saddam, Still," *Time*, March 29, 1993.

Nelson, Mike. 2002. Interview by Michael Knights. March 6. Washington,
D.C.

O'Rourke, Ronald. *Iraq War: Defense Program Implications for Congress.*
Washington, D.C.: Congressional Research Service, 2003.

Ockmanek, David. "The Air Force: The Next Round." In *Transforming
America's Military*, edited by Has Binnendijk. Washington, D.C.:
National Defense University, 2002, pp. 159–184.

*Operation DESERT FOX—December 1998—Bomb Damage Assessment
Imagery,* Global Security, July 29, 2004, http://www.globalsecurity.org/
intell/library/imint/desert_fox.htm

Pape, Robert. *Bombing to Win: Airpower and Coercion in War.* Ithaca, N.Y.:
Cornell University Press, 1996.

———. "The True Worth of Air Power." *Foreign Affairs* 83, no. 2
(March/April 2004): pp. 127–128.

Parris, Mark. 2004. Interview by Michael Knights. July 18. Washington,
D.C.

Peko, Miquel. 2002. Interview by Michael Knights. February 23. Maxwell Air Force Base, Ala.

Peters, Ralph. "How Saddam Won This Round," *Newsweek*, November 30, 1998.

Petraeus, David. 2004. Interview by Michael Knights. April 7. Washington, D.C.

Phillips, Ryan, and Jeffrey White. "Sadrist Revolt Provides Lessons for Counterinsurgency in Iraq." *Jane's Intelligence Review* 16, no. 8 (August 2004): pp. 22–28.

Plummer, Stephen. 2002. Interview by Michael Knights. July 5. Washington, D.C.

Pokrant, Marvin. *Desert Shield at Sea: What the Navy Really Did*. Westport, Conn.: Greenwood, 1999.

———. *Desert Storm at Sea: What the Navy Really Did*. Westport, Conn.: Greenwood, 1999.

Pollack, Kenneth. 2004. Interview by Michael Knights. September 2. Washington, D.C.

Pollack, Ken. *The Threatening Storm: The Case for Invading Iraq*. New York: Random House, 2002.

Pollack, Kenneth. *Arabs at War: Military Effectiveness, 1948–1991*. London: University of Nebraska Press, 2002.

Powell, Colin. *My American Journey*. New York: Random House, 1995.

"Power Strugle Behind Iraq's Policy Muddle?" *Middle East Mirror*, October 21, 1994.

Powers, John. "Mass Graves Testify to Saddam's Evil." *Insight Magazine*, March 16, 2004.

Priest, Dana, Rick Atkinson, Vernon Loeb, David Hoffman, and Peter Finn. "Albright: U.S. May Attack Iraq Again," *Washington Post*, December 20, 1998.

Priest, Dana, and Bradley Graham. "Airstrikes Took a Toll on Saddam, U.S. Says Iraqi Army's Loyalty, Size Appear Changed," *Washington Post*, January 9, 1999.

Priest, Dana, and Howard Schneider. "Over Iraq, US Fights a Quiet War," *Washington Post*, March 7, 1999.

Putney, Diane T. "From Instant Thunder to Desert Storm: Developing the Gulf War Air Campaign's Phases." *Air Power History* 41, no. 3 (1994): pp. 38–50.

———. *Telephone Interview: General Norman H. Schwarzkopf*. Maxwell, Ala.: AFHRA, 1992.

Putney, Diane, and Richard Reynolds. *Interview with Lieutenent Colonel Sam Baptiste*. Edited by Oral History Interview. Maxwell, Ala.: AFHRA, 1992.

Ralston, Joseph. 2003. Interview by Michael Knights. *Telephone interview*. May 10. Washington, D.C.

Rathmell, Andrew. "Iraq's Military: Waiting for Change." *Jane's Intelligence Review* 7, no. 2 (February 1995).

Riedel, Bruce. 2004. Interview by Michael Knights. *Telephone interview*. May 15. Washington, D.C.

Renuart, Gene. 2003. Interview by Michael Knights. *Telephone interview*. July 10. Washington, D.C.

Reynolds, Richard. *Interview with Lt. Commander Mike Casey*. Edited by Desert Story. Maxwell, Ala.: AFHRA, 1991.

Reynolds, Richard T. *Heart of the Storm: The Genesis of the Air Campaign against Iraq*, vol. 1. Maxwell Air Force Base, Ala.: Air University Press, 1995.

Rice, Donald B. "Air Power in the New Security Environment." In *The Future of Air Power in the Aftermath of the Gulf War*, edited by Richard Shultz and Robert Pfalzgraff. Maxwell Air Force Base, Ala.: Air University Press, 1992.

Ricks, Thomas. "Bombs in Iraq Fell Wide of Targets: New Navy Weapon Blamed for Misses," *Washington Post*, February 22, 2002.

———. "U.S. Army Changed by Iraq, but for Better or Worse?" *Washington Post*, July 6, 2004.

Ricks, Thomas, and Alan Sipress. "Cuts Urged in Patrols over Iraq," *Washington Post*, May 9, 2001.

Rip, Michael, and James Hasik. *The Precision Revolution: GPS and the Future of Aerial Warfare*. Annapolis, Md.: Naval Institute Press, 2002.

Ripley, Tim. "Iraqi Missile Forces Failed to Impact on Iraqi Freedom." *Jane's Intelligence Review* 14, no. 4 (April 2003): pp. 1–6.

————. *Scud Hunting: Counter-Force Operations against Theater Ballistic Missiles*. Center for Defense and International Security Studies, June 24, 2004, http://www.cdiss.org/scudnt3.htm.

Ritter, Scott. *Endgame: Solving the Iraq Problem—Once and for All*. New York: Simon & Schuster, 1999.

Robbins, Carla Ann, and John Fialka. "Iraq Repairs Air Defenses, Defying Clinton," *Wall Street Journal*, September 11, 1996.

Roberson, Anthony. 2003. Interview by Michael Knights. Telephone interview. *August 12*. Washington, D.C.

Roberts, Ross. "Desert Fox: The Third Night." *U.S. Naval Institute Proceedings* 125, no. 4 (April 1999): pp. 36–38.

Rosenau, William. *Special Operations Forces and Elusive Enemy Ground Targets: Lessons from Vietnam and the Persian Gulf War*. Santa Monica, Calif.: RAND, 2001.

Scales, Robert. "Accuracy Defeated Range in Artillery Duel." *Jane's International Defense Review* 24, no. 5 (May 1991): pp. 4–8.

Schmidt, John W., and Clinton L. Williams. "Disjointed or Joint Targeting?" *Marine Corps Gazette* 76, no. 9 (1992): pp. 67–71.

Schmidt, Mark. 2002. Interview by Michael Knights. June 17. Washington, D.C.

Schmitt, Eric. "Clinton, Claiming Success, Asserts Most Iraqi Troops Have Left Kurds' Enclave." *New York Times*, September 5, 1996.

————. "In the Skies over Iraq, Silent Observers," *New York Times*, April 18, 2003.

Schneider, Howard. "Clashes Reported in Iraq," *Washington Post*, February 24, 1999.

Schwartz, Michael. "The Taming of Sadr City," *Asia Times*, January 12, 2005.

Scully, Megan. "U.S. Army Rushes Helo Defense Systems to Iraq," *Defense News*, March 17, 2003.

Seib, Gerald. "Iraq Is Warned Not to Employ Ground Forces," *Wall Street Journal*, August 31, 1992.

————. "Iraq Restores Air Network, US Sources Say," *Wall Street Journal*, August 19, 1992.

————. "Saddam Hussein Seen Trying to Boost Posture of Iraq in Dealing with Clinton Administration," *Wall Street Journal*, January 12, 1993.

Seroka, Steve. 2004. Interview by Michael Knights. June 16. Washington, D.C.

Shaffer, Glen. 2002. Interview by Michael Knights. Tape recording (author's collection). May 23. Washington, D.C.

Shaffer, Glen. 2003. Interview by Michael Knights. May 10. Washington, D.C.

Shellum, Brian G. *Defense Intelligence Crisis Response Procedures and the Gulf War,* Defense Intelligence Agency, http://www.dia.mil/History. Histories/response.html.

Sigler, John. 2003. Interview by Michael Knights. June 10. Washington, D.C.

Silliman, Scott L. "JAG Goes to War: The Desert Shield Deployment." *The Air Force Law Review* 37 (1994): pp. 85–96.

Smith, Jeffrey. "'Cheat and Retreat' Familiar by Now," *Washington Post*, January 9, 1993.

Socolovsky, Jerome. "Iraq Reports Fresh Clashes with Kurds, Blames US," Associated Press, March 7, 1995.

Speier, Richard. *Iraq's Al-Samoud: A Missile with Great Possibilities*. Washington, D.C.: Washington Institute for Near East Policy, 2002.

Steinberg, James. 2002. Interview by Michael Knights. Tape recording (author's collection). March 7. Washington, D.C.

Stewart, John. *Operation Desert Storm: The Military Intelligence Story: A View from the G-2, U.S. Third Army.* Washington, D.C.: Department of Defense, 1991.

Swanneck, Chuck. 2004. Interview with by Michael Knights. June 30. Washington, D.C.

Sykes, Roy. 2002. Interview by Michael Knights. January 30. Maxwell Air Force Base, Ala.

Third Infantry Division (Mechanized). *After-Action Report: Operation Iraqi Freedom.* February 18, 2004.

Tyler, Patrick. "U.S. Said to Plan Raids on Baghdad over Inspections," *New York Times*, August 16, 1992.

Ullman, Harlan, and Jim Wade. *Shock and Awe: Achieving Rapid Dominance.* Washington, D.C.: NDU Press, 1996.

United Kingdom House of Commons. *Review of Intelligence on Weapons of Mass Destruction*. London: House of Commons, 2004.

United Nations. *Resolution 687: Iraq-Kuwait*, http://ods-dds-ny.un.org/doc/RESOLUTION/GEN/NR0/596/23/IMG/NR059623.pdf?OpenElement.

————. *Resolution 688: Iraq*, http://ods-dds-ny.un.org/doc/RESOLUTION/GEN/NR0/596/24/IMG/NR059624.pdf?OpenElement.

————. *Resolution 707: Iraq*, http://ods-dds-ny.un.org/doc/RESOLUTION/GEN/NR0/596/43/IMG/NR059643.pdf?OpenElement.

————. *Resolution 715: Iraq*, http://ods-dds-ny.un.org/doc/RESOLUTION/GEN/NR0/596/51/IMG/NR059651.pdf?OpenElement.

U.S. Air Force. *Air Force Doctrine Document 2–1.2: Strategic Attack.* Washington, D.C.: Department of the Air Force, 1998.

U.S. Army Center for Lessons Learned. *On Point: The United States Army in Operation Iraqi Freedom*, August 23, 2004, http://onpoint.leavenworth.army.mil.

"U.S. Artillery Demonstrates Flexible Fires in Iraq." *Jane's International Defense Review* 37, no. 3 (March 2004), p. 4.

"U.S. Armor in Combat: The Iraqi Lessons." *Military Technology* 27, no. 11 (2003): pp. 54–55.

U.S. Central Intelligence Agency. *Comprehensive Report of the Special Advisor to the DCI on Iraqi WMD,* February 26, 2005, http://www.cia.gov/cia/reports/iraq_wmd_2004/chap1.html.

U.S. Congress. House. Armed Services Committee. *Operational Lessons Learned from Operation Iraqi Freedom*, October 2, 2003.

————. Senate. Committee on Armed Services. *Joint Chiefs of Staff Briefing on Current Military Operations in Somalia, Iraq and Yugoslavia.* 1st sess., January 29, 1993.

————. Senate. Committee on Armed Services. *The "Threat and Forget" Approach Is No Answer*, July 30, 1992.

————. Senate. Committee on Intelligence. *U.S. Intelligence Community's Pre-War Intelligence Assessments on Iraq*, 2004.

U.S. Defense Intelligence Agency. *Point Paper on BDA: Day Six—Operator's Outlook.* Washington, D.C.: Defense Intelligence Agency, 1991.

U.S. Department of Defense. *Conduct of the Persian Gulf War. Final Report to Congress.* Washington, D.C.: Department of Defense, 1992.

————. "Coalition Forces Air Component Command Briefing April 5, 2003." News Transcript, April 5, 2003, http://www.defenselink.mil/news/Apr2003/t04052003_t405mose.html.

———. *Defense Department Briefer: Iraq*, June 26, 1993, http://www.fas.org/man/dod-101/ops/docs/dod_930626.htm

———. *Defense Department Briefer: Iraq*, October 11, 1994, http://www.defenselink.mil/transcripts/1994/t101194_t1011asd.html.

———. *Defense Department Briefer: Iraq,* December 19, 1998, http://www.defenselink.mil/news/Dec1998/t12191998_t1219fox.html.

———. *Iraq: Country Handbook.* Washington, D.C.: Department of Defense, 1994.

U.S. General Accounting Office. *Operation Desert Storm: Operation Desert Storm Air War.* Washington, D.C.: U.S. General Accounting Office, 1996.

Wadhams, Nick. "Iraq Car Bombings up under Interim Gov't," Associated Press, January 13, 2005, http://www.cleveland.com/lake/plaindealer/index.ssf?/base/iswar/110561733925420.xml.

Waite, Mark. 2002. Interview by Michael Knights. Tape recording (author's collection). February 20. Maxwell Air Force Base, Ala.

Wald, Charles. 2002. Interview by Michael Knights. Tape recording (author's collection). June 19. Washington, D.C.

Wall, Robert. "Cobras in Urban Combat," *Aviation Week and Space Technology*, April 14, 2003.

———. "Fight Control," *Aviation Week and Space Technology*, June 16, 2003.

———. "Lessons Emerge," *Aviation Week and Space Technology*, April 14, 2003.

———. "New Weapons Debut in Attacks on Iraq," *Aviation Week and Space Technology*, December 21, 1998.

———. "Super Hornets at Sea," *Aviation Week and Space Technology*, March 17, 2003.

———. "Time Runs Short," *Aviation Week and Space Technology*, March 17, 2003.

———. "US to Replenish Missile Stocks, Steps Up Strikes against SAMs." *Aviation Week and Space Technology*, January 18, 1999.

Warden, John. 2002. Interview by Michael Knights. March 1. Maxwell Air Force Base, Ala.

Warden, John A. "Employing Air Power in the 21st Century." In *The Future of Air Power in the Aftermath of the Gulf War*, edited by Richard Shultz and Robert Pfalzgraff. Maxwell Air Force Base, Ala.: Air University Press, 1992.

Warnock, Timothy. *Short of War: Major USAF Contingency Operations*. Maxwell, Ala.: Air Force Historical Research Agency, 2000.

Warren, Patrick, and Keith Barclay. "Operation Airborne Dragon, Northern Iraq." *Military Review* (November/December 2003): pp. 1–2.

Weber, Bruce A. *Combined Task Force Provide Comfort: A New Model for 'Lead Nation' Command?* Naval War College, 1994, pp. 12–25.

Welsh, Mark. "Day of the Killer Scouts." *Air Force Magazine* 75, no. 4 (April 1992): pp. 6–8.

White, Jeffrey. 2004. Interview by Michael Knights. August 12. Washington, D.C.

———. *Faces of Battle: The Insurgents at Fallujah*. Washington, D.C.: Washington Institute for Near East Policy, 2004.

———. *Iraq Fights Its War 'Outside-In'*. Washington, D.C.: Washington Institute for Near East Policy, 2003.

———. *War in Iraq: A Preliminary Assessment*. Washington, D.C.: Washington Institute for Near East Policy, 2003.

White, Paul. *Crises after the Storm: An Appraisal of U.S. Air Operations in Iraq since the Persian Gulf War*. Washington, D.C.: Washington Institute for Near East Policy, 1999.

White, Paul, and Daniel Byman. *Air Power and U.S. Policy towards Iraq*. Washington, D.C.: Washington Institute for Near East Policy, 1999.

Williams, Daniel. "Cleric's Killing Arouses Shiites: Iraqi Officials Nervous About Turmoil in the South," *Washington Post*, March 16, 1999.

Wilson, Charles. *Strategic and Tactical Aerial Reconnaissance in the Near East*. Washington, D.C.: Washington Institute for Near East Policy, 1999.

Winnefield, James, Preston Niblack, and Dana Johnson. *A League of Airmen: U.S. Air Power in the Gulf War*. Santa Monica, Calif.: RAND, 1994.

Wood, David. "U.S. Will Miss Having Its Nose inside Iraq," *Cleveland Plain Dealer*, January 6, 1999.

Woodward, Bob. *The Commanders*. New York: Simon & Schuster, 1991.

———. *Plan of Attack*. New York: Simon & Schuster, 2004.

————. *Veil: The Secret Wars of the CIA 1981–87*. New York: Simon & Schuster, 1988.

Woolsey, James. 2004. Interview by Michael Knights. July 1. Washington, D.C.

Zinni, Anthony. 2003. Interview by Michael Knights. Telephone interview. July 12. Washington, D.C.

Zucchino, David. *Thunder Run: The Armored Strike to Capture Baghdad*. New York: Atlantic Monthly Press, 2004.

Index

Killer Scouts, 89–90, 94, 105, 314, 315
kinetic operations, 252
Kolchuga early warning system, 232
KRG. *See* Kurdistan Regional
   Government
KTO. *See* Kuwait Theater of Operations
Kurdish civil war, 153–56; Saddam
   invited in, 154; US intelligence, 155
Kurdish factions, 154; U.S. relations
   with, 169. *See also specific factions*
Kurdistan Regional Government
   (KRG), 127
Kurdistan Worker's Party (PKK), 219
Kurdistant Democratic Party (KDP),
   151, 152
Kurds, 265; after Desert Storm, 127;
   Mukharabat and, 141; 1991 uprisings
   and, 123–24; post–Iran–Iraqi war, 6;
   separatist movements in, 19. *See also*
   Operation Desert Strike
Kuwait: detainees, 11; inter-Arab
   solidarity and, 8; international
   solidarity, 11; Iraqi 1994 feint,
   146–50; Iraqi claims against, 6; Iraqi
   lack of business credit-worthiness,
   11; loans to Iraq, 7; negotiations for
   withdrawal, 95; post–Cold War
   context of, 11; pre–war saber-rattling
   toward, 7–12; reaction to British press
   corps visit, 214; reparations to, 152;
   royal family assassination attempts, 9,
   10; shared Iraqi oil resevoirs, 7; U.S.
   air bases in, 150; willingness to host
   strike forces, 161. *See also* Operation
   Desert Shield
Kuwait Theater of Operations (KTO),
   21

Lamoureux, Cherry, 203
land-warfare doctrine, 24
LANTIRN pods, 92
laser-guided bombs (LGBs), 28, 46, 91
Latifah phosgene plant, 317
Latifyah fuel facility, 68
Law of Armed Conflict Risks, 215
LGBs. *See* laser-guided bombs
Libya, 142, 145

lines of communications (LOCs),
   308–9
lines of operations, 252
linguists per battalion, 339
LOCs. *See* lines of communications;
   logistics and lines of communications
logistical bunkers, 82. *See also* igloos
logistics and lines of communications
   (LOCs), 81
long range navigation (LORAN), 99
looting, 154–55, 333
LORAN. *See* long range navigation
low-altitude navigation and targeting
   infrared for night (LANTIRN)
   targeting pods, 59
Luttwak, Edward, 361

MAGTF. *See* Marine Air-Ground Task
   Force
Mahmoud, Abid Hamid, 190
MANPADS. *See* manportable air
   defense systems
manportable air defense systems
   (MANPADS), 25, 84
maps, 86–88, 100; timeliness of, 96;
   updating of, 17–18; urban sprawl and,
   288, 299, 314
MARCENT, 94, 95
March on Baghdad, 280–327; distance
   per day, 287; divided
   zones-objectives, 309; entering the
   cities, 307–11; Iraqi operational
   movements during, 292; media and,
   293; northward lunge, 283–87;
   Objective Firebird, 282; Objective
   Liberty, 282, 283; operational tempo
   of, 287–94, 302; *On Point* review of,
   292; reducing resistance v. masking,
   308; resiliency of the regime,
   unexpected, 293; US casualties, 294;
   willingness to die, 283. *See also*
   Baghdad, Battle for; irregulars;
   smackdown
Marine Air-Ground Task Force
   (MAGTF), 38, 303
Marine Expeditionary Unit (MEU), 41
Maverick missiles, 91

TAC. *See* U.S. Air Force Tactical Air
  Command
TACC. *See* Tactical Air Command
  Center
TACSAT, 287
Tactical Air Command Center (TACC),
  59
tactical air-launched decoys (TALDs),
  53
tactical intelligence, timeliness of, 100
tactical reserves, 23
Tactical Review Board, 215
Talabani, Jalal, 153
TALDs. *See* tactical air-launched decoys
Tamara early warning system, 232
tank plinking. *See* plinking
target sets, 191–92, 276; C3 networks,
  273; cruise missiles and, 163;
  expansion of strategic set, 69–72;
  high-value targets, 267, 337;
  industrial sites, 69; inside-out
  warfare, 44, 72–73, 323; in KTO,
  96–2; leadership targets, 72, 74, 78,
  195, 273, 325; logistical bunkers, 82;
  matching of missile and target types,
  165; no-target lists of civilian
  facilities, 274. *See also* sensitive
    targets, *specific operations, targets*
targeting models, 45; bottleneck
  targeting, 188, 189, 203; centers of
  gravity, 251; Cold-war approaches
  and, 45, 45; commander's intent and,
  193; Desert Thunder I, 179; direct
  attack, 268; limiting damage to
  long-term assets, 45; nodal analysis,
  195; qualitative v. quantitative strikes,
  162; ring model, 72–73; smackdown
  and, 268. *See also* effects-based
    targeting
targeting systems, 83; C3 targets, 258;
  centers of gravity, 271; concentric
  ring model, 271; direct attack, in
  smackdown operation, 306; dynamic
  targeting, 204; effects-based
  targeting, 273; federated targeting
  system, 193; information
  technologies and, 160; Iraqi emigres

and, 48; mobile-target tracking, 137;
  nodal analysis, 258; Operation
  Southern Focus, 257; Operation
  Southern Watch and, 215–16;
  over-the-horizon targeting, 22;
  stratification of Iraq armed forces,
  192; targeting cycles, 137; virtual
  targeting staff, 193; website for
  nominating no-strike locations, 275.
  See also specific systems
Task Force Normandy, 51, 58
Task Force Proven Force, 52
TELS. *See* transporter erector launchers
TERCOM. *See* terrain contour matching
terrain, 223; cluttered battlefields,
  86–87; load-bearing capacites, 18; oil
  fields. *See* oil fields; reconnaissance
  of, 99; urban, 310; western desert,
  252–53
terrain contour matching (TERCOM),
  164
terrorism, xix; asymmetric warfare and,
  361; global war on, 251; suicide
  vests, 331; terrorist groups, 332; U.S.
  state-sponsors list, 4; US
  state-sponsors-of list, 5. *See also*
    insurgency, *specific groups*
Time-on-Targets (ToTs), 14
Time-Phased Force Deployment
  Directive, 14
time-sensitive targeting (TST), 62,
  64–65, 312
TLAM. *See* Tomahawk land-attack
  missile
Tomahawk land-attack missiles
  (TLAMs), 42, 51–52, 68, 139;
  casualty aversion and, 139; diplomacy
  and, 139, 140, 141–46, 167–70;
  fallout from era of, 167–70; first use
  of Block III GPS-guided, 164; June
  1993 strike, 141; limited objectives
  school, 140; US polls, 167
ToTs. *See* Time-on-Targets
Touted Gleam exercise, 63
TR-1 reconnaissance aircraft, 61
TRADOC. *See* U.S. Army Training and
  Doctrine Command

About the Author

Dr. Michael Knights earned his doctorate at the Department of War Studies, King's College London. Since 2003, Knights has been an associate of The Washington Institute for Near East Policy, specializing in the security and military affairs of Iraq, Iran, Saudi Arabia, and the smaller Gulf Cooperation Council (GCC) states. Working with the U.S. Department of Defense, Dr. Knights has undertaken extensive interview-based research on lessons learned from U.S. military Operations in Iraq since 1990. Knights is also the editor of *Operation Iraqi Freedom and the New Iraq: Insights and Forecasts* (The Washington Institute, 2004). He is a senior political risk consultant for Jane's Information Group, Oxford Analytica, and a wide range of other business intelligence providers. He can be contacted at michaelk@outremerconsulting.com